GENESIS

Books in the PREACHING THE WORD Series:

EXODUS:
Saved for God's Glory
by Philip Graham Ryken

JEREMIAH AND LAMENTATIONS:
From Sorrow to Hope
by Philip Graham Ryken

DANIEL:
The Triumph of God's Kingdom
by Rodney D. Stortz

MARK, VOLUME ONE:
Jesus, Servant and Savior

MARK, VOLUME TWO:
Jesus, Servant and Savior

LUKE, VOLUME ONE:
That You May Know the Truth

LUKE, VOLUME TWO:
That You May Know the Truth

JOHN:
That You May Believe

ACTS:
The Church Afire

ROMANS:
Righteousness from Heaven

EPHESIANS:
The Mystery of the Body of Christ

COLOSSIANS AND PHILEMON:
The Supremacy of Christ

1 & 2 TIMOTHY AND TITUS:
To Guard the Deposit
by R. Kent Hughes and Bryan Chapell

HEBREWS, VOLUME ONE:
An Anchor for the Soul

HEBREWS, VOLUME TWO:
An Anchor for the Soul

JAMES:
Faith That Works

THE SERMON ON THE MOUNT:
The Message of the Kingdom

Unless otherwise indicated, all volumes are by R. Kent Hughes

PREACHING THE WORD

GENESIS

Beginning and Blessing

R. Kent Hughes

CROSSWAY BOOKS

A DIVISION OF
GOOD NEWS PUBLISHERS
WHEATON, ILLINOIS

Genesis

Copyright © 2004 by R. Kent Hughes.

Published by Crossway Books
    a division of Good News Publishers
    1300 Crescent Street
    Wheaton, Illinois 60187

Cover banner by Marge Gieser

Art Direction: David LaPlaca

First printing, 2004

Printed in the United States of America

Library of Congress Cataloging-in-Publication Data

Hughes, R. Kent
 Genesis : beginning and blessing / R. Kent Hughes
   p. cm. — (Preaching the word)
 Includes bibliographical references and index.
 ISBN 1-58134-629-8 (hc : alk. paper)
 1. Bible. N.T. Genesis Commentaries. I. Title. II. Series.
 BS1235.53H84 2004
 222'.1107—dc22   2004007199

RRD		16	15	14	13	12	11	10	09	08	07	06	05	04
15	14	13	12	11	10	9	8	7	6	5	4	3	2	1

For

Paul and Heather House

חברים נאמנים

"faithful friends"

Table of Contents

Acknowledgments

My best asset in the long task of writing these expositions of Genesis has been Barbara, my soul-mate of forty-four winters — first, because of her willingness to free me to do the necessary work, and second, because of her knack of "cutting to the chase" in matters of clarity and relevance. Her "so whats" have been salutary and saving.

Thanks must go to my administrative assistants Mrs. Sharon Fritz (now retired) and Mrs. Pauline Epps for their cheerful assiduousness and concern for accuracy and detail. As always, Herb Carlburg's proofreading and cross-checking of references is a great gift to me and to the reader. Likewise, Ted Griffin's masterful editing has much improved this work.

Lastly, I must express my appreciation to the congregation of College Church whose prayers and careful listening have elevated the Word preached.

A Word to Those Who Preach the Word

There are times when I am preaching that I have especially sensed the pleasure of God. I usually become aware of it through the unnatural silence. The ever-present coughing ceases, and the pews stop creaking, bringing an almost physical quiet to the sanctuary — through which my words sail like arrows. I experience a heightened eloquence, so that the cadence and volume of my voice intensify the truth I am preaching.

There is nothing quite like it — the Holy Spirit filling one's sails, the sense of his pleasure, and the awareness that something is happening among one's hearers. This experience is, of course, not unique, for thousands of preachers have similar experiences, even greater ones.

What has happened when this takes place? How do we account for this sense of his smile? The answer for me has come from the ancient rhetorical categories of *logos*, *ethos*, and *pathos*.

The first reason for his smile is the *logos* — in terms of preaching, God's Word. This means that as we stand before God's people to proclaim his Word, we have done our homework. We have exegeted the passage, mined the significance of its words in their context, and applied sound hermeneutical principles in interpreting the text so that we understand what its words meant to its hearers. And it means that we have labored long until we can express in a sentence what the theme of the text is — so that our outline springs from the text. Then our preparation will be such that as we preach, we will not be preaching our own thoughts about God's Word, but God's actual Word, his *logos*. This is fundamental to pleasing him in preaching.

The second element in knowing God's smile in preaching is *ethos* — what you are as a person. There is a danger endemic to preaching, which is having your hands and heart cauterized by holy things. Phillips Brooks illustrated it by the analogy of a train conductor who comes to believe that he has been to the places he announces because of his long and loud heralding of them. And that is why Brooks insisted that preaching must be "the bringing of truth through personality." Though we can never *perfectly* embody the truth we preach, we must be subject to it, long for it, and make it as much a part of our ethos as possible. As the Puritan William Ames said, "Next to the Scriptures, nothing makes a sermon more to pierce, than when it comes out of the inward affection of the heart without any affectation." When a preacher's *ethos* backs up his *logos*, there will be the pleasure of God.

Last, there is *pathos* — personal passion and conviction. David Hume, the Scottish philosopher and skeptic, was once challenged as he was seen going to hear George Whitefield preach: "I thought you do not believe in the gospel." Hume replied, "I don't, but *he does*." Just so! When a preacher believes what he preaches, there will be passion. And this belief and requisite passion will know the smile of God.

The pleasure of God is a matter of *logos* (the Word), *ethos* (what you are), and *pathos* (your passion). As you *preach the Word* may you experience his smile — the Holy Spirit in your sails!

R. Kent Hughes
Wheaton, Illinois

1

Beginning

GENESIS 1:1, 2

It was the custom in ancient times to name a book by its opening word, which is what the Hebrews did in titling this initial Bible book *Bereshith*, which means "in the beginning." When the Old Testament was translated into Greek about 250 B.C. the Greek equivalent of the title was rendered Genesis, which both the Latin and English translations have adopted letter for letter. It is an exquisitely perfect title because this book gives us the genesis (the beginning) of the doctrine of God, which rose to tower high over the pagan notions of the day. It is the genesis of the doctrine of creation, which likewise rose far above the crude mythologies of the surrounding nations. Genesis gives us the doctrine of man, demonstrating that from the beginning we are both wonderful and awful. The doctrine of salvation too has its genesis in Eden and its grand development throughout the whole book.

Astounding! What we know about God, about creation, about ourselves, and about salvation begins in Genesis. It provides the theological pillars on which the rest of the Bible stands. Jesus, the Messiah, has his prophetic genesis in the opening chapters of Genesis (cf. 3:15). The importance of Genesis for the believing heart can hardly be overstated.

At the same time, as deep and weighty as the book of Genesis is, it is no dry textbook. Its narratives of the garden, the flood, and the tower of Babel have captivated hearts for over three millennia and have provided inspiration for the world's greatest poetry. The earthy, epic lives of Abraham and Isaac, and Jacob and Esau, and Joseph in Egypt are so primary and universal and so skillfully told that they have never ceased to enthrall listeners. The last decade of the twentieth century and the opening years of the twenty-first century produced a renewed public interest in the narratives of Genesis, and even a PBS special, and numbers of books on the shelves of popular bookstores. Genesis is *in* as literature. And what grand preaching material it is!

An overview of Genesis reveals neatly structured themes. It is widely accepted that chapters 1 — 11 cover primeval history (the early history of Planet Earth) and chapters 12 — 50 patriarchal history (the history of Israel's founding fathers). The famous Hebrew term *toledoth*, literally translated "generations of," occurs ten times in Genesis. Five refer to primeval history and five to patriarchal history.[1] Closer examination reveals that five of them variously introduce narratives, and five introduce genealogies.[2] Genesis is finely crafted.

Primeval history. The first eleven chapters, which give us the primeval history (universal history) of the world, do so by relating five stories that all have the same structure. The stories are of the fall, Cain, the sons of God marrying the daughters of man, the flood, and the tower of Babel. All five stories follow this fourfold pattern: a) *Sin*: the sin is described; b) *Speech*: there is a speech by God announcing the penalty; c) *Grace*: God brings grace to the situation to ease the misery due to sin; and d) *Punishment*: God punishes the sin. See an instructive chart on this in the footnotes.[3]

Here is amazing grace — amazing because though in all five stories there is an increasing avalanche of sin and resulting punishment that necessarily becomes increasingly severe, there is always more grace. Adam and Eve are punished, but God graciously withholds the death penalty. Cain is banished from his family, but God graces him with a mark of protection. The flood comes, but God graciously preserves the human race through Noah. Only in the case of Babel is the element of grace muted.[4]

Patriarchal history. But this lack serves to set up the continuation of grace during the following patriarchal section of Genesis 12 — 50. In this section Abraham receives the gracious promise that through him all the peoples of the world will be blessed (cf. 12:3). And then the patriarchal period unfolds the fulfilling of that gracious promise. Despite the patriarchs' repeated sins, God's promise stands. The salvation history of the patriarchal narratives functions as the gracious answer to mankind's scattering at Babel.[5]

Genesis is about grace. The Apostle Paul's aphorism, "where sin increased, grace abounded all the more" (Romans 5:20) sums up this major theme of Genesis. Genesis, far from being a faded page fallen from antiquity, breathes the grace of God. What a time we're going to have as our souls are worked over by the sin-speech-grace-punishment pattern of chapters 1 — 11, and by the overall "where sin increases, grace abounds" theme of the whole book. This is good soul medicine — strong meat. It was grace from the beginning — in both primeval and patriarchal history. It always will be grace.

Genesis also provides us with a grand revelation of God's faithfulness as it recounts God's fidelity over and over again in the lives of the patriarchs. We see that God remains faithful even when the people to whom the promises are made become the greatest threat to the fulfillment of the promise. Such is God's faithfulness that the sinful, disordered lives of the promise-bearers can't abort the promises. This is the way God has always been. The New Testament puts it this way:

> *If we are faithless, he remains faithful —*
> *for he cannot deny himself. (2 Timothy 2:13)*

Faithfulness is a primary reality about God — the Genesis reality. It's nothing new, but it is everything.

In regard to man, Genesis is eloquent: He is at the same time truly wonderful and truly awful. The bulk of Genesis affirms our terrible sinfulness. Even the best of the patriarchs are helpless, hopeless sinners. Not one ever comes to merit salvation. So we understand that from the first, salvation could come only through faith. Moses makes it clear that is how Abraham, the greatest of the patriarchs, was saved: "And he believed the LORD, and he counted it to him as righteousness" (Genesis 15:6). Paul would allude to this multiple times in the New Testament, saying of Abraham in Romans, "The purpose was to make him the father of all who believe . . . so that righteousness would be counted to them as well" (4:11). There is only one way that fallen humanity can be saved — the Genesis way — by faith. There never has been another.

Who wrote Genesis? The Scriptures, both Old Testament and New Testament, affirm that Moses was the author of the first five books of the Bible (Genesis through Deuteronomy; cf. Exodus 17:14; Deuteronomy 31:24; Joshua 8:31; 2 Kings 14:6; Romans 10:5; and 2 Corinthians 3:15). Most significantly Jesus himself confirms Mosaic authorship (cf. John 5:45-47). Of course, Moses' writing was somewhat revised and added to by others. Moses would have had a hard time writing Deuteronomy 34, the last chapter of the book, which describes his death![6]

Internal biblical dating points to the late fifteenth century B.C. at the time of or following the exodus when Israel wandered in the wilderness.[7] In the dynamic context of the wilderness journey, as God's people dreamed of the promised land, they would naturally ask about Abraham and the patriarchs who had brought them down to Egypt. And beyond that they would ask about their ultimate origins. Thus God met Moses with his Word, giving him not only Genesis but what we call the Pentateuch, the first five books of the Bible.

As we now consider the opening lines of Genesis, we must carefully note that Israel had just escaped the oppressive polytheism of Egypt's temples and pyramids with its solar and lunar gods. In Egypt, the pagan mythologies had opposed Israel's monotheism. In opposition to a single creator, the Egyptians taught pantheism and shored up their beliefs with elaborate myths of love affairs and reproduction among the gods, of warfare marking out the heavens and the earth. Their priests annually mimed their myths, hoping that by reenacting them they would create life. And that was not without effect. Some of God's people had succumbed to the lavish liturgies of the Nile.

So Moses took them on. These opening lines would forever establish a true understanding about God, the universe, and humanity. Moses began with a radical and sweeping affirmation of monotheism over polytheism.[8]

His style was one of calm, majestic, measured grandeur. Moses did not condescend to mention the pagan worldviews but answered them through deliberate, solemn utterances that dismissed the opposing cosmologies by silence and subtle allusion:[9] "In the beginning, God created the heavens and the earth. The earth was without form and void, and darkness was over the face of the deep. And the Spirit of God was hovering over the face of the waters" (vv. 1, 2). The emphasis is threefold: first God, then the universe, and then the earth.

GOD AND THE BEGINNING

Derek Kidner, one-time warden of Tyndale House, Cambridge, has pointed out that it is no accident that God is the subject of the first sentence of the Bible because his name here, *Elohim*, dominates the whole chapter — occurring some thirty-five times in all, so that it catches the reader's eye again and again. Kidner's point is that this section and indeed the entire book of Genesis is about God from first to last — and to read it any other way is to misread it.[10] We will keep this advice in the forefront, especially as Genesis begins to focus on God the Son as the beginning and end of history.

Remarkably, the mystery of the Holy Trinity is embedded in the first three Hebrew words of the text (*Bereshith bara Elohim*) because the name "God," *Elohim*, is in the plural, and the verb "created" (*bara*) is in the singular, so that God (plural) created (singular). On the one hand the Bible teaches that God is a unity: "Hear, O Israel: the LORD our God, the LORD is one" (Deuteronomy 6:4; cf. 1 Corinthians 8:6). On the other hand, it is equally as explicit that God is three persons (cf. Matthew 28:19; 2 Corinthians 13:14) — and that all three Persons were active in creation (God and the Spirit in Genesis 1:1, 2; God and the Son in John 1:1-3, 10; and the Son in Colossians 1:15-17 and Hebrews 1:1-3).[11] So it is that we meet the awesome Triune God in the first three words of Biblical revelation!

God was there in the beginning. And here the context means "the beginning" of time itself, not sometime within eternity.[12] Later Moses would give God's presence at the beginning wonderful poetic expression when he sang,

Before the mountains were brought forth,
or ever you had formed the earth and the world,
from everlasting to everlasting you are God. (Psalm 90:2)

Whichever way we look — to the vanishing points of the beginning or the end — God is there, having always been there.

And even more, God created everything out of nothing. "It is correct to say that the verb *bara*, 'create,' contains the idea both of complete effortlessness and *creatio ex nihilo*, since it is never connected with any statement of the material" (Von Rad).[13] Believing God's word, the writer of Hebrews gave it precise explanation, "By faith we understand that the universe was created by the word of God, so that what is seen was not made out of things that are visible" (11:3; cf. Isaiah 40:26; Revelation 4:11).

Moses' assertion that nothing existed before God spoke it into existence was an attack on the polytheism and pantheism from which his people had just escaped. Today it stands as the answer to philosophical materialism and naturalism, which hold that the only real things are material, physical things — or as the opening line of Carl Sagan's best-seller *Cosmos* puts it: "The cosmos is all there is, or has been, or will be" — matter is God! As we all know, this worldview has dominated the sciences for the last one hundred years. And it is defended, by some, against all logic — for fear that a Divine Foot might get in the door.[14] In particular, absolute devotion to materialism has been the creed of Darwinian evolution and its dubious and increasingly discredited doctrine of natural selection.

Significantly, the emergence of the Intelligent Design Movement and the appearance of books the caliber of Michael Behe's *Darwin's Black Box* have moved some old-line Darwinists to retreat. Intelligent Design asks questions that the Darwinists can only answer *by faith* in metaphysical materialism. Thus William Dembski writes in his introduction to *Mere Creation*:

> Darwin gave us a creation story, one in which God was absent and undirected natural processes did all the work. That creation story has held sway for more than a hundred years. It is now on the way out. . . . In *The End of Christendom* Malcolm Muggeridge wrote, "I myself am convinced that the theory of evolution, especially to the extent to which it has been applied, will be one of the greatest jokes in the history books of the future. Posterity will marvel that so very flimsy and dubious an hypothesis could be accepted with the incredible credulity it has."[15]

Well, what do you know? The Bible was right. Creation could not happen without God!

In the beginning God existed in plural unity as the Holy Trinity. In the beginning God was existing from eternity to eternity. In the beginning was God — before there was as much as a material atom of the cosmos.

GOD AND THE UNIVERSE (v. 1)

"In the beginning," says Moses, "God created the heavens and the earth" (v. 1). Moses uses very specialized and honed vocabulary here. "Created" is only used of God in the Bible. Only God creates. And in Genesis 1 the verb "created" is reserved only for the most crucial items in God's plan: the universe (1:1), animate life (1:21), and man (1:27).[16] The combination of the words "heavens and earth" is also very specialized. It is a merism (a statement of two opposites to indicate a totality), so that the sense is, "In the beginning God created the cosmos."[17] God created everything there is in all creation.

Cambridge University physicist Stephen Hawking, who has been called "the most brilliant theoretical physicist since Einstein," says in his bestselling *A Brief History of Time* that our galaxy is an average-sized spiral galaxy that looks to other galaxies like a swirl in a pastry roll and that it is over 100,000 light-years across[18] — about six hundred trillion miles. He says, "We now know that our galaxy is only one of some hundred thousand million that can be seen using modern telescopes, each galaxy itself containing some hundred thousand million stars."[19] It is commonly held that the average distance between these hundred thousand million galaxies (each six hundred trillion miles across and containing one hundred thousand million stars) is three million light-years! On top of that, the work of Edwin Hubble, based on the Doppler effect, has shown that all red-spectrumed galaxies are moving away from us — and that nearly all are red. Thus, the universe is constantly expanding.[20] Some estimates say that the most distant galaxy is eight billion light-years away — and racing away at two hundred million miles an hour. Finally, the fact of the expanding universe demands a beginning, though Hawking now doubts that a Big Bang was its beginning.[21]

Not only that — God created every speck of dust in the hundred thousand million galaxies of the universe. He created every atom — the submicroscopic solar systems with their whimsically named quarks (from James Joyce's *Three Quarks for Master Mark*) and leptons (the same Greek word used for the widow's mite) and electrons and neutrinos ("little neutral ones") — all of which have no measurable size.

The awesomeness of creation has been the subject of famous biblical poems like Job 38, Psalms 19, 33, 136, and Isaiah 45. Isaiah 40 references creation repeatedly, culminating in this expression:

> *To whom then will you compare me,*
> *that I should be like him? says the Holy One.*
> *Lift up your eyes on high and see:*

> *who created these?*
> *He who brings out their host by number,*
> *calling them all by name,*
> *by the greatness of his might,*
> *and because he is strong in power*
> *not one is missing. (vv. 25, 26)*

The force of Moses' words, "In the beginning, God created the heavens and the earth" was not lost on the children of the exodus. The night skies of Sinai, the diaphanous veil of the Milky Way, the paths of the comets, and the intermittent meteor showers sang to them of an omnipotent Creator who cared for his people. No wonder the poetry! How we need to rise above the congestion and smog of our existence and see our Creator, our cosmic caregiver.

GOD AND THE EARTH (v. 2)

The second half of Moses' introduction brings us down to earth: "The earth was without form and void, and darkness was over the face of the deep. And the Spirit of God was hovering over the face of the waters" (v. 2). The perspective is geocentric — from earth level — and from that view earth is seen as uninhabitable. The Hebrew of "without form and void" is rhythmic (*tohu wabohu*) and served as a common expression for a place that is disordered and empty[22] and therefore uninhabitable and uninhabited — the very opposite of what the earth would be after the six days of creation.

Spread over the uninhabitable earth was "darkness," serving to emphasize the emptiness. Darkness is impenetrable to man but transparent to God (cf. Psalm 139:12). God was there. And under the darkness and covering the earth was "the deep," the primeval ocean. The famed Genesis commentator Umberto Cassuto provides this picture:

> Just as the potter, when he wishes to fashion a beautiful vessel, takes first of all a lump of clay, and places it upon his wheel in order to mould it according to his wish, so the Creator first prepared for Himself the raw material . . . with a view to giving it afterwards order and life. . . . It is this terrestrial state that is called *tohu* and *bohu*.[23]

However, above the primeval chaos floated unutterable beauty — "and the Spirit of God was hovering over the face of the waters." The verbal picture comes clear in the final Psalm of Moses where he uses the same word to describe "an eagle that stirs up its nest, that flutters over its young" (Deuteronomy 32:11). We have seen it when a bird suspends itself stationary in the sky by fluttering its wings. The Spirit of God fluttered like a nurturing bird over the dark in preparation for day one.[24]

The beauty and spiritual symmetry of the Bible's opening words become even clearer as we see that the word "Spirit" in Hebrew also means "breath." God's creative breath hovered over the water, and on day one his breath would come forth as speech — his word. Psalm 33:6 makes this connection:

> By the word of the LORD the heavens were made,
> and by the breath of his mouth all their host.

The Spirit is to God's word as breath is to speech.

On day one the miracle would begin with God speaking light into existence and that light shining in the darkness. None less than the Apostle Paul made the application of this truth to our dark hearts: "For God, who said, 'Let light shine out of darkness,' has shone in our hearts to give the light of the knowledge of the glory of God in the face of Jesus Christ" (2 Corinthians 4:6). Just as the Spirit of God fluttered over the dark waters, so he does over the dark hearts of humanity, preparing them for the word of God that will make them into new creations in Christ.

God created the heavens and the earth, the universe! He can make you new as well.

In the beginning was God. In the end God will be.

Genesis is about God, the universe, and you.

Genesis is about grace.

May his grace abound to you and me as we study the book of beginnings.

2

Forming the Earth

GENESIS 1:3-13

Through the centuries Christians who have held that the Scriptures are inerrant and wholly true have differed over the interpretation of the six days of creation. Bryan Chapell, president of Covenant Seminary, has noted that those who believe that the Bible teaches that creation took place in six twenty-four-hour solar days include such greats as John Calvin (though Warfield says he was open to other views), William Henry Thornwell, and Louis Berkhof. Others of equal stature have believed that the six days of Genesis did not limit God's creating actions to the 144 hours of six days. These include the ancients Augustine and Aquinas, the Puritan William Ames, the great nineteenth-century defenders of orthodoxy Charles Hodge, A. A. Hodge, and B. B. Warfield, and prominent twentieth-century defenders of the faith such as J. Gresham Machen, J. Oliver Buswell, Donald Grey Barnhouse, and Francis Schaeffer.[1]

It is therefore an established fact that godly, Scripture-loving people who have given their lives to God's Word have differed over the opening verses of the Bible. What they have not differed on is the utter truth of God's Word and that the Genesis accounts are factual and historical. Neither have they differed over the historicity of Adam and Eve as special creations of God and the truth of the fall.

This ought to give pause to those who employ a particular view of creation as a litmus test for orthodoxy. Furthermore, the remarkable diversity of the major views of the six days ought to make us cautious and humble in our judgments.

There are at least six views of the six days, namely: 1) the twenty-four-hour solar day view (creation took place in 144 hours); 2) the punctuated activity view (the twenty-four-hour days of creation activity were separated by indefinite periods); 3) the gap view (there is a gap between Genesis 1:1 and 2, wherein a primeval rebellion took place, and the creation week is a remaking of the earth after the rebellion); 4) the day-age view (which understands the days as corresponding to geological ages); 5) the framework view (the days are a literary structuring device to convey the truth of creation, and not consecutive days); and 6) the analogical day view (the days are God's workdays). Certainly these six views cannot all be correct. In fact, only one can be right. And it is our duty to seek it. But in the seeking and finding and holding of our view we ought to employ good-will and magnanimity.

A model for this is the way we hold our millennial views. Here Dr. Chapell offers some seasoned advice:

> Some of us are pre-millennial, some are amillennial, some are post-millennial. There are serious questions among us about the timing of the events that will end the world. Still, we recognize that people can differ over the timing issues and still believe the Bible is entirely true, and we accept these differences without accusing one another of being unorthodox. The same ought to be possible in the discussions we are having over the timing of the days at the beginning of the world.[2]

Hopefully, this is the spirit in which this exposition of the days of creation will be conducted. The interpretive goal is to say no more and no less than what Scripture says. We must stay on the line of Scripture.

MOSES' INTENT

Moses' careful intent is evident in the majestic arrangement, symmetry, and subtle craft of his writing.

Arrangement. A quick read reveals that the six days of creation are perfectly divided, so that the first three days describe the *forming* of the earth and the last three its *filling*. The two sets of days are a direct echo and remedy to the opening statement that the earth was "without form and void." The earth's formlessness was remedied by its forming in days one to three, and its emptiness by its filling on days four to six. This is exactly what happened, and Moses was at pains to make sure his hearers did not miss it.

Correspondence. There is also a remarkable correspondence between the first three days and the last three. Day four corresponds to day one, day five to day two, and day six to day three.

It is all so beautiful! On day one the light was created. On the corresponding day four there came the sun and moon to rule the light. On day two God created the expanse that he called the sky, separating the waters above from the waters below. And on the parallel day five God filled the sky and waters with fowl and fish. On day three God separated the water and dry land and created vegetation. On the matching day six God filled the land with animal life and created man to rule over it all.

	FORM		**FILLING**
DAY 1	Light	DAY 4	Luminaries
DAY 2	Sky (waters below)	DAY 5	Birds and fish
DAY 3	Land (plants)	DAY 6	Animals and man (plants for food)

On days three and six the correspondence is especially emphasized by the double repetitions of "God said" and of "it was good" — emphasizing a formal correspondence between the final days of forming and filling the earth. These correspondences reveal an astonishing record of the symmetries of creation.

Perfection. The late Hebrew University professor Umberto Cassuto points out that the structure of the days of creation is based on a system of numerical harmony, using the number seven. He wrote, "The work of the Creator, which is marked by absolute perfection and flawless systematic orderliness, is distributed over seven days: Six days of labour and a seventh day set aside for the enjoyment of the completed task."[3]

And then he made these observations: The words "God" (*Elohim*), "heavens" (*samayim*), and "earth" (*eretz*), which are the three nouns of the opening verse, "In the beginning, *God* created the *heavens* and the *earth*," are repeated in this creation account in multiples of seven. "God" occurs thirty-five times (5 x 7), "heavens" twenty-one times (3 x 7), and "earth" twenty-one times. In addition to this, in the Hebrew original the first verse has seven words, and the second fourteen words. The seventh paragraph (the seventh day) has three sentences, each of which has seven words, and contains in the middle the phrase, "the seventh day." Cassuto concludes: "This numerical symmetry is as it were, the golden thread that binds together all the parts of the section and serves as a convincing proof of its unity."[4] So Genesis 1 is remarkable literature as to its arrangement, its correspondences and symmetries, and its literary-numerical perfection.

History. However, this said, it is not poetry but narrative prose. The whole account is written in the normal Hebrew narrative tense.[5] There is no question that the Genesis account is written as history. "Moses presents the creation story as what actually happened in the time space world we experience."[6] And that is the way that every Biblical author who looks back to it treats it (cf. Exodus 20:11; Isaiah 40:26; Jonah 1:9; Hebrews 11:3; Revelation 4:11). Thus Francis Schaeffer writes:

> The mentality of the whole Scripture . . . is that creation is as historically real as the history of the Jews and our present moment of time. Both the Old

and the New Testaments deliberately root themselves back into the early chapters of Genesis, insisting that they are a record of historical events.[7]

Genesis 1 is therefore exalted, carefully structured and worded narrative *prose — history*. Certainly it is not meant to be an exhaustive account of creation. It is only one page long! It must not be treated as a photograph of creation but rather as a broad-stroked painting of what happened when God created the heavens and the earth.

The narrative tense presents a sequence in those six days that demands chronological reality.[8] Day two followed day one, etc. Derek Kidner writes: "The march of the days is too majestic a progress to carry no implication of ordered sequence; it also seems over-subtle to adopt a view of the passage which discounts one of the primary impressions it makes on the ordinary, reader."[9]

So then, how did Moses' hearers understand the days of creation as he read them the account? Certainly they did not understand it as myth! It was a polemic against the pagan mythologies of the surrounding nations. Each day of creation attacks one of the gods in the pagan pantheons of the day and declares that they are not gods at all. On day one the gods of light and darkness are dismissed. On day two, the gods of sky and sea. On day three, the earth gods and gods of vegetation. On day four, the sun, moon, and star gods. Days five and six dispense with the ideas of divinity within the animal kingdom. Finally, it is made clear that humans and humanity are not divine, while also teaching that all, from the greatest to the least, are made in the image of God.[10] Thus Biblical reality replaced myth.

Neither did Moses' hearers regard the days as metaphorical or literary. The Hebrew tense used here is the *wayyiqtol*, that of narrative history. Elevated, sonorous, primeval history is what they heard in the six days of creation.

Could the Israelites have understood the days as geological ages? Impossible. What ignorant arrogance people bring to the text when they imagine that God directly referenced the shifting scientific paradigms of the last hundred years.

Possibly the Israelites understood Moses as describing creation in six twenty-four-hour days. Genesis can reasonably be interpreted as reading this way.[11] But I do not think that is how the Israelites heard it.

Most probably the six days of creation are *God's workdays*, which are not identical to ours but are analogous to ours. We understand something about God's days from our experience of living in earth days. The six days are not solar days but God's days because: 1) the first three days couldn't have been solar because God made the sun and moon on the fourth day, and 2) the seventh day has no end. The phrase "and there was evening and there was morning" does not appear with day seven (see 2:2, 3).

Those who hold that the word "day" here must be a twenty-four-hour day do so by arguing that every place in Scripture that the word "day" (*yom*) is used with a designating number, it is a solar day. But they ignore a cardinal rule of biblical interpretation — namely, when a word like *yom* appears in a text (a word that has a wide range of meanings), the context must determine the word's meaning. Here, in the immediate context, the seventh day is not a twenty-four-hour day. Thus it indicates that the preceding six days must be similarly understood.[12]

As a matter of fact God still is in the seventh day, the day of rest. He has been so since the creation of the world. Significantly, the writer of Hebrews bases his whole argument regarding God's people entering the rest by faith upon the fact that God is still resting, though also at work (Hebrews 4:3-11; cf. Psalm 95:11).

Therefore, Genesis 1 is history, the literal history of what God did when he created the heavens and the earth. He did it in six days, *his* days. He did it in the order described. The Genesis account is a majestic, finely-wrought telling of what God did in time and space. It is our history.

FORMING THE WORLD

Day one. As mentioned, the first three days remedy the fact that "the earth was without form." The formless world, covered with primeval sea, was floating in space, like an unformed lump of clay on the potter's wheel. The Spirit of God fluttered over the dark waters in anticipation.

His word. His only tool was his word, the revelation of his will — "And God said" — his speech. That is all. In creating everything through his word, God's thought shaped itself exactly to the least cell and atom. The vast universe was shaped by his thought and will, as was each of the trillions of cells in our body, each cell's nucleus containing a coded database larger in information content than all thirty volumes of the *Encyclopedia Britannica*.[13] There is such intimacy and immediacy in his knowledge in the willing of creation that we might say he knows each aspect of creation by experience. But, as Kidner says, "experience is too weak a word."[14] This is not pantheism. This is taking creation seriously!

And God does it all with such ease. A "mere" utterance. C. S. Lewis attempted to capture God's ease and joy in creation by his word in his Narnia Chronicles where he has Aslan creating the universe. Aslan's mouth is wide-open in song, and as he sings, the color green begins to form around his feet and spreads out in a pool. Then flowers and heather appear on the hillside and move out before him. As the tempo of the music picks up, showers of birds fly out of a tree, and butterflies begin to flit about. Then comes great celebration as the song breaks into even wilder song.[15]

The fanciful figure fits. In Genesis, God is like the soloist — "Let there be light," and the narrator is like the accompanist — "and there was light."

Light. The first day reads, "And God said, 'Let there be light,' and there was light. And God saw that the light was good. And God separated the light from the darkness. God called the light Day, and the darkness he called Night. And there was evening and there was morning, the first day" (vv. 3-5). For the first three days light shone from a source other than the sun. Thus we observe that the Bible begins with light but no sun and ends the same way — "And night will be no more. They will need no light of lamp or sun, for the Lord God will be their light, and they will reign forever and ever" (Revelation 22:5). Calvin said of this, "Therefore the Lord, by the very order of creation, bears witness that he holds in his hands the light, which he is able to impart to us without the sun and moon."[16] The rhythm of evening beginning the day, in Jewish reckoning, begins here because the darkness over the face of the earth was followed by the first light for the first day.

The pronouncement "good" is the first of seven such benedictions. The great artist admires his handiwork. It is good and perfect and will accomplish what he desires. As for the pagan cosmologies? The gods of light and darkness are dismissed without mention.

This is the beginning of the motif of darkness and light in Scripture, in which darkness and light are mutually exclusive realms. Ultimately Christ will bring eternal light to his people and to all creation. The end will be an explosion of light.

Day two. Light shone on the glistening deep of the unworked, unordered earth. Then God spoke again: "And God said, 'Let there be an expanse in the midst of the waters, and let it separate the waters from the waters.' And God made the expanse and separated the waters that were under the expanse from the waters that were above the expanse. And it was so. And God called the expanse Heaven. And there was evening and there was morning, the second day" (vv. 6-8).

The expanse (*raqia*) signifies a kind of horizontal area, extending through the very heart of the mass of water and dividing it into two layers, one above the other, creating upper and lower layers of water (Cassuto).[17] It was the visible expanse of sky with the waters of the sea below and the clouds holding water above. It is the blue we see. God called it "Sky" (alternate translation of the word "Heaven" in verse 8). This is a phenomenological description of the earth's atmosphere as viewed from earth.

The naming that took place of the "Day" and the "Night" on the first day and the "Sky" on day two was understood in biblical culture to be an act of sovereign dominion. Later God would entrust his dominion over the earth to Adam by letting him name all living creatures. Here the naming dismisses the pagan gods of sky and sea without a word.

Day three. During the first two days of creation God had brought increasing form and order to creation. The earth, warmed by light, was now robed in blue and dappled with clouds floating over a sparkling sea. The picture is increasingly inviting. Now, on day three God spoke twice more. His first speech completed the forming of earth — "And God said, 'Let the waters under the heavens be gathered together into one place, and let the dry land appear.' And it was so. God called the dry land Earth, and the waters that were gathered together he called Seas. And God saw that it was good" (vv. 9, 10). There was no new creation here, but a final ordering. The world as we know it had been given shape. The chaos had disappeared.

Then, with his second word on the third day, the emphasis began to switch toward the theme of fullness as he spoke plant life into existence:

> And God said, "Let the earth sprout vegetation, plants yielding seed, and fruit trees bearing fruit in which is their seed, each according to its kind, on the earth." And it was so. The earth brought forth vegetation, plants yielding seed according to their own kinds, and trees bearing fruit in which is their seed, each according to its kind. And God saw that it was good. And there was evening and there was morning, the third day. (vv. 11-13)

Here the gods of earth and vegetation, the gods of fertility, are powerfully dismissed. There is no sea god, only the seas that God controls, as he likewise controls the earth and its harvest.

The earth is now ready for animate, mobile life. The fixed forms are in place. God has sublimely ordered the chaos by his word. This is the history of the world's first three days.

CHRIST AND CREATION

Christ is the light. Because the Bible begins and ends by describing an untainted world that is filled with light but no sun and shows God as the source of light, it was fitting that Jesus called himself the light, saying "I am the light of the world." And he would continue by saying, "Whoever follows me will not walk in darkness, but will have the light of life" (John 8:12). It was an audacious claim because as Jesus spoke these words he was standing in the temple treasury by the massive extinguished torches that had burned that very night in the ceremony of the Illumination of the Temple, which celebrated the *Shekinah* glory that led Israel for forty years in the wilderness. It was a solemn declaration of his divinity as "the light of the world." This divine-light declaration ultimately identified him with the giver of light in Genesis 1. Indeed Revelation says of Jesus, "And the city has no need of sun or moon to shine on it, for the glory of God gives it light, and its lamp is the Lamb" (21:23). It was also an unfailing promise because Jesus needs merely to speak, and men and women receive his light.[18]

Christ the Creator. Jesus the light was present when creation was spoken into existence. The Scriptures are explicit. John's Gospel begins, "In the beginning was the Word, and the Word was with God, and the Word was God. He was in the beginning with God. All things were made through him, and without him was not any thing made that was made. In him was life, and the life was the light of men" (1:1-4). Nothing was made without Christ! Paul likewise affirms, "yet for us there is one God, the Father, *from whom are all things and for whom we exist,* and one Lord, Jesus Christ, *through whom are all things and through whom we exist*" (1 Corinthians 8:6, italics added). All things came, at once, from God the Father and God the Son, the Lord Jesus Christ. And again Paul says of Jesus, "For by him all things were created, in heaven and on earth, visible and invisible, whether thrones or dominions or rulers or authorities — all things were created through him and for him" (Colossians 1:16). And then hear the twenty-four elders as they cast their crowns before him: "Worthy are you, our Lord and God, to receive glory and honor and power, for you created all things, and by your will they existed and were created" (Revelation 4:11).

Christ brings order. The grand point is that it is Christ the light, Christ the Creator, who brings order out of the dark chaos of our lives — who brings form to the chaos of our lives. If your life is dark and desolate, if your life is out of control, if there is no light in your life, but only darkness, and there seems to be no hope — there is!

The very same power that flung the stars out into the unfathomable, expanding universe while orchestrating life in the irreducible complexity of the cells of your body will act on your behalf if you come to him. He will turn your night into day with a word. He will reorder your broken life with a word. He will bring form out of chaos with a word. It is his specialty.

He is not only the light, the Creator, and the Son of God — he is the Savior of the World. This very one who created the fleeing constellations, who orders the cell, who sustains every atom, came and died on the cross for your sins. This one will save you. He can bring a genesis to your life. That is what he came to do!

If you have never understood this before, realize that there is hope for you. There is creation power that can re-create your life. There is eternal life that will turn the midnight of your life into dawn and daylight and life and spring.

This is our God. He gives form. He reorders life. He will do it for you.

3

Filling the Earth

GENESIS 1:14-31

The first three days of creation describe the *forming* of the earth, and the second three describe its *filling*. And together they remedy earth's initial condition of being "without form and void." The correspondence of each set of days is immediately apparent as we see that day one, which describes the creation (*forming*) of light, is matched by day four, which describes the *filling* of earth with light.

FILLING THE EARTH

Day four. This filling with light on day four is given full expression by Moses' telling it twice, the second telling being the reverse of the first.[1] Both tellings doubly emphasize the functions of the sun, moon, and stars in respect to the earth. The description is geocentric — from earth's vantage point.

> And God said, "Let there be lights in the expanse of the heavens to separate the day from the night. And let them be for signs and for seasons, and for days and years, and let them be lights in the expanse of the heavens to give light upon the earth." And it was so. And God made the two great lights — the greater light to rule the day and the lesser light to rule the night — and the stars. And God set them in the expanse of the heavens to give light on the earth, to rule over the day and over the night, and to separate the light from the darkness. And God saw that it was good. And there was evening and there was morning, the fourth day. (vv. 14-19)

Notice that the sun and moon are identified as "two great lights." Moses consciously avoids using their names because they are gods in the Egyptian pantheon. Moses is saying that the sun, moon, and stars are not gods, but God's creations! He asserts Israel's majestic monotheism over the degraded pagan polytheism of his day.

With just a "mere" word — the expression of God's will — the solar system was set like a jeweled watch in the midst of the universe. The focus is geocentric indeed! The universe gets only a throwaway line — "Uh, he also made the stars."

And what a wonder the earth and its environs are! The seventeenth-century mathematician and philosopher Sir Isaac Newton had a mechanical replica of our solar system made in miniature. At its center was a large golden ball representing the sun, and revolving around it were smaller spheres attached at the ends of rods of varying lengths. They represented Mercury, Venus, Earth, Mars, and the other planets. These were all geared together by cogs and belts to make them move around the sun in perfect harmony. One day as Newton was studying the model, an unbelieving friend stopped by for a visit. Marveling at the device and watching as the scientist made the heavenly bodies move in their orbits, the man exclaimed, "My, Newton, what an exquisite thing! Who made it for you?" Without looking up, Sir Isaac replied, "Nobody." "Nobody?" his friend asked. "That's right! I said nobody! All of these balls and cogs and belts and gears just happened to come together, and wonder of wonders, by chance they began revolving in their set orbits and with perfect timing." His friend undoubtedly got the point. The existence of Newton's machine presupposed a maker, and even more so the earth and its perfectly ordered solar system.

The chances against such an ordered cosmic machine just happening are overwhelming. For example, if I take ten pennies, number them one to ten, and put them in my pocket, then put my hand back in my pocket, my chances of pulling out the number one penny would be one in ten. If I place the number one penny back in my pocket and mix all the pennies again, the chances of pulling out penny number two would be one in a hundred. The chances of repeating the same procedure and coming up with penny number three would be one in a thousand. To do so with all of them (one through ten in order) would be one in ten billion! Noting the order and design of our universe, Johannes Kepler — the founder of modern astronomy, discoverer of the "Three Planetary Laws of Motion," and originator of the term *satellite* — said, "The undevout astronomer is mad."

The slant of the earth, tilted at an angle of 23°, gives us our seasons. If it was not tilted exactly at 23° we would not only lose our seasons but life itself — as the vapors from the ocean would move north and south, piling up continents of ice. If our moon were closer, our tides would daily inundate whole continents.

Charles Colson reported in his *BreakPoint Commentary* that in April 1999 astronomers at Harvard and San Francisco State University announced they had discovered evidence of three planets orbiting a nearby star, Upsilon Andromedae, some forty-four light years away. What they found countered previously held theories about planetary formation. The standard theory derived from our solar system is that the small dense planets like Mercury, Venus, Earth, and Mars are closest to the sun, and that the large gaseous planets like Jupiter, Saturn, Uranus, and Neptune are farthest away (the only exception is Pluto).

But this simply is not so with Upsilon Andromedae's massive close-in planets. "This will shake up the theory of planetary formation," said astronomer Geoffrey Marcy to the *Washington Post*. Astronomers are learning that our solar system is even more remarkable and unique than thought before. And there is more. In the past four years some twenty planets have been discovered outside our solar system, and half of them move in egg-shaped "killer orbits" that lead to cosmic collisions. But in respect to our solar system, Dr. Marcy says, "It's like a jewel. You've got circular orbits. They're all in the same plane. . . . It's perfect, you know. It's gorgeous. It's almost uncanny." Colson comments: "Dr. Marcy may not realize it, but his language echoes that of the great Isaac Newton more than 300 years ago. Newton likewise found our solar system beautiful, but he took that insight to its logical conclusion. 'This most beautiful system of the sun, planets, and comets,' he wrote, 'could only proceed from the counsel and dominion of an intelligent and powerful Being.'"[2]

Joseph Addison was right in Newton's day, and it is still true in ours:

> *The spacious firmament on high,*
> *With all the blue, ethereal sky,*
> *And spangled heavens, a shining frame,*
> *Their great Original proclaim!*
>
> JOSEPH ADDISON,
> "THE SPACIOUS FIRMAMENT ON HIGH"

God thought it and willed it, and it was! The stars were flung in their fleeing courses. The sun was set in its galaxy. The earth began to revolve around the sun — and the moon around the spinning earth — like a jeweled watch. As we saw before, this was Christ's handiwork. The constellations speed away because Christ tells them to. The earth and moon waltz because Christ commands them to. The natural laws work because Christ ordains it. The earth was filled with rotating light. "And there was evening and there was morning, the fourth day" (v. 19).

Day five. On day two God had divided the primeval waters by creating an expanse, which he called "Heaven" or "Sky," separating the waters above and below. Now on the corresponding day five he filled the waters and the skies with animate life.

And God said, "Let the waters swarm with swarms of living creatures, and let birds fly above the earth across the expanse of the heavens." So God created the great sea creatures and every living creature that moves, with which the waters swarm, according to their kinds, and every winged bird according to its kind. And God saw that it was good. And God blessed them, saying, "Be fruitful and multiply and fill the waters in the seas, and let birds multiply on the earth." And there was evening and there was morning, the fifth day. (vv. 20-23)

The seas literally swarmed with living things — the monsters of the deep. There were whales, sharks, leviathan (crocodiles); swordfish reigned amidst schools of tuna and dolphin and thousands of lesser colorful finned creatures — many unknown until the twentieth century. And above, an ornithologist's delight filled the skies — eagles, cormorants, ravens, gulls, geese, ducks, woodpeckers, finches, cardinals, indigo buntings. The skies and seas teemed with astonishing variety, all from the mind of God. The waving, undulating beauties seen first by the sea diver and the gliding, iridescent arrays of the heavens exist because of God's thought and at his pleasure — "And God saw that it was good."

As a result he blessed his new creatures and commanded them to increase and grow, infusing them with the ability to reproduce. And we, too, must celebrate his extravagant hand, as Hopkins did with this joyous poem:

> *Glory be to God for dappled things —*
> *For skies of couple-colour as a brindled cow;*
> *For rose-moles all in stipple upon trout that swim;*
> *Fresh-firecoal chestnut-falls; finches' wings;*
> *Landscape plotted and pieced — fold, fallow,*
> *   and plough;*
> *And all trades, their gear and tackle and trim.*
>
> *All things counter, original, spare, strange;*
> *Whatever is fickle, freckled (who knows how?)*
> *With swift, slow; sweet, sour; adazzle, dim;*
> *He fathers-forth whose beauty is past change:*
> *Praise Him.*
>
> GERARD MANLEY HOPKINS,
> PIED BEAUTY[3]

Day six. On day three God had caused the dry ground to appear and covered it with vegetation, and now on the corresponding day six he filled it with land creatures.

And God said, "Let the earth bring forth living creatures according to their kinds — livestock and creeping things and beasts of the earth according to their kinds." And it was so. And God made the beasts of the earth according to their kinds and the livestock according to their kinds, and everything that creeps on the ground according to its kind. And God saw that it was good. (vv. 24, 25)

The categories are generic and are meant to encompass every terrestrial beast. Livestock means domesticated animals, creatures that move along the ground signify all manner of small animals, and wild animals represent game.[4] *"All creatures great and small/The Lord God made them all."*

We must never forget that the mind of God created all of this. So when we contemplate the heavens, we learn something of God. "Day to day pours out speech, and night to night reveals knowledge" (Psalm 19:2). Ride the Hubble telescope across the galaxies and learn something of him. Travel in the microscope into the complexity of the human cell and learn more. Go deeper into the atom and its quarks and leptons and learn more. Likewise, that which we touch, taste, and feel does the same. Remember William Blake's poem?

> *Tyger, Tyger, burning bright*
> *In the forests of the night,*
> *What immortal hand or eye*
> *Could frame thy fearful symmetry?*
>
> *In what distant deeps or skies*
> *Burnt the fire of thine eyes?*
> *On what wings dare he aspire?*
> *What the hand dare seize the fire?*[5]

We must never stop our mind at what we see. We must think on to the Immortal Hand and Eye that made it all and "saw that it was good." Certainly we must never worship nature as the pantheists do, but we worship the Creator of the material universe. He called his handiwork "good," and thus it represents his thought — so varied and beautiful and joyous. The God who created all this did it to form an environment for man. And as his children we must understand that it hints at the depth of his care for us.

God had formed the world in three days, and now in three parallel days he had wonderfully filled it with the light of the sun and moon and stars and trees and plants and creatures of the deep and the winged creatures of the sky and a zoo of wondrous earth-treading beasts. Creation was full and ready for its ultimate fullness with the creation of man. Here the narrative slows down during the sixth day (like slow motion), because it is here with the creation of man that we come to the apex of the narrative.

FILLING THE EARTH WITH MAN

The specialness of this section is immediately apparent because in verse 26 the narrative changes from the third person to the first person plural — "Then God said, 'Let us . . .'" — which indicates divine dialogue. Some have tried to sidestep this by seeing it as a conversation with the angels. But that is impossible because angels are not in the image of God. Besides, angels can add nothing to God's omniscient wisdom. Others have attempted to prove it is a plural of majesty such as was used by ancient potentates. But this idea is flawed because the point of the verse is not God's majesty.

In truth it is the plural of deliberation, here divine deliberation. Henri Blocher explains: "God addresses himself, but this he can do only because he has a Spirit who is both with him and distinct from him at the same time. Here are the first glimmerings of a Trinitarian revelation."[6] The reference to "the Spirit of God" in 1:2, hovering over the waters, demonstrates a co-participant in creation. And the New Testament gives the full meaning (the *sensus plenior*) when it teaches the radical involvement of Christ in creation (cf. John 1:1-3; 1 Corinthians 8:6; Colossians 1:15-18; Hebrews 1:1-3; Revelation 4:11).

So now we see that an awesome declaration about man is made by God in consultation with himself (Father, Son, and Holy Spirit):

> *Then God said, "Let us make man in our image, after our likeness. And let them have dominion over the fish of the sea and over the birds of the heavens and over the livestock and over all the earth and over every creeping thing that creeps on the earth."*

> > *So God created man in his own image,*
> > *in the image of God he created him;*
> > *male and female he created them. (vv. 26, 27)*

Verse 27 is the first poetry in the Bible, consisting of three lines, each with four stresses and three repetitions of the verb *bara* ("created").[7] This is the high point toward which God's creativity from the opening verse is directed.[8] So consider this: Though you could travel a hundred times the speed of light, past countless yellow-orange stars, to the edge of the galaxy and swoop down to the fiery glow located a few hundred light-years below the plane of the Milky Way, though you could slow to examine the host of hot young stars luminous among the gas and dust, though you could observe, close-up, the protostars poised to burst forth from their dusty cocoons, though you could witness a star's birth, in all your stellar journeys you would never see anything equal to the birth and wonder of a human being. For a tiny baby girl or boy is the apex of God's creation! But the greatest wonder of all is that the child is created in the image of God, the *Imago Dei*. The child once was not; now, as a created soul, he or she is eternal. He or she will exist forever. When the stars of the universe fade away, that soul shall still live.

How are we in God's image? Certainly the church fathers and Reformers were correct in viewing the image of God in us as essentially spiritual, though some Reformers erred in supposing that it was completely destroyed in the fall. What was destroyed in the fall was man's original righteousness. That part of the image of God was eradicated. Nevertheless, even after the corruption of the world and the flood's judgment, man was regarded as in God's image.

The post-flood prohibition of murder was based on the fact that man is in the image of God (cf. Genesis 9:6). The Apostle James also understood that sinners still bear the image of God: "With [the tongue] we bless our Lord and Father, and with it we curse people who are made in the likeness of God" (James 3:9).

The image of God still persists in sinful men and women, though marred and sometimes even a caricature — and a witness against itself.[9] Nevertheless, the image of God that we all bear is wondrous and holds eternal potential.

Hearers. Significantly, immediately after God had created man and woman in his image, he spoke to them: "And God blessed them. And God said to them . . ." (v. 28). This means that as image-bearers we can hear and receive God's word. No other creature can do that. This also means that we are responsible, moral, spiritual beings. The continental divide is the question of God's grace. If by his grace we respond, we can live in accord with his word. By his grace we can live nuanced lives of the deepest morality. His grace can enable us to hold forth his word. And we can live with him eternally.

Rulers. It is also most significant that God calls his image-bearers to rule over the earth in verses 26 and 28. God views his image-bearers as royal figures, his vicegerents over creation. This is what astonished the psalmist in Psalm 8:

> *When I look at your heavens, the work of your fingers,*
> *the moon and the stars, which you have set in place,*
> *what is man that you are mindful of him,*
> *and the son of man that you care for him?*
> *Yet you have made him a little lower than the heavenly beings*
> *and crowned him with glory and honor.*
> *You have given him dominion over the works of your hands;*
> *you have put all things under his feet. (vv. 3-6)*

There is vast dignity attached to being made in God's image, though marred by the fall.

Sons. Elsewhere in Genesis we see more about the image of God that distinguishes human life — namely, that it suggests sonship for both men and women. In Genesis 5:3 we read that Adam fathered a "son" in his own "likeness" and "image." Although biological descent was in view, the passage also links image with sonship. This idea is picked up in Luke's Gospel, which calls Adam "the son of God" (3:38). Being in God's image indicates God's paternity and a filial relationship.[10]

So with these realities about the *Imago Dei* the spiritual potential of humanity is immense. Image-bearers can hear God's word and ride it to untold spiritual heights. Image-bearers are innately regal beings meant to rule over all creation. Image-bearers are the created offspring of God, with real possibilities of eternal sonship.

We see man as the apex of a fully formed and filled creation made by God for him. Man and woman are glorious indeed. There they stood before the fall — vicegerents of creation in a state of spiritual, social, and ecological perfection. God had given every seed-bearing plant and fruit-bearing tree for food (cf. vv. 29, 30). They were at peace with God and nature. "And God saw everything that he had made, and behold, it was very good. And there was evening and there was morning, the sixth day" (v. 31).

But as we know, the fall did come. No category can adequately express the tragedy. Mankind remains in the image of God, but as a "grisly shadow of himself."[11]

Where is our hope? It is in Christ who is "the image of the invisible God, the firstborn of all creation" (Colossians 1:15). He is the exact image of God's being (cf. Hebrews 1:3). Jesus' incarnation resulted in a formal correspondence with the first Adam by virtue of his humanity. But Christ, the second Adam, did not sin. So he can make all those who are in him alive (cf. Romans 5:12ff.).

What awaits the Christian is the likeness (*eikon*, image) of Christ: "Just as we have borne the image of the man of dust, we shall also bear the image of the man of heaven" (1 Corinthians 15:49). The destiny of believers in Christ is to be in his image, and this includes everything that was suggested in our being created in God's image. We will rule in and with Jesus, whom the writer of Hebrews shows is the one who fulfilled Psalm 8: "But we see him who for a little while was made lower than the angels, namely Jesus, crowned with glory and honor because of the suffering of death, so that by the grace of God he might taste death for everyone" (2:9).

Again, all our hope rests on Jesus, the perfect bearer of the *Imago Dei*. Note well that Colossians 1:15 ("He is the image of the invisible God, the firstborn of all creation") is followed by verses 16-18, which depict him as the Creator, Sustainer, and Goal of the universe!

As he was the one who formed the universe, he can restore form to broken lives. And more, he who filled the earth with light, the seas with fish, the air with birds, and the land with its denizens specializes in giving his righteousness to sinful, vacuous humanity. He only has to say the word, and it is done.

Long ago Blaise Pascal (following Augustine) said that there is an abyss within fallen man that "can only be filled by an infinite and immutable object, which is to say only by God himself."[12] Do you know this vacuum? Is there emptiness within you — some uncomfortable space — due to your sin? *If so, all you have to do is come to him believing and say, "Here's my cup, Lord/fill it up, Lord" — and he will.*

Will you bring your emptiness to Christ? In that marvelous section in Colossians 1, verse 15 states that Christ is "the image of . . . God"; then verses 16-18 affirm that he is the Creator, Sustainer, and Goal of the universe; and finally, verse 19 includes that he is the Savior: "For in him all the fullness of God was pleased to dwell, and through him to reconcile to himself all things, whether on earth or in heaven, making peace by the blood of his cross" (vv. 19, 20). So Paul could say to believers, "For in him the whole fullness of deity dwells bodily, and you have been filled in him, who is the head of all rule and authority" (Colossians 2:9, 10).

Are you empty, in need of God's forgiveness and righteousness? Then come to him. His fullness will become yours with a "mere" word!

4

God Rests

GENESIS 2:1-3

The opening verse of chapter 2 should have been included at the end of chapter 1 because it completes the account of the six days of creation. Stephanus, the sixteenth-century printer-scholar who introduced the verse divisions of the Bible that we use today, simply blew it. He should have seen this because Genesis 2:1 is an echo of Genesis 1:1, which begins, "In the beginning, God created the heavens and the earth." And 2:1 concludes, "Thus the heavens and the earth were finished, and all the host of them." The echo is technically called an *inclusio*, which indicates the conclusion of the six days of creation. The story is that Stephanus made his verse divisions while riding horseback. So we must go easy on him.

Stephanus aside, the reading of 1:31 and 2:1 together express the contented satisfaction of God at the conclusion of day six: "And God saw everything that he had made, and behold, it was very good. And there was evening and there was morning, the sixth day. Thus the heavens and the earth were finished, and all the host of them." So we have here the complete picture of the heavens and the earth and all they contain in their harmonious perfection — *Rare Earth* as scientists are now calling it in the title of a best-selling book that argues that our position in the Milky Way, the juxtaposition and size of the planets in our solar system (especially Jupiter), the function of the Earth's moon, and numerous other factors make it likely that earth is the only place in the universe where there is life.[1]

However that may be, the first three days of forming creation and the concluding three days of filling it, capped by the creation of man, left creation lacking nothing. All that God had made was worthy of praise, and as such he gave it his highest commendation: "it was very good." The earth spun perfectly in its orbit around the sun in majestic twenty-four-hour rotation. The well-ordered planet swarmed with life under the joyous watch of the first couple.

GOD RESTS

God had formed and filled the earth, and now on the seventh day he rested: "And on the seventh day God finished his work that he had done, and he rested on the seventh day from all his work that he had done. So God blessed the seventh day and made it holy, because on it God rested from all his work that he had done in creation" (2:2, 3). This seventh day was significantly different from the first six days of creation, as Kenneth Mathews has so clearly noted: 1) There was no creation formula — "And God said" — because his creative word was not required. 2) The seventh day did not have the usual closing refrain — "and there was evening and there was morning" — to indicate the day's end. 3) The seventh day was the only day to be "blessed" and "made . . . holy" by God. 4) The seventh day stood outside the paired days of creation because there was no corresponding day to it in the preceding six. And 5) unlike the six creative days, the number of the day (the seventh day) is repeated three times.[2]

This is given dramatic significance because verses 2, 3 contain four lines, and the first three are parallel (each having seven words in the Hebrew), with the midpoint of each line being the phrase "the seventh day." Here's how the Hebrew word order has it:

> Line one: So God finished by *the seventh day* his work which he did,
> Line two: and he rested on *the seventh day* from all his work which he did,
> Line three: and God blessed *the seventh day* and sanctified it,
> Line four: because on it he rested from all his work that God created to do.[3]

The seventh day stands apart in solitary grandeur as the crown to the six days of creation. This indicates not only immense literary craft but deep theological significance. From the beginning of creation the seventh day was central, not only to creation, but to the ultimate destiny of God's people, as we shall see.

God rested. Verses 2 and 3 each state that God rested: Verse 2 says, "he rested . . . from all his work," and verse 3 adds, "[he] rested from all his work that he had done in creation." Why did God rest? Certainly not from fatigue. Omnipotence needs no rest because regardless of the amount of power that goes forth from him, his power is not depleted one whit. His omnipotent creating power is infinite. God did not need a breather. Actually the word "rest" means "to cease from."[4] God simply stopped his creating activity. In fact, though God rested (ceased his creating activity), he still worked. Jesus said exactly that when he healed a crippled man on the Sabbath: "My Father is working until now, and I am working" (John 5:17). God rested from creating but works in sustaining the world by his power, governing it by his providence, and insuring the propagation of its creatures. In fact, if he stopped working, everything would dissolve into nothing.

God's rest was one of deep pleasure and satisfaction at the fruit of his labor. This joyous rest of the Creator certainly extended to Adam and Eve in paradise as, in their state of innocence, they lived in blessed peace with their Creator. And this original rest was the beginning of a type of the rest that was lost at the fall but will be restored through redemption and its final consummation.[5]

God blessed. God took such pleasure in the seventh day that he blessed it — "So God blessed the seventh day" — which means that he made it spiritually fruitful. We know that the two preceding blessings in the creation account, first on living creatures and then on Adam and Eve, bestowed fertility because in both instances God said, "Be fruitful and multiply" (1:22, 28). The meaning here is essentially the same but in the spiritual realm. "God's blessing bestows on this special, holy, solemn day a power which makes it fruitful for human existence. The blessing gives the day, which is a day of rest, the power to stimulate, animate, enrich and give fullness to life."[6] The seventh day is one of perpetual spiritual spring — a day of multiplication and fruitfulness. This would become of great importance and benefit to God's people.

God made it holy. So God ceased from his creation labors on the seventh day, pronounced it "blessed" (spiritually life-giving), and then "made it holy." The seventh day was the first thing to be hallowed in Scripture. It was therefore elevated above the other days and set apart for God himself.

This blessed and holy day has no end. There is no morning and evening. It has existed from the completion of creation and still is. God still rests after the great event.

SABBATH REST

Generations later — following the fall, the flood, Babel, the lives of the patriarchs, the captivity in Egypt, and the exodus — the seventh day was given preeminence in Israel by becoming the text for the fourth commandment:

> *Remember the Sabbath day, to keep it holy. Six days you shall labor, and do all your work, but the seventh day is a Sabbath to the LORD your God. On it you shall not do any work, you, or your son, or your daughter, your male servant, or your female servant, or your livestock, or the sojourner*

who is within your gates. For in six days the LORD made heaven and earth, the sea, and all that is in them, and rested the seventh day. Therefore the LORD blessed the Sabbath day and made it holy. (Exodus 20:8-11)

The Sabbath day was to be one of complete rest, cessation from life's labors. Like God's rest, it was "blessed," and thus its observation by God's people was essential to their spiritual health and growth.

Creation celebrated. By keeping the Sabbath, God's people entered into the seven-day rhythm of work and joyful rest. The seventh day pointed the Hebrew worshiper to a day of rejoicing over the created work of God. Jewish theologian Abraham Heschel writes: "It is a day on which we are called upon to show what is eternal in time, to turn from the results of creation to the mystery of creation; from the world of creation to the creation of the world."[7] The Sabbath implicitly instructed all humanity that there is more to life than work. It afforded God's people the time to hear and meditate on God's Word, to contemplate eternal things, and to pray. Isaiah sang of it:

If you turn back your foot from the Sabbath, from doing your pleasure on my holy day, and call the Sabbath a delight and the holy day of the LORD honorable; if you honor it, not going your own ways, or seeking your own pleasure, or talking idly; then you shall take delight in the LORD, and I will make you ride on the heights of the earth; I will feed you with the heritage of Jacob your father, for the mouth of the LORD has spoken. (Isaiah 58:13, 14)

Salvation celebrated. The Sabbath was also a day to remember and celebrate redemption. In Deuteronomy's extended version of the Fourth Commandment, Moses adds, "You shall remember that you were a slave in the land of Egypt, and the LORD your God brought you out from there with a mighty hand and an outstretched arm. Therefore the LORD your God commanded you to keep the Sabbath day" (5:15). In Egypt Israel had been cruelly overworked, even forced to make bricks without straw. And Pharaoh only let them go when God wrought his mighty deliverance at the Passover. With their redemption from Egypt came the rest that had not been theirs for hundreds of years. So on the Sabbath, as they rested, they were to reflect on their miraculous redemption.

These two versions of the Fourth Commandment give the twofold meaning of the seventh day for Israel: 1) the celebration of God as Creator, and 2) the celebration of God as Redeemer.[8] The Sabbath's purpose was to grace God's people — to grace their bodies with the rest of the Genesis rhythm and to grace their souls with Heaven's rhythm, providing Israel with respite from their labors so they could focus on God and gratefully celebrate him as their Creator and Redeemer.

Covenant sign. The Sabbath and its ritual observance became the pre-eminent sign of God's covenant with Israel.[9] After the tabernacle was built, the Sabbath was regarded as the sign of the covenant between God and his people: "And the LORD said to Moses, 'You are to speak to the people of Israel and say, "Above all you shall keep my Sabbaths, for this is a sign between me and you throughout your generations, that you may know that I, the LORD, sanctify you"'" (Exodus 31:12, 13). And again, "The people of Israel shall keep the Sabbath, observing the Sabbath throughout their generations, as a covenant forever. It is a sign forever between me and the people of Israel" (31:16, 17a).

No other people had the Sabbath. None but Israel had this blessed law, enforced by the gracious threat of death should one fail to keep it. God meant them to be his people. So the Sabbath persisted through the centuries as a covenantal sign and grace for God's people.

And what a grace it was. The compulsory rest of the Sabbath gave God's people time to reflect on eternal things. Indeed, life was more than work. On that day their minds were drawn to the initial rest of God after the creation. As they gazed up to the stars, they saw "his invisible attributes, namely, his eternal power and divine nature" (Romans 1:20). As they rested they were also reminded that the Creator had redeemed them forever from slavery. They sometimes sang the song of Moses and Miriam, which catalogs their multiple deliverances (cf. Exodus 15). The Sabbath thus afforded them time to celebrate and worship God as Creator and Redeemer. The quietness of the Sabbath allowed them time to reflect on the Law. Its statutes became their delight and their counselors (cf. Psalm 119:24). The Sabbath was indeed a grace and a preeminent sign of the covenant.

CHRIST'S REST

With the coming of Israel's long-awaited Messiah, Jesus, the Creator-Redeemer completed his work of redemption on the cross and cried out, "It is finished" (John 19:30). It was only then that Jesus rested from his great work. His work on the cross *created* salvation and the possibility of entering his rest.

Present rest. Since the "seventh day" has no closing refrain — no "And there was evening and there was morning" — the seventh day has no end and is eternal. And this Sabbath rest is taken up in the New Testament and interpreted in the context of Jesus as one greater than Moses. The writer of Hebrews therefore speaks of "a Sabbath-rest for the people of God," using Israel's history to demonstrate that the rest can only be entered by faith (4:9; cf. vv. 1-11). And he warns, "For good news came to us just as to them, but the message they heard did not benefit them, because they were not united by faith with those who listened" (v. 2).

Mere intellectual belief will not bring rest to any soul. Acknowledging that Jesus Christ is the Son of God and Savior of the world will not bring rest. Trust in him is what gives rest to our souls. True faith is belief plus trust. When you truly trust in Christ as Savior, rest comes because the burden of your sins is lifted. You rest from your works. And because you are in Christ, you enter the Sabbath rest of God. You know that he is your Creator and Redeemer.

Everyone who has truly come to Christ has experienced that rest. All the impossible striving to gain salvation was then over. You rested in Christ, not in yourself. The burden of guilt was lifted. Your soul was light with rest.

And now as a believer the principle is: the more trust, the more rest. Our belief or unbelief makes all the difference. Few have lived as stressful a life as Hudson Taylor, founder of China Inland Mission. But Taylor lived in God's rest, as his son so beautifully attests:

> Day and night this was his secret, "just to roll the burden on the Lord." Frequently those who were wakeful in the little house at Chinkiang might hear, at two or three in the morning, the soft refrain of Mr. Taylor's favorite hymn ["Jesus, I Am Resting, Resting"]. He had learned that for him, only one life was possible — just that blessed life of resting and rejoicing in the Lord under all circumstances, while He dealt with the difficulties, inward and outward, great and small.[10]

It is possible to live a life as harried and busy as Hudson Taylor and yet be resting. Resting is trusting. Believer, you can have perpetual rest by resting in him.

The rest that the Scriptures offer is the rest that God entered when he finished creating the universe. The fact that in Genesis 2:2 there is no morning or evening means that the seventh day continues even now. God's rest began with the completion of the cosmos and continues on and on — and therefore is available to all his children. The question is: Are you resting in the joy of what Christ is?

The character of God's rest is the ideal of all rests.

First, it is *joyous*. Job 38:7 tells us that at creation, "the morning stars sang together and all the sons of God shouted for joy." They were echoing the "very good" of the Creator. And they were, of course, voicing the joy that he carried into his Sabbath rest.

Second, his rest is *satisfying*. His eternal satisfaction is understood from his multiple assertions that creation was "good." When he smote his anvil the final time, sparking his final star a million million million light-years away, and put his final luminous touch on the firefly, he sat back in everlasting satisfaction.

Third, it is a *working* rest. God finished his great work and rested, but it was not a cessation from work. Rather it was a repose that came from completing a great work. God's repose is full of active toil. God rests, and in his rest he keeps working, even now.

Fellow Christians, God does not offer us just any rest. He offers us *his* rest — the repose of his soul — divine rest. It is cosmic in its origination, as old as creation. And as such, a continuing Sabbath is available to all. It is the ideal rest, for it comes from our perfect, almighty God.

There is a *now* and a *then* to our rest. *Now*, in Christ, we have entered and are entering our rest. Our experience of rest is proportionate to our trusting in him. A wholehearted trust brings his rest to our souls in all its divine, cosmic, and ideal dimensions, just as Hudson Taylor experienced.

But there is also a *future* rest in Heaven — the repose of soul in God's rest, forever *joyous*, forever *satisfied*, and forever *working*. "'Blessed are the dead who die in the Lord from now on.' 'Blessed indeed,' says the Spirit, 'that they may rest from their labors, for their deeds follow them!'" (Revelation 14:13).

Today Jesus — the Creator, Sustainer, and Goal of the universe, the Redeemer — says, "Come to me, all who labor and are heavy laden, and I will give you rest. Take my yoke upon you, and learn from me, for I am gentle and lowly in heart, and you will find rest for your souls. For my yoke is easy, and my burden is light" (Matthew 11:28-30).

> *Lord Sabaoth His name*
> *From age to age the same.*
> MARTIN LUTHER

St. Augustine said, "Our hearts are restless 'til they find their rest in Thee."[11] He knew from experience that life apart from Christ is striving, that men and women will remain restless regardless of what they attain or obtain in this world. You will never find rest apart from redemption in Christ.

But when you come to him in faith as your Creator and Redeemer, you find a Sabbath rest for your soul — his own rest that he has enjoyed from creation. This same Jesus said, "Whoever believes in me, as the Scripture has said, 'Out of his heart will flow rivers of living water'" (John 7:38). His Spirit will indwell you. You will find rest for your soul.

Will you come in faith, believing and trusting in him?

5

East, in Eden

GENESIS 2:4-17

Genesis 2:4 begins a new section of the primeval history of the world. The six days of forming and then filling the earth had left a dazzling, complete creation under the benign rule of Adam and Eve. Upon the seventh day (the number of perfection), "God rested from all his work that he had done in creation." And because there was no evening or morning that day, he still rests. Today his children partake of his "Sabbath rest" through faith (cf. Hebrews 4:1, 2, 9).

SOME INTRODUCTORY THOUGHTS

Yahweh-Elohim. Up to this point in the story, Moses has used only one designation for God, the name *Elohim*. And he has used it with studied care some thirty-five times (five times seven, the number of perfection). *Elohim* is the appropriate word for the majestic portrayal of God as Creator of the universe, signifying omnipotent deity. The thirty-five repeated use of this name is metered praise for the perfect creation of the perfect Creator.

But now at 2:4 (where chapter 2 should actually begin), the name for God switches to *Yahweh-Elohim*, "the LORD God" as our translations have it. *Yahweh-Elohim* is the dominant name from here to the end of chapter 4, which concludes this second section of the creation account. The reason for this is that *Yahweh* is the personal covenant name of God who relates to and redeems his people (cf. 15:7 and Exodus 3:14, 15). Significantly, the only place in chapters 2 — 4 that it is not used is 3:2-5, when the serpent and Eve consciously avoid the personal name of God as she is lured toward sin. Gordon Wenham, the eminent Genesis commentator, remarks, "The god they are talking about is malevolent, secretive, and concerned to restrict man:

his character is so different from that of Yahweh Elohim that the narrative pointedly avoids the name in the dialogue."[1]

Beautifully, *Yahweh-Elohim* combines the Creator and Covenant-Redeemer aspects of God into one magnificent name. Here, in the immediate context of the Sabbath, which for Israel became a day to celebrate God as Creator (cf. Exodus 20:11) and as Redeemer (cf. Deuteronomy 5:15), the name *Yahweh-Elohim* — "the LORD God" — proclaims both these realities. So for our own hearts, we must remember that whenever we come across the title "the LORD God" in Scripture, it signifies God our Creator and our Covenant-Redeemer. How utterly beautiful "the LORD God" is!

The appropriateness of this name to this section is everywhere apparent, because Genesis 2 — 4 focuses on man and woman's relationship with God. We see it immediately in 2:4-17, which deals with *man's nature, position,* and *responsibility* to God in creation.

Toledot. Another reason chapter 2 ought to begin at 2:4 is the telltale phrase "These are the generations [Hebrew, *toledot*] of the heavens and the earth," which is used ten times in Genesis to introduce major divisions (cf. 2:4; 5:1; 6:9; 10:1; 11:10, 27; 25:12, 19; 36:1 and 9 repeated for emphasis; and 37:2). "These are the generations" followed by the duplication here of the phrase from 1:1 ("the heavens and the earth") informs us that we are about to read another narrative about creation. It is not a second creation account because it centers on a localized scene, moving from the cosmos to "a garden in Eden, in the east" (v. 8). Everything here happens in Eden.

We must also note that verse 4 is a unit and must not be divided. The verse is written in Hebrew chiastic parallelism (ABBA) which forbids separation:

> A *the heavens and the earth*
> B *when they were created (bara)*
> B' *when the LORD God made (asa)*
> A' *the earth and the heavens.*[2]

Verse 4 is an independent sentence, just like 1:1. Verses 5, 6 then describe the condition of the land when God formed the man (2:7).[3]

The earth. Verses 5, 6 describe the *untended* condition of the earth prior to man's creation, "when no bush of the field was yet in the land and no small plant of the field had yet sprung up — for the LORD God had not caused it to rain on the land, and there was no man to work the ground, and a mist was going up from the land and was watering the whole face of the ground." The ESV's marginal reading, "spring" is to be preferred over "mist" and is the rendering of the ancient Septuagint and Vulgate as well as most modern translations.[4] Thus the picture here is of subterranean springs rising up from the ground and watering the arid earth.

The noes in these verses tell us why the earth was untended: There was "no bush" — "no small plant" — no "rain" — and "no man to work the ground." Significantly, day three of creation, which described the earth's production of vegetation, did not include the Hebrew words for "bush" and "small plant." This is because, as Cassuto explains, "These species did not exist, or were not found in the form known to us, until after Adam's transgression, and it was in consequence of his fall that they came into the world or received their present form."[5] Thus bushes and small plants are post-fall phenomena that occurred when Adam began to tend the earth. Indeed, after the fall of Adam, the Lord told Adam regarding the land, "thorns and thistles it shall bring forth for you; and you shall eat the plants of the field" (3:18). "The plants of the field" were those that would grow under Adam's cultivation. And the bushes? Cassuto equates them with weeds and explains again: "In areas, however, that were not tilled, the earth brought forth of its own accord, as a punishment to man, *thorns* and *thistles* — that . . . *siah of the field* that we see growing profusely to this day in the land of Israel *after the rains.*"[6]

The absence of rain is accounted for in verse 6: "and a mist [read "streams"] was going up from the land and was watering the whole face of the ground." The mention of streams watering the earth is likely a reference to recurrent flooding of the Tigris and Euphrates. Without man to irrigate the land, the rising streams were useless.[7] All this — the lack of rain and shrubs and plants — points to the untended condition of the earth.

Thus the essential missing element was man. The untended creation needed man to rule and subdue it.

MAN'S NATURE (v. 7)

Whereas the initial description of man's creation is poetry in 1:27 — "So God created man in his own image, / in the image of God he created him; / male and female he created them" — the account in chapter 2 is equally powerful prose.[8] "The LORD God formed the man of dust from the ground and breathed into his nostrils the breath of life, and the man became a living creature" (v. 7).

Adam: God-formed. "The LORD God formed the man of dust from the ground." The term "formed" indicates that the act of creation was by careful design. The same Hebrew word is used later in Genesis to indicate the "intention" of the thoughts of our heart (6:5). Here it conveys divine intentionality.[9] God is the potter, so to speak, who perfectly works out his designs. Man is no afterthought, but rather the intentional product of the infinite mind that designed the atom and the cosmos. Infinite intention was focused on the creation of man.

At the same time man is of the earth, "dust" in fact. This is emphasized by a beautiful play on words: "The LORD God formed the man [*ha adam*] of dust from the ground [*ha adama*]."[10] "The dust of earth" is in his very name. Calvin remarks here: "The body of Adam is formed of clay and destitute of sense; to the end that no one should exult beyond measure in his flesh. He must be excessively stupid who does not here learn humility."[11] Yes, Calvin! The truth is, though we are wonderfully conceived and formed by God, yet because of sin we will return to dust.

> *By the sweat of your face*
> *you shall eat bread,*
> *till you return to the ground,*
> *for out of it you were taken;*
> *for you are dust,*
> *and to dust you shall return. (3:19; cf. Job 34:15).*

Adam: God-breathed. ". . . and breathed into his nostrils the breath of life." There is such intimacy here, as Kidner memorably explains: "*Breathed is warmly personal, with the face-to-face intimacy of a kiss and the significance that this was an act of giving as well as making; and self-giving at that.*"[12] Furthermore, "breathed" (literally, "blew") suggests a good puff, as one that would revive a fire (cf. Isaiah 54:16; Haggai 1:9).[13] It is very much like what happened in Ezekiel's vision of the dry bones when the reconstructed skeletons of the slain were brought to life by the inbreathing of the Spirit:

> *"Prophesy to the breath; prophesy, son of man, and say to the breath, Thus says the Lord GOD: Come from the four winds, O breath, and breathe on these slain, that they may live." So I prophesied as he commanded me, and the breath came into them, and they lived and stood on their feet, an exceedingly great army. (Ezekiel 37:9, 10)*

Here the metaphor of shared "breath" suggests a correspondence between Adam and his Maker that was expressed in Genesis 1:27 in the language of "image." This man of dust is in the image of God! Only he of all creation can hear the word of God. Under God, he is to rule creation itself.

Adam: a living being. ". . . and the man became a living creature." Like the animals, he is a "living creature" (*nepesh hayya*), the same term used to describe the living creatures in 1:20, 24. He is of a similar makeup and draws his breath and life the same way. But God breathed life into him, making him unlike the animals. Man is immortal. He has immense capacities. He is responsible. And as such he has great potential for glory — and for disaster!

MAN'S POSITION (vv. 8-14)

In Eden. God positioned Adam in Eden: "And the LORD God planted a garden in Eden, in the east, and there he put the man whom he had formed" (v. 8). The designation "in Eden, in the east" is from the perspective of Moses, in the Sinai. So the garden was most probably in the area of Mesopotamia in modern Iraq. Eden, then, would be a geographical area in which the garden was placed. Eden itself was not the garden.

Verses 10-14 contain a digression about the garden that seems very clear in what it says but is nearly impossible to make any sense of. What is clear according to verse 10 is that a river rose from a subterranean source, perhaps as already described — "a mist [or river] was going up from the land" (v. 6). Eden's abundant river then watered the garden and flowed out and then separated into the headwaters of four rivers: the Pishon, the Gihon, the Tigris, and the Euphrates.

Here is the insoluble problem: While the Tigris and Euphrates are identifiable with rivers today, the Pishon and Gihon are totally unknown. Efforts to equate them with other rivers in the area fail, and identifying them with man-made canals in the area is impossibly anachronistic.

The mystery of the garden has invited incredible fancies. When Christopher Columbus passed the mouth of the Orinoco River in South America, he surmised that its waters came down from the garden of Eden. Of course, he thought he was on the east coast of Asia.[14]

Nineteenth-century author W. F. Warren outdid everyone by locating Eden at the North Pole! He contended, "In northern Greenland and in Spitsbergen abundant remains of fossil plants show that during the middle of the Tertiary period the whole circumpolar region manifested a climate similar to that occurring at present in southern Europe."[15]

But the most exotic assertion came from the great British General Charles George Gordon, who fought in the Crimean War and then in China where his exploits earned him the popular title "Chinese Gordon." Later he served as governor of Sudan, and he died defending Khartoum in 1885. Gordon was also a devout student of the Bible. His answer? The Garden of Eden was located on one of the one hundred beautiful islands in the Indian Ocean that make up the Seychelles. Specifically, he pinpointed the location of the garden in the valley of Mai on Praslin Island. As one British officer quipped, "Whether Chinese Gordon was right or wrong, you must admit that Eden should have been there."[16]

Responsible guessers place it in Mesopotamia near the head of the Persian Gulf.[17] But it was so long ago, we cannot be sure. We must allow for topographical change like what might have come from the great flood.

In paradise. What is sure is that "in Eden, in the east," Adam was in paradise! The presence of a great river flowing from Eden is indicative of the life-giving presence of God (cf. Psalm 46:4 and Ezekiel 47:1-12). Later in Genesis it is called "the garden of the LORD" (13:10). God's presence was concomitant with the garden.

The common Hebrew meaning of Eden is "delight," and "the sound play of 'Eden' suggests even by its name that the garden was luxuriant."[18] Verdant, luscious trees were the signature of the garden. "And out of the ground the LORD God made to spring up every tree that is pleasant to the sight and good for food" (v. 9a). Such extravagance for the eye and for the body.

Naked Adam lacked nothing. He was made in the image of God. God had kissed life into him. He was perfect. He was the human sovereign of creation. He had the blessing of God and the unparalleled presence of God. Adam "speaks and walks with God as if they belong to one another," writes Bonhoeffer.[19] Paradise it was.

MAN'S RESPONSIBILITY (vv. 9b, 15-17)

His incredible position did bring with it singular responsibility.

The two trees. The last half of verse 9 introduces this: "The tree of life was in the midst of the garden, and the tree of the knowledge of good and evil." The two trees stood side by side in the very center of the garden. And through those two trees the destiny of man would be decided.

Life was at the center of the garden, and eating fruit from "the tree of life" would result in continued life. After the fall Adam was excluded from the garden "lest he reach out his hand and take also of the tree of life and eat, and live forever" (3:22b). But at the consummation the tree will appear again: "To the one who conquers I will grant to eat of the tree of life, which is in the paradise of God" (Revelation 2:7; cf. 22:2, 14, 19). The tree of life gives life — and grows in eternity. Adam was not tempted to partake of the tree of life because he had life.

The commandment. Adam's responsibility was made clear by the commandment of God himself: "The LORD God took the man and put him in the garden of Eden to work it and keep it. And the LORD God commanded the man, saying, 'You may surely eat of every tree of the garden, but of the tree of the knowledge of good and evil you shall not eat, for in the day that you eat of it you shall surely die'" (vv. 15-17). The verb "put," which describes God's placing Adam in the garden, carries the nuance of rest and suggests a connection to God's Sabbath rest.[20] His tending the garden and caring for it was an act of rest.

God's word to him was first *permissive*: "And the LORD God commanded the man, saying, 'You may surely eat of every tree of the garden'" (v. 16). Adam was to partake of everything in the garden to his heart's content, which included the tree of life. This is lavish, extravagant abundance, and Adam could take from the tree of life if he wanted it. Everything was there for him — everything he could possibly want.

But God's permission was paired with his *prohibition*: "but of the tree of the knowledge of good and evil you shall not eat, for in the day that you eat of it you shall surely die" (v. 17). To disobey and eat from this tree would bring sure death.

Here we must note that this passage does not suggest that Adam was immortal and that, had he not sinned, he would live forever in the garden. There is a difference between man's creation when he received life by God's inbreathing (2:7) and the perpetuation of that life by appropriating from the tree of life (cf. 3:22). Adam was not intrinsically immortal. Only God is immortal (1 Timothy 6:16). John Calvin explains this, saying of Adam, "His earthly life truly would have been temporal; yet he would have passed into heaven without death, and without injury."[21] Perhaps the translation of Enoch, who "was taken up so that he should not see death" (Hebrews 11:5), shows what God would have done with Adam.

So what was the temptation for Adam in light of the "every tree" abundance of the garden and the "surely die" threat of the forbidden tree? Simply this: The temptation to eat from "the tree of the knowledge of good and evil" was to seek wisdom without reference to the word of God. It was an act of *moral autonomy* — deciding what is right without reference to God's revealed will. This is confirmed by Ezekiel 28 (the closest parallel to Genesis 2 — 3), which tells how the King of Tyre was expelled from Eden for his pride and for claiming that his heart was "like the heart of a god" (cf. 28:6, 15-17).[22] Adam and Eve desired wisdom, but they sought it outside of the word and will of God. They usurped God's role in determining what is right and wrong. So here we get to the very heart of original sin. It was to sidestep God and his word and will in order to become wise. Moral autonomy brings death. "I did it my way" is an autonomous dirge of death.

In contrast Jesus, the second Adam, lived by "by every word that comes from the mouth of God." Jesus lived every second of his life in radical dependence on God's word (cf. Matthew 4:4). He believed the bare word of God. But the first Adam decided to be autonomous, to willfully disregard God's revealed will and seek wisdom on his own. And Adam did obtain "the knowledge of good and evil," but it killed him — because he got his wisdom his way.

And so it is with us. What we do with the word of God is everything. Imagine for a moment you do not know how this is going to end. Adam has the whole garden before him. He could have partaken of the tree of life and all that it promised! But he decided to seek wisdom from the tree of knowledge, apart from God's word and God's will. And in doing so he died.

And that is the great temptation for all of us today — to establish our wisdom apart from God's word. This is intensified by postmodernism, which centers authority in the autonomous self. As fallen men and women, our only hope is to trust in the bare word of God.

And the choice remains — the tree of life or the tree of knowledge of good and evil. We know how the story ends. But the great question is, how does *our* story end?

Man does not live by bread alone, but by every word that proceeds from the mouth of God (Deuteronomy 8:3; Matthew 4:4). Let us believe the bare word of God.

6

Man and Woman

GENESIS 2:18-25

I have committed a line from the *Merchant of Venice* to memory because it expresses my regard for my wife.

> *For she is wise, if I can judge of her,*
> *And fair she is, if that mine eyes be true,*
> *And true she is, as she hath prov'd herself,*
> *And therefore, like herself, wise, fair, and true,*
> *Shall she be placed in my constant soul.*
> —II.VI

Not only does this express my esteem for her — it also expresses my resolve to place her at the heart of my life — in "my constant soul" — as my Eve, my one flesh, consonant with the Genesis pattern for man and woman.

This text, which recounts the divine provision of a helper for Adam and of the two becoming "one flesh," is the deep well from which is drawn all biblical teaching on the covenant of marriage. As with everything else thus far in Genesis, all of it is from God. Divine initiative is at the root of everything, as we see in the God-initiated verbs: "The LORD God *said*" (v. 18), "the LORD God *formed*" (v. 19), "the LORD God *caused*" (v. 21), and "the LORD God . . . *made*" (v. 22, emphasis added throughout). In each case the Lord God, *Yahweh-Elohim*, the Creator, the covenant-making God, takes the initiative to shape man and woman and their relationship. Everything here is directly from him. The instruction here is primary and vital to all human existence.

MAN NEEDS WOMAN (ADAM'S NEED) (vv. 18-20)

The six joyous refrains ("And God saw that it was good"), capped by the satisfied perfection of the seventh refrain ("and it was very good"), leaves the first-time reader unprepared for the "not good" of this section: "Then the LORD God said, 'It is not good that the man should be alone'" (v. 18a). This startles us. Professor Cassuto points out that "not good" here is strong language. It indicates not only the absence of something good but a substantial deficiency.[1]

The observation and declaration of Adam's need is all God's. God did not consult Adam. Indeed, Adam may not have had any idea that it was "not good" for him to be alone. He may not even have known that he was alone! Remember, he was in Eden with every bountiful provision his heart could desire, including a whole zoo of pets that adored him as their ruler. God was not responding to a complaint by Adam. "Not good" was God's sovereign, unilateral assessment. Perhaps since God is a plurality and Adam was created in his image, the image demanded plurality (cf. 1:27).[2]

God's resolve. Whatever the exact reasons for man's aloneness being "not good," God's sovereign, unilateral resolve was unequivocal: "I will make him a helper fit for him" (v. 18b). Lest any imagine that "helper" is a diminishing or servile term, it must be understood that it is the name used to describe God as the helper of Israel (cf. Exodus 18:4; Deuteronomy 33:7; 1 Samuel 7:12). Often "helper" was used to reference God's aid against Israel's enemies (cf. Psalm 20:2; 121:1, 2; 124:8). Moses referred to God as his "helper" who delivered him from Pharaoh (cf. Exodus 18:4). So man's "helper" would be no "weak sister" by any stretch of a misogynist's imagination.

The function of the helper would be complementary to the man's — "a helper fit for him" — literally, "like opposite him"[3] or "according to his opposite."[4] The woman would be a corresponding counterpart. As a counterpart she would share in his nature. Male and female were created in the image of God (cf. 1:27). And as his matching opposite, she would supply what was lacking in him.

So God declared that help was on the way from one who would be both like and unlike the man — one whose corresponding differences would make man complete for what God intended him to do. This is why the Apostle Paul would say that the man was not made for the woman "but woman for man" (1 Corinthians 11:9). The woman would make it possible for man to do what he could never do alone. And likewise for the woman.[5] Something "very good" would fill man's aloneness.

Adam's awareness. To prepare the needy bachelor, God initiated an awareness program.

So out of the ground the LORD God formed every beast of the field and every bird of the heavens and brought them to the man to see what he would call them. And whatever the man called every living creature, that was its name. The man gave names to all livestock and to the birds of the heavens and to every beast of the field. But for Adam there was not found a helper fit for him. (vv. 19, 20)

The considerable menagerie was likely drawn from Eden rather than from the entire earth. Even so, the process would have been daunting. And whereas before God had been the namer of creation, conferring the names "Day" and "Night" and "Earth" as an indication of his sovereignty over creation, now Adam performed the sovereign naming function.

The process challenged Adam's intellectual capacities. Naming demanded acquaintance and understanding of the animals. It was not a whimsical process of reviewing a ten-mile pet parade and saying, "Um, let's see . . . I've got it! Aardvark! Ah . . . Chimpanzee. Oh yes, Zebra. There, you're Pelican. I like that."

> *A wonderful bird is the Pelican,*
> *His bill will hold more than his belican.*
> —DIXON LANIER MERRITT

No, Adam wasn't Dr. Doolittle on amphetamines. The classic work of Keil and Delitzsch points out that we must not regard the names that Adam gave the animals as merely denoting their outward characteristics, "but as a deep and direct insight into the nature of the animals,"[6] which penetrated far deeper than knowledge that comes from simple reflection.

As Adam fulfilled his kingly responsibility of interpreting the animals for what they were and giving them appropriate names, his differentiating power became acute. He saw there was none that corresponded to him. In the process he also realized that many of the animals had a social companionship that he lacked. So Adam began to long for companionship with a being like himself. It is reasonable to surmise that the man began to ache for a corresponding other. God was preparing him to value his helper.

GOD MAKES WOMAN (GOD'S SUPPLY) (vv. 21-23)

Woman created. Adam was ready. The five short clauses of verses 21, 22 describe *Yahweh-Elohim's* work: "So the LORD God caused a deep sleep to fall upon the man, and while he slept took one of his ribs and closed up its place with flesh. And the rib that the LORD God had taken from the man he made into a woman and brought her to the man." A deep or heavy sleep like that of Adam is often divinely induced in Scripture. Such was Abraham's slumber when God made the Abrahamic covenant, passing between the pieces of the sacrifice as "a smoking firepot and a flaming torch" (Genesis

15:12-19). Jonah apparently experienced a similarly induced sleep (cf. Jonah 1:1-5). Von Rad gives the implications: "God's miraculous creating permits no watching. Man cannot perceive God 'in the act,' cannot observe his miracles in their genesis; he can revere God's creative activity only as an actually accomplished fact."[7]

The rib is not metaphorical as some have suggested[8] but actual — and for immense theological reasons, as we shall see. As to whether the rib refers to the side (as it does in other Scriptures) or a specific rib is open to debate. But "rib" seems correct here because the Scripture clearly states that God took "one of his ribs," whereas one of his sides does not make sense. The language pictures a long, curved, glistening rib still moist with Adam's fluids and warm with his marrow. And no, men do not have one less rib than women. When God closed Adam back up, he was missing a rib, but his children can "count 'em all."

The significances of this are several and profound. Adam was not created *ex nihilo* (out of nothing) but out of the dust of the earth, and neither was Eve made *ex nihilo*. "The rib that the LORD God had taken from the man he made [literally, "built"] into a woman" (v. 22a.). She was made of the same stuff as the man — the same bone, the same flesh, the same DNA. Her correspondence in form, her femaleness, her estrogens were shaped and constituted from the man. Eve was the first person to be created from a living being. Because she came from Adam, she perfectly shared the image of God. Their mutual flesh lies behind 1:27: "So God created man in his own image, in the image of God he created him; male and female he created them."

The woman's creation out of Adam is the basis for her equality. As the Puritan Matthew Henry quaintly coined it: "not made out of his head to top him, not out of his feet to be trampled upon by him, but out of his side to be equal with him, under his arm to be protected, and near his heart to be beloved."[9] So here it is: Eve was taken out of Adam so that he might embrace with great love a part of himself.

The fifth clause, which is the last line of verse 22, completes the Lord God's work: He "brought her to the man." "God himself, like a father of the bride, leads the woman to the man" (Von Rad).[10]

The woman was stunning. She was the prototype of all women fresh from the well of creation. Every aspect of her was perfect. She was perfect in body and perfect in soul. She was perfectly sinless. And as she stood on the arm (so to speak) of her Father God, she was there for Adam to see.

Adam's response. Remember now, Adam had been acquainted with his need. His powers of discernment had been elevated by his close evaluation of God's creatures. So Adam's response was a shout of ecstasy:

> *Then the man said,*
> *"This at last is bone of my bones*

> *and flesh of my flesh;*
> *she shall be called Woman,*
> *because she was taken out of Man." (v. 23)*

Adam's rapturous cries are the first human words quoted in the Bible.

This is also the first poetic couplet in God's Word (the first poem was in 1:27). Gordon Wenham points out that the five short lines of this poem employ the standard techniques of Hebrew poetry: "parallelism (lines 2-3; 4-5), assonance and word play (woman/man); chiasmus (ABC/C'B'A') and verbal repetition."[11]

The couplet has a pronounced rhythmic pattern. The first line consists (in Hebrew) of three parts with two stresses each:

> *Then the man said,*
> *"This at last is bone of my bones*
> *and flesh of my flesh."*

The second line has two parts of three stresses each:

> *She shall be called Woman,*
> *because she was taken out of Man.*

And more, the rhythm belongs to the very form of the cry. The first verse's two-beat rhythm comes from Adam's explosive surprise, while the second verse's three-beat rhythm gives the thought solemnity.[12]

Adam's explosive astonishment, "This at last is bone of my bones and flesh of my flesh," voiced the traditional kinship formula of Israel. Whereas English speaks of "blood" relationships, Hebrew speaks of "flesh and bone." He saw her as a mirror of himself, with some very agreeable differences! Calvin beautifully puts words into Adam's mouth: "Now at length I have obtained a suitable companion, who is part of the substance of my flesh, and in whom I behold, as it were, another self."[13] Such astonished ecstasy! He had found his companion and his longed-for love. He was no longer alone.

Because God had honed Adam's naming powers, the man spontaneously declared, "She shall be called Woman [*isha*], because she was taken out of Man [*ish*]." The sound play celebrates their relationship. Adam restated his own name imbedded in hers. Adam anticipated the deepest intimacy.

MARRIAGE ORDAINED (vv. 24, 25)

Adam's joyous shout echoes down to the present day, proclaiming the joy and intimacy of marriage. Here in the text Adam's voice subsides, and the voice of Moses concludes, "Therefore a man shall leave his father and his mother and hold fast to his wife, and they shall become one flesh" (v. 24). Moses' words were divine revelation, and Jesus himself would quote them as the very Word of God (cf. Matthew 19:5). These words, this Word of God, became the deep well for the Bible's teaching on marriage and family.

Leave. Neither before Moses nor after Moses was it ever the custom for a man to leave his father and mother when he took a wife. It just was not done. In fact, the custom was for a man to marry and remain in his father's household, as did Jacob's sons who remained with him though they founded their own families and fortunes. Rather, custom called for the wife to join the family of her husband. So Moses' declaration, "Therefore a man shall leave his father and his mother" must be understood *relatively* and as a prescription for the loyalty and intimacy that a man must give his wife — he must "leave" his family. The union with his wife is so profound that he leaves his family even though he remains with them. His first obligation and loyalties are to his wife.

So many marriages fail today at precisely this point: Husbands and wives fail to leave their parents. First loyalties are not established. The creation norm is ignored — and marriage perverted. Any man or woman who believes that first loyalties belong to their parents believes a perversion.

Cleave. The following requirement, "and hold fast to his wife" has been made much too tame in our translation. The exact sense is, "and sticks to his wife," even as Israel was repeatedly urged to stick to the Lord in covenantal relationship (cf. Deuteronomy 10:20; 11:22; 13:4).

The term "leave" ("stick") here indicates that marriage is to be viewed as a covenant.[14] Leaving and cleaving involves a public declaration in the sight of God. Marriage is not a private matter. It involves a declaration of intention and a reorganizing of relationship. The idea of a purely private marriage is a recent aberration spawned by the culture of individualism and the demise of community. Christian marriage calls for a public covenant before God, the church, the family, and the state.[15]

It is of utmost importance that we understand and hold before us that what is taught about man and woman and marriage here was given at and rooted in the very act of creation. The creation of Eve and the command to leave and cleave occurred on the sixth day as the culmination of the creation process. This is radically primary to creation and civilization. Jesus himself called on this passage to establish the fact that marriage is an ordinance of God,

> He answered, "Have you not read that he who created them from the beginning made them male and female, and said, 'Therefore a man shall leave his father and his mother and hold fast to his wife, and they shall become one flesh'? So they are no longer two but one flesh. What therefore God has joined together, let not man separate." (Matthew 19:4-6)

Likewise Paul made it foundational to marriage: "'Therefore a man shall leave his father and mother and hold fast to his wife, and the two shall become one flesh.' This mystery is profound, and I am saying that it refers to Christ and the church" (Ephesians 5:31, 32). Human marriage illustrates something of the union between Christ and his people. "One flesh" expresses deepest intimacy. Everything is shared. And this is so between Christ and the church. That is why a marriage that rises to the creational intention is so important. It is a human window into how Christ and his bride relate. This makes the quality of our marriages of great importance. To abuse marriage is to abuse Christ and the church!

Now the obvious thing must be stated: Monogamous heterosexual marriage was always viewed as the norm from the time of creation. The account is about Adam and Eve; there is no Adam and Steve! Legislators who would legitimize same-sex marriage, giving it the putative status of heterosexual marriage, are attacking a creation ordinance and are reproaching God himself. What unmitigated Dante's terror awaits such presumption. God will not be mocked!

For Adam and Eve, sexuality and God were all a part of the same fabric. God defined humanity, sex, and love — and elevated them all. But this is not so in our reductionist age. Men and women have become sexual users and consumers rather than participants in a holy union with God at the center. Love without God has reduced love to an inner feeling. When love becomes a feeling, anything goes. Extramarital sex and multiple partners is the outcome — even same-sex marriages. And why not if our feelings are autonomous and imperial?

But how lovely it all is with God at the center and his primeval instruction the rule and guide. Adam and Eve were truly in paradise. Fellowship with God was as natural as breathing. They lived in one-flesh harmony. She was placed in his constant soul, and he in hers.

At the end of the sixth day *Yahweh-Elohim's* "not good" became "very good. And there was evening and there was morning, the sixth day" (1:31).

When God's word informs your life and love — when God is your center — it is very good.

7

Paradise Lost: The Fall

GENESIS 2:25 — 3:7

As we come to the third chapter of Genesis, Adam and Eve are living in unparalleled splendor amidst the crystal waters and green forests of Eden in delightful concert with each other and with the animals God had placed in the garden. The magnificent couple shared the same bones and same flesh in naked majesty. She was at once his daughter (she came out of him), his sister (she had the same Creator-Father), and his "one flesh" wife. Their one-flesh relationship reflected the eternal intimacy and order of the Holy Trinity and foreshadowed the intimacy and order of Christ and his bride, the church (cf. Ephesians 5:31, 32). Their intimacy was a substantial glory to God as a reflection of what always was and a glimpse of what was to come.

Adam's authority in the order of the husband-and-wife relationship was part of creation *before* sin and the fall entered the picture. This is evident because: 1) Adam was created first, a fact that Paul makes central in his argument for maintaining creation order in 1 Timothy 2:13 — "For Adam was formed first, then Eve."[1] 2) Eve was taken out of man, which Paul likewise notes in a similar argument in 1 Corinthians 11:8, 9 — "For man was not made from woman, but woman from man. Neither was man created for woman, but woman for man." 3) Eve was designated Adam's "helper" (2:18), whereas this could not be said of Adam. And 4) the authority structure of Genesis 2 — 3 rests on the careful order of God, the man, the woman, and the animal (serpent). This, of course, was tragically reversed by the fall, as Kenneth Mathews points out: "The woman listens to the serpent, the man listens to the woman, and no one listens to God."[2] This usurping of authority will be addressed immediately after the fall in God's successive judgment speeches to the serpent, to the woman, and to the man.

But now, before the fall, Adam and Eve have listened only to God. The sinless pair ride the pinnacle of innocence and openness. "And the man and his wife were both naked and were not ashamed" (2:25). They were spiritually naked before God. God came first in their love and in their thoughts, "and that without painful effort" (C. S. Lewis).[3] There was no need for disciplined devotion. All of life was devotion. Loving God was as natural as breathing, and as effortless!

Domestically, they were naked with one another. Clothing had never occurred to them. There was nothing to hide or protect. The gravitational pull of self did not exist. Neither one was the center of his or her own life. God and each other were their centers. They were, in today's parlance, "other-directed." All that they were was simply there for the other to see and love. Eve was placed in Adam's "constant soul" (*Merchant of Venice*), and he in hers. They were both naked in their environment — ecologically at home in the garden and with its denizens.

Here at the pinnacle in 2:25 we should note that 2:25 and 3:7 enclose a unit, because both focus on the couple's nakedness, but in radical contrast. Whereas 2:25 pictures Adam and Eve at the pinnacle of innocence and intimacy, 3:7 describes them in the pit of guilt and estrangement. This section describes the first couple's descent from innocence to guilt. It is real history.[4] But as primal history, it describes what has happened countless times down through the ages. It is universal. And wise people will listen well.

THE DIALOGUE OF DESCENT (vv. 1-5)

Verses 1-5 describe the dialogue that leads to the descent of Adam and Eve, and verses 6, 7 describe the couple's actual descent into the pit. The surprise here is that the initiator of the dialogue is a talking snake! And more, it is not a bad snake — because everything that God created he called "good." Neither is it a good snake gone bad. Sin had made no entrance into the world at this point. Its description as "crafty" (or "shrewd") does not imply evil. The word has the idea of being wary and of knowing when dangers lurk.[5] The Scriptures encourage the naive and simple to cultivate such an attitude (cf. Proverbs 1:4), but if it is misused it becomes guile (cf. Job 5:12; 15:5; Exodus 21:14; Joshua 9:4).[6]

This is a snake, a naturally shrewd creature, under the control of Satan — and a natural tool. The New Testament identifies this serpent as the devil, referring back to this scene in paradise (cf. Revelation 12:9; 20:2).[7] The snake's designation as "more crafty than any other beast of the field that the LORD God had made" may suggest that it was not a common part of the garden's pet population and may also explain why Eve was not put off by its talking.

God's word attacked. Did the snake suddenly drop from a tree *Tumbling in twenty rings/ Into the grass* (*Eve*, Ralph Hodgson)? Did the serpent extend itself upright so that it could address Eve forked tongue to tongue — "Good morning, fair lady. Mind if I recoil here awhile?" Did it hiss or lisp its words or speak with a voice like Eve's husband? We do not know. But we do know that through its voice Satan attacked God's word.

Here we must remember that God's word was responsible for everything Eve enjoyed — day and night, the sun and the moon, the dappled blue of the sky, the exotica of the garden, the flowers, the singing rainbows of birds, the adoring creatures, her Adam — all came from God's good word, which Satan now attacked. It would seem that Satan's attack would not have a chance. But appearances are sometimes deceiving.

The serpent's question. The serpent opened the dialogue with a surprised, incredulous tone. "He said to the woman, 'Did God actually say, "You shall not eat of any tree in the garden"?'" (v. 1b). Satan was so subtle. He did not directly deny God's word, but he introduced the assumption that God's word is subject to our judgment.[8] Such a thought had never been verbalized before. It was enticing.

The serpent also carefully avoided the use of God's covenant name, "the Lord" (*Yahweh*). In chapter 1 *Elohim* (signifying God as Creator) was used in every instance to refer to God, but in chapters 2 — 4 the title *Yahweh-Elohim* is everywhere employed (combining his Creator and Covenant-Redeemer names) — everywhere except here in the deadly dialogue of 3:1-5. Satan was careful not to mention God's personal covenant name but stuck to *Elohim*, the more remote designation. Ominously, Eve followed his lead as she too only used *Elohim* in their dialogue.

Satan's incredulous tone and conscious disuse of God's personal name set up his studied distortion of God's word. Whereas in 2:16 the Lord God had generously commanded, "You may surely eat of every tree of the garden," Satan now asks, "Did God [*Elohim*] actually say, 'You shall *not* eat of any tree in the garden'?" (emphasis added). That was a complete distortion and travesty of God's word. God's generosity was perverted by Satan's question to suggest divine stinginess!

Satan's approach was so subtle that Eve did not suspect that God's word was being attacked. It was just an "innocent question." But a seed of doubt about God's word had been planted in Eve's heart that would bear immediate fruit.

Eve's revisions. The snake's distorted question provided Eve with a memorable chance to set the serpent straight. But our mother failed. Instead, as Moses carefully records, she descended to her own revisions of God's word in three sad instances in which she first *diminished* God's word, then *added* to his word, and then *softened* his word.[9]

God had said in 2:16, "You may surely eat of *every* tree of the garden" (italics added), but now Eve leaves out the "every," simply saying, "We may eat of the fruit of the trees in the garden" (3:2). Thus she minimized the provision of the Lord. Her inexact, unenthusiastic rendition of God's word discounted his generosity. She was in tacit agreement with the serpent. Something bad was happening in her heart.

Eve's subtle shift in heart was further revealed in her telltale addition to God's word: "But God [*Elohim*] said, 'You shall not eat of the fruit of the tree that is in the midst of the garden, *neither shall you touch it*'" (v. 3a, italics added). God never said, "neither shall you touch it"! Eve magnified God's strictness — "Just touch the tree, and zap! — you're dead!" Her comment suggested that God is so harsh that an inadvertent slip would bring death.

This is so typical of us sons and daughters of Eve. A father says to his young daughter, "You and your friend Katie have been too noisy — so Katie will have to go home." Then his daughter runs to her mother crying, "Daddy says I can't ever have Katie over again!" The boss calls in an employee who's been late several times and says, "I think this is something you need to give attention to. It's important." The employee walks out of the office and says to his coworkers, "You know what that stuffed shirt said? If I'm late again, I'm fired!" When we don't like a prohibition or a warning, we magnify its strictness. The suggestion that our superior is unjust mitigates our culpability. And if we do not perform, we may imagine that we have a morally superior way out.

We must beware, lest we begin to think that God's word is unreasonable or too requiring. Do we find ourselves overstating Scripture's call to purity as "unrealistic"? Have we represented the Bible's teaching on forgiveness as impracticable? If so, we need to take a step back and a deep breath — and pray.

Lastly, Eve paradoxically softened God's word by merely saying, "lest you die." She left out the word "surely" (2:17). The certitude of death was removed. So in the extended sentence that makes up verses 2, 3, Eve, in a breath, at once *diminished, added to*, and *softened* God's word. Her revisionist approach to the holy word of God put her in harm's way. And it likewise does so today.

Satan's contradiction. It also emboldened the snake's blasphemous contradiction: "But the serpent said to the woman, 'You will not surely die'" (v. 4). This is an in-your-face to God. The Hebrew places the word *lo* ("not") in front of God's declaration: "not — you shall surely die."[10] "Take that, God!" It is the serpent's word versus God's word — an absurd juxtaposition.

Note, too, that the doctrine of divine judgment is the very first doctrine to be denied. Satan attacked it from the beginning. Modern culture's loathing for the doctrine comes from the fact that this is the devil's world, the *cosmos diabolicus*. Satan is "the prince of the power of the air, the spirit that is now at work in the sons of disobedience" (Ephesians 2:2).

Nevertheless, divine judgment has fallen and will fall as surely as it did for Adam and Eve.

The pathology of this dialogue of descent is so clear: Satan offers a question based on the perversion of God's word. Eve then begins to question it herself, as is evidenced by her revisions of God's word. And then Satan is free to declare God's word as wrong. He who has ears to hear, let him hear!

Eve should have recoiled in horror and run screaming — a buff streak through the garden to Adam. And Adam should have stepped forth to uphold the good word of God. But Eve was "buying it." She remained entranced before the serpent, flushed with excitement. Anticipation consumed her.

God's goodness attacked. Encouraged by Eve's revisions, Satan went after God himself, attacking his goodness: "For God knows that when you eat of it your eyes will be opened, and you will be like God, knowing good and evil" (v. 5).

God was cast in an ugly light. According to the serpent, the threat of death was nothing more than a scare tactic to keep Adam and Eve in their place. God was repressive, and obviously jealous that they might ascend too high. What an incredible attack in light of the fact that the thousand "goods" of creation, not to mention the gift of each other and their rulership of the earth as well, came from God. Such a blatant slur on God's character! But Eve was believing it. If you are going to lie, it might as well be a big one, big enough to totally reinterpret life. This was big. It would alter life forever.

The lie bore the lure of divinity for Eve — "you will be like God." Sin has an intrinsic spiritual lure. It holds a seemingly golden promise. I remember as a young high school boy sitting in front of my locker tying my shoes slowly as I listened to the older boys describe their backseat exploits. Its lure was the gnostic promise of elevation to the elite realms of another world, which God's word withheld, I thought. But it was actually the lure of Hell. If you are in the thrall of sin, you will see God's prohibitions as barriers for the "strong" to climb. If Eve would just stretch forth her lovely hand and resolutely take the fruit, divinity would be hers.

The lie also held out the lure of moral autonomy — "you will be like God, knowing good and evil." By taking the fruit she would become wise. Equal with God, she would autonomously decide what was right and wrong. How intoxicating! She would make the rules. She would do it her way. That promise still intoxicates. A funeral director told me that among the unbelieving population Frank Sinatra's "My Way" is in first place as a funeral favorite:

> But best of all
> I did it my way.

Another funeral director confirmed this, saying that he witnessed the very nadir when *"My Way"* was used as the musical motif for a funeral Communion. But the truth is, *"My Way"* is the dirge of death, marking the implosion of the autonomous self. But what deadly magnetism it carries.

THE DESCENT (vv. 6, 7)

During the dialogue of descent Satan attacked God's word and then God's goodness. And Eve had stood still for it. She was at the abyss.

Eve's descent. The serpent now departs from our view. Eve is alone. Moses provides a brilliant picture of Eve's descent in verse 6, in which there is no dialogue — only Eve's thoughts. She saw that "the tree was good for food" (physically appealing) and "a delight to the eyes" (aesthetically appealing) and "to be desired to make one wise" (this is the great enticement — wisdom apart from God's word). The prospect of God-like moral autonomy drew her ineluctably.

God's command seemed insubstantial. She could see no reason not to eat. So "she took of its fruit and ate." Moses expresses no shock here. "On the contrary," says Von Rad, "the unthinkable and terrible is described as simply and unsensationally as possible."[11] From the human perspective, it is all so natural and undramatic. But it was cosmic and eternal.

> *Earth felt the wound, and Nature from her seat*
> *Sighing through all her works, gave signs of woe*
> *That all was lost.*
>
> —JOHN MILTON,
> *PARADISE LOST*, BOOK IX, II, 784)

Adam's descent. With Eve's sin, the narrative quickens with a rapid sequence of verbs — "she took of its fruit and ate, and she also gave some to her husband who was with her, and he ate" (v. 6b).

Here is a shocker: Adam was apparently privy to the conversation between Eve and the snake! The text says that he was "with her" (though that in itself does not prove he was with her during the temptation). What is decisive is that during the temptation in verses 1-5 Satan addressed Eve with the plural "you," which implies Adam's presence.[12] Adam passively watched everything.

And Adam was not deceived by the snake. He'd had his powers of discernment honed by the naming of the animals, a rigorous intellectual process that probed the essence of each animal. Adam was no ignorant rustic as we patronizing moderns like to imagine. "His mental powers," surmised St. Augustine, "surpassed those of the most brilliant philosopher as much as the speed of the bird surpasses the tortoise."[13] Milton insisted that Adam had insight into the mysteries of the soul.[14] The Apostle Paul was insistent that "Adam was not deceived, but the woman was deceived" (1 Timothy 2:14; cf. Romans 5:12, 17-19).

Adam sinned willfully, eyes wide-open, without hesitation. His sin was freighted with sinful self-interest. He had watched Eve take the fruit, and nothing happened to her. He sinned willfully, assuming there would be no consequences. Everything was upside-down. Eve followed the snake, Adam followed Eve, and no one followed God. The result was seismic:

> *Earth trembled from her entrails, as again*
> *In pangs, and Nature gave a second groan;*
> *Sky loured, and muttering thunder, some sad drops*
> *Wept at completing of the mortal sin*
> *Original. . . .*
>
> —JOHN MILTON,
> *PARADISE LOST*, BOOK IX, II, 782-784

The pit! Adam and Eve had fallen from the pinnacle of innocence and intimacy into the pit of guilt and estrangement: "Then the eyes of both were opened, and they knew that they were naked. And they sewed fig leaves together and made themselves loincloths" (v. 7). What Satan had told them was true — *half* true. They did not die that day, as they supposed they might. Indeed Adam lived another 930 years. Yet they did die. Their constant communion with God underwent death. They would go to earthly graves. They would need a Savior. Their eyes were opened — grotesquely. They got the knowledge they sought, but they got it the wrong way. They saw evil. And they saw themselves. They realized they were naked and desperately sought to cover themselves. Their innocence evaporated. Guilt and fear gripped their hearts. Now they would have to labor to love God and each other.

The New Testament encourages us not to be unaware of Satan's schemes (cf. 2 Corinthians 2:11). And Genesis is packed with primary wisdom in this regard. From Eve and Adam's sin we learn that sin takes hold when we begin to doubt God's word and God's goodness.

Growing doubt about God's word naturally spawns biblical revisionism, both conscious and unconscious. We tend to minimize Scripture's great promises by our less than enthusiastic rehearsal of their benefits. We discount God's largesse to us. Our colorless renditions of God's glorious promises blanches their polychrome wonders to a dull monochrome "Ho hum . . ." Thus we feel justified in ignoring his word.

We not only minimize his word, but we exaggerate what we do not like by adding to his word. His commands become absurd caricatures that no one can be expected to obey. And we count ourselves off the hook. Then our minimizing and adding to his word leaves us free to subtract from his word. The Scripture's teaching on sensuality is said to be culturally bound and unrealistic for today's urbane man and woman. And thus it is jettisoned. The same is done with the Bible's teaching on materialism and business ethics. Ultimately such *minimizing*, *adding*, and *subtracting* leaves us without the word — and free-falling into temptation.

The free fall is enhanced by doubts about God's goodness. "How can God be good and not give me the person or thing or position or experience that I deem essential to my happiness? God is keeping me from being all I can be." When we doubt both God's word and his goodness, the ground is coming up fast!

Moses, who gave us this account, was ever so passionate about the necessity of God's people being people of God's word. In Deuteronomy, his fifth and final book of the Pentateuch, in the chapter following the giving of the Ten Commandments (sometimes called the Ten Words), Moses eloquently called his people to put God's word at the center of their existence:

> *And these words that I command you today shall be on your heart. You shall teach them diligently to your children, and shall talk of them when you sit in your house, and when you walk by the way, and when you lie down, and when you rise. You shall bind them as a sign on your hand, and they shall be as frontlets between your eyes. You shall write them on the doorposts of your house and on your gates. (6:6-9; cf. vv. 14-25)*

Then at the end of Deuteronomy, after Moses had completed his writing of the Torah and placed it beside the Ark of the Covenant, he sang his final song, ending with these words: "Take to heart all the words by which I am warning you today, that you may command them to your children, that they may be careful to do all the words of this law. For it is no empty word for you, but your very life" (32:46, 47a).

This "your very life" attitude became the standard for all the Old Testament. The Psalter opens with a call to make the word central: "Blessed is the man who walks not in the counsel of the wicked, nor stands in the way of sinners, nor sits in the seat of scoffers; but his delight is in the law of the LORD, and on his law he meditates day and night" (Psalm 1:1, 2). The 176 verses of Psalm 119 were divided into twenty-two parts in an acrostic poem based on the twenty-two letters of the Hebrew alphabet, from *aleph* to *tau* — saying in effect that God's word is "everything from A to Z!" The final chapter of Isaiah records, "This is the one to whom I will look: he who is humble and contrite in spirit and trembles at my word" (66:2b). God's word was the life of God's people.

When we come to the New Testament, Jesus, the second Adam, is the man of the Word *par excellence*. When Jesus was tempted, he, unlike the first Adam, threw himself on God's Word, defeating Satan with three deft quotations from Deuteronomy. Astounding! *The eternal Word of God resisted temptation by turning to the written Word of God.*

Principal among the Scriptures that Jesus quoted to Satan was Deuteronomy 8:3 — "'Man shall not live by bread alone, but by every word that comes from the mouth of God'" (Matthew 4:4). Jesus said that the Word must be our food.

Moses, the earthly savior of Israel who delivered them from slavery in Egypt, said the word of God is our life. Jesus the eternal Savior said it must be our food. The Word must be our *life* and *food*.

This same Jesus, the second Adam, through massive dependence on God's Word, triumphed over the tempter, living a perfect life, and died victoriously with the cry, "It is finished!" Jesus rested everything on God's good word and on the good God of the Word.

8

Paradise Lost:
The Confrontation

GENESIS 3:8-13

Dietrich Bonhoeffer describes in his little book *Temptation* how temptation works:

> With irresistible power desire seizes mastery over the flesh. . . . It makes
> no difference whether it is sexual desire, or ambition, or vanity, or desire
> for revenge, or love of fame and power, or greed for money. . . . Joy in
> God is . . . extinguished in us and we seek all our joy in the creature. At
> this moment God is quite unreal to us, he loses all reality, and only desire
> for the creature is real. . . . Satan does not here fill us with hatred of God,
> but with forgetfulness of God. . . . The lust thus aroused envelops the
> mind and will of man in deepest darkness. The powers of clear discrimi-
> nation and of decision are taken from us. The questions present themselves:
> "Is what the flesh desires really sin in this case?" "Is it really not permit-
> ted to me, yes — expected of me, now, here, in my particular situation, to
> appease desire?" . . . It is here that everything within me rises up against the
> Word of God.[1]

This is precisely what happened to Eve in her treatment of God's word
in the dialogue with the serpent. She first *minimized* the freedom God had
given them to eat from the trees of the garden, then *added* a strictness to his
word that simply was not there, and finally *softened* his word in regard to
the certainty of death should they sin. Eve's revisionism left her open to
believe the lie of Satan against all her experience of God's goodness. Thus

she rose up against his word, took the fruit and ate it, and gave it to her husband. Her husband's transgression of God's word had greater culpability because: 1) God's word had been given directly to him before Eve's creation, 2) he was present with Eve during the temptation (as evidenced by Satan's consistent address of Eve with the plural "you"), and 3) Adam, in self-serving passivity, allowed his wife to partake while he looked on. Then, seeing that she did not die, he partook. Adam was not fooled, as was Eve (cf. 1 Timothy 2:14). His rebellion was an informed, eyes-wide-open, self-serving rejection of God and his word. Unspeakable rebellion.

Paradise lost! The carefree nakedness that went with their perfectly transparent character and their unfettered harmony with God and each other dissolved. "Then the eyes of both were opened, and they knew that they were naked. And they sewed fig leaves together and made themselves loincloths" (v. 7).

Both Adam and Eve, in fact, died right there at the tree of the knowledge of good and evil, while the taste of the fruit was yet on their lips. Henri Blocher explains: "In the Bible, death is the reverse of life — it is not the reverse of existence. To die does not mean to cease to be, but in biblical terms it means, 'cut off from the land of the living.' . . . It is a diminished existence, but nevertheless an existence."[2] Since dying is existing, Adam and Eve's existence was now one of death. And not only that — sin immediately penetrated every sphere of their being, like a drop of dye in a pail of water. They were at once utterly sinful.

Paul was probably thinking of Genesis 2:17 ("you shall surely die") when he wrote Romans 6:23, "For the wages of sin is death." And he certainly had in mind this very instance when he wrote, "sin came into the world through one man, and death through sin, and so death spread to all men because all sinned" (Romans 5:12). Paul's assertion that "all sinned" describes an action that was completed in past time. We "all sinned" in Adam when Adam sinned. And because of this we also died, as also seen in Paul's words elsewhere: "And you were dead in the trespasses and sins in which you once walked, following the course of this world, following the prince of the power of the air, the spirit that is now at work in the sons of disobedience" (Ephesians 2:1, 2). We, too, entered the world dead and depraved, since sin colors every part of our existence, so that we hide from God rather than seek him (cf. Romans 3:9-18).

In an instant the original couple passed from life to death, from sinlessness to sin, from harmony to alienation, from trust to distrust, from ease to dis-ease. It did not take a day. It happened in a millisecond!

Adam and Eve, as our parents, were genetically, historically, and theologically every man and every woman. They are paradigmatic of all of us — not only in their original sin, but because the way they attempted to deal with their sin is the pattern with which we attempt to deal with it today. And the way that God dealt with Adam and Eve is the way he deals with us.

So there the first couple were, in their ridiculous fig leaves, slouching around paradise lost. God then confronted them in a graciously gentle, remedial way. And in their confrontation we see our confrontation.

SEEK AND HIDE (vv. 8-10)

God seeks. Though God is everywhere present in creation, the garden of Eden was the special place of God's presence on earth, much like the later tabernacle and temple. Eden contained the garden of God's presence, and the garden of Eden was prophetic of and will be ultimately fulfilled in a new and universalized garden where God dwells (cf. Revelation 22:15). Here in Moses' writings the garden-tabernacle (and by implication temple) association is especially evident in the fact that when Adam and Eve were cast from the garden, cherubim were placed at its entrance to prevent their access (3:24), and in the later tabernacle statues of cherubim were placed on either side of the ark in the holy of holies. Significantly, the function of the cherubim as guardians of the divine sanctuary reappears in the holy of holies of the Jerusalem temple.

Therefore, because God was present in the garden, we must not imagine that the opening line, "And they heard the sound of the LORD God walking in the garden in the cool of the day" (v. 8a), indicates that God came down to the garden. He was already there. It was his earthly palace, his garden-temple. What the couple heard was "the rustle of God's step" (Von Rad).[3] It was the sacred sound that they had heard before and that had so filled them with joy but now brought dread.

They hide. "And the man and his wife hid themselves from the presence of the LORD God among the trees of the garden" (v. 8b). At the sound of God's approach, they sensed that their fig leaves were not enough and crouched deeper among the good trees of God's bounty. What a pathetic delusion for anyone, then or today, to imagine that it is possible to hide from God. The psalmist tellingly asks:

> *Where shall I go from your Spirit?*
> *Or where shall I flee from your presence?*
> *If I ascend to heaven, you are there!*
> *If I make my bed in Sheol, you are there! (139:7, 8)*

We all know this, but when we disobey we naturally succumb to Jonah's folly and hop Tarshish ships "to flee . . . from the presence of the LORD" (Jonah 1:3). Unbelief spawns the ontological delusion that we can be where God is not. And more, we think we can privatize our thoughts, denying the fact that "You know when I sit down and when I rise up; you discern my thoughts from afar" (Psalm 139:2). Sin brings hiding and its multiple pathologies. Even as Christians, we can become mastered by the we-can-hide-from-God delusion.

How utterly pathetic Adam and Eve were because they were literally hiding from the "face" ("presence," v. 8) of God whom they had regularly seen, and whose face all believers will see in the new universalized garden where "they will see his face, and his name will be on their foreheads" (Revelation 22:4). Paradise was lost!

God finds. God sought — they hid — and God found. "But the LORD God called to the man and said to him, 'Where are you?' And he said, 'I heard the sound of you in the garden, and I was afraid, because I was naked, and I hid myself'" (vv. 9, 10). God's "Where are you?" was remedial, like a father's question to a naughty child hiding behind a door to avoid his face. The "where are you?" asks "why are you there? Is that where you should be? Come out and face me!" So Adam, realizing that God had found him, rose from his hiding-place, shamefaced, wearing his ridiculous fig leaves, mumbling his reply. And his wife crept out slowly after him.[4] God drew Adam from hiding rather than drove him from it. The initial question was not an indictment like "where are you hiding?" but simply "where are you?" There was no hint of accusation. God nudged Adam to come to his senses. The process was graced.

Notice that Adam's response contained no admission of wrongdoing. He only said, "I was afraid, because I was naked, and I hid myself." It is apparent that at that moment he was more aware of his nakedness and shame than of his sin against God. Adam had undergone a profound change, but all he could do was express his fear and shame. The only thing that Adam truly confessed to was a *feeling* — fear. Of course, he knew he had broken God's command, but in his new self-focused state he was more concerned about how he felt than about his sin against God.

This self-focus and shrinking from God remains part and parcel of our fallen condition. No one seeks God; every one flees God (cf. Romans 3:11). Even fallen man's apparent seeking is not after God but after the idolatrous god of his own making. Fear and shame and flight are the incurable stigmata of the fall.[5] We only begin to deal with them when God says, "Where are you?"

Perhaps God is calling you from your hiding — "Come out of your hiding place, from your self-reproach, your covering, your secrecy, your self torment, from your vain remorse" (Bonhoeffer).[6]

FUTILE EXCUSES (vv. 11-13)

As we shall see, God addressed the man, then the woman, and then the snake in the order of their responsibility. Adam bore the primary responsibility.[7] Having begun gently, God then pressed the issue with two questions. First, "Who told you that you were naked?" (v. 11a). Was it the serpent? Was it the woman? Was it a glance in a pool? Someone or something told him that he was naked. Then came a second question: "Have you eaten of the tree of which I commanded you not to eat?" (v. 11b). The question was a graced arrow.

Adam's excuse. Satan originated the lie, a real whopper, in his temptation of Eve. But here Adam told a shameful whopper of his own: "The woman whom you gave to be with me, she gave me fruit of the tree, and I ate" (v. 12). These are the words of a man who was spiritually dead. This is wicked! Remember Adam's ecstasy when he first laid eyes on Eve?

> *This at last is bone of my bones*
> *and flesh of my flesh;*
> *she shall be called Woman,*
> *because she was taken out of Man. (2:23)*

These are the first human words recorded in Scripture and the initial poetic couplet. She was at once his sister, his daughter, and his one-flesh wife. Such a helper — such intimacy — such oneness — such joy. She was his human universe. But now — "she gave me fruit of the tree, and I ate." What infamous treachery! "It's her fault, God. Don't blame me." Adam was so calculated and so cold.

So long, marital bliss. Adam would live for nearly 930 years more. They would settle things. But paradise was lost!

But the blame didn't stop with Eve, because Adam also accused God: "The woman *whom you gave to be with me*, she gave . . ." (emphasis added). "God, you put this dangerous creature at my side. I'm not guilty, God. You're guilty!" In doing this Adam was like Satan, who had argued that a better God would not withhold anything from his people. Here Adam implied that a better God would not have given him Eve. Implicit blasphemy. And Eve's excuse followed the pattern of Adam's shift of blame — "The serpent deceived me, and I ate." But her excuse is not as ignominious as that of Adam. She did not say "It's this 'man' that you gave me," and she didn't insinuate that God was at fault. Still she, like Adam, did not accept blame. Note at this point that neither Adam nor Eve showed a hint of contrition.

Passing the buck. Will Rogers once remarked that there are two eras in American history — "the passing of the buffalo and the passing of the buck." Actually, the passing of the buck took place in primeval history as well. And it has remained endemic to the human race. With a wry smile the Metropolitan Insurance Company once listed these among its clients' excuses: "An invisible car came out of nowhere, struck my car, and vanished." "The other car collided with mine without warning me of its intention." We all understand from this (and from our own hearts) that to err is human; to blame it on others and upon God is more human.

Circumstances. We sometimes blame God for placing us in circumstances that we regard as too much for us. Some students cheat, rationalizing that God is to blame for giving them a difficult professor *and* a busy schedule. Some thieves steal, blaming life and God for their stealing, "God, you know my weaknesses, but there it was. Why did you allow it?" Consider the adulterous man who blames God for the ingredients that led to his sin — his depression, his poor self-image, that woman, the faraway place, his loneliness.

Disposition. The commonest delusion is that "God has given me passions and appetites so strong that I can only yield to them."

> *Thou know'st that Thou hast formed me*
> *With passions wild and strong;*
> *And list'ning to their witching voice*
> *Has often led me wrong.*[8]
>
> ROBERT BURNS

"It's my God-given hormones. My passions, my appetites, my exquisite tastes, my intelligence, my proclivities, my insecurities, my experience, my energy — these together leave me subject to sins that barely tempt others. God made me this way, so what can I do?" Such thinking is from below.

Victimhood. If you read Adam's sin through the lens of today's world, you see the language of victimhood — Adam as the poor victim of the woman and of the God who gave her to him. The modern version goes like this: "God, you're responsible for my situation that has left me so susceptible to sin — my upbringing, my abuse, my inept parents and teachings." And it plays in our culture in therapeutic exculpation like that of the Menendez brothers who murdered their parents and then asked the court for mercy on the grounds that they were orphans! Given this thinking, only God is responsible for sin — if there is a God.[9]

But according to Scripture no one from Adam to the last man on earth will ever get away with passing the buck. Listen to James, the Lord's brother: "Let no one say when he is tempted, 'I am being tempted by God,' for God cannot be tempted with evil, and he himself tempts no one" (James 1:13). The perverse intellectualizings of poets, writers, analysts, lawyers, and preachers will not hold water. Adam's pathetic attempt, no matter how deceptively rephrased by us, will not suffice. We must never say, or even *imagine*, that God is tempting us.

The Genesis reality and the New Testament reality is this: "But each person is tempted when he is lured and enticed by his own desire. Then desire when it has conceived gives birth to sin, and sin when it is fully grown brings forth death" (James 1:14, 15). We cannot blame God. We cannot blame anyone else. And we cannot blame the devil.

So what are we sons and daughters of Adam to do since we share such solidarity with him in our sins that we are thoroughly sinful and utterly responsible and blamable? What is the answer? May I suggest that in a sense we are to blame Jesus! Or more accurately, we are to rest all our blame on him. How so? Paul explains, "If, because of one man's trespass, death reigned through that one man [the first Adam], much more will those who receive the abundance of grace and the free gift of righteousness reign in life through the one man [the second Adam] Jesus Christ" (Romans 5:17). Our second Adam was the one man in history who never tried to pass the buck, because as a sinless man he never needed to pass on the responsibility for sin. Rather, as our sinless God-man and Messiah and Savior he said, "Pass the blame to me." The buck stopped with Jesus.

We see this so clearly on Calvary's three crosses. Blameless Jesus hung between two blameworthy thieves. Christ hung as the innocent among the guilty. But on that hill a miracle happened. One of the thieves ceased cursing and began to listen. And before he died he declared Jesus to be guiltless, saying, "Jesus, remember me when you come into your kingdom" (Luke 23:42).

During the ensuing darkness of Calvary, that guilty man's sins were lifted from him and placed on Jesus. His blame stopped when it rested on Jesus. The so-called buck of our guilt stopped with Jesus, the second Adam.

Have you stopped passing the buck? Have you said the guilt for your sin is yours alone? And then, have you passed it on to Jesus?

9

Paradise Lost:
Curse and Judgment

GENESIS 3:14-16

$\mathbf{C}$alvin and Hobbes provided one of the great cartoons of the 1990s because it so perfectly captured the growing no-fault ethos of the decade. The cartoon is mostly a monologue by Calvin, the little boy, to his tiger friend Hobbes. It begins with the two walking along and Calvin musing, "Nothing I do is my fault." The next frame shows Hobbes scratching his whiskers as Calvin expostulates, "My family is dysfunctional and my parents won't empower me! Consequently, I'm not self-actualized!" Then we see Calvin, eyes shut and arms crossed, doing a poor me: "My behavior is addictive functioning in a disease process of toxic codependency! I need holistic healing and wellness before I'll accept any responsibility for my actions!" Hobbes responds, "One of us needs to stick his head in a bucket of ice water." The strip ends with Calvin walking on saying, "I love the culture of victimhood."[1]

"Victimhood" has become the fantasyland refuge of everyone from criminals to presidents to theologians who imagine that the blame for their conduct can be placed on some other person or thing or group. Buck-passing is the therapeutic trademark of the new millennium. Of course, as we saw in Genesis 3:8-13, the culture of victimhood has primeval roots in original sin. It is nothing new. Adam's sin brought *instant* death and *instant* sinfulness. In the bat of an eye, every part of the couple's beings was diffused with the tincture of sin — and in a nanosecond they were utterly dead in their transgressions and sins. Then came instant guilt and instant victimhood as Adam pointed a treasonous finger at the woman and at God himself and as the woman pointed to the snake.

And so it has been throughout history until the cross of Christ, when the sinless Son of God, the second Adam, became the willing victim of our sins. Significantly, in the garden God did not question the serpent but straightaway cursed him — there was no hope for Satan. Yet in that cursing of Satan there was imbedded a hope of grace for the couple. And when God judged Eve and then Adam, the judgments were again laced with grace.

The divine oracles — the curse and the judgment — in the garden were strangely interwoven with grace. Indeed, paradise was lost. Depravity and death became the lot of all humanity. But the curse and the judgments given as they were meant that paradise could be regained — by grace.

CURSE (vv. 14, 15)

As already noted, God made no remedial gesture to the serpent. There was only a curse. The curse had two objects, first the reptile itself (v. 14) and then Satan who controlled the reptile (v. 15). The curse is typical of prophetic language that addresses an object or person and then moves beyond the object to the source.

Reptile cursed.

God said to the serpent:

> *Because you have done this,*
> *Cursed are you above all livestock*
> *and above all beasts of the field;*
> *on your belly you shall go,*
> *and dust you shall eat*
> *all the days of your life. (v. 14)*

The cursing of the snake is consistent with the fate of other animals in Scripture that caused injury to humans and were therefore put to death. Exodus 21:28 states, "When an ox gores a man or a woman to death, the ox shall be stoned." Beasts used for immoral purposes were also put to death, not because they were accountable, but because they were used to abuse men and women made in the image of God (cf. Leviticus 20:15, 16).[2] Every animal was made *for* man and was subject *to* him as its head. Thus any abuse or perversion of the order called for strict judgment.

This is one of the two places in the Bible where God himself verbalized a curse. The other is in Genesis 4:11, where we read that God cursed Cain for the murder of Abel. In all other instances men invoke curses in God's name. Here the fact that God made the curse means that the curse was completely certain. The idea of this curse is banishment from the place of blessing, the garden. All of animate creation would be banished from the fertility and harmony of the garden, but the serpent was cursed "above all" the rest of the animals. His exile was permanent and inviolable — eternal.

The curse upon the serpent is stated in physical terms — the snake crawling on its belly and eating dust. Does this suggest a new way of travel for the serpent, say, from an upright posture to its belly? Possibly, but probably not. Derek Kidner argues "that the crawling is henceforth symbolic (cf. Isaiah 65:25) — just as in 9:13 a new significance, not a new existence will be decreed for the rainbow."[3] Thus through God's curse, a new significance was given to the serpent's distinctive posture. Eating dust variously signifies abject humiliation in Scripture. "May . . . his enemies lick the dust" (Psalm 72:9). "They shall lick the dust like a serpent, like the crawling things of the earth; they shall come trembling out of their strongholds" (Micah 7:17; cf. Isaiah 49:23). The image was so fitting. The snake had exalted itself above man. Therefore it would go upon its belly.

And what a fittingly repulsive image a snake is. I know some people delight in snakes, including my grandsons. But that is an acquired taste. Even Indiana Jones feared snakes! John Calvin had it right when he said, "It is regarded, as among prodigies, that some take pleasure in them; and as often as the sight of a serpent inspires us with horror, the memory of our fall is renewed."[4] Serpents continue to keep the revolting image of Satan before our eyes. Isaiah 65 pictures the whole of creation delivered from the effects of the fall, except for the serpent, which lives in perpetual degradation, fulfilling the sentence "all the days of your life" — and therefore prophesying the fate of the ultimate serpent for whom there will be no deliverance![5]

Satan cursed. As God addressed the reptile, his speech moved beyond the snake, and the referent became Satan himself:

> *I will put enmity between you and the woman,*
> *and between your offspring and her offspring;*
> *he shall bruise your head,*
> *and you shall bruise his heel. (v. 15)*

What we have here is an astounding gospel prophecy because God's curse upon the serpent turned into a word of grace, giving what has been recognized from the second century A.D. as the "first gospel," the *protevangelium,* when the post-apostolic fathers Justin Martyr and Irenaeus preached that the woman's offspring (literally, "seed") here referred to Christ who would crush Satan's head. This has been the church's position, with little variation, until the rise of modern biblical criticism, which views it as nothing more than a statement that there would be perpetual conflict between humanity and the snake population in which humanity would ultimately triumph.

But we know such thinking is wrong, for several good reasons. Most tellingly, in 250 B.C. when Jewish scholars translated the Bible into Greek, giving the world the Septuagint translation, they interpreted the word "seed" ("offspring" in the ESV) as a single individual — "*he* will crush your head." The Septuagint translators, who could not possibly have had any Christian presuppositions, understood the seed of the woman to be a future individual who would deal a deathblow to the serpent. Later rabbinic commentators saw it otherwise, but not the original Septuagint translators.[6] Recently Hebrew scholar Jack Collins examined every use of the word "seed" when it means offspring and found that when the word is singular (as it is here in Genesis 3:15) it always denotes a specific descendant and that when it is an individual, the pronoun will be masculine. Thus, in the broader context of Genesis Collins argues that "it would be fair to read this as God's threat to the snake, of an individual who will engage the snake in combat and win."[7]

This view is sustained by the fact that in Galatians 3:16 Paul argues, on the basis of the use of the singular "seed" in God's promise to Abraham, that the word "seed" refers to Christ: "Now the promises were made to Abraham and to his offspring. It does not say, 'And to offsprings,' referring to many, but referring to one, 'And to your offspring,' who is Christ." Here in Genesis 3:15 we have a prophecy of the cross when Satan would *strike* the heel of Christ (the suffering on the cross), but Christ would *strike*[8] Satan's head (through his death and glorious resurrection). All Christians (those who are in Christ) participate in the crushing through Christ, so that Paul could write in the conclusion of the book of Romans, "The God of peace will soon crush Satan under your feet" (16:20).

Those who argue that the author of Genesis could not have known or meant this betray their naturalistic presuppositions. God is the author of Scripture, and this prophecy is a direct quotation of his words. God knew what he meant. He meant to communicate that his Son, the second Adam, as the ultimate offspring of Eve, would be wounded in his destruction of Satan. Certainly Moses got the gist of God's words. Read the rest of Genesis and the Pentateuch and observe the theology — all of which came through Moses' hand. Amazing! Here is the gospel in paradise just lost. God cursed Satan and in the process proclaimed grace through his Son, the second Adam, who crushed Satan by his great work on the cross.

And there is more, because when Christ came, he understood the "first gospel" in Genesis. He understood that he himself was the antidote to the serpent's venom. In fact just prior to declaring "For God so loved the world, that he gave his only Son, that whoever believes in him should not perish but have eternal life" (John 3:16) Jesus said, "And as Moses lifted up the serpent in the wilderness, so must the Son of Man be lifted up, that whoever believes in him may have eternal life" (vv. 14, 15). His reference, of course, was to Numbers 21, where due to Israel's sin God sent venomous snakes into the camp so that many people died and were dying. As Moses prayed amidst the death, "the LORD said to Moses, 'Make a fiery serpent and set it on a pole, and everyone who is bitten, when he sees it, shall live.' So Moses made a bronze serpent and set it on a pole. And if a serpent bit anyone, he would look at the bronze serpent and live" (vv. 8, 9).

The details of the event are remarkable. The snakes were the result of sin — in fact, the perfect expression of sin because it was a serpent who tempted Adam and Eve in the garden, thereby bringing sin into the world. Our very natures have been polluted by the serpent's venom. Paul says, "as it is written: 'None is righteous, no, not one'" (Romans 3:10).

Above the dying people we see the likeness of a serpent lifted up on a pole, foreshadowing Christ who was "made . . . to be sin for us" (2 Corinthians 5:21). And it is significant that Moses elected not to use an actual serpent but a likeness! The symbolism would not have been so exact and perfect if he had used a literal snake. Our Lord became sin (or a serpent) for us. Romans 8:3 says, "God . . . [sent] his own Son in the likeness of sinful flesh and for sin." Second Corinthians 5:21 adds, "For our sake he made him to be sin who knew no sin, so that in him we might become the righteousness of God." And Galatians 3:13 states, "Christ redeemed us from the curse of the law by becoming a curse for us." With all the animal realm from which to choose, God chose the perfect representation — the serpent. On the cross our Lord took the sins of the world upon himself as symbolized by the writhing serpent.

We dare not miss the importance of the gaze of faith. Numbers 21:9 says, "If a serpent bit anyone, he would look at the bronze serpent and live." The command to look to that uplifted serpent was a gracious foreshadowing of looking to the crucified Christ for our salvation. No wonder our Lord said, "And as Moses lifted up the serpent in the wilderness, so must the Son of Man be lifted up" (John 3:14). Moses raised that serpent up high in the camp, and all the dying Israelites had to do was look to that pole and be saved. No matter how horribly they were bitten, no matter how many times they had been bitten or how sick they were, the opportunity for salvation was there.

Even the most degraded and miserable sinner who looks to Christ alone for salvation will be saved. This great grace had its origins and image in the "first gospel" in the garden. There was hope in paradise lost!

JUDGMENT (v. 16)

This unexpected intermingling of grace continued in the judgments upon the woman in her two primary roles of childbearing and her relationship to her husband.

Childbearing. First, the intrinsically joyous area of her life was invaded by pain. "To the woman he said, 'I will surely multiply your pain in childbearing; in pain you shall bring forth children'" (v. 16a). The pain of child-birth, unrelieved by modern medicine, is a bitter pill. Maternity and suffering became coextensive. And her pain was not limited to the physical because pain here means "painful toil" and refers to the emotional as well as the physical. Mothering itself, with its attendant joys, was also a source of painful labor.

Marriage. Marriage was also struck with a corresponding pain: "Your desire shall be for your husband, and he shall rule over you" (v. 16b). The woman's desire would be very much like the desire of sin to master Cain because the same word is used in 4:7, where God says to Cain, "Sin is crouching at the door. Its desire is for you." The woman would now desire to control her husband, but she would fail because God had ordained that man should lead. Nevertheless strife would persist in domestic relationships. John Sailhamer writes, "Thus the Lord affirms in the oracles of judgment the creation order: the serpent is subjected to the woman, the woman to the man, and all to the Lord. In those moments of life's greatest blessing — marriage and children — the woman would serve most clearly the painful consequences of her rebellion from God."[9]

The grace in all of this is a sense of dis-ease and dissatisfaction in what ought to be the most rewarding areas of life. Bliss, perfect peace, is no woman's lot in this world. And as we shall see, the center of the man's life will also know the same striving. These punishments are God's graces. Marriage alone will give no woman all she wants. Mothering is fraught with pain from birth onward. To be a mother is to experience a new and ongoing index of pain. "Joy and woe are woven fine" (William Blake) at the very center of domestic life. Nothing completely satisfies. This is a grace because it will drive the willing soul to seek God. Augustine praised God in retrospect for this uncomfortable grace, saying, "Your goad was thrusting at my heart, giving me no peace until the eye of my soul could discern you without mistake."[10]

It was midnight in the garden of Eden. Curses and judgments rained down. Paradise was lost.

Yet there was grace. God's curse upon Satan meant that his own Son would one day become a curse for us. Satan would strike his heel, but the wound received would mean that the Son would strike a deathblow to Satan. Grace is rooted in Christ's victory.

God's judgments would fall on the very center of the woman's existence. But in those judgments there was grace. Nothing would satisfy her but God. And Jesus' gracious words often would have powerful appeal to such needy hearts: "Come to me, all who labor and are heavy laden, and I will give you rest" (Matthew 11:28).

Have you seen the "first gospel" in the garden of Eden?

I will put enmity between you and the woman,
and between your offspring and her offspring;
he shall bruise your head,
and you shall bruise his heel. (v. 15)

If you see this "first gospel," you will understand Jesus' words: "And as Moses lifted up the serpent in the wilderness, so must the Son of Man be lifted up, that whoever believes in him may have eternal life. For God so loved the world, that he gave his only Son, that whoever believes in him should not perish but have eternal life" (John 3:14-16).

This is grace indeed!

10

Paradise Lost: Judgment and Sin

GENESIS 3:17-24

When we began our study of Genesis, we emphasized that Genesis is about grace — that the book of Genesis, far from being a faded page from antiquity, actually breathes the living grace of God. We pointed out that the first eleven chapters, especially, give us the primeval (universal) history of the world by relating five stories that all have the same fourfold structure. The five stories are: the fall, Cain, the sons of God marrying the daughters of man, the flood, and the tower of Babel.

And the four-part structure by which they are told is: 1) *sin*, as sin is initially described; 2) *speech*, as there is a speech by God announcing the penalty for sin; 3) *grace*, as God brings grace to the situation to mitigate the misery caused by sin; and 4) *punishment*, as God punishes sin. Here in chapter 3, the story of the fall, the pattern runs like this: *sin* (vv. 1-13, esp. v. 6, which describe the temptation, the sin, and God's confrontation of the sinners); *speech* (vv. 14-19, which quote the judgment oracles of God to the snake, the woman, and the man); *grace* (vv. 20, 21, mainly v. 21, which records the mitigating grace of God); and *judgment* (vv. 22-24, which describe the exile from the garden).

Thus God's amazing grace looms prominent in the fall. And in fact we have already seen that there have been flashes of grace in the *Sin* and *Speech* sections of the story. On the occasion of Adam's sin God did not destroy him but graciously engaged the fallen man in conversation. Also, the ensuing judgment speech to the snake and to the woman shone with grace. God cursed the snake, but the curse also contained the "first gospel," indicating that the woman's seed would crush the serpent's head, while the serpent would strike his heel (cf. 3:15). God's judgment on Eve's fundamental roles as wife and mother meant that nothing in life would satisfy her apart from God himself. This perpetual discomfort in life was a grace insofar as it would drive her to God.

Now as we take up the remainder of God's speech and move on to the concluding punishment, grace will shine ever brighter — amazing, astounding, abounding grace — primeval and eternal.

JUDGMENT AND GRACE (vv. 17-19)

God was explicit about the reason for his judgment oracle to Adam: "And to Adam he said, 'Because you have listened to the voice of your wife and have eaten of the tree of which I commanded you, "You shall not eat of it," cursed is the ground . . .'" (v. 17a). God cursed the ground because Adam *obeyed* his wife. (Here "listened to" is an idiom meaning "obey.") Thus the curse fell because Adam abdicated his headship as he, in passive self-interest, observed the tempting of his wife and her eating without even voicing an objection. He was not fooled as she was but knowingly and willfully hearkened to her voice and partook (cf. 1 Timothy 2:14). That is why God cursed the earth and judged Adam.

Judgment. The judgment oracles regarding Adam continue in the parallelism of Hebrew poetry:

> Cursed is the ground because of you;
> in pain you shall eat of it all the days of your life;
> thorns and thistles it shall bring forth for you;
> and you shall eat the plants of the field.
> By the sweat of your face
> you shall eat bread,
> till you return to the ground,
> for out of it you were taken;
> for you are dust,
> and to dust you shall return. (vv. 17b-19).

Here we must observe that in the same way that "the woman's punishment struck at the deepest root of her being as wife and mother, the man's strikes at the innermost nerve of his life: his work, his activity, and provision for sustenance" (Von Rad).[1] The "pain" that verse 17 describes as Adam's lot is the same word twice used for the woman's "pain" in verse 16. Both of them would experience perpetual pain in the centers of their existence. Ironically, the very ground that had been such a source of joy when

Adam cared for the garden now became the source of his ongoing pain. The earth became an enemy.

Note that work itself was not cursed. Work, in fact, had been a gift from God (cf. 2:15). God's curse was upon the ground. God's oracle anticipated Adam's expulsion from the garden, when the man would have to battle "thorns and thistles" to "eat the plants of the field." This applies to all work involved in human culture. Painful toil will assault every soul who attempts to produce in this world. We may imagine exceptions such as royalty or the super-rich. But even the rich are made for work. The bored, indolent Prince of Wales, Edward VI, hitting a thousand golf balls into the sea from the deck of his yacht, knows he is not meant to do nothing. Nevertheless, anyone who works to produce in this world knows pain and frustration. This condition is irrevocable. It is for "all the days of your life" (v. 17), "till you return to the ground" (v. 19). No repentance — nothing — will remove the curse on the ground. Only death can provide a respite. So all men submit to "the law of the dust" (Blocher).[2]

Grace. But even grace shines here. For apart from God, no man's work, no man's achievements, fully satisfy — whether it be as a farmer or artist or craftsman or executive or teacher — regardless of his accomplishments. That from which we seek fulfillment is a perpetual source of pain. The gift of work is good, but it is covered with thorns. Writing from the perspective of life apart from God, the writer of Ecclesiastes reflects:

> *What does man gain by all the toil*
> *at which he toils under the sun?*
> *A generation goes, and a generation comes,*
> *but the earth remains forever. (Ecclesiastes 1:3, 4)*

> *And whatever my eyes desired I did not keep from them.*
> *I kept my heart from no pleasure,*
> *for my heart found pleasure in all my toil,*
> *and this was my reward for all my toil.*
> *Then I considered all that my hands had done*
> *and the toil I had expended in doing it,*
> *and behold, all was vanity and a striving after wind,*
> *and there was nothing to be gained under the sun.*
> *(Ecclesiastes 2:10, 11)*

Today both creation and the children of God groan as with birth pangs for the dawning of a new day (cf. Genesis 3:15, 16). And this groaning paradoxically confirms the hope of God's children. Final and full liberation for Adam and the earth will come in Christ at the end of the age (cf. Romans 8:19-22).[3] Our groaning is a palpable grace.

MITIGATING GRACES (vv. 20, 21)

Adam's faith. Now the first two parts of the *Sin, Speech, Grace, Punishment* structure of the story are complete, and in verse 20 mitigating grace begins to glow as Adam exhibits faith by renaming his wife. "The man called his wife's name Eve, because she was the mother of all living" (v. 20). "Eve" means "life"[4] or "life-giver."[5] Adam named his wife *Life* because she would become the mother of all the living! Adam was able to do this because he had a very precise awareness of the overall significance of God's words to his wife.[6] Adam had listened closely to God's speech to his spouse. He understood that one of her offspring would crush the head of the snake (v. 15). He knew that his wife's pain in childbearing meant that a people would follow. Indeed, the tense Adam used to declare his faith is the prophetic perfect, indicating that her becoming the mother of all the living "is as good as done."[7] Adam's declaration was an overwhelming shout of hope. The name *Eve* celebrates the survival of the human race and victory over death. The reformer Philip Melanchthon called Eve "the seal of grace."[8] Certainly Adam's hope yielded a prophetic glimpse of grace.

Graced garments. Now God performed an act of mitigating grace: "And the LORD God made for Adam and for his wife garments of skins and clothed them" (v. 21). It is clear that this is a sovereign work of God, conceived and executed by God alone. It is a work that Adam and Eve would never have conceived of because it involved the unprecedented taking of life. Their self-made attempts to cover themselves in inadequate fig-leaf loincloths were replaced by clothing made by God. They had attempted to cover themselves, but this covering was from God — a tunic that reached to their knees or ankles.[9] God's provision here of robes of animal skin both recognized their sin and was an act of grace.

Marcus Dods, the brilliant nineteenth-century Scottish preacher and scholar, and principal of New College, Edinburgh University, makes these remarkably penetrating observations:

> It is also to be remarked that the clothing which God provided was in itself different from what man had thought of. Adam took leaves from an inanimate, unfeeling tree; God deprived an animal of life, that the shame of His creature might be relieved. This was the last thing Adam would have thought of doing. To us life is cheap and death familiar, but Adam recognized death as the punishment of sin. Death was to early man a sign of God's anger. And he had to learn that sin could be covered not by a bunch of leaves snatched from a bush as he passed by . . . but only by pain and blood. Sin cannot be atoned for by any mechanical action nor without expenditure of feeling. Suffering must ever follow wrongdoing. From the first sin to the last, the track of the sinner is marked with blood. . . . It was

made apparent that sin was a real and deep evil, and that by no easy and cheap process could the sinner be restored. . . . Men have found that their sin reaches beyond their own life and person, that it inflicts injury and involves disturbance and distress, that it changes utterly our relation to life and to God, and that we cannot rise above its consequences save by the intervention of God Himself, by an intervention which tells us of the sorrow He suffers on our account.[10]

God's action here in primeval history was a gracious foreshadowing of his ultimate sovereign provision for sin. Certainly the first couple would have only understood this in faint principle. But the foundation was mightily laid. Later no Levitical priest could read this passage without making the connection with atonement because the skins of the animals slain in sacrifice were given to the priests for their use (cf. Leviticus 7:8).[11]

The divine provision was a telling illustration of the method of grace in response to sin and its consequences. God covers sin and its degradation. The biblical picture of justification is the gift of the robe of righteousness (cf. Zechariah 3:4ff.; Matthew 22:11; Luke 15:22).[12] Believers are described as clothed with Christ (cf. Galatians 3:27). In a passage on the wedding of the Lamb and his bride, we read how God's righteousness produces the saints' righteousness:

> *"It was granted her to clothe herself*
> *with fine linen, bright and pure" —*
> *for the fine linen is the righteous deeds of the saints.*
> *(Revelation 19:8)*

This is grace abounding! This is again the gospel in Genesis.

EXILE AND GRACE (vv. 22-24)

Verse 22 records divine deliberation as God dialogues with himself (as he had done in 1:26): "Then the LORD God said, 'Behold, the man has become like one of us in knowing good and evil'" (v. 22a). What Satan had promised Eve had become *partially* true. Man had become *like* God. But the couple's likeness to God was not glorious, as they had supposed, but ignominious.

They had sought moral autonomy, the power to decide what was right and wrong apart from God and his word. And all humanity has done this ever since. Henri Blocher writes: "The word implies the achievement of autonomy in a certain way. But only in a certain way, for the father of lies only ever speaks the truth by perverting it. In reality, the autonomy is illusory, a mere, pitiful aping of God."[13] Because God is sovereign, man's supposed autonomy is an illusion. He cannot escape the lordship of God. "The crazy little god with his absurd pretensions is not God and never shall be. All he can do is die," writes Blocher.

In fact, he *is* dead. He died when he sinned, becoming "dead in . . . trespasses and sins" (Ephesians 2:1) and utterly sinful (cf. Romans 3:9-18). Adam and Eve's bodies were alive, but they were dead. As residents of the garden, they could have eaten from the tree of life and perpetuated their bodily existence indefinitely. Thus the garden would have become Hell on earth, populated with the undying dead — forever living and forever dead.

Exile. God forestalled their inevitable "next step toward self-divinization by his own preemptive first strike" (Wenham).[14] "Therefore the LORD God sent him out from the garden of Eden to work the ground from which he was taken. He drove out the man, and at the east of the garden of Eden he placed the cherubim and a flaming sword that turned every way to guard the way to the tree of life" (vv. 23, 24). The couple were exiled forever from the garden. Cherubim were stationed at the east side of the garden. A flaming sword, representing the justice and holiness of God at work in his judgments, flashed to and fro (cf. Jeremiah 47:6; Ezekiel 21). Adam, the garden's caretaker, was now excluded, like a thief, never to enter it again.

The exile was terrible, but it was also a grace. The garden had been the Holy of Holies of God's presence, the original divine space. Adam and Eve had lived gazing on God's face as he walked in the garden. They had breathed the air of God's presence. Now it was impossible. For them, their new state must have been like life without oxygen. They were perpetually short of spiritual breath. They could never get enough of God.

Eve found pain at the very center of her domestic existence, and so did Adam in all his labors, all the days of his life. They fought. Their children fought. They saw a son violently die by the hand of his brother. After Eden, they were never truly at home again.

But Adam's 930 years and the long years of Eve's life were a grace. There was plenty of time to seek God and to proclaim his word. Did they do so? Very likely they did, because the desire for God and his presence must have become more dear with the centuries. If they did, there awaits them the garden of the eternal city where the tree of life will continually grant its fruit to all who believe (cf. Revelation 22:2, 14, 19). They will again see the face of God.

ULTIMATE GRACE

The Bible (from the garden of Eden to the ultimate garden in the Holy City at the end) is a story of grace. The garden as a holy space, together with the tabernacle and temple with their successive Holy of Holies and the ultimate city of God, form an exquisite spiritual unity. The continuity between the garden and Israel's future tabernacle and temple are apparent to the observant reader for several reasons: 1) Both the garden and the tabernacle/temple were filled with the special presence of God. 2) Both featured cherubim; the garden had cherubim guarding its entrance, and in the tabernacle and temple the curtains of the Holy of Holies featured embroidered cherubim. There were also sculpted cherubim above the mercy seat (cf. Exodus 25:18-22; 36:35; 37:7-9). In the later temple a huge sculpted pair of cherubim stood guard in the inner sanctuary of the temple (cf. 1 Kings 6:23-28). Significantly, the language used in Genesis 3:24 (God "placed" the cherubim on the east side of the garden) is particularly associated with God's camping in the tabernacle among his people (cf. Exodus 25:8).[15] Even the mention of the east side of the garden is associative, because the entrances of the tabernacle and temple were from the east.[16]

3) God's provision of garments for Adam and Eve, which covered them fully, parallel the full garments required of the priests who served in the tabernacle. Kenneth Mathews says: "Since the garden narrative shares in tabernacle imagery, it is not surprising that allusion to animal sacrifice is found in the garden too. Through an oblique reference to animal sacrifice, the garden narrative paints a theological portrait familiar to the recipients of the Sinai revelation who honored the tabernacle as the meeting place with God."[17] In the tabernacle and temple, access to God's presence came only by the shedding of blood and the mediation of a priest (cf., e.g., Leviticus 16).

As we know, this tabernacle/temple system pointed to Jesus Christ. John 1:14 says, "And the Word became flesh and dwelt [literally, "tabernacled"] among us." Jesus saw himself as the fulfillment of the tabernacle and the temple. In the very next chapter of John's Gospel Jesus said, "Destroy this temple, and in three days I will raise it up" (v. 19). Jesus saw his own body as the temple, and the resurrection as proving his authority (v. 22). Finally Revelation 21:22 tells us that God himself is the temple (cf. 21:3).

When Jesus died on the cross, the veil of the temple was torn from top to bottom (cf. Matthew 27:51). Access into the presence of God no longer required sacrifice or a priest or a temple — because Jesus was at once the sacrifice, the priest, and the temple. This is the argument of Hebrews 6 — 10. Hebrews 9:11, 12 alludes to all three aspects:

> *When Christ appeared as a high priest of the good things that have come, then through the greater and more perfect tent (not made with hands, that is, not of this creation) he entered once for all into the holy places, not by means of the blood of goats and calves but by means of his own blood, thus securing an eternal redemption.*

Listen to Hebrews 6:19, 20: "We have this as a sure and steadfast anchor of the soul, a hope that enters into the inner place behind the curtain, where

Jesus has gone as a forerunner on our behalf, having become a high priest forever after the order of Melchizedek."

Christians, the amazing reality is this: We have access to the presence of God — which was first experienced in the holy space of the garden, then in the Holy of Holies of the tabernacle and temple — and all this comes through the work of Jesus Christ! In fact, all true believers are presently in heaven: "[God] raised us up with him and seated us with him in the heavenly places in Christ Jesus, so that in the coming ages he might show the immeasurable riches of his grace in kindness toward us in Christ Jesus" (Ephesians 2:6, 7). Now that is access!

For Adam and Eve (and us), there is no going back to the garden. But through Christ, the second Adam, these realities lie ahead of us, as seen in these excerpts from the book of Revelation:

> *And I saw the holy city, new Jerusalem, coming down out of heaven from God, prepared as a bride adorned for her husband. And I heard a loud voice from the throne saying, "Behold, the dwelling place of God is with man. He will dwell with them, and they will be his people, and God himself will be with them as their God." (Revelation 21:2, 3)*

> *And I saw no temple in the city, for its temple is the Lord God the Almighty and the Lamb. And the city has no need of sun or moon to shine on it, for the glory of God gives it light, and its lamp is the Lamb. (Revelation 21:22, 23)*

> *Then the angel showed me the river of the water of life, bright as crystal, flowing from the throne of God and of the Lamb through the middle of the street of the city; also, on either side of the river, the tree of life with its twelve kinds of fruit, yielding its fruit each month. The leaves of the tree were for the healing of the nations. No longer will there be anything accursed, but the throne of God and of the Lamb will be in it, and his servants will worship him. They will see his face, and his name will be on their foreheads. And night will be no more. They will need no light of lamp or sun, for the Lord God will be their light, and they will reign forever and ever. (Revelation 22:1-5)*

The gospel has always been this: ". . . that Christ died for our sins in accordance with the Scriptures, that he was buried, that he was raised on the third day in accordance with the Scriptures" (1 Corinthians 15:3, 4). "In accordance with the Scriptures" means "according to the Old Testament Scriptures" and naturally takes us to Genesis 3:15, 16, the initial prophecy that Jesus would crush Satan's head by his death and resurrection. "In accordance with the Scriptures" takes us to the flash of grace in 3:21, where God took the life of animals to provide tunics to cover Adam and Eve's sin.

The exile itself was a grace, because the only way future generations could get access into the presence of God was through shed blood and the offices of a priest. Access to the presence of God was lost in the garden and then was only possible for the priest who entered the Holy of Holies in the tabernacle and the temple. But now it is possible through the person of Jesus Christ — who is at once priest, sacrifice, and temple.

If you want to have your sins forgiven and receive the robe of righteousness, the only way is through the blood of Jesus. This great gospel was announced in the beginning in Genesis and is consummated in the end in Revelation. All of Scripture points to the gospel in Christ. If you are apart from Christ, you are lost; if you are in Christ, you have life. Indeed, if you are a believer, Christ — the priest, sacrifice, and temple — is in you. And ultimately you are going to see the garden and the tree of life and the face of God and live forever in his presence. If you want the gift of eternal life, there is only one thing to do. You must say in your heart, "Not what these hands have done / Can save this guilty soul" (Horatius Bonar). You must simply believe the great, ravishing reality that "Christ died for our sins in accordance with the Scriptures, that he was buried, that he was raised on the third day in accordance with the Scriptures" (1 Corinthians 15:3, 4).

This is the gospel. Do you believe it? Are you just now believing it? If you are, congratulations because you have received access to the holy presence of God! In fact, in an instant you were seated in heaven and in heavenly places in him. He is your priest, your temple, and your Savior.

11

The Way of Cain

GENESIS 4:1-16

A few years ago the *Chicago Tribune* carried a news brief that began: "HOUSTON (Reuters) — A Texas mother was so intent on making sure her daughter made the cheerleading squad that she was willing to hire a hit man to kill a competitor's mother, police said Friday." The woman's hope was that her daughter's thirteen-year-old competitor would be so overwhelmed with grief by her mother's death that she would drop out of competition for the cheerleading spot. Detectives said that at first the woman plotted to hire a hit man to kill both the girl and her mother but decided the double murder was too expensive. So she opted for the girl's mother for $2,500.[1] Again reality trumps the imagination! Cheerleading on the cheap. All that is required is an inexpensive homicide. "Give me an M . . ." Our imaginations reel.

But we should not be surprised. The twentieth century stood as the unchallenged century of violence (and the twenty-first century is continuing in the same vein). The modern state has proven itself the greatest killer of all time. By 1990 state violence (war, collectivist pogroms, revolution, and "ethnic cleansing") had been responsible for the unnatural deaths of 125 million people during that century, which is more than the state had succeeded in destroying in all of human history up to 1900.[2] Much of the blame for violence — for example, the genocide in Cambodia — can be laid on intellectual godfathers like Marx and Sartre.

But our own culture leads the way in homicide. The March 1993 issue of *Chicago Magazine* noted that 936 people were murdered in Chicago alone in 1992, establishing the highest murder rate ever for the city — 33 per 100,000.[3]

Today more children than ever are dying at the hands of their abusive parents. Feticide is booming, with over thirty million abortions since 1973.

John Wayne Gacy, Jeffrey Dahmer, and Ted Bundy are part of our national vocabulary. So we as a culture (and especially we Christians who have the revelation of God's Word regarding the heart) cannot turn our backs on these grim realities. Most of us have personally known someone who has suffered a violent death. I have personally seen it in the church I pastor.

Here in Genesis 4 homicide is the centerpiece. But this is far more than a record of the first murder. It is about "the way of Cain" (Jude 11) — the corruption and slide of a heart away from God into notorious sin. The story reveals something of the essential nature of all mankind by presenting an unforgettable picture of elementary, primal power. It is a story of depravity *and* grace.

Moses has exercised great literary care in constructing the story because again, as in the Creation account, sevens and multiples of sevens are used to shape the narrative symmetry. Within verses 1-17, the name "Abel" and the important designation "brother" each occur seven times. "Cain" occurs fourteen times. And whereas in 1:1 — 2:3 (the first *toledot*) the name "God" (*Elohim*) occurred thirty-five times, from 2:4 to the end of chapter 4 (the second *toledot*) the words "God," "the LORD," or "the LORD God" occur a total of thirty-five times. The careful Hebrew scholar Gordon Wenham observes: "The last verse of chapter 4, 'At that time people began to call on the name of the LORD,' thus contains the seventieth mention of deity in Genesis."[4] Conclusion: There is vast intentionality in this narrative as it instructs us about the essential nature of all mankind. The story of Cain and Abel calls for us to observe well and to take its instruction to heart.

The account begins with a burst of exuberant optimism: "Now Adam knew Eve his wife, and she conceived and bore Cain, saying, 'I have gotten a man with the help of the LORD'" (v. 1). Eve's pregnancy certainly must have been a source of joyous wonder to the couple. Like millions of her daughters to follow, Eve likely placed Adam's hand on her tummy so he could feel the stirring life. Perhaps he even listened in awe to the busy heartbeat within. Eve's was the first pain ever in childbearing. But those terrible pangs gave way to a joy so deep that it subsumed her pain. The Hebrew for "man" (*ish*) is not used anywhere else in Scripture to describe a baby boy. The baby's gender was that of Adam. This was another *ish*! Eve said in effect, "God made man, and now with the help of the Lord, I have made a second man!"[5] She rightly saw Cain as a work of God.

Her words were an implicit declaration of faith. Adam had believed the promise of Genesis 3:15 and so had named her Eve: "The man called his wife's name Eve ["Life"], because she was the mother of all living" (3:20). And the new mother praised God with a newly charged faith.

Eve conceived again and "bore his brother Abel" (v. 2a). His name signified a lack of permanence or meaning and alluded unwittingly to his life being cut short (cf. Ecclesiastes 1:2; 12:8 which employs the same word).

Nevertheless, Abel's birth doubled her joy. Eve had become the mother of two sons. Three men filled the earthly horizons of the mother of all the living. Hope welled high in the first family.

PRELUDE TO MURDER (vv. 2b-7)

We know nothing of the boys' growing-up years other than that Cain followed in his father's footsteps as firstborn, becoming a farmer, while his little brother became a shepherd. So both had honorable professions.

Crisis. We don't know if the brothers were in the habit of making offerings or if the text describes their initial presentation of offerings. Very likely this was not the first occasion because the opening words of verse 3 — "In the course of time" — nearly always denote a precise period of time, here likely referring to the end of an agricultural year when sacrifices would be presented.[6]

In any event, their offerings perpetuated a crisis:

> *Now Abel was a keeper of sheep, and Cain a worker of the ground. In the course of time Cain brought to the LORD an offering of the fruit of the ground, and Abel also brought of the firstborn of his flock and of their fat portions. And the LORD had regard for Abel and his offering, but for Cain and his offering he had no regard. So Cain was very angry, and his face fell. (vv. 2b-5)*

Why, we wonder, was Abel's offering accepted while Cain's was not? And why did Cain become so angry? It is often supposed that the answer is simply that animal offerings were more acceptable to God than grain offerings, that blood sacrifices are superior to harvest offerings. But this is certainly mistaken, because the Old Testament Scriptures honor both types of offerings. Moreover, the context says nothing about the priority of blood sacrifice. The answer lies in the text of verses 3, 4 because whereas Cain only brought "an offering of the fruit of the ground," Abel brought the best of the flock — "the firstborn of his flock and of their fat portions" (v. 4). Cain evidently was indifferent about his offering, but Abel was careful about his. The rabbinic commentators note that "fat" and "firstborn" mean that Abel gave God the pick of the flock.[7]

The difference was that of heart attitude. Cain came to God on Cain's own self-prescribed terms, but Abel came to God on God's terms. Cain's spirit was arrogant, as the subsequent story will reveal.

The writer of Hebrews provides further insight into the brothers' hearts, indicating that Abel's offering was one of faith. "By faith Abel offered to God a more acceptable sacrifice than Cain, through which he was commended as righteous, God commending him by accepting his gifts. And through his faith, though he died, he still speaks" (11:4).

Cain's was not an offering from faith. He presumed to define what his sacrifice would be. He was the captain of his own heart. God would have to take him and his offering as it was. Cain's error was what latter prophets such as Micah would rail against. "Will the LORD be pleased with thousands of rams, with ten thousands of rivers of oil? Shall I give my firstborn for my transgression, the fruit of my body for the sin of my soul? He has told you, O man, what is good; and what does the LORD require of you but to do justice, and to love kindness, and to walk humbly with your God?" (Micah 6:7, 8). But Cain was singularly unjust, unmerciful, and unhumble!

The giveaway as to Cain's sinful attitude was his countenance: "So Cain was very angry, and his face fell" (Genesis 4:5). Cain could have taken the divine disapproval of his offering as the gracious communication that it was and humbly asked for God's forgiveness, promising never again to fall to such sin. But he did not.

Blazing resentment toward God welled in Cain, which strangely (or should we say predictably?) was directed at his brother Abel. And Cain's hatred was so intense that it distorted his body. No one could miss it.

Intervention. God gently responded to the seething man with remedial questions. "The LORD said to Cain, 'Why are you angry, and why has your face fallen? If you do well, will you not be accepted?'" (vv. 6, 7a). Literally God said, "If you do right, there is uplift."[8] That is, "If you do well, will not *your countenance* be lifted up?" (NASB). The downcast lines of Cain's mouth could yet become a happy face!

In a last-ditch attempt to deter Cain, God painted for him a frightening but hopeful picture: "And if you do not do well, sin is crouching at the door. Its desire is for you, but you must rule over it" (v. 7b). God personified sin as a beast crouching at the door about to pounce on him. If Cain did not master it, he would be its victim.

The sin at the door was Cain's own sin (the beast was within him), and its interior growth cycle would do him in. "But each person is tempted when he is lured and enticed by his own desire. Then desire when it has conceived gives birth to sin, and sin when it is fully grown brings forth death" (James 1:14, 15). The consequences of Cain's action would be more far-reaching than the initial sin itself.

Cain stood at the edge of Hell. But sadly, God's graphic words about sin as a crouching beast bounced off his hardening heart, and in monumental willfulness he began his descent into the pit.

MURDER (v. 8)

The stark simplicity of the homicide accentuates the horror of the deed. "Cain spoke to Abel his brother. And when they were in the field, Cain rose up against his brother Abel and killed him" (v. 8). Haste and violence pulse in this short description.

"Brother" is twice used in the text. This is not only a homicide but a fratricide. This was Cain's little brother who, no doubt, was very much like him since both were direct offspring of the mother and father of the human race. Abel's flesh felt the same. Abel's eyes were mirrors of his own. Abel's breath bore the same aroma.

There were no guns or bombs to depersonalize Cain's murder of his brother. Did he crush his skull and watch him die like a bug in the dust? Did he cut his throat with Abel's sacrificial knife and bleed him like a sacrifice? Did he choke Abel with his own hands until his eyes lost their light and there was no breath?

His young brother was a good man, a "righteous" man according to Hebrews 11:4 (cf. Matthew 23:35). Jesus would even call him a prophet (cf. Luke 11:50, 51). But Cain killed him with his own bloody hands.

Why? Because he hated Abel? Yes, but also no. "Why does Cain murder?" asks Bonhoeffer rhetorically. "Out of hatred for God," he answers.[9] Murder is an act of hatred toward God for making or accepting another who offends us or troubles us or is favored with gifts and honors we do not have or stands in our way.

That's precisely the way it was with King David, the murderer of Uriah the Hittite, as evidenced by his astonishing confession to God: "Against you, you only, have I sinned" (Psalm 51:4). David's God-awareness was not because he was unaware of his guilt toward Uriah and Bathsheba. Rather, King David saw within himself the cause of his horrendous crime: It was with God that he was offended because God had limited his freedom by forbidding him the wife of Uriah the Hittite. David's crime was directed at his restricting God.[10]

According to Jesus we are likewise exposed by our own hatreds because they are spiritual homicides ultimately directed at God — however private they may seem (cf. Matthew 5:21-26).

POSTLUDE TO MURDER (vv. 9-12)

Confrontation. God was immediately on the spot, just as he had been with Adam and Eve after the fall. When God challenged Adam, Adam told the truth, if not the whole truth (cf. 3:10). But Cain told an outright lie. "Then the LORD said to Cain, 'Where is Abel your brother?' He said, 'I do not know; am I my brother's keeper?'" (4:9).

Cain's flip, indifferent reference to his dead brother revealed a heart hardened in its depravity. Wit became the murderer's refuge. Paul would write, "Since they did not see fit to acknowledge God, God gave them up to a debased mind to do what ought not to be done. They were filled with all manner of unrighteousness, evil, covetousness, malice. They are full of envy, murder, strife, deceit, maliciousness" (Romans 1:28, 29).

Then the voice of God thundered over Cain: "And the LORD said, 'What have you done? The voice of your brother's blood is crying to me from the ground'" (v. 10). Abel's cry would not be silenced. In Scripture, this cry is like the cry of desperate men without food (cf. Genesis 41:55). It is the scream for help by a woman being raped (cf. Deuteronomy 22:24). It will not be silenced.

Now Cain learned something he had not previously considered: Abel's body, though covered with earth, could not be hidden, for his blood screamed to God. "My soul in fumes of Blood Cries for Vengeance . . . Blood on Blood . . . Compelled I cry, O Earth, cover not the blood of Abel!"[11] Von Rad writes, "According to the Old Testament view, blood and life belong to God alone; wherever a man commits murder he attacks God's very own right of possession. To destroy life goes far beyond man's proper sphere. Spilled blood cannot be shoveled underground; it cries aloud to heaven and complains directly to the Lord of life."[12]

Judgment. So the curse fell: "And now you are cursed from the ground, which has opened its mouth to receive your brother's blood from your hand. When you work the ground, it shall no longer yield to you its strength. You shall be a fugitive and a wanderer on the earth" (vv. 11, 12). This is the first instance in Scripture where a human is cursed. Cain now shared this tragic distinction with the serpent (the language is the same as in 3:14).

But he would not merely become a wandering bedouin — the curse went beyond that. All his relationships with his family were broken. He was a lifelong pariah. The earth itself would be his enemy. Cain, who had once worked the soil, had watered it with his brother's blood. That blood had cried against him from the soil, so that he was banned from it forever — to wander over it as an enemy of the earth.

GRACE TO THE MURDERER (vv. 13-15)

Cain's response provides the first lament recorded in Scripture: "My punishment is greater than I can bear. Behold, you have driven me today away from the ground, and from your face I shall be hidden. I shall be a fugitive and a wanderer on the earth, and whoever finds me will kill me" (vv. 13, 14). Poor Cain falls to pieces! But not because he felt any compassion for Abel and his parents, or even because he had sinned against God. His cry was one of terror and self-pity. He, the wolf, feared that he would be devoured. He knew that with the expansion of civilization, some during his long life would seek to avenge Abel's blood. He felt fear and self-pity, but no remorse.

God's mark. Yet amazingly God heard him and responded, "'Not so! If anyone kills Cain, vengeance shall be taken on him sevenfold.' And the LORD put a mark on Cain, lest any who found him should attack him" (v. 15). God promised Cain that any vigilante would be severely judged, and then he marked Cain with a distinctive sign. In one sense the mark did not lighten his punishment, because a premature death would have shortened his awful sentence. Nevertheless, the fear of a violent death was removed.

The nature of Cain's sign has been the subject of endless speculation. Some have supposed a tattoo, others a special hairstyle. One of the ancient rabbis argued that the sign was a dog that accompanied Cain on his wanderings. The dog assured Cain of God's protection and frightened attackers.[13] In my mind I see a giant bull mastiff with a spiked collar!

By all estimates God's mark, whatever it was, was an amazing grace. Cain was cursed and separated from God, yet guarded by God. Cain's life still belonged to God. He bore God's image, however disfigured that image was. This was the utmost mercy that God could do, and does, for the unrepentant.

"Then Cain went away from the presence of the LORD and settled in the land of Nod, east of Eden" (v. 16).

There is astounding grace right here in one of the darkest scenes in Genesis. Observe that the Lord did not abandon guilty Cain. When Cain arrogantly brought his sparse offering to God, and God saw his evil anger, God did not turn away from him. That is grace. God, in fact, engaged Cain in a fatherly manner with probing, remedial questions. God did not leave him exposed to Satan without recourse. Such grace. God then exhorted Cain to withstand temptation. Again, grace. After the murder, the Lord listened to Cain's unrepentant, self-pitying plea. Finally, God placed a sign upon Cain that protected him for the remainder of his natural life. Amazing grace!

Did Cain repent? Probably not. The New Testament Scriptures uniformly speak of Cain in the negative with phrases like "the way of Cain" (Jude 11) and one "who was of the evil one and murdered his brother" (1 John 3:12). His life is contrasted with "righteous Abel" (Matthew 23:35, NIV).

Nevertheless, we do not know what ultimately happened to him. He may have responded to God. Cain was not beyond God's grace.

On this side of the cross, the Scriptures tell us that in coming to Christ, we come "to Jesus, the mediator of a new covenant, and to the sprinkled blood that *speaks a better word than the blood of Abel*" (Hebrews 12:24, italics added). Abel's blood rightly calls for vengeance. But Jesus' shed blood shouts forgiveness to all who come to him.

So there is great hope for us all. Jesus' blood will wash away all the hidden sins of those who come to him. And his blood also atones for our public sins, whatever they may be.

No one is beyond grace because "the sprinkled blood [of Jesus] . . . speaks a better word than the blood of Abel."

Not what these hands have done
Can save this guilty soul;
Not what this toiling flesh has borne,
Can make my spirit whole.

Thy grace alone, O God,
To me can pardon speak;
Thy power alone, O Son of God,
Can this sore bondage break.

HORATIUS BONAR,
"NOT WHAT THESE HANDS HAVE DONE," 1861

12

The Song of Lamech

GENESIS 4:17-26

Wiliam Ernest Henley's poem "Invictus" ("Unconquered") is drenched with the spirit of Cain:

> *Out of the night that covers me,*
> *Black as the Pit from pole to pole,*
> *I thank whatever gods may be*
> *For my unconquerable soul.*
>
> *In the fell clutch of circumstance*
> *I have not winced nor cried aloud.*
> *Under the bludgeonings of chance*
> *My head is bloody, but unbowed.*
>
> *Beyond this place of wrath and tears*
> *Looms but the Horror of the shade,*
> *And yet the menace of the years*
> *Finds, and shall find, me unafraid.*
>
> *It matters not how strait the gate,*
> *How charged with punishments the scroll,*
> *I am the master of my fate:*
> *I am the captain of my soul.*[1]

Cain's fierce anger at the rejection of his offering betrayed his self-right-eous independence and smoldering disdain for God. His murder of his brother was in actuality a strike at God who had shown favor to Abel's offering instead of his. He killed his righteous brother, who, of the two of them, most represented the image of God. This Cain did without the slightest hint of remorse. His only emotion was self-pity.

So when Cain went out from the Lord's presence to live in the land of Nod (Nod means "wandering") east of Eden, his head was "bloody, but unbowed." Though he bore the gracious mark of protection, he left Eden full of disdain and anger toward God. The taste of anger, bitter and sweet, mixed with blood, energized him. He would show God! He would show them all! His anger was electric and exhilarating. Molten energy shot through his veins. He was Captain Cain.

> *It matters not . . .*
> *How charged with punishments the scroll.*
> *I am the master of my fate:*
> *I am the captain of my soul.*

So what happened to Cain after he left God and family in such angry defiance? He prospered! As Allen Ross has noted, his posterity "took the lead in producing cities, music, weapons, agricultural implements — in short, civilization."[2] But it was a dark prosperity.

Paradoxically, civilization descended as it ascended. Culture fell even as it rose. In this section of Genesis, we see civilization's grim demise in its glorious rise. But we also get a glimpse of grace.

THE RISE OF CAINITE CIVILIZATION (vv. 17-22)

City. Cain's history is highly compressed here: "Cain knew his wife, and she conceived and bore Enoch. When he built a city, he called the name of the city after the name of his son, Enoch" (v. 17). Cain apparently wandered for several decades before settling down because we must assume that Cain's wife was one of Adam's other daughters or granddaughters. (Genesis 5:4 informs us, "The days of Adam after he fathered Seth were 800 years; and he had other sons and daughters.")

Cain's building a city at the time of Enoch's birth was a defiant, in-your-face violation of God's revealed will for Cain. This willful act is consonant with the record of his behavior. Cain had not changed at all. The city probably was not much, because the Hebrew for "city" here can be applied to any settlement, small or great. But his city was his statement to God, his family, and his replacement-brother Seth that in his mind he was the captain of his soul. And the city's name, "Enoch," which means "dedicated," was his attempt to perpetuate the name of his son. The psalmist later wrote of the futility of this:

Their graves are their homes forever,
their dwelling places to all generations,
though they called lands by their own names. (49:11)

As it was, Cain's decision to settle down and establish his own line of descent indicates that he was determined to go his own way, rejecting the word of God.

Civilization. Nothing else is said of Cainite culture except to list the names of five generations up to and including the infamous Lamech and his two wives. "To Enoch was born Irad, and Irad fathered Mehujael, and Mehujael fathered Methushael, and Methushael fathered Lamech. And Lamech took two wives. The name of the one was Adah, and the name of the other Zillah" (vv. 18, 19).

Here we see in the initial growth of civilization the first sign of degeneration (civilization's demise in its rise) with the tragic institution of polygamy. God's will had been given to Adam and Eve as part of creation: "Therefore a man shall leave his father and his mother and hold fast to his wife, and they shall become one flesh" (Genesis 2:24). Polygamous departures from the divine norm came to dominate both Cainite and Sethite culture, as the rest of Genesis records. And its disastrous effects are seen often in Genesis. Jesus himself would call believers back to the creational ideal, warning that in regard to divorce, "from the beginning it was not so" (Matthew 19:8). So note well that as civilization advanced, rebellion against God's word advanced.

Nevertheless, the description here is one of singular prosperity:

And Lamech took two wives. The name of the one was Adah, and the name of the other Zillah. Adah bore Jabal; he was the father of those who dwell in tents and have livestock. His brother's name was Jubal; he was the father of all those who play the lyre and pipe. Zillah also bore Tubal-cain; he was the forger of all instruments of bronze and iron. The sister of Tubal-cain was Naamah. (vv. 19-22)

A biased account would have managed to say nothing positive about the achievements of Cain's descendants. But, as Derek Kidner has noted, "The truth is more complex: God was to make much of Cainite techniques for His people."[3] Take, for example, animal husbandry: The greatest of God's people tended livestock — Abraham, Moses, David. And concerning the gift of music, read the book of Psalms. Also note that technically gifted craftsmen are described as people "in whom the LORD has put skill and intelligence" (Exodus 36:1). Godless, Cainite civilization birthed massive cultural advances that have enriched all of life. Of course, this does not mean that godly Sethite culture was not making similar advances, but merely that Cain's progeny distinguished themselves in this.

Adah's two sons by Lamech excelled, one in the pastoral life (livestock and agribusiness, we might say), and the other in music arts. Jubal's name bears an etymological connection with Israel's delightful concept of Jubilee and with words that indicate joy and happiness.[4] Indeed, Jubal's name also corresponds with the melodic ram's horn (the *yôbēl*), which in later Israel was used to joyously announce the Year of Jubilee.[5] Jabal and Jubal made quite a pair. Bring on the lamb chops and the music!

Zillah's son Tubal-cain (the half-brother of Jabal and Jubal) is described as "the forger of all instruments of bronze and iron" (v. 22). Tubal-cain is the ancestor of technology and industry. However primitive his work was (his name literally means "hammer, sharpen"), his work no doubt included making weapons as well as farming tools. This dark side of technology is suggested by the fact that he is not simply called Tubal (which would give a nice domestic rhyme — Jabal, Jubal, Tubal), but Tubal-cain. Mathews notes, "With the appendage of 'Cain' the grim side of his craft comes to mind first."[6] The double name that Lamech gave him anticipated the terrifying song that was to follow.

These cultural skills (the production of food, the arts, and technology) should be and can be devoted to the highest interests of human life, and to the glory of God. However, civilization's advances apart from God have untold potential for evil. Nuclear technology, for example, is a double-edged sword. Today thousands of lives are being saved by diagnostic procedures only possible through nuclear medicine. What a boon it has been and will become. The potential for good is staggering. However, in a flash an H-bomb could kill more people than nuclear medicine could save in a generation — and maim generations to follow. Oppenheimer's quotation of the Bhagavad Gita at Alamogordo as he watched the initial explosion of the neutron bomb comes to mind: "the radiance of a thousand suns . . . I am become as death, the destroyer of the worlds."[7] A microchip can be used to help you find your dog or to guide a smart bomb through your bedroom window.

Can we imagine a life without drugs? Without painkillers? Without estrogens? Without antibiotics? At the same time, can we today imagine life without whole neighborhoods under the control of cocaine and heroin, the victims lying about wrapped in greasy newspapers like fish and chips?

What a gift music and the arts are! But what power for evil they have if misused. The stage and the screen regularly portray evil as exciting, and goodness as dull and boring. Reality is, in fact, the very opposite: Life in the grip of sin is tedious and unfulfilling, whereas a life full of God's goodness is bright and polychrome — and full of new adventure.

We all understand that some types of music (due to the combination of lyrics and melody) are debasing. But we must also understand that high culture — for example, the music of Bach and Beethoven — can be used to romanticize an adulterous or a homosexual affair. Virtually any evil can be made to appear morally compelling by the skillful use of script, music, and cinematography.

One more thing: "Culture, used or abused, offers no redemption" (Kidner).[8] Neither low culture, nor pop culture, nor high culture (apart from God) can redeem. No combination of agricultural abundance, the arts, and technology can save society. Nazi Germany in its day considered itself the repository of *Kultur* (high art), the leader in technology, and the master of abundance. All the while the Third Reich enslaved helpless people and performed unspeakable barbarisms.

Here the story of Cainite civilization saves us from overvaluing culture. The descendants of Cain through Lamech could manage their surroundings in order to prosper, but they could not manage their lives. Today there are millions who indulge their families in abundance, the arts, and all the boons of high-tech culture, even as their lives spin more and more out of control.

THE SONG OF CAINITE CIVILIZATION (vv. 23, 24)

Vengeance. The picture darkens here. I see Lamech naked or in a loincloth, sword in hand, strutting before his wives and thumping his bare chest as he shouts this savage song. Though no sword is mentioned in the poem, the dark double name of Tubal-cain implies that Lamech's craft had made weapons that escalated violence.[9] Traditionally Lamech's poem has been called "The Song of the Sword."

> *Adah and Zillah, hear my voice;*
> *you wives of Lamech, listen to what I say:*
> *I have killed a man for wounding me,*
> *a young man for striking me.*
> *If Cain's revenge is sevenfold,*
> *then Lamech's is seventy-sevenfold. (vv. 23, 24)*

If the song were to be sung today, it would probably be by a man naked or in his designer briefs, with barbed-wire bandoliers tattooed across his bare chest, gripping an Uzi, as he intones the Sword Song rap style.

> *Lamech said to his wives,*
> *Said to his wives,*
> *Said to his wives,*
> *Yeah, said to his wives,*
> *Listen to me . . .*

Lamech's song must be a woman's worst dream. The reference to his wives in this violent context points to the worst outworking of the judgment oracle of Genesis 3:16: "Your desire shall be for your husband, and he shall rule over you." Adah and Zillah suffered the humiliation of polygamy in their marriage to a brutal, remorseless male.

The Sword Song gloried in violence: "I have killed a man for wounding me, a young man for striking me." The "savage disposition of killing a mere lad (Hebrew *yeled*, 'child') for a mere wound is the whole point of his boast" (Kidner).[10] Rather than shame, Lamech wore violence as a badge of honor. This was a remorseless, carnivorous man.

Just as marriage was debased with the rise of Cainite civilization, life was devalued. And can we say otherwise of our advanced culture with its violent icons, violent music, and violent streets? In a 1994 *Time* magazine article ("Dances with Werewolves"), the author stated, "Public fascination with serial killers is at an all time high." The curious, the author noted, could at that time call 1-900-GACY to listen for $1.99 per minute as John Wayne Gacy argued against the death penalty. Serial killer collectibles — trading cards, T-shirts, and a comic book — celebrated the mass murderer's exploits. Most bizarre, Gacy's paintings of eerie clowns were selling for up to twenty thousand dollars in elite galleries.[11] I recall a young woman telling me that *Silence of the Lambs* (the subject of which is murder and cannibalism) was her favorite movie. She had watched it six times!

The empirical evidence is that the twentieth century, despite its massive advances in agribusiness, the arts, and technology, was the most violent of centuries (and we are not doing any better in the twenty-first century). So much for *civilization*.

The final stanza of Lamech's song gloried in exponential vengeance — "If Cain's revenge is sevenfold, then Lamech's is seventy-sevenfold." God's vengeance upon anyone killing Cain was sevenfold, meaning a perfect measure, appropriate to the crime.[12] But Lamech threatened that he would take vengeance seventy-seven fold — an avalanche of vengeance. The descendants of Lamech would come to regard vengeance in terms of duty. Vengeance formally became a part of human tradition.[13] Today civilization stockpiles reservoirs of exponential vengeance, and when the time is "right," it unleashes it in toxic devastation.

Lamech, of course, did not hear Christ's words, and if he could have he probably would have stopped his ears anyway. Significantly, Jesus referenced this very text and Lamech's merciless song as a backdrop to teach Peter about the necessity of mercy and forgiveness. When Peter came to Jesus and asked, "'Lord, how often will my brother sin against me, and I forgive him? As many as seven times?' Jesus said to him, 'I do not say to you seven times, but seventy times seven'" (Matthew 18:21, 22). Exponential forgiveness! An avalanche of grace.

Jesus presented the ideal in direct contrast with that of so-called civilization. He rained down grace and forgiveness on the toxic waste of our souls. His followers must do the same. He said, "For if you forgive others their trespasses, your heavenly Father will also forgive you, but if you do not forgive others their trespasses, neither will your Father forgive your trespasses" (Matthew 6:14, 15; cf. 18:21-35). Lamech's ecstasy of anger was answered by the graced ecstasy of Christ's forgiveness.

THE BEGINNING OF SETHITE CIVILIZATION (vv. 25, 26)

Faith. This section concludes with the birth of Seth, and again, as in the case of Cain, God's grace became explicit: "And Adam knew his wife again, and she bore a son and called his name Seth, for she said, 'God has appointed for me another offspring instead of Abel, for Cain killed him'" (v. 25). Seth means "granted." So the sense of verse 25 is that she named him "Granted," saying, "God has granted me another child. . . ."[14] Thus Eve attributed the birth of her child to the grace of God.

Eve's faith also shined because "another offspring" is literally "another seed," which references the promise of 3:15 about how her seed would crush the serpent's head. The gift of baby Seth ensured that the promise would stay alive in Eve, who was indeed "the mother of all living" (3:20).

Again, the birth of this third son must have been particularly sweet to the virtually sonless couple. Eve had another man, an *ish* to coddle and love — and she knew that great things would happen through him.

Worship. The grace of God was not in vain in the line of Seth, because "To Seth also a son was born, and he called his name Enosh. At that time people began to call upon the name of the LORD" (v. 26). Kenneth Mathews beautifully captures the significance of men beginning "to call upon the name of the LORD," saying, "Cain's firstborn and successors pioneer cities and civilized arts, but Seth's firstborn and successors pioneer worship."[15] That is exactly what Seth's children did. They worshiped. And they did more than what the rendering "call upon the LORD" suggests, because in Moses' writings "call upon" regularly means *proclaimed.* The idea is that the people began to make proclamation about the *nature* of the Lord.[16]

So in earth's earliest ages, a special people began to develop, and they proclaimed the name of the Lord. When Cainite civilization began to rise and worship at the shrines of abundance and art and technology — when abuse and violence and the devaluation of life became commonplace — when vengeance became exponential — when men fancied that they were captains of their souls — Sethite civilization began to proclaim the name of the Lord, the Captain of their salvation!

Christians, we must understand that during primeval history, before the Abrahamic covenant, before the Law, before the Davidic covenant, God's people were known for this: They proclaimed the name of the Lord! This is the distinctive of God's people. They proclaim the character of the Lord; they sing his praises. That is what God's people have always done through all the periods of sacred history. Thus this section of Scripture concludes with a shout of grace.

Our text provides us a paradigm, an outline to understand civilization and culture today and its ostensible rise with the increase in abundance, music, arts, and technology. It rises impressively, but in its rise there is demise because of sin. The only hope is to call upon the name of the Lord. This is the only hope for culture. This is the only hope for your soul. This is the only hope for the church — to call upon the name of the Lord, who is Jesus Christ.

And there is salvation in no one else, for there is no other name under heaven given among men by which we must be saved. (Acts 4:12)

13

He Was No More

GENESIS 5:1-32

Genesis 4 provides a record of human degeneration — first with Cain's personal, cold-blooded, hands-on murder of his younger brother, Abel. Cain showed no remorse, but only fear and self-pity. He left bloodied but unbowed, to wander the earth.

The record of degeneration that began with Cain is rounded out in the second half of the chapter with the account of its flowering among Cain's descendants — especially Lamech and his children Jabal, Jubal, and Tubalcain — the fathers of agribusiness, the arts, and technology. Lamech's "Sword Song" was a chest-thumping revel in exponential violence — "If Cain's revenge is sevenfold, then Lamech's is seventy-sevenfold" (4:24). And so it has been in the succeeding generations. People and nations have answered slights with swords and spears and machine guns and missiles. Civilization, with its abundance and arts and technologies, does not save. In fact, these very boons can be used for exponential evil.

But this dark picture was not devoid of hope because in contrast to the Cainite line, a new line was raised up, the Sethite line: "And Adam knew his wife again, and she bore a son and called his name Seth, for she said, 'God has appointed for me another offspring instead of Abel, for Cain killed him.' To Seth also a son was born, and he called his name Enosh. At that time people began to call upon the name of the LORD" (vv. 25, 26). This godly line called on and proclaimed the name of the Lord. They declared the wonders of his name. They sang of his excellencies.[1]

With this bright event, chapter 5 introduces a new section in Genesis, the second of the ten *toledots*, the ten "These are the generations of" divisions of Genesis. This account runs from 5:1 — 6:8, and its first part, which makes up chapter 5, is the Sethite genealogy that extends from Adam through

Seth on to Moses. And how different it is from the Cainite genealogy! The
genealogy of Cain gives no ages, since his line, being cursed by God, would
have no eternal history. But Seth's genealogy not only gives the age of each
patriarch at the time of the firstborn (by whom the line would be continued), but the number of years that he lived after the birth, and then the total
years of his life. Each individual is important to God's eternal economy.

DAZZLING PROMISE: CREATED AND BLESSED BY GOD (vv. 1, 2)

The Sethite genealogy is introduced in verses 1, 2 with the dazzling retrospect that recalls that the descendants of Adam and Seth have been created in
the image of God and blessed by him.

His image. The opening line ("This is the book of the generations of
Adam. When God created man, he made him in the likeness of God," v. 1)
references the Bible's first poem in Genesis 1:27:

> *So God created man in his own image,*
> *in the image of God he created him;*
> *male and female he created them.*

This retrospect reminded the descendants of Seth that the fall had not
obliterated the image of God in them (cf. 9:6). And because they were image-
bearers, they had unparalleled privilege and potential. First, as image-bearers they had the capacity to hear God's word, which is something no other
creature, except angels, could do. Second, as image-bearers they were
charged to rule the earth in God's stead (cf. 1:26, 28). And third, the image
of God in them suggested the possibility of an intimate spiritual relationship as children of God.

His blessing. Similarly, as the image of God had not been obliterated
by the fall, neither had the blessing been abrogated. Thus the Sethite line was
reminded in verse 2, "Male and female he created them, and he blessed
them and named them Man when they were created." The blessing had
been defined in 1:28 as physical procreation and multiplication: "And God
blessed them. And God said to them, 'Be fruitful and multiply.'" The Sethites
were to get with it and fill the earth.

The genealogy in Genesis 5 demonstrates that they did so, because it
suggests extraordinary multiplication. The ten-generation structure of the
genealogy indicates that it is a selective genealogy with gaps between the
ancestors, which leaves room for substantial increase in population. The
other Genesis genealogy, from Shem to Abram, also includes ten generations
(counting Abram; cf. 11:10-26). King David's genealogy in Ruth 4:18-22
also is given in the form of ten names. These ten-name structures telescope

the number of descendants in order to create a compressed history.[2] Therefore we understand that the flexibility of this genealogy, plus the repeated emphasis that the patriarchs "had other sons and daughters," plus their amazing longevity (their average age at death was about nine hundred years, and this included their offspring) all together argues for rapid multiplication!

Thus Seth's genealogy shows the patriarchs living out God's blessing — and multiplying and spreading the image of God in humanity — especially as many had begun "to call upon the name of the LORD" (4:26).

DARK CLOUD: UNIVERSAL DEATH (vv. 3-20, 25-32)

So the descendants of Adam and Seth had substantial reasons for optimism. They fathered thousands of offspring to whom they passed on the *Imago Dei*, people who despite the fall and their sinfulness could hear God's word, could rule and subdue the earth, and could live in relationship to God. Some did, and some did not. Yet, as they multiplied, the possibilities were immense.

Nevertheless, the Sethites' optimism was always clouded because the genealogy continually repeats the depressing phrase, "and he died." Adam lived some 930 years, "and he died." His dear son Seth lived 912 years, "and he died." It was 905 years for Enosh, "and he died." Methuselah came to within thirty-one years of a millennium, "and he died." The Hebrew for these three words is a resounding single word. Thus the Sethites lived under the double-edged sword of human experience. "Life produces hope only to see it dashed by the all too real finality of death."[3]

And so it has been since the fall. A great plow furrows the earth, plowing men and women and their children under. As Mike Mason says, this awareness is "like the unfolding of a murder mystery in which we ourselves turn out to be the victim."[4] The day is coming when the earth will not know us. We will be gone.

The day came fast for the long-lived patriarchs. At death, life is short for all. "Where did it all go?" we wonder. "Only yesterday I was young and running through the fields." Vast multitudes of people have been born bearing the image of God, originals all, so beautiful, so full of potential — but they have been plowed under. The rains have washed their names from the tombstones. Their bones are no more.

Death spread its dark cloud over the patriarchs' bright hopes, and the cycle went on and on and on — "and he died" — "and he died" — "and he died."

BRIGHT HOPE: ENOCH WAS NO MORE (vv. 21-24)

But then we come to the seventh generation from Adam and the man Enoch. "This astonishing paragraph shines like a single brilliant star above the earthly record of this chapter" (W. R. Bowie).[5] Its light illuminates the dark rhythm of Seth's genealogy. The placement of Enoch's name could not be more intentionally dramatic. Evil Lamech, the man who worshiped his sword, was number *seven* in the Cainite genealogy, while here, Enoch, the man who "walked with God," is number *seven* in the Sethite genealogy. These two are placed in eternal antithesis. They are Hell and Heaven — exponential death and unbounded life. There is wisdom for all in the life of Enoch.

Walked with God. This phrase "walked with God" is only applied to Enoch and Noah (cf. 6:9) and describes the closest personal communion with God — as if walking at the side of God. It must be distinguished from other Old Testament phrases such as walking before God (cf. 17:1; 24:40) and walking after God (cf. Deuteronomy 13:4), which describe blameless moral and ethical conduct. Walking with God is far more intimate. The minor prophets use this phrase, in fact, to describe the intimate walk of priests who entered the Holy of Holies to speak directly with God.[6] The phrase also indicates the deepest obedience, for the metaphor of walking suggests walking along God's path, in the same direction. As Allen Ross says, "The expression became a common description of the life of fellowship and obedience with the Lord, as if to say that walking with the Lord was a step above mere living."[7]

As to the question of how Enoch's walk with God worked out and what characterized it in life, we have an answer in Hebrews 11:5, which tells us that Enoch's walk was one of faith: "By faith Enoch was taken up so that he should not see death, and he was not found, because God had taken him. Now before he was taken he was commended as having pleased God." So his faith pleased God. The next verse tells us what this God-pleasing faith was like: "And without faith it is impossible to please him, for whoever would draw near to God must believe that he exists and that he rewards those who seek him" (v. 6).

First, such God-pleasing faith literally believes that God is — that the awesome, sovereign God of creation is God. Because Enoch was made in God's image, he could hear and respond to God's word. And so he did, believing with all his heart that God is who he says he is. This pleases God. It is the same today. God is pleased with those who wholly believe what his Word says about him.

Second, Enoch believed that God "rewards those who seek him" — that God is positively equitable. Enoch also believed the negative side of this — that God judges those who reject him and continue to go their own way. Jude 14, 15 reveals that Enoch (just like Noah after him) preached this: "It was also about these that Enoch, the seventh from Adam, prophesied, saying, 'Behold, the Lord came with ten thousands of his holy ones, to execute judgment on all and to convict all the ungodly of all their deeds of ungodli-

ness that they have committed in such an ungodly way, and of all the harsh
things that ungodly sinners have spoken against him.'"

What we see in sum is that Enoch's walk with God subsumed all of
life. His walk was rooted in deepest intimacy with God; he knew God. His
walk rested on great faith; he believed in God with all his heart. And he
believed that God would judge and reward all who live. So he preached the
righteousness of God. This describes not the high point of his life but his
entire life for three hundred years — three centuries! It describes three hundred years of a progressively closer walk with God.

God took him. And so at the age of 365 (while still a young man), "he
was not, for God took him." How did God do this? Perhaps it was as God
later did with Elijah as Elijah walked along with his successor Elisha: "And
as they still went on and talked, behold, chariots of fire and horses of fire separated the two of them. And Elijah went up by a whirlwind into heaven.
And Elisha saw it and he cried, 'My father, my father! The chariots of Israel
and its horsemen!' And he saw him no more" (2 Kings 2:11, 12). What a
way to go! Or perhaps he just disappeared, was "beamed up," so to speak.
One thing is sure — his walk with God extended into eternity. As Luci
Shaw states in her poem *Enoch*, he

> *crossed the gap*
> *another way*
> *he changed his pace*
> *but not his company*[8]

We do know what ultimately did happen. He was taken up from this
earthly life and transposed to life eternal, exempted by God from the law of
death and decay — just as it will be for the faithful who will be alive at the
coming of Christ for judgment. Those in like manner shall not taste death and
corruption but will be changed in a moment, in the twinkling of an eye.

As to why God took Enoch, we have only to look at our passage. Enoch
was translated up to eternal life with God and was spared disease, death,
and corruption for the consolation and encouragement of believers, and to
awaken them to hope of life after death. God took Enoch about halfway
between Adam and the flood. Some of the patriarchs in this genealogy, and
the hosts they represent, were alive at that time. They had whole centuries
to reflect upon and discuss Enoch's translation. How they must have been
heartened to what awaited them as they faithfully followed God. Did many
of Enoch's peers and descendants begin to listen to God's word and walk
with him and call upon his name? We think not a few.

Certainly such hopes were rooted in the hearts of the great ones in the
Old Testament. Listen to Job: "For I know that my Redeemer lives, and at the
last he will stand upon the earth. And after my skin has been thus destroyed,

yet in my flesh I shall see God, whom I shall see for myself, and my eyes shall behold, and not another. My heart faints within me!" (Job 19:25-27). And listen to Daniel: "Many of those who sleep in the dust of the earth shall awake, some to everlasting life, and some to shame and everlasting contempt. And those who are wise shall shine like the brightness of the sky above; and those who turn many to righteousness, like the stars forever and ever" (Daniel 12:2, 3). This all foreshadows the New Testament promises of Christ's return — promises with which we are to comfort one another (cf. 1 Thessalonians 4:13-18).

The question for us is, how do we walk with God today? And the answer is this: The image of God has been passed on to us through natural birth, so that it is possible for us to hear and obey God's Word and to live as his children. We may have further marred the image by our sin, but the likeness persists.

The wondrous fact is that by God's grace we can know God intimately. Jesus said, "And this is eternal life, that they know you the only true God, and Jesus Christ whom you have sent" (John 17:3). Jesus also said, "Whoever has seen me has seen the Father" (John 14:9). So we see God in his Son, and we see him best in his Son's death. The cross is God's supreme revelation of himself: "For God so loved the world, that he gave his only Son, that whoever believes in him should not perish but have eternal life" (John 3:16).

When you see God in Christ pouring forth his love for the world, you begin to understand. And when you believe it, you know him! When by faith you receive Christ, you receive God. By growing in Christ, you become more like God. And when this happens you can begin to walk with God. As you draw nearer through the gift of divine intimacy, you will walk closer and closer to the heart of God.

And one day you will be no more, for God will take you to himself!

14

Great Sin, Greater Grace

GENESIS 6:1-8

Jones Very's poem "Enoch" ends with the depiction of mankind's universal and tragic habit of building temples to God while making no room for him in their hearts.

> *God walked alone unhonored through the earth;*
> *For Him no heart-built temple open stood,*
> *The soul forgetful of her nobler birth*
> *Had hewn him lofty shrines of stone and wood,*
> *And left unfinished and in ruins still*
> *The only temple he delights to fill.*[1]

That was the problem before Enoch and after Enoch despite the temporary spiritual boost his contemporaries experienced when they realized that he had been taken up to heaven. Not a few, we think, responded well and began to walk with God, and as a result they went on to die in belief and faithfulness. But with the passing of time and the growth of population, the ancient culture's memory of Enoch began to fade, so that they came to regard the whole episode with a dismissive incredulity. *It was so long ago*, they thought, *and life was different then. We've got our own living to do.* And so the whole pre-flood culture began a headlong plunge into depravity so deep that it deserved to die. The account is, frankly, appalling — and sobering.

HUMAN DEGENERATION (vv. 1-4)

Verses 1-4 of Genesis 6 record the degeneration of primeval culture — marriage was demonized, life shortened, and violence idolized.

Marriage demonized. The story opens with what all agree is the most debated text in Genesis: "When man began to multiply on the face of the land and daughters were born to them, the sons of God saw that the daughters of man were attractive. And they took as their wives any they chose" (vv. 1, 2). I used to think this passage was not so difficult. In fact, I thought the answer was rather apparent from the context. Recall that chapter 4 gives the genealogy of the ungodly Cainite line (vv. 17-22) and that the whole of chapter 5 is about the godly Sethite line. Therefore, I reasoned, these verses describe "the sons of God" (the godly Sethites) sizing up "the daughters of man" (the beautiful but ungodly Cainite women) and marrying them, which, of course, promoted the Sethites' degeneration. Nice and neat. In biblical interpretation, context is king.

But then I was made aware of the New Testament passages that link fallen angels and the flood. For example, 1 Peter 3:19, 20 alludes to Christ preaching upon his death "to the spirits in prison, because they formerly did not obey, when God's patience waited in the days of Noah, while the ark was being prepared, in which a few, that is, eight persons, were brought safely through water." The word for "spirits" (*pneumata*) is used in the Bible only to describe supernatural beings — here the fallen angels of Genesis 6.[2] And 2 Peter 2:4, 5, 9 references the same fallen angels in the context of the flood, as Peter warns that God will also hold the unrighteous for judgment:

> *For if God did not spare angels when they sinned, but cast them into hell and committed them to chains of gloomy darkness to be kept until the judgment; if he did not spare the ancient world, but preserved Noah, a herald of righteousness, with seven others . . . then the Lord knows how to rescue the godly from trials, and to keep the unrighteous under punishment until the day of judgment.*

Similarly Jude 6 references these same angels: "And the angels who did not stay within their own position of authority, but left their proper dwelling, he has kept in eternal chains under gloomy darkness until the judgment of the great day."

In addition to these New Testament references, I have learned that the angel interpretation of Genesis 6 is the oldest view. The earliest Jewish exegetes held this view as represented in such sources as 1 Enoch, the Book of Jubilees, the Septuagint (LXX), the writings of Philo and Josephus, and the Dead Sea Scrolls. The same position was held by the early Christian writers Clement of Alexandria, Tertullian, and Origen.[3]

I also learned that although the Old Testament sometimes declares God's people to be his sons (cf. Deuteronomy 14:1; Isaiah 1:2; Hosea 1:10), the normal meaning of "sons of God" is angels. Job's usage of the term is normative: "Now there was a day when the sons of God came to present themselves before the LORD, and Satan also came among them" (1:6). "Again there was a day when the sons of God came to present themselves before the LORD, and Satan also came among them to present himself before the LORD" (2:1). "On what were its [earth's] bases sunk, or who laid its corner-stone, when the morning stars sang together and all the sons of God shouted for joy?" (38:6, 7; cf. Daniel 3:25).

I also saw, with a closer look at the account, that "the sons of God" were not godly Sethite choirboys. Rather, as Allen Ross says, "The story describes these 'sons of God' as a lusty, powerful lot, striving for fame and fertility."[4] And I also recalled that the Gospels record demons as craving for bodies (cf. Mark 5:11-13; Luke 8:31-33; 11:24-26).

Therefore, understanding that "the sons of God" are angels (here in Genesis 6, fallen angels), and also understanding that angels are sexless and cannot marry and procreate (cf. Luke 20:34-36), what we must have here in "the sons of God" marrying "the daughters of man" is fallen angels (demons) commandeering the souls of men (demon-possession, in modern parlance), and these demonized men marrying the daughters of other men. It is these same angelic lowlifes whom Peter and Jude reference as having been imprisoned at the time of the flood and as now being kept in dungeons for ultimate judgment. Unbelievable? I think not. As the highly respected Old Testament scholar Gordon Wenham has said, "If the modern reader finds this story incredible, that reflects a materialism that tends to doubt the existence of spirits, good or ill. But those who believe that the creator could unite himself to human nature in the Virgin's womb will not find this story intrinsically beyond belief."[5]

Commentators have long seen that the wording of Genesis 6:2 parallels the fall of Eve in the garden (3:6). There Eve "*saw* that the fruit was good for food" and pleasing to the eye, and she took and ate. Here in the demonized replay of the fall, the object of lust is not fruit but the bodies of beautiful women that the sons of God "saw" and took for themselves. The picture is one of unmitigated lust. What would give a fallen spirit more pleasure than having sex through the body of the demonized human body? Perhaps only this — taking the whole thing to the lowest levels of perversion. I wonder if we have here the demonic beginning of harems? Given the fact that God will shorten life, as we will see in the next verse, it also appears that these marriages were an attempt to grasp something of divinity and to achieve immortality.

Just how low culture had gotten is evidenced by the apparent parental complicity in the marriage of their daughters to the demonic "sons of God." There is no hint that these were anything but proper marriages. In the ancient world there were not supposed to be any marriages apart from parental approval. Therefore, we must understand the girls' fathers as encouraging these unions, just as pagan fathers pushed their daughters into fertility cults.

Chilling! Genesis 6 gives us nothing less than the demonization of marriage and primeval culture itself. We will consider its individual implications below. But what we see here is the takeover of culture by Satan and his hosts. Evil has multiplied faster than the population, so that it has spread through the entire people of earth.

But more important than the details of this episode is that man was beyond self-help. Demonic powers were in the driver's seat.

Life shortened. As we said, these demonized marital unions intended, as with eating from the tree of life, to secure eternal life for humanity. But God drastically reduced man's life span from some nine hundred years to a little over a hundred: "My Spirit[6] shall not abide in man forever, for he is flesh: his days shall be 120 years" (v. 3). Having sought immortality through his liaisons, man was sentenced to live a maximum of 120 years — roughly a sevenfold reduction of the average life span of the antediluvians. This is problematic in the wider setting of Genesis because Noah and many of his descendants lived hundreds of years (cf. Genesis 11). Abraham lived to be 175, Isaac 180, and Jacob 147 years. However, it may simply be that 120 years as a life span was gradually implemented. As Wenham points out, "In the post-flood period, the recorded ages steadily decline (chap. 11), and later figures very rarely exceed 120. After the time of Jacob, the longest-lived include Joseph (110, Gen. 50:26), Moses (120, Deut. 34:7), and Joshua (110, Josh. 24:29). Only Aaron (123, Num. 33:39) exceeds 120."[7] So much, then, for man's attempt at superhumanity. He not only fell short of immortality — his mortality shrank!

Violence idolized. Verse 4 introduces the Nephilim (literally, "fallen ones"): "The Nephilim were on the earth in those days, and also afterward, when the sons of God came in to the daughters of man and they bore children to them. These were the mighty men who were of old, the men of renown." The Nephilim were the offspring of the demonized marriages. Older translations of this verse translated Nephilim as "giants" because the only other reference to the Nephilim is Numbers 13:33 where they are described as so tall that the Israelites felt like grasshoppers. A direct genetic link is impossible because all the pre-flood Nephilim perished. Perhaps they were giants (the products of demonized eugenic breeding — "we breed horses; why not people?"); perhaps they were not.

But one thing is sure — these fallen ones were the heroes (the mighty men) of old, "men of renown" — and men of violence. The same word is used in 10:8 to describe "Nimrod; he was the first on earth to be a mighty man." If the Nephilim were giants, they were all the more fearsome. So we see that the "men of renown," the idols of pre-diluvian culture, were violent men. The ESV "sons of God came in to the daughters of man" captures an animalistic expression for sexual relations.[8] Sexual violence was a certitude.

The portrait that Moses gives of pre-flood culture is that of a thoroughly demonized civilization. It was, of course, destroyed by the flood. But it has enjoyed mini-recurrences throughout subsequent history. Canaanite Baal worship is an infamous example of phallic violence. The Herodians during Christ's life were a cesspool of sensuality and violence. Nero's and Caligula's Roman courts come to mind, as does the depravity of the Third Reich.

Today, though I would not go as far as to say that western culture is demonized, I will say that the signs are growing more ominous. Certainly a demonization of sexual relations has taken place. How can you conclude otherwise when at given times on the major networks you can view men on top of women and women on top of men and same-sex individuals engaged in *faux* sexual intercourse (and is it all pretend?)? How can you think otherwise when the daytime talk shows will plumb any subject, with the most appalling bathos? How can you think otherwise when the holy name of God is blasphemed *de rigueur*, while the most holy things (from the virgin birth to the sexuality of Jesus) are the subject of obscene jokes? How can you suppose otherwise when so many of the heroes of our culture, our "men of renown," are violent?

I once heard ex-heavyweight champion Mike Tyson talk up his upcoming fight by saying that he would kill his opponent and that he would do anything because he (Tyson) was a convicted rapist! Here was a man gleefully referencing his sexual violence before the world. This is the same man who bit off part of an opponent's ear! Do we think the WWF (World Wrestling Federation) is a joke? I hope not! Sensuality, violence, comic-book fantasy, testosterone, steroids, Viagra, blood — that is what the voyeurs drink. The next time you read of someone beaten to death or dragged to death, remember all the negative models. Video stores rent movies of animal attacks on people so you can view the real thing — humans being torn apart — while you eat popcorn. Truly a feast of demons.

I could not guess who they are, but demonized men and women are at the controls of all this — Nephilim. "For we do not wrestle against flesh and blood, but against the rulers, against the authorities . . . against the spiritual forces of evil in the heavenly places" (Ephesians 6:12).

HUMAN DEPRAVITY (v. 5)

What does God think of this? The Genesis account tells us in dramatic terms, set up by the repeated phrase in chapter 1 of God's assessment of creation — "And God saw that it was good" (1:9, 18, 21, 25), concluding with "it was very good" (v. 31). Now here we read in stark contrast, "The LORD saw that the wickedness of man was great in the earth, and that every intention of the thoughts of his heart was only evil continually" (v. 5).

It is hard to conceive of a more emphatic statement of the wickedness of the human heart. The words "every . . . only . . . continually" leave nothing out. The term "every intention" is literally "every forming," which comes from the metaphorical sense of the verb that describes a potter in the act of forming and molding his vessel (cf. Isaiah 29:16; Genesis 2:7, 8). "It means even the reflections of fantasy, the rising and freely formed movements of the will were 'only evil continually'" (Von Rad).[9] Their depravity was not a temporary state. There were no relentings, no repentances, no hesitations. Lust was their medium, violence their method. This was total, inveterate depravity.

DIVINE JUDGMENT (vv. 6, 7)

The relentless depravity of the primeval race set divine judgment on its inevitable course.

God's grief. Moses first gives us a peek at God's heart: "And the LORD was sorry that he had made man on the earth, and it grieved him to his heart" (v. 6). We must not imagine that God was surprised or taken unaware. Elsewhere he said, "And also the Glory of Israel will not lie or have regret, for he is not a man, that he should have regret" (1 Samuel 15:29). Though God's eternal joy and happiness cannot be disturbed, he is not a disinterested observer of the human scene. One of the marks of personality is feeling, and here in Genesis we read that God's heart was filled with pain. The word expresses the most intense form of human emotion, "a mixture of rage and bitter anguish" — like Jonathan experienced when he learned of Saul's plan to kill David (cf. 1 Samuel 20:34; 2 Samuel 19:2).[10]

God's plan. So God responded with a declaration of irrevocable judgment: "So the LORD said, 'I will blot out man whom I have created from the face of the land, man and animals and creeping things and birds of the heavens, for I am sorry that I have made them'" (v. 7). His judgment would involve a complete erasure of man and all accompanying creatures from existence. The destruction of everything from man to animals had to do with man's given sovereignty over the earth, for the irrational creatures were created for him and therefore were involved in the fall.[11] There would be no half-measures in dealing with sin. God's terrible resolution was grounded in the promise he had made that the seed of the woman would crush the serpent's head (cf. 3:15). The race was thoroughly demonized and incapable of delivering such a seed, and thus it was only right that humanity be destroyed.

DIVINE GRACE (v. 8)

But just as there were no half-measures in executing judgment, there were no half-measures in effecting salvation: "But Noah found favor in the eyes of the LORD" (v. 8). It was all of grace. Noah had responded like Enoch to the grace of God. The Scriptures say of Noah that he, like Enoch, "walked with God" (v. 9). Like Enoch, he walked in deepest intimacy and obedience with God. Noah knew God.

Now Noah was a wretch like the rest. He was not saved by his righteousness. He was saved by grace. Left to himself, he would have perished like the rest.

This side of the flood, we don't have to fear a universal deluge (cf. 9:12-16). Nevertheless we must fear a more lethal flood — that of being forever drowned beneath the cold waves of our own sin. Our only hope is in God's great grace.

> *Sin and despair, like the sea waves cold,*
> *Threaten the soul with infinite loss;*
> *Grace that is greater, yes, grace untold,*
> *Points to the refuge, the mighty cross.*
> JULIA H. JOHNSTON,
> "GRACE GREATER THAN OUR SIN"

Today our world rightly sits under the judgment of God. Perhaps it is not thoroughly demonized, but the signs are there. Who can doubt it as they look at popular culture? Who can doubt it when so many of our heroes are people of violence?

We, despite the flood and the cross of Christ, are a profoundly sinful people in soul and word and deed.

- *Souls*: "'None is righteous, no, not one; no one understands; no one seeks for God. All have turned aside; together they have become worthless; no one does good, not even one'" (Romans 3:10-12).
- *Words*: "'Their throat is an open grave; they use their tongues to deceive.' 'The venom of asps is under their lips.' 'Their mouth is full of curses and bitterness'" (vv. 13, 14).
- *Deeds*: "'Their feet are swift to shed blood; in their paths are ruin and misery, and the way of peace they have not known'" (vv. 15-17).

Such are we if left to ourselves. There is always room for de-provement — if we refuse the grace of God.

Just how relevant is this primeval story? Jesus thought it highly so and said:

> *As were the days of Noah, so will be the coming of the Son of Man. For as in those days before the flood they were eating and drinking, marrying and giving in marriage, until the day when Noah entered the ark, and they were unaware until the flood came and swept them all away, so will be the coming of the Son of Man. (Matthew 24:37-39)*

Our only hope is the marvelous grace of God. "For by grace you have been saved through faith. And this is not your own doing; it is the gift of God, not a result of works, so that no one may boast" (Ephesians 2:8, 9). "He saved us, not because of works done by us in righteousness, but according to his own mercy, by the washing of regeneration and renewal of the Holy Spirit" (Titus 3:5).

15

De-creation:
The Biblical Flood

GENESIS 6:9 — 7:24

The Genesis assessment of the sinfulness of pre-flood humanity astounds us: "The LORD saw that the wickedness of man was great in the earth, and that every intention of the thoughts of his heart was only evil continually" (6:5). As bad as our world is today, this cannot be said of it. It is true that every aspect of our personalities is tainted with sin (cf. Romans 3:9-18). But it is not true that "every intention" of the thoughts of every man's and every woman's heart are "only evil continually" — at least not yet. But this was, indeed, the pre-flood assessment and forecast. Every forming, every purposing of their thoughts (as the Hebrew stresses) was evil all the time.

Pre-flood culture had undergone a thorough demonization. Fallen angels (demons) had taken over the souls and bodies of men and through marriage had produced Nephilim (fallen ones) who became the violent "mighty men who were of old, men of renown" (6:4). Marriage had been demonized, and violence was idolized. Sexual violence was *de jure*. Therefore God decided to wipe the world clean of every trace of humanity, except for the man Noah: "But Noah found favor in the eyes of the LORD" (v. 8). So ends the second *toledot* ("These are the generations of" section) of Genesis.

Toledot three. This third section of Genesis, which recounts the flood of judgment, runs from 6:9 to the end of chapter 9. It is the longest of the ten sections of Genesis and serves as the centerpiece of primeval history. This section provides an "interpretive bridge between the shadowy past before the flood and the nearer more comprehensible era of the fathers following the deluge" (Mathews).[1] It is key to understanding ourselves today because we see how a soul is saved from destruction and is instructed in the doctrine of salvation. And we also see what kind of man Noah was, because though Noah was exemplary throughout the flood, Noah's behavior was disappointing after the deluge. The story actually ends on a lower note than it begins. Furthermore, the sin of Noah's son Ham foretells the moral setting of the world into which Abraham was born and ultimately in which we live. It explains life.

Structure. The shape of the flood account indicates exacting care by Moses as to its content and literary style. In literary terms it is a chiasmus. That is, the flood story divides into halves, with the second half being a mirror image of the first, but in reverse order. The first half, which describes the beginning and the 150-day rise of the flood, is a kind of *de-creation*, while the second half, which gives the 150-day receding of the floodwater and its end, is a kind of *re-creation*. The center of this mirror-imaged structure is in the opening line of chapter 8, "But God remembered Noah." Allen Ross has provided this helpful diagram:

Title: "These are the generations of Noah."

Introduction: Noah's righteousness and Noah's sons (6:9-10).

A God resolves to destroy the corrupt race (6:11-13).

B Noah builds an ark according to God's instructions (6:14-22).

C The Lord commands the remnant to enter the ark (7:1-9).

D The flood begins (7:10-16).

E The flood prevails 150 days, and the mountains are covered (7:17-24).

F God remembers Noah (8:1a)

E ' The flood recedes 150 days, and the mountains are visible (8:1b-5).

D ' The earth dries (8:6-14).

C ' God commands the remnant to leave the ark (8:15-19).

B ' Noah builds an altar (8:20).

A ' The Lord resolves not to destroy humankind (8:21-22).[2]

Obviously Moses has not given us a stream-of-consciousness rendition of the flood, but a highly nuanced historical and theological account.

Noah and Adam. The de-creation/re-creation theme creates a deliberate parallel between Adam and Noah and between Adam's world and Noah's world. As Kenneth Mathews observes:

> Noah is depicted as Adam *redivivus* (revived). He is the sole survivor and successor to Adam; both "walk" with God; both are the recipients of the promissory blessing; both are caretakers of the lower creatures; both father three sons; both are workers of the soil; both sin through the fruit of a tree; and both father a wicked son who is under a curse.[3]

Just as Adam's conduct accounted for the spiritual shape of the pre-flood world, so Noah's conduct accounts for the spiritual contours of the post-flood world.

Noah and Moses. As Moses compiled the Genesis account, and then the account of Exodus, he must have marveled at the parallels with his own life. The Hebrew word for "ark" was used in Genesis to refer to Noah's ship. The only other place that Hebrew word appears in the Old Testament is in Exodus 2:3, 5 when it is translated "basket" — the basket into which Moses' mother placed him to drift down the Nile. Just as the great pitch-covered ark preserved Noah and his family from a watery death, so the tiny pitch-covered ark/basket preserved Moses (cf. Genesis 6:14 and Exodus 2:3).[4] Moses, the greatest man of the old covenant, experienced a salvation through an ark parallel to that which saved Noah, the man who "found favor in the eyes of the LORD."

Then later, as Moses opposed Pharaoh, he witnessed God's judgment by water when God unleashed the waters of the Red Sea, flooding destruction over the armies of Egypt (cf. Exodus 14:26-31). That was a microcosm of the original deliverance of Noah, and it likewise preserved a people to serve God.

Lastly, Moses was given explicit instructions for building the tabernacle, just as Noah had been given detailed instructions for the ark, even down to specifications regarding clean and unclean animals. These parallels suggest that Moses saw a comparison between the salvation in the ark of Noah during the forty days and forty nights of rain and the salvation in the presence of the tabernacle during the forty years in the wilderness.[5]

Because the flood story is a carefully crafted, perfectly constructed chiastic account featuring intentional parallels with the great saving figures of Adam, Noah, and Moses, we need to pay careful attention to its message. But we must understand that the message is *not the flood* — though it is one of the most gripping accounts of Scripture. Neither is the message one of judgment, though it describes an awful judgment. Rather the story focuses on Noah as the kind of man who is saved out of a lost world. The message is salvific. Here we find out why God saved Noah.

NOAH AND MANKIND (vv. 9-12)

Righteous Noah. Moses describes Noah in terms of a fully-dimensioned man of God. "These are the generations of Noah. Noah was a righteous man, blameless in his generation. Noah walked with God. And Noah had three sons, Shem, Ham, and Japheth" (vv. 9, 10). "Noah was a righteous man" not because he was perfect or had an antecedent righteousness, but because he believed God. Like Abram after him, who "believed the LORD, and he counted it to him as righteousness" (Genesis 15:6), Noah believed. The fact that his righteousness came by faith is made unmistakably clear in the New Testament. "By faith Noah, being warned by God concerning events as yet unseen, in reverent fear constructed an ark for the saving of his household. By this he condemned the world and became an heir of the righteousness that comes by faith" (Hebrews 11:7).

The statement that "Noah was a righteous man" is the first mention of righteousness in the Bible and sets the standard that righteousness comes by faith. The biblical doctrine of imputed righteousness began before the flood. This is the first of the Old Testament expressions that are made more explicit in subsequent Old Testament texts (cf. Genesis 15:6; Psalm 32:2) and are given full flower in the New Testament (cf. Romans 1:17; 3:21, 22; 5:17, 19; 2 Corinthians 5:21; Philippians 3:9; Titus 3:5; Hebrews 11:7; 2 Peter 1:1).

That he was also "blameless in his generation" (Genesis 6:9) describes his moral conduct. He, of course, was not sinless, but his conduct was blameless despite the evil context. The demonized culture did not divert or pervert him, nor could it indict him. He was the one bright spot among the numberless darkened souls of the primeval world.

And like Enoch he "walked with God." Enoch and Noah were the only primeval patriarchs to walk with God. They experienced a taste of the intimacy and obedience that pre-fallen Adam and Eve knew when God walked with them in the garden. Noah was a full-dimensioned, remarkably complete man of God. He had "found favor [grace] in the eyes of the LORD" (v. 8).

Sinful mankind. In contrast, sin is flat and monotonous, and the author describes the world and its people with two dimensions — "corrupt," "corrupted," and "filled with violence." "Now the earth was corrupt in God's sight, and the earth was filled with violence. And God saw the earth, and behold, it was corrupt, for all flesh had corrupted their way on the earth" (vv. 11, 12). This is the tragic bookend to 6:5: "The LORD saw that the wickedness of man was great in the earth, and that every intention of the thoughts of his heart was only evil continually." The Nephilim, violent warriors, were the "men of renown" (v. 4). It was a bloody culture in the grasp of demonic aliens.

Preached righteousness. Surrounded by corruption, righteous Noah not only stood alone but very tall. Second Peter 2:5 reveals that Noah was "a herald of righteousness." Since Genesis does not say what he preached, later Jewish imagination filled in the lines. The *Sibylline Oracles* imagined these impassioned words:

> Faithless men, maddened by passion, do not forget the great things God has done; for the immortal all-provident Saviour knows all things, and he has commanded me to be a messenger to you, lest you be destroyed by your madness. Sober yourselves, cease from your evil practices and from mur-

derous violence against each other, soaking the earth with human blood. Reverence, my fellow mortals, the supreme and unassailable Creator in heaven, the imperishable God who dwells on high. Call upon him, all of you (for he is good) to be merciful to you all. For this whole vast world of men will be destroyed with water and you will then utter cries of terror. Suddenly the elements will turn against you and the wrath of Almighty God will come upon you from heaven.[6]

Preaching righteousness in any way, however measured or impassioned, would not have gone down well in the violence-ridden, pre-flood culture. Noah would not have survived had not God, as Peter says, "preserved Noah, a herald of righteousness, with seven others" (2 Peter 2:5).

ARK OF SALVATION (vv. 13-22)

Ark of salvation. Having described Noah in his inhospitable context, God speaks, framing his instructions for the ark with declarations of utter judgment in verses 13 and 17:

> *And God said to Noah, "I have determined to make an end of all flesh, for the earth is filled with violence through them. Behold, I will destroy them with the earth. Make yourself an ark of gopher wood. Make rooms in the ark, and cover it inside and out with pitch. This is how you are to make it: the length of the ark 300 cubits, its breadth 50 cubits, and its height 30 cubits. Make a roof for the ark, and finish it to a cubit above, and set the door of the ark in its side. Make it with lower, second, and third decks. For behold, I will bring a flood of waters upon the earth to destroy all flesh in which is the breath of life under heaven. Everything that is on the earth shall die." (vv. 13-17)*

The ark was of incredible size, especially in its ancient setting. When Noah laid out its keel at 450 feet, the pre-diluvians must have laughed themselves silly. We can visualize it by imagining the length of one and a half football fields! It was 238 feet longer than the *Cutty Sark*, the largest wooden boat ever built, at 212 feet. Of course, in modern times the advent of steel has made possible much larger vessels. The *Queen Elizabeth* was over 1,000 feet in length.[7]

What a monster the ark was! As best we can tell, the ark was shaped like a shallow box topped with a roof, with an eighteen-inch space under the roof interrupted only by the roof supports, so light could get into the vessel from every side. Noah had more than enough work to keep him and his three sons occupied for a century. Remember, there were no trucks, no chain saws, and no cranes.

Covenant of salvation. The only thing that Noah had to sustain him was the bare word of God, God's promise — the so-called Noahic covenant, here given in abbreviated form as part of further instructions for the ark:

> *But I will establish my covenant with you, and you shall come into the ark, you, your sons, your wife, and your sons' wives with you. And of every living thing of all flesh, you shall bring two of every sort into the ark to keep them alive with you. They shall be male and female. Of the birds according to their kinds, and of the animals according to their kinds, of every creeping thing of the ground, according to its kind, two of every sort shall come in to you to keep them alive. Also take with you every sort of food that is eaten, and store it up. It shall serve as food for you and for them. (vv. 18-21)*

Certainly more was said to Noah than the cryptic message of verse 18, because Noah went into the ark knowing that he was not only to be a survivor but "the bearer of God's promise for a new age."[8] The specifics of the covenant were unfolded at the end of the flood, as 9:1-17 will show. This promise, this bare word of God, was what sustained Noah for a century of labor and the final seven days of gathering the animals and then seeing the door slammed tight.

The promise of God's word is the sustenance of his people. But our advantage is incomparable because we have *all* the promises of the vast corpus of God's Word, Holy Scripture. And more than that, they are all "Yes" in Christ (2 Corinthians 1:20). Every promise is fulfilled in him. How much greater, then, should our obedience be!

Obedience of salvation. God had given Noah two things in his communication to that patriarch — a detailed design for the ark and the covenant promise of salvation. But as important as those are, the one thing we must fasten onto is the brief descriptive statement that caps God's speech: "Noah did this; he did all that God commanded him" (v. 22). In an epic biblical account like that of the flood, it is the repetitions that most clearly convey the author's message. Variations of this description of Noah occur four times in the subsequent text, and they are carefully placed. Genesis 7:5 records that in response to God's instructions for the final seven days, "Noah did all that the LORD had commanded him." Verse 9 records that the animals entered the ark "as God had commanded Noah." And again in verse 16, before the door was shut, "those that entered, male and female of all flesh, went in as God had commanded him."

This refrain of obedience represented Noah's long life — "he did all that God commanded him" — "Noah did all that the LORD had commanded him." An amazing man had risen out of the heart-dead wastes of primeval culture. Here was a man who knew who God was, knew who he himself was, and obeyed God's word. Noah was a man alive to God. Here was monumental obedience. Calvin gets to the point:

> First, the prodigious size of the ark might have overwhelmed all his senses, so as to prevent him from raising a finger to begin the work. Let the reader reflect on the multitude of trees to be felled, on the great labour of conveying them, and the difficulty of joining them together. The matter was also long deferred; for the holy man was required to be engaged more than a hundred years in most troublesome labour. Nor can we suppose him to have been so stupid, as not to reflect upon obstacles of this kind.[9]

Building the ark required careful planning and engineering and a century of sweat, but "Noah did this; he did all that God commanded him" (v. 22). When Noah finished laying out the incredible 450-foot keel and began to install the ark's ribs, imagine the abuse he took! How many Noah jokes do you think people could come up with in a century? Imagine the taunts that came at the expense of Noah and his own: "How many of Noah's sons does it take to drive a spike? One to hold the spike, and one to . . ." But Noah remained obedient, doing exactly what God said, for twenty-five . . . fifty . . . seventy-five . . . a hundred years — until the ark lay like a huge coffin on the land.

And beyond the ridicule there was the settled hatred of a demonized culture and its fallen ones, the violent "men of renown." When they saw that the ark was meant to save Noah and his family, some undoubtedly flew into a homicidal rage. Noah's preaching of righteousness would have brought death apart from God's protective hand. Finally at the end, as Noah brought supplies into the high and dry ark and collected the animals, we read twice that it all happened "as God had commanded Noah" (7:9, 16). The words *everything* and *all* describe Noah's obedience.

So now we begin to see what it means to be righteous. The righteous person rests everything on the bare word of God and obeys it. We also glimpse what it means to walk with God, because to walk with him is not a stroll. It means to go the same way in obedience — even as the culture marches the other way. What is the person God saves like? He believes in God's promise to him, and it is counted as righteousness. As a righteous man he lives not a perfect but a blameless life. He walks with God. And everything about him is covered by obedience to God's perfect word.

THE DELUGE (7:1-24)

Final instructions. The opening paragraph of chapter 7 (vv. 1-4) contains God's final words to Noah just seven days prior to the flood. And the following paragraphs up to verse 16 review and reiterate what God had said.

Each of the brief paragraphs reveals something more about the event. Verse 2, which commands Noah to "Take with you seven pairs of all clean animals," anticipates Noah's offering sacrifices at the end of the voyage and also anticipates the sacrificial system that would develop after the flood. Noah and his family were sinners who would carry into the new world the sin of the old.[10] Verse 4 records God's final spoken sentence before the flood, one of total destruction: ". . . and every living thing that I have made I will blot out from the face of the ground" (v. 4). The seven-day pause recorded in verse 10 was, according to the Jewish midrash, a period of mourning for the death of Methuselah who died in the year of the flood (cf. 5:27, 28).[11] Lastly, verse 16 reveals, "And the LORD shut him in." The single heavy, pitched-over door of the ark was locked by an act of God. There Noah and his family sat in darkness, lighted first on one side, then the other by the lolling sun in its course from east to west.

Universal flood. And then down came torrential rains.

> *The flood continued forty days on the earth. The waters increased and bore up the ark, and it rose high above the earth. The waters prevailed and increased greatly on the earth, and the ark floated on the face of the waters. And the waters prevailed so mightily on the earth that all the high mountains under the whole heaven were covered. The waters prevailed above the mountains, covering them fifteen cubits deep. (vv. 17-20)*

The language is evocative of a violent, churning, whirling maelstrom. The repetitions in these brief verses of "waters" (5x), "increased" (2x), "rose"(3x, NIV), and "greatly" (3x in the Hebrew)[12] portray a wild "water, water everywhere" ride. The earlier description in verse 11 ("on that day all the fountains of the great deep burst forth, and the windows of the heavens were opened") describe a great rending of the beds of the seas and torrential rain and makes us recall chapter 1 when the waters above and below the firmament were separated (cf. 1:6, 7). Now in a massive act of *de-creation* they were unleashed back into chaos.

The forty days and forty nights picture floods raging over vast continents, unleashing total destruction. The famous and older Gilgamash Epic, which certainly references the flood, describes the flood as "Gathering speed as it blew, [submerging the mountains], overtaking the [people] like a battle" (Tablet XI, lines 109, 110).[13] The storm was supernatural. Only the coffin-like ark survived.

Universal death. Other than Noah and his family, there were no survivors.

> *And all flesh died that moved on the earth, birds, livestock, beasts, all swarming creatures that swarm on the earth, and all mankind. Everything on the dry land in whose nostrils was the breath of life died. He blotted*

out every living thing that was on the face of the ground, man and ani-
mals and creeping things and birds of the heavens. They were blotted out
from the earth. (vv. 21-23a)

This was the terminal reiteration of God's initial declaration of 6:7: "So the LORD said, 'I will blot out man whom I have created from the face of the land, man and animals and creeping things and birds of the heavens, for I am sorry that I have made them.'" The picture is one of total, unexceptionable death. Moses says, "Everything on the dry land in whose nostrils was the breath of life died" (7:22), which especially references man, into whose "nostrils" God had breathed "the breath of life" (2:7). All living souls in the pre-flood world died. Their corruption and violence could only be met with death.

No doubt there were people who felt they had no warning and shook angry, incredulous fists at Heaven. But the judgment was not a divine whim. Peter reveals that "God's patience waited in the days of Noah, while the ark was being prepared" (1 Peter 3:20). Noah had been warning mankind for over a century! Today, through the cross, Jesus has provided an ark of salvation from the coming judgment. He has warned explicitly of the coming judgment, and so have his apostles and prophets (cf. Matthew 24:36-44 and 2 Peter). Only those who enter the ark through his redeeming blood will be saved. This has been the message in these last days — for more than two thousand years.

As to the question of whether the flood was universal or local, this must be said: The Scriptures present the flood as universal, a cataclysm that was worldwide in scope. This is the sense of 6:7, 12, 13; 7:4, 19, 21-23; 8:21; 9:11, 19 and of the New Testament — "For they deliberately overlook this fact, that the heavens existed long ago, and the earth was formed out of water and through water by the word of God, and that by means of these the world that then existed was deluged with water and perished. But by the same word the heavens and earth that now exist are stored up for fire, being kept until the day of judgment and destruction of the ungodly" (2 Peter 3:5-7).

The only way you can read a local flood in the Genesis account is to read it phenomenologically as describing what Noah saw, from his limited viewpoint. But this is not the way the writers of the Old and New Testaments understood the flood, nor the rabbinical exegetes, nor the church until the nineteenth century. As for myself, I will read it as the writers of Scripture, including Moses, read it. I am wary of scientific certitudes that purport to tell how things have always been and must be. I am also wary of the certitudes of creation scientists, so-called, who use the same methods as scientific naturalism in an attempt to prove their case.

But if you want a certainty, here it is. The text is not concerned to discourse on geography or meteorology or paleontology. It is concerned rather to demonstrate what kind of man or woman is saved from judgment. And Noah provides the answer! "By faith," says the writer of Hebrews, "Noah, being warned by God concerning events as yet unseen, in reverent fear constructed an ark for the saving of his household" (11:7a). Being warned by God of coming destruction and being called to build an ark, Noah believed and became certain of what he did not see — namely, a terrible mountain of water engulfing the earth with an ark riding high — *visual certitude* (cf. Hebrews 11:1b). As this *visual certitude* combined with *future certitude*, he became sure of what he hoped for (cf. Hebrews 11:1a) — namely, the promise of salvation for him and his family. This dynamic certitude swept his soul. *Noah believed God.*

Therefore, "By this he condemned the world and became an heir of the righteousness that comes by faith" (Hebrews 11:7b). Like Abram, he "believed the LORD, and he counted it to him as righteousness" (Genesis 15:6). God found Noah "righteous" in his generation (Genesis 7:1). Such righteousness produced a life of obedience — a life that "walked with God" — as Noah did for the rest of his long life.

This life has "found favor in the eyes of the LORD" and will walk with him forever!

16

Re-creation:
The World Restored

GENESIS 8:1 — 9:17

The rise of the Genesis flood was a divine act of de-creation. At creation, God had made an expanse that he called "sky" to separate the watery chaos into waters above the sky and under the sky (cf. 1:6, 8). But the flood acted to effect a reversal of creation when "all the fountains of the great deep burst forth, and the windows of the heavens were opened" (7:11), engulfing the earth again in a wild watery chaos. The hydrological violence continued for forty days as water raged from great fissures in the seabeds and heaven's cataracts, while the rolling ark rode the dark valleys and steeps of the watery death like a gigantic sealed coffin.

Cosmic drama! But as gripping as the account is, its focus is not on the flood or on judgment but on Noah as the kind of person God saves from judgment. Noah was saved by faith, as the writer of Hebrews makes so clear: "By this he condemned the world and became an heir of the righteousness that comes by faith" (11:7b). Noah believed God, and righteousness was imputed to him. He is the first man in the Bible to be described as righteous: "Noah was a righteous man, blameless . . ." (6:9; cf. 7:1). And his faith and righteousness produced towering obedience in him. Four times the account gives variations of the declaration that "Noah . . . did all that God commanded him" (6:22; cf. 7:5, 9, 16). So we see that the person God saves is the one who believes the bare word of God — so that it changes his life. Whenever we read this story, we must see above the churning drama the arching faith and obedience of one man. Noah was the *only* figure of his time to experience the grace of God.

As we saw in the preceding chapter, the flood story divides into perfect halves of de-creation and then re-creation, with the second half providing a mirror image of the first half, but in reverse order. The symmetries in this re-creation half of the account are astounding because it not only mirrors the events of the first half but also presents a mirror-image repetition in the use of the numbers of days, as Wenham's chart shows:

> 7 days of waiting for flood (7:4)
> > 7 days of waiting for flood (7:10)
> > > 40 days of flood (7:17a)
> > > > 150 days of water triumphing (7:24)
> > > > 150 days of water waning (8:3)
> > > 40 days of waiting (8:6)
> > 7 days of waiting (8:10)
> 7 days of waiting (8:12)[1]

Moses' attention to detail amazes us. And if that is not enough, this re-creation half of the account not only mirrors the de-creation of the flood's rise but parallels the events of creation in Genesis 1 — the re-creation parallels the original creation![2] The implication for us readers is apparent, because such care means that essential theology and primary directives for living are here for us, if we will pay attention.

NOAH'S FAITHFULNESS (8:1-20)

The hinge between the two halves of the flood story is in 8:1, "But God remembered Noah . . ." And the function of that hinge is this: God's remembering is more than a recollection because when God remembers, he acts. When God remembered Abraham, he saved Lot (19:29). When he remembered Rachel, she conceived (30:22). As Brevard Childs said, "God's remembering always implies his movement toward the object. . . .The essence of God's remembering lies in his acting toward someone because of a previous commitment."[3]

So now God acted to bring restoration and re-creation to the flooded world: "But God remembered Noah and all the beasts and all the livestock that were with him in the ark. And God made a wind blow over the earth, and the waters subsided" (8:1). This wind echoed "the Spirit" ("wind" and "Spirit" are the same Hebrew word) in Genesis 1 hovering over the waters at creation.

Voyage ends. Here, as the author describes the flood's abatement, he gives great care to recording the exact calendar days. When God remembered Noah, the earth had already been flooded for 150 days or five months. Think of it — a five-month lock-in with Mrs. Noah, his three sons and their three wives, and a complete menagerie of the world's animals, birds, and crawlers. Five months of stable muck and bilgewater, daughters-in-laws and mother-in-law, and seasickness. There must have been times when Noah wished they would hit an iceberg!

The effect of the God-ordered wind caused enough abatement that "At the end of 150 days the waters had abated, and in the seventh month, on the seventeenth day of the month, the ark came to rest on the mountains of Ararat" (vv. 3b, 4) — somewhere in Armenia. And there the ark sat for over two more months, until "in the tenth month, on the first day of the month, the tops of the mountains were seen" (v. 5). They sat in the grounded ark for sixty days plus as they waited for the land to dry out, now some seven months in all.

In verses 6-12 the story focuses on the patience of Noah as he waited for God's deliverance in mounting monotony. After forty more days Noah sent out a raven that did not return. Then he sent out a dove on three journeys, waiting seven days between each of the journeys for a total of fifty-four days, as the dove returned once, returned again with an olive leaf, and then did not return.

What awesome faith! Righteous Noah not only displayed scrupulous obedience when he did everything God commanded him over a hundred-year period while building the ark but then displayed astounding endurance and faith as in the midst of confinement and discomfort he waited patiently for God's deliverance. There is no recorded evidence that God spoke to him during the months on the ark or that Noah had a new word from God. But he persevered in faith, manifested by his amazing obedience and patience — "walking with God."

Noah also learned as he went. He released the raven first because as an unclean bird it was expendable since it was good for neither food nor sacrifice (cf. Leviticus 11:15; Deuteronomy 14:14). But the dove was an altogether different bird. It was white and clean and often used for sacrifice (cf. Leviticus 1:14; 12:6). Because it was from among the clean animals, a dove would be sacrificed in Noah's post-flood burnt offerings (cf. 8:20).

"Noah with the dove in hand reflects the religious interests of the passage: the raven, an unclean bird departs from the ark, but the dove, indicative of purity (cf. Matt. 10:16), is a welcomed resident upon the vessel" (Mathews).[4] The picture of the dove's repeated returns and final release is one of lingering sweetness and beauty.

The primeval voyage concludes, "In the six hundred and first year, in the first month, the first day of the month, the waters were dried from off the earth. And Noah removed the covering of the ark and looked, and behold, the face of the ground was dry. In the second month, on the twenty-seventh day of the month, the earth had dried out" (vv. 13, 14).

Exit effected. Now the LORD spoke, evidently breaking his voyage-long silence, and he did so in the style of epic repetition:

> *Then God said to Noah, "Go out from the ark, you and your wife, and your sons and your sons' wives with you. Bring out with you every living thing that is with you of all flesh — birds and animals and every creeping thing that creeps on the earth — that they may swarm on the earth, and be fruitful and multiply on the earth." So Noah went out, and his sons and his wife and his sons' wives with him. Every beast, every creeping thing, and every bird, everything that moves on the earth, went out by families from the ark. (vv. 15-19)*

The effect of this kind of epic repetition is to slow down the pace of the story so that "It holds the picture a little longer and enforces it on the mind."[5] It is a kind of Hebraic slow motion. So we see Noah, almost as a second Adam, as he steps into a virgin world washed clean by judgment — amidst colorful birds filling the air and great animals lumbering forth and busy creatures scurrying about. There he stands with his family in the sunlight of a new world.

Altar built. It was glorious. But the first thought of Noah was Godward: "Then Noah built an altar to the LORD and took some of every clean animal and some of every clean bird and offered burnt offerings on the altar" (v. 20). Joyous worship, surrender, and atonement were in this offering. The burnt offering described here represented Noah's total surrender and dedication to God (cf. Leviticus 1). The offering was totally incinerated to picture the total giving of oneself. At the same time it was wholly celebratory — thanking God for the salvation just rendered. As it burnt and then incinerated to ashes, Noah was indicating in effect, "All my life is yours — everything!"

GOD'S RESPONSE (8:21 — 9:17)

From here on to 9:17 the story switches from Noah's faithfulness to God's response to Noah — a response of *grace, blessing,* and *covenant* — three words for the new world.

Grace. God's response to Noah's offering was one of grace: "And when the LORD smelled the pleasing aroma, the LORD said in his heart, 'I will never again curse the ground because of man, for the intention of man's heart is evil from his youth. Neither will I ever again strike down every living creature as I have done'" (8:21). The aroma pleased God, signaling his acceptance.

Noah's offering propitiated (turned aside) God's righteous wrath. Noah himself was not under God's wrath. He was already "righteous" and "blameless" (6:8, 9; 7:1) and "walked with God" (6:9). Therefore we understand that his offering propitiated God's wrath against sinful mankind in general.

Though man has not changed, though he still naturally gravitates to sin, God will not again curse the ground any further.[6] In respect to the flood, God responded with the gracious stanza,

> *While the earth remains,*
> *seedtime and harvest,*
> *cold and heat,*
> *summer and winter,*
> *day and night,*
> *shall not cease. (v. 22)*

Despite man's sin, God elected to be gracious and forbearing. God responded to Noah's sacrifice with grace to humanity for reasons totally within himself. Today we all live under this grace, though the world's sin seems to compound.

Blessed multiplication. Next God responded to Noah by repeating the blessing first given to Adam (cf. 1:22-25, 28-30), but with some qualifications due to human sin. God charged Noah's family to multiply and by implication to exercise dominion over the earth. "And God blessed Noah and his sons and said to them, 'Be fruitful and multiply and fill the earth'" (9:1). The blessing still is intact. It has been true, and always will be, that children are a blessing from God (cf. Psalm 127:3-5). God's people are charged to procreate and fill the earth.

But as they fill the earth and their dominion spreads, they are advised that while Adam enjoyed relationship with the animals, "The fear of you and the dread of you shall be upon every beast of the earth and upon every bird of the heavens, upon everything that creeps on the ground and all the fish of the sea. Into your hand they are delivered. Every moving thing that lives shall be food for you. And as I gave you the green plants, I give you everything" (vv. 2, 3).

The animals' fear of man had naturally developed after the fall, and now after the flood such fear was a part of everyday life. Humans were enjoined to eat the flesh of animals, which may or may not have been a new freedom. Meat was to be a normal part of the human diet.

Respect for animal life. This said, humans do not have wholesale rights over God's creatures since their life (blood) is God's possession: "But you shall not eat flesh with its life, that is, its blood" (v. 4). Humans are not to devour animals the way animals devour one another, while the blood is pulsing in the flesh. The reason for this is respect for life and beyond that the respect for the giver of life.[7] Life is in the blood, and God is the giver of life. Disregard for the gift of life is an affront to the giver of life. This divine prohibition against eating blood also prepared humanity to appreciate the use of blood in sacrifice because "Belonging to God, it could be seen as his atoning gift to sinners, not theirs to him" (Kidner).[8] Ultimately, we can understand that it is the life (blood) of the Lamb of God that is God's atoning gift to us.

Respect for human life. Before the flood, not only was humanity thoroughly corrupted, but the earth was "filled with violence" (6:13). Murder was a ho-hum, everyday occurrence. Violent men were "men of renown" (6:4). After the flood, Noah's descendants had the potential to descend to the same levels of violence — especially with the increase in population. Thus the Lord moved in his speech from respect of animal life to respect for human life: "And for your lifeblood I will require a reckoning: from every beast I will require it and from man. From his fellow man I will require a reckoning for the life of man" (v. 5).

No sin shows a greater contempt for life than homicide. Whereas an animal's blood may be shed but not consumed, human blood must not be shed. Any animal that shed human blood was summarily executed (cf. Exodus 21:28, 29). Similarly, God also demands "from his fellow man [Hebrew, "his brother"] . . . a reckoning for the life of man." God stated the accounting with *a fortiori* logic (from the greater to the lesser). As Cassuto renders it, "How much more so shall I require a reckoning for the blood of a man in this instance, seeing that the slain person is the brother of the slayer."[9] There is a double entendre here, because "from his brother" echoes the first human murder, when Cain murdered his brother. But also by virtue of our shared humanity in the image of God, all murder is fratricide.[10] The Lord then put his law in a compelling poetic stanza:

> *Whoever sheds the blood of man,*
> *by man shall his blood be shed,*
> *for God made man in his own image. (v. 6)*

Since man is created in the image of God and as such is of immense value, and since the blood (life) of man is God's alone, to take human life is to usurp God's sovereignty over life and death — and thus merits death itself. Precisely because life is so precious, the one who willfully takes another's life must suffer death at the hands of man.

Exacting retribution is not a personal matter but a societal obligation. Certainly we live in a day when there are judicial abuses, and the death penalty is sometimes politically and even racially motivated. Such abuses are an abomination. Woe to a system that wrongly administers the death penalty. Woe to the society who allows that to happen. Woe to judges who are culpable. God will not be mocked.

But to argue against the death penalty on humane grounds is to argue against God's Word. It exists precisely because of God's humane concerns.

To ignore it is to despise life. This was, and is, God's word to a violent world. This was meant and is meant to protect human life. To ignore God's teaching is to descend ever more into a society of violence.

Having given his advice about respecting life, the Lord closed this section of his speech to Noah with the same words with which he began: "And you, be fruitful and multiply, teem on the earth and multiply in it" (v. 7). Respect life and multiply!

Covenant. With this, God went on to declare the Noahic covenant, the very first covenant in the Bible, and as such one that informs every covenant to follow (the Abrahamic, Mosaic, Davidic, and new covenants):

> *Then God said to Noah and to his sons with him, "Behold, I establish my covenant with you and your offspring after you, and with every living creature that is with you, the birds, the livestock, and every beast of the earth with you, as many as came out of the ark; it is for every beast of the earth. I establish my covenant with you, that never again shall all flesh be cut off by the waters of the flood, and never again shall there be a flood to destroy the earth." (vv. 8-11)*

This grand covenant was/is *universal*, *unilateral*, and *unconditional*. Its universality is evident because it encompasses not only every human being (good or evil) but every living creature on the planet. It is unilateral in that God alone is the sole initiator. He twice calls it "my covenant" (vv. 8, 11). It does not require any assent, action, or ratification from mankind — not even acknowledgment. It is unconditional because there will never be another cosmic destruction by water no matter what we earthlings do. The covenant is the self-motivated promise of an unconditional mercy throughout human history.

The sign of the covenant was a rainbow, which is described here in joyous repetitions that "serve to underline the message, pealing like bells reverberating into the future" (Westermann).[11]

> *And God said, "This is the sign of the covenant that I make between me and you and every living creature that is with you, for all future generations: I have set my bow in the cloud, and it shall be a sign of the covenant between me and the earth. When I bring clouds over the earth and the bow is seen in the clouds, I will remember my covenant that is between me and you and every living creature of all flesh. And the waters shall never again become a flood to destroy all flesh. When the bow is in the clouds, I will see it and remember the everlasting covenant between God and every living creature of all flesh that is on the earth." God said to Noah, "This is the sign of the covenant that I have established between me and all flesh that is on the earth." (vv. 12-17)*

Beautifully, God called the rainbow simply "my bow." And twice Scripture associates a rainbow with God's glory, once to speak of his brightness (Ezekiel 1:28) and once to describe the light around his throne (Revelation 4:3). There was no suggestion that the bow was a new phenomenon. Rather, it was divinely owned as a sign for future generations.

One summer my wife, Barbara, and I stopped our car on a rise in northern Wisconsin, and we spent the better part of an hour observing a huge rainbow that arched across the sky. We could see both ends on the ground illuminating whole fields of grain within a shimmering, golden aura. It was God's dazzling bow — his universal, unilateral, unconditional sign of his grace. When God saw it, as he does all his bows (and he saw many that day across his cosmos), he remembered his covenant (cf. vv. 15, 16) — which means he acted to keep his gracious promise never to flood the world again.

We call this common grace. As believers we understand this forbearance and wait patiently for all things to be made new. Rainbows remind us that divine wrath gave way to peace and that judgment is God's "strange . . . work" (Isaiah 28:21).

It reminds us, too, of the ultimate work of the new covenant, when God's wrath was propitiated by his own Son on the cross, so that all who are in Christ find grace instead of wrath (cf. Romans 3:25; 1 John 2:2). Christ, the greater Noah, saves his people from the waters of death by his faithful obedience and atoning sacrifice.

Praise be to his name!

17

Noah:
Curse and Blessing

GENESIS 9:18-29

The biblical picture of Noah and his family standing resplendent in the sunlight of the new world as the ark's animal life emerged by families was given in the slow-motion style of Hebrew epic repetition so that it would impress our imaginations. It represented a new beginning, with magnificent Noah as the human centerpiece.

And Noah was magnificent indeed. The first thing he did was build an altar to the Lord and sacrifice burnt offerings, signifying the complete giving of his life to God. The aroma of Noah's total commitment pleased God. God then blessed Noah, calling for him to multiply so that his offspring would again fill the earth. The sacredness of human life was affirmed. Lastly, God established a covenant with Noah, promising that he would never again destroy the earth with a flood. The sign of the covenant was a shimmering rainbow, "my bow" as God literally termed it.

Noah stood resplendent, arched by the splendor of the spectrumed glory of God's bow. The sign of the covenant stood incandescent over Noah and his three sons Shem, Ham, and Japheth and their wives, from whom the whole earth would be populated (cf. vv. 18, 19). We can see them backlit by the pink and turquoise and gold of God's bow as the day fades.

What a day! And what a promise. Noah was a man of faith. And because of that, he was a righteous man. "By faith Noah," says the writer of Hebrews, " . . . became an heir of the righteousness that comes by faith" (11:7). Not only was he righteous — he was also "blameless in his generation," and he "walked with God" (Genesis 6:9) — just like Enoch who did not see death.

Further, God's call for Noah to build the ark and endure the voyage became the occasion for his amazing obedience — "He did all that God commanded him" (6:22; cf. 7:5, 9, 16) — and also the occasion for a remarkable patience of faith.

How would this great man fare? Surely, after his grand voyage, it would be something to see!

NOAH'S SIN (vv. 20, 21)

And it was — but not in the way we would expect: "Noah began to be a man of the soil, and he planted a vineyard. He drank of the wine and became drunk and lay uncovered in his tent" (vv. 20, 21). Righteous, rescued Noah lay passed out in a drunken stupor on the floor of his tent. Some commentators (especially the older ones) have tried to mute the scene. For example, Delitzsch said, "In ignorance of the fiery nature of wine, Noah drank and was drunken, and uncovered himself in his tent."[1]

But the reality is that Noah was not ignorant. He was over six hundred years old, and this event was some time after the flood because it takes years for a vineyard to produce, not to mention that he now had numerous grandsons because Ham's son Canaan was the youngest of four (cf. 10:6).[2] He was a seasoned man of the soil, and he knew what wine could do. He was no helpless victim. He passed out because his drinking had gone out of control. Noah had wrought his own degradation. The Hebrew "lay uncovered" is reflexive, which emphasizes that he "uncovered himself."[3] He was so utterly inebriated that he stripped himself naked and passed out. Having uncovered himself, he therefore had covered himself with shame and disgrace (cf. Habakkuk 2:15; Lamentations 4:21).

Sin was alive and well in the new world. Graeme Goldsworthy comments, "The flood did not purge the earth of wickedness and we cannot suppose that such was its purpose."[4] Indeed, if God wanted to eradicate evil, he would have had to eradicate the entire human race. But this God would not do — because he had promised that the offspring of Eve would one day crush the head of Satan (cf. 3:15).

Nonetheless, the virulence of sin is astounding. Noah was the one righteous man on the face of the earth. His righteousness was not self-generated, but God-given imputed righteousness that came by faith. His blameless life had been a thing of wonder in the depraved pre-diluvian world. But sin at that moment had conquered him. This helpless drunk, fallen unconscious in his tent, is as significant a warning to us as the flood. Noah could not make it on his own. He was terribly flawed. He needed help from beyond himself. He needed God's grace.

Noah's folly is recorded to make us wise. His pathetic example demonstrates that people in their prime, and even in their old age, are sometimes overtaken by sensualities that they before had avoided. I have known this because it has been told to me for years. But now I can feel it — the tendency to allow myself indulgences that I avoided when younger, be they visual or mental or physical, with the dismissive line that "I'm too old for these things to harm me." The tendency is to ease up when the conflicts lessen. When all the world was against Noah, he faced scorn and violence straight-up. But in his vineyard among his own who needed no proof of his virtue, he relaxed. Marcus Dods observed, "Noah is not the only man who has walked uprightly and kept his garment unspotted from the world so long as the eye of man was on him, but who has lain uncovered on his own tent floor."[5] We can become so careless in our home life that we forgo spiritual disciplines around those we trust. All too often the walls of our homes witness irritabilities and anger and slanderous words and laziness and sensualities that — if the walls could speak — would take our gray hairs down to Sheol.

Remember Robertson McQuilkin's words in "Let Me Get Home Before Dark":

> *The darkness of a spirit*
> *grown mean and small,*
> *fruit shriveled on the vine,*
> *bitter to the taste of my companions,*
> *burden to be borne by those brave few*
> *who love me still.*
> *No, Lord. Let the fruit grow lush and sweet,*
> *A joy to all who taste;*
> *Spirit-sign of God at work,*
> *stronger, fuller, brighter at the end.*
> *Lord, let me get home before dark.*

Noah's failure stands as a witness to the dangers that await the faithful with the passing of years. His sorry lassitude is a call to vigilance. But even more, the Scriptures here record Noah's fall in order to instruct us that this great pre-diluvian who had so honored God was a flawed man — *a sinner* — and thus in need of continual grace. Sin came with him into the new world. The human predicament survived intact. This was the painful new-world reality.

SONS' RESPONSES (vv. 22, 23)

Sin was alive and well in Noah — and also among his offspring. "And Ham, the father of Canaan, saw the nakedness of his father and told his two brothers outside. Then Shem and Japheth took a garment, laid it on both their shoulders, and walked backward and covered the nakedness of their father. Their faces were turned backward, and they did not see their father's nakedness" (vv. 22, 23).

Ham. Ham took a sniggering delight in the spectacle of his aged father sprawled naked in his tent. He also took perverse pleasure in exposing his father's folly to his brothers. His action mocked and ridiculed. It was a proto-abrogation of what would be the fifth commandment to "Honor your father and your mother" — and a heinous breach of the hierarchical order of creation. Ham desecrated his filial relationship, sinning against both his father and God. He, in effect, further *uncovered* his father's nakedness.

Shem and Japheth. In marked antithesis, Shem and Japheth acted to cover their father's nakedness by covering him with "*the* garment" (as the Hebrew literally reads).[6] Evidently Ham had completed Noah's uncovering of himself by bringing the discarded garment out to show his brothers. The Scriptures take great care to show that the brothers did not see their father's nakedness. Keeping their backs turned to Noah, they spread the garment across both their shoulders, then slowly backed into the tent and laid it upon him without looking. Thus they "covered the nakedness of their father." Truly, "love covers a multitude of sins" (1 Peter 4:8).

Here we must take careful note that the sons' covering of Noah's nakedness bears monumental spiritual implications, because their actions unwittingly imitated God. Remember that when Adam and Eve sinned, "The LORD God made for Adam and for his wife garments of skins and clothed them" (3:21). Noah's sons now covered his sin and nakedness.

The sons of Noah — Ham on the one hand, and Shem and Japheth on the other — are representative of two groups of mankind: those like Adam and Eve who with God's help have their nakedness covered, and those like Ham who make no attempt to cover their nakedness, even shamelessly exposing it.[7] To one group, the line of Shem, there will be blessing; but to the others, the Canaanites, there will only be a curse.

So right here we learn of the great demarcation that divides all humanity into those who are blessed in that their sins have been covered and those who are cursed because their sins lay uncovered. The then-future beatitude of King David voices the divine reality: "Blessed is the one whose transgression is forgiven, whose sin is covered" (Psalm 32:1).

NOAH'S ORACLES (vv. 24-27)

How Noah learned what had transpired, we do not know. Obviously someone had covered him up. Most likely he inquired and was told. No doubt he was provoked as much by Ham's words as he was by his actions because Ham's mocking words could well have caused fraternal division like that between Cain and Abel.[8] Noah's oracles here are his only recorded words in Scripture. His curse on Ham's son Canaan and his blessing on Shem and Japheth are in effect his last will and testament because the next verses report his death, bringing an end to ancient Sethite lineage.[9]

Curse. The curse came first:

> *When Noah awoke from his wine and knew what his youngest son had done to him, he said,*
>
> > *"Cursed be Canaan;*
> > *a servant of servants shall he be*
> > *to his brothers." (vv. 24, 25)*

The curse fell not on Ham, the perpetrator, but on the youngest of his four sons, who in order were, "Cush, Egypt, Put, and Canaan" (10:6).

Why did the curse fall on Canaan? First, because Noah likely detected in Canaan the evil traits he had seen in his father. Canaan was a bad apple who did not fall far from the tree. He was already walking in his father's footsteps.

Second, this curse was a prophetic oracle. Delitzsch writes:

Noah, through the Spirit and power of that God with whom he walked, discerned in the moral nature of his sons, and the different tendencies which they already displayed, the germinal commencement of the future course of their posterity, and uttered words of blessing and of curse, which were prophetic of the history of the tribes that descended from them.[10]

Such curses had no power in themselves, unless the Lord fulfilled them. God would bring this curse about only if it was his desire to do so — which it was.

Third, Canaan was the father of the Canaanites, the depraved nemesis of Israel. Therefore the curse fell on Israel's future enemies. The Canaanites were a sensually depraved people. Everything the pagan Canaanites did was an extrapolation of Ham's lurid sensuality. From the moment Abram entered the land, the Canaanites were there spreading corruption (cf. Genesis 13, 15, 18, 19, 38). Leviticus 18 describes the degenerate practices of the Canaanites with a litany of euphemisms so as not to offend the reader, employing "nakedness" twenty-four times (cf. vv. 7-23, RSV and NASB).[11]

The curse upon Canaan had immense contemporary relevance for the original readers of the Torah as they sojourned for forty years in the desert. Their orders were to drive out the Canaanites. Noah's oracle had prophesied the bitter fruit that all now could see. The Canaanites were naked, shameless, and uncovered. They would become the "servant of servants" (9:25) to Shem and Japheth — that is, to Israel and the Indo-Europeans and sea peoples as they swept over Canaan.

Blessings. Noah's "cursed be" was matched by "blessed be." Aged Noah looked again to the future in prophetic vision and saw the rich blessings that would be experienced by Shem and his descendants, the Israelites — and what he saw so elevated his soul that he burst forth in doxology.

> *"Blessed be the LORD, the God of Shem;*
> *and let Canaan be his servant." (v. 26)*

Just as we were surprised to see the curse go to Canaan instead of Ham, we are now surprised that the blessing is directed not to Shem, but to his Lord, Yahweh. Hamilton notes that "by directing the blessing to Yahweh instead of to Shem, the narrator subordinates the human actors to the divine actor. It is Yahweh, rather than Shem, who is praised."[12] What is most remarkable here is that the use of God's covenant name suggests that Shem (the ancestor of Israel) was already in covenant relationship with the Lord and that his blessing was found wholly in the Lord.[13] This special relationship with God is indeed the highest and greatest blessing anyone can experience. The way had been prophetically paved for Abram through the line of Seth to establish a people in special covenant relationship with Yahweh.

Noah's oracle then went on to extend the blessing to Japheth.

> *May God enlarge Japheth,*
> *and let him dwell in the tents of Shem,*
> *and let Canaan be his servant. (v. 27)*

A glance at the table of nations in 10:2-4 indicates that the Japhethites are what we would call Indo-Europeans, encompassing vast territories extending to whole continents. Noah's wish that "Japheth . . . dwell in the tents of Shem" involves the sharing of the blessings of Shem. But while the Israelites and Hamitic people from Egypt and Indo-Europeans from Asia Minor did regularly subjugate the Canaanites, there is no substantial evidence in the Old Testament of these Japhethite Gentiles living in the tents of the Shemites so as to share their blessings.

But the New Testament reveals otherwise! Through Christ, the Gentiles (both Hamitic and Japhethite) came to be the true seed of Abraham. "If you are Christ's, then you are Abraham's offspring, heirs according to promise" (Galatians 3:29). Regarding this, Calvin comments:

> This is done by the sweet and gentle voice of God, which he has uttered
> in the gospel; and this prophecy is still daily receiving its fulfillment,
> since God invites the scattered sheep to join his flock, and collects on every
> side, those who shall sit down with Abraham, Isaac, and Jacob, in the
> kingdom of heaven. It is truly no common support of our faith, that the call-

ing of the Gentiles is declared by the mouth of the Patriarch Noah; lest we should think it to have happened suddenly, or by chance, that the inheritance of eternal life was offered generally to all.[14]

The gospel is not new. It was declared first to Adam and Eve at the fall: "I will put enmity between you and the woman, and between your offspring and her offspring; he shall bruise your head, and you shall bruise his heel" (3:15). It was foreshadowed in God's covering their nakedness (cf. 3:21). It was pictured in Noah's deliverance from the waters of judgment (cf. 1 Peter 3:20).

Nevertheless, when Noah stepped into the new world washed clean by the flood, he brought sin with him. Its astounding virulence left him drunk and naked in his tent. Ham then made his father's sin the occasion for his own savage, sensual delight and the desecration of God's good order in creation.

Noah saw the same sin welling in Ham's youngest son, Canaan, and uttered an oracle that foresaw the degradation of Canaanites as enemies of God's people. But Noah's oracle also foresaw the blessing of Shem and his descendants, the Israelites, who would live in covenant relationship with Yahweh. Noah's oracle anticipated God's covenant with Abram:

And I will make of you a great nation, and I will bless you and make your name great, so that you will be a blessing. I will bless those who bless you, and him who dishonors you I will curse, and in you all the families of the earth shall be blessed. (12:2, 3)

That ultimate blessing came from the tents of Shem to the Gentiles through Christ. "If you are Christ's, then you are Abraham's offspring, heirs according to promise" (Galatians 3:29).

And today the gospel knows no boundaries. It goes to the children of Ham, Shem, and Japheth with saving power. "Here there is not Greek and Jew, circumcised and uncircumcised, barbarian, Scythian, slave, free; but Christ is all, and in all" (Colossians 3:11).

The gospel is not new. The unfolding of God's program of grace began with God's declaration to Adam and Eve. It was then heralded by Noah and Abram and Moses and David and the prophets — and ultimately fulfilled in Christ. All the promises — from Adam to John the Baptist — have been fulfilled in Christ. "For all the promises of God find their Yes in him. That is why it is through him that we utter our Amen to God for his glory" (2 Corinthians 1:20).

He is the ultimate covering for our sin. He is "the Lamb of God, who takes away the sin of the world!" (John 1:29).

18

Hope for the Nations

GENESIS 10:1-32

The names of Genesis 10 provide an exotic verbal map of the known world at the dawn of history. Three times (once for Japheth, then for Ham, and then for Shem), the author states that the Table was composed according to "their clans, their languages, their lands, and their nations" (v. 31; cf. vv. 5, 20) — which creates for our minds a baffling mishmash of ethnic, linguistic, geographical, and political designations. The descendants of Canaan listed in verse 17 sound to our ears like an entomologist's list of something for the pest controller — "Hivites, Arkites, Sinites," and termites!

Actually, however, this Table of Nations has carefully structured symmetries. For example, when we add up the nations that came from Noah's sons, we discover that they total seventy — another example of the multiples of sevens, tens, and seventies that we have seen so often in Genesis. Here it suggests totality — all the nations of the earth.

What is clear to everyone is that despite its complexity, the Table of Nations is structured on the familial symmetry of Noah's three sons Shem, Ham, and Japheth. The Japhethites made up "the geographical horizon"[1] of Moses' world, the outer fringes of the known world. Japheth's seven sons — "Gomer, Magog, Madai, Javan, Tubal, Meshech, and Tiras" (v. 2) — lived mostly to the north and east of Canaan and spoke the Indo-European languages.[2] Gomer dwelt north of the Caspian Sea. Tubal and Meshech settled around the southern shores of the Black Sea. Tiras lived west of the Black Sea in Thrace. Madai occupied the area south of the Caspian in what became Media. And Javan populated Ionia, the southern part of Greece. The sons of Javan spread around the northern Mediterranean as far west as Tarshish or southern Spain.

Ham's four sons — "Cush, Egypt, Put, and Canaan" (v. 6) — settled primarily in northeast Africa and Egypt, the eastern Mediterranean, and Southern Arabia. Cush populated the territory of the upper Nile south of Egypt. "Egypt" here really means "Egypts" and indicates Upper and Lower Egypt. No one is sure where Put was put! But Canaan settled in what was later called "Palestine," after the Philistines. The descendants of Canaan noted in verses 15-19 read like a "most wanted" list of Israel's inveterate enemies.

The five sons of Shem — "Elam, Asshur, Arpachshad, Lud, and Aram" (v. 22) — are the Semitic peoples. Elam's descendants lived between the Medes to the north and the Persian Gulf to the south. Asshur's descendants were the Assyrians in northern Mesopotamia. Arpachshad was the father of the Chaldeans in southern Mesopotamia. Lud's descendants were the Lydians of Asia Minor. And the Arameans dwelled in today's Syria. Of greatest significance among Shem's descendants was Eber (cf. vv. 24, 25). The name *Eber* is related to the word *Hebrew* — so that Eber is understood to be the ancestor of the Hebrew people. Ultimately "Abram the Hebrew" (14:13) shared descent from Eber through Peleg as the genealogy from Shem to Abram will show (cf. 11:16-26). It is through Abram that Noah's blessing of Shem would be ultimately realized.

What we have in the Table of Nations is the response to God's charge to Noah after the flood to "Be fruitful and multiply and fill the earth" (9:1). And thus the Table of Nations concludes expansively, "These are the clans of the sons of Noah, according to their genealogies, in their nations, and from these the nations spread abroad on the earth after the flood" (v. 32). It was from these geographical horizons that the world's population spread over the continents of the world — to India, Asia, the islands of the sea, and the continents beyond the setting sun.

The transcending truth of the Table of Nations is that it gives "an unparalleled ecumenical vision of human reality" (Brueggemann).[3] The Table declares the interrelatedness of all peoples. We all have the same ancestry. We all — "red and yellow, black and white" and pink and beige and piebald — share the dual paternity of Adam and Noah. Our DNA comes from the same source.

The Table also declares that all people derive their existence from the life-giving power of God and are responsible to him. The Apostle Paul used this truth in his famous sermon at the Areopagus in Athens when he called the idolatrous Athenians to seek the one true God:

> *And he made from one man every nation of mankind to live on all the*
> *face of the earth, having determined allotted periods and the boundaries*
> *of their dwelling place, that they should seek God, in the hope that they*
> *might feel their way toward him and find him. Yet he is actually not far*
> *from each one of us, for "In him we live and move and have our being";*

as even some of your own poets have said, "For we are indeed his off-spring." (Acts 17:26-28)

The divinely ordered juxtaposition of nations was set to enhance their turning to God.

All people are *united* to one another both by their ancestry and by their responsibility to their Creator God. But at the same time all the world's people are *divided* by geography and language and ethnicity and culture — and most of all by their fallenness and sin, which separates them both from God and each other. So, what is the answer for a people so united and yet profoundly divided? The answer is embedded deep in Genesis where Adam and Eve suffered division from God and each other through their sin, and God responded to Satan with an oracle that promised that one of her offspring would undo his work by crushing his head:

> *I will put enmity between you and the woman,*
> *and between your offspring and her offspring;*
> *he shall bruise your head,*
> *and you shall bruise his heel. (3:15)*

That was a divine prophecy of the cross, describing how Satan will strike the heel of Christ (the suffering of the cross) and how Christ will crush Satan's head (through Christ's death and glorious resurrection). The only hope for Adam and Eve, who were so sundered from God and each other (and from the whole world, which would be likewise divided), is through the offspring of Adam and Eve — and ultimately Jesus Christ.

How God preserved this unbroken line to Christ through primeval and patriarchal history is one of the great themes of Genesis — as evidenced in a series of dramas where the covenant line was almost wiped out and then saved by events both ridiculous and sublime. We will examine first how the primeval preservations were carried out through chapter 11, and then the patriarchal preservations in chapters 12 — 50. Lastly we will see what this preservation of the covenant line means to the Table of Nations.

PRIMEVAL PRESERVATIONS

Seth (chaps. 3 — 4). Adam had listened closely to God's speech to his spouse. He understood that one of her offspring would crush the head of the snake (cf. 3:15). So "the man called his wife's name Eve, because she was the mother of all living" (3:20). Eve means "life." He was so sure that she would bear offspring that he called his wife *Life*! Hope welled in the primeval couple.

And then when Eve gave birth to her first son, Cain, she said, "I have gotten a man with the help of the LORD" (4:1). Her words were an implicit declaration of faith. Adam had believed the promise of Genesis 3:15 and so had named her Life. And now she praised God with a newly charged faith for her *ish*, her man just like Adam. Later the advent of their second son, Abel, again buoyed their hope.

But all was not well. A dark shadow moved over the offspring. Ungodly Cain refused to bring an offering that would please God, whereas "By faith Abel offered to God a more acceptable sacrifice than Cain" (Hebrews 11:4). Seething, unbowed, Cain rejected God's remediation — and murdered his brother! As life faded from Abel's eyes, the promise went dark. With Abel's death there was no heir, no seed who would challenge, much less strike the head of the serpent.

Predictably, Cainite civilization went "the way of Cain" (Jude 11), as epitomized in the brutal Song of Lamech.

> *I have killed a man for wounding me,*
> *a young man for striking me.*
> *If Cain's revenge is sevenfold,*
> *then Lamech's is seventy-sevenfold. (4:23, 24)*

Darkness had gone to midnight. Exponential vengeance was customary.

But in this violent, seedless night there flashed light: "Adam knew his wife again, and she bore a son and called his name Seth, for she said, 'God has appointed for me another offspring instead of Abel, for Cain killed him'" (4:25). Eve's faith also shined bright because "another offspring" is literally "another seed," which references the promise of 3:15 that her seed would crush the serpent's head. How sweet it must have been for the mother of all living as she held the promise in her arms. And more, the grace of God was not in vain in the line of Seth, because "to Seth also a son was born, and he called his name Enosh. At that time people began to call upon the name of the LORD" (4:26). Seth's children worshiped — more exactly, they *proclaimed* — the name of the Lord. One day a child would come from Seth's descendants who would strike the snake. God was preserving his covenant line.

Flood (chaps. 5 — 9). Both the Cainite and Sethite lines multiplied. The apex of the long-lived Sethite patriarchs was Enoch who "walked with God, and he was not, for God took him" (5:24). Nevertheless, despite the elevating example of Enoch, Cainite civilization increased in dominance over the Sethites. Through the agency of fallen angels, men gave themselves over to demonization, so that marriages and children were conduits to sensuality and violence. The heroes of old were the violent Nephilim. Sethite civilization became indistinguishable from Cainite culture, so that "The LORD saw that the wickedness of man was great in the earth, and that every intention of the thoughts of his heart was only evil continually" (6:5). With this the Lord determined to put an end to all people save one (and his family) (cf. 6:6-8; 7:13).

The covenant hope had reduced to a single pinpoint in all humanity. Only one Sethite remained untarnished: "Noah was a righteous man, blameless in his generation. Noah walked with God" (6:9). This one man "did all that God commanded him" (6:22; cf. 7:5, 9, 16) during a century of preparation and on the incredible voyage. When the flood was over (cf. 8:15-18), Noah and his three sons Shem, Ham, and Japheth stood as the only hope for the fulfillment of the covenant promise of Genesis 3:15. The godly line was intact.

But it was hardly safe! Noah's drunken display demonstrated that (cf. 9:20-23). And the danger was confirmed by his son Ham's leering delight in his father's folly, desecrating his filial relationship and assaulting the good order of creation. If Shem and Japheth had followed suit, the covenant promise would have been nullified. But, of course, they did not, because they took their father's garment from Ham and covered Noah without looking upon his nakedness. This was an unwitting reenactment of God's earlier covering of the sin and nakedness of Adam and Eve (cf. 3:21). As such it portrayed two groups of mankind: those like Adam and Eve who by God's grace have their sins covered, and those like Ham who make no attempt to cover their nakedness, even exposing it. Divine judgment followed as Noah cursed Canaan, the youngest son of Ham who would become the father of the Canaanites — a people infamous for their violence and sensuality — perennial enemies of God's people.

Noah then countered with a blessing: "Blessed be the LORD [*Yahweh*], the God of Shem" (9:26). By blessing the covenant name of God, we see that Shem (the father of the Semitic peoples and Israel) was already in covenant relationship with God. It was through Shem that the line of Adam's son Seth would continue on to Abram, the father of Isaac, the father of Jacob. Among Shem's offspring came Eber, from which the name *Hebrew* was derived (cf. 10:21). And it is also through Shem that the Gentile Japhethite peoples would enjoy spiritual blessings "in the tents of Shem" (9:27) — a reference to the blessings that ultimately came through Christ: "And if you are Christ's, then you are Abraham's offspring, heirs according to promise" (Galatians 3:29).

The primeval preservations of God's promise to Eve astound us. The promise appeared to be finished with Cain's murder of Abel. But then came baby Seth — and people "called upon the name of the LORD" (4:26). With time, however, Seth's line became all but buried by the demonized Cainite civilization with its Nephilim, and "every intention of the thoughts of [their] heart was only evil continually." Such depravity. But God answered with Noah and the flood.

Righteous Noah and his three sons and their spouses were all who survived. And then the promise was narrowed to Shem (the Semites), from whom would come Abram the Hebrew. The promise would narrow down to one man again, father Abraham, but it would be for the benefit of all seventy of the Table of Nations.

PATRIARCHAL PRESERVATIONS

Abram's bloodline went back through Shem to Noah, the one remaining righteous Sethite, and through Seth to Adam and Eve and the promise — and thus God's promise to Eve came through him to the Table of Nations, "all the families of the earth." God's covenant to Abram reads:

> And I will make of you a great nation, and I will bless you and make your name great, so that you will be a blessing. I will bless those who bless you, and him who dishonors you I will curse, and in you all the families of the earth shall be blessed. (Genesis 12:2, 3)

The only problem was that Abram was childless, and after some years he expressed his despair to God:

> But Abram said, "O Lord GOD, what will you give me, for I continue childless, and the heir of my house is Eliezer of Damascus?" And Abram said, "Behold, you have given me no offspring, and a member of my household will be my heir." And behold, the word of the LORD came to him: "This man shall not be your heir; your very own son shall be your heir." And he brought him outside and said, "Look toward heaven, and number the stars, if you are able to number them." Then he said to him, "So shall your offspring be." And he believed the LORD, and he counted it to him as righteousness. (15:2-6)

That night God dramatically confirmed the promise when his fiery presence passed figure-eight-style around the halves of sacrifice (cf. 15:9-18).

Isaac (chaps. 15 — 21). Years passed and still no child. So Sarai and Abram took it upon themselves through Sarai's maidservant Hagar. Abram was eighty-six years old when Ishmael was born (cf. 16:16). But Ishmael was not to be the answer. In Abram's ninety-ninth year God ordered the circumcision of Abram and his clan as the sign of his covenant promise, also ordering him to rename Sarai Sarah, promising that she would have a son. Abraham laughed (cf. 17:17), but God persisted, instructing him to name the yet unconceived child Isaac. When the circumcisions were complete, Sarah herself overheard God's messengers again affirm that she would have a son within the year. "So Sarah laughed to herself, saying, 'After I am worn out, and my lord is old, shall I have pleasure?'" (18:12).

So although Abraham laughed incredulously and then Sarah laughed incredulously, they laughed together in great joy when baby Isaac (Hebrew for "laughter") was born. "And Sarah said, 'God has made laughter for me; everyone who hears will laugh over me'" (21:6). Amazing! God had taken an old couple who were "as good as dead" (Romans 4:19) in respect to child-bearing and gave them a son whose descendants would be as numerous as the stars, among whom would spring the bright morning star!

Jacob (chaps. 25 — 33). When Isaac, the sole heir of the promised seed, grew to his manhood and married Rebekah, she was at first barren (cf. 25:21). But in answer to Isaac's prayers Rebekah conceived twins who prophetically jostled in her womb. Esau was born first, with Jacob grasping his heel (cf. 25:26). Neither of the sons was honorable. Esau despised his birthright (cf. 25:34), and Jacob schemed to steal it, first by manipulating Esau to sell it and then by fooling his father Isaac into blessing him when he thought he was blessing Esau (cf. chaps. 25, 27).

Jacob did in fact become the legitimate heir through his dishonest deal-ings — and had to flee Esau's homicidal intentions (cf. 27:41ff.). It was in the land of Paddan-aram that Jacob met his match in double-dealing Laban, for whom he worked fourteen years in order to marry his beloved Rachel (cf. chaps. 29 — 31). When Jacob finally fled from Laban, it was as a chas-tened, much sobered man. And he would have to face Esau at the other end of the flight home. But first he was appointed to wrestle God in the night. When that was over, newly-crippled Jacob was renamed Israel (cf. 32:22-31). Then God gave Israel mercy from Esau. Finally, back in the land, he built an altar to God (cf. 33:20). This man Jacob, now Israel, had been pre-served and disciplined and sanctified by God so that he might become the father of the tribes of Israel. God's promise to Eve was alive in Jacob, the son of Isaac, the son of Abraham.

Judah and Tamar (chap. 38). The Bible places Jacob's son Judah fully in the line of Christ. At the end of Jacob's life he would prophesy concern-ing Judah,

> *The scepter shall not depart from Judah,*
> *nor the ruler's staff from between his feet,*
> *until tribute comes to him;*
> *and to him shall be the obedience of the peoples. (49:10).*

But Judah was an unlikely candidate if there ever was one! For starters Judah married a Canaanite. By her he had three sons — Er, Onan, and Shelah. Judah found a wife for his son Er named Tamar, but the marriage was short-lived due to Er's sin: "But Er, Judah's firstborn, was wicked in the sight of the LORD, and the LORD put him to death" (38:7). Judah then commanded his second oldest, Onan, to fulfill husband-obligations to Tamar. And when he disobeyed, God put him to death, leaving only one son, Shelah, who was yet a boy. When Shelah matured, Tamar was not given as a wife. The biological possibilities for the covenant line to continue through Judah were about zero.

Then Tamar, motivated only by concern for her status (certainly not by covenant responsibilities!), disguised herself as a Canaanite prostitute and sat by the roadside, where her widowed father-in-law Judah propositioned her. Tamar conceived, escaped death by revealing Judah's culpability, and gave birth to twins. The firstborn Perez, son of Judah, is listed with his father in the bloodline of Christ (cf. 38:29; Matthew 1:3; Luke 3:33).

So we see that God even overruled the compounded miseries of human sin to work his plan. There is a flash of grace here though, because the very bloodline of the Messiah has sinners in it who are as bad as we are. This prophesies hope for us all!

Joseph (chaps. 37, 39-48). The story of Joseph has a similar "sin used for good" twist. Joseph's near-murder by his older brothers and his subsequent sale into slavery in Egypt represents the height of treachery. What a great group the patriarchs were! Who would ever have guessed that Joseph would rise to become vicegerent of Egypt? And that he would wisely store supplies for a famine? And that his brothers would journey there to seek relief? And that he would recognize them? And forgive them? And that Jacob's family would be saved in and through Egypt? And that the covenant line would be preserved so that the world would have a Messiah? Who would ever have guessed that such evil would be used for such good? As Joseph himself said, "You meant evil against me, but God meant it for good, to bring it about that many people should be kept alive, as they are today" (50:20).

What a God we have! God works his plan out in and not apart from human history — right in the middle of the politics, tragedies, surprises, and schemings of fallen man. History has two authors — man and God, but it is God who sovereignly directs everything. Our mighty God keeps his promises. We can trust him even if all of life seems out of control. And we can expect him to deliver by the unexpected.

As already mentioned, there are seventy nations listed in the Table of Nations in Genesis 10. The selective list was composed because seventy is meant to convey totality, all the nations of the earth. It conveys a vast ecumenical unity of all humanity. And it was out of this one humanity that Abraham was called. The reason God chose Abraham is so that through his seed God's blessing would go to "all the families of the earth" (12:3).

And it is with this purpose in mind that Moses reminds his readers that the total number of Abraham's seed (that is, Jacob and his sons and their families) was seventy when they went down to Egypt (cf. 46:27; Exodus 1:5).

Before Abraham, the nations numbered seventy. After Abraham, at the close of Genesis, his seed numbered seventy — exactly parallel to the number of nations.[4] Moses is taking care to let us know that God has a special role for the seed of Abraham, which is to bring blessing to the whole earth. Jesus himself was aware of this, and that is why he once sent out seventy disciples.[5]

The answer for the world — which is so *united* in its humanity and its responsibility to God but so *divided* from God and one another by sin — comes through the ultimate seed of Abraham, Christ the Messiah. It was this Jesus who said, "All authority in heaven and on earth has been given to me. Go therefore and make disciples of all nations, baptizing them in the name of the Father and of the Son and of the Holy Spirit, teaching them to observe all that I have commanded you. And behold, I am with you always, to the end of the age" (Matthew 28:18-20).

19

All Man's Babylons

GENESIS 11:1-9

A few years ago the *Arizona Republic* carried this local profile by columnist E. J. Montini:

> It is dusk. Gordon Hall stands at an overlook on his 55,000-square-foot mansion in Paradise Valley, a structure built by Pittsburgh industrialist Walker McCune and now owned and being renovated by Hall. He is 32 years old and a millionaire many times over. He stares at the range of lights stretching before him from horizon to horizon and breathes a deep, relaxed sigh.
>
> The lights of the city are like the campfires of a great army to Hall, who sees himself as its benevolent general. They are like the flashlights of the world's fortune seekers, and Hall is their beacon to riches. They are, for Hall, like the stars of the firmament. And he is above them.
>
> He is worth more than $100 million, he says, because it was his goal to be worth more than $100 million before the age of 33. . . There are other goals. By the time he is 38, he will be a billionaire. By the time his earthly body expires — and he is convinced he can live to be 120 years old — he will assume what he believes to be his just heavenly reward: Gordon Hall will be a god.
>
> "We have always existed as intelligences, as spirits," he says. "We are down here to gain a body. As man is now, God once was. And as God is now, man can become. If you believe it, then your genetic makeup is to be a god. And I believe it. That is why I believe I can do anything. My genetic makeup is to be a god. My God in heaven creates worlds and universes. I believe I can do anything, too."
>
> He looks to the horizon, and then he looks behind him, where his great dark house seems to drift like a ship in the night sky.[1]

Gordon Hall's delusion is only another expression of humanity's primeval desire to displace God, even becoming as God himself. Hall's pathetic thinking calls for Francis Thompson's clearheaded lines:

> *And all man's Babylons strive*
> *but to impart*
> *The grandeurs of*
> *his Babylonian heart.*[2]

History demonstrates that Babylonian hearts are endemic to humanity. Centuries after the fiasco at Babel, Nebuchadnezzar strode over the ramparts of his royal palace and declared, "Is not this great Babylon, which I have built by my mighty power as a royal residence and for the glory of my majesty?" (Daniel 4:30). Centuries later when King Herod, decked out in royal livery, addressed his people, they shouted, "The voice of a god, and not of a man!" (Acts 12:22). The litany of history's Babylonian hearts roll easily from our lips. Alexander the Great. Caesar Augustus — when he died, some feared that God had died. Louis XIV, the sun king. Stalin, who encouraged those who were weary to think of him. Of course, we do not need history to understand this. We have the imperial self — our tendency to become mini-potentates — to exalt our little Babylonian hearts to the thrones of our lives.

What does God think of this? And what does he do? This is what this story is all about. And it is told with remarkable skill and care.

The literary structure of this account is another example of a perfectly balanced story in which the second half is a reversed mirror-image of the first half — an extended chiasmus. The story's central hinge is in verse 5, where the Lord comes down "to see the city and the tower, which the children of man had built." From there on the story becomes a point-for-point inversion of the first half.

A "The whole earth had one language" (v 1)
B   "there" (v. 2)
C   "each other" (v 3)
D   "Come, let us make bricks" (v 3)
E   "let us build for ourselves" (v 4)
F   "a city and a tower"
G   "the LORD came down . . . " (v 5)
F¹   "the city and the tower"
E¹   "which mankind had built"
D¹   "come . . . let us mix up" (v 7)
C¹   "each other's language"
B¹   "from there" (v 8)
A¹ "the language of the whole earth" (v 9)[3]

We see here: Human Arrogance (vv. 1-4), Heaven's Awareness (v. 5), and Heaven's Reversal (vv. 6-9).

The careful structure is matched by a painstaking use of words and wordplays through assonance (words that sound the same), rhyme, and alliteration, which of course are hidden in the Hebrew.[4] The result is a remarkably subtle and powerful story that leaves its mark on the hearers. This story of Babel also mirrors humanity's attempt in Eden to grasp power apart from God. The tower builders' attempt to exceed proscribed human limits is much like Eve's desire for the tree (cf. 3:5, 6). The use of the divine plural ("Come, let us go down," v. 7) reflects similar language in Eden ("The man has become like one of us," 3:22), and both instances focus on God's concern about what will happen to humanity. Both Babel and Eden are in roughly the same setting between the Tigris and Euphrates Rivers on the plain of Shinar (cf. 2:14 and 11:2). "Genesis 1—11 then has come full circle from 'Eden to Babel,' both remembered for the expulsion of their residents" (Mathews).[5] This sameness of message underlines the importance of the message for us. There is primary, essential teaching here, parallel to that of the fall.

Perhaps you have noticed that the Babel story in chapter 11 pictures everyone in the world as gathered in one place speaking one language, while chapter 10 gives the Table of Nations in which everyone is described as scattered "in their lands, each with his own language, by their clans, in their nations" (10:5; cf. vv. 20, 32). Logically, the gathered world in 11:1-9 ought to precede the scattered world in chapter 10. And, in fact, it does because the order here is thematic and not chronological. And the reversed order is a stroke of genius because the absurdity of the attempt to build the tower and remain as one people (chapter 11) is framed by the present reality of nations spread over the whole earth (chapter 10).

Though the Table of Nations sequentially follows Babel, the Table serves to inform the story of Babel. The mention in 10:8-12 of Nimrod's kingdom in connection with Babylon and Shinar is revealing because Nimrod's name means "we shall rebel," which perfectly characterizes the heart of the builders of Babel. Also the mention in 10:25 of Peleg in whose days "the earth was divided" places the scattering from Babel chronologically during Peleg's time.[6]

HUMAN ARROGANCE (vv. 1-4)

The human situation. Moses' description of humanity's settlement is brief but informative: "Now the whole earth had one language and the same words. And as people migrated from the east, they found a plain in the land of Shinar and settled there" (vv. 1, 2). "One language" is literally "one lip," and "the same words" is "words, one." So the story's beginning stresses that the picture is universal, including all of humanity in original linguistic solidarity. This communion of language ought to have promoted a godly one-ness of faith, but sin was alive and well among Noah's descendants.

The mention that they moved "from the east" indicates trouble because in Genesis "east" or "from the east" suggests movement away from God. When Adam and Eve were expelled from the garden, cherubim guarded the entry at the "east of the garden of Eden" (3:24). When Lot left Abraham, he traveled "eastward," where he met disaster in Sodom and Gomorrah (13:10-12). Abraham's sons by his concubine Keturah were sent "away from his son Isaac, eastward to the east country" (25:6). Jacob fled his homeland to "the land of the people of the east" (29:1). Here in the tower story the people's eastern migration depicts universal rebellion. They have moved outside the place of blessing (Mathews).[7]

As they wandered eastward from Ararat (Armenia), they settled in Mesopotamia on the broad, flat plain of Shinar in what the Talmud would call the "valley of the world."[8] Moses' clear statement that they "settled there" (v. 2) is not incidental, because "settled" is the opposite of "dispersed" (v. 8), which is the story's dramatic outcome. Their settling was in direct opposition to God's post-flood command to "fill the earth" (9:1).

Humanity's resolve. Having established humanity's rebellious direction, Moses treats us to some well-chosen sound bites from their community dialogue that indicates their sinful resolve. "They said to one another, 'Come, let us make bricks, and burn them thoroughly.' And they had brick for stone, and bitumen for mortar" (v. 3). This quotation in effect mocks the would-be tower builders because sun-dried or kiln-baked bricks set with tar was a Babylonian invention, whereas Israel used stone and mortar. The implication is, "We use stone; they have only brick!"[9] Only fools would choose brick in preference to good Palestinian stone.

Also, since the use of brick to build a Mesopotamian ziggurat or sacred mountain is in view, the mockery extends to the mythic theology of the ancient world, mocking the present myths of Mesopotamia that describe their ziggurats as being built by their gods. The famous Babylonian poem *Enuma Elish* describes the gods as molding bricks for a year to build Babylon's ziggurat. There is a scene on a cylinder seal that portrays their gods mixing clay, climbing ladders, carrying mortar, and passing bricks to the top.[10] Moses mocks all such foolishness. He sees it as laughable folly.

Humanity's arrogation. Though the story is satiric, the arrogance of the tower builders was no laughing matter. "Then they said, 'Come, let us build ourselves a city and a tower with its top in the heavens, and let us make a name for ourselves, lest we be dispersed over the face of the whole earth'" (v. 4). The intent behind building "a tower with its top in the heavens" was to join or displace God. The ziggurat was a lofty, massive, solid brick struc-ture — multi-staged (like giant porch steps) up to heaven. Nahum Sarna writes in his Torah commentary:

Rooted in earth, with its head lost in the clouds, it was taken to be the meeting point of heaven and earth and, as such, the natural arena of divine activity. On its heights the gods were imagined to have their abode. Constituting the obvious channel of communication between the celestial and terrestrial spheres, the sacred mountain was looked upon as the center of the universe, the "navel of the earth."[11]

But the Bible regarded all such towers as pitiful symbols of human arrogance (cf. Isaiah 2:12-15; 30:25; Ezekiel 26:4, 9).

The problem with the tower as such lay not in the desire to be in touch with God but in its underlying suppositions and approach. Its builders supposed that God was localized, in direct contradiction to the explicit teaching of Genesis. The post-diluvians had created a god in their own image. Also, the unadorned belief that man by his superior effort could reach God betrays the fatal delusion of all man-made religion. This delusion is at the heart of every religious enterprise apart from the gospel because the world's religions all teach that works bring spiritual advance — as in an improved karma or works-righteousness. Collective apostasy had engulfed the descendants of Shem, Ham, and Japheth as they stacked their bricks up to heaven.

> *"Brick on brick," the hunter*
> *Muttered to the mass, "and soon*
> *We'll reach the porches of the moon*
> *Where heaven and the angels are."*[12]

The tower builders were clear about what drove them — "and let us make a name for ourselves." Their desire to "make a name" was ominous because the only previous mention of name in this way was of the Nephilim, who were "the mighty men who were of old, the men of renown" (Hebrew, "men of name") (6:4). The tower builders were motivated by the same base desire for renown as the pre-diluvians.

Negatively, they were driven by the fear of anonymity. Today this same will to fame is everywhere. It drives politicians and preachers and athletes and actors. If we can make a name for ourselves so people esteem us, we will have succeeded, we think. We have seen this in Olympic commentators' use of "immortal" to describe athletic feats. Immortal? How language suffers! A disgraced president works to shore up his "legacy" (codeword: name). "Ah," we say, "he's made a name for himself," implying something transcendent. The artful black-and-white film sparkles as Humphrey Bogart toasts Ingrid Bergman with "Here's looking at you" — and we are told that we have seen the immortal.

This drive to make a name for ourselves can drive us to re-create ourselves. And the effect can be so tragic that neither we nor anyone else knows who we are. Alan Richardson says it well: "The hatred of anonymity drives men to heroic feats of valour or long hours of drudgery; or it urges them to spectacular acts of shame or of unscrupulous self-preferment. In its worst forms it tempts men to give the honour and glory to themselves which properly belong to the name of God."[13]

Indeed, the tower builders were going to make a name for themselves, but not the one they had hoped for. Their name would become a joke. The only name that counts is that which God gives, as when he said to Abraham, "I will . . . make your name great" (12:2). The fame that lasts comes from God. "They will see his face, and his name will be on their foreheads" (Revelation 22:4).

The tower builders were a broken people. And the fact that they feared being scattered is proof that their fellowship with God and their unity with each other had been shattered by sin.[14] Centripetal spiritual forces were at work. Their attempt to preserve their unity by outward means would not be successful apart from coercion, as world history so sadly proves. And here God would graciously work to effect their scattering.

HEAVEN'S AWARENESS (v. 5)

Now the scene switches from earth to heaven, the hinge on which the Babel story turns: "And the LORD came down to see the city and the tower, which the children of man had built" (v. 5). Here the satire peaks. The tower's top was in the sky where God ostensibly dwelt. But this was Yahweh, the infinitely transcendent and incomparably supereminent God of the whole Old Testament, of whom Isaiah declared, "It is he who sits above the circle of the earth, and its inhabitants are like grasshoppers; who stretches out the heavens like a curtain, and spreads them like a tent to dwell in" (40:22). This "Yahweh must draw near, not because he is near-sighted, but because he dwells at such tremendous height and their work is so tiny" (Procksch).[15] Their tower was so microscopic that the all-seeing omnipotent God had to come down to see. It was as if God stooped down like a man on his hands and knees and lowered his face to the earth to see the great tower. The psalmist says, "He who sits in the heavens laughs; the Lord holds them in derision" (Psalm 2:4). Great peals of laughter echoed in the heavens. So much for the aspirations of men's Babylonian hearts.

HEAVEN'S REVERSAL (vv. 6-8)

Divine assessment. Next comes the record of God's investigation: "And the LORD said, 'Behold, they are one people, and they have all one language, and this is only the beginning of what they will do. And nothing that they propose to do will now be impossible for them'" (v. 6). God was not threatened by humankind's corporate potential — "Oh no, if they band together, what shall I do?" Instead, he was troubled by what would happen to humanity if the human family was left unchecked. They would build up a delusion of self-sufficiency through their false religion, corporate security, and political uniformity. They would throw off God and attempt to rule the universe. And in their delusion they would never turn to God. Their Babylonian hearts would become impenetrable and irredeemable.

Divine judgment. The hammer fell in the LORD's concluding words: "'Come, let us go down and there confuse their language, so that they may not understand one another's speech.' So the LORD dispersed them from there over the face of all the earth, and they left off building the city" (vv. 7, 8). The confusion of language may have been God's sending a judgment of misapprehension to the people that, in turn, drove them away, alienated from each other. Or it may be that they simply awakened to the world as a foreign movie — without subtitles! In any event, the thing that they feared most fell upon them as they were scattered over all the earth. Deprived of community and cooperative technology, the project fell by the wayside. Whole tribes fled to the horizons. But this all was grace.

God's judgment was complete. And Moses concludes, "Therefore its name was called Babel, because there the LORD confused the language of all the earth. And from there the LORD dispersed them over the face of all the earth" (v. 9). Babel no longer meant "the gate of God," as the tower builders had it, nor was it "the navel of the earth" as Moses' pagan contemporaries liked to call it, but it came to mean "mixed-up, confused," signifying a place of meaningless babble, the site of alienation and scattering.

Throughout Scripture Babylon became evocative of the human pride and godlessness that attracts the judgment of God (cf. Isaiah 14:3, 4, 13-15). Genesis links the fate of Sodom with that of Babylon (cf. 10:10-19; 11:7; 18:21). Isaiah wrote:

> *And Babylon, the glory of kingdoms,*
> *the splendor and pomp of the Chaldeans,*
> *will be like Sodom and Gomorrah*
> *when God overthrew them. (13:19)*

Isaiah's prophesies were later taken up and reapplied to the neo-Babylonian empire by Jeremiah (50, 51). The book of Daniel records the glory and demise of the evil Babylonian empire (Daniel 1 — 5). Likewise, the New Testament describes Babylon as the great harlot, the persecutor of God's people, and the embodiment of pride and vice (cf. Revelation 18:1-4, 19-24).

Yet the reality of Babel's long influence in history is also the source of a great hope. A final reversal was promised by the prophet Zephaniah: "For at that time I will change the speech of the peoples to a pure speech, that all of them may call upon the name of the LORD and serve him with one accord" (3:9). Zephaniah answers the effects of Babel. And then came the Messiah and his death and resurrection and Pentecost, when "each one was hearing them speak in his own language" — a reversal of Babel and a sign of the last days when all who call upon the name of the Lord will be saved (cf. Acts 2:6-21). The hopelessness of Babel was not God's last word.

The day is coming when sin will be destroyed and perfect unity will be restored among the nations. In the book of Revelation the holy city (the antithesis to Babel) is seen as coming down out of heaven, with gates open to unite the nations:

> And he carried me away in the Spirit to a great, high mountain, and showed me the holy city Jerusalem coming down out of heaven from God. . . . By its light will the nations walk, and the kings of the earth will bring their glory into it, and its gates will never be shut by day — and there will be no night there. They will bring into it the glory and the honor of the nations. (21:10, 24-26)

Then, and today, the message is the same: We must leave Babel with its proud dreams and God-defying ways if there is to be any hope. We must abandon our Babylonian hearts' search for security in the city of man with its collective delusions. Man's Babylonian heart may meld political philosophy and economic theory and technology and psychology and religion into a mighty, self-elevating ziggurat — but it will never effect the autonomy or security we long for. We will never scale heaven. We must leave off chasing after a name and find our identity in Christ.

> But to all who did receive him, who believed in his name, he gave the right to become children of God. (John 1:12)

20

From Shem to Abraham

GENESIS 11:10-32

Following the confusion of language at the tower of Babel, wave after wave of warriors, shepherds, and builders left the plain of Mesopotamia for the rims of the world. As they swarmed out, they pushed one another further west and east through their commerce, adventure, conquest, and appetites. And as they went, they took their Babylonian hearts with them. The scattering was by and large a scattering of idolatrous pagans, regardless of whether they were descendants of Shem or Ham or Japheth. Here and there were some exceptions who maintained the true worship of God — for example, Melchizedek in Canaan and Job in Arabia. But the apostasy was universal, and the spreading waves blanketed the earth with darkness. Babel concluded with the scattered human race estranged from God much as before the flood when the godly Sethite line had been polluted and subsumed by the evil Cainite line.

Genesis 11:10-32, which takes us from Noah's son Shem to Abram, reveals how God again took steps to save a people: 1) preserving the line of Shem through one man (parallel to the way God had done it through one man in his use of Noah), and 2) again doing it through one man's faith (as God had also done through Noah).

THE GENEALOGY OF FATHER ABRAM (vv. 10-26)

Though humanity had become idolatrous, God's promised blessing on the descendants of Shem (the Semitic peoples) still remained. So Moses here records the genealogy of Shem. This is meant to be a counterpart to the earlier genealogy of Seth in chapter 5, which names the ten generations from Adam's son Seth to Noah. Here in chapter 11 we also have ten generations, extending from Noah's son Shem to Abram.[1] The two parallel genealogies together record a total of twenty generations from Adam to Abram.

As you read through this genealogy, the most notable difference is the absence of the refrain "and he died," which occurs eight times in chapter 5. Genesis 5 stressed that death prevailed in the race, whereas Genesis 11 "stresses a movement away from death toward the promise, and it stresses life and expansion" (Ross).[2] The other obvious difference between the genealogies is the shrinking life span of the patriarchs after the flood. The 438 years of Arphachsad's life is only about two-thirds of his father Shem's six hundred years. Peleg's 239 years is about half the 464 years of his father Eber. Toward the end of the genealogy Nahor lives some 138 years — so that the predicted shortening of man's life span to 120 years is realized (cf. 6:3).

Man's sin diminished his longevity. But at the same time, the genealogy testifies to a rising optimism by the deletion of "and he died." The genealogy is moving toward a great hope. This genealogy begins another of the ten *toledots* ("These are the generations of" sections) in Genesis, and it concludes at the end of the genealogy with verse 26. This is because it completes primeval history. Patriarchal history begins in verse 27 with *toledot* six: "Now these are the generations of Terah." Therefore Shem's genealogy stands as a bridge of hope to a new era.

The midpoint and dividing line of Shem's genealogy is the birth of Peleg in verse 16: "When Eber had lived 34 years, he fathered Peleg." Peleg occupies place number five in the ten generations that run from Shem to Abram — the five generations being Shem, Arpachshad, Shelah, Eber, and Peleg. These five represent a concise recapitulation of Shem's genealogy as it was given in the Table of Nations in 10:21-25, except that there the genealogy also includes Peleg's brother Joktan and his descendants. But here in chapter 11 Joktan is not mentioned and Peleg's descendants are listed all the way to Terah and Abram.

Why? The answer is that Joktan's line leads up to the fiasco at Babel, while Peleg's line results in the great man Abram, the hope of God's people (cf. 11:17-26). As Kenneth Mathews says, "This highlights the difference in the two inner branches of the Shemite family — one leading to *disgrace* and the other to *grace*."[3]

We should also note that Eber, the father of Peleg, is prominent in the genealogy. He is the ancestor of the Hebrews, and the name *Hebrew* comes from Eber. Significantly, Eber is fourteenth from Adam (two times seven), and Abram is seventh from Eber, making him Adam's twenty-first descendant (three times seven) — all suggesting the perfections of the divine plan.

Peleg to Abram. The second half of the genealogy, which extends from Peleg through Terah to Abram, places Abram only five generations away from Babel because the tower was built in Peleg's time — "in his days the earth was divided" (10:25). Lastly, the genealogy ends with Terah fathering three sons — Abram, Nahor, and Haran — so that the genealogy ends just like the ten generations from Adam to Noah ended when Noah fathered three sons — Shem, Ham, and Japheth (cf. 5:32). Though Abram, like Shem, was named first in the list over his three brothers, he, like Shem, was not the firstborn. He was named first because of his prominence. And whereas Noah was the hero of the following account, Terah was not. It was Terah's son Abram who became the great man. Abram means "he is exalted as to his father," as in noble birth, or more likely "the father [i.e., God] is exalted." Later his name would be changed to Abraham, which as Genesis 17:5 explains means "father of many nations."

So we see that hope abounds with the conclusion of this genealogy. Moses has shown that God's promise to Eve of a seed who will crush the head of the snake (cf. 3:15) could not be thwarted by the confusion and scattering of the nations. Even though the seed was scattered from Babel, God had preserved ten great men from Noah to Abram. And furthermore, the line of Peleg brought grace in place of Joktan's line of disgrace. How gracious God was going to be to the nations!

THE FAITH OF FATHER ABRAM (vv. 27-32)

Abram's pagan milieu. Like all families, domestic complications developed, as is implicit in the "who married who" generations of Terah.

> *Now these are the generations of Terah. Terah fathered Abram, Nahor, and Haran; and Haran fathered Lot. Haran died in the presence of his father Terah in the land of his kindred, in Ur of the Chaldeans. And Abram and Nahor took wives. The name of Abram's wife was Sarai, and the name of Nahor's wife, Milcah, the daughter of Haran the father of Milcah and Iscah. Now Sarai was barren; she had no child. (vv. 27-30)*

"Haran fathered Lot," the nephew who would give Abram so much worry in future years. Nahor married Milcah, his niece, the orphaned daughter of his departed brother Haran. And we learn two things about Abram's wife Sarai — first by the extraordinary omission of any information about her being a daughter of Terah and thus the half-sister of Abraham. Moses withholds this information so as not to ruin the suspense in chapter 20 when Abraham, in order to save his own skin, reveals to Abimelech that Sarai is his half-sister. Also, we learn that Sarai was barren — which sets up the huge challenges that would come to Abraham's faith. This challenge of barrenness will occur again for the matriarchs Rebekah and Rachel, and later for the mothers of Samson and Samuel.

Most important is that we understand that at this time Terah's tiny, inbred family were moon worshipers residing in the leading center of lunar religion.

The city was dominated by a massive, three-staged ziggurat built by Ur-Nammu during the beginning of the second millennium B.C. Each stage was colored distinctively, with the top level bearing the silver one-roomed shrine to Nanna, the moon-god. The royal cemetery reveals that ritual burials were sealed with the horrors of human sacrifice.[4]

If there be any doubt that this was Abraham's context, Joshua removes it with his words to Israel during the covenant renewal in Shechem: "Joshua said to all the people, 'Thus says the LORD, the God of Israel, "Long ago, your fathers lived beyond the Euphrates, Terah, the father of Abraham and of Nahor; and they served other gods"'" (Joshua 24:2). Abram's family, including Abram himself, were polytheistic idolaters. Their names come right out of the cult of moon worship. Terah's name is related to the word *yārēah*, "moon" and *yerah*, "lunar month." Sarai is the equivalent to the Akkadian *sarratu*, "queen," and was the name of the wife of the moon god Sin. Milcah is the same as the goddess *Malkâtu*, a title of Ishtar, daughter of the moon god.[5]

As a moon worshiper, Abram had stood atop the ziggurat's stargazing platform on night watches and offered his obeisance. He may well have witnessed the dark side of moon worship at the silver room of Nanna. At times he may have mused that there must be something greater than the order of nature and that the waxing and waning of the moon evidenced a power beyond Nanna.

Abram's faith and the family move. The final verses record a family move: "Terah took Abram his son and Lot the son of Haran, his grandson, and Sarai his daughter-in-law, his son Abram's wife, and they went forth together from Ur of the Chaldeans to go into the land of Canaan, but when they came to Haran, they settled there. The days of Terah were 205 years, and Terah died in Haran" (vv. 31, 32). If we had only this, we would conclude that Terah moved his family to Haran where he lived for some time and then died at age 205, after which God called Abram.

But neither Genesis nor the rest of the Old Testament or the New Testament allow this. Rather it was while Abram was in Ur that he was called. When God later affirmed his covenant with Abram he said, "I am the LORD who brought you out from Ur of the Chaldeans to give you this land to possess" (15:7). Similarly, the Levites made this corporate confession: "You are the LORD, the God who chose Abram and brought him out of Ur of the Chaldeans and gave him the name Abraham" (Nehemiah 9:7). The most explicit account of Abram's call while in Ur came from Stephen when he began his defense before the Sanhedrin:

> *"Brothers and fathers, hear me. The God of glory appeared to our father Abraham when he was in Mesopotamia, before he lived in Haran, and said to him, 'Go out from your land and from your kindred and go into*

the land that I will show you.' Then he went out from the land of the
Chaldeans and lived in Haran. And after his father died, God removed
him from there into this land in which you are now living." (Acts 7:2-4)

The way we get this to square with the age data in Genesis 11, 12 is to understand that Abram was not the firstborn of Terah's three sons when Terah began having children at age seventy (similarly, note that Shem heads the list of Noah's three sons but is younger than Japheth; cf. 10:1, 21, NIV).[6] So it is best to understand that Terah was 130 when Abram was born and that he lived seventy-five more years until the age of 205 (cf. 11:32). Therefore Abram was, as 12:4 says, "seventy-five years old when he departed from Haran."

The point here is that it was in darkest Ur that Abram saw the glory of God and heard the call to depart and go to a land that God would show him. And he convinced Terah to leave with him. But when they got to Haran (another center of moon worship), Terah would not budge. So dutiful Abram bid his time until Terah's death, after which he was off again to the promised land.

We say all of this to underline that Abram's obedience was a monumental act of faith. He was a pagan. He was advanced in years. He was prosperous and settled in his pagan world. He was the only one in his culture who heard God's word. But on the basis of hearing alone, he risked everything to follow God. None of us has ever done anything comparable to this. We trivialize it if we imagine that we have.

How did he do it? Happily, we know the answer because the author of Hebrews chose to use Abraham as an illustration of his definition of faith. Hebrews defines faith like this: "Now faith is the assurance of things hoped for, the conviction of things not seen" (11:1). Biblical faith possesses *a future certainty*, "the assurance of things hoped for," coupled with *a visual certainty*, "the conviction of things not seen." Thus faith produces *a dynamic certainty* that gives the reality of actual existence to the things for which we hope.

Therefore when Abram heard God's call, he became so certain that God would lead him to a land where he would establish a great people that the future promise was transposed to the present. Philo of Alexandria said Abram considered "the things not present as beyond question already present by reason of the sure steadfastness of him that promised them."[7]

The result in Abram was immediate obedience. Abraham's obedience was an outward evidence of his inward faith. His obedience was so prompt, as described in Hebrews 11:8 where it says that he "obeyed" and "went," that he seems to have set out while the command yet rang in his ears. It was not until later that his destination was revealed as Canaan. Faith steps out. Faith and obedience are inseparable in man's relation to God. We must never imagine that we have faith if we do not obey.

Here is the beautiful thing in Genesis: The two greatest persons of primeval and patriarchal times were Noah and Abram — and both were paragons of faith. Of Noah, Hebrews says, "By faith Noah, being warned by God concerning events as yet unseen, in reverent fear constructed an ark for the saving of his household. By this he condemned the world and became an heir of the righteousness that comes by faith" (11:7). Of Abram, Hebrews follows by saying, "By faith Abraham obeyed when he was called to go out to a place that he was to receive as an inheritance. And he went out, not knowing where he was going" (11:8).

Both men's faith produced amazing obedience. "Noah . . . did all that God commanded him," the Genesis text emphasizes four times (cf. 6:22; 7:5, 9, 16). Abraham immediately "obeyed" and "went," says the writer of Hebrews. Thus we see that both men were used to effect salvation for others by their faith. Noah's faith wrought salvation for his family and preserved the promise of the seed of Eve. Abram's faith created a people through whom the promise would be fulfilled.

And the way Abram's faith began in Ur is the way it continued. Later it was the same faith by which he received his righteousness. Faith does not *earn* righteousness; it *receives* righteousness. Faith is the instrument by which we receive the righteousness that God gives. "He believed the LORD, and he counted it to him as righteousness" (Genesis 15:6).

May we believe the bare word of God. May we believe so that the promises not present become as present by reason of the sure steadfastness of him who promised them. May we enjoy the promises now because we believe in God. And because we do, may we obey every word that comes from the mouth of God!

21

The Life of Abraham: Faith Answers the Call

GENESIS 12:1-9

S ir Leonard Woolley's excavation of the ancient Mesopotamian city of Ur in the 1920s and early 1930s was a media event. During the thirteen years of excavations, the great newspapers of the world followed his progress in countless articles. Woolley's discovery of the royal cemetery of Ur with its large cache of gold objects and evidence of human sacrifice attracted travelers from around the world, including mystery writer Agatha Christie.[1] Young Agatha married Woolley's assistant, M. E. L. Mallowan, and set her 1936 mystery *Murder in Mesopotamia* in an excavation in Iraq. Later she wrote in her autobiography:

> Leonard Woolley saw with the eye of imagination: the place was as real to him as it had been in 1500 B.C., or a few thousand years earlier. Wherever he happened to be, he could make it come alive. While he was speaking I felt in my mind no doubt whatever that the house on the corner had been Abraham's. It was his reconstruction of the past and he believed in it, and anyone who listened to him believed in it also.[2]

Having seen the traveling exhibition of "Treasures from the Royal Tombs of Ur" at the University of Chicago's Oriental Institute, I can testify to Woolley's ability to make the past real. His scaled map of the city of Ur in the time of Abraham with its ziggurat topped with the temple of Nanna (the moon god), the palace of Ur-Nammu, the temples of Ningal and Enki surrounded by the city's walls and harbors, his schematic drawings and photographs of the "Great Death Pit" with seventy-three bodies of servants arranged in sacrifice around Queen Puabi's gorgeously decorated corpse — all serve to make the past come alive.

But most of all the artifacts themselves make Abraham's context live. Puabi's incredible golden headdress and beaded cape, the gold and lapis lazuli headbands of her attendants, the gold beech leaf wreaths beaded with carnelian, the gold, silver, and ivory vessels, and the great lyre with the golden bull's head portray the ruler's vacuous hopes of a good life to come. Puabi's body, and those of her unfortunate servants, as well as her gold and silver all lay for over three thousand years in the Death Pit until unearthed by Sir Leonard.

These treasures of Ur tell us that Abraham's social and religious context was as sophisticated and pagan and claustrophobic as that of any Babylonian or Egyptian dynasty. Ur was desolate and barren of knowledge of the true God. Ur's intrusive, lunar religion dominated life from birth to the grave.

During the ten generations from Noah through Shem to Abram the whole family of earth had played out its future and had nowhere to go. The culture of Babel, though dispersed, had triumphed. There was no foreseeable future other than darkness. And there was certainly no human power to invent a future. Mankind was hopelessly lost, except for the distant promise to Shem that blessing would come through his line (cf. 9:26, 27).

ABRAM'S CALL AND PROMISE (vv. 1-3)

Call. So Abram, a descendant of Shem, lived on in dark Ur until God spoke, as the famous opening verse of chapter 12 recalls: "Now the LORD said to Abram, 'Go from your country and your kindred and your father's house to the land that I will show you.'" The shocking immensity of God's command and the agonizing nature of Abram's decision are indicated by the ascending order of Abram's personal sacrifice: Leave your country — leave your people — and leave your father's household (nuclear family).

His agonizing decision was further compounded by the vagueness of God's order — "go . . . to the land that I will show you." Abram was not told that Canaan was the land God was talking about until he got there! Calvin observed that this uncertainty forced Abram to trust God's word even more. Calvin comments that God said in effect, "I command you to go forth with closed eyes, and forbid you to inquire where I am about to lead you, until, having renounced your country, you shall have given yourself wholly to me."[3] Abram was asked to believe and obey the bare word of God — the *verbum nudum* as Calvin has it — the naked word of the Lord.

This call to forsake all is very much like the call of the gospel. Jesus said, "Whoever loves father or mother more than me is not worthy of me"

(Matthew 10:37a), and "For whoever would save his life will lose it, but whoever loses his life for my sake and the gospel's will save it" (Mark 8:35). The gospel calls us to rest all our hope on the word of Christ, and nothing else!

When Jesus calls us, he does not guarantee the future or even tell us what it will be like. He does promise that he will take us to be with him — which is the ultimate land! He does promise forgiveness and inner peace. He does promise that he will be with us through thick and thin. He does promise our ultimate good. But Jesus does not say that it will be smooth here on earth. He does not say that your problems will be solved. Nor does he promise a life of peace and ease. If you are looking for these kinds of up-front promises before turning to Christ, you will never get them. And if you persist in your requirements, you will never come to Christ. He calls you to trust his word alone.

Promise. Of course, remarkably rich promises were made to Abram, but they were promises that he would never experience in full because their ultimate fulfillment would come through his offspring, first in believing Israel and then in the church (cf. Galatians 3:16, 29). The famous expression of the promise in Genesis 12:2, 3 is magnificent. As you can see, it is poetry. But because it uses the word "bless" or "blessing" or "blessed" five times, you may not have noticed that it actually contains seven expressions of blessing that thereby indicate that "the Bible intended by this formulation to set before us a form of blessing that was perfect in every respect" (Cassuto).[4] Note also that the whole promise is full of divine assertion as God promises five times, "I will." Everything is from God himself.

Personal blessings. The first half of the great promise prophesies personal blessings upon Abram.

> *And I will make of you a great nation,*
> *and I will bless you and make your name great,*
> *so that you will be a blessing. (v. 2)*

God's promise that Abram would become a great nation assaulted reality, because Abram was childless and Sarai was barren — a painful reality in antiquity and doubly painful in the throw-away world of Ur. Abram was asked to believe in the dark. And more, Abram was promised that he would not merely become a great people but "a great nation"! The Hebrew word here for nation is *gôy*, which is a word used frequently in the Old Testament to describe the Gentile nations of the world (cf. 10:5, 20, 31, 32). Today the Hebrew word for Gentiles is still *gôy* (singular) or *gôyim* (plural). Abram's offspring would be a *gôy* among the *gôyim*[5] — a powerful political entity with a land and language and government. Believe that, Abram!

And there was yet more. God promised to make Abram's "name great."

Ironically, this is what the builders of the tower of Babel sought — "let us make a name for ourselves" (11:4). By faith Abram was going to get what never truly comes by self-serving effort. His great name was a gift. This endowment with a name is clearly royal language, and Abram is viewed here as a regal figure.[6] Later Abram will be promised that "kings" will come from him, and Sarah will be called the mother of "kings" (cf. 17:6, 16). Still later the Hittites hailed Abram as a "prince" (23:6). A millennium later King David would be his royal heir *par excellence.* And, of course, there would come the ultimate King to whom God gave "the name that is above every name, so that at the name of Jesus every knee should bow" (Philippians 2:9, 10).

Global blessings. The second half of the promise moves from personal blessings for Abram to specific global blessings.

> *I will bless those who bless you,*
> *and him who dishonors you I will curse,*
> *and in you all the families of the earth*
> *shall be blessed. (v. 3)*

There is more than the law of retribution at work in God's curse-for-curse, blessing-for-blessing promise. True, those who bless Abram will be blessed. But "him who dishonors you [literally, "disdains you"] I will curse," says God. That is, there will be heightened, disproportionate punishment for merely disdaining Abram.[7] Abram saw this principle worked out in his own life. Melchizedek and Abimelech were blessed for honoring Abram. But Hagar was cut off from Abram's family for despising Sarah. The Canaanites who so distressed and persecuted Israel are no more. Today those who align themselves against the church ("Abraham's seed, heirs according to the promise," Galatians 3:29) will not fare well. The defunct USSR, which so oppressed the church, is a case in point. God's people may suffer slight and discrimination. They may be characterized and despised. But let the despisers beware. Retribution and justice will not be left to the impersonal operation of fate. The Lord himself says, "him who disdains you *I* will curse" (italics added).

Abram's call ends with the soaring promise that "all the families of the earth" will be blessed through him. The buildup to this blessing is explicit: Abram alone is blessed — then Abram's name is used as a blessing — next Abram's blessers are blessed — and finally all families find blessing in Abram![8]

Sadly, Abram's descendants, the children of Israel, never really did rise to the glorious task. Kidner summarizes:

Blessing for the world was a vision fitfully seen at first (it disappears between the patriarchs and the kings, apart from a reminder of Israel's priestly role in Ex. 19:5, 6). Later it reappeared in the psalms and prophets, and perhaps even at its faintest it always imparted some sense of mission to Israel; yet it never became a programme of concerted action.[9]

It was only with Christ, the ultimate seed of Abram, that the fulfillment came and blessing went out to all people. The Apostle Paul explains, "And the Scripture, foreseeing that God would justify the Gentiles by faith, preached the gospel beforehand to Abraham, saying, 'In you shall all the nations be blessed.' So then, those who are of faith are blessed along with Abraham, the man of faith" (Galatians 3:8, 9). So the gospel, our good news, was announced four thousand years ago to Abram in darkest Ur with the shadow of the great ziggurat above and the death pits below. This gospel announced in advance to Abram and fulfilled in Christ is now the church's responsibility to proclaim, so that the so-called Gentile Psalm (the shortest Psalm in the Psalter) will be sung by multitudes of the *gôyim*.

> *Praise the LORD, all nations!*
> *Extol him, all peoples!*
> *For great is his steadfast love toward us,*
> *and the faithfulness of the LORD endures forever.*
> *Praise the LORD! (Psalm 117)*

ABRAM'S OBEDIENCE (vv. 4, 5)

There has been a lot of speculation as to how long Abram sojourned with his father Terah in Haran after leaving Ur. Did he leave Haran immediately upon Terah's decision to stay there, or did he linger until Terah died? The answer is indifferent. The point is that he obeyed God's call. He left Ur and Haran. He succeeded in rising above the idolatrous notions of his moon-worshiping environment and recognized the voice of the Lord, Yahweh, "God Most High, Possessor of heaven and earth" (14:22) — so that without argument or questioning on his part, we read of his obedience.

> *So Abram went, as the LORD had told him, and Lot went with him. Abram*
> *was seventy-five years old when he departed from Haran. And Abram*
> *took Sarai his wife, and Lot his brother's son, and all their possessions*
> *that they had gathered, and the people that they had acquired in Haran,*
> *and they set out to go to the land of Canaan. (vv. 4, 5)*

Though the text does not give the details, the 800-mile route would have taken them near some of the great urban centers of the day. Abram likely traveled over to Carchemish and down to Aleppo and through Damascus to Canaan.[10] Abram's migrant entourage included "the people that they had acquired in Haran," who were *not* slaves, as we might naturally suppose. Cassuto translates the phrase as "the souls that they had won in Haran," arguing that this translation is better exegetically and in line with rabbinic interpretation. Therefore the text likely refers to making proselytes. Abram had been actively sharing his story and faith in the Lord.[11]

ABRAM'S SOJOURN (vv. 6-9)

Abram's sojourn in Canaan supplies essential instruction about the life of faith. The authentic life of faith demands that we be pilgrims in this world. The letter to the Hebrews is specific about Abram's relationship to the promised land: "By faith he went to live in the land of promise, as in a foreign land, living in tents with Isaac and Jacob, heirs with him of the same promise. For he was looking forward to the city that has foundations, whose designer and builder is God" (11:9, 10). Abram's clear vision of God's call and the future detached him from the world, just as it will always detach God's people from grounding their lives too deeply in the present.

That idea is radical because it challenges "the dominant ideologies of our time which yearn for settlement, security and placement" (Brueggemann).[12] Everything around us tells us to hunker down, save everything, hedge ourselves about with every protection. Our natural desires are for more comforts. Our culture celebrates great homes and dynastic families. But God's Word says otherwise, instructing us to "seek the things that are above, where Christ is, seated at the right hand of God. Set your minds on things that are above, not on things that are on earth. For you have died, and your life is hidden with Christ in God. When Christ who is your life appears, then you also will appear with him in glory" (Colossians 3:1-4).

In Shechem. As Abram traveled the promised land from end to end, he symbolically took possession of it for his descendants, lingering at holy places and building altars. His first stop was Shechem, in the geographical center of the promised land. "Abram passed through the land to the place at Shechem, to the oak of Moreh. At that time the Canaanites were in the land. Then the LORD appeared to Abram and said, 'To your offspring I will give this land.' So he built there an altar to the LORD, who had appeared to him" (vv. 6, 7).

The presence of Canaanites indicated opposition that was going to be a reality as Abram continued in his life of faith. A godly life must always be lived out in the middle of misunderstanding and temptation and even persecution. Likewise the mention of "the oak of Moreh" strikes an ominous note. Moreh means "teacher, oracle giver."[13] The great tree of Moreh was the place where the Canaanites assembled to hear the oracles that soothsayers received from the rustling of the leaves. So there, in the very heart of the land promised to Abram, idolatry was alive and well. Abram had traveled all the way from Ur to find something very similar to home!

But there also in the heartland Abram experienced a theophany: "The LORD appeared to Abram and said, 'To your offspring I will give this land.'" This, the shortest of all promises, was monumental. From here on the Jewish people and the land were bound inseparably together. The history of the world had received a constant.

It is noteworthy that God chose to appear to Abram in the land. Abram, who had followed his unseen God to an unknown destination, was granted a vision of his Lord. Pilgrims who leave all and follow God see more and more. "For to the one who has, more will be given, and he will have an abundance" (Matthew 13:12). "In your light do we see light" (Psalm 36:9b).

"Abram the pilgrim became Abram the builder" (Hamilton),[14] building neither a tower nor a city, but an altar. "So he built there an altar to the LORD." And then, like Noah fresh from the ark, he offered sacrifice (cf. 8:20). We can presume that he offered consumed offerings like those of Noah, which symbolized the complete offering of his life to God. Abram would build altars in Bethel, Hebron, and Mount Moriah (cf. 12:8; 13:18; 22:9). How beautiful — the only architecture that remained from Abram's life were altars.

In Bethel. Abram's next stop was some twenty-one miles to the south, midway between Bethel and Ai, a mile from his tent to each town: "From there he moved to the hill country on the east of Bethel and pitched his tent, with Bethel on the west and Ai on the east. And there he built an altar to the LORD and called upon the name of the LORD. And Abram journeyed on, still going toward the Negeb" (vv. 8, 9). Bethel, like Shechem, was home to an important Canaanite sanctuary to the god El, head of their pantheon. But, as in Shechem, Abram ignored this and built an altar to Yahweh[15] "and called upon the name of the LORD." Abram publicly proclaimed the name of the Lord (cf. remarks on 4:26). He proclaimed his faith. Luther translated this "preached" to convey the idea here.[16] Abram's entourage was quite large (cf. Genesis 14:14). So this was a very public event. The locals knew what was happening. Proclaiming Yahweh's name would include extolling his great attributes and mighty works. Preach it, Abram!

Again, how beautiful this life of faith was. The Lord had promised to make Abram's *name* great, and Abram responded by proclaiming the *name* of the Lord! How far he had come from Babel — the tower builders who wanted to make their name great.[17] Abram spent his time making God famous in Canaan.

The brief itinerary of Abram has taken him from the northern to the southern border of the land. He not only saw what had been promised to his offspring — he had walked through it and lived and worshiped in it. Symbolically he has taken possession of it.

Abram's initial walk of faith had set the standard. In dark, dark Ur he believed the bare word of God. He believed the *personal promises* that he would become a great nation and that his name would be great. He believed

the *global promises* that his offspring would mediate the blessing and cursing of God and that all the world would be blessed through his life. So he
left Ur — "By faith Abraham obeyed when he was called to go out to a
place that he was to receive as an inheritance. And he went out, not knowing where he was going" (Hebrews 11:8). Abram became a sojourner: "By
faith he went to live in the land of promise, as in a foreign land, living in tents
with Isaac and Jacob, heirs with him of the same promise. For he was looking forward to the city that has foundations, whose designer and builder is
God" (Hebrews 11:9, 10). Faithful Abram worshiped wherever he went. All
of his life became worship. The artifacts of his worship stood in the land. And
as a man of faith, he proclaimed the name of the Lord.

Indeed, the gospel was announced in advance in Abram.
- True faith believes the bare word of God.
- True faith steps out on God's word.
- True faith follows wherever God's word directs.
- True faith builds altars and worships wherever it goes.
- True faith proclaims the name of the Lord.

*And there is salvation in no one else, for there is no other name under
heaven given among men by which we must be saved. (Acts 4:12)*

22

Starting and Stumbling

GENESIS 12:10-20

The immensity of Abram's faith-response to God's call is meant to remain as a perpetual wonder to us in the community of faith. Two millennia before Christ, as Abram dwelt in the moon-worshiping context of the storied city of Ur, he heard the voice of Yahweh call him to an unspecified land where he would bless him, and through him bless the whole world. And Abram believed God, ultimately leaving Ur and Haran "not knowing where he was going" (Hebrews 11:8). As Abram followed God's direction, he trekked a great 800-mile arc that took him east to west across Mesopotamia and down the east end of the Mediterranean, where he descended through Damascus into Canaan, which God then promised to him (cf. 12:7). There Abram's trek of faith became a tour of faith as he traveled the length of the promised land, building altars in its very heart and calling upon (that is, proclaiming) the name of the Lord in the midst of the land's pagan inhabitants.

Once again the immensity of his faith stands as a wonder because he was not allowed to take immediate possession of the land. Rather, as Hebrews explains, "By faith he went to live in the land of promise, as in a foreign land; living in tents . . ." (11:9). Abram believed that the land would go to his offspring. His journey from north to south served as a tour of inspection, but not outright possession. The writer of Hebrews explains, "For he was looking forward to the city that has foundations, whose designer and builder is God" (v. 10). What a great man! What faith! He had nothing but God's word. And he believed it.

Abram's sojourn was not easy. Naturally his initial expectation when he departed from Ur was to take possession of the land. But that was not to be. He remained an interloper in pagan territory. Everywhere he went he found Canaanites. Debauchery was *de jure* in Canaan, and he had seen enough of that in Ur. They likely scoffed at his altars and his preaching. He certainly met no righteous Melchizedeks.

And on top of all this, "there was a famine in the land" (12:10). As to whether Abram was surprised at this, we cannot know. Famine is always a possibility for those who live close to the earth. But certainly this is not what we would expect after such a protracted and stellar display of faith. We would expect some tangible rewards, or at least a pleasant respite. After believing in Christ and exercising my newfound faith, I expected nothing but blue skies. But this was not God's way with this progenitor of faith or with his children. And because of the story's primary importance, we learn that faith is regularly followed by famine, even severe trial. That is God's way.

Faith is always tested. The tests may not be as immediate as Abram's, but they always come. Experience and God's Word taught James, the Lord's brother, to advise, "Count it all joy, my brothers, when you meet trials of various kinds, for you know that the testing of your faith produces steadfastness. And let steadfastness have its full effect, that you may be perfect and complete, lacking in nothing" (James 1:2-4). Here faithful Abram, who had left all to follow the bare word of God, who had been outstanding in his 800-mile trek to the promised land and in his tour of inspection, got whacked. He was literally starved out of the land.

FAITH LAPSES (vv. 10-13)

Abram's flight. There was nothing remarkable in Abram's decision to go down to Egypt for help, nor is there any portent in the description of this: "Now there was a famine in the land. So Abram went down to Egypt to sojourn there, for the famine was severe in the land" (v. 10). All Abram intended was a temporary stay in Egypt until the famine ended. He was not abandoning the promised land. If that had been his intention, he would have gone back to Ur. Going to Egypt was the natural thing to do. Those in Canaan and especially the Negev did this regularly because the Nile always guaranteed food. An Egyptian inscription reads: "Certain of the foreigners who know not how they may live have come . . . their countries are starving."[1]

Abram did the natural thing, and herein the problem lies. There is no mention that he sought God's will in the matter. The famine had created the fear of starvation, and Abram then instinctively moved to allay his fear, without reference to God's will. Given what then befell him, it is apparent that if he had solicited God's will, the story would have been quite different. Abram's going to Egypt was not so much an intentional sin as it was a reflexive turn to his own devices. He did not deny God; he simply forgot him. He forgot how great God is.

How like Abram we are! Trials come, and we automatically go into survival mode. We scheme, we prognosticate, we run through the "what ifs," we shore up our position, we pile sandbags. And God? Oh yes. We ask him to bless our ways.

Abram's deception. The problem with going down to Egypt was that Sarai was a woman of legendary beauty. If the face of Helen of Troy could launch a thousand ships, Sarai's could launch a thousand caravans. What are we to make of her beauty? Some liberal critical scholars say that she was not beautiful and in fact did not even exist. Rather, they say that she is the product of the cultural tendency to glorify the national mother figure.[2] Of course, these same critics also say Abram did not exist!

Some have suggested that her beauty was in the eye of the beholder — namely, her lovestruck husband Abram. Such loving delusion is not uncommon. James Boswell's *Life of Samuel Johnson* records Boswell's amusement that Johnson always thought his wife was beautiful — "that the impressions which her beauty, real or imaginary, had originally made upon his fancy, being continued by habit, had not been effaced, though she herself was doubtless much altered for the worse."[3] All of us, if we live long enough, will be "much altered for the worse" — but not in the eyes of love. No doubt Abram always saw Sarai as an unfaded beauty. But the story also reveals that here, with Sarai sixty-five years old, the Egyptians thought the same (cf. 12:14)!

Evidently Sarai was a knockout and remained the same for a long time. We must remember that the patriarchal life span was still about double our own. Abraham died at 175, Sarah at 127. Jacob thought that 130 years were "few and evil" (Genesis 47:9). Sarai's sixties would be equivalent to our thirties and forties, and her ninety years at the birth of Isaac to our fifties.[4] Sarai's eye-stopping Mesopotamian beauty no doubt dazzled the Egyptians, and that could be a problem. Abram had substantial reason to fear. The law of hospitality that was so central in biblical thought did not necessarily apply in Egypt, or so Abram feared.

All this ran through Abram's mind as his family and servants crossed the Sinai Peninsula toward Egypt. "When he was about to enter Egypt, he said to Sarai his wife, 'I know that you are a woman beautiful in appearance, and when the Egyptians see you, they will say, "This is his wife." Then they will kill me, but they will let you live. Say you are my sister, that it may go well with me because of you, and that my life may be spared for your sake'" (vv. 11-13). This deception was not new to Abram's thinking. Earlier, when Abram left Haran, he had said to Sarai, "This is the kindness you must do me: at every place to which we come, say of me, He is my brother" (20:13). Now, at the border of Egypt, Abram put the deceit to work. And he would do it again (cf. chap. 20). "This man of God, being a man still, appears in a new light, or rather in the old light, the light of his old nature" (Candlish).[5] Abram, by nature, was a cunning man.

Those who imagine that he knowingly was risking Sarai fail to understand that posing as brother and sister was designed to buy time so they could escape. Abram was playing off the well-known custom of fratriarchy, as Nahum Sarna has explained: "Where there is no father, the brother assumes legal guardianship of his sister, particularly with respect to obligations and responsibilities in arranging marriage on her behalf. Therefore, whoever wished to take Sarai to wife would have to negotiate with her 'brother.' In this way, Abram could gain time to plan escape."[6] Just as Laban, the brother of Rebekah, would use his position as brother to put off Eliezer's approach, so Abram hoped to forestall Sarai's suitors. It was brilliant. No one would get hurt, apart from the feelings of Sarai's would-be husbands.

And besides, it was only a half-lie because Sarai was his half-sister (cf. 11:27-30; 20:2). Abram could ease his conscience in saying "truthfully" that she was his sister, while also knowing how the Egyptians would take it. Pretty smart! Abram probably congratulated himself for being so wise and forward-looking. He was a responsible man. And he was helping God. After all, if something happened to him, God's promise would be undone. Clever man, Abram.

There were only a few little problems. This trickery was not an act of faith. Abram was living as if the God who had spoken to him in Ur, who had promised those incredible personal and global blessings, who had led him to and through Canaan and promised it to his descendants, did not exist. God was not in the driver's seat — Abram was. And more, he was using a lie to promote God's work. George Burns was joking when he said that the key to his success was first learning honesty; once he could fake that, he could achieve anything.[7] Abram had mastered the art of fake honesty in Ur, and it was no joke.

How the great man had stumbled. And he did not even suspect it — yet.

TRAGEDY IN EGYPT (vv. 14-16)

Abram had forgotten one thing: *Pharaoh.* The average Egyptian would have happily negotiated for his sister. But not Pharaoh. Abram never thought of that.

Sarai suffers. Everything disintegrated in an instant.

> When Abram entered Egypt, the Egyptians saw that the woman was very beautiful. And when the princes of Pharaoh saw her, they praised her to Pharaoh. And the woman was taken into Pharaoh's house. And for her sake he dealt well with Abram; and he had sheep, oxen, male donkeys, male servants, female servants, female donkeys, and camels. (vv. 14-16)

Great! Sarai became a part of Pharaoh's harem. What was going on in those chambers? Was she now in Pharaoh's arms? "Oh, Pharaoh, Pharaoh . . . let my Sarai go!" Sarai, so beautiful, would surely become one of Pharaoh's favorite entertainments. And from then on, life would have taken its natural course. She well could have lived and died in Egypt, had her place in a royal tomb — and her excavated mummy would be grinning up at us in the British Museum. Good job, Abram.

Abram prospers. And then there was an excruciating moral twist. Pharaoh was so pleased with obtaining Sarai that he made Abram a very rich man. Two of the gifts tell all — the female donkeys and the camels. Female donkeys were far more controllable and dependable for riding and therefore the ride of choice of the rich (the Lexuses and BMWs of the Nile).[8] The camels (note the plural) had just been introduced as domesticated animals and were a rarity. They were prestige symbols, for show by the very rich, not for utility (the equivalent in my mind of a Ferrari Testarosa).[9] And Abram now had several in his stable. So faithless, deceitful Abram was inundated with luxurious things, while his beloved spent frantic days and sleepless nights in Pharaoh's harem.

GOD INTERVENES (vv. 17-20)

There was absolutely nothing that Abram could do except perhaps die in a futile attempt to save his wife. Maybe it would come to that. It appeared that all was lost.

Then it was that God sovereignly acted: "But the LORD afflicted Pharaoh and his house with great plagues because of Sarai, Abram's wife" (v. 17). Literally, Yahweh inflicted great plagues on Pharaoh and his household. The Hebrew construction stresses the severity of the plagues; so we understand that Pharaoh's household was overwhelmed by them. But Sarai was untouched.[10] The word translated "plagues" often refers to skin diseases. So possibly the Egyptian court suffered from something akin to a plague of boils (cf. Exodus 9:9).[11]

Abram reproached. We surmise that because Sarai suffered no affliction, Pharaoh's servants questioned her and learned of the deception and reported it to Pharaoh. Thus came Pharaoh's stinging reproach. "So Pharaoh called Abram and said, 'What is this you have done to me? Why did you not tell me that she was your wife? Why did you say, "She is my sister," so that I took her for my wife? Now then, here is your wife; take her, and go'"(vv. 18, 19). The concluding line is staccato — just four Hebrew words: "Here . . . wife . . . take . . . go."[12] Such disdain. Pharaoh assumed the moral high ground. Abram appeared the sinner, Pharaoh the saint.

Had Sarai been in Pharaoh's bed? Some scholars think so because Pharaoh says, "I took her for my wife," indicating actual adultery,[13] and the plagues seem to indicate that Pharaoh actually did commit adultery.[14] More likely Sarai escaped undefiled, as Allen Ross explains: "The words of

Pharaoh need not be interpreted to mean that there had been sexual contact. He simply stated that he took her for a wife. In a royal household, it would take time for her to come before the monarch (note the twelve months for Esther's preparation [Esther 2:12]). Moreover, the statement 'Here is your wife' strongly suggests that she was returned unharmed, as his wife."[15] Also, if Sarai had been defiled, she would never again consent to do the same deception later with King Abimelech — and neither would Abram (cf. chap. 20)!

Abram expelled. Abram's exit from Egypt was in ignominy: "And Pharaoh gave men orders concerning him, and they sent him away with his wife and all that he had" (v. 20). Abram remained silent under Pharaoh's reproach, uttering not a word. What could he say? He would build no altars in Egypt. Neither would he proclaim the name of the Lord. Abram and his entourage humbly crept out of Egypt.

Abram's lack of trust in God (doubting that he would keep his promises) had reduced him to a scheming, little man. This great giant of faith had become, for the present, a very small man. And he felt it.

If we wonder why Pharaoh did not punish them but rather sent them off with their new riches, it is because Pharaoh was still suffering the effects of the plagues. He never again wanted to be on the receiving end of the power behind Abram. Significantly, those new riches were no blessing to Abram. The ill-gotten gain caused huge trouble in the following years, first in the strife with Lot's herdsmen, and then through a young Egyptian woman named Hagar, who was likely one of the maidservants given to Abram by Pharaoh.

Having dissected Abram's failure, we must again affirm that he stands as a man of faith and among the greatest of men. If we doubt it, we must read on through chapter 22, or the celebration of his faith in Hebrews 11:8-12, 17-19, the longest section devoted to anyone in that famous chapter.

Abram started so magnificently but stumbled in ignominy because he did not expect the famine, the trial that came after his experience of faith. But famines are God's way. Trials are what produce perseverance and maturity so that we may become complete, not lacking anything.

Abram stumbled because, when testing came, he forgot God. He did not disbelieve in God. He forgot how great God is. And forgetting God, he resorted to his own devices, his stealth and manipulation. And then his world graciously fell in. But this was allowed by the goodness of God, because God had greater things for Abram to do.

The message for us who have believed God and trusted him for salvation and life is this: Expect trials as a part of God's plan, just as they were for Jesus who was made "perfect through suffering" (Hebrews 2:10; cf. 5:7-10).[16] We say this because the Apostle Paul reveals that God's promise to Abram in Genesis 12:7 ("To your offspring [literally, "seed," singular] I will give this land") actually had Christ in view. He argues this in Galatians 3:16, explaining, "Now the promises were made to Abraham and to his offspring. It does not say, 'And to offsprings,' referring to many, but referring to one, 'And to your offspring,' who is Christ."

Therefore Christ is the one through whom the whole world will be blessed. He is the one through whom the global blessings will be fulfilled. Also, as the ultimate heir of Abram, he is the man of faith *par excellence*.[17] Jesus did not stumble when trials came. His faith never wavered. He did not look to his own devices but only to God. Abram was a great man of faith, but Christ is the perfect man of faith. Abram left his home and family in Ur to go to an unknown land, but Christ left heaven in obedience to the Father's call. Abram is known for both his great faith and great failure. Jesus' life was one of unexceptionable faith. His life was all in faith and by faith from beginning to end.

Here is the great benefit: As Christians who have experienced the regenerating power of Christ, we are *in* Christ (cf. 2 Corinthians 5:17). And, therefore, because we are *in* the man of faith, he not only saves us but empowers us to live a life of faith! The very one to whom Abram's faith pointed, the very one to whom the promises pointed and who fulfilled the promise, is the one who enables us to live by faith. Jesus is the beginning and end of faith.

So when trials come, as they must, do not turn to your own resources but to Christ. And he will sustain your faith.

23

Magnanimous Faith

Genesis 13:1-18

The record of Abram's fiasco in Egypt is the story of a man of faith. His scandalous attempt to represent Sarai as his sister was not the act of a man devoid of real faith, but of a man who had succumbed to doubt, whose trust had devolved to distrust. Despite the fact that he had descended to such self-serving deception, Abram was yet a man of faith. Abram's faith was not window dressing or a rabbit's foot or fire insurance. It was the real thing, but in temporary retreat.

On the momentous day when he left Ur, he had rested everything on the bare word of God. He obeyed and went out, though he had no idea where he was going. He believed God's promise that great blessing would come both *upon* him and *through* him. Then, in Canaan, he believed God when God said, "To your offspring I will give this land" (Genesis 12:7). But in Egypt he exhibited a distrust that was not consonant with the faith in his heart of hearts.

Abram was like us, a paradoxical mixture of self-centered reliance and trust in God. And the author Moses makes no attempt to gloss over Abram's failures. In fact, the stories, first of Abram's *failure* in Egypt with Pharaoh and then his *success* in Canaan with Lot, explore the contradictions within this man of faith. By this studied contrast Moses will help us explore our own hearts.

Back to Bethel. Abram left Egypt chastened and silent. His journey from Egypt to the Negev to Bethel was apparently a conscious pilgrimage through which he desired to recapture his previous walk with God, because he ultimately returned to the altar where he first called on the name of the Lord. The account reads:

So Abram went up from Egypt, he and his wife and all that he had, and
Lot with him, into the Negeb [Negev]. Now Abram was very rich in live-
stock, in silver, and in gold. And he journeyed on from the Negeb as far as
Bethel to the place where his tent had been at the beginning, between
Bethel and Ai, to the place where he had made an altar at the first. And
there Abram called upon the name of the LORD. (vv. 1-4)

The intentional contrast with Abram's failure in Egypt is clear from the
parallel use of the Hebrew word *kābhōdh,* "heavy," both at the beginning of
the previous account about Egypt and now here at the beginning of this
account. Whereas in the Negev "the famine was severe" ("heavy," 12:10),
"now Abram was very rich ("heavy") in livestock, in silver, and in gold"
(13:2).[1] This indicates that we are to read the present success story keeping
in mind his failure in Egypt.

Indeed, Abram had become very wealthy because he not only had
female donkeys (the transportation of the rich) and camels (the prestige symbols of the super-rich), but he was also heavy in silver and gold. This was
extraordinary for the wandering shepherd culture. Abram, in fact, prefigured the Israelites' exodus from Egypt when they carried out the voluntary
plunder of their Egyptian masters (cf. Exodus 12). Similarly, as Abram left
the Negev, the account says that "he journeyed on from the Negeb as far as
Bethel" (v. 3), which is similar terminology to Israel's journey from Egypt
in the exodus — and therefore a further foreshadowing of that event (cf.
Exodus 17:1 and Numbers 10:12).[2] Later the Israelites were heartened by this
story as they wandered in the wilderness, because they realized that their
great forefather had a similar experience when he left Egypt.

Ultimately, Abram's pilgrimage culminated at Bethel, "the site he loved
so dearly because on it stood the altar, the second monument . . . to the symbolic conquest of the land and its consecration to YHWH, his God"
(Cassuto).[3] And there in Bethel Abram renewed his spiritual connection
with God and the land. Again "Abram called upon the name of the LORD."
He renewed his lapsed obedience. He proclaimed that Yahweh was Lord in
dark, pagan Canaan, just as his Sethite forebears had done amidst the darkness of the pre-flood world (cf. 4:26). The sin and fiasco of Egypt was now
behind Abram. This was a fresh start.

Abram worshiped at Bethel's altar. Here again he would offer whole
burnt offerings like those of Noah (cf. 8:20), declaring, as the smoke rose
upward, that all of his life was God's. It is very important that we take careful notice that the account will end with Abram's building a third altar at
Hebron (v. 18), so that the whole story here is clothed in authentic worship.
All of Abram's dealings with Lot were an act of worship. Abram's knee
remained bent to God. By faith he saw the unseen and acted accordingly.
He believed God's word.

ABRAM TESTED (vv. 5-7)

Abram's nephew Lot had played no significant role in Egypt and so received no mention. He now appears because of his role in the following episode. The tag voiced in verse 1, "and Lot with him," hints at estrangement. So here we read:

> And Lot, who went with Abram, also had flocks and herds and tents, so that the land could not support both of them dwelling together; for their possessions were so great that they could not dwell together, and there was strife between the herdsmen of Abram's livestock and the herdsmen of Lot's livestock. At that time the Canaanites and the Perizzites were dwelling in the land. (vv. 5-7)

Lot had piggy-backed on Abram's wealth so that both men were rich. No doubt Abram's possessions were far more substantial, and thus Lot's considerable flocks, plus Abram's, plus the fact that the local Canaanites and Perizzites already had their own pasturage made the situation tense. The result was a range war — the kind of western-movie scenario with which we're so familiar. The only thing missing here is Gene Autry's background music — "Oh, give me a home where my shepherds can roam."

The irony (and it is an irony of human existence) is that the material blessing of God upon Abram and Lot fueled the problem. The New Testament, through the Apostle Peter, tells us that Lot was a "righteous" man (2 Peter 2:7); otherwise we would not have guessed it. Lot had not learned at all from Abram's debacle in Egypt. He remained a greedy, scheming man. And Lot and his herdsmen (who took their cues from him) behaved poorly. Thus Abram's and Lot's prosperity, rather than pulling them together, divided them. We imagine that need and want will divide us. But it is not true. Believers who sense their need will naturally draw close to God and each other. Need produces a poverty of spirit that reaches up for help and out to one another. But assailed by prosperity, Abram and Lot drew apart. We must consider ourselves forewarned as we prosper.

What a test this conflict must have been for Abram's recharged faith. Initially, the first time in Bethel when he had called on the name of the Lord, he was tested by famine. Here when he again called on the Lord's name, he was tested by another trial. But now Abram was up to the test.

ABRAM'S MAGNANIMITY (vv. 8, 9)

Abram's response is a study in magnanimity. "Then Abram said to Lot, 'Let there be no strife between you and me, and between your herdsmen and my herdsmen, for we are kinsmen. Is not the whole land before you?

Separate yourself from me. If you take the left hand, then I will go to the right, or if you take the right hand, then I will go to the left'" (vv. 8, 9).

Abram, not Lot, took the initiative. He nipped potential catastrophe in the bud. Perhaps Solomon had Abram's example in mind when he penned the proverb, "The beginning of strife is like letting out water, so quit before the quarrel breaks out" (Proverbs 17:14). Abram's words were explicitly tender. Twice he says in the Hebrew, "I pray you" (please).[4] He appealed to their kinship. The sense is, "men should not quarrel, let alone brothers."[5] Unlike Cain, Abram saw himself as his brother's keeper (cf. 4:9).

Such nobility of character! Abram, as the older man and the leader of the faith expedition, the one to whom the promises were made, could have appealed to his position, which was unassailable in Semitic culture. But he did not. Confident and unthreatened, he was selfless and generous — "Take your choice, my nephew and brother."

What a change from the calculating, self-serving schemer that he was in Egypt. In Egypt he had trusted nothing but his own shrewdness. Now Abram is so remarkably different. He takes no thought for tomorrow (cf. Matthew 6:25-34). The contrast between the two narratives could not be more defined. In the former, Abram was consumed with survival. In the present, he risks all in light of the promise.[6]

By faith. How had Abram ascended to such heights? He believed God's word, the very word upon which he had rested everything. God had said, "To your offspring I will give this land" (12:7) — and therefore Abram knew that even if he gave the land away a thousand times, it would go to his descendants. By his faith Abram's vision of the unseen was renewed. Abram was not living by sight. What difference does the geography make when our vision is that of a city whose architect and builder is God? Abram's renewed faith had made all the difference!

Abram experienced an astonishing ascendancy of soul. Amidst this miserable conflict with Lot, Abram's total trust had catapulted him to the likeness of his ultimate seed and heir, the Lord Jesus Christ, who did not look out for his own interests but the interest of others — who did not grasp what was his but gave himself (cf. Philippians 2:4-8). Abram foreshadowed the very spirit of Christ.

Fellow believers (Abram's spiritual seed), when we truly believe the promises that are ours in Christ, when we truly understand and believe that we are seated right now in him in the heavenly places, when we understand that all things are ours in Christ, we will cease our grasping. As Alexander Maclaren put it:

> The less of our energies are consumed in asserting ourselves, and scrambling for our rights, and cutting in before other people, so as to get the best places for ourselves, the more we shall have to spare for better things;

and the more we live in the future, and leave God to order our ways, the more shall our souls be wrapped in perfect peace.[7]

SEPARATION (vv. 10-13)

Whereas Abram was living by faith, Lot was living by sight, much as Abram had lived in Egypt.

Lot's choice. Bethel is situated on a hill almost three thousand feet high. And less than one mile to the southeast is the famous prominence of Burj-Beitin, which affords a magnificent view of the Jordan Valley.[8] From this vantage point, "Lot lifted up his eyes and saw that the Jordan Valley was well watered everywhere like the garden of the LORD, like the land of Egypt, in the direction of Zoar. (This was before the LORD destroyed Sodom and Gomorrah)" (v. 10). The language makes it clear that Lot intensely surveyed the Jordan Valley — "Lot lifted up his eyes and saw" — he took it all in.[9] There scarce could be more lavish and evocative allusions than Eden and Egypt. The great river that flowed from Eden divided into four famous headwaters that watered Mesopotamia. The Nile was the life of Egypt. Lot saw the well-watered plain as paradise — though the very references to Eden and Egypt themselves also foreshadowed judgment. And, of course, the parenthetical "This was before the LORD destroyed Sodom and Gomorrah" is ominous. But what Lot saw with his eyes was stupendous — a verdant plain brightly dotted with inviting cities.

Catastrophe. The choice was as easy as falling off a log. "So Lot chose for himself all the Jordan Valley, and Lot journeyed east. Thus they separated from each other. Abram settled in the land of Canaan, while Lot settled among the cities of the valley and moved his tent as far as Sodom. Now the men of Sodom were wicked, great sinners against the LORD" (vv. 11-13). Here is the tragedy: Though Lot was offered a share in the land of Canaan, he rejected it and moved to its very edge — "at the end of its border," according to Cassuto.[10] His journey "east" was a dark echo of the way Cain had departed (cf. 3:24; 4:16). Genesis 19 will reveal that Lot would eventually dwell outside the border of Canaan in the hill country on the eastern side of the Jordan (cf. 19:30).[11]

The description of the Sodomites as "wicked, great sinners" is a rare phrase that suggests they were living at a level lower than normal sinners.[12] Chapter 19 will grotesquely bear this out.

Dazzled by the ostensible prosperity of Sodom, Lot pitched his tent "as far as Sodom." Lot was the kind of man who would certainly choose Heaven over Hell if given the choice, but not Heaven over earth. Material prosperity was the bottom line. He was the example of believers who choose professions for their children or encourage marriages that will elevate the family's prosperity and power — with no thought of what it will do to their souls and the souls of their children. Lot's descendants testified to this as they became enemies of God's people.

Again, Lot's choice was by sight alone. It was the biggest mistake of his life.

GOD SPEAKS (vv. 14-17)

Certainly Abram did not expect what followed. But subsequent to his magnificent display of faith and the departure of Lot, God again spoke, reaffirming and further defining his promise of both a land and a people.

Land. Using the same language that described Lot's intense look at the Jordan Valley, God told Abram, "Lift up your eyes and look from the place where you are, northward and southward and eastward and westward, for all the land that you see I will give to you and to your offspring forever" (vv. 14, 15). According to the Genesis Apocryphon (21:8-15), they were at Ramath Hazor, about five miles northeast of Bethel and the highest spot in central Israel, well over three thousand feet. From there Abram could view Mt. Hermon in the north, the Dead Sea and the hills of Hebron to the south, the Jordan to the east, and the Mediterranean Sea in the west.[13] As Abram gazed at the four respective points of the compass, he heard God audibly promise the land to him. The promise was unconditional and "forever." And so the sure word of God was made more explicit to the heart of faith!

People. God here referenced Abram's descendants three times, using the same word, "offspring" (literally, "seed," singular), that he had used in the original promise in 12:7. "All the land that you see I will give to you and to your *offspring* forever. I will make your *offspring* as the dust of the earth, so that if one can count the dust of the earth, your *offspring* also can be counted" (vv. 15, 16, italics added). Later in 15:5 God would promise that Abram's offspring would be as numerous as the stars. So whether he looked down as he traversed the land by day or whether he looked up at the stars at night, he was reminded that he and his barren wife would become a great nation (cf. 12:2).

Tour. Earliest Jewish commentaries, in concert with the practice of the ancient world, understood that God's directive — "Arise, walk through the length and the breadth of the land, for I will give it to you" (v. 17) — was a symbolic act signifying legal acquisition of the land.[14] As Abram walked the land, the great promises — personal and global — coursed through his soul. He believed. He was seeing the unseen.

And when his faith walk was completed, the narrative concludes, "So Abram moved his tent and came and settled by the oaks of Mamre, which are at Hebron, and there he built an altar to the LORD" (v. 18). The aroma of worship has enveloped the whole passage. Abram's encounter with Lot and his response were worship from first to last.

A look at Abram and Lot side by side is instructive. Lot chose the things that are seen and found them corrupting. Abram looked and saw through the eyes of faith the things that are unseen, and he found great assurance and peace. He could even give away the promised land, because he knew it was his by God's word. Thus he lived in royal magnanimity, like Christ.

And because he walked in faith, God made the promise even clearer. As he looked north, south, east, and west, Abram took it all into his heart. Whether he looked up at the stars or down at the dust, he was assured that he would be the father of a great nation. His tour of the land was a victory tour. He worshiped God.

How this calls us to believe God's word, to see the unseen, and to live in magnanimity!

Yet there is a further point that is instructive — Abram's conduct with Pharaoh in contrast to Abram's conduct with Lot. The two Abrams represent what we are — people of faith, but strange mixtures of trust and distrust. Abram in Egypt descended to a small, shriveled heart, but Abram back in Canaan elevated to a great, magnanimous heart. The heart-difference in this man of faith depended upon whether he trusted or distrusted God's word.

Distrusting God's word will constrict your soul. It will reduce you to a smallest compass, and your life will be of very little use, much like that of Lot. But when you believe God's word and rest your faith on his promises with all your heart, there will rise in you a greatness of soul that will enable you to live in a magnanimity not unlike the Lord Jesus Christ himself.

People of faith are truly a mixture of trust and distrust. Distrust in a believer is folly; trust in a believer is divine.

24

Magnanimous Living

GENESIS 14:1-24

The dictionary tells us that the word *magnanimous* is a combination of two Latin words — *magnus* (great) and *animus* (spirit) — suggesting a lofty and courageous spirit, a nobility of feeling, and a generosity of mind.[1] In a word, bigheartedness. A magnanimous person is able to face trouble calmly, to set aside meanness and revenge, and to make sacrifices for worthy ends.

Magnanimous perfectly describes Father Abram *after* his experience in Egypt. Down in Egypt his lack of trust in God had reduced him to a small-hearted, self-focused man. But back in Canaan, repentant and trusting God, he exemplified a greatness of spirit and generosity of soul in his dealings with his nephew Lot. Now the story of Abram's rescue of Lot provides us with an instructive sequel to chapter 13 as we see Abram, the man of faith, living magnanimously in a sinful, violent world — as he trusts God. Such living would bring Abram unique rewards, as his recompense and mighty declaration will show.

INTERNATIONAL CONFLICT (vv. 1-12)

Due to Abram's generosity, the parting with Lot had been peaceful. And with Lot's departure a temporary calm graced their lives. Abram settled contentedly in Hebron and worshiped God at his newly-built altar. Lot, who had pitched his tents *near* Sodom, was now living *in* Sodom as he pursued his prosperity (cf. 13:12 and 14:12). Likely, Lot did not know how endangered the place was when he made his initial move to Sodom. But the reality was that Sodom was part of a pentapolis (a group of five cities, each with a petty king) located at the southern end of the Dead Sea, which had been paying tribute for twelve years to a coalition of four kings from the east.

Rebellion and war. Moreover, the five Dead Sea kings rebelled, pro-
voking invasion by the eastern coalition:

> *In the days of Amraphel king of Shinar, Arioch king of Ellasar, Chedorlaomer*
> *king of Elam, and Tidal king of Goiim, these kings made war with Bera*
> *king of Sodom, Birsha king of Gomorrah, Shinab king of Admah, Shemeber*
> *king of Zeboiim, and the king of Bela (that is, Zoar). And all these joined*
> *forces in the Valley of Siddim (that is, the Salt Sea). Twelve years they had*
> *served Chedorlaomer, but in the thirteenth year they rebelled. (vv. 1-4)*

The eastern coalition was international in scope. Chedorlaomer of Elam
was from modern Iran, Amraphel of Shinar (= Babylon) was from modern
Iraq, and the two other kings, Arioch and Tidal, represented the Hurrians
and Hittites (peoples from areas within modern Turkey).

Their war plan was twofold — first, to subdue the Transjordan and the
Sinai, and second, to subdue the Dead Sea kings. Chedorlaomer led his
cohorts to a sweeping victory in accomplishing the first objective. His invasion route was the same taken by Terah and Abram in their migration, first
traveling west along the Euphrates to Carchemish and then down through
Damascus to Canaan and the Transjordan. The campaign went as planned.

> *In the fourteenth year Chedorlaomer and the kings who were with him*
> *came and defeated the Rephaim in Ashteroth-karnaim, the Zuzim in Ham,*
> *the Emim in Shaveh-kiriathaim, and the Horites in their hill country of Seir*
> *as far as El-paran on the border of the wilderness. Then they turned back*
> *and came to En-mishpat (that is, Kadesh) and defeated all the country of*
> *the Amalekites, and also the Amorites who were dwelling in Hazazon-*
> *tamar. (vv. 5-7)*

The first tribe to fall were the Rephaites who, like the Anakim, were
famous for their height (cf. Deuteronomy 2:11). These Rephaites were called
"Zamzummim" by the Ammonites (Deuteronomy 2:20) and "Emim" by
the Moabites (Deuteronomy 2:11). Thus the first stroke subdued the most
intimidating of their opponents, the giants of the Transjordan. The Horites
lived in the hill country of Seir, the mountainous region east of the Rift Valley
(the Arabah), which runs between the Dead Sea and the Gulf of Akaba.
Chedorlaomer and his hordes subdued everything in this area as far as El
Paran, thus covering most, if not all, of the Sinai Peninsula and part of the
Negeb and the Arabah.[2]

Then, turning northwest, they took the strategic oasis of Kadesh-barnea,
whipping the Amalekites and Amorites in Hazazon-tamar, which we know
as Engedi on the western side of the Dead Sea.[3] This well-conceived and executed strategy left the five kinglets at their mercy. No tribe could be sum-

moned to help them, and they had nowhere to flee. The Transjordan was so crippled that when the coalition nations returned back to their eastern kingdoms, none would have the capacity to attack them. On top of this, they had secured the trading route between Mesopotamia and Egypt — the link between the Euphrates and the Nile. It was an awesome achievement.

Pacification. Now they were ready for the plum, the rebellious five, the Dead Sea kings — and they fell to them like overripe fruit from a tree.

> *Then the king of Sodom, the king of Gomorrah, the king of Admah, the king of Zeboiim, and the king of Bela (that is, Zoar) went out, and they joined battle in the Valley of Siddim with Chedorlaomer king of Elam, Tidal king of Goiim, Amraphel king of Shinar, and Arioch king of Ellasar, four kings against five. Now the Valley of Siddim was full of bitumen pits, and as the kings of Sodom and Gomorrah fled, some fell into them, and the rest fled to the hill country. (vv. 8-10)*

The mention of the king of Sodom and his confederates first suggests that they were ready and even took the initiative. But they were no match for the experienced, confident troops of Chedorlaomer. Tar and asphalt are native to the Dead Sea, which Josephus actually called the Asphalt Sea. Asphalt still oozes in heavy liquid form in the southern part of the sea, where the five towns once lay.[4] Many of the defenders met a horrific death in the tar pits in the Valley of Siddim, falling headlong into the black ooze as they fled. Calvin writes: "I, however, understand them to have exchanged one kind of death for another, as is common in the moment of desperation; as if Moses had said, the swords of the enemy were so formidable to them, that, without hesitation, they threw themselves headlong into the pits."[5]

And Lot? What painful irony. He had greedily chosen the best part of the land, and his choice had proven disastrous. "So the enemy took all the possessions of Sodom and Gomorrah, and all their provisions, and went their way. They also took Lot, the son of Abram's brother, who was dwelling in Sodom, and his possessions, and went their way" (vv. 11, 12). Lot and everything he possessed was carted off to who knows where. Turkey? Read between the lines. Lot had seen agonizing deaths and rapes, the traditional wake of ancient victory. Perhaps he had lost children and loved ones. Perhaps a daughter was now the prize of some Hittite. As he trudged across the Transjordan toward Canaan's borders, all his hopes were dead.

ABRAM'S MAGNANIMITY (vv. 13-16)

Those who escaped the mayhem at Sodom fled to the hills. And sometime, perhaps after nightfall, one stumbled to Abram's camp, because Abram was only about twenty miles away.

*Then one who had escaped came and told Abram the Hebrew, who was
living by the oaks of Mamre the Amorite, brother of Eschol and of Aner.
These were allies of Abram. When Abram heard that his kinsman had
been taken captive, he led forth his trained men, born in his house, 318 of
them, and went in pursuit as far as Dan. (vv. 13, 14)*

Abram's pursuit. Here Abram was magnificent. Iain Duguid sees the
event as a kind of epiphany: "The veil is lifted for a moment, and we see
Abram in his true colors, acting as the king of the land that is his by right
and that will be inherited by his offspring. This is Abram's mount of trans-
figuration, when his glory is clearly — if brightly — revealed to those closest to him."[6] We see Abram in stunning magnanimity.

Abram could easily have elected to do nothing. Lot had made his choice.
He had cared for no one but himself. Lot had pitched his tent near Sodom and
then moved into town! Besides, wisdom is the better part of valor. People
would get further hurt if he got involved. And what if something happened
to him? He was the one indispensable man.

But Abram chose to take action. He was the original Braveheart — the
real thing! "He led forth his trained men, born in his house, 318 of them."
These were servants from birth, not acquired servants, and therefore the most
loyal and dependable. The Hebrew here is dynamic. "He led forth . . . 318
of them" is literally, "drew out 318 men," as you would draw out a sword
from its sheath.[7] His 318 loyal men were his sword unsheathed and ready
for war! Out came the quivers and bows; swords were whetted to a razor's
edge; spears were thrust into the sky.

Abram trembled like every man has who has mounted for battle.
Napoleon often referred to Marshall Nay as the bravest man he had ever
known. Yet Nay's knees trembled so badly one morning before a battle that
he had trouble mounting his horse. When he was finally in the saddle, he
shouted contemptuously, "Shake away, knees, you would shake worse than
that if you knew where I am going to take you!"[8] Abram surely trembled,
but there was no way he would turn back.

> *If I falter, push me on.*
> *If I stumble, pick me up.*
> *If I retreat, shoot me.*
> MOTTO, FRENCH FOREIGN LEGION

Abram the shepherd, the wanderer, the man of peace, was now General
Abram. And amidst war cries Abram and his valiant men were off in a cloud
of dust on the trail of the kings of the east — the Elamites and Babylonians,
the Hurrians and Hittites. One hundred and twenty miles later at Dan, the
northernmost reach of the promised land, they caught the four kings.

Before we move on, take note that this brave heart, this great heart, was at this very moment like that of Jesus. As Abram was to Lot, so Christ is to us. Jesus did not sit idly by in Heaven waiting for us to deserve redemption. Neither was our redemption painless. Christ left the glories of heaven to come after us.[9]

Abram's victory. The enemy was evidently unaware of the interception. They had no reason to worry, they thought. Every people from Moab to the Gulf of Akaba had been dealt with. No doubt after their nightly revels, they slept well around their fires. Perhaps Abram's stealth is here what later informed Gideon's victory. "And he divided his forces against them by night, he and his servants, and defeated them and pursued them to Hobah, north of Damascus. Then he brought back all the possessions, and also brought back his kinsman Lot with his possessions, and the women and the people" (vv. 15, 16).

Swords rang in the night. And the combination of Abram's well-planned attack and the surprise routed the evil armies of the east. The pursuit bore them well out of the promised land above Damascus. What an incredible feat! And Moses wants us to see it and marvel. That is why he so carefully chronicles the brilliant campaign of the kings of the east — their flattening of the giants of the Transjordan and the peoples of the mountain and desert. See Braveheart and his victory — and wonder!

How had Abram done this? From whence came his courage? It was his faith. He believed God's word — that the land would go to his descendants — and therefore knew that God was with him. Even if he met defeat, he knew that God would keep his promise. Whereas in Egypt he had fallen to *distrust* and smallness, now he was living in profound *trust* and an elevation of heart as king of the land. We see Christ in this man.

Those 120 miles back to Hebron must have been intoxicating. Winston Churchill recalled that when the British people learned of their victory in World War II, "I heard the cheers of the brave people who had borne so much and given all; who had never wavered, who had never lost faith in their country or its destiny, and who could be indulgent to the faults of their servants when the hour of deliverance had come." According to Churchill, one simple cheer, an eight-word antiphon now locked in the memory of history, was heard that Monday night and throughout the following day wherever London crowds gathered — in Mayfair and White Chapel, Leicester Square and Regent's Park. It echoed and reechoed, repeated by tearful, proud, exultant Britons who rejoiced in the evidence that they had prevailed. Someone in a throng would chant, "Who won the war?" And the rest would roar back, "We won the war!" Eventually they grew hoarse, until at last all had fallen silent.[10]

Similar euphoric, incredulous ecstasy rang from the valiant men and the repatriated captives from the pentapolis. Abram's name would become commonplace from the Euphrates to the Nile. An authentic hero!

But here lay a further testing — *the test of success.* So often those who have been stellar in adversity are derailed by success. Their behavior changes in order to take advantage of their fame. Faith in God reverts to faith in self. They begin to believe the good press. And so weakened, they succumb to temptations they had easily resisted before. How would Abram fare?

ABRAM'S RECOMPENSE (vv. 17-20)

The setting was the Valley of Shaveh, the King's Valley, a brief distance south of Jerusalem.[11] There two kings greeted Abram and his warriors, the king of Sodom and the king of Salem. Both were Canaanite kings. The kings are a study in contrast. The king of Sodom viewed Abram's victory as a human feat, but the king of Salem saw it as divine. The king of Sodom made a businesslike offer to Abram. But the king of Salem "offered him, in token, a simple sufficiency from God, pronounces an unspecified blessing (dwelling on the Giver, not the gift), and accepts costly tribute" (Kidner).[12]

Melchizedek. The king of Salem was none other than the mysterious Melchizedek, actually the king of Jerusalem. Both etymology and rabbinic commentary as well as Psalm 76:2 confirm that Salem is Jerusalem.[13] So he was king of what would become the Holy City. Melchizedek means "king of righteousness" or "my king is righteous." Either way his name stresses his righteous character. And in addition to his royalty and righteousness, he was a priest of the Most High God. Add to this the fact that he was a Canaanite, and you have the reality: *Melchizedek was the God-fearing, Canaanite priest-king of Jerusalem.* He was a Canaanite like the king of Sodom, a descendant of Canaan, the cursed son of Ham. He was not a physical descendant or relative of Abram. Yet he was like Abram in this: He believed that there is one God, God the Most High. Unlike Abram, he did not know that God's name is Yahweh. But he would know immediately (cf. v. 22). Gordon Wenham explains:

> Within Genesis, however, Melchizedek is primarily an example of a non-Jew who recognizes God's hand at work in Israel: like Abimelech (21:22), Rahab (Josh. 2:11), Ruth (1:16) or Naaman (2 Kings 5:15). Similarly, he may be seen as a forerunner of the Magi (Matt. 2:1-12), centurions (Matt. 8:5-13; Mark 15:39; Acts 10), or the Syro-Phoenician woman (Mark 7:26-30), let alone the multitude of Gentile converts mentioned in Acts. They are those who have discovered that in Abram all the families of the earth find blessing.[14]

This union of *priest* and *king* at *Jerusalem* will move David, the first Israelite *priest*[15] (or at least having priestly functions) and *king*, to sit on a throne in *Jerusalem* to sing of a greater Melchizedek to come (cf. Psalm 110:4). The significance of this is explained in depth in Hebrews 7, as we shall see in our next study.

What did this God-fearing Canaanite priest-king do? First, he refreshed Abram: "And Melchizedek king of Salem brought out bread and wine" (v. 18a). This expressed his goodwill and his generosity. Bread and wine was royal fare (cf. 1 Samuel 16:20). He laid out a royal banquet for the returning conquerors in the valley of the kings.

Melchizedek's blessing. Secondly, while his hands were full of gifts, his lips were full of blessing.

> *And he blessed him and said,*
> *"Blessed be Abram by God Most High,*
> *Possessor of heaven and earth." (v. 19)*

This looks back to 12:1-3 when God promised Abram that he would be a blessing and that all the families of the earth would be blessed in him. This was the initial fulfillment of that promise, as Melchizedek, one of the families of the earth, blessed Abram. This suggests that Melchizedek himself would be blessed through Abram. This was in stark contrast to the king of Sodom who was outside the blessing.

Melchizedek's identification of God Most High as "Possessor of heaven and earth" grounded the blessing in the ultimate power in the universe. These blessings "invite us to take creation faith out of the arena of 'origins' and see it as source for life buoying, and joy in the trials of the day" (Brueggemann).[16] God's cosmic power is the ultimate ground of faith.

Then as Melchizedek's blessing echoed over Abram, Melchizedek blessed God:

> *". . . and blessed be God Most High,*
> *who has delivered your enemies into your hand!" (v. 20)*

Melchizedek understood what was lost on the king of Sodom — that the source of Abram's victories was God. His doxologies flowed not only outward but upward. This mysterious Canaanite was himself a man of faith. And he was now living under God's blessing. He was the prime example of God's promise, "and in you [Abram] all the families of the earth shall be blessed" (12:3b).

Abram tithes. Abram recognized Melchizedek's blessing as the voice of God and implicitly that Melchizedek, too, was a man of faith. "And Abram gave him a tenth of everything" (v. 20b). Abram validated Melchizedek's priesthood by his tithe, as was customary for priestly services. At the same time he was giving his tenth to God.

ABRAM'S DECLARATION (vv. 21-24)

Seeing the exchange, the king of Sodom offered his own deal: "Give me the persons, but take the goods for yourself" (v. 21). Sodom gave nothing, whereas Melchizedek brought a banquet. Melchizedek blessed Abram, but Sodom offered a crude, rude deal that can be summarized in six words: "Give me people; take property yourself."[17] As rescuer, Abram was entitled to all. Sodom's deal was an ungracious, self-serving demand.

But observe Abram's response to him, which he delivered in the form of an oath before "the LORD [Yahweh], God Most High, Possessor of heaven and earth." Now Melchizedek learned that the Lord Most High is Yahweh. From now on, he would know of and believe in the name of God. Abram's oath closes the account:

> But Abram said to the king of Sodom, "I have lifted my hand to the LORD, God Most High, Possessor of heaven and earth, that I would not take a thread or a sandal strap or anything that is yours, lest you should say, 'I have made Abram rich.' I will take nothing but what the young men have eaten, and the share of the men who went with me. Let Aner, Eshcol, and Mamre take their share." (vv. 22-24)

This oath, this refusal, was Abram's declaration of dependence upon God. Abram knew the name of God and lifted it high. He believed God's word with all his heart. He risked everything because of his trust in God's word. He was at that moment a victorious king. His faith had made him so. This closing oath was a militant statement of faith and also a polemic against the perspective of the king of Sodom[18] — and all who trust in the things of this world.

Such magnanimity! Such greatness of soul! Again the veil is lifted. We see Abram in his true colors. He is living as king of the land. Abram's glory is briefly and clearly seen by those closest to him. He is riding a faith ascendancy that will take him to Genesis 15:6 — "he believed the LORD, and he counted it to him as righteousness." Abram trusted God's word implicitly. That is the great continental divide in our lives as believers. Do we really trust his word? Distrust will implode us, shrink us, compact us, reduce us, and hermetically seal us in the smallest compass of self. But if we truly believe God's word, that will enlarge our souls, not just in generosity, not just in opening our hands, but in moving us to sacrifice for the welfare of others — to be like Jesus himself. In this great moment, Abram foreshadowed his great heir and ultimate seed who said, "Man shall not live by bread alone, but by every word that comes from the mouth of God" (Matthew 4:4). Abram believed the words that came from the mouth of God. His heart became great. He lived in magnanimity.

25

Melchizedek
the Priest-King

GENESIS 14:18-20 WITH PSALM 110
AND HEBREWS 7:1-10

On June 27, 1976, armed operatives for the Popular Front for the Liberation of Palestine (PFLP) surprised the twelve crew members of an Air France jetliner and its ninety-one passengers, hijacking it to a destination unknown. The plane was tracked heading for Central Africa, where indeed it did land under the congenial auspices of then Ugandan President Idi Amin. And there it remained apparently secure at Entebbe Airport, where the hijackers spent the next seven days preparing for their next move. The hijackers were by all estimations in the driver's seat.

However, 2,500 miles away in Tel Aviv three Israeli C-130 Hercules transports were secretly boarded by a deadly force of Israeli commandos who within hours attacked Entebbe under cover of darkness. In less than sixty minutes the commandos rushed the old terminal, gunned down the hijackers, and rescued 110 of the 113 hostages. The next day, July 4, Israel's Premier Yitzhak Rabin triumphantly declared the mission "will become a legend" — which it surely has.[1] Israel's resolve and stealth in liberating her people is admired by her friends and begrudged by her enemies.

Actually, Israel's resolve is nothing new because the same quality can be traced all the way back to the very beginning of the Hebrew nation in the prowess of their father Abraham. The kidnappers in his day (the Middle Bronze Age) were an international coalition of four eastern kings headed by King Chedorlaomer who attacked the Transjordan, defeating the city states of Sodom and her neighbors, carrying off a large number of hostages that included Abraham's nephew Lot (cf. Genesis 14:5-13). Undaunted, Abraham recruited "318 trained men" (proto-commandos!) from his own household and took off in hot pursuit — until he closed in on the kidnappers some 120 miles later at the northernmost border of Canaan. And there, under the cover of night, Abram deployed his small forces in a surprise attack. His troops, riding slathering mounts, bore down on the hijackers and their hostages. Deadly arrows flew in the night, and bloody swords were raised gleaming in the dusty moonlight — and the four kings were put to flight. The Genesis account gives this Entebbe-like summary of Abram's success: "Then he brought back all the possessions, and also brought back his kinsman Lot with his possessions, and the women and the people" (Genesis 14:16). Abram could be formidable. It was not wise to fool with Father Abram.

So when Abram returned to his home after the defeat of the kings, he was a hero at the pinnacle of martial success. Can you see him proudly astride his lumbering mount, smeared with the dirt and blood of battle, leading his 318 proud men plus Lot and *all* the captives and all the plunder through Salem? If so, you have the feel necessary to begin to appreciate Abram's strange, mystic encounter with a shadowy figure of immense grandeur — Melchizedek, the priest-king of Salem. Genesis says:

> *And Melchizedek king of Salem brought out bread and wine. (He was priest of God Most High.) And he blessed him and said,*
>
> > *"Blessed be Abram by God Most High,*
> > *Possessor of heaven and earth;*
> > *and blessed be God Most High,*
> > *who has delivered your enemies into your hand!"*
>
> *And Abram gave him a tenth of everything. (Genesis 14:18-20)*

So mysterious. And think of this — this is the *only* historical mention of Melchizedek in the Old Testament. Puzzled, some ancient Jewish commentators identified Melchizedek with Shem, who was thought to have lived until Abram's time (Targum Neofiti I).[2] But if this was so, certainly Moses or David or the writer of Hebrews would have made much of it. Also such speculations are based on a very constrained reading of the genealogies of Genesis. Others have theorized that Melchizedek was a Christophany (a pre-incarnate appearance of Christ) rather than a historical person. But the statement of Hebrews 7:3, which refers to Melchizedek as "resembling the Son of God," will not allow this because the Greek verb translated "resembling" always assumes two distinct and separate identities.[3] The Son of God and Melchizedek were distinct persons.

The truth is that Melchizedek was the godly, residing Canaanite priest-king of Jerusalem. Whereas Abram was a descendant of the blessed Shem, Melchizedek was a descendant of the cursed Canaan (cf. Genesis 9:24-27). Nevertheless, Melchizedek, like Abram, had come to believe in the one true God. Abram had found him to be a true spiritual brother and therefore accepted his provision and blessings — and then gave Melchizedek a tenth of everything. In effect, Abram bowed before Melchizedek in paying him tithes. "Abram bows only to Melchizedek, in a story filled with kings" (Von Rad).[4] Abram bowed before the one who was holding the place for the future Davidic dynasty and its ultimate son.

That was around 2000 B.C., and for a millennium there was no mention at all of Melchizedek, not even in retrospect. But in the tenth century B.C., when the psalmist David became King of Israel and made Jerusalem the royal city (making his house, in effect, the successor to Melchizedek's earlier dynasty of priest-kings),[5] David gave the famous oracles of Psalm 110:

> The LORD says to my Lord:
> "Sit at my right hand,
> until I make your enemies your footstool." (110:1)

> The LORD has sworn
> and will not change his mind,
> "You are a priest forever
> after the order of Melchizedek." (v. 4)

Here, though David was celebrating his own ascendancy to the throne, he also had in view one greater than himself because the Psalm begins with David calling him "LORD" — "The LORD says to my Lord . . ." (cf. Mark 12:35-37). David was indicating that the ultimate application of Melchizedek extended beyond himself. Psalm 110 declared that God was going to do something *new* by bringing into history a priest-king like Melchizedek. His priesthood would last "forever." He would be appointed directly by God. A divine oath guaranteed it: "The LORD has sworn and will not change his mind." What an intriguing prophecy! God was going to establish a totally new priesthood.

Now let your mind course ahead another thousand years to the apostolic age and imagine for a moment that you are the writer of the book of Hebrews, whose purpose in writing was to encourage the soon-to-be persecuted Jewish church. Also imagine yourself reflecting on Melchizedek's *history* and *prophecy* and the apostolic teaching that connects Genesis 14 and Psalm 110, showing that they point to Christ (cf. Christ's teaching in Matthew 22:44 and Luke 20:41-44 and Peter's teaching in Acts 2:34, 35). You begin to muse and pray, and then everything falls into place.

Now in Hebrews 7 you write out what you have learned as a means of encouragement to the storm-tossed church. There is no teaching like it anywhere. This is, as we say today, *heavy.*

THE SIGNIFICANCE OF MELCHIZEDEK (HEBREWS 7:1-3)

In the writer's opening statement, he concisely lays out the significance of the historical Melchizedek as a type of the ultimate priesthood of Christ.

> *For this Melchizedek, king of Salem, priest of the Most High God, met Abraham returning from the slaughter of the kings and blessed him, and to him Abraham apportioned a tenth part of everything. He is first, by translation of his name, king of righteousness, and then he is also king of Salem, that is, king of peace. He is without father or mother or genealogy, having neither beginning of days nor end of life, but resembling the Son of God he continues a priest forever." (vv. 1-3)*

Foreshadowing Christ's character. For starters, the author of Hebrews has noted that Melchizedek's titles foreshadowed the character of Christ. Melchizedek bore the title of king, which is mentioned four times in verses 1, 2. Jesus is, of course, the ultimate "King of kings and Lord of lords," as will be written bold on his robe and thigh when he returns (Revelation 19:16). Significantly, Melchizedek was a priest-king, something that, by law, no Levitical priest could ever be. But Jesus became the ultimate priest-king, fulfilling to the letter what was promised through Zechariah regarding the Messiah: "Yes, it is He who will build the temple of the LORD, and He who will bear the honor and sit and rule on His throne. Thus, He will be a *priest on His throne*, and the counsel of peace will be between the two offices" (Zechariah 6:13, NASB, italics added; cf. Psalm 110:1, 4).

The title "Melchizedek," our author explains, means "king of righteousness," and the title "king of Salem" means "king of peace." Significantly here, we should note that both the qualities of righteousness and peace were prophesied about the coming Messiah in Isaiah 9:6, 7, where his fourth title is "Prince of peace" (v. 6), and he is said to go on to rule with "righteousness" (v. 7). The New Testament identifies Jesus specifically as "Jesus Christ the righteous" (1 John 2:1). Jesus is the King of righteousness! Likewise the New Testament says of Jesus, "For he himself is our peace" (Ephesians 2:14). Jesus is the King of peace! So Jesus brings righteousness and peace together in his person. As the psalmist so beautifully had sung, in the Lord "righteousness and peace kiss each other" (Psalm 85:10). Righteousness and peace form the telltale kiss of his character.

But he is more: Jesus is *King*, the sovereign of righteousness and peace. As such, he is the bestower of all righteousness and peace. He is the sovereign giver of the kisses of peace and righteousness. As we shall see, he is the only one in whom peace and righteousness can be found. Therefore, we see that Melchizedek foreshadowed the *character* of Christ — his priesthood, his kingship, his righteousness, and his peace. Jesus came as a perfect king, a perfect priest, perfect righteousness, and perfect peace.

Foreshadowing Christ's qualifications. Going deeper, the writer of Hebrews also sees a foreshadowing of Christ's qualifications, because he writes that Melchizedek was "without father or mother or genealogy, having neither beginning of days nor end of life, but resembling the Son of God he continues a priest forever" (v. 3). As we have noted, some have inferred from these words that Melchizedek must have been an angel who took on human form for Abram, or even a pre-incarnate appearance of Christ himself. But such interpretations are unnecessary, because the writer is simply using a rabbinical method of interpretation from silence. His point is that the Genesis account does not mention Melchizedek's parents or genealogy or when he was born or died, thereby giving a type of what would be fleshed out in the qualifications of Christ.[6]

No genealogy. All Levitical priests had to have a priestly genealogy that could be traced all the way back to Aaron. But Melchizedek was "without father or mother or genealogy" — he had no priestly genealogy through Levi or Aaron. Likewise, while Jesus' bloodline could be traced to Judah, he had no priestly genealogy. Jesus was in effect "without genealogy." The point is, Jesus' priesthood, just like Melchizedek's, was based solely on the call of God, not on heredity. Jesus and Melchizedek were appointed as "priest[s] of the Most High God."

No beginning/end. Secondly, all Levitical priests served limited terms of office — no more than thirty years.[7] But with Melchizedek, there was no set beginning or end of his life. As William Lane says, "Melchizedek's sudden appearance and equally sudden disappearance from recorded history awakens within a sensitive reader the notion of eternity."[8] What was foreshadowed in Melchizedek's being without beginning or end was fully realized in Christ's eternal priesthood. The writer of Hebrews caps his thoughts at the end of verse 3, saying, "resembling the Son of God he continues a priest forever"; or more exactly, "but being *made like* the Son of God he remains a priest continuously." The silence of the Biblical record regarding Melchizedek's days suggests a continuous priesthood for Melchizedek that foreshadows what perfectly was, and is, fulfilled in Christ, who ministers continually without interruption.[9]

Whereas the earthly high priest could only enter the Holy of Holies once a year and with great trepidation, Jesus lives in the heavenly Holy of Holies. There he perpetually prays for us. His whole being is one unceasing intercession for more life, for more blessing, for more holiness, for more love. There is no interruption. Just as the sun does not exist for one moment without pouring out its light, so our Lord Jesus, our Priest, cannot exist a single moment without interceding for his children — "he always lives to make intercession for them" (Hebrews 7:25).

The big picture that the writer wants us to see is that Jesus perfectly fulfills what was foreshadowed in the Genesis account of Melchizedek. Melchizedek's *character* type as king, priest, righteousness, and peace was fulfilled to perfection in Christ. Melchizedek's *qualifications*, being without genealogy and without beginning or end, prefigured Jesus' who had no priestly genealogy or priestly term of service but was appointed by God and ministers eternally.

No one had ever brought all of this together in writing as the writer of Hebrews presented it. His heart was full, and he expected that his Jewish hearers would feel the same as they reflected on their unsure situations. So brimming over with joy, he then took them even higher in presenting the superiority of Melchizedek over the Levitical priesthood.

SUPERIORITY OF MELCHIZEDEK (HEBREWS 7:4-10)

Melchizedek's superiority is presented through two events in his meeting with Abraham — *tithing* and *blessing*.

Tithing and superiority. In the ancient world, paying tithes to another was recognition of the other's superiority and a sign of subjection to that person. In the event of Abram's presenting his tithe to Melchizedek, we must remember that when Abram returned from his victory over the four kings, he was on a personal mountaintop. He had proven himself a man of great courage and of considerable capability. Moreover, in the eyes of succeeding generations of Jews he was considered to be the greatest of men. He was called "a friend of God" (James 2:23; cf. 2 Chronicles 20:7; Isaiah 41:8). He was the father of the nation of Israel — *the* patriarch.

But when he met Melchizedek, he recognized that personage's greatness and paid him a "tenth part of everything" — literally, "the top of the heap" — the choicest spoils of war. It was a reasoned recognition by Abram that he was in the presence of one greater than himself. Our writer expresses proper astonishment: "See how great this man was to whom Abraham the patriarch gave a tenth of the spoils!" (v. 4). Melchizedek was a person of arching superiority.

The author has made a powerful point, but he realizes that some may diminish it in their minds by saying, "What's the big deal? Levitical priests collect tithes too!" So in anticipation he further argues, "And those descendants of Levi who receive the priestly office have a commandment in the law to take tithes from the people, that is, from their brothers, though these also are descended from Abraham. But this man who does not have his descent from them received tithes from Abraham" (vv. 5, 6a). His point is that the

Levites' ability to collect tithes came from the provision made by the Law and not from any natural superiority. But Melchizedek was different. He did "not have his descent from them," and yet as a figure of immense superiority he collected tithes not from his people, *but from Abram*!

The author further builds on Melchizedek's established superiority through tithing by noting that since the Scriptures do not list his end, he represents a living superior priesthood: "In the one case tithes are received by mortal men, but in the other case, by one of whom it is testified that he lives" (v. 8).

For the final expression of the superiority of Melchizedek's priesthood over the Levitical priesthood due to Abram's tithing to Melchizedek, the writer appeals to the common belief that an ancestor contains all his descendants within himself. Thus he argues, "One might even say that Levi himself, who receives tithes, paid tithes through Abraham, for he was still in the loins of his ancestor when Melchizedek met him" (vv. 9, 10).

Even the Levitical priesthood acknowledged the superiority of Melchizedek's priesthood — because it paid tithes to Melchizedek in advance.[10] Our writer has taken the common Hebrew understanding that tithing to another established his superiority and has demonstrated from every angle that Melchizedek is superior.

Blessing and superiority. The other principle he uses to establish Melchizedek's superiority is that in the matter of a formal biblical blessing, the superior always blesses the inferior. Just as Abram knew he should present a tithe to Melchizedek, he knew that he must bow and receive his prayer of blessing. Therefore, verses 6b, 7 tell us that Melchizedek "received tithes from Abraham and blessed him who had the promises. It is beyond dispute that the inferior is blessed by the superior."

What a stupendous act on Abram's part. Remember, God had told Abram, "in you all the families of the earth shall be blessed" (Genesis 12:3). Abram was the supreme blesser. All the rest of mankind were blessees! But he saw himself as inferior to Melchizedek who towered above him with mystic grandeur and received his blessing.

So we must conclude that Melchizedek's priesthood, though it has only briefest mention in Scripture, is superior in every biblical and logical way to the Old Testament Levitical priesthood. Yet, realizing that, we must note that it was only a type of the ultimate superior priesthood of our Lord Jesus Christ who is "a priest forever after the order of Melchizedek" (Psalm 110:4). And as the antitype to the type, he supersedes it, just as living reality supersedes a photograph!

Though Melchizedek was "king of righteousness" and "king of peace," he could never make men righteous or give them peace. He was only a type.

Righteousness. But Jesus — the grand, the true, the eternal Melchizedekian Priest-King — gives righteousness and peace. As to righteousness, we understand this: First, he *is* righteousness incarnate — "Jesus Christ the righteous" (1 John 2:1). He is intrinsically righteous, the essence of righteousness, the source of righteousness, the sum of righteousness. Second, Jesus is the *bestower* of righteousness. "But now the righteousness of God has been manifested apart from the law, although the Law and the Prophets bear witness to it — the righteousness of God through faith in Jesus Christ for all who believe" (Romans 3:21, 22; cf. Romans 1:17; 1 Corinthians 1:30; Philippians 3:9). Third, he is the priestly *mediator* of righteousness. In bestowing it, he becomes our personal Melchizedekian priest who prays for the working out of his righteousness in every area of our lives. He remains forever our King and Priest of righteousness.

Peace. But he is also the King of Peace, of which we understand this: His peace comes with the gift of righteousness — and never before it. The sequence is always righteousness, then peace. We understand, first, that he *is* peace — the "Prince of Peace" (Isaiah 9:6) — that he is the source and sum and essence of all peace — and that there is no peace without him. We understand, too, that he is the *bestower* of peace. When he came to earth the angels sang, "peace among those with whom he is pleased" (Luke 2:14). On the eve of his death he said, "Peace I leave with you; my peace I give to you" (John 14:27). And after his glorious resurrection, he came to his disciples again with the words "Peace be with you" (John 20:19). And finally, as our eternal priest he *mediates* our growth in peace as he prays for us. Jesus, our High Priest forever in the order of Melchizedek, is praying for our *shalom* — our wholeness and well-being. He is praying for it now!

Righteousness and peace have kissed in Christ — and that is the kiss that the King repeatedly bestows on his bride.

And this is what our gospel offers today to every heart that comes to Christ by faith.

• *Righteousness*, the King's righteousness, which he will give to every heart that believes, so that person becomes the very righteousness of God.

• *Peace*, the King's peace, that will become your constant possession in both good times and bad. Peace with God. Peace with yourself. Peace before your enemies.

• *Prayer,* the King's prayers — unceasing unending, unrelenting.

> *Intercessor, friend of sinners,*
> *Earth's Redeemer, plead for me,*
> *Where the songs of all the sinless*
> *Sweep across the crystal sea.*
> WILLIAM C. DIX, 1866

26

Faith and Righteousness

GENESIS 15:1-6

According to the writers of Hebrews and the Genesis record, the link between faith and righteousness was not a New Testament invention, nor was it even a patriarchal innovation. Instead, the dynamic connection between faith and righteousness is rooted in primeval history well before the flood. The lives of three famous pre-diluvians — Abel, Enoch, and Noah — make this very clear.

Of Abel we read, "By faith Abel offered to God a more acceptable sacrifice than Cain, through which he was commended as righteous, God commending him by accepting his gifts. And through his faith, though he died, he still speaks" (Hebrews 11:4). Faith-righteousness was exemplified in earth's first family by the second son of Adam and Eve.

Of Enoch Genesis says, "Enoch walked with God, and he was not, for God took him" (5:24). The metaphor "walked" indicates closest communion and intimacy — a righteous life. Enoch's godly walk grew out of his faith, as Hebrews makes so clear: "By faith Enoch was taken up so that he should not see death, and he was not found, because God had taken him. Now before he was taken he was commended as having pleased God" (11:5). According to verse 6, his God-pleasing faith believed that "God is" (literal translation of the Greek) — that the sovereign God of creation is God. He also believed that God "rewards those who seek him" — that God is positively equitable. As a result, Jude 14, 15 records that he became a preacher of righteousness, apparently for his entire life, for some three centuries! Enoch's life demonstrated a righteousness based on faith.

Of Noah Genesis says, "Noah was a righteous man, blameless in his generation. Noah walked with God" (6:9). That Noah "walked with God" identifies him with the godly character of Enoch. But even more significant, the statement that "Noah was a righteous man" is the first occurrence of the word righteous (*tsadiq*) in the Bible. Noah's righteousness was not derived from his being perfect or any antecedent righteousness, but because he *believed* God, as the writer of Hebrews explains: "By faith Noah, being warned by God concerning events as yet unseen, in reverent fear constructed an ark for the saving of his household" (11:7). The biblical doctrine of imputed righteousness (a righteousness from God) began here in primeval history before the flood!

We must keep this in mind as we examine Genesis 15:1-6, which is the Bible's landmark text for understanding the relationship between faith and righteousness. Righteousness through faith was not new with Abram. It was intrinsic in primeval, pre-flood history — in the lives of Abel, Enoch, and Noah.

Primeval history ended with the flood and the rise and fall of the tower of Babel. Patriarchal history began with Abram's father Terah. And Abram became the great exemplar of faith — "the father of all who believe" (Romans 4:11). The curve of Abram's faith graphs unevenly. It soars when he hears God's word and leaves Ur, traveling west across the Fertile Crescent and down its side, south into Canaan. It spikes higher when Abram travels the land, building altars and calling on the name of the Lord. But the curve dives dramatically in his disastrous trip to Egypt. After Egypt, it gently rises when he returns to Canaan repentant and rises more in his generous faith-based dealings with Lot. Then in chapter 14 the faith-curve again sweeps upward with his magnanimous rescue of Lot from the kings of the east and his continual magnanimity as he is blessed by Melchizedek, gives him gifts, and refuses to keep the plunder of the eastern kings. Abram models faith to the entire world.

ABRAM AND FAITH: THE LANDMARK PRINCIPLE (vv. 1-6)

Now, in the aftermath, Abram's great heart slows and spasms with doubt and fear. This is not uncommon to human experience following strenuous victories. Elijah suffered similar effects after his victory over the priests of Baal at Mt. Carmel, even fleeing to the wilderness and asking God to let him die (cf. 1 Kings 18, 19). Abram was tired, fearful, and despondent. Humanly, Abram had reasons to fear reprisals from the eastern coalition. Bigger armies might return.

Abram also had plenty of time for reflection in the postbellum quiet — his great victory had not brought him any nearer his promised inheritance. Long ago when he first responded to God's call, Sarah was barren (cf. 11:30). Their journey had begun in barrenness, but with hope in God's promise. But the thousand-mile journey, the sojourn in Canaan, the fiasco in Egypt, the return to Canaan, and the victory over the kings were all carried out under the shadow of barrenness. Now barrenness persisted. Abram's servants had children. Other men's children clung to his garments. Likely, Abram mused, "So what if everybody knows my name from the Nile to the Euphrates? So what if I'm rich? What difference does it make if I have no children?" Restless, dark doubt gripped his faltering heart. Fearless Abram feared.

God speaks. Abram may have suffered his doubts in silence. The text does not say. But God knew what was going on inside Abram. And the close connection with the preceding text suggests the immediacy of God's response:[1] "After these things the word of the LORD came to Abram in a vision" (v. 1a). Visions (in contrast to dreams) in Scripture are for the purpose of communicating the word of God.[2] Abram had a vision in the night, but what he saw was not important. What he heard was: "Fear not, Abram, I am your shield; your reward shall be very great" (v. 1b).

The divine greeting ("Fear not, Abram") shook him because it revealed that God knew all. Abram shivered in the nakedness of his exposed unbelief. This was a grace.

Next Abram, whose foes now extended from the Euphrates to the Nile, heard God say, "I am your shield" against every enemy (cf. Psalm 3:3; 18:2; 28:7; 84:9; 91:4). And then, in reference to Abram's magnanimous refusal to have any share of the plunder he secured from the four kings, God said, "your reward shall be very great." All Abram got for his labors was God. That's all! God was teaching Abram to be satisfied with him alone. This demonstrates, of course, what God desires to give us as we submit to the disciplines of a life of faith. He teaches us to be satisfied with him as enough — our all in all.

Abram's response. Exposed, Abram was stung into verbal lament and protest. This is the first time Abram speaks to God, his first dialogue. "But Abram said, 'O Lord GOD, what will you give me, for I continue childless, and the heir of my house is Eliezer of Damascus?' And Abram said, 'Behold, you have given me no offspring, and a member of my household will be my heir'" (vv. 2, 3). Abram was unhappy, but he was careful to address God as "Lord GOD," which emphasized that God was Master and he was the servant. Abram would not allow his distress to compromise his respect and reverence for God.[3] Yet his skepticism in the light of the divine promise of "shield" and "great reward" edged toward blasphemy. His apparent conclusion was that God's promise had been of no effect, so that a household servant like Eliezer would be his heir. Such adoption was common where he came from.[4] So be it! *C'est la vie.* Abram was on the edge.

God's assurance. Now God dealt so tenderly and lovingly with his stumbling servant. First, God said, "This man shall not be your heir; your very own son shall be your heir" (v. 4). Three times previously God had promised Abram a multitude of descendants — initially when he called him in Ur (12:2), then in Canaan at Shechem where he built an altar (12:7), and last from the highest spot in central Palestine as Abram was surveying the promised land in every direction (13:14-16).

But what God now said was new. "It was not an argument but a revelation" (Kidner)[5] — a son from his own body would be his heir! The heir would be his congenital son. A further question would arise later in chapters 16, 17 having to do with whether barren Sarah could possibly be the mother. But Abram was rocked and captivated by the present revelation.

Again God spoke: "And he brought him outside and said, 'Look toward heaven, and number the stars, if you are able to number them.' Then he said to him, 'So shall your offspring be'" (v. 5). Numerous times during the summer nights at our vacation place in Door County, Wisconsin, my wife and I have led our grandchildren and dogs out by flashlight to a dark road amidst the fields, turned the flashlights off, and gazed from horizon to horizon at the planets, the Milky Way of our galaxy, and the stars beyond. It is always an awesome family experience. The only unawed among us are the dogs, who never look up. They are occupied with their own universe of smells. We always talk about God. Such times are salutary for our souls.

Remember here that Abram had been a moon worshiper who had earlier stood atop the ziggurat in Ur topped with the temple of Nanna, the moon god. He was familiar with the planets and the astral trails. Now he was alone in the silence with God Almighty, who spoke. Abram was humbled, awed, and hushed. He said nothing. He was speechless. There were only stars and silence.

Abram's belief. What was happening here? Though Abram did not speak, Scripture does: "And he believed the LORD" (v. 6a.). The Hebrew sense is that he believed and continued believing the Lord.[6] W. H. Griffith Thomas observes, "The original Hebrew for 'believed' comes from a root whence we derive our 'Amen,' and we might paraphrase it by saying that 'Abraham said Amen to the Lord.' 'Amen' in Scripture never means a petition ('May it be so'), but is always a strong assertion of faith ('It shall be so,' or 'It is so')."[7]

What happened within Abram? How did his faith come? Certainly it was not because he suddenly felt potent or that his expectations were raised. He simply rested on God's promise. In this moment God's word was not a theory about how things would turn out, but "the voice around which his life is organized" (Brueggemann).[8] We know that Abram must also have repented. But ultimately his fresh faith can only be attributed to God. His faith was not a human achievement or the result of his moral will. It came from God, like Peter's later confirmation of Christ: "You are the Christ, the Son of the living God" (Matthew 16:16). How had Peter come to this? "And Jesus answered him, 'Blessed are you, Simon Bar-Jonah! For flesh and blood has not revealed this to you, but my Father who is in heaven'" (v. 17). In the same way Abram moved from protest to confession by the power of God.[9] As the

Apostle Paul said, "For by grace you have been saved through faith. And this is not your own doing; it is the gift of God, not a result of works, so that no one may boast" (Ephesians 2:8, 9).

This was, of course, not the first time that Abram had put his faith in God's word. He had believed for over a decade (cf. 12:1ff.). But here his faith was defined.

This clarification is a landmark in our understanding of faith: "And he believed the LORD, and he counted it to him as righteousness" (15:6). No other Old Testament text has exercised such an influence in understanding faith and on the New Testament itself. The verb *hāšab* means, as our text has it, "counted [or reckoned or imputed] it to him as righteousness"[10] (cf. Leviticus 7:18; Numbers 18:27; 2 Samuel 19:19; Psalm 32:2; and 106:31, which is the closest parallel). Note that Abram is not described as doing righteousness, but his faith was credited as righteousness. Abram, who was originally destitute of righteousness, was now counted as righteous through faith in God. As Von Rad has said, "But above all, his righteousness is not the result of any accomplishments, whether of sacrifice or acts of obedience. Rather, it is stated programmatically that belief alone has brought Abraham into a proper relationship to God."[11]

This understanding is revolutionary! Circa 2000 B.C., Abram was declared righteous because of his belief. This declaration was in profound accord with the primeval fathers Abel, Enoch, and Noah. Furthermore, the principle has remained operative through both primeval and patriarchal history and the entire old-covenant era and is the foundation of the new covenant.

PAUL AND FAITH: THE UNIVERSAL PRINCIPLE

Genesis 15:6 is quoted in full in three New Testament passages — Romans 4, Galatians 3, and James 2.

Romans 4. This chapter is an extended exposition of Genesis 15:6 in which the text is quoted three times and the Greek equivalent to the Hebrew word *hāšab* (Greek *logizomai*) — "counted" — is quoted eleven times. In this chapter Paul argues that salvation comes only through faith for Abraham, then David, then the Gentiles, then for those under the Law.

David. In the case of King David, Paul refers to David's blessedness and joyous relief at having his sins against Bathsheba and Uriah forgiven and an undeserved righteousness bestowed upon him, as described in Psalm 32:1, 2. Paul introduces this penitential Psalm in verse 6 and quotes its opening two verses in verses 7, 8:

David also speaks of the blessing of the one to whom God counts righteousness apart from works:

> *"Blessed are those whose lawless deeds are forgiven,*
> *and whose sins are covered;*
> *blessed is the man against whom the Lord will*
>   *not* count *his sin." (emphasis added)*

Ostensibly, Paul turned to this Psalm because of the rabbinical principle of interpretation that when the same word is used in two Biblical passages, each can be used to interpret the other. (Genesis 15:6 and Psalm 32:2 both contain the same word — *hāšab*, MT and *logizesthai*, LXX).[12]

But the burning reason Paul points to Psalm 32:2 and its use of *hāšab/logizomai* is that David had broken three of the Ten Commandments outright when he coveted Bathsheba, committed adultery, and murdered Uriah — and the Old Testament sacrificial system made no provision for such premeditated sin (cf. Numbers 15:22-31, esp. v. 30).[13] This is why David cried in the parallel penitential Psalm 51:16, 17:

> *For you will not delight in sacrifice, or I would give it;*
> *you will not be pleased with a burnt offering.*
> *The sacrifices of God are a broken spirit;*
> *a broken and contrite heart, O God, you will not despise.*

David's case was hopeless. There was nothing he could do but cast himself on God's mercy. And this is what David did by faith — and thus God forgave his transgressions, covered his sin, and did not count his sins against him. In effect God credited him as righteous apart from works, as Paul said in Romans 4:6. Regarding this, F. F. Bruce says of Psalm 32: "And if we examine the remainder of the psalm to discover the ground on which he was acquitted, it appears that he simply acknowledged his guilt and cast himself in faith upon the mercy of God."[14]

Paul here calls David blessed, and David twice calls himself "blessed" in Psalm 32 because when there was no work that could possibly atone for his sins, he was forgiven on the basis of faith. So the principle of imputed righteousness was mightily illustrated in the life of Israel's greatest king — "a man after [God's] own heart" (1 Samuel 13:14). Likewise, nothing you and I can ever do can atone for our sins. Our only hope is "the righteousness of God [that] has been manifested apart from the law, although the Law and the Prophets bear witness to it — the righteousness of God through faith in Jesus Christ for all who believe" (Romans 3:21, 22).

Gentiles. In respect to Gentiles, Paul argues in verses 9-12 that Abram was saved by faith while he was a Gentile, and therefore the faith principle is universal. Paul shows that Genesis 15:6 occurred at least fourteen years before Abram was circumcised, and thus he was still a Gentile (cf. Genesis 15:6; 16:16; 17:24). Therefore both Jews and Gentiles have always been saved by faith.

Law. Paul also makes a similar argument in respect to those under the Law. Paul explains in verse 13, "For the promise to Abraham and his offspring that he would be heir of the world did not come through the law but through the righteousness of faith." The historical fact is, as Paul has written in Galatians 3:17, the Law came 430 years after Abraham was made heir to the promise by faith — and there is thus no way the Law could invalidate or restrict the scope of that promise.

To make the promise conditional on obedience to the Law, which was not even hinted at when the promise was given, would nullify the whole promise. Righteousness, and its promised benefits, has always come by faith to those who live by faith! "Don't be fooled," says Paul in effect, "the principle of faith transcends the Law."

Abram was credited as righteous because of his faith. So was David. Righteousness through faith preceded the Jewish people and the Law. Salvation comes only through faith. That is the way it has always been.

Galatians 3. The second place in the New Testament where Paul makes major reference to Genesis 15:6 is Galatians 3:6-9:

> Abraham *"believed God, and it was counted to him as righteousness."* . . . *Know then that it is those of faith who are the sons of Abraham. And the Scripture, foreseeing that God would justify the Gentiles by faith, preached the gospel beforehand to Abraham, saying, "In you shall all the nations be blessed." So then, those who are of faith are blessed along with Abraham, the man of faith.*

Paul brilliantly argues here that the faith principle is what makes possible the blessing of all nations through Abraham. Thus the gospel is part of God's initial call to Abraham.

James 2. Finally, James the Lord's brother quotes Genesis 15:6 in developing a balanced doctrine of faith that Paul in his passion did not assert:

> *Do you want to be shown, you foolish person, that faith apart from works is useless? Was not Abraham our father justified by works when he offered up his son Isaac on the altar? You see that faith was active along with his works, and faith was completed by his works; and the Scripture was fulfilled that says, "Abraham believed God, and it was counted to him as righteousness"* — *and he was called a friend of God. You see that a person is justified by works and not by faith alone. (James 2:20-24)*

James argues that authentic faith is a faith that works. James never confused faith and works. He understood them to be separate. James would agree that we are justified by faith alone, but not by faith that is alone! He would say that if your faith is alone, you are in the grip of an eternal delusion, and he would urge you to real faith — a faith that works.

It has always been the same — in primeval times and patriarchal times — under the old covenant and the new covenant: Faith brings righteousness and salvation.

So it was for Abel: "By faith Abel offered to God a more acceptable sacrifice than Cain" (Hebrews 11:4). Abel was saved by faith, a faith that was not alone because it produced better works than Cain.

So it was for Enoch: "By faith Enoch was taken up so that he should not see death" (Hebrews 11:5). But Enoch's faith was such that he "walked with God" (Genesis 5:22) before he was no more. His faith was a real faith — a faith that worked.

So it was for Noah: "By faith Noah, being warned by God concerning events as yet unseen, in reverent fear constructed an ark for the saving of his household. By this he condemned the world and became an heir of the righteousness that comes by faith" (Hebrews 11:7). Noah's profound faith produced a profound obedience. And his works were monumental: "He did all that God commanded him" (Genesis 6:22; cf. 7:5, 9, 16). His was a faith that worked.

So it was with Abram: "By faith Abraham obeyed when he was called to go out to a place that he was to receive as an inheritance. And he went out, not knowing where he was going" (Hebrews 11:8). "By faith Abraham, when he was tested, offered up Isaac" (v. 17a.). Abraham was saved by faith alone — a faith that was not alone — a faith that works!

We conclude this study with two penetrating questions. Have you rested your faith on God the Son, Jesus Christ, alone for your salvation? That is the first question. Are you trusting your works or Christ? Now if you answer, "I am trusting Christ alone," then the second question is, has your faith produced works? Is your faith real enough that it has changed your life? These are salutary questions because you are saved by faith alone. But if it is true faith, it is faith that is not alone but a faith that works.

Salvation is in no other name but Jesus. Have you believed and trusted him alone for your salvation? And if you say you have, has your life changed? May this landmark text dominate your understanding of God's revelation about faith and righteousness because it comes from his Word.

27

God's Covenant with Abram

GENESIS 15:7-21

As Abram gazed up to the starry vault of the night and contemplated God's promise — "So shall your offspring be" (Genesis 15:5) — Abram believed the Lord. He saw the stars, and beyond the stars the promise, and beyond the promise, God himself. Abram believed with all his heart that a vast people would come from his own body. And on that silent night, that holy night, he inwardly breathed and, likely, voiced[1] an audible "Amen" ("It is so") to God. And God credited his belief to him as righteousness. Whatever translation is used, whether "credited" it, "reckoned" it, "counted" it, or "imputed" it, the meaning is the same. Abram's righteousness was all God's doing. As we saw in the previous chapter, this landmark text informs the Scriptures of both the old and new covenants and is our singular hope (cf. Romans 3:27-30).

God's great promise to Abram, as it has been rolled out in chapters 12, 13, had two parts: a *people* (cf. 12:2; 13:16) and a *land* (12:1, 7; 13:14, 17). So now God proceeded to encourage Abram's heart and faith by raising the issue of the land: "And he said to him, 'I am the LORD who brought you out from Ur of the Chaldeans to give you this land to possess'" (15:7).

The opening phraseology ("I am the LORD who brought you out") is monumental language because God would later use an almost identical formula to introduce the Mosaic covenant at Sinai: "I am the LORD your God, who brought you out of the land of Egypt, out of the house of slavery" (Exodus 20:2). Thus the two most formative events in the history of the Jewish people — Abram's exodus from Ur and Moses' exodus from Egypt

— were prefaced with identical language.[2] Also, both the Abrahamic covenant and the Mosaic covenant were based on sovereign acts of salvation: first in Abram's deliverance from Ur and then in Moses' deliverance from Egypt. As we proceed we will see that what happens here with Abram in Canaan neatly foreshadows the setting for Moses at Sinai.

Prompted by God's declaration, Abram naturally inquired about the land: "But he said, 'O Lord GOD, how am I to know that I shall possess it?'" (v. 8). It was the question of a believing heart, and consistent with the strongest faith that God, of course, knew full well was in Abram. In a later similar situation, when Zechariah, the father of John the Baptist, asked the same question when he was told by Gabriel that he and his barren Elizabeth would have a son — "How shall I know this?" (Luke 1:18) — he was struck dumb for his unbelief. Abram's question was more in the attitude of "I believe; help my unbelief!" (cf. Mark 9:24).

Covenant preparation. Abram's humble request was followed by a divine order and his obedient preparation. "He said to him, 'Bring me a heifer three years old, a female goat three years old, a ram three years old, a tur- tledove, and a young pigeon'" (v. 9). Abram understood exactly what God was ordering him to do because this custom was common in Abram's Mesopotamian homeland where when two parties solemnized a promise/covenant, they would kill a donkey, divide it in two, and arrange the halves so that the covenanting parties could walk between the sundered body of the animal.[3]

The ceremony dramatized a self-imposed curse should either of the covenanting parties break the pledge. The sense was: "If I break my word, may I become like this severed animal!" The nearest scriptural parallel to this would come later from the time of Jeremiah, when the leaders of Jerusalem proclaimed the freeing of their slaves and then went back on their word. To these promise-breakers Jeremiah, speaking for God, cried:

> *You have not obeyed me by proclaiming liberty, every one to his brother and to his neighbor; behold, I proclaim to you liberty to the sword, to pesti- lence, and to famine, declares the LORD. I will make you a horror to all the kingdoms of the earth. And the men who transgressed my covenant and did not keep the terms of the covenant that they made before me, I will make them like the calf that they cut in two and passed between its parts — the officials of Judah, the officials of Jerusalem, the eunuchs, the priests, and all the people of the land who passed between the parts of the calf. And I will give them into the hand of their enemies and into the hand of those who seek their lives. Their dead bodies shall be food for the birds of the air and the beasts of the earth. (Jeremiah 34:17-20)*

Here in Genesis, Abram was directed to use five distinctive animals, all of which would become standard sacrifices when the Mosaic covenant was instituted. Though slaughtered and sundered, the animals were not sacrificed. There was no altar, no fire, no burning. Their symbolic purpose was to represent God's covenant people much as in the same way these animals would represent them before God in the future sacrificial system. So Abram killed the animals and arranged the halves of the heifer, goat, and ram to line a gruesome covenant path. Apparently the dove and young pigeon were not halved because they were so small but were placed on opposite sides of the path facing each other.

The assault by the carrion-eating birds of prey and Abram's driving them away foreshadowed the attacks that would come upon Abram's offspring from the nations and God's protection (both of which will be described in part in God's following covenant promises).

Evidently the daylight following Abram's belief under the stars had been spent in his carrying out God's directives — slaughtering the animals, arranging them into the covenant path, and fending off the birds — as he awaited further directions for the covenantal pageant. However, the weary patriarch was not conscious for the covenant ceremony because "As the sun was going down, a deep sleep fell on Abram. And behold, dreadful and great darkness fell upon him" (v. 12). Abram's sleep engulfed him in terrifying darkness, which "reflects a human emotion that is inspired most often by Yahweh's presence" (Hamilton).[4] Later the covenant at Sinai would be inaugurated in a similar darkness (cf. Exodus 19:16-18), and ultimately the new covenant of Christ's blood would spring from the darkness over the cross (cf. Matthew 27:45). Here in Genesis amidst the initial darkness God would encourage Abram with a meticulously crafted promise about the land, which then would be followed by a spectacular ratification of the promise.

LAND COVENANT DETAILED (vv. 12-16)

God's promise was described in sequence — how, to whom, when, and why the land would be given.

How. The means by which Abram's descendants would come to possess the land would be a terrible ordeal. "Then the LORD said to Abram, 'Know for certain that your offspring will be sojourners in a land that is not theirs and will be servants there, and they will be afflicted for four hundred years. But I will bring judgment on the nation that they serve, and afterward they shall come out with great possessions'" (vv. 13, 14). Prophesying in round numbers, God foretold Abram that his followers would be enslaved for four hundred years in an undesignated land (which we know to be Egypt).[5] The word "afflicted" is the same Hebrew word used in Exodus to describe the oppression that the Israelites experienced in Egypt as they built the store cities for Pharaoh (cf. 1:11). This was the historical outworking of Abram's vision of birds of prey descending on the slain animals. And it is possible that the carrion birds directly referenced his descendants' abuse at the hands of the Egyptians because the Egyptian falcon god Horus was a carrion-eating bird.[6]

As we know, Egypt would be severely punished for its mistreatment of Israel through the ten plagues that culminated with the death of their firstborn sons as the death angel passed over (cf. Exodus 6:6; 7:4; 12:12). When Israel left in the exodus, the Egyptians were so eager that they go that Israel actually "plundered" the Egyptians: "The people of Israel had also done as Moses told them, for they had asked the Egyptians for silver and gold jewelry and for clothing. And the LORD had given the people favor in the sight of the Egyptians, so that they let them have what they asked. Thus they plundered the Egyptians" (Exodus 12:35, 36). These explicit prophecies of a captivity and exodus must have been shocking knowledge for Abram. But the information was also helpful. The long Egyptian captivity could not block the fulfillment of the promises! Moses, especially, would find strength in this knowledge as he led the revolt and exodus from Egypt.

To whom. Abram must have been further shocked by the next line: "As for yourself, you shall go to your fathers in peace; you shall be buried in a good old age" (v. 15). Abram had to accept the fact that he would *not* possess the land. Hard knowledge. But that was also good for him to know — especially with what lay ahead in his long life. This knowledge also promoted a calm certitude for the aging patriarch in knowing that he would die "in peace," *shalom*. As Abram aged and his skin wrinkled and his eyes dimmed, his gaze turned even more to the city whose architect and builder is God.

When, and why the 400 years? There is no contradiction between "four hundred years" (v. 13) and the statement in verse 16, "And they shall come back here in the fourth generation, for the iniquity of the Amorites is not yet complete." This is because a "generation" could mean a lifetime, and during the patriarchal period that equaled at least a hundred years. So the round number 400 and the four generations of our text and the 430 years specified in Exodus 12:40 all describe the same long period ending with the exodus.[7]

The 400 years, of course, was important as a mark by which to count the progress of history. But of far greater significance is the reason for the four centuries — namely, "the iniquity of the Amorites is not yet complete" (v. 16b). God was revealing to Abram that he is patient beyond human calculation. This long-suffering on the part of God was memorialized by Paul in this question: "Or do you presume on the riches of his kindness and forbearance and patience, not knowing that God's kindness is meant to lead you to repentance?" (Romans 2:4). Long-suffering is God's *modus operandi* in history.

And the Amorites (the inhabitants of Canaan) would take full advantage of the divine patience. According to W. F. Albright, the three principal goddesses of the Canaanite pantheon — Astarte (Ashtaroth), Anath, and Asherah — were primarily concerned with sex and war. "Sex was their primary function."[8] Leviticus 18:1-24 lists twelve variations of incest that were endemic to Canaan along with adultery, child sacrifice, sexual perversion, and bestiality, concluding with this warning: "Do not make yourselves unclean by any of these things, for by all these the nations I am driving out before you have become unclean" (v. 24; cf. v. 27).

There ultimately would come a day when the Amorites had reached the point of no return — their cup would be full. And that is when God unleashed a flood of Israelites out of Egypt and across the Jordan. In truth, Joshua's invasion was actually "an act of justice, not aggression" (Kidner).[9] And the universal fact is, the history of the world is under the moral governance of God. The displacement of the Amorites by Israel was not simply the result of divine favoritism.[10] They had long flaunted God's moral law.

Again the emphasis here in Genesis is not on the wrath of God, but on the patience of God. We may look at the prosperity of the wicked. We may look at the rise of Hitlers and Stalins and Pol Pots and genocide around the world and the puerile depravity of our own media and call out to God, "O Sovereign Lord, holy and true, how long . . . ?" (Revelation 6:10). But we must remember, as Donald Grey Barnhouse said, "If the iniquity of the world had been full a hundred years ago, none of us would have been born to be born again."[11] Bless God for his patience!

God's purpose behind this meticulous revelation to Abram was to strengthen his faith and to encourage him regarding the truth that the land would one day go to his descendants. Certainly as he observed the decadence of the Amorites over his long life, this teaching would hearten him.

Yet there was more here. Abram learned that suffering would precede glory. This is the abiding order that Paul reminded believers of on his first missionary journey: "through many tribulations we must enter the kingdom of God" (Acts 14:22). Even though Abram would die in peace, God's great promise to him was ultimately on the other side of the grave. Abram's life had one trial after another. Isaac was not yet born. Think of the tests that were coming! Nevertheless, "by faith he went to live in the land of promise, as in a foreign land" (Hebrews 11:9).

This divine preview of history with its precise predictions and explicit dating taught Abram that God is sovereign in history. Process Theology and Openness Theology have no place here. God controls every detail of history. The forty-fifth chapter of Isaiah, which so magnificently chronicles God's sovereignty and direction of history, bears this divine query:

> *Who told this long ago?*
> *Who declared it of old?*
> *Was it not I, the LORD?*
> *And there is no other god besides me,*
> *a righteous God and a Savior;*
> *there is none besides me. (Isaiah 45:21)*

LAND COVENANT RATIFIED (vv. 17-21)

Abram had taken in all the varied details of the promise in the thick and
dreadful darkness of his deep sleep. They were filed in his slumbering mind
and would inform his future actions.

Unilateral ratification. But Abram was certainly not prepared for the
fireworks that came in the pyrotechnic confirmation of the covenant. "When
the sun had gone down and it was dark, behold, a smoking fire pot and a flaming torch passed between these pieces" (v. 17). God made a fiery appearance as a smoking firepot radiating orange in the darkness. It was a
theophany, a visual manifestation of God! Moses would view a similar phenomenon in the burning bush (cf. Exodus 3:2). Israel would see it at Sinai
when they "came near and stood at the foot of the mountain, while the mountain burned with fire to the heart of heaven" (Deuteronomy 4:11). "The LORD
had descended on it in fire. The smoke of it went up like the smoke of a
kiln" (Exodus 19:18). Israel saw it again in the pillar of cloud by day and
the cloud of fire by night (cf. Exodus 13:21). It symbolized God's unap-
proachable holiness.

Then the glowing furnace moved, gliding down the aisle lined with the
animal parts that glistened in the fire's light. Surely an ecstasy gripped
Abram's soul! He had not been asked to join in the pageant — to pass with
God between the pieces. It was God alone. This was an unconditional, unilateral covenant. God (with astounding condescension) was symbolizing that
if he were to break his word, he would be sundered like the butchered animals. It was an acted-out curse, a divine self-imprecation guaranteeing that
Abram's descendants would get the land or God would die. And God cannot die.

Then God spoke. Perhaps his words emanated from the blazing furnace,
just as when God spoke to Moses from the burning bush. His voice conveyed the most specific delineation of the land and its inhabitants in Scripture.
"To your offspring I give this land, from the river of Egypt to the great river,
the river Euphrates, the land of the Kenites, the Kenizzites, the Kadmonites,
the Hittites, the Perizzites, the Rephaim, the Amorites, the Canaanites, the
Girgashites and the Jebusites" (vv. 18-21). This promise would be actual-
ized briefly during the apex of David's reign, only to dissolve under
Solomon.[12] And today modern Israel approximates the ancient designations.

Think what elevation this stunning revelation brought to Abram's soul. First, under the stars Abram had believed that a countless people would come from his own body — and God credited it to him as righteousness. Now with the same faith he believed that the land would someday go to his people. The darkness was gone. All was light. His fears and doubts fled. Abram was at the pinnacle. Joy flooded his soul. God's fiery presence departed, and Abram awoke.

Today some 4,000 years have passed since that wondrous event. And what does it mean to us? Iain Duguid answers:

> By what figure could God have demonstrated his commitment more graphically to Abram? How could it have been displayed more vividly? The only way would have been for the figure to become a reality, for the ever living God to take on human nature and taste death in the place of the covenant-breaking children of Abram. And that is precisely what God did in Jesus Christ. On the cross, the covenant curse fell completely on Jesus, so that the guilty ones who place their trust in him might experience the blessings of the covenant. Jesus bore the punishment for our sins, so that God might be our God and we might be his people.[13]

Fellow Christians, "If you are Christ's, then you are Abraham's offspring, heirs according to promise" (Galatians 3:29). By God's Word you are now part of Abram's offspring, his *people*. And there is an ultimate *land* awaiting you, the same land to which Abram went, full of years and in peace.

Again, what more could God do than this theophany? Could there be a greater condescension than his self-curse should he break his word? Yes! He could become incarnate among us, and he could become a curse for us, that we might become the righteousness of God. The Scriptures say, "Christ redeemed us from the curse of the law by becoming a curse for us — for it is written, 'Cursed is everyone who is hanged on a tree' — so that in Christ Jesus the blessing of Abraham might come to the Gentiles, so that we might receive the promised Spirit through faith" (Galatians 3:13, 14). And again, "For our sake he made him to be sin who knew no sin, so that in him we might become the righteousness of God" (2 Corinthians 5:21).

What a God and Savior we have! Abram's God is the God of creation, the God of the universe. He is the sovereign God who scripts history. He is the long-suffering God whose kindness reaches out today to the lost. He is the One who has extended history so that we might be born so that we could be born again. He is the One who guides us through the sufferings by which we enter the kingdom. He is the One upon whom the covenant curse fell, so that we guilty ones who trust him might be heirs of the blessings.

Fellow believers, I am convinced that our view of God is everything. Some Christians, because they believe in the God of Scriptures (the God of

Abraham), have a big God. But others have a small God. I believe that what you think about God is everything, because if you have a big God, then you have a God who, through his Son, redeemed you to be his people.

• You have a God who will give you the land.

• You have a God who will lead you through much suffering into the kingdom.

• You have a God who will do miracles in your life.

• You have a God to direct your life.

• You have a God who will answer prayers.

• You have a God to whom you must give all your love.

The question is, is your God the God of Abraham, the God of this text? Or is he a God of your own puny imagination or your sinful reductionism? If you have the God of the Bible, you will be able to stand tall, even until the sin of our culture has reached its full measure.

28

Shortcutting Faith

GENESIS 16:1-16

We would reasonably think that the two preceding faith-events in Abram's life, through which he was promised both a land and a people, would have steeled him against the slightest distrust in God. Remember that Abram's experience had been crowned by God's unilateral, unconditional ratification of his promise when he appeared to Abram in a flaming theophany and passed between the sundered pieces of animals — indicating that if he did not keep his word, he would become as those animals. Imagine the elevation that then coursed through Abram's soul. His faith naturally soared off the charts. Surely this would render him impervious to distrust — we think. Now he would never fail to trust God — we think. Perpetual obedience would characterize Abram — we think.

How wrong we are! Genesis 16's story of Abram and two women, Sarai and Hagar, showcases falling faith and distrust and shocking expediencies. The result was the first marital triangle in biblical history. Here we have the multiplication of rejection, anger, hurt, jealousy, and vicious cruelty. Life complicated itself exponentially, and there was no resolution. The following is a warning to all children of faith. "No perfect feet walk the path of faith" (Barnhouse).[1] As Paul would warn, "Let anyone who thinks that he stands take heed lest he fall" (1 Corinthians 10:12). Are you a person of faith? Then pay attention.

HUMAN CHAOS (vv. 1-6)

Aging Sarai was a magnificent woman who had been exemplary — and would be so again as a woman who did not give way to fear (cf. 1 Peter 3:6). But at this time she had been in Canaan for ten years and was seventy-five years old (cf. 12:4, 5 and 17:17). Her barrenness was deemed a tragedy in ancient culture, where it was a mark of success to have many children and a sad failure to have none. From Sarai's perspective, the flower was fading, and time was running out. Anguished humiliation throbbed within her. Significantly, she knew that God had promised Abram that a son coming from his own body would be his heir (cf. 15:4), but it had not yet been explicitly revealed to her that she would be the mother. That would happen when her name would be changed to Sarah (cf. 17:15, 16). At present she was still Sarai, who only knew the former.

Scheming. So Sarai began to scheme. "Now Sarai, Abram's wife, had borne him no children. She had a female Egyptian servant whose name was Hagar. And Sarai said to Abram, 'Behold now, the LORD has prevented me from bearing children. Go in to my servant; it may be that I shall obtain children by her.' And Abram listened to the voice of Sarai" (16:1, 2).

Almost surely Sarai had acquired Hagar the Egyptian (*misrit*) while in Egypt (*Misrayim*; cf. 12:16). As an Egyptian, Hagar was a descendant of Ham, and not a descendant of Shem (as were Abram and Sarai), upon whom the primal blessings were prophesied by Noah (cf. 9:26, 27). Hagar was also Sarai's personal property, in accord with both Mesopotamian and Egyptian culture. Sarai's fatal choice of Hagar as the answer to her barrenness discounted the power of God, Hagar's Hametic descent, and, possibly, Hagar's wishes.

While we are scandalized by Sarai's polygamous solution, it was perfectly logical and acceptable in the culture from which she had come as well as in the culture that surrounded her. And it had been so for a thousand years from Babylon to Egypt.[2] Nuzi tablet Number 67 (which describes a marriage arrangement in ancient Mesopotamia) alludes to the surrogate custom: "If Gilimninu bears children, Shennima shall not take another wife. But if Gilimninu fails to bear children, Gilimninu shall get for Shennima a woman from the Lullu country (i.e., a slave girl) as concubine. In that case, Gilimninu herself shall have authority over the offspring."[3] Clearly, Sarai's polygamous solution was conventional and proper in the eyes of everyone but God, whose will had been expressed at creation (cf. 2:24; Matthew 19:5).

As best we can tell, Sarai's heart at this time was a mixture of both good and bad. She so wanted God's promise to Abram to be fulfilled that she was willing to sacrifice the specialness of her intimacy with her husband. She was the monogamous wife of his youth. He was the love of her life. Sarai for love did violence to love. At the same time, there is explicit blame and implicit anger in her directive: "The LORD has prevented me from bearing children. Go in to my servant." She would take care of what God had not done. As Griffith Thomas has it:

Though Sarah's motive was good, genuine, and involved self-sacrifice, the proposal was wrong in itself, and, at the same time, wrong in its method of obtaining the end sought. It was wrong against God, Whose word had been given and Whose time should have been waited. It was wrong against Abraham, leading him out of the pathway of patient waiting for God's will. It was wrong against Hagar, and did not recognize her individuality and rights in the matter. It was wrong against Sarah herself, robbing her of a high privilege as well as leading to disobedience.[4]

There is also an ironic reversal here. Down in Egypt, trustless Abram had given Sarai over to the Egyptian Pharaoh. Now in Canaan untrusting Sarai gave Abram over to her Egyptian servant. Abram's fiasco in Egypt was costly indeed.

If we are scandalized by Sarai's volunteering Hagar as her surrogate, Abram's passive, compliant conduct is even more offensive. He, not Sarai, had heard the voice of God. He had led them from Ur. He had had no divine directive to employ Hagar. Otherwise he would have led the way. And Abram was fresh from the fiery theophany. But he did not question her idea. He did not demur. Rather, as the Hebrew blandly says, "Abram listened to the voice of Sarai." Is this passive, pliant man the same one who chased the four eastern kings for 120 miles and whipped them above Damascus? Yes. But there his faith was soaring. Now it is plunging.

Fall! Abram's taking Hagar as his wife was nothing less than a fall. "So, after Abram had lived ten years in the land of Canaan, Sarai, Abram's wife, took Hagar the Egyptian, her servant, and gave her to Abram her husband as a wife. And he went in to Hagar, and she conceived" (vv. 3, 4a). The whole matter was so ugly. Normally the girl's father gave the woman to be married, but Sarai gave her away. And Hagar had no say in the matter. She was taken and given. Virgin Hagar was treated as a commodity.

Moses wrote the account as a parallel to the fall in the garden. Sarai's action was parallel to that of Eve. Here Abram *listened* to his wife (v. 2), just as Adam listened to his (3:17). Here Sarai *took* Hagar (v. 3a), just as Eve took the fruit (3:6a). Here Sarai *gave* Hagar to her husband (v. 3b), just as Eve gave the fruit to hers (3:6b). And in both cases the man willingly and knowingly partook.[5]

Their lives were in a free fall, and the bottom was coming up fast! "Do not be deceived," says the Scripture. "God is not mocked, for whatever one sows, that will he also reap. For the one who sows to his own flesh will from the flesh reap corruption" (Galatians 6:7, 8). They will reap the whirlwind.

Chaos. Proverbs 30:21-23 says:

Under three things the earth trembles;
under four it cannot bear up:
a slave when he becomes king,
and a fool when he is filled with food;
an unloved woman when she gets a husband,
and a maidservant when she displaces her mistress.

Now the earth began to quake. Abram and Sarai had treated Hagar like an inanimate, unfeeling instrument — a soulless baby machine. But Hagar became proudly pregnant. And because she had succeeded where Sarai had not, she began to look down on her mistress. Hagar "enjoys it as a triumph over Sarah" (Von Rad).[6] Haughty looks were cast Sarai's way. Hagar strutted her round profile.

Sarai became volcanic. The shaking ground erupted in anguished jealousy and bloodcurdling blame. "And Sarai said to Abram, 'May the wrong done to me be on you! I gave my servant to your embrace, and when she saw that she had conceived, she looked on me with contempt. May the LORD judge between you and me!'" (v. 5). Logically Sarai was wrong to place all the blame on Abram. After all, it was her idea. But actually she was right. He was the patriarch. He was the head of the house. God had spoken to him, not to her. He should never have allowed the situation. Abram was truly responsible for the "wrong" (Hebrew, "violence") she was suffering. Her soul felt as if she were a victim of homicide (cf. 49:5). Such misery! "Abram," she cried, "may the LORD judge between you and me!'" She appealed to the highest Judge, who sees everything in secret. And God was watching, as we shall see.

Here is where Abram should have been the man. He should have taken his Sarai aside and assured her of his love and that she was first. He should have accepted the full blame and responsibility. He should have dealt kindly and firmly with Hagar. Tellingly, he, like Sarai, never refers to Hagar by name in the account but only by label ("your servant," v. 6).[7] It is so much easier when you depersonalize those you abuse.

Abram should have sought God's wisdom in repentant prayer. Instead, he capitulated again to Mesopotamian social convention. "Behold, your servant is in your power," Abram said. "Do to her as you please" (v. 6a). He hid behind the conventions of the Code of Hammurabi (Law 146), which stipulates that if a concubine claims equality with her mistress because she bore children, her mistress may demote her to her former status.[8] Abram impotently abdicated any responsibility for the situation, or for that matter for poor Hagar who had recently become his wife, and said, "Do with her what you want, dear." This Sarai did with a vengeance. "Then Sarai dealt harshly with her, and she fled from her" (v. 6b). The word translated "mistreated" is used later of what the Egyptian slave masters would do to Israel.

The thing that shouts loudest here in the story is that there was not an honorable character in the lot. All were ignoble. Abram was the worst. He was pathetic, passive, impotent, and uncaring of either woman. Neither woman had any compassion on the other. Sarai was worse, but you get the idea that Hagar would have done the same if she could. Notwithstanding, Hagar was the prime victim. And Sarai was a not-so-distant second.

Remember that it all began when people of faith began to distrust God's word. It took shape when they decided that God needed help in fulfilling his word. It took off when Abram and Sarai took a shortcut to obtain what they knew God had promised, the good promise. Their expedience brought degeneration both to the perpetrators and the victim.

What a mess this original triangle was! So complicated, so impossible, so painful — and, I must say as a pastor now for some forty years, so true to life. Not a few times I have had believers in my office whose resort to expediencies in order to hurry what they have believed to be God's will has resulted in humanly unsolvable problems. In fact, some situations have been so complicated that there can be no solution in this life. There is grace, of course. But some sins are such that the results cannot be taken back. And the pain goes on and on in this world. Believers, beware.

DIVINE INTERVENTION (vv. 7-16)

Poor, abused, pregnant Hagar fled a great distance from Sarai's wrath. The location of "Shur" (v. 7), according to Genesis 25:18 and 1 Samuel 15:7, was near the border of Egypt. Likely she had traveled from Abram's camp to Beersheba and through Kadesh-barnea to the Bitter Lakes. Shur is the name of the desert in northwestern Sinai, next to Egypt. Hagar was going home to her people, the descendants of Ham, bearing her half-Shemite baby. And she was almost there.

Divine discovery. There, alone by a spring, Hagar was surprised by a stranger — "the angel of the LORD" (v. 7), whom Hagar would learn was God himself.[9] Some think this was the Second Person of the Trinity, Christ the Son. The angel of the Lord does, indeed, have Christological qualities. In 48:16 Joseph describes him as "the angel who has redeemed me from all evil." Whether he was the Son or not, the divine ministration was at least a shadow of Christ.[10]

It was obvious from the onset that this angel knew everything about Hagar and that he was authoritative. "The angel of the LORD found her by a spring of water in the wilderness, the spring on the way to Shur. And he said, 'Hagar, servant of Sarai, where have you come from and where are you going?' She said, 'I am fleeing from my mistress Sarai.' The angel of the LORD said to her, 'Return to your mistress and submit to her'" (vv. 7-9). The reason for his surprising directive became clear in the subsequent revelations.

Divine revelation. The first sentence of revelation to Hagar was astounding. "The angel of the LORD also said to her, 'I will surely multiply your offspring so that they cannot be numbered for multitude'" (v. 10). The patriarchal stories in Genesis feature numerous instances where individuals are promised descendants. There are six such promises to Abram (12:2; 13:14-16; 15:5; 17:8; 18:14; 22:17). There is one each to Isaac and Jacob (26:4; 28:3, 4). But Hagar is the only matriarch to receive such a promise. This places her alone among the matriarchs.[11] Hagar's descendants would be included in Abram's descendants — as numerous as the stars. She was an honored woman.

Having prophesied Hagar's matriarchal glory, the Lord delivered the following oracle informing her of the gender, name, character, and future of her child.

> And the angel of the LORD said to her,
> "Behold, you are pregnant
> and shall bear a son.
> You shall call his name Ishmael,
> because the LORD has listened to your affliction.
> He shall be a wild donkey of a man,
> his hand against everyone
> and everyone's hand against him,
> and he shall dwell over against all
> his kinsmen." (vv. 11, 12)

The name Ishmael means "God has heard." Its very sound commemorated God's remembrance of Hagar in her oppression. Whenever she murmured or sang it to her baby, she would commemorate this event. Even when he was so difficult that she shouted his name ("Ishmael!"), she recalled God's intervention.

As to her son's character, the wild donkey is a desert animal that looks more like a horse than a donkey and is "used in the O.T. as a figure of an individualistic lifestyle untrammeled by social convention"[12] (cf. Jeremiah 2:24; Hosea 8:9). He would be a wild, free bedouin. Ishmael's character portended his destiny. He would live in perpetual conflict with those around him. Note well that there is not a word here about the great promise to Abram. Ishmael's prophecy is apart from the promised land, apart from the great promise to Abram. Derek Kidner writes: "To some degree this son of Abram would be a shadow, almost a parody, of his father, his twelve princes notable in their times (17:20; 25:13) but not in the history of salvation; his restless existence no pilgrimage but an end in itself; his nonconformism a habit of mind, not a light to the nations."[13]

The historical reality is that Ishmael's offspring became a thorn to God's people both under the old and new covenants. Through Ishmael, the firstborn, they claim Abram as their father and affirm that they are his truest representations. Little did Abram and Sarai imagine that their shortcut would originate a conflict that would run for millennia and that oceans of blood would be spilt. Abram, the father of the faithful, had begotten a wild man instead of a child of grace. How tragic was Abram's expediency.

Hagar's response. Young Hagar's response to the Lord's oracles was remarkable. "So she called the name of the LORD who spoke to her, 'You are a God of seeing,' for she said, 'Truly here I have seen him who looks after me.' Therefore the well was called Beer-lahai-roi; it lies between Kadesh and Bered" (vv. 13, 14). Surprisingly, Hagar did not revel in the information about the child she would bear but rather in God. In amazement she bestowed two names — one on God and the other on the place. Both celebrate the same reality — God's omniscience. She named God, "You are a God of seeing." She named the well "Beer Lahai Roi" which means "well of the living one who sees me."

Hagar realized that all her knowledge of God depended on his initiative in knowing her. When she felt as if God were absent, she learned that he was watching over her (cf. Psalm 139:1-12). Her soul sang. She was the only person, male or female, in the Old Testament who conferred a name on God.[14] She also obeyed God, traveling all the way back through Kadesh-barnea to Beersheba to Abram's tents in Mamre. And there she submitted to Sarai. The sense here is that she believed God and remained a child of grace, dwelling in the tents of Shem (cf. 9:27).

Thus we come to the factual, colorless epilogue, "And Hagar bore Abram a son, and Abram called the name of his son, whom Hagar bore, Ishmael. Abram was eighty-six years old when Hagar bore Ishmael to Abram" (vv. 15, 16). The absence of Sarai's name is significant. Hagar's child was intended to be Sarai's, but three times the text emphasizes that Hagar bore a son *for* Abram. Moreover, Sarai did not name the child. Abram did. And he confirmed the name Ishmael ("God has heard"), recognizing God's intervention. It seems, too, that Sarai's intervention and Abram's acquiescence may have delayed the promise for some thirteen years. Shortcuts do not promote God's purpose.

What a mess life had become. The two women would never get along, and there was nothing Abram could do. And the conflict escalated with the birth of Isaac. The Genesis account tells us, "And the child grew and was weaned. And Abraham made a great feast on the day that Isaac was weaned. But Sarah saw the son of Hagar the Egyptian, whom she had borne to Abraham, laughing. So she said to Abraham, 'Cast out this slave woman with her son, for the son of this slave woman shall not be heir with my son Isaac'" (21:8-10). Hagar and Ishmael were put out, and both almost died. But again God protected Hagar and her son. The account concludes, "And God was with the boy, and he grew up. He lived in the wilderness and became an expert with the bow. He lived in the wilderness of Paran, and his mother took a wife for him from the land of Egypt" (21:20, 21). Ishmael went back to his Hametic roots.

Finally, we read in Genesis 25 that Ishmael fathered twelve tribal rulers who would become a spiritual antithesis to the later twelve tribes of Israel, and the account ends, "They settled from Havilah to Shur, which is opposite Egypt in the direction of Assyria. He settled over against all his kinsmen" (25:18).

How tragic the expediencies, compromises, and shortcuts of real life can be. True, there is grace and forgiveness for all who turn to Christ. Christ comes to Hagars in the wilderness, and also to miserable Abrams and Sarais in the camp, and ministers grace. Very often God restores the years the locusts have eaten up. God gives his repentant children joys along the way, laughter and serendipities. But some sins cannot be undone in this world. There are times when life moves from bright color to monochrome — and never back to its original vividness.

Christian, are you contemplating an expediency to obtain what you imagine to be God's will in your most treasured relationship — in a friendship — in a professional pursuit — in your career — in your education — in your ministry? If so, take a deep breath.

Stand back.

Take some time.

Read God's Word.

Think.

Pray.

And obey the revealed will of God.

29

Covenant Confirmed

GENESIS 17:1-27

The bleakness of Abram and Sarai's shortcut attempt to obtain an heir through Hagar is meant to provide the spiritual background for the story of covenant renewal. The interconnectedness of the two accounts is clear because the final verse of chapter 16 indicates that "Abram was eighty-six years old when Hagar bore Ishmael to Abram," whereas the opening verse of chapter 17 emphasizes that he "was ninety-nine years old" when the Lord appeared to him. Moses intends that the reader understand that for some thirteen years now a cloud of domestic gloom and growing darkness about the promise had hung over the tents of Abram.

Familial frictions continued unabated. Ishmael, the shortcut heir (the child of fleshly expediency), was rushing toward manhood. Though he was certainly loved by Abram and Hagar, his untamed, contrary nature was evident to all. Sarai (a decade younger than Abram) was eighty-nine. She had always been barren and was well past childbearing years. And the thirteen years of Ishmael's childhood had only increased the tension between her and Hagar. Ishmael's innate insolence had not helped matters. And, in fact, it would be his undoing (cf. 21:8ff.). Abram, a year shy of the century mark, believed that God would fulfill his promise. He also inwardly hoped that dashing Ishmael, despite his insolent ways, would somehow live under God's blessing (cf. v. 18). The boy was Abram's flesh and blood and thus lodged deep in his affections.

If Ishmael was not the answer, how then would Abram become the father of a vast people and his heirs inherit the land? It had been some twenty-three years since the initial promise. And now, with the bleakness of the last thirteen years, the promise seemed more distant than ever. God had given Abram a lot of time to think about his sin and his lapse of trust — and the living consequences. God was growing the patriarch's faith. Great days lay ahead. But Abram did not know it.

Chapter 17 is about how God came to Abram and elevated his faith by confirming the promise with the covenant of circumcision, which was then sealed by Abram's obedience. Abram's covenant faith and obedience were encouraged by God's revelation of four new names: "God Almighty" (v. 1), "Abraham" (v. 5), "Sarah" (v. 15), and "Isaac" (v. 19).

GOD HIMSELF AND ABRAM (vv. 1-8)

God Almighty. The first name that the Lord called forth was his own name — *El-Shaddai*, "God Almighty." "When Abram was ninety-nine years old the LORD appeared to Abram and said to him, 'I am God Almighty; walk before me, and be blameless, that I may make my covenant between me and you, and may multiply you greatly'" (vv. 1, 2). This is the very first use of this divine designation in the Pentateuch. *El-Shaddai* signifies God's power (omnipotence) and sovereignty. The rendering "All Mighty" is the best English translation of this name because "it describes the God who makes things happen by means of his majestic power and might" (Youngblood).[1] It is the name by which the patriarchs came to know God. As God later explained to Moses, "I appeared to Abraham, to Isaac, and to Jacob, as God Almighty" (Exodus 6:3). It is the name that is used some thirty-one times in Job to encourage that man amidst his trials. Here in Genesis the name regularly occurs with the divine promise of descendants (cf. 17:1, 2; 28:3; 35:11; 48:3, 4).[2] Its final occurrence in Genesis speaks eloquently of

> . . . *the Almighty who will bless you with . . .*
> *blessings of the breasts and of the womb. (49:25)*

God was saying, by this initial invoking of his name *El-Shaddai*, "I am able to fulfill the awesome hopes that I have set before you of a *people* and a *land*. There is no need to let go of the promise because of your old age. There is no need to succumb to passive desperation. There is no need to scale down the promise to match your puny thoughts — no need to resort to fleshly expedience — no need of trying to fulfill the promise in any second-rate way. Everything — all your life, all your future — lies in this: I am God Almighty!"[3]

Christians, it is the same for us. The way we live is determined by what we think of God. If our God is *El-Shaddai*, the awesome, mighty God of this account, then our lives will live out the fullness of God's promises to us. What you truly believe about God is the most important thing in your life. Any thoughts of a God less potent than the God of Abram will shrink your soul and neutralize your faith.

Abraham. Next God Almighty proceeded to explain the covenant to Abram. And in this first section (vv. 3-8) we see that he renamed Abram "Abraham" — "No longer shall your name be called Abram, but your name shall be Abraham, for I have made you the father of a multitude of nations. I will make you exceedingly fruitful, and I will make you into nations, and kings shall come from you" (vv. 5, 6).

It was a momentous act. Nahum Sarna explains, "In the psychology of the ancient Near Eastern world, a name was not merely a convenient means of identification but was intimately bound up with the very essence of being and inextricably intertwined with personality."[4] And more, the Bible itself views name-giving as symbolizing the transformation of character and destiny. The Bible also presents name-giving as an exercise of sovereignty or lordship (cf. 2 Kings 24:17). Indeed name-giving is a lordly, authoritative act in any context. Imagine me as pastor taking an infant boy in my arms at his dedication or baptism and saying, "Your parents named you Caleb, but from now on God has named you Elijah." Next, I hold a baby girl and say, "Melissa just won't do! Your name is Claire." Many of my hearers would be heading to the exits with Bibles clasped tightly! That would be nothing less than a cultic exercise of power. But God's renaming of Abram and Sarai was nothing less than a blessed reassertion of divine sovereignty over their lives.

Abram's name meant "exalted father" and referred *not* to the patriarch but to God as exalted Father. But when Abram's name was changed to Abraham, it referred to the man himself as "father of a multitude" (literal Hebrew). The effect was that every time people called him "Abraham," they reiterated God's promise that he would be a father of a multitude! How many times did that happen each day? Fifty? A hundred? "Good morning, father of a multitude." "Here's lunch, father of a multitude." "Good night, father of a multitude." Get the point, Abe?

In addition, Abraham's astonishing name ("father of a multitude") was matched by another astounding revelation — "and kings shall come from you" (v. 6b). It was beyond tent-dwelling Abraham's dreams that such a thing could be! But one thousand years later the founding of a line of kings in the Davidic dynasty began the fulfillment of this promise, which was ultimately fulfilled another thousand years later in the advent of Jesus Christ, King of the Jews. This is what Matthew celebrates in the opening verse of his Gospel: "The book of the genealogy of Jesus Christ, the son of David, the son of Abraham." Here in Genesis is the first prediction of the ultimate "King of kings and Lord of lords" (Revelation 19:16). This phrase, "and kings shall come from you" is the genesis of Palm Sunday. From here on the royal reality would also echo in his heart every time he was called Abraham, "father of a multitude."

GOD COMMANDS CIRCUMCISION (vv. 9-14)

The next section of God's speech details and proscribes the covenant of circumcision.

Sign of the covenant. Specifically, God said, "This is my covenant, which you shall keep, between me and you and your offspring after you: Every male among you shall be circumcised. You shall be circumcised in the flesh of your foreskins, and it shall be a sign of the covenant between me and you" (vv. 10, 11). As to its function as a sign, Ronald Youngblood explains:

> As the rainbow is the sign of the Noahic covenant (Gen. 9:13), and as the Sabbath is the sign of the Sinaitic covenant (Exod. 31:16-17), so circumcision became the sign of the Abrahamic covenant (Gen. 17:11). The rainbow and the Sabbath already existed prior to the institution of the covenants they came to signify. So also circumcision did not originate with Abraham. It was practiced in Egypt and elsewhere centuries before his time, but it received new meaning in Genesis 17. Similarly, thousands of people were crucified before the time of Jesus, but the cross took on a vastly new and different meaning when our Lord was crucified.[5]

Early on, circumcision came to symbolize the spiritual commitment of one's life to God. Moses wrote, "And the LORD your God will circumcise your heart and the heart of your offspring, so that you will love the LORD your God with all your heart and with all your soul, that you may live" (Deuteronomy 30:6). Likewise Jeremiah challenged the people, "Circumcise yourselves to the LORD; remove the foreskin of your hearts, O men of Judah and inhabitants of Jerusalem" (Jeremiah 4:4). As a sign, circumcision functioned much as a wedding ring symbolizes commitment. The external sign signified a whole life commitment. But unlike a wedding ring, circumcision could not be cast aside. It was a permanent, ineradicable sign. It would bear terrible, unremitting witness against a sinful, unconsecrated heart.

Significantly, circumcision involved Abraham's powers of procreation — the area of life in which he had resorted to fleshly expediency — and had so failed. Man's best plans and strength of will would never bring about the promise. For Abraham circumcision was an act of repentance and a sign of dependence upon God for the promise.

The rite of circumcision itself is a reminder that covenants are solemnized through blood. Circumcision inflicts blood and pain. Every Hebrew male from Abraham to Isaac to Moses to Jesus underwent the operation. Every instance symbolized the enduring, irrevocable nature of the covenant.

The Almighty's word of instruction on circumcision concluded as he stated that it was the essential sign: "Any uncircumcised male who is not circumcised in the flesh of his foreskin shall be cut off from his people; he has broken my covenant" (v. 14). There was only one way — *God's way.* Circumcision was not an institution that could be dismissed as Cain had attempted to disregard God's will regarding sacrifice. Cain thought that God had no business in picking or choosing what was acceptable to him — "It's God's business to accept whatever sacrifice is offered."

Here in circumcision we have an early warning that there is no way but God's way. How this flies in the face of conventional religious culture, which imagines that it is God's duty to accept us apart from his directives as long as we are doing our best. Iain Duguid notes that many people approach God as if they were interviewing him for a job position for "personal deity in my life."[6] If the man in the sky fits the job description, being nonjudgmental and accepting, and allows us to determine what is right and wrong — he's got the job. Lucky God!

Let the ostensible believer beware. Just as there was only one way under the old covenant, so there is only one way under the new. Jesus, who made the new covenant with his blood, said that he is the *only* way (cf. John 14:6)!

COVENANT SPECIFICITY (vv. 15-19)

In the next section the covenant promise gathers intense specificity as Sarai is renamed and designated the matriarch of the covenant, Abraham responds, and Isaac is named.

Sarah. God's revelation regarding Sarai was incredible. "And God said to Abraham, 'As for Sarai your wife, you shall not call her name Sarai, but Sarah shall be her name. I will bless her, and moreover, I will give you a son by her. I will bless her, and she shall become nations; kings of peoples shall come from her'" (vv. 15, 16). Sarai meant "princess," and the modernization of her name to Sarah also meant "princess." It was God's plan all along that she would be a princess — because princesses have kings! Not only would Sarah bear a child as an old woman, but the sacred, royal dynasty would have her blood in its veins — and ultimately the Lion of the tribe of Judah (cf. 49:10). So now Abraham, "the father of many," has his "princess" confirmed as Sarah. A spiritual springtime was mounting in Abraham's soul. God Almighty had revealed himself with his awesome name, Abraham had a new name, the sign of the covenant had been commanded, and Sarah had her new name.

Laughter. And what was the patriarch's response? "Then Abraham fell on his face and laughed and said to himself, 'Shall a child be born to a man who is a hundred years old? Shall Sarah, who is ninety years old, bear a child?' And Abraham said to God, 'Oh that Ishmael might live before you!'" (vv. 17, 18). Abraham began well enough by falling to the ground on his face in the prostrate posture of deepest respect, just as he initially had done when the Lord said, "I am God Almighty" (v. 3). But as he lay in reverence, the old boy began to involuntarily convulse with laughter so that he laughed out loud! And as he laughed he thought to himself, *She'll be ninety and I'll be a hundred.* Perhaps he burst out laughing again. And then he addressed God, suggesting Ishmael's name.

Was Abraham disbelieving the Almighty? Evidently not, because God voiced no disapproval of his laughter. In contrast, in the next episode when Sarah laughed at the same promise, the Lord rebuked her — "Why did Sarah laugh?" (18:13). Her laughter reflected her ongoing lack of belief in the promise that she would bear a son — despite what God had said to Abraham. The absence of any correction for Abraham implied not that he lacked faith, but rather that his faith was limited. He was believing, but his faith was pushed to the limits of credulity. Nevertheless Abraham's faith held. Listen to St. Paul's commentary:

> *In hope he believed against hope, that he should become the father of many nations, as he had been told, "So shall your offspring be." He did not weaken in faith when he considered his own body, which was as good as dead (since he was about a hundred years old), or when he considered the barrenness of Sarah's womb. No distrust made him waver concerning the promise of God, but he grew strong in his faith as he gave glory to God, fully convinced that God was able to do what he had promised. (Romans 4:18-21)*

That is the divine commentary on Genesis 17. The aged patriarch did believe. Abraham's faith was a great thing. It is so easy to say we believe in something that is far-off — like Heaven. But when we are asked to believe that God will do a certain thing within a specific time, we find believing much more difficult. Abraham believed God.

Isaac. And God's response? The Almighty named their coming son "Isaac," which means "laughter."

> *God said, ". . . Sarah your wife shall bear you a son, and you shall call his name Isaac. I will establish my covenant with him as an everlasting covenant for his offspring after him. . . . But I will establish my covenant with Isaac, whom Sarah shall bear to you at this time next year." When he had finished talking with him, God went up from Abraham. (vv. 19, 21, 22)*

Laughter would ironically engulf Isaac's existence, beginning with his birth. The laughter was an expression of God's blessing and their joy, and also a reminder of the aged couple's doubts.[7]

Obedience. What a dynamic event! In establishing the covenant of circumcision, the Lord had announced his name as *El-Shaddai*, the almighty, omnipotent, sovereign God who can do anything. Abram became Abraham, "father of a multitude." Sarai became Sarah, "the princess." Together they would birth a royal dynasty of kings. Their yet-to-be-conceived son was named Isaac — "laughter" — a sweet symbol of faith's struggle.

And so it was that all of this converged on Abraham's soul, and Father Abraham lived out the obedience of faith on that very day (cf. vv. 23-27). Ninety-nine year-old Abraham and thirteen-year-old Ishmael and every male in his household were circumcised. It was the birthday of God's covenant people. Not all were saved that day. Ishmael received the sacred rite but showed no evidence of grace. Although he bore the ineradicable sign of the covenant, Ishmael did not ultimately remain a part of God's covenant people. But on that day there was blood and pain, and there was laughter among the people of God!

THE CIRCUMCISION DONE BY CHRIST

King. Kings did come out of Abraham and Sarah. At the end of Genesis, Jacob prophesied that the King would come from the tribe of Judah: "The scepter shall not depart from Judah" (49:10). Balaam would later cry:

> *I see him, but not now;*
> *I behold him, but not near:*
> *a star shall come out of Jacob,*
> *and a scepter shall rise out*
> *of Israel. (Numbers 24:17)*

When King David came, God promised him, "Your house and your kingdom shall be made sure forever before me. Your throne shall be established forever" (2 Samuel 7:16). After David's death, God's people began to look for the ultimate messianic David. Four hundred years later Ezekiel recorded God's words, "I will set up over them one shepherd, my servant David, and he shall feed them: he shall feed them and be their shepherd" (Ezekiel 34:23). Isaiah prophesied of a coming "Prince of Peace" who would establish an endless government and rule on David's throne (cf. 9:6, 7). Then Zechariah prophesied, "Rejoice greatly, O daughter of Zion! Shout aloud, O daughter of Jerusalem! behold, your king is coming to you; righteous and having salvation is he, humble and mounted on a donkey, on a colt, the foal of a donkey" (Zechariah 9:9). Israel continued to look. And on Palm Sunday Jesus rode into Jerusalem as the crowds shouted, "Hosanna to the Son of David! Blessed is he who comes in the name of the Lord! Hosanna in the highest!" (Matthew 21:9).

Faith. That week brought to its culmination Jesus' life of perfect faith. What Abraham had begun was completed by his ultimate seed, Christ the

King (cf. Galatians 3:16). Jesus would say of his life, "When you have lifted up the Son of Man, then you will know that I am he, and that I do nothing on my own authority, but speak just as the Father taught me. And he who sent me is with me. He has not left me alone, for I always do the things that are pleasing to him" (John 8:28, 29).

Obedience. Jesus in perfect obedience said on the eve of his crucifixion, "This cup that is poured out for you is the new covenant in my blood" (Luke 22:20). There was pain and blood that Good Friday as Jesus was nailed to the cross, and the new covenant was launched. Jesus underwent the ultimate circumcision, that we might receive the ultimate circumcision of the heart (cf. Romans 2:29).

Listen to Paul on what this means to us:

> *In him also you were circumcised with a circumcision made without hands, by putting off the body of the flesh, by the circumcision of Christ, having been buried with him in baptism, in which you were also raised with him through faith in the powerful working of God, who raised him from the dead. And you, who were dead in your trespasses and the uncircumcision of your flesh, God made alive together with him, having forgiven us all our trespasses, by canceling the record of debt that stood against us with its legal demands. This he set aside, nailing it to the cross. (Colossians 2:11-14)*

Jesus' body was cut away for our sin. He was cut off from God for our sin and cried out, "My God, my God, why have you forsaken me?" (Matthew 27:46; cf. Psalm 22:1). And all of this was so that we might be "circumcised with a circumcision made without hands, by putting off the body of the flesh, by the circumcision of Christ."

The question is, have you been made a new creation? "Neither circumcision counts for anything, nor uncircumcision, but a new creation" (Galatians 6:15). The question is, have you believed, do you have faith in him? "For in Christ Jesus neither circumcision nor uncircumcision counts for anything, but only faith working through love" (Galatians 5:6).

> *Tell out, my soul, the greatness of his name!*
> *Make known his might, the deeds his arm has done;*
> *His mercy sure, from age to age the same;*
> *His holy name, the Lord, the mighty one.*
>   TIMOTHY DUDLEY-SMITH, 1961

30

Is Anything Too Hard for the Lord?

GENESIS 18:1-15

The writer of Hebrews commemorates Abraham's hospitality with this famous advice: "Do not neglect to show hospitality to strangers, for thereby some have entertained angels unawares" (13:2). Such was Abraham's experience. It was only at the conclusion of his hospitality that he came to understand what had transpired.

The sun sat high over Abraham's encampment under the great trees of Mamre outside Hebron. The morning chores were complete, and workers had returned to their tents for the customary siesta. The sheep, donkeys, and camels were clumped under the shade of the trees in midday languor. And Abraham was sitting at the shaded entrance of his tent enjoying the respite. Perhaps he had nodded off because as he looked up he saw three men standing nearby. Abraham had neither seen nor heard their approach. They were simply there, looking at him.

Abraham's response was spontaneous and from the heart as, despite his hundred years, he ran toward the men and bowed low to the ground before them in warm respect. The patriarch apparently sensed from their appearance that the visitors must be honored. He even granted them the respect that is due those of higher rank, as he addressed the leader as "my lord" (ESV margin; *ădōnāy*),[1] saying, "O my lord, if I have found favor in your sight, do not pass by your servant" (v. 3). Abraham's insistence prevailed, and the trio consented to his offer of water for their feet, rest in the trees' shade, and something to eat — "a morsel of bread" — some pita-like flat bread.

The sleepy camp flew into fast-forward as Abraham hurried to Sarah, told her to be quick, and then ran to a servant, who then hurried off. The minimalist "something to eat" became a huge feast. There were only three guests, but three seahs (six gallons) of fine flour were baked, plus a whole calf, and the meal was served along with curds (yogurt) and milk as a compliment to the savory fare. It was a royal feast. As the three feasted, Abraham, the good host, stood discreetly by, willing to assist in any way.

VISITATION (vv. 1-8)

We know that Abraham's guests were the Lord (Yahweh) and two angels. But Abraham had no idea of this — at first. In retrospect, there were indications. The initial hint may be that he did not see them approach him. In Old Testament times, supernatural visitors often appeared from nowhere and then disappeared (cf. Judges 6:11-21).[2] Next, Abraham's bowing low was an unwittingly proper honoring of deity, because the word for "bowed" is also translated "worship" when God is the object (cf. 24:26).[3] Also, Abraham's singular address "O Lord" (Lord = sovereign) was unknowingly appropriate in respect to God. And, finally, as Abraham watched his guests he no doubt witnessed their otherworldly character and saw that one of them commanded a reverence far above the others. In retrospect, Abraham realized that his generous banquet had been eaten by the Lord and his attending angels!

Covenantal meal. The divine visitation and feast was nothing short of a covenantal meal. This is the only place in Scripture before the Incarnation that the Lord ate a meal with a human being. Robert Candlish, the eminent nineteenth-century principal of New College Edinburgh, explains:

> It is a singular instance of condescension — the only recorded instance of the kind before the incarnation. On other occasions, this same illustrious being appeared to the fathers and conversed with them; and meat and drink were brought out to him. But in these cases, he turned the offered banquet into a sacrifice, in the smoke of which he ascended heavenward (Judges vi. 18-24, xiii. 15-21). Here he personally accepts the patriarch's hospitality, and partakes of his fare, — a greater wonder than the other; implying more intimate and gracious friendship, — more unreserved familiarity. He sits under his tree, and shares his common meal.[4]

The meal with Abraham was an exercise of spiritual intimacy. To dine with Yahweh at the table was and is the ultimate honor any mortal could have in this world. As a grade-school boy, I was awed as I watched the coronation of Queen Elizabeth II. And in the months that followed, I fancied what it would be like if our family hosted her for dinner. Of course, she would love my mother's cooking — because common food would be so unique to her! I dreamed of how we would all behave perfectly, and the queen would notice it. And best of all, I imagined what my friends would say of our (*my!*) great honor. It was all so logical to my seven-year-old mind. Here Abraham's exponentially superior honor was no schoolboy's dream. *God* came to dinner.

As we will see, the covenantal function of this meal was to restate the promise of a son through Sarah. What better way could there be than the familial intimacy of a meal to communicate the close relationship on which the promise was based.[5] Later the same day, when the two angels departed for Sodom, the Lord stayed behind with Abraham, and they talked face to face as the Lord explained what was to follow (cf. vv. 16-33). Such intimacy! Significantly, Abraham received the title "friend of God" (James 2:23; cf. 2 Chronicles 20:7; Isaiah 41:8). A friend is someone to whom you open your heart. A friend is someone you understand and who understands you.[6] Abraham and God were friends.

We should note that four hundred years later the Lord held a covenantal meal with the family of Abraham on the eve of the fulfillment of the covenant of the Law (cf. Exodus 24:5). We should note even more that the new covenant was celebrated with a covenantal meal when Jesus took the cup and said, "This cup . . . is the new covenant in my blood" (Luke 22:20).

Abraham needed the assurance of this first covenantal meal because in the next hours he would experience the final separation from his nephew Lot. Lot would come to the edge of doom, his wife would be judged, his family lost, and his possessions stripped away. In anticipation of these harrowing experiences, God gave himself afresh to Abraham — his friend.

ANNUNCIATION (vv. 9-15)

But this meal was not just for Abraham alone — it was also for his wife Sarah who had prepared it. The feast was as much or more for her than it was for Abraham. Sarah, as a married woman, was inside the tent out of the sight of the male visitors. But she could hear everything.

Sarah addressed. So with the meal over, the trio addressed Sarah through Abraham. "They said to him, 'Where is Sarah your wife?' And he said, 'She is in the tent.' The LORD said, 'I will surely return to you about this time next year, and Sarah your wife shall have a son.' And Sarah was listening at the tent door behind him" (vv. 9, 10). Instantly Abraham understood that his visitors were not ordinary men. They had used the *new* divinely given name of his wife (formerly Sarai, now Sarah), and they had also repeated almost word for word the announcement of El Shaddai about the birth of a son about the same time the following year. And more, the Lord had said, "I [singular] will surely return to you about this time next year." This was the Lord God himself! God had again appeared to Abraham in the form of a stranger — and they had just dined together. Suddenly all the lights went on, drawing full wattage. Abraham's soul soared.

Nevertheless the focus of the story is upon Sarah who was listening in the tent directly *behind* the Lord. Yahweh had his back to Sarah. There was no human way that he could see how she reacted to the news. And Sarah? Moses adds the narrative note, "Now Abraham and Sarah were old, advanced in years. The way of women had ceased to be with Sarah" (v. 11). Not only had Sarah been infertile all her life — she was now ninety and post-menopausal. She was doubly dead in respect to childbearing. The promise that she would be a mother next year was absurd.

Sarah responds. Sarah's response was silent and inward. "So Sarah laughed to herself, saying, 'After I am worn out, and my lord is old, shall I have pleasure?'" (v. 12). It was melancholy, hopeless, and nonbelieving laughter. She thought of herself as a decrepit, old woman married to an old man. "She could certainly not expect to enjoy the pleasures of younger women in being a mother or perhaps even sexual intercourse with her husband" (Wenham).[7] Sarah's unbelief suggests that Abraham had either not told her of the promise (17:16, 19) or that he had failed to convince her. The fact that she would be rebuked (however mildly) indicates that she had heard the promise from her husband but persisted in unbelief. For the present, Sarah's faith did not match that of her husband. She inwardly laughed in unbelief.

Sarah reproved. But in a blessed moment it was stripped away. "The LORD said to Abraham, 'Why did Sarah laugh and say, "Shall I indeed bear a child, now that I am old?"'" (v. 13). In a graced instant Sarah understood that her unuttered thought was fully known to the Lord. Whereas Hagar had learned that God sees her, Sarah now learned that God sees *inside* her. Sarah was doused with the reality that God is omniscient or all-knowing. Sweetly and ironically, her future son David would put this reality in unforgettable verse:

> *O LORD, you have searched me and known me!*
> *You know when I sit down and when I rise up;*
> *you discern my thoughts from afar. . . .*
> *Even before a word is on my tongue,*
> *behold, O LORD, you know it altogether.*
> *(Psalm 139:1, 2, 4)*

Similarly, the Apostle John would say, "God is greater than our heart, and he knows everything" (1 John 3:20). And Hebrews gives it classic expression: "And no creature is hidden from his sight, but all are naked and exposed to the eyes of him to whom we must give account" (4:13). God knows every inner thought whether they be the thoughts of humans or angels. No human, whether in a dark rain forest or atop a Manhattan skyscraper, has a thought that is not known to God. He perfectly knows all things. He has never wondered at anything. He has never been taken by surprise. He has never forgotten anything. He has never been mistaken.

A. W. Tozer has summed up the truth of divine omniscience in lyrical cadences:

> God knows instantly and effortlessly all matter and all matters, all mind and every mind, all spirit and all spirits, all being and every being, all creaturehood and all creatures, every plurality and all pluralities, all law and every law, all relations, all causes, all thoughts, all mysteries, all enigmas, all feelings, all desires, every unuttered secret, all thrones and dominions, all personalities, all things visible and invisible in heaven and in earth, motion, space, time, life, death, good, evil, heaven, and hell.[8]

We can fool others, but not the unblinking, omniscient eye of God. He sees how our shoes fit and the soap residue on our hands. He knows our unspoken thoughts.

Surely Sarah did not take this thought to such elegant dimensions. But she did experience the essential benefit, which is: *If God knows me like this, then he can do anything!* Thus Sarah's soul was instantly plowed for the promise, "Is anything too hard for the LORD? At the appointed time I will return to you about this time next year, and Sarah shall have a son" (v.14). Sarah came to believe that nothing was "too hard" (literally, "too wonderful" or "too surpassing" or "too incredible") for the Lord. Twelve months later she experienced the incredible. Beautifully, her ultimate Son, Christ the Messiah, bore the title "wonder" or "wonderful" (Isaiah 9:6).

This is the Lord's question for us: Is anything too hard for the Lord? Is anything too incredible for the Lord? There can only be one answer: *Nothing is too hard for the Lord!*

Allen Ross says rightly that the message of this account could be summarized like this: "Nothing is incredible for those in covenantal fellowship with the Lord, because nothing is too marvelous for him."[9]

Those under the new covenant of the blood of Christ (believers) possess joyous realities that are parallel to these experienced by Abraham and Sarah. First, we see that the Lord's Table memorializes the fact that we are participants in his covenantal meal. As such, we are in deepest spiritual connection with him, as Jesus so graphically explained:

> *Truly, truly, I say to you, unless you eat the flesh of the Son of Man and drink his blood, you have no life in you. Whoever feeds on my flesh and drinks my blood has eternal life, and I will raise him up on the last*

day. For my flesh is true food, and my blood is true drink. Whoever feeds
on my flesh and drinks my blood abides in me, and I in him.
(John 6:53-56)

The gruesome metaphorical language of Christ speaks of the deepest
spiritual exchange. He is the meal. As partakers of the covenantal meal, we
are in deepest intimacy with him. When we obey, we sit at the table with him.
That is why he called the lukewarm church of Laodicea to repent, saying,
"Behold, I stand at the door and knock. If anyone hears my voice and opens
the door, I will come in to him and eat with him, and he with me" (Revelation
3:20). The repentant believer has a perpetual meal before him — perpetual
intimacy with Christ. And the meal is eternal — to be drunk anew in the
Father's kingdom (cf. Matthew 26:29).

The other parallel that we believers have in common with Abraham
and Sarah are promises that are humanly impossible, except that nothing is
too hard/incredible for the Lord! There was no way that Sarah could give
birth apart from God's power — which was precisely the situation that later
faced Mary, the mother of our Lord. Her response to Gabriel's announcement
was, "How will this be, since I am a virgin?" (Luke 1:34). And Gabriel's
answer — "the power of the Most High will overshadow you" (v. 35) —
was parallel to what God said to Sarah. But whereas aged, barren Sarah
became pregnant by Abraham, young Mary would be with child without ever
knowing a man sexually! Why? Because nothing is too hard/wonderful for
the Lord! The Christ-child was, in fact, a wonder (cf. Isaiah 9:6, same root
word).

Likewise the impossibility of rebirth takes place through God's power.

Jesus answered, "Truly, truly, I say to you, unless one is born of water
and the Spirit, he cannot enter the kingdom of God. That which is born of
the flesh is flesh, and that which is born of the Spirit is spirit. Do not mar-
vel that I said to you, 'You must be born again.'" (John 3:5-7)

Lastly, there is no way that we can possibly experience the resurrection
— except for the fact that nothing is too hard for God. As Jesus testified, "For
this is the will of my Father, that everyone who looks on the Son and believes
in him should have eternal life, and I will raise him up on the last day"
(John 6:40).

God calls his people to respond with faith, not doubt, because he always
keeps his word. The truth is, if God's people, those who are in covenantal
relationship with him, fully believed that what he said, he will do, their
lives would be so different. We do not need greater things to believe. His
promises to us are stupendous. We simply need to believe that he will do

them — because nothing is too hard for God. He can give you new birth right now. He can seat you at his table. He can raise you up.

This section has a postscript that was at first embarrassing to Sarah, but then a source of ongoing joy: "But Sarah denied it, saying, 'I did not laugh,' for she was afraid" (v. 15). But God had the last laugh, so to speak. "No, but you did laugh," he said. Thus Yahweh ended the dialogue with a subtle reference to Isaac, whose name means "laughter." The great laugh would be Isaac, Sarah's firstborn.

God smiled on Sarah — and on all who believe.

31

God, Righteous and Just

GENESIS 18:16-33

The covenant meal was over. Honored Abraham had become the only mortal to ever dine with God prior to the incarnation of God the Son. Over that meal Abraham heard Yahweh reaffirm his covenant promise to *doubting* Sarah, saying, "Is anything too hard for the LORD? At the appointed time I will return to you about this time next year, and Sarah shall have a son" (v. 14). This announcement would have its messianic denouement in the announcement to the Virgin Mary that she would bear Abraham's ultimate seed, Christ Jesus. *Believing* Mary asked, "'How will this be . . . ?' And the angel answered her, 'The Holy Spirit will come upon you, and the power of the Most High will overshadow you'" (Luke 1:34, 35). Clearly, again, this was because nothing was too hard for God!

Abraham, ever the good host, escorted his guests as they departed from his tents. Thus, having just *dined* with God, he then literally *walked* with God like Enoch of old (cf. 5:24). Joyous, as no doubt the departure was, it was also ominous because as his heavenly guests got up to leave, "they looked down toward Sodom" (v. 16). The traditional site for this is the mountain-top village of Beni Na'im, three miles east of Hebron where the Dead Sea and its surrounding plains are visible through gaps in the hills.[1]

The covenant feast had extended late into the afternoon, so that the sun hung low in the west, radiating off the golden, leathered faces of Abraham and his heavenly guests. Below them sparkled the turquoise of the Dead Sea. Just to the south of the sea, the western façades of Sodom and Gomorrah could be seen in the slanting rays. The next time Abraham is recorded to have looked down from this vantage is at the end of the episode, when "he looked down toward Sodom and Gomorrah and toward all the land of the valley, and he looked and, behold, the smoke of the land went up like the smoke of a furnace" (19:28).

ABRAHAM INFORMED (vv. 17-21)

Apparently Abraham did not have the slightest inkling of what was coming because as the parting company surveyed the Jordan Valley's cities glowing in the setting sun, the Lord raised the question, "Shall I hide from Abraham what I am about to do . . . ?" (v. 17). Answering his own question, Yahweh proceeded to give weighty reasons why Abraham must be informed of the impending destruction of Sodom and Gomorrah. The first two had to do with Abraham's responsibility, and the third with the condition of Sodom and Gomorrah.

Abraham's responsibility. First, Abraham was to become a channel of blessing to the world: "Abraham shall surely become a great and mighty nation, and all the nations of the earth shall be blessed in him" (v. 18). As such Abraham had been "chosen" (literally, "known") by God (v. 19). He had then *dined* with God face to face and finally *walked* with him. He was accorded the singular title "friend of God" (James 2:23). Servants may not know their master's purposes, but friends do. So as God's friend and conduit of blessing to the whole world, it was essential that Abraham know what was going down in respect to the neighboring cities where his nephew Lot dwelt.

In addition to this, Abraham was also responsible to teach righteousness and justice to his offspring. "For I have chosen him, that he may command his children and his household after him to keep the way of the LORD by doing righteousness and justice, so that the LORD may bring to Abraham what he has promised him" (v. 19).

God desired that his covenant people be a people who did righteousness and justice to everyone, regardless. This would become a major purpose of the law — to love your neighbor as yourself (cf. Leviticus 19:18; Galatians 5:14). It is here that Sodom and Gomorrah provide the starkest, darkest contrast because their lifestyle was the absolute antithesis of righteousness and justice. And when God judged Sodom and Gomorrah, their ruins would become a powerful teaching tool to Abraham and his descendants. There on the border of Israel, the eerie, burnt-out, sulphur-stenched remains of Sodom and Gomorrah permanently testified to what happens to a people who reject righteousness and justice.

Atop Beni Na'im, Yahweh elected to apprise Abraham of what he was going to do to these wicked cities in order to strengthen Abraham's resolve and ability to instruct his children in godliness. "My children, do you want to know what God thinks of an unjust culture? Take a look! Do you want to know what God does to such a people? Take a walk through the ruins." The example was still powerful in Jesus' day as the apostle Peter explained that God burned Sodom and Gomorrah as "an example of what is going to happen to the ungodly" (2 Peter 2:6). Today the grave-like mounds of those cities under the surface of the southern waters of the Dead Sea testify to the permanence of God's judgment.

Sodom's condition. Having thus far underlined Abraham's responsibility to bless the nations and to teach his own children to do righteousness and justice, Yahweh next emphasized the depth of Sodom's sin, perhaps gesturing toward the cities as he spoke. "Then the LORD said, '. . . the outcry against Sodom and Gomorrah is great and their sin is very grave'" (v. 20). We naturally think of the sins of these cities as largely sexual in nature. Sodom provides the basic word (sodomy) for sins outside normal sexuality.

But if we imagine the sins of these cities only in sexual terms, we miss the depth of their depravity. The Hebrew word for "outcry" is used in Scripture to describe the cries of the oppressed and brutalized. It is used for the cry of the oppressed widow or orphan (cf. Exodus 22:22, 23), the cry of the oppressed servant (cf. Deuteronomy 24:15), and the cries of the Israelites in Egypt (cf. Exodus 2:23; 3:7, 9). Jeremiah uses it to refer to the scream of terror by an individual or city when it is attacked (cf. Jeremiah 18:22; 20:16; 25:36; 48:3-5, 34; 49:21; 50:46; 51:54). Such an outcry is the miserable wail of the oppressed and brutalized.[2] Nahum Sarna says of the terms as used here:

> They connote the anguished cry of the oppressed, the agonized plea of the victim for help in the face of some great injustice. In the Bible these terms are suffused with poignancy and pathos, with moral outrage and soul-stirring passion. . . . The sin of Sodom, then, is heinous moral and social corruption, an arrogant disregard of basic human rights, a cynical insensitivity to the sufferings of others.[3]

This is confirmed by Ezekiel who described the inhabitants of Sodom: "she and her daughters had pride, excess of food, and prosperous ease, *but did not aid the poor and needy*" (16:49, italics added).

Sodom and Gomorrah were terrible little towns in which the inhabitants cared only for themselves while they brutalized and oppressed each other. Social violence was *de jure*. There were no human rights. The poor and needy and defenseless were especially brutalized. Tellingly, the great outcry against Sodom and Gomorrah came from the inhabitants of the cities *themselves!*[4] Unpunished sin cried out to heaven for vengeance, like the blood of Abel (cf. 4:10). Ominously, the Lord described "the outcry" as "very grave" (vv. 20, 21). Terrifying little towns indeed. And so reminiscent of today, as historian David Wells has written:

There is violence on the earth. The liberated search only for power. Industry despoils the earth. The powerful ride roughshod over the weak. The poor are left to die on street grates. The unborn are killed before they can ever see the rich and beautiful world that God has made. The elderly are encouraged to get on with the business of dying so that we might take their places. The many forms that violence takes in our world provide stunning reminders of how false have been the illusions about freedom with which we have, for two centuries, been enticed in the West.[5]

We still see Sodom and Gomorrah today.

There are real terrors here for all who take God's word seriously. But those who take God's word to heart are not the ones who ought to shake. Sadly, it is those who believe nothing — who fear nothing — until it is too late!

Investigation. Earlier that day Yahweh had confirmed his omniscience, that he knows everything, when he revealed Sarah's hidden thoughts while dining with Abraham. And a God who knows "all thoughts, all mysteries, all enigmas, every unuttered secret" (Tozer)[6] has no trouble understanding the depth of people's sins. Indeed, Jesus would say, "I tell you, on the day of judgment people will give account for every careless word they speak, for by your words you will be justified, and by your words you will be condemned" (Matthew 12:36, 37).

God knows everything! But through a huge act of condescension, the Lord responded anthropomorphically to Abraham (like a mere human being) saying, "I will go down to see whether they have done altogether according to the outcry that has come to me. And if not, I will know" (v. 21). By this he assured Abraham that he would base his judgment on full, accurate information. God would send his angels on a fact-finding mission — to gather information he already perfectly knew.

ABRAHAM INTERCEDES (vv. 22-33)

On this great day Abraham had *dined* with God (the only man to do so in the old covenant), he had *walked* with God (joining the select company of Enoch and Noah), and here atop Beni Na'im he *interceded* with God face-to-face.

Bold intercession. Verses 23-25 record his beautiful but flawed intercession.

> *Then Abraham drew near and said, "Will you indeed sweep away the righteous with the wicked? Suppose there are fifty righteous within the city. Will you then sweep away the place and not spare it for the fifty righteous who are in it? Far be it from you to do such a thing, to put the righteous*

*to death with the wicked, so that the righteous fare as the wicked! Far be
that from you! Shall not the Judge of all the earth do what is just?"*

There was so much that was right about Abraham's prayer. The forthright passion with which Abraham interceded for the cities on the plain
showed a new side of Abraham. Earlier he had stepped up to save Lot from
the invading kings from the east, selflessly risking everything for his kinsman. The deliverance of the Dead Sea kings had been a side effect of saving Lot. But here he prayed not for Lot but for the sinful inhabitants of
Sodom. He demonstrated a God-like compassion for others. Abraham, the
friend of God, has become a true friend of men. He acted as a morally compassionate man. He knew people in those wicked cities, and he cared for
them despite their paganism and depravity.

Abraham was also bold, but not too bold because he based his approach
upon his absolute confidence in the righteousness of God. His confidence
was this: "Shall not the Judge of all the earth do what is just?" (v. 25b). He
has no doubt that God is the author and arbiter of all righteousness and justice. He was convinced that God cannot and will not do wrong. His understanding anticipated Moses' declaration:

> *The Rock, his work is perfect,*
> *for all his ways are justice.*
> *A God of faithfulness and without iniquity,*
> *just and upright is he. (Deuteronomy 32:4)*

God is righteous in his being and just in his actions. Abraham's whole
intercession rested on this awesome understanding of God. This is so beautiful! This said, Abraham was wrong in supposing that the righteous cannot
suffer the same tragedies as sinners. Abraham was wrongheaded (not wrong-
hearted) in his bold admonishment, "Far be it from you to do such a thing,
to put the righteous to death with the wicked, so that the righteous fare as
the wicked! Far be that from you!" (v. 25a). Abraham's bold charge came
from his having never imagined that it could be possible for the righteous and
sinners to fall to the same trauma at the sovereign hand of God. Abraham
thought he was appealing to an immutable law.

Unlike us, Abraham did not have the benefit of all the Scriptures. He
did not have Psalm 73, which wonders at the prosperity of the wicked and the
difficulties of the righteous, nor did he have the marvelous answers that
God there provides. It is apparent that Abraham had not reflected that, as
Alexander Maclaren put it:

> In widespread calamities the righteous are blended with the wicked in one
> bloody ruin; and it is the very misery of such judgments that often the

sufferers are not the wrongdoers. . . . The whirlwind of temporal judgments makes no distinctions between the dwellings of the righteous and the wicked, but levels them both.[7]

Neither did Abraham have the words of Christ explaining that the victims of the fallen tower of Siloam were not greater sinners than the rest of Jerusalem's populace (cf. Luke 13:4, 5). And, of course, he did not have the benefit of the new-covenant teaching that earthly judgment cannot touch the righteous in the ultimate sense because they are in Christ. Abraham was wrong, but the spirit of his intercession was so right!

Bold exploration. As Abraham explored the fate of Sodom with God, beautiful things emerged about him and his God. The six "what ifs" — What if . . . fifty? . . . forty-five? . . . forty? . . . thirty? . . . twenty? . . . ten? — are instructive. In all of this Abraham "hangs on to God's skirt like a burr."[8] He wrestled with God like Jacob later did with the angel (cf. Genesis 32). And amazingly, Abraham's boldness grew, for notice that the last three petitions lowered the number of the necessary righteous by tens! Jesus would teach his disciples that "they ought always to pray and not lose heart" (Luke 18:1). This first patriarch and disciple set the pace. And we should note that Abraham's prayers were not without effect. As the cities of the plain went up in flames, we read tellingly that "God remembered Abraham and sent Lot out of the midst of the overthrow" (19:29). Lot, the alien, was the only righteous person in Sodom. And God saved him because God remembered Abraham.

Along with this we learn that God would have spared Sodom if anyone apart from Lot was righteous (Lot was only an alien, and not a full citizen; cf. 19:9). The lurid details of the following episode indicate that there simply were no righteous people in Sodom — not one! When Abraham realized where the statistics were going, coupled with Yahweh's introduction of the word "destroy" into the final phrases of the exchange, he ceased his intercession, and Yahweh departed.[9] Yahweh disappeared into the lengthening shadows, and Abraham descended the heights for the lights of his camp. The Lord would have shown mercy if there had been anyone upon whom he could bestow it. Such is the heart of God.

Now darkness had fallen, and the two angels had arrived in Sodom for its final black night.

The essential truth that transcends everything in this section is that God is righteous and just — "Shall not the Judge of all the earth do what is just?" Righteousness is an attribute of God's moral being, and because of that, all his actions are just. It is impossible for God to do anything that is unjust. His judgments are righteous and just. His mercies are righteous and just. We can rest everything in life on this truth. It will never change. The Judge of all the earth will do right!

Next we must understand that God hears the outcries of humanity. He hears the cry of the baby as it suffers abuse. He hears the cry of an old man beaten on the street. He hears the cries of the teenage girl as she is compromised. He hears the tears of the abandoned wife. He hears the bitter moans of the man stripped of his dignity and humiliated by the system. The cries of painful silence go up all at once in a deafening roar, and God hears them all — even the whimpers and the silent screams.

Because God hears all and knows all, judgment is coming — as sure as God is righteous and just. Still, nothing is more offensive to the unbelieving heart than the coming judgment. No doubt, the inhabitants of Sodom would have shouted God down for being so unfair. *Why should you single us out for punishment?* they would have thought. But God must act in a way consonant with his perfections, for such action is always right.

Jesus, Abraham's seed *par excellence* (cf. Galatians 3:16), did what Abraham could never do. He became sin on the cross, bearing all the unrighteousness and injustices of those who come to him. Our sins were focused on Christ on the cross. On the cross Christ was robed in all that is heinous and hateful as the mass of our corruption poured over him. With horror Christ found his entire being to be sin in the Father's sight. "Christ redeemed us from the curse of the law by becoming a curse for us — for it is written, 'Cursed is everyone who is hanged on a tree'" (Galatians 3:13). On the cross Christ suffered the fiery wrath of God's righteous judgment. This he did to redeem us from our sins. As Paul explained, "For our sake he made him to be sin who knew no sin, so that in him we might become the righteousness of God" (2 Corinthians 5:21).

In this world it is God's people who are called to mediate his hope — like Abraham in his day. Jesus has become for them the righteousness of God (cf. 1 Corinthians 1:30). As his people, we are to live lives of *righteousness* and *justice*. As God's people we reach out to the needy, we love the sinner, we give of our resources, we sacrifice ourselves for the lost, we petition Heaven for their souls. And through Christ God calls a people to himself.

32

Molten Rain

GENESIS 19:1-29

When the Lord had finished his exchange with Abraham atop the promi-nence where they together gazed down on the cities of Sodom and Gomorrah, he then left, and Abraham returned to the lights of his camp in the falling darkness. This would have been about the same time that the two angels, who had left earlier, arrived in Sodom for its final dark night. As Abraham fell asleep, he surely reflected long and hard on what he had learned during the mountaintop exchange. First, he had learned that God intended to destroy Sodom and Gomorrah because of their utter sinfulness. And sec-ond, Abraham's intercession for Sodom had progressively taught him that there were no righteous in the city except Lot. We conclude this because the conversation ended when the Lord declared that he would not destroy Sodom if there were ten righteous people. It was clear where the math was going, and the Lord ended the conversation.

Abraham was given this revelation so that he would learn (in the words of his own question, "Shall not the Judge of all the earth do what is just?" [18:25b]) that God is righteous and just. It was essential that Abraham under-stand and believe this with all his heart, both because of his position in sal-vation history and his responsibility to teach his descendants to "keep the way of the LORD by doing righteousness and justice" (18:19). Come sun-rise he would begin to understand God's righteousness in a way that was before impossible.

When the angels earlier had approached Abraham, he was sitting in his tent in the heat of midday. Here in Sodom at the end of the day, it was likely still hot due to its below-sea-level elevation — which probably accounts for Lot still being outside in the gate of the city, the spacious area where people lounged by the towers and guardrooms of the city's entrance and gossiped and did business. Lot's position in the gate indicates that he was a major player in Sodom. Significantly, Genesis records the progression of Lot's assimilation into Sodom. Initially he had "moved his tent *as far as* Sodom" (13:12), next he is described as "dwelling *in* Sodom" (14:12), and here he is pictured as "*sitting* in the gate of Sodom" (19:1, italics added in all). Lot had become a prominent man in Sodom. He was well-known in the gates. Evidently the angels had traveled by supernatural means to Sodom because the journey could not have been made unassisted in the waning hours of the day.

Although Lot had become a city-dweller, he still practiced the grand hospitality that was typical of Abraham's family. Like Abraham, he bowed low to the ground. And because of the late hour, he offered appropriate hospitality — a bed instead of rest under a tree and a meal. The angel's unexpected turndown of his hospitality — "No; we will spend the night in the town square" (v. 2) — left Lot shocked and frightened. Custom demanded that you must offer strangers a bed for the night, and custom likewise demanded that you accept such offers (cf. 24:23; Judges 18:2; 19:4-21). Besides, this was Sodom, and Lot knew what happened to defenseless strangers at night. So he "pressed them strongly" (v. 3), or as Gordon Wenham translates it, "manhandled" them![1] He did some major arm-twisting till they said yes. And when he got them safe inside his home, he "made a feast"[2] for them of *matzah* that could be prepared quickly for unexpected guests. Lot rolled out the red carpet as best he could.

SODOM'S ASSAULT (vv. 4-9)

Homosexual practice had become a dominant way of life in Sodom. Such texts as Leviticus 18:22, 24 and 20:13, 23 reveal that homosexuality had become one of the common perversions of the Canaanites.[3]

Attempted rape. Here in Sodom, Canaanite culture had descended into the added depths of sexual violence: "But before they lay down, the men of the city, the men of Sodom, both young and old, all the people to the last man, surrounded the house. And they called to Lot, 'Where are the men who came to you tonight? Bring them out to us, that we may know them'" (vv. 4, 5).

It is apparent that in Sodom homosexual and bisexual men (like the men pledged to Lot's daughters) eagerly participated in the communal rape of visiting men. The celebrated critic and Old Testament scholar Gerhard Von Rad writes:

> One must think of the heavenly messengers as young men in their prime, whose beauty particularly incited evil desire. . . . In Canaan, where civilization at that time was already old, sexual aberrations were quite in vogue. . . . This was especially true of the Canaanite cult of the fertility gods Baal and Astarte, which was erotic and orgastic at times (Lev. 18:22ff.; 20:13-23).[4]

The black rain of violent sexual perversion had fallen on all the men of Sodom. Moses' choice of words is deliberate: "the men of the city, the men of Sodom, *both young and old, all the people to the last man,* surrounded the house" (italics added). Sexual orientation aside, such violence was anathema to all oriental culture.[5] The violent depravity of the Sodomites was extraordinary. Lot's home was encircled by a vast, gibbering mob of lusting men of every age, howling for perverted satisfaction.

In ironic contrast to the men of Sodom stood righteous Lot. I say righteous not because of what we see here, but on the basis of New Testament revelation, which tells us:

> If by turning the cities of Sodom and Gomorrah to ashes he [God] condemned them to extinction, making them an example of what is going to happen to the ungodly; and if he rescued righteous Lot, greatly distressed by the sensual conduct of the wicked (for as that righteous man lived among them day after day, he was tormenting his righteous soul over their lawless deeds that he saw and heard); then the Lord knows how to rescue the godly from trials. (2 Peter 2:6-9)

Notice that Peter called Lot "righteous" three times so that his readers could not miss it. He also described Lot as "distressed" — literally, "worn down" by the filthy lives of the Sodomites — and tormented or *continually tortured* (imperfect tense) in his "righteous soul."

How so? we wonder. Obviously *righteous* does not mean perfect! We must understand that Lot was righteous in a way comparable to that of Noah and Abraham. Scripture affirms that Noah's righteousness had come by faith: "By this he condemned the world and became an heir of the righteousness that comes by faith" (Hebrews 11:7). And the Scripture says of Abraham, "And he believed the LORD, and he counted it to him as righteousness" (Genesis 15:6). Yet both these men were flawed, as Noah's drunkenness and Abraham's expediency with Hagar and later with Abimelech demonstrate.

Therefore we must understand that Lot was a believer, though a man of far less character and commitment than Noah and Abraham. In contrast to Abraham's magnanimity, Lot had chosen for himself the well-watered plain of the Jordan. He was attracted to the glitz and materialism of Sodom. Even after Abraham delivered him and his fellow Sodomites from the kings of the east, Lot returned to Sodom to ultimately sit in its gates. Clearly Sodom had gotten inside of him. It is probable (though not provable) that he married a Sodomite woman. His daughters were betrothed to pagan Sodomites (who were surely part of "the men . . . young and old" who pursued the gang rape of Lot's guests). Later, while in a drunken stupor in a mountain cave, Lot would fall to Sodom-like sin.

In a word, Lot was a conflicted soul, at the same time both offended and allured by Sodom. He liked the prosperity, the comforts, the "culture," and the prestige. But he was worn down by the filthy lives of lawless men and perpetually tortured in his righteous soul by the deeds he saw and heard. As such, he is the prototype and paradigm of so many believers today. He is not a caricature, a joke written on the pages of antiquity. Lot is for real!

Lot's resistance. Lot's initial response evokes a sense of gallantry: "Lot went out to the men at the entrance, shut the door after him, and said, 'I beg you, my brothers, do not act so wickedly'" (vv. 6, 7). With the closed door behind him, Lot stood as the human insulation between his guests and the wild mob. His plea — "I beg you, my brothers, do not act so wickedly" — was a moral judgment, however gently expressed.

But any hint of gallantry was eclipsed by his craven proposal: "Behold, I have two daughters who have not known any man. Let me bring them out to you, and do to them as you please. Only do nothing to these men, for they have come under the shelter of my roof" (v. 8). Conflicted, compromised Lot placed the sanctity of hospitality above the sanctity of his family. Even if he thought that his daughters would suffer no harm, because they were betrothed as virgins to their fellow Sodomites (and the Mesopotamian law code made betrothal as sacrosanct as a consummated marriage — the offender would incur the death penalty), the offer was a monstrous breach of fatherly duty.[6] Had this plan been somehow carried out, a ghastly result like that of the parallel account in Judges 19 would have been effected.

Fortunately, Lot's foolishness was overridden by the mob's contemptuous response. "But they said, 'Stand back!' And they said, 'This fellow came to sojourn, and he has become the judge! Now we will deal worse with you than with them.' Then they pressed hard against the man Lot, and drew near to break the door down" (v. 9). Lot's assertion of morality into the melee offended the Sodomites. *How dare he play the judge! He came here an alien — and that he is!* Evidently Lot's muffled testimony and the fact that he did not run with the Sodomites or participate in their wicked deeds offended them. Peter said much the same of his own day: "With respect to this they are surprised when you do not join them in the same flood of debauchery, and they malign you" (1 Peter 4:4). Little has changed today. Sinners (especially people involved in these kinds of sins) are offended because you do not give hearty approval to their actions (cf. Romans 1:32). In their eyes, absence of approval is unforgivably judgmental.

My emotional response to Lot here is probably pretty much like yours. What a disgusting little man. And he was. But at the same time Peter reveals that he was "greatly distressed by the sensual conduct of the wicked (for as that righteous man lived among them day after day, he was tormenting his righteous soul over their lawless deeds that he saw and heard)" (2 Peter 2:7, 8). Are we tortured by the sin around us like this? Truthfully, some Christians are not. They watch the same movies and television as everyone else. They witness the same debaucheries impassively, without even a hint of indignation. At least Lot *felt* something.

ANGELIC DELIVERANCE (vv. 10-22)

Blindness. Second Peter 2:9 says, after referencing Lot's rescue, "then the Lord knows how to rescue the godly from trials, and to keep the unrighteous under punishment until the day of judgment."

Indeed he does! An angel's arm reached out and yanked bumbling Lot back into his home and slammed the door. Then, as the Hebrew word suggests (v. 11), there came a blinding flash of light, leaving every man in Sodom dazzled, temporarily blinded like Paul on the road to Damascus.[7] But to our astonishment we read that the divinely given blindness did not cool their lust. There is grim comedy here as blind, unseeing, lust-crazed men stumble about in vain in search of the door. If there had been any doubt as to God's declaration that there were no righteous Sodomites, it was now gone. Every mother's son, and by implication every daughter of Sodom, was an unrepentant, hardened sinner.

Warning. This final confirmation evoked an angelic warning: "Then the men said to Lot, 'Have you anyone else here? Sons-in-law, sons, daughters, or anyone you have in the city, bring them out of the place. For we are about to destroy this place, because the outcry against its people has become great before the LORD, and the LORD has sent us to destroy it'" (vv. 12, 13).

Of course, the angels confirmed what Yahweh already knew (cf. 18:20, 21). Naturally, Lot rushed to warn his pledged sons-in-law. But to no avail. Despite the fact that they along with Lot had been divinely delivered by God from the eastern kings through the agency of Abraham, despite the fact that they had been struck with blindness that very night, despite the fact that they had seen something of Lot's righteousness, they rejected Lot's warning. They thought he was joking (v. 14). In their fleshly security, they did not believe in divine judgment. Men like that think all such talk is a joke. Thus they establish their guilt beyond all doubt.

Flight. The picture that focuses before us in verses 15-17 is backlit by the appearance of the dawn, that time when the blackness of night begins to lighten before the sunrise.[8] The final dark night of Sodom had come to an end. The common biblical image of salvation coming with the sunrise was now established (cf. Isaiah 9:2; Malachi 4:1-3; Luke 1:78). Silhouetted against the red dawn, two angels, each grasping the hesitant hand of two people, could be seen running through the dark streets, through the gates, and out toward the rising dawn.

The reason for this is sublimely stated in the last part of verse 16: "the LORD being merciful to him." The angels' use of force was an act of mercy.

Lot's deliverance was a divine exercise of grace and was due to no merit of his own. It was completely undeserved. This grace came from Abraham's prayers, as the final verse of this section makes so clear (v. 29).

Outside the city in the dawn's scarlet light the angels shouted, "Escape for your life. Do not look back or stop anywhere in the valley. Escape to the hills, lest you be swept away" (v. 17).

Condescension. There are many weird and wonderful things in the Sodom narrative, but nothing is more astonishing than Lot's self-centered wheedling with God as the sun rose, and then God's astounding concession.

> *And Lot said to them, "Oh, no, my lords. Behold, your servant has found favor in your sight, and you have shown me great kindness in saving my life. But I cannot escape to the hills, lest the disaster overtake me and I die. Behold, this city is near enough to flee to, and it is a little one. Let me escape there — is it not a little one? — and my life will be saved!" He said to him, "Behold, I grant you this favor also, that I will not overthrow the city of which you have spoken. Escape there quickly, for I can do nothing till you arrive there." Therefore the name of the city was called Zoar. (vv. 18-22)*

Lot's whimpering speech astounds us because he first acknowledged that he had found favor (grace) in God's eyes and that God had kindly spared his life. And then Lot went on to state that he doubted God's ability to preserve his life in the flight to the mountains! Unbelievably he had the nerve to ask God to send him to Zoar (Hebrew, "small"), which was a mini-Sodom itself. As Kidner well says, "Not even brimstone will make a pilgrim of him: he must have his little Sodom again if life is to be supportable."[9] We might think, *Come on, God, strike this simpering, whimpering, wheedling weasel dead!* But God astonished again by granting Lot his request. Such mercy and grace — even to people who fall so short of Noah and Abraham. Divine grace, not human righteousness, is the ultimate basis of salvation.

One more astonishment: God spared Zoar because of righteous Lot — the one righteous man in town. Abraham's intercession was answered in the preservation of Zoar.[10]

JUDGMENT (vv. 23-29)

Sodom and Gomorrah. The favored naturalistic explanation for the destruction that followed is this (favored by Delitzsch, Von Rad, and Sarna): The Jordan Valley is part of the great Syrian-African Rift that stretches from Syria, through Palestine, down the Arabah to the Gulf of Akaba, through the Red Sea to the Upper Nile Valley, through the Rift

Valley in Kenya, on to Lake Nyasa in eastern Africa. This great rift in the earth was caused by a series of earthquakes. And here, four thousand years ago, a quake opened a fissure, releasing gases that then ignited, setting the sulfur and petroleum deposits aflame, resulting in a catastrophic firestorm.

That may be. But what is sure is that the firestorm was entirely due to God's directive, because the text twice says the Lord did it: "Then the LORD rained on Sodom and Gomorrah sulfur and fire from the LORD out of heaven. And he overthrew those cities, and all the valley, and all the inhabitants of the cities, and what grew on the ground" (vv. 24, 25). The judgment had its origin in God, it was decided by God, and it was executed by God.

The other sure thing is that when the sun was fully up, God extended the red arm of his vengeance, and molten rain fell upon the land, incinerating all plant and animal life, so that the cities of the plain became a scorched graveyard.

Lot's wife. A final certitude of the judgment is that "Lot's wife, behind him, looked back, and she became a pillar of salt" (v. 26). As they were fleeing toward Zoar, Lot's wife stopped on the plain. Her backward look was far more than momentary because the destruction of the cities did not begin until Lot and his daughters were safe in Zoar. Evidently she refused all encouragements to leave and lingered far behind. There were no angels to grasp her unwilling hand as the deathly rain rushed toward her.

Why did she fatally linger? Was it because of family? Or pleasure? Or delights? Jesus provided the cue in his warning to be prepared for the coming of the Son of Man: "On that day, let the one who is on the housetop, with his goods in the house, not come down to take them away, and likewise let the one who is in the field not turn back. Remember Lot's wife" (Luke 17:31, 32). Apparently she lost her life because of her reluctance to let go of her household stuff. In a word: "She was a wife after Lot's own heart"[11] — but without the grace. Her sorrow over her goods so fixated her that she could not or would not move. Perhaps she decided that she would be better dead than separated from her possessions.

How did she become a pillar of salt? Was it like the B-rated movie version? The four of them are running together, and she casts a wistful glance back, and her eyes become salt, and then her face is frozen in grinning saline horror. Mrs. Lot becomes a sodium chloride monument that generations of Israelites will view. We smile, but Josephus claimed to have seen the pillar in his day.[12] Reality was probably more like this: As she tarried, she succumbed to the sulfurous gases. And then as her corpse lay exposed, it was encrusted in salt and debris so that she became a pillar of salt.

Whatever the exact details, her example is meant to instruct us. An angel of grace had taken her by the hand, led her away from certain destruction, and charged her to flee. But having been dragged away from the city of destruction, she returned in heart. For her, it was possessions. For others, it can be many other things — a reputation, a relationship, a particular lust, a comfort. To all Jesus calls, "Remember Lot's wife. Whoever seeks to preserve his life will lose it, but whoever loses his life will keep it" (Luke 17:32, 33).

> *Like Lot's wife,*
> *I'm sometimes loath*
> *to turn my eyes from my possessions,*
> *even knowing fully*
> *that my true treasures are in heaven.*
> *Lord, there's a looking back*
> *on your leading that's pleasing.*
> *But there is another kind of past-clinging*
> *that's soul and body petrifying.*
>
> ANITA DEYNEKA

There is silence as we come to the conclusion of this amazing story: "And Abraham went early in the morning to the place where he had stood before the LORD. And he looked down toward Sodom and Gomorrah and toward all the land of the valley, and he looked and, behold, the smoke of the land went up like the smoke of a furnace" (vv. 27, 28). The night was over; the sun was up and shining as the smoke rose from the land in the south.

The sunrise had brought both judgment and salvation. But Abraham did not know that. We are not told what he was thinking as he watched the smoke rise from the cities. "Abraham was silent. His thoughts were his own" (Sailhamer).[13] However, because the writer has directed our thoughts back to the promontory where Abraham the day before had interceded with God for the people of Sodom, the big question returns to the justice of God: "Shall not the Judge of all the earth do what is just?" (18:25).[14]

The answer is a resounding yes! And the narrator supplies what Abraham will learn: "So it was that, when God destroyed the cities of the valley, God remembered Abraham and sent Lot out of the midst of the overthrow when he overthrew the cities in which Lot had lived" (19:29). There was not a single righteous soul in Sodom except Lot. And righteous Lot, conflicted and compromised as he was, was saved not on his own merits but through grace effected by Abraham's intercession. God remains just and the justifier of all those who come to him.

Of course, the ultimate sunrise, bearing salvation and judgment, came with Christ. Isaiah sang of it: "The people who walked in darkness have seen a great light; those who dwelt in a land of deep darkness, on them has light shined" (9:2). Malachi declared it as well:

For behold, the day is coming, burning like an oven, when all the arrogant and all evildoers will be stubble. The day that is coming shall set them ablaze, says the LORD of hosts, so that it will leave them neither root nor branch. But for you who fear my name, the sun of righteousness shall rise with healing in its wings. You shall go out leaping like calves from the stall. (4:1, 2)

When Jesus came, the rising sun came to us from Heaven and shined on those living in darkness and in the shadow of death and set their feet on the path of peace (cf. Luke 1:78, 79).

All glory to his name!

33

Finishing Un-well

GENESIS 19:30-38

In the fall of 2001 an important book appeared by Robert Gundry, New Testament scholar and scholar-in-residence at Westmont College, with the daunting title *Jesus the Word According to John the Sectarian: A Paleofundamentalist Manifesto for Contemporary Evangelicalism, Especially Its Elites, in North America*. I suspect that the publisher did not choose this title, but that it was at the author's insistence. Titles like this do not sell books, though this may well be the exception.

In clearest terms his argument is this: The instincts of early fundamentalism were right in its attempt to maintain theological orthodoxy and separation from the world, but it was sidetracked by the fundamentalism of the twenties and forties into a shallow separatism. And, therefore, what is needed today is a new old fundamentalism that is in line with the paleofundamentalism of John's Gospel that while being in the world is morally separated from the world and that unashamedly preaches the gospel.

Dr. Gundry states his concern in very specific terms:

The "seeker sensitivity" of evangelicals — their practice of suiting the gospel to the felt needs of people, primarily the bourgeoisie — contributes to their numerical success but can easily sow the seeds of worldliness (broadly conceived). How so? Well, in a society such as ours where people do not feel particularly guilty before God (though in fact they are), seeker-sensitivity — if consistently carried through — will soft-pedal the preaching of salvation from sin, for such preaching would not meet a felt need of people. As a result, the gospel *message* of saving, sanctifying grace reduces to a gospel *massage* of physical, psychological, and social well-being that allows worldliness to flourish.[1]

By worldliness Gundry means "not merely the disregard of fundamentalist taboos against smoking, drinking, dancing, movie-going, gambling and the like, but more expansively such matters as materialism, pleasure-seeking, indiscriminate enjoyment of salacious and violent entertainment, immodesty of dress, voyeurism, sexual laxity, and divorce."[2] Who can deny that this is modern evangelicalism — that materialism does not grip the church — that pleasure-seeking is not common among us — that evangelicals do not watch sensuality and violence like everyone else — that modesty has not been minimized — and that voyeurism and pornography and sexual laxity and divorce are not on the rise? Know for certain that what is *not* needed today is a massage, but rather the disquieting message of a believer who finished un-well.

As we observed in our study of the destruction of Sodom, if we only had the Old Testament we would never have imagined that Lot was a true believer. But 2 Peter 2 three times tells us that this conflicted, compromised little man was "righteous," and that he was distressed and tormented by life in Sodom. Ironically, though Lot was revolted by Sodom, Sodom was in his soul. It is possible, then, to be distressed by the world while hanging on to it for dear life.

LOT'S DESCENT (vv. 1, 30)

The Genesis account gives us a subtly crafted portrait of Lot. Lot had left Ur as part of Abram's faithful entourage and trekked the full eight hundred miles to Canaan (cf. 12:4ff.). But with the passing of time, he perceptibly loosed himself from God's grasp, allowing the fingers of Sodom to close ever tighter around his convulsing soul. Given his choice of land by Abram, he succumbed to the lures of the Jordan Valley, pitching his tents "as far as Sodom" (13:12), next living "in Sodom" (14:12), and finally "sitting in the gate of Sodom" (19:1) — having become a prominent man in that wicked city.

Lot proved himself feckless and impotent during the melee over his angel-guests — offering his daughters to appease the Sodomites and balking at the angels' call to flee so that they had to grasp his family's hands while he whimpered to be exempted from fleeing to the mountains so he could take refuge in the nearby mini-Sodom, Zoar.

Then, ensconced in Zoar, he did not trust the implied divine guarantee of safety. Consumed by fears, he fled with his two daughters to the mountains of the Dead Sea and became a cave-dweller (v. 30). "When a man is out of the will of God, he is haunted by the bogeys of his own imagination" (Barnhouse).[3] Perhaps Lot feared reprisals from his new neighbors or trembled at the thought of another earthquake. It is intriguing that he did not return to the tents of Abraham, where he surely would have been welcome. Perhaps this was due to shame. Or maybe even pride.

Fear and depression can cloud judgment. Perhaps he projected his own sinful delusions upon his godly uncle. However it was, the cave was more than metaphorical of his descent. Lot and his daughters lived in dark isolation in the musty, dank chambers of a cave. Caves were often tombs. Abraham purchased a cave in Machpelah for Sarah's tomb and was later buried there himself (25:9, 10).

Spiritually entombed, Lot lived a degenerated, death-like existence, sinking into ever deeper depression and corruption.

THE DAUGHTERS' DESCENT (vv. 31, 32)

Lot's corruption had consequences for his family because we read, "And the firstborn said to the younger, 'Our father is old, and there is not a man on earth to come in to us after the manner of all the earth. Come, let us make our father drink wine, and we will lie with him, that we may preserve offspring from our father'" (vv. 31, 32).

Incest was considered wrong in Near-Eastern culture, as Harry Hoffner has shown in his *festschrift* for Cyrus Gordon, *Orient and Occident*. And Hebrew culture explicitly forbade a man's having relations with his daughters or daughters-in-law (Leviticus 20:12; Ezekiel 22:10, 11). The penalty for such sin was death (Leviticus 20:11-13). Mesopotamian culture similarly forbade such incest in the Code of Hammurabi (Paragraphs 154-158). Likewise Hittite laws forbade such sins, punishing them either by death or banishment and, later, by paying a fine and sending an animal out of the town bearing the guilt on the analogy of Israel's scapegoat.[4] On the basis of this evidence I think that father-daughter incest was an aberration even in the Dead Sea cultures of Sodom and Gomorrah — and that Lot's daughters knew it to be sinful.

Some who read the account argue that the story was handed down from the Moabites and Ammonites as a record of their mothers' heroic actions, thus seeing the sisters' act as comparable to that of Tamar with her father-in-law Judah. Such an interpretation is a stretch, although it does correctly emphasize that the seduction was motivated by economic desires and not by perverted sensuality. Lot's daughters sought the social security that only children could provide. But in contrast to the Tamar-Judah episode, Lot was the girls' flesh-and-bone father! And more, the fact that they had to get their father drunk to do it shows that they were abusing moral conventions. Besides, though the phrase "lie with" may sound like an innocent euphemism, it is unusual for it to be used except to describe illicit relationships (e.g., 34:2, 7) or desperation (cf. 30:15, 16).[5] Also the girls' names being withheld implies censure.[6] Lot's daughters sinned intentionally.

MUTUAL DESCENT (vv. 33-35)

Lot's descent and his daughters' descent coalesced in an act of mutual degeneration.

> *So they made their father drink wine that night. And the firstborn went in and lay with her father. He did not know when she lay down or when she arose. The next day, the firstborn said to the younger, "Behold, I lay last night with my father. Let us make him drink wine tonight also. Then you go in and lie with him, that we may preserve offspring from our father." So they made their father drink wine that night also. And the younger arose and lay with him, and he did not know when she lay down or when she arose.*

This is dark. The deeds took place at night in a cave. There could scarce be a darker context on earth.

It is evident that Lot's life choices had promoted his daughters' absorbing of the spirit of Sodom into their souls. Life in Sodom had repeatedly demonstrated before his daughters' eyes how wine and sensuality worked together — weakening a man's inhibitions so that he was capable of anything. Deception, of course, was a way of life in Sodom. And Lot was part of it. But his deception was so spiritually charged and therefore so domestically lethal. Inwardly he was "distressed by the sensual conduct of the wicked" and was "tormenting his righteous soul over their lawless deeds," says Peter (2 Peter 2:7, 8). But outwardly he said little or nothing as he became a prominent man in town. Forthrightness would have jeopardized his standing. Lot had mastered the craft of turning a blind eye and a deaf ear to the social and sexual abuses of Sodom. He did not do them. He did not approve of them. But he did not speak out against them. Blasphemies and filthy speech were met by Lot's benign smile and deft deflection.

His daughters saw his feckless character that so shrewdly masked what he really thought. Lot the survivor was a master. His girls could not forget that he had offered them in order to appease the inflamed men of Sodom in a monstrous betrayal of fatherly duty.

So when the successive father-daughter seductions took place, his girls used the craft he had bequeathed them. It was his wine, his deceit, his betrayal mixed together and served in an infamous cup in the depths of the cave. Their dishonor of him was brilliant — because with cruel irony he himself carried out the shameful act he had first suggested to the men of Sodom. Lot had effectively allowed Sodom into his daughters' souls.

And understand this: Lot was drunk, but Lot was culpable for what he did. Unconscious drunks cannot do what Lot did. As Delitzsch says, the words "He did not know" (Genesis 19:33) do not affirm that he was in an unconscious state — "they merely mean, that in his intoxicated state, though not entirely unconscious, yet he lay with his daughters, without clearly knowing what he was doing."[7] In the morning he did not recall what he had done. But he was guilty, just as any father would be today. Alcohol was no excuse. Lot's drunkenness simply facilitated the working out of the dark side of his own heart.

While the Bible does not forbid wine, it repeatedly warns of its abuse. The parallels with Noah's drunkenness in the final episode of his life are so clear. But here is the greatest lesson: At the conclusion of the two storied narratives of divine judgment (one the primeval flood and the other patriarchal judgment in the destruction of Sodom), those who had been spared God's wrath (Noah and Lot) succumbed to sins similar to those who died in the judgments.[8] And here we witness the rebirth of Sodom in the cave. Sodom was alive and well in "righteous" Lot's family. And he was the father of it all!

LOT'S DESCENDANTS (vv. 36-38)

The story's conclusion carries the last mention of Lot in the Old Testament. He is of no further importance to the history of salvation. His death receives no mention. So much for the "righteous" man who was sucked into the world.

Here is the end: "Thus both the daughters of Lot became pregnant by their father. The firstborn bore a son and called his name Moab. He is the father of the Moabites to this day. The younger also bore a son and called his name Ben-ammi. He is the father of the Ammonites to this day" (vv. 36-38). The names the daughters gave their sons immortalized Lot's paternity. "Moab" is based on the Hebrew, "from [my] father." And "Ben-ammi" means literally, "son of my [paternal] kinsman."[9] The Moabites inhabited the territory between the Arnon and the Zered Rivers east of the Dead Sea. And the Ammonites were located generally in the eastern part of the same region between the Jabbok and the Arnon.

Here we must understand that this account and its designations did not give rise to Israel's national hatred of the Moabites and Ammonites, nor was it placed here to stigmatize those tribes. Their origin was not held against them. Deuteronomy regarded their territories as God-given and affirmed the right of these peoples to live peaceably in their homelands (cf. Deuteronomy 2:9, 19).

Deuteronomy also tells us that it was the Moabites' and Ammonites' later inhospitality to the wandering Israelites that brought the animosity (cf. Deuteronomy 23:3, 4). The king of Moab's enlistment of Balaam to curse Israel did ultimately eventuate in the carnal seduction of Israel (Numbers 25, 31). But it should also be remembered that King David and ultimately the Messiah was descended from Ruth the Moabite, as so beautifully told in Ruth 4. Today every Jew and Gentile can become a true son or daughter of Abraham through Christ, his ultimate seed (cf. Galatians 3:16, 29).

Lot's immortal folly was this: Though the worldliness of Sodom vexed his righteous soul, he lived as close to the world as he could, hanging on to it for dear life until the bitter end. And the result was that though God judged all of Sodom except Lot and his daughters, *Sodom was reborn in their very lives.* So we see that it is possible for believing people like us who are truly distressed by the course of this world to live lives that are so profoundly influenced by culture that Sodom is reborn in the lives of those we love the most.

The enticements to yield to this syndrome have never been more powerful than they are right now because of our prosperity, cyber-options, and the powers of the media. I sense that these are crucial days politically, culturally, and spiritually. And we are the only ones who can do anything about it. And we must! God help us if while decrying sin, we are sprinting headlong after it because we will not deny ourselves.

• *Materialism.* Whether we are wealthy or not, we must say no to materialism. We know it is bad. But we are not saying no when we deny nothing to ourselves. We are not saying no when we give our children whatever they want — if they pester us long enough. And we are not saying no if our giving does not affect our lifestyles. We simply must not be worldly materialists who are only offended by those whose lifestyles are more lavish than ours. We must say no! We must not participate in Lot's folly.

• *Pleasure-seeking.* Nothing is more despotic than pleasure-seeking, and few things control our families more than pleasure. Certainly we must know how to abound. And as Christians in a sense our pleasures are more acute. But to determine our actions by a desire for the greatest pleasure is to surrender to Hell — and to bring the ways of Hell on our offspring. Lot could never say no — even in that dark cave. We must.

• *Entertainment.* Despite the pundits' demurrals, we become what we focus on in the same way that we are what we eat. I would like to call men (because we are the biggest offenders) to take control of what comes into our houses. We must become biblically discriminating. Some need to put the TV in the closet for a season. TV violence is *de jure* in most homes. Sensuality is *de jure* on every network following the evening news. Today is the day to say no and take control of our own minds and souls — for the sake of our sons and daughters.

• *Immodesty.* Modesty must be essential in every Christian life not because we think we are good, but because we know how bad we are. We must celebrate the differences between men and women not with lewdness but with the respect that honors the God who made us.

The example for all of life is our Lord Jesus Christ. Jesus came into the world and therefore *engaged* it. Jesus sanctified himself and thus (unlike Lot) *separated* himself from it. Jesus explained God and therefore preached the gospel.

If we look to Christ for our example and strength to live as we ought, we will finish well.

34

Old Sins

GENESIS 20:1-18

The effect of the comparative portraits of Abraham and Lot in Genesis 12 — 19 is that Abraham towers over Lot. Lot shrinks as he chooses the well-watered Jordan plain for himself and is progressively absorbed into Sodom and ultimately the ignominy of the cave. Abraham, despite some bumps along the way (for example, when he passed off Sarah as his sister to Pharaoh and the Hagar affair), grows ever-larger — building altars in the land; magnanimously giving Lot his choice of the land; rescuing kidnapped Lot from an invading coalition of kings; receiving Melchizedek's blessing; believing the Lord's promise that a son would come from him and that his progeny would be like the stars and having it credited to him as righteousness; witnessing the flaming presence of God pass between the flayed sacrifices in unilateral covenant; undergoing the covenant of circumcision; having his name changed from Abram to Abraham and Sarai's to Sarah as God promises that Sarah will bear a son by Abraham; feasting the Lord and two angels in his camp; hearing the Lord promise that Sarah would have a child at the same time next year; and then passionately pleading with God for Sodom, which brought about Lot's preservation. In all of this Abraham rises as the towering man of faith whom the writer of Hebrews so eloquently celebrates.

It is this height that provides the background for Abraham's shameful conduct with the pagan king Abimelech. And his failure came so fast, before Sarah was even pregnant with Isaac, who was born a year later as chapter 21 records. Shortly after the destruction of Sodom and the Dead Sea cities, Abraham pulled up stakes and began the wanderings described in verse 1, first traveling south into the Negev and then spending some time farther south in the line between the oasis of Kadesh and Shur that formed the Egyptian defense wall in the eastern Nile Delta. After some time Abraham

left the Kadesh-Shur grazing area to visit the royal city of Gerar back north
on the fringes of the promised land.[1]

SIN (vv. 1, 2)

We are amazed to read, "And Abraham said of Sarah his wife, 'She is my sister.' And Abimelech king of Gerar sent and took Sarah" (v. 2). Our astonishment is this: Abraham resorted to the same sin that he had committed in
Egypt right after receiving the promise of posterity that had precipitated his
leaving Ur by faith. Now, decades later, not long after receiving the explicit,
dated promise of a son by Sarah, he commits the same old sin! Our amazement is compounded when we remember his embarrassment and the stinging reproach of Pharaoh when he booted Abraham out of Egypt: "Why did
you not tell me that she was your wife? Why did you say, 'She is my sister,'
so that I took her for my wife? Now then, here is your wife; take her, and
go" (12:18, 19). That concluding staccato line has just four Hebrew words:
"Here . . . wife . . . take . . . go." Such disdain.

So we have to ask ourselves, "What has happened here in Gerar?" And
we know part of the answer from our own hearts. There are certain old sins
to which each of us are uniquely susceptible — "sin which clings so closely"
(Hebrews 12:1). We each have our unique susceptibilities. Sins that may
not appeal to others maintain a deadly lure for us and promote a tragic recidivism. Abraham's clinging sin when pressured was to trust himself rather than
God. Generally he trusted God. Abraham believed the divine promise, and
it was credited to him as righteousness (15:6). But sometimes when pushed,
he decided to give God a little help with a "little" lie. Inarticulate musings
like, "Lord, I trust you, but I just want to make sure that things work out
right" accompany such sins.

But such self-trust (which is really distrust of God) can have no place
in a believer's life if he or she desires maximum use by God. As Oswald
Chambers wrote:

> God can achieve his purpose either through the absence of human power
> and resources, or the abandonment of reliance on them. All through his-
> tory God has chosen and used nobodies, because their unusual depend-
> ence on him made possible the unique display of his power and grace. He
> chose and used somebodies only when they renounced dependence on their
> natural abilities and resources.[2]

Abraham was God's friend, a "somebody" who had to learn to trust
God alone. And God was working to that end.

Isn't life beautiful! Abraham is alive. And Abimelech, believing that
Sarah is Abraham's lovely sister (remember she will soon bear a child

despite her age), has taken her into his harem. Sleep well, Father Abraham, man of God.

We know how it was for Abraham because we have all known the angst that comes from our deceptions — the times we have misled others in order to maintain control of a situation — or lied in order to insure our comfort — or allowed a false impression to persist so that others would think well of us.

INTERVENTION (vv. 3-7)

Of course, we know in light of salvation history that God would not allow Abraham's lie to follow its inevitable course to tragedy. God had made an unconditional, unilateral covenant with Abraham. And Abraham's faithlessness could not abrogate it. God had recently said, "I will surely return to you about this time next year, and Sarah your wife shall have a son" (18:10) and "Is anything too hard for the LORD? At the appointed time I will return to you about this time next year, and Sarah shall have a son" (18:14). God would not allow Sarah in the arms of any man but Abraham.

Therefore God came suddenly to Abimelech in a dream with these shocking words, literally translated: "You are a dead man because of the woman whom you have taken, for she is a man's wife."[3] God had Abimelech's undivided attention. And though dreaming, the king began to sweat as he responded, "Lord, will you kill an innocent people? Did he not himself say to me, 'She is my sister'? And she herself said, 'He is my brother.' In the integrity of my heart and the innocence of my hands I have done this" (vv. 4, 5). Sarah had been in on the deception too, having identified Abraham as her "brother." And seeing that Sarah had no children, how was he to imagine that what they said was untrue? Abimelech's heart and hands were clean. He'd had no relations with her.

Abimelech was indeed telling the truth. So God informed the king that it was his omniscience (his all-knowingness) and his omnipotence (his all-powerfulness) that had kept Abimelech from violating Sarah, and further that the king must return Sarah — "Now then, return the man's wife, for he is a prophet, so that he will pray for you, and you shall live. But if you do not return her, know that you shall surely die, you, and all who are yours" (v. 7). This is the first use of the word *prophet* in the Bible. Abraham's intercession for Sodom and Lot installed him as the forerunner of the great prophetic intercessors like Moses and Samuel and Jeremiah. The return of Sarah to her husband and her husband's prayers were Abimelech's only hope.

CONFRONTATION (vv. 8-13)

Now the story begins to throb with mounting irony because Abimelech, the pagan Canaanite, acted more righteously than righteous Abraham.

Abimelech's speech. After assembling his people and relating his dream, the king summoned Abraham and implored him with a speech full of moral shock and indignation, as its questions so clearly indicate: "'What have you done to us? And how have I sinned against you, that you have brought on me and my kingdom a great sin? You have done to me things that ought not to be done.' And Abimelech said to Abraham, 'What did you see, that you did this thing?'" (vv. 9, 10). Abimelech's references to "us" and "me and my kingdom" demonstrated his concern for others endangered by Abraham's lie. Abimelech's "How have I sinned against you?" was freighted with moral earnestness. His "You have done to me things that ought not to be done" assumed the moral high ground. And his concluding "What did you see, that you did this thing?" allowed Abraham to explain. In that moment Abraham's towering spirituality had shrunk low before the pagan Abimelech.

Abraham's reply. Abraham's reply was lame, to say the least:

> *I did it because I thought, There is no fear of God at all in this place, and they will kill me because of my wife. Besides, she is indeed my sister, the daughter of my father though not the daughter of my mother, and she became my wife. And when God caused me to wander from my father's house, I said to her, "This is the kindness you must do me: at every place to which we come, say of me, He is my brother." (vv. 11-13)*

Abraham had completely misread Abimelech and Gerar. There was fear of God among these pagans. The irony lay in his heart — because Abraham's fears were grounded in his own momentary lack of respect and reverential awe of God. Had he exhibited a proper fear of God, he would never have lied!

And more, Abraham's deceit pulled Sarah down with him. His sorry request — "This is the kindness you must do me: at every place to which we come, say of me, He is my brother" (v. 13b) — was a kind of domestic blackmail. How could Sarah do otherwise in the face of such a plea? Evidently this "she is my sister" deception had been a regular part of Abraham's life ever since God had called him to leave his father's house in Ur. Father Abraham was less of a saint than we might have concluded from the preceding chapters. And here he had little or no witness with Abimelech and his people, who were, after all, a microcosm of the nations that were to be blessed through Abraham! This was a very low time indeed. And it was all Abraham's fault.

This, coupled with righteous Lot's catastrophic demise, is very sobering. Lot was so attached to the world that, though vexed by its violence and sin, he hung on to it for dear life right to the bitter end. Abraham was the righteous man of faith *par excellence*. But in Gerar his besetting sin overcame him and erased his witness.

Both their lives are ominous warnings to those in the train of faith, the church. It is entirely possible for the righteous through their sins to nullify their witness to the world permanently (as did Lot) or temporarily (as did Abraham).

As we know, it is never again recorded that Abraham descended to such deception, and his life increasingly became one of deep dependence on God, resulting in an ultimate display of faith: "By faith Abraham, when he was tested, offered up Isaac. . . . He considered that God was able even to raise him from the dead" (Hebrews 11:17-19).

GRACE (vv. 14-17)

All was not lost because of Abraham's lapse into a besetting sin. The remainder of the account drips with grace. Abimelech showered Abraham with gifts.

> *Then Abimelech took sheep and oxen, and male servants and female ser-vants, and gave them to Abraham, and returned Sarah his wife to him. And Abimelech said, "Behold, my land is before you; dwell where it pleases you." To Sarah he said, "Behold, I have given your brother a thousand pieces of silver. It is a sign of your innocence in the eyes of all who are with you, and before everyone you are vindicated." (vv. 14-16)*

In offering Abraham land, the king removed Abraham's alien status. It was now impossible for Abraham to fear in Gerar. The thousand shekels of silver was an awesome monetary gift. Fifty shekels was the most that could be offered for a bride. This was the price of twenty brides! Abraham's folly was met by amazing grace.

And grace also went out to Abimelech. "Then Abraham prayed to God, and God healed Abimelech, and also healed his wife and female slaves so that they bore children. For the LORD had closed all the wombs of the house of Abimelech because of Sarah, Abraham's wife" (vv. 17, 18). Perhaps this healing grace was a demonstration and precursor of grace to some in that Philistine village. Certainly they saw the awesome power of God.

And there was graced hope for Sarah as well. Some years earlier Sarah had said, "Behold now, the LORD has prevented [literally, "closed"] me from bearing children" (16:2). And now her words were echoed in the final words of the account: "For the LORD had closed all the wombs of the house of Abimelech because of Sarah, Abraham's wife" (v. 18).

Certainly the Lord could open Sarah's womb just as he did for the Philistine women. Sarah, take heart — Laughter is coming soon!

Iain Duguid's study of Abraham, *Living in the Gap Between Promise and Reality*, makes this observation:

> God's ability to use even our sins for his own purposes shows that he doesn't love us simply for the great things we can do for him. There's an additional verse to the children's hymn "Jesus Loves Me" that we don't sing very often, but that captures this aspect of God's love perfectly:
>
> > *Jesus loves me when I'm good,*
> > *When I do the things I should.*
> > *Jesus loves me when I'm bad,*
> > *Though it makes him very sad.*[4]

It is so common to think that God will love us more if we perform some great work, some external achievement. But the Bible (and here the story of Abraham and Abimelech) focuses on making a great heart. Here God was working in Abraham to create an unusual dependence upon him, because "He chose and used somebodies only when they renounced dependence on their natural abilities and resources."[5]

This is why God's plan so often seems to be different from our own script for our lives. The stress that comes when you are doing your best to serve God — the interruptions that plague your prayers — the family times that are ruined by illness — the letter to a missionary that gets lost — in these, you wanted to do something for God. But even more, he is doing something in your heart.

Duguid concludes:

> One of the ways in which he does that is by showing us, and others, our sin. Often that will be embarrassing for us, even humiliating, especially if we are in positions of Christian leadership. But in that way he gives us an opportunity to repent publicly, to speak plainly about the gospel that is the only hope for sinners like us. Jesus loves us when we are bad, as well as when we are good, and our public sins give us ample opportunity to testify to that amazing fact.[6]

The story of Abraham and Abimelech showcases the grace and goodness of God to his sinful children as God works to develop great hearts. Let us offer deep praise to our good God.

35

Two Laughters

GENESIS 21:1-34

The first car my wife, Barbara, and I purchased after our marriage was a pale green 1959 Volkswagen. Perhaps some of you recall the factory color, a kind of washed-out, pea-soup green. The car's color had been further dulled by oxidation and sixty thousand miles of road film. How pleased and proud I was to find that a little rubbing compound and lots of elbow grease could make that old Beetle shine — still a pale, pea-soup color, but lustrous and shiny — absolutely VW cool. I also discovered that the paint required regular attention, and I gave it.

Like many everyday things in life, my experiences suggested some spiritual wisdom to my budding preacher's mind — namely, that as believers who are indwelt by Christ we have the inner potential to shine for him. In fact, Christ calls us to do so (cf. Matthew 5:14-16). However, as we go through life, the sheen gets dulled by the road film we accumulate from our self-centeredness, unconfessed sin, and worldly accretions. And chief among God's ways of bringing out the shine is the buffing function of trials, which cause us to see ourselves for what we are and then cause us to confess our sins and turn to him. The result, of course, is a renewed, buffed-out luster that shines with the character of Christ. The abiding truth is that for every believer, the frictions of adversity are used to polish the soul. As King David said, "Before I was afflicted I went astray, but now I keep your word" (Psalm 119:67), and "It is good for me that I was afflicted, that I might learn your statutes" (v. 71).

This process of knocking off our rough edges and polishing our character through repeated trials and buffetings is as old as Father Abraham and his father's fathers. Though Abraham's character and devotion to God towered over that of Lot, he had his weaknesses. His capitulation to Sarah's insistence that he take her servant girl Hagar as a wife demonstrated a lack of faith in God's word, not to mention an abdication of his patriarchal leadership (cf. 16:2b and 3:17a). Most recently, he had tried to pass Sarah off as his sister to the Philistine king Abimelech to save his own skin, and this was not the first time he had tried that ploy (cf. 12:10-20). Pagan Abimelech had rightly taken the moral high ground in reproving Abraham. Abraham's failure, his failure to shine, was the cloud that preceded Genesis 21:1-34. But the patriarch was in process. And from here on he began to shine ever brighter. The present chapter records both Abraham's and Sarah's growth in grace as he moved toward his ultimate test.

We must understand that Abraham was a believer, the father of the faithful, "the man of faith" (Galatians 3:9). "He believed the LORD, and he counted it to him as righteousness" (Genesis 15:6). Works follow faith. But Abraham was saved by faith, not by works (Romans 4:2, 3).

As a man of faith, Abraham was subject to a polishing process (so to speak) whereby God worked through the ups and downs of life (awful times and blessed times) to make him more and more godly and more usable to God. The process was one of grace from beginning to end.

As believers, saved by grace through faith, we are subject to the same gracious polishing. Genesis 21 is for believers, not for humanity at large. In general, people often become stronger through hardships. But this is about grace to serve.

ISAAC'S ARRIVAL A GRACE (vv. 1-7)

This account opens on a soaring note. "The LORD visited Sarah as he had said, and the LORD did to Sarah as he had promised. And Sarah conceived and bore Abraham a son in his old age at the time of which God had spoken to him" (vv. 1, 2).

Sarah's pregnancy was, at the time, certainly the most celebrated of all pregnancies. Pregnant at ninety with baby number one! It was, of course, initially her secret — and then she informed Abraham in hushed excitement. Did Sarah at first try to hide her pregnancy from the camp? She may well have been too sick to hide anything! Besides, everyone knew everything in Tent City. Sarah went on to radiant full-bloom and then to the discomforts of full-term. All the preparations had been long made when her labor began — at four score and ten years. When the baby's cry rose across the camp, there were tears and festive shouts that all would long remember.

God had been faithful to his word. This is stressed three times in the first two verses so that we would not miss it. "The LORD visited Sarah *as he had said*, and the LORD did to Sarah *as he had promised*. And Sarah conceived and bore Abraham a son in his old age *at the time of which God had spoken to him*" (vv. 1, 2, emphasis added). Specifically God had told

Abraham a year earlier that Sarah would bear a son within a year and that he was to name the son "Isaac" (cf. 17:15-22, esp. v. 21). Abraham had laughed at this revelation with incredulous belief. Sarah laughed too as she overheard a second assertion that she would give birth within a year (cf. 18:10-15, esp. v. 12).

But now both Abraham and Sarah knew that God had been faithful in every detail of his word. The birth of Isaac was a precise, empirical validation of God's promise. A ninety-year-old mother (the only ninety-year-old nursing mother in history!) and her baby boy bore proud evidence. Thus here in Genesis we get a sampling of what has been the experience of God's people in all ages: *God is true to his word.* Jesus would declare, "Truly, I say to you, until heaven and earth pass away, not an iota, not a dot, will pass from the Law until all is accomplished" (Matthew 5:18). This solemn declaration by the One who is himself the "Yes" to all the promises of Scripture (2 Corinthians 1:20) means that you and I can, and must, trust every syllable of God's word. This is the way every Christian is meant to live — in deepest trust in all of God's word — just as Jesus lived.

The depth of Abraham's joyous belief was immediately evident in his naming and circumcising the child. "Abraham called the name of his son who was born to him, whom Sarah bore him, Isaac. And Abraham circumcised his son Isaac when he was eight days old, as God had commanded him. Abraham was a hundred years old when his son Isaac was born to him" (vv. 3-5). The divinely given name Isaac means "laughter," and the name recalls the initial incredulity of the parents at the idea that a son would be born within a year. As to Abraham, the earlier account says, "Then Abraham fell on his face and laughed and said to himself, 'Shall a child be born to a man who is a hundred years old? Shall Sarah, who is ninety years old, bear a child?'" (Genesis 17:17). God countered by further informing him that his son's name would be Isaac ("laughter") (17:19, 21). God would have the last laugh, so to speak.

Next, when Sarah heard that she was to give birth within a year, she too laughed. This brought a divine challenge. "The LORD said to Abraham, 'Why did Sarah laugh and say, "Shall I indeed bear a child, now that I am old?" Is anything too hard for the LORD? At the appointed time I will return to you about this time next year, and Sarah shall have a son.' But Sarah denied it, saying, 'I did not laugh,' for she was afraid. He said, 'No, but you did laugh'" (18:13-15). Their son Laughter was coming.

And now new mother Sarah gave a joyous utterance that had the form of a song:[1] "And Sarah said, 'God has made laughter for me; everyone who hears will laugh over me.' And she said, 'Who would have said to Abraham that Sarah would nurse children? Yet I have borne him a son in his old age'" (vv. 6, 7). There was laughter everywhere. The old man and his wife laughed and continued to laugh as they held tiny Laughter in their arms. Baby Isaac cooed and laughed. The camp chuckled out loud. Heaven smiled.

The true heir of the Abrahamic covenant had been born. Isaac was the first person reported to have been circumcised at birth. His spiritual destiny was therefore separate from that of Ishmael who was circumcised at age thirteen.[2] Grace rained down on Abraham and his people. God had kept his word. They had obeyed, and their hearts sang.

And their faith went even deeper. From the onset Abraham had believed God. That is why he left Ur and later gave Lot his choice of the land and then went after the kings of the north when they kidnapped Lot. But now Abraham was ascending to such a level of unwavering belief that God would keep his word that later Abraham would be willing to sacrifice his Laughter, his Isaac.

ISHMAEL'S DEPARTURE A GRACE (vv. 8-21)

Predictably, with the demise of Ishmael's heirship the rise of baby Isaac's star soon followed. Isaac's name has appeared three times in Genesis 21, while Ishmael's never once appears, though he is a central subject.

Another laughter. By verse 8 we know that at least three years had passed, because that was the traditional time for weaning a child in ancient Israel (see 1 Samuel 1:23ff.; cf. 2 Maccabees 7:27 in the Apocrypha). Isaac was a toddler. And Ishmael was about sixteen years of age.

Tellingly, the account contains a new instance of laughter because the word "mocking" (v. 9, NIV; ESV, "laughing") is actually an intensive form of Isaac's name — the verb "to laugh." Here Ishmael, firstborn but not Abraham's heir, laughs. As Moses recorded this, "And the child [Isaac] grew and was weaned. And Abraham made a great feast on the day that Isaac was weaned. But Sarah saw the son of Hagar the Egyptian, whom she had borne to Abraham, laughing. So she said to Abraham, 'Cast out this slave woman with her son, for the son of this slave woman shall not be heir with my son Isaac'" (vv. 8-10). Here the NIV's "mocking" rightly catches the malicious sense of the laughter because Paul in Galatians 4:29 says that Ishmael "persecuted" Isaac.[3] Understandably, young Ishmael felt jealousy at being displaced. Envy always magnifies the importance of the other and belittles our own.

Ishmael's mocking laughter does not suggest violence, but Sarah imagines the ominous trajectory and proportions to which the laughter could go. However, there is simply no warrant for thinking that Sarah was acting righteously here. She had no affections for Hagar and Ishmael, even though they had been a part of the family for years. Nor did she seem to care at all what happened to them. Sarah was a noble woman (cf. 1 Peter 3:6), and her instincts were sound. But her actions at that time were far from noble. Sarah would brook no possible sharing of the inheritance. She wanted the problem uprooted and cast away.

Abraham was, of course, distressed. Ishmael was his son and had been the sole focus of his fatherly love until the arrival of Isaac. What heartache. How welcome, then, God's intervention must have been! "But God said to Abraham, 'Be not displeased because of the boy and because of your slave woman. Whatever Sarah says to you, do as she tells you, for through Isaac shall your offspring be named. And I will make a nation of the son of the slave woman also, because he is your offspring'" (vv. 12, 13). Abraham's breaking heart was comforted by the promise that great futures awaited both his boys. Isaac was the one through whom the promise would be realized. And Ishmael would father a great nation. Both boys had prodigious futures.

God was graciously addressing the self-created mess of Abraham and Sarah because he "was taking up the tangled threads of His servant's life, weaving them into his own divine pattern, and overruling everything for good" (Griffith Thomas).[4] This is God's way. This is what would later be realized in Joseph's life when he addressed his brothers: "you meant evil against me, but God meant it for good" (Genesis 50:20). The truth is, without affliction and hardship we would be trivial, superficial, flat-sided beings — people without depth or substance — with shallow faith. This truth is a life-changing revelation when taken to heart. God works in and through the vicissitudes of life to mature our faith. Take this to heart!

Separation and provision. Hagar and Ishmael's bleak departure the next morning with only Abraham bidding farewell — and then their apparent tragic end in the wilds of the desert as Ishmael lay dying a bowshot away from his distraught mother — was a prelude to divine grace. Ishmael, like Isaac after him, was saved by a sudden voice from Heaven (vv. 17, 18; cf. 22:11). God promised an awesome posterity to the boy: "A great nation" (v. 18) would come through him. God informed Hagar of a well of water, a well of salvation, close by. And God declared himself to be "with the boy" (v. 20).

Specific graces had fallen. The separation left Isaac free to pursue the promise of the land and his call to a special relationship with God — a necessary grace. And God's protecting hand rested on Ishmael from then on as he pursued a life separate and distinct from the patriarchs — a grace also. And there was grace upon Abraham's soul as God was preparing him for an ultimate act of faith when he would offer up Isaac on Mt. Moriah.

GRACE AT BEERSHEBA (vv. 22-34)

The chapter ends with another meeting between Abraham and Abimelech. The encounters with Abimelech recorded earlier in chapter 20 and here in chapter 21 serve as bookends to this section. In the first encounter Abraham disgraced himself, but now he stood tall and was respected as Abimelech sought Abraham's favor.

> *At that time Abimelech and Phicol the commander of his army said to Abraham, "God is with you in all that you do. Now therefore swear to me here by God that you will not deal falsely with me or with my descendants or with my posterity, but as I have dealt kindly with you, so you will deal with me and with the land where you have sojourned." And Abraham said, "I will swear." (vv. 22-24)*

Abraham had risen from disgrace to having a positive witness for God. The Philistine's observation, "God is with you" says it all. And Abraham, in response to his imploring, swore to a nonaggression pact. Abraham had now set the "God is with you" standard that would also become that of Isaac (26:28), Jacob (30:27), and Joseph (39:3).

Resolution of conflict. Abraham also now had a new sense of confidence. He no longer was timid and evasive in dealing with royalty. Thus Abraham put Abimelech's nonaggression proposal to the test by charging that Abimelech's servants were stealing one of his wells. The result was the Treaty of Beersheba, in which Abimelech acknowledged the well to be Abraham's by receiving seven of Abraham's lambs and making a solemn oath (vv. 25-31). Abimelech then went back to his own people in peace (cf. v. 32).

And Abraham? "Abraham planted a tamarisk tree in Beersheba and called there on the name of the LORD, the Everlasting God. And Abraham sojourned many days in the land of the Philistines" (vv. 33, 34). His planting of the tree was a symbol of fruitfulness and prosperity. Abraham memorialized God as the source of his prosperity.[5] It also demonstrated his rootedness in the land where he indeed stayed "many days." The title "Everlasting God" (*el olam*) as a divine designation is unique in the Bible. Abraham's use of it has to do with the eternal nature of the events in chapters 20, 21 — namely, Isaac's birth and a covenant relationship that is eternal. Abraham's God was the Everlasting One whose will for man cannot be thwarted.[6] This awesome view of God would now inform all of Abraham's dealings. It was this exalted understanding that would be tested in his offering up of Isaac, and that also would help him to stand.

There had been grace in the birth of Isaac, grace in the departure of Ishmael, and grace in the treaty of Beersheba.

The grinding and polishing of old Abraham had been going on for years. The frictions of adversity had been polishing his soul. And it was becoming luminous. And it is going to dazzle us with divine light! But what about us? Frederick Buechner writes:

> We believe in God — such as it is, we have faith. . . . We work and goof
> off, we love and dream, we have wonderful times and awful times, are
> cruelly hurt and hurt others cruelly, get mad and bored and scared stiff
> and ache with desire, do all such human things as these, and if our faith is
> not mainly just window dressing or a rabbit's foot or fire insurance, it is
> because it grows out of precisely this kind of rich human compost.[7]

Faith does not grow in a hothouse but in the unpredictable climates of
life. When we believe and step out in faith to follow Christ, we step into a
process in time and space under the tutelage and sovereign direction of
God, a process that is meant to pour repeated mercies and graces into our
lives, which then make us more and more able to rest everything in Christ
and therefore live even more for his glory.

This was true for scheming, grasping Jacob who, after wrestling with
God, was a changed man whom God renamed "Israel" (cf. Genesis 32:28-31).

The same was true for Moses who after his flight for killing an Egyptian
spent forty years in the wilderness and emerged to lead Israel as a man who
was "very meek, more than all people who were on the face of the earth"
(Numbers 12:3).

Job was a man who was "blameless and upright, one who feared God
and turned away from evil" (Job 1:1). But after his long afflictions he said
of his spiritual growth, "I had heard of you by the hearing of the ear, but
now my eye sees you" (42:5).

In Jesus' time Peter's innate confidence in his own abilities caused him
to declare to Christ, "I will lay down my life for you" (John 13:37). But
after his failure (cf. Luke 22:60-62) came his great faith and strength as displayed from Pentecost onward to his death.

The Apostle Paul's given name was Saul, after Israel's proud warrior
king. But following his conversion he renamed himself *Paulos*/Paul, which
means "small" — as a witness to what the gospel and life's disciplines had
taught him.

This was true for Jacob, true for Job, true for Moses, true for David,
and true for Peter and Paul. Our calling, like that of those who have gone
before, is to submit to the friction and polishing for what it is — the sweet
grace of God.

36

The Lord Will Provide

GENESIS 22:1-19

Abraham's life of faith was launched when he left Ur in obedience to God's promise that he would make Abram into a great nation and bless him and that all the nations of the earth would be blessed through him (cf. Genesis 12:1-3). Over the years that great promise was repeated and reiterated with remarkable drama and specificity. At the onset, as Abram, fresh from Ur, traveled through central Canaan, the Lord appeared to him, promising the land to his offspring, and there the patriarch built an altar in the heart of the land (cf. 12:7). Next, after Lot separated from Abram and took for himself the best portion of the land, God commanded Abram from Ramath Nazor (the highest spot in central Israel) to look north, south, east, and west — promising everything in the 360-degree radius to Abram's offspring forever, also indicating that his children would number like the dust of the earth (cf. 13:14-17).

Sometime later, after Abram had rescued Lot from the kings of the north and lay fretting one night over his childless state, God dramatically promised him an heir. God took Abram out under the stars and challenged him to look up and count them, if he could. Then God said to Abram, "So shall your offspring be" (15:5). Awed and humbled, Abram was silent under the stars. But the Scripture speaks for him: "And he believed the LORD, and he counted it to him as righteousness" (v. 6). Abram said a silent amen to the promise of God. He was absolutely sure that he would have a son. "Faith is the assurance of things hoped for" (Hebrews 11:1).

The next day Abram obeyed God's directives as God told him to arrange the parts of slain animals for a covenantal sacrifice. And when the sun set, God appeared as a flaming furnace radiating orange in the darkness. Then the glowing furnace moved — gliding down the macabre path lined with glistening animal parts (cf. vv. 17-21). Abram saw God *alone* pass between the pieces. This, then, was a unilateral, unconditional covenant that announced that if Abram's descendants did not get the land, God himself would be sundered. So we see that on succeeding nights Abram was assured first by God that a countless *people* would come from his body and then that the *land* would go to his people.

Years later, when Abram was ninety-nine years old and God was preparing Abraham's heart for the covenant of circumcision, God changed the patriarch's name from Abram to Abraham ("father of many"), again signifying that the old man would be fruitful and that nations and kings would come from him and that Canaan would be their possession (cf. 17:1-8). Sarai was also renamed Sarah, reaffirming her role as "princess" because she would have Abraham's son from whom kings would come — and ultimately the Lion of the tribe of Judah (cf. 49:10). God also named their yet-to-be-conceived son Isaac ("laughter"), promising that he would be born within a year (vv. 17-21). Upon bestowing these new names, circumcision (the sign of God's promise) was instituted, and Abraham and all his house were circumcised. Aged Sarah would also herself laugh at the promise, but baby Laughter was coming (cf. 18:10-15).

During those long years that the great promise of a people and a land and a blessing was being reiterated, Abraham's growth in faith had been uneven. Faith's mountaintops were always edged by dark valleys such as Abraham's identical lies to Pharaoh and Abimelech about Sarah and the Hagar affair, which precipitated some sixteen years of domestic misery. But with the birth of Isaac (and the necessary departure of Ishmael) and the treaty of Beersheba, Abraham was reassured of a people and a land. Abraham's faith in God's word therefore soared as evidenced by his calling upon the Lord as *El Olam*, "the Everlasting God." This designation of the Lord as Everlasting God or Enduring God says it all because it is evocative of the "stability, security, and permanence"[1] that Abraham now felt in the covenant and in his relationship with God.

The landmark statement and restatements of God's promise came, first, when Abraham first set foot in Canaan, second, when under the stars he believed the Lord, third, when he saw the fiery presence of God glide between the flayed parts, fourth, when he heard the renamings "Father of a multitude," "Princess," and "Laughter" and was circumcised, and finally when he and Sarah held baby Laughter in their arms and he called the Lord *El Olam* ("Everlasting God"). These restatements of the promise initiated Abraham's long, secure stay in the land of the Philistines (the promised land) — until the test.

The announcement in the opening line of chapter 22 that God was testing Abraham serves to cushion the reader from the shock that follows. How painful this story would be to read for the first time without the knowledge that it was a test. Also, the understanding that this is a test alerts us to the truth that growth in faith involves testing. As God tests our faith, it is stretched and thereby grows. Here Abraham's faith was going to be stretched to the utter limit, and because he held firm, his faith has become the grand faith-example in history. We see from this that the way to increase faith is to exercise faith. Trust God as you can, and he will give you so much more than you expected — and then you will trust him even more! It is also important to see that this test came *after* substantial spiritual growth and blessing. Abraham's recent success and growth was the ground for greater testing and growth.

We know it was a test, but Abraham did not — and the hearing of God's command must have been excruciating beyond words because it began with terms of family endearment: "Take your son, your only son Isaac, whom you love, and go to the land of Moriah" (v. 2a). He was Abraham's only son by virtue of Ishmael's departure some fourteen to sixteen years earlier. (Significantly the same word — "boy" (vv. 5, 12) — is here used for Isaac as was used for Ishmael when he was a teenager.) Teenager Isaac had been his laughter for a decade and a half. And as the child of the promise, everything was focused on him. Abraham loved him with aching parental love, the kind that hurts.

Those sweet, endearing terms are followed by unmitigated horror: "Offer him there as a burnt offering on one of the mountains of which I shall tell you" (v. 2b). Three simple unqualified imperatives — "Take," "go," "offer him" — are the bare structure of the command.[2] To an ancient Middle Easterner, "burnt offering" suggested a process: first cutting the offering's throat, then dismemberment, and then a sacrifice by fire in which the body parts were completely consumed on the altar. This is the horror Abraham imagined, with his own son the sacrifice. And more, it was not beyond the range of Abraham's experience or credulity. Human sacrifice took place in Ur, and it was also a part of Canaanite culture. Human sacrifice was therefore familiar to his conceptual worldview, however dumbfounding and repulsive it may have been to him.[3] Remember, he did not have the yet-to-be-written Torah to inform his worldview or his doctrine of God. Yet Abraham did not for a moment doubt God's command.

God was asking him to act against common sense, his natural affections, and his lifelong hope. The author does not tell us how Abraham felt. The reader will look in vain for an explicit indication of his inner thoughts. Moses leaves us to fill in the lines. The account is artfully minimalist. Also note that Abraham was told to do it with his own hands. Light had fled his life. Laughter was only a memory.

ABRAHAM'S OBEDIENCE (vv. 3-10)

Initial obedience. Astounded by God's command to Abraham, we are even more astounded by his immediate obedience. "So Abraham rose early in the morning, saddled his donkey, and took two of his young men with him, and his son Isaac. And he cut the wood for the burnt offering and arose and went to the place of which God had told him" (v. 3). At the crack of dawn he was up and at it. No hesitation whatsoever. However, there is a subtle hint that his sorrow may have numbed his mind, as Gordon Wenham notes, because of the order of action — first saddling his donkey and then cutting wood is illogical.[4] Though possibly disoriented, Abraham nevertheless obeyed with alacrity.

The wonders increase, because after three days' journey Abraham looked up and saw in the distance the place where he was to sacrifice Isaac and said to his two servants, "Stay here with the donkey; I and the boy will go over there and worship and come again to you" (v. 5). "I and the boy will . . . worship" was, of course, intentionally vague because "offer a burnt offering" could have raised further questions. What amazes us is that Abraham was totally sincere and convinced that after offering Isaac as a burnt offering they would return together.

We know this because the writer of Hebrews comments, "By faith Abraham, when he was tested, offered up Isaac, and he who had received the promises was in the act of offering up his only son, of whom it was said, 'Through Isaac shall your offspring be named.' He considered that God was able even to raise him from the dead, from which, figuratively speaking, he did receive him back" (Hebrews 11:17-19). Abraham so utterly believed God's promise that Isaac's children would carry on the bloodline that he reasoned that God would have to raise Isaac from the dead. Abraham envisioned the doctrine of the resurrection when as yet there had been nothing in history to suggest it. In this way he perhaps began to see Christ's day (cf. John 8:56). Here was a bold, original, informing faith!

Continuing obedience. The ascent to the place of sacrifice was too steep for the donkey. So "Abraham took the wood of the burnt offering and laid it on Isaac his son. And he took in his hand the fire and the knife" (v. 6a). Significantly the *Genesis Rabbah*, a pre-Christian Jewish midrash, commented that Isaac with the wood on his back was like a condemned man, carrying his own cross.[5] Indeed the image was truly prophetic of Jesus, who John's Gospel describes as "bearing his own cross, to the place called the place of a skull" (John 19:17).

The ascent, with the son carrying the wood and the father carrying the implements of sacrifice, evidently went on for a while in silence. "They went both of them together. And Isaac said to his father Abraham, 'My father!' And he said, 'Here am I, my son.' He said, 'Behold, the fire and the wood, but where is the lamb for a burnt offering?'" (vv. 6b, 7). Isaac's breaking the silence underscores the father's silent grief. The literal Hebrew parallel addresses — "my father"/"my son" — emphasizes their tender and mutual affection. And Isaac's question, "where is the lamb . . . ?" indicates not only his naivete but his absolute trust in his father. He did not have a hint of what awaited him. How could he? There was nothing in his short, joyous life to suggest it.

Isaac's trust also foreshadowed the greater partnership of the cross expressed in the familiar words of Isaiah 53: "He was oppressed, and he was afflicted, yet he opened not his mouth; like a lamb that is led to the slaughter, and like a sheep that before its shearers is silent, so he opened not his mouth" (v. 7). "Yet it was the will of the LORD to crush him; he has put him to grief; when his soul makes an offering for sin, he shall see his offspring; he shall prolong his days; the will of the LORD shall prosper in his hand" (v. 10). Here in our story, the descriptive "they went both of them together" (repeated in verses 6 and 8) twice emphasize the victim and the offerer willingly ascending the hill together — again a shadow of Calvary.

Abraham's immortal answer to Isaac — "God will provide for himself the lamb for a burnt offering, my son" (v. 8) — is the turning point of the story. "God will provide for himself" states Abraham's absolute trust in God but also allows for God to be God. Abraham cannot tell Isaac all that he would like to know because Abraham truly does not know what God will do. Abraham's "God will provide for himself" is at the same time a declaration of trust, an expression of hope, and a prophecy of the future. And it is breathed in a submissive spirit of prayer. As we shall see, Abraham's declaration of faith is going to effect a mighty echo in our doctrine of God. John Calvin wisely observes: "This example is for our imitation. . . . In such straits, the only remedy . . . is to leave the event to God, in order that he may open a way for us when there is none." Calvin concludes, "We pay Him the highest honour, when, in affairs of perplexity, we nevertheless entirely acquiesce to his providence."[6]

Ultimate obedience. One thing is very clear: Abraham could not have offered Isaac without Isaac's consent and cooperation. Isaac, as the bearer of the wood, was the stronger of the two. As a young man he was also the quickest and fastest of the two. Apparently Isaac had decided to obey his father whatever the cost, just as his father had decided to obey God whatever the cost. Perhaps Abraham persuaded Isaac by rehearsing the story of his son's supernatural birth and then by enumerating the reaffirmations of the great promises to him and therefore reasoning that God would have restored Isaac to life, even though his body was reduced to ashes. The father's faith was alive in his son! They were heroes in soul.

In quick order Abraham built an altar, arranged the wood into a proper pyre, bound his beloved son hand and foot so that he might not flee in sudden fear, hoisted him up on the wood, and then reached for the blade. His trembling fingers convulsed as they tightened about the handle for the sacrificial cut. True faith produces amazing works. Real faith is a faith that works, just as the Apostle James said in referencing Abraham's sacrifice:

Was not Abraham our father justified by works when he offered up his son Isaac on the altar? You see that faith was active along with his works, and faith was completed by his works; and the Scripture was fulfilled that says, "Abraham believed God, and it was counted to him as righteousness" — and he was called a friend of God. You see that a person is justified by works and not by faith alone. (2:21-24)

DIVINE RESPONSE (vv. 11-18)

Divine intervention. Abraham's will was in motion. In a split second the sacrifice would be done. "But the angel of the LORD called to him from heaven and said, 'Abraham, Abraham!' And he said, 'Here am I.' He said, 'Do not lay your hand on the boy or do anything to him, for now I know that you fear God, seeing you have not withheld your son, your only son, from me'" (vv. 11, 12). Never was there a more welcome voice! Abraham's old heart soared, as did that of young Isaac.

Divine provision. The hearing of God's voice and Abraham's seeing a substitute offering took place in an instant because the account says that "Abraham lifted up his eyes and looked, and behold, behind him was a ram, caught in a thicket by his horns. And Abraham went and took the ram and offered it up as a burnt offering instead of his son" (v. 13). Never was there a more joyous and eager sacrifice. As the flames consumed the ram, Abraham and Isaac were offering their hearts to God. The burnt offering declared to God, "All we have and all we are, God, is upon the altar. Consume our lives to your glory."

In ecstasy "Abraham called the name of that place, 'The LORD will provide'; as it is said to this day, 'On the mount of the LORD it shall be provided'" (v. 14). His initially ambiguous, "God will provide" (v. 8) had now been fulfilled more perfectly than he had ever dreamed. Abraham's declaration of faith — "God will provide" — as he and Isaac ascended toward sacrifice had now become the story's end. We see that the God who tests is also the God who provides — the Tester is the Provider. Both truths are actual fact, but they must be appropriated by faith. When God tests you, he will provide for you.

So we see that the Lord who tests is the Lord who provides. That is what we need to see about God. As we go through the tests of growing a greater faith, as God tests us and stretches us, we believe, and he provides. He always has provided. He provides for every believer. He always has. So when we are called to give our "Isaacs" — those things that are most precious to us — we need to understand when we do it that God is *Jehovah Jireh* — God provides.

Divine oath. Abraham's extraordinary act of faith prompted God to do something that he had never before done. He swore an oath by his *own* name.

And the angel of the LORD called to Abraham a second time from heaven and said, "By myself I have sworn, declares the LORD, because you have done this and have not withheld your son, your only son, I will surely bless you, and I will surely multiply your offspring as the stars of heaven and as the sand that is on the seashore. And your offspring shall possess the gate of his enemies, and in your offspring shall all the nations of the earth be blessed, because you have obeyed my voice." (vv. 15-18)

With this oath Abraham had every possible assurance from God — the initial promise made to him in Ur, the promise made to him when he first visited Canaan, the promise made to him again when Lot took the best land, the promise that he believed under the stars, the promise confirmed by God's unilateral covenant when his flaming presence passed through the sacrifice, the promise in the new names (Abraham, Sarah, and Isaac), and the promise in the person of Isaac himself.

And now God had sworn an oath by himself that every promise would come to pass! Again the writer of Hebrews explains the weight of God's action: "For when God made a promise to Abraham, since he had no one greater by whom to swear, he swore by himself, saying, 'Surely I will bless you and multiply you.' And thus Abraham, having patiently waited, obtained the promise" (Hebrews 6:13-15).

The great encouragement is, God always keeps his word. He keeps every word — every promise of God is kept. God has sworn — he keeps his promises. He has made a unilateral covenant. He will be flayed before his word is not carried out.

From here on, it is only necessary to refer back to this oath to say all that needs to be said about the promises of God.

It is all so simple. We grow in faith as we believe the bare word of God. The process is this: God comes to us with his word, and we are challenged to believe. When we believe his word, he tests us by stretching our faith so it can grow to greater dimensions than before. There are always valleys next to the hilltops of faith. There are ups and downs. But God grows our faith incrementally, so that we are enabled to give our "Isaacs" to God.

37

Promise and Purchase

GENESIS 23:1-20

Among my treasured memories of growing up on the West Coast is attending the seventy-fifth wedding anniversary of Grandpa and Grandma Bandy, aged ninety-seven and ninety-eight. When it was my turn to congratulate them, Grandpa Bandy took my hand in his old working-man's hands and drawing me close whispered, "Seventy-five years is a long time to be married to one woman." After a dramatic pause came the punch line — "this close to Hollywood!"

When Sarah died, we calculate that Abraham and Sarah had been married well over a hundred years, and we know that it had been exactly sixty-two years since she and Abraham had left Ur. According to the opening line of our text, "Sarah lived 127 years; these were the years of the life of Sarah. And Sarah died at Kiriath-arba (that is, Hebron) in the land of Canaan, and Abraham went in to mourn for Sarah and to weep for her" (vv. 1, 2). Sarah had died in the very heart of the promised land, leaving her bereaved husband at age 127 and her Isaac at thirty-seven years.

Sarah had been Abraham's soul-mate on his epic journey from Ur to Canaan and then down to Egypt and back again as they sojourned in and around the promised land. Sarah was at hand for every pinnacle of Abraham's life — the repeated covenant promises; the defeat of the invading coalition of kings and Abraham's victorious return when he was greeted by Melchizidek, king of Salem; the covenant of circumcision and the dramatic renamings; Abraham's intercession for Sodom; and, of course, the offering of Isaac. Sarah was also there for all Abraham's failures as she was twice cajoled into complicity in perpetrating the deception that she was not his wife but his sister. And, of course, she was principal to some failures of her own — in the Hagar affair and mocking the Lord's promise of

Isaac. But above it all, in her old age she had been the mother of Laughter, the son of promise.

In and through all of this Sarah was a woman of faith. The prophet Isaiah urged his countrymen to "look to the rock from which you were hewn, and to the quarry from which you were dug. Look to Abraham your father and to Sarah who bore you" (51:1, 2). Similarly, the writer of Hebrews includes Sarah in the list of the faithful (11:11). Abraham and Sarah had been soul-mates in the journey of faith for over sixty years. And when Abraham offered Isaac, they had together learned that "The LORD will provide" — Jehovah-Jireh — that this is God's pattern in dealing with his people. God tests, and then God provides. The faith of the old couple was brilliantly informed and reformed in those post-Moriah years as young Isaac grew to full manhood.

Now Sarah, Abraham's princess, his soul-mate of over a century, was dead. The pall of death enshrouds this passage. It begins with "Sarah died" and ends with "Abraham buried Sarah his wife" and is laced in between with variations of "bury . . . dead" seven times. Sarah's death was a numbing blow to Abraham, "and Abraham went in to mourn for Sarah and to weep for her" (v. 2). His tears were not perfunctory. Abraham cried aloud over his princess, the wife of his youth.

The death of a loved one has always been a time to think about the eternal. The Preacher (Solomon) would write, "It is better to go to the house of mourning than to go to the house of feasting, for this is the end of all mankind, and the living will lay it to heart" (Ecclesiastes 7:2). Sarah's passing pierced him afresh with his temporal status as a "stranger and exile" (Hebrews 11:13) not only in Hittite culture but in the very land promised to him.

Sarah had died in the land, in Hebron, the heart of the promised land, without receiving the promised land. Indeed, she was first among generations who would die without receiving the promise (cf. Hebrews 11:13). Clearly the promise of the land was not going to be effected in Abraham's lifetime either. Nevertheless, in the face of Sarah's death Abraham believed the promise with all his heart. At Sarah's side, the echoes of God's voice reverberated afresh in his mind: "To your offspring I will give this land" (12:7). "All the land that you see I will give to you and to your offspring forever" (13:15). "Arise, walk through the length and the breadth of the land, for I will give it to you" (13:17). "To your offspring I give this land, from the river of Egypt to the great river, the river Euphrates" (15:18). "And I will give to you and to your offspring after you the land of your sojournings, all the land of Canaan, for an everlasting possession" (17:8).

There was no doubt at all in Abraham's mind that the land would go to his descendants. What ought he to do? Kneeling next to his wife, a mighty resolve welled in his soul.

SARAH'S TOMB PURCHASED IN HEBRON (vv. 3-16)

Abraham requests a burial site. "And Abraham rose up from before his dead and said to the Hittites, 'I am a sojourner and foreigner among you; give me property among you for a burying place, that I may bury my dead out of my sight'" (vv. 3, 4). Abraham was so sure that his descendants would get the land that he wanted Sarah's bones to be there when they got there! By owning a part of the land he was prophesying its ultimate ownership. "The legal action of a purchase was a full investment in a promise against the present circumstance" (Brueggemann).[1] His beloved wife's body entombed in Hebron, the center of the land, was his public stake in God's promise — against all present appearances.

Abraham saw far beyond the present. "By faith he went to live in the land of promise, as in a foreign land, living in tents with Isaac and Jacob, heirs with him of the same promise. For he was looking forward to the city that has foundations, whose designer and builder is God" (Hebrews 11:9, 10). So it is with us. "Our citizenship is in heaven, and from it we await a Savior, the Lord Jesus Christ" (Philippians 3:20). Abraham's bold example calls us to the same unflinching faith! The deaths that touch our lives, especially those that are close to us, are meant to make us look by faith beyond the present material world to the architectures of Heaven, to the eternal foundations laid by God.

The Hittites,[2] the dominant group in Canaan at that time, were quick to answer, "Hear us, my lord; you are a prince of God among us. Bury your dead in the choicest of our tombs. None of us will withhold from you his tomb to hinder you from burying your dead" (vv. 5, 6). The answer was at once high-mannered and insincere. No one had any intention of giving Abraham anything for free.

Yet, at the same time, calling Abraham "a prince of God among us" does indicate respect, even if a bit disingenuous. And for us it suggests a deep spiritual truth — namely, that the landless sojourner is the true heir of the promises of God and is "a prince of God."[3] This public recognition of Abraham's greatness by pagan Canaanites foreshadowed the covenant promise of blessing to all the nations.[4]

Abraham secures a burial site. Abraham's request initiated a customary protocol indicated by his bowing and asking for Ephron's cave at Machpelah (Abraham bows nowhere else to anyone in Canaan).

> *Abraham rose and bowed to the Hittites, the people of the land. And he said to them, "If you are willing that I should bury my dead out of my sight, hear me and entreat for me Ephron the son of Zohar, that he may give me the cave of Machpelah, which he owns; it is at the end of his field. For the full price let him give it to me in your presence as property for a burying*

place." Now Ephron was sitting among the Hittites, and Ephron the Hittite
answered Abraham in the hearing of the Hittites, of all who went in at the
gate of his city, "No, my lord, hear me: I give you the field, and I give you
the cave that is in it. In the sight of the sons of my people I give it to you.
Bury your dead." (vv. 7-11)

Despite his three "I gives" Ephron was extorting Abraham. All Abraham
wanted was the cave, but Ephron added the field. More real estate, more
money! Abraham knew it, but there was nothing he could do. Abraham had
been sincere in his offer to pay "full price" (literally, "full silver") for the
grave, but Ephron had just a wee bit more in mind.

Following the elaborate protocol, "Abraham bowed down before the
people of the land. And he said to Ephron in the hearing of the people of the
land, 'But if you will, hear me: I give the price of the field. Accept it from me,
that I may bury my dead there.' Ephron answered Abraham, 'My lord, listen to me: a piece of land worth four hundred shekels of silver, what is that
between you and me? Bury your dead'" (vv. 12-15).

If Abraham had been given to quick retorts, he could have answered
Ephron's "What is that between you and me?" with "A whole lot, Ephron!
You're taking me to the cleaners." Indeed, four hundred shekels of silver was
extortionate. During patriarchal times the shekel was a weight, not a coin.
Coinage was not invented until centuries later.[5] Four hundred shekels of sil-
ver was about six and a quarter pounds of silver.

Ephron likely anticipated that Abraham would bow again and make a
counteroffer. But Abraham accepted Ephron's price. And note well that the
patriarch got just what he wanted. First, the deal was transacted in the gate
of Ephron the Hittite's city, in full public view and full disclosure. Second,
the agreement was struck in the hearing of all the Hittites, who watched as
the six plus pounds of silver were measured out "according to the weights
current among the merchants" (v. 16) — that is, in strict conformity to the
practices that were common in the business world of that day. Third, the price
was high, so that no subsequent Hittite could dispute Abraham's ownership. And furthermore, no price was too high for a resting place for his
bride and princess. All was done with patriarchal dignity.

SARAH'S BURIAL IN HEBRON (vv. 17-20)

As it turned out, Abraham purchased considerably more property than the
cave he initially sought.

So the field of Ephron in Machpelah, which was to the east of Mamre, the
field with the cave that was in it and all the trees that were in the field,
throughout its whole area, was made over to Abraham as a possession in

the presence of the Hittites, before all who went in at the gate of his city. After this, Abraham buried Sarah his wife in the cave of the field of Machpelah east of Mamre (that is, Hebron) in the land of Canaan. The field and the cave that is in it were made over to Abraham as property for a burying place by the Hittites. (vv. 17-20)

In this way a large burial plot was ceded to Abraham and his descendants. The cave of Machpelah has never been conclusively identified, though the traditional tomb of Sarah and the patriarchs is located beneath the Mosque of Abraham, a Muslim shrine in Hebron, and is not open to modern investigation.[6]

From Sarah's time on, the cave at Machpelah became an ossuary, a depository for the bones of the patriarchs. By insisting that their bones be buried in Canaan, the patriarchs gave their last and ultimate witness to the promise. As Calvin so well put it, "While they themselves were silent (in death) . . . the sepulchre cried aloud, that death formed no obstacle to their entering in possession of it."[7]

Machpelah in Hebron became a monument to Abraham's faith in God's sure word of promise.

• By faith Abraham believed God's promise that his descendants would inherit the land (cf. 12:1-3; 13:14-17; 15:17-21; 17:3-8).

• By faith Abraham sojourned in the land for almost a century, living as one to whom it would belong (cf. 13:7, 8; 18:1; 21:34).

• By faith Abraham purchased the cave at Machpelah in Hebron (23:19, 20).

• By faith Abraham buried Sarah in the cave at Hebron (23:19, 20).

• By faith Isaac buried Abraham with Sarah at Hebron (Genesis 25:9).

• By faith Jacob buried his father Isaac at Hebron (cf. 49:31).

• By faith, while in Egypt, Jacob charged his sons to bury him in Hebron (cf. 49:29, 30).

• By faith Jacob's sons had him embalmed and took his remains to Hebron for burial (cf. 50:1, 2, 12-14).

• By faith, as the very last lines in Genesis record, "Then Joseph made the sons of Israel swear, saying, 'God will surely visit you, and you shall carry up my bones from here.' So Joseph died, being 110 years old. They embalmed him, and he was put in a coffin in Egypt" (50:25, 26).

• By faith Moses, 430 years later, at the exodus took Joseph's bones up out of Egypt (cf. Exodus 13:19) and then for forty years bore his mummified remains throughout Israel's wanderings.

• By faith when Joshua conquered the promised land, he buried Joseph's body in fulfillment of the same principle in a plot of land earlier purchased by Joseph's father Jacob (cf. Joshua 24:32).

It is of abiding spiritual significance that two of the twelve spies sent out to scout the promised land *after* visiting Hebron (cf. Numbers 13:21, 22) declared it could be taken. Those two men were Joshua and Caleb, men of faith (Numbers 14:5-9). Later by faith Caleb, at eighty-five years of age, took Hebron (cf. Joshua 14:6-15). Hear his words of faith:

> *I am still as strong today as I was in the day that Moses sent me; my strength now is as my strength was then, for war and for going and coming. So now give me this hill country of which the LORD spoke on that day, for you heard on that day how the Anakim were there, with great fortified cities. It may be that the LORD will be with me, and I shall drive them out just as the LORD said. (Joshua 14:11, 12)*

Ultimately David was anointed king over the house of Judah in Hebron (cf. 2 Samuel 2:3, 4). Thus we see that the bones of the patriarchs shouted from the cave of Machpelah that God would give Israel the land — which then culminated through the lives of Joshua and David and David's son Solomon.

We must keep in mind that though Abraham bought the tomb for Sarah in the heart of the promised land as a declaration of his faith in the promise, he was not looking for an earthly homeland for himself. Hebrews, speaking of the faith of Abel, Enoch, Noah, and Abraham, says:

> *These all died in faith, not having received the things promised, but having seen them and greeted them from afar, and having acknowledged that they were strangers and exiles on the earth. For people who speak thus make it clear that they are seeking a homeland. If they had been thinking of that land from which they had gone out, they would have had opportunity to return. But as it is, they desire a better country, that is, a heavenly one. Therefore God is not ashamed to be called their God, for he has prepared for them a city. (Hebrews 11:13-16)*

Specifically, Hebrews says of Abraham, "By faith he went to live in the land of promise, as in a foreign land, living in tents with Isaac and Jacob, heirs with him of the same promise. For he was looking forward to the city that has foundations, whose designer and builder is God" (vv. 9, 10). Tragically, ancient Israel gained the land and then lost it — when they became more interested in the land than in the One who had promised it.

But the mark of true believers has always been that "they desire a better country, that is, a heavenly one." Brothers and sisters, "our citizenship is in heaven, and from it we await a Savior, the Lord Jesus Christ, who will transform our lowly body to be like his glorious body, by the power that enables him even to subject all things to himself" (Philippians 3:20, 21). Longing for Heaven is the signature of the believing soul.

As it was with Abraham, times of bereavement, and even our own deaths, are times to declare our hope. Just as Abraham bought the cave in hope, we must substantively declare our hope in the stupendous benefits of salvation beyond this life. As Allen Ross says, "The time of death (when the natural inclination is to mourn as the world mourns) should be the time of our greatest demonstration of faith, for the recipient of God's promises has a hope beyond the grave."[8]

As Christians, we are prisoners of hope! We are chained and barred in by hope. We cannot escape hope. We declare at death:

> *I know that my Redeemer lives,*
> *and at the last he will stand upon the earth.*
> *And after my skin has been thus destroyed,*
> *yet in my flesh I shall see God. (Job 19:25, 26)*

We accept the challenge of Colossians 3: "If then you have been raised with Christ, seek the things that are above, where Christ is, seated at the right hand of God. Set your minds on things that are above, not on things that are on earth. For you have died, and your life is hidden with Christ in God. When Christ who is your life appears, then you also will appear with him in glory" (vv. 1-4). We feed on the reality that God "raised us up with him and seated us with him in the heavenly places in Christ Jesus" (Ephesians 2:6). We focus on the eternal because all that is not eternal is eternally out-of-date, "for the things that are seen are transient, but the things that are unseen are eternal" (2 Corinthians 4:18).

And like Abraham, by faith we invest in the promise — giving generously of our possessions and wealth for the preaching of the Word to the ends of the earth, laying up indestructible treasures, investing our time and our whole lives in kingdom expansion.

In so doing, we declare by faith that we are heirs of the promise, even if our circumstances declare it is not so.

38

Faith and Providence

GENESIS 24:1-67

The death of Abraham's beloved Sarah and her interment in the purchased cave of Machpelah in the very heart of the promised land trumpeted to the world Abraham's faith that his descendants would one day possess the land. Machpelah would become the magnificent by-faith repository for the bones of the patriarchs. For Abraham, Sarah's death was also a fresh awakening to his own advanced age and his responsibility to make sure that his forty-something son, Isaac, would marry well and produce heirs. The matter was of such momentous importance to Abraham that he summoned his chief servant to make a vow unique to Genesis, in which his servant was asked to place his hand under Abraham's thigh, near the patriarch's powers of pro-creation, formalizing the purpose and importance of his task (cf. 47:29).

Very likely, the hand-under-thigh referenced circumcision, "the sign of the covenant" (cf. 17:11) that had been given to all the males of Israel in conjunction with the expansive renaming of Abraham and Sarah and the prophetic naming of Isaac, the heir of the covenant who would be born a year later. The oath therefore invoked the power and presence of the Lord God Almighty who gave the covenant.[1] The highly personal formalizing of this oath by his servant suggests that for Abraham the fulfillment of the vow was as important as life itself.

And of first importance, Abraham demanded that Isaac's wife must not be a Canaanite — "that I may make you swear by the LORD, the God of heaven and God of the earth, that you will not take a wife for my son from the daughters of the Canaanites, among whom I dwell, but will go to my country and to my kindred, and take a wife for my son Isaac" (vv. 3, 4). Father Noah's primeval oracle, "Cursed be Canaan" (cf. 9:25) was being lived out by the present Canaanite depravities that would curse them for generations to come (cf. 15:16). There could be no mixing of Abraham's off-spring with these cursed people.

Neither would Abraham allow Isaac to be taken out of the land because his very presence in Canaan was a living declaration that the land would belong to his descendants. Therefore when the servant suggested that perhaps Isaac could go back to Ur to find a wife, Abraham said, "See to it that you do not take my son back there. The LORD, the God of heaven, who took me from my father's house and from the land of my kindred, and who spoke to me and swore to me, 'To your offspring I will give this land,' he will send his angel before you, and you shall take a wife for my son from there. But if the woman is not willing to follow you, then you will be free from this oath of mine; only you must not take my son back there" (vv. 6-8). Significantly, Isaac was never once permitted to leave the land, even in time of famine (cf. 26:2). Isaac encapsulated the divine promise of a people and a land.

What stands out above all else in these words (Abraham's final words in Scripture) is Abraham's faith. Abraham's first recorded words in Scripture had been expressive of his doubts to God when he said, "you have given me no offspring" (15:3). But here his last recorded words declared unwavering faith in God as he said, "he will send his angel before you, and you shall take a wife for my son from there" (v. 7). So here, as Calvin says, we have "simple reliance on the providence of God."[2] Abraham believed that God's unseen hand would do all. God's hand may be hidden, but his effective power is absolute. Abraham believed this with all his heart.

There will be no miracle in this story, as we usually think of miracles. No rearrangement of molecules — no sun standing still — no healing — no river stopped up. Rather, God will bring about the acquiring of Isaac's bride through the "normal" events of life — the delays, the customs, the stresses, the chance meetings. As J. I. Packer says, believers "are never in the grip of blind forces (fortune, chance, luck, fate); all that happens to them is divinely planned, and each event comes as a new summons to trust, obey, and rejoice."[3]

In Genesis 24, the structure of this twice-told story of Isaac and Rebekah gives us the advantage of knowing what happens before the main characters do and thereby observing the providential workings of God in everyday life. The position of this great story in Genesis at the end of Abraham's life serves, in effect, to tell us that this is the way God works day in and day out in our lives. Such a God, of course, is great beyond our imaginings because he *maintains* all of life, *involves* himself in all events, and *directs* all things to their appointed end while rarely interrupting the natural order of life.[4]

This is an awesome thought. The God of Scripture is not simply a God of miracles who occasionally injects his power into life. He is far greater because he arranges all of life to suit and effect his providence. This makes all of life a miracle. God is over all. He is all-powerful, all-knowing, all-present, and all-controlling. This is the God of Scripture. Anything less is an idolatrous reduction of our puny imaginations.

We must also take careful note that Abraham's servant was also himself a man of remarkable faith and, as Derek Kidner says, one of the most attractive minor characters of the Bible.[5] If this was Eliezer of Damascus, he had been at one time a potential heir of Abraham, who had been now displaced by the birth of Abraham's sons (cf. Genesis 15:2). In character he was like the future John the Baptist who declared, "He must increase, but I must decrease" (John 3:30). So it was with profound covenantal faith that the servant obediently placed his hand under Abraham's thigh (v. 9) and swore in magnificent oath "by the LORD, the God of heaven and God of the earth" (v. 3) that he would carry out Abraham's wishes.

A SERVANT'S FAITH (vv. 10-27)

Verse 10 encompasses a thousand miles and several months as the servant assembled a sizable caravan — no doubt to make a grand impression on Isaac's future wife — and traveled north and then east to Aram Naharaim, "the land within the river" bounded on three sides by the great Euphrates.[6] There in the slanting rays of evening when women came out to draw water, Abraham's servant directed his camels to kneel near the town well.

A servant's prayer. With his camels positioned, his very first action was a humble prayer for guidance: "O LORD, God of my master Abraham, please grant me success today and show steadfast love to my master Abraham. Behold, I am standing by the spring of water, and the daughters of the men of the city are coming out to draw water. Let the young woman to whom I shall say, 'Please let down your jar that I may drink,' and who shall say, 'Drink, and I will water your camels' — let her be the one whom you have appointed for your servant Isaac. By this I shall know that you have shown steadfast love to my master" (vv. 12-14).

Notably, this unnamed servant is the first person described in Scripture as asking for divine guidance at a critical juncture. His prayer will also be described later as a spontaneous prayer — "in my heart" (v. 45). But what is most remarkable is that in keeping with the passage's emphasis on providence, the servant did not ask for a miraculous sign from God. Rather, he sought guidance in the regular way, the ordinary events of life. As Nahum Sarna observes, "Nothing is more characteristic of biblical man than a profound and pervasive conviction about the role of divine Providence in everyday human affairs. It should be noted that the servant does not ask for a miraculous divine intervention or for a revelation that would designate Isaac's bride-to-be. He prays, rather, that the rational criteria of suitability that he himself determines might be in accordance with God's will and be effective."[7]

To be sure the criterion was demanding — the bride must say, "Drink, and I will water your camels." But it is not extraordinary or miraculous to the context. This was not a fleece (cf. Judges 6:36-40). The servant did not ask that the normal effects of nature be suspended. And what the servant asked was brilliantly revealing. A woman who would volunteer to do this would be remarkably kind, generous, and industrious. Above all, the faithful servant placed himself in unbounded reliance upon God. Only God could effect such a providence.

Amazing answer. It is reasonable to conclude that Rebekah had left her house *before* the servant had begun to pray. Therefore we are meant to see that the providence was all of God. That is, as the servant humbly prayed, God directed him to ask for specific providences that God was at the same time orchestrating as Rebekah arrived at the well amidst his prayers — and in a cheerful, self-giving humor.

Note the text carefully: "Before he had finished speaking, behold, Rebekah, who was born to Bethuel the son of Milcah, the wife of Nahor, Abraham's brother, came out with her water jar on her shoulder. The young woman was very attractive in appearance, a maiden whom no man had known. She went down to the spring and filled her jar and came up" (vv. 15, 16). What is most astonishing is that Rebekah volunteered to water his ten camels! To grasp what a wonder this was, we must understand that the ancient well was a large, deep hole in the earth with steps leading down to the spring water — so that each drawing of water required substantial effort. And more, a camel typically would drink about twenty-five gallons of water, and an ancient water jar held about three gallons of water. This means that Rebekah made between eighty to one hundred descents into the well.[8] As to the amount of time she gave to this, a camel takes about ten minutes to drink its full complement of water. Rebekah's labors filled one and one half to two sweaty hours! And all the while the servant watched without saying a word, to see whether or not the Lord had made his journey successful.

That the servant remained quiet is extraordinary, especially as Rebekah came up with the last few jars of water. The old servant's pulse had to be racing as he at last took out costly gifts of a gold nose ring and two gold bracelets and asked whose daughter she was and if there was room at her father's house. Her answer that she was the granddaughter of Abraham's brother Nahor and that he was indeed welcome in her father's home left the servant overcome. His soul soared in an ecstasy of thankfulness. "The man bowed his head and worshiped the LORD and said, 'Blessed be the LORD, the God of my master Abraham, who has not forsaken his steadfast love and his faithfulness toward my master. As for me, the LORD has led me in the way to the house of my master's kinsmen'" (vv. 26, 27). God's providential answer to his prayer was beyond doubt. There could be no mistake here. Rebekah was the answer to his prayers. What an awesome God.

GOD'S FAITHFULNESS (vv. 28-60)

The sight of the servant's intense worship charged the girl's heart, and the mention of Abraham's name, which she had heard so many times as part of the household lore, filled her with expectancy and awe. So off she ran to her mother's household.

Laban's hospitality. The name of Rebekah's older brother, Laban, means "the white one" and is a poetic term for the moon, which was in keeping with Abraham's moon-worshiping origin.[9] This Laban is the same man who would shamefully deceive Isaac's son Jacob when Jacob came seeking the hand of his daughter Rachel. Laban was a man who loved money and advantage. Though Laban would not be able to take advantage of Abraham's servant, his materialism was implicit in the exchange.

> *Rebekah had a brother whose name was Laban. Laban ran out toward the man, to the spring. As soon as he saw the ring and the bracelets on his sister's arms, and heard the words of Rebekah his sister, "Thus the man spoke to me," he went to the man. And behold, he was standing by the camels at the spring. He said, "Come in, O blessed of the LORD. Why do you stand outside? For I have prepared the house and a place for the camels." So the man came to the house and unharnessed the camels, and gave straw and fodder to the camels, and there was water to wash his feet and the feet of the men who were with him. Then food was set before him to eat. But he said, "I will not eat until I have said what I have to say." He said, "Speak on." (vv. 29-33)*

At this the servant launched into a lengthy retelling of Abraham's *commission* to find a wife, his wife-finding *mission* to Mesopotamia, and his amazing *encounter* with Rebekah. The rehearsal of the story may be tedious to our western ears, but by ancient conventions it was essential. And as the servant told the story, recorded in verses 34-49, he repeated the central points of the narrative while adding and subtracting minor points to maximize the effect on Laban and his father Bethuel.[10] His purpose was, of course, to convince them of God's providential guidance so that they would consent to sending Rebekah to Isaac.

Marriage secured. The servant's speech was brilliantly effective.

> *Then Laban and Bethuel answered and said, "The thing has come from the LORD; we cannot speak to you bad or good. Behold, Rebekah is before you; take her and go, and let her be the wife of your master's son, as the*

LORD has spoken." When Abraham's servant heard their words, he bowed himself to the earth before the LORD. And the servant brought out jewelry of silver and of gold, and garments, and gave them to Rebekah. He also gave to her brother and to her mother costly ornaments. And he and the men who were with him ate and drank, and they spent the night there. (vv. 50-54a)

God's amazing providence could not be denied. For the moment Laban's mouth was muzzled. Both father and brother agreed to the marriage. And for the third time the servant again bowed low to the ground in profound worship and prayer. Then out came princely treasures, and rich gifts were bestowed without reserve — even to Laban.

But predictably, despite the servant's great generosity, when morning came, Laban and his mother demurred, asking that Rebekah remain ten more days. Such a postponement could well have proved costly, given Laban's deviousness. But the servant remained steadfast — "Send me away that I may go to my master" (v. 56).

God honored the servant's resolve because the family's attempt to stonewall him occasioned another joyous providence — the public declaration of Rebekah's faith. "They said, 'Let us call the young woman and ask her.' And they called Rebekah and said to her, 'Will you go with this man?' She said, 'I will go'" (vv. 57, 58). Her simple "I will go" states the nature of her trust in the God of Abraham. Young Rebekah willingly left her father's house — recognizing the call of the same Lord who called Abraham, casting herself on him alone, with a noble confidence worthy of the woman who was to be Abraham's daughter.

Upon Rebekah's faithful "I will" the departure was secured.

So they sent away Rebekah their sister and her nurse, and Abraham's servant and his men. And they blessed Rebekah and said to her,

> *"Our sister, may you become*
> *thousands of ten thousands,*
> *and may your offspring possess*
> *the gate of those who hate them!" (vv. 59, 60)*

This blessing of Rebekah by her family was parallel to the blessing given to Abraham by the Lord after his offering of Isaac: "Your offspring shall possess the gate of his enemies" (22:17). Now in God's plan we see that the same blessing was given to both Isaac and his bride.[11]

FAITH'S REWARD (vv. 61-67)

The meeting of Isaac and Rebekah was one of storied beauty. The long journey of the gold-adorned bride had afforded her ample time to meditate over the servant's words in anticipation of meeting her God-chosen husband. And if Isaac was merely walking in the field as some suggest, he still had ample time to ponder the sure return of the servant and his future bride. Apparently Isaac and Rebekah saw each other at the same time, though they could only recognize one another as they were identified. But when she knew it was him, she donned a wedding veil, signifying that she was his bride.[12]

Then Isaac heard all the amazing details from the servant himself. Isaac, Laughter himself, must have laughed in delight at the account of Rebekah's watering the camels. All this, and she was such a beauty to boot! Joy was everywhere.

The marriage was immediate. "Then Isaac brought her into the tent of Sarah his mother and took Rebekah, and she became his wife, and he loved her. So Isaac was comforted after his mother's death" (v. 67). Rebekah replaced Sarah by entering the deceased matriarch's tent. Rebekah became at once the new matriarch of Israel.

"And he loved her" is the first reference to marital love in the Bible. They had married in the Lord. They were one flesh.

The scriptural doctrine of divine providence is that God has total hands-on control of the world. And as the hymn says, we are to:

> *Judge not the Lord by feeble sense,*
> *But trust Him for His grace;*
> *Behind a frowning providence*
> *He hides a smiling face.*
> WILLIAM COWPER, 1774

God provides and controls in three grand arenas — history, nature, and the lives of individual people. God's providential control of life is illustrated by virtually every narrative in the Bible.[13]

The lesson from the story of Isaac and Rebekah is certainly not that we are to lay out criteria that God must fulfill as a way to determine his will, but rather that the Lord will guide us as we are faithful to his word. Proverbs 3:5, 6 puts it in memorable form: "Trust in the LORD with all your heart, and do not lean on your own understanding. In all your ways acknowledge him, and he will make straight your paths." Providence is God's gracious outworking of his purpose in Christ in his dealings with man. As God's children, we must take to heart that it is God's day-in, day-out providence that perpetuates the promise of Scripture's famous "Golden Chain":

And we know that for those who love God all things work together for good, for those who are called according to his purpose. For those whom he foreknew he also predestined to be conformed to the image of his Son, in order that he might be the firstborn among many brothers. And those whom he predestined he also called, and those whom he called he also justified, and those whom he justified he also glorified. (Romans 8:28-30)

This story, and all of Scripture, teaches us that our lives are not ruled by chance or fate but by God. God is always faithful to his children — always! Our challenge is to be faithful to him. God does not help those who help themselves. He helps those who entrust themselves completely to him, as did Abraham and his servant.[14]

> *Sing, pray, and keep His ways unswerving,*
> *Perform thy duties faithfully,*
> *And trust His Word: though undeserving,*
> *Thou yet shalt find it true for thee.*
> *God never yet forsook in need*
> *The soul that trusted Him indeed.*
> GEORG NEUMARK, 1641

39

The Death of Abraham

GENESIS 25:1-18

Marvin R. O'Connell shares some thoughts by Blaise Pascal, the great mathematician and Christian philosopher, concerning the death of his beloved father:

> We who are bereaved by the death of our father will find no "solid relief" unless we acknowledge that what has occurred is a result "not of chance, nor of some fatal necessity of nature, nor of the interplay of the elements or parts of the human condition"; it is rather "an event indispensable, inevitable, just, holy, and useful for the well-being of the Church and for the exaltation of the name and of the glory of God, an intervention of Providence decreed from all eternity to take place in the fulness of time, in such a manner." What is left for us is "to unite our will to that of God himself, to will in him, with him, and for him the thing that he has eternally willed in us and for us."[1]

Pascal thus took comfort in two things: first, that the very year, day, hour, place, and manner of his father's death was a providence lovingly decreed by God from all eternity; and second, he took comfort to his heart as he aligned his will to what God had eternally willed for his father. In doing this, Pascal displayed a profoundly biblical perspective about death and life. It is the same providence-laced perspective that graced Father Abraham's death: "These are the days of the years of Abraham's life, 175 years. Abraham breathed his last and died in a good old age, an old man and full of years, and was gathered to his people" (vv. 7, 8). Abraham's 175 years were metered and measured out by the perfect hand of Providence.

The careful observer of Abraham's death will see that the account of his death and burial is framed on either side by genealogies. Immediately before his death are listed the names of Abraham's six sons by his wife Keturah (vv. 1-4), and following his death come the names of Ishmael's twelve sons (vv. 12-18). These genealogies answer the covenant promise that God made to him of untold offspring through phrases like "I will make your offspring as the dust of the earth" (13:16) and "Look toward heaven, and number the stars, if you are able to number them. . . . So shall your offspring be" (15:5) and "I will make you exceedingly fruitful, and I will make you into nations" (17:6). By bookending Abraham's death with genealogical lists, the narrator Moses demonstrates God's faithfulness to his promises of unnumbered descendants. Abraham's multiple descendants at his death thus declared that God was faithful to his word. And as a corresponding subtext, we also see that Abraham had been faithful to God.

LIFE AFTER SARAH (vv. 1-6)

Sarah's death naturally brought about momentous changes in the patriarch's family structure. Isaac's position as heir and progenitor of the chosen people was strengthened by the epic search for and finding of Rebekah in faraway Paddan-aram under the guiding providence of God. Widowed Abraham also took a new wife. We do not know whether this was before or after Isaac's marriage. But depending upon the time that Abraham married Keturah, we surmise that at his death they would have been married some thirty-five to thirty-eight years. Because Keturah's name means "spices," and because several of her sons' names are associated with the Arabian Peninsula, especially the territory east of the Gulf of Aqaba in Arabia, most Bible scholars believe that her sons became principals in the international spice trade — the gathering and distribution of frankincense and myrrh and other aromatic substances.[2] These six sons (v. 2) plus the twelve sons of Ishmael (vv. 13-15) would come to occupy the region over toward Egypt and would truly make Abraham the father of many tribes and nations.

There is no record as to how these six sons of Abraham and Keturah interacted with their much older half-brother Isaac, the son of the promise. Certainly no conflict is mentioned or implied. In fact, Abraham's sunset years are described in idyllic terms of blessing and peace. Nevertheless Abraham believed that God's promise was through Isaac alone. The faith in the promise by which he had offered Isaac and sent his servant to search out a wife for Isaac did not waver in his declining years. So with immense resolve, "Abraham gave all he had to Isaac" (v. 5). No secondary heirs are listed. But though everything went to Isaac, yet Abraham gave his heart and largesse to his six later-in-life sons: "But to the sons of his concubines

Abraham gave gifts, and while he was still living he sent them away from his son Isaac, eastward to the east country" (v. 6).

The Scriptures are silent about the inevitable emotion of the parting. How was it for the old couple, especially Keturah? Did the six sons go reluctantly, or with a spirit of adventure, thankful for their father's gifts? One thing is clear: Isaac, the one through whom a people and a place would be secured for God's people, remained with his father as the unchallenged sole heir and prince of the promise.

We wonder about the spiritual destiny of the departed sons. Was there spiritual hope for them and their progeny? Yes, because as Kidner explains, "In God's plan, these sons were sent away that there might be a true home, in the end, to return to."[3] Indeed, their descendants' return was joyfully prophesied by Isaiah as part of the future glory of Israel:

> *A multitude of camels shall cover you,*
> *the young camels of Midian and Ephah;*
> *all those from Sheba shall come.*
> *They shall bring gold and frankincense,*
> *and shall bring good news, the praises of the LORD.*
> *All the flocks of Kedar shall be gathered to you;*
> *the rams of Nebaioth shall minister to you;*
> *they shall come up with acceptance on my altar,*
> *and I will beautify my beautiful house. (Isaiah 60:6, 7)*

Today the offspring of those six sons may come just as it always has been — through faith. This side of the cross, the way is so clear because those who trust in Christ actually become Abraham's spiritual offspring and heirs of the promise (cf. Galatians 3:29).

ABRAHAM'S DEATH (vv. 7-10)

How was it for Abraham in his final golden years? Perhaps Alexander Solzhenitsyn's gentle musings about his own aging can give us an idea. These smiling thoughts come from his "Growing Old":

> Aging is in no sense a punishment from on high, but brings its own blessings and a warmth of colors all its own. There is warmth to be drawn from the waning of your own strength. . . . You can no longer get through a whole day's work . . . but how good it is to slip into the brief oblivion of sleep, and what a gift to wake up once more to the clarity of your second or third morning of the day. . . . You are still of this life, yet you are rising above the material plane. Growing old serenely is not a downhill path but an ascent.[4]

The great novelist was, of course, writing from the perspective of a man of faith whose hope is in Christ and the resurrection.

Very likely, Abraham's final years brought him similar experience, because his end is given unusual space as scriptural death notices go, as well as presenting a picture of completeness and satisfaction. "These are the days of the years of Abraham's life, 175 years. Abraham breathed his last and died in a good old age, an old man and full of years, and was gathered to his people" (vv. 7, 8). Abraham lived 175 years (one and three-quarter centuries!), and since he was seventy-five when he left Ur, his last hundred years were lived as a pilgrim and a sojourner. The patriarch had learned through his long experience that he must never imagine that his final abode was on earth. Abraham truly looked beyond this world, to the ultimate city.

He died as "an old man and full of years" — an expression that indicates that life is limited, that a span of life is allotted to us all.[5] Abraham's time had come, to borrow Pascal's phrase, as "an intervention of Providence decreed from all eternity to take place in the fulness of time." And so it will be for all of us. All our days are numbered. Our full complement of years is already determined. None of us die too soon, whether we die at nine months or ninety years. As the psalmist wrote:

> *In your book were written, every one of them,*
> *the days that were formed for me,*
> *when as yet there were none of them. (Psalm 139:16)*

Scriptural wisdom demands that we number our days.

> *So teach us to number our days*
> *that we may get a heart of wisdom. (Psalm 90:12)*

> *O LORD, make me know my end*
> *and what is the measure of my days;*
> *let me know how fleeting I am! (Psalm 39:4)*

What a gift it is to embrace our mortality and to understand that we have an allotted number of days, especially for those who are young. Such understanding can serve to bring a graced wisdom to our lives and to focus our energy so as to yield eternal fruit. Further, Abraham's satisfaction did not come from living 175 years but from a century of faith.

Abraham's epitaph ends with this soaring note: "and [he] was gathered to his people" — not to his tomb, not to Sarah's bones, but "to his people," the living fellowship of the redeemed. He was "gathered to his people," just as the beggar in Christ's parable was said to be carried to "Abraham's bosom" (Luke 16:22, KJV). "The patriarch was 'gathered to his people,' until that day when the dust shall live again at the sound of the last trumpet, and all the buried dead — Abraham and his people to whom he is gathered — shall hear the voice of the Son of Man, and shall come forth" (Candlish).[6]

The account of Abraham's death closes with the estranged half-brothers Isaac and Ishmael reunited in their grief and love for their father. "Isaac and Ishmael his sons buried him in the cave of Machpelah, in the field of Ephron the son of Zohar the Hittite, east of Mamre, the field that Abraham purchased from the Hittites. There Abraham was buried, with Sarah his wife" (vv. 9, 10). Machpelah was opened as it had been almost three decades earlier when Sarah was interred. Now, by faith, Abraham's body was placed next to Princess Sarah's bones. Abraham's body was a reminder that his descendants would one day possess the land.

Father Abraham's flesh would fall away before the tomb was again opened and by faith the remains of their son Isaac, their Laughter, their child of promise, would be laid by their grinning bones. Ironically, it would be Isaac's estranged sons Jacob and Esau who would join together in that task (cf. 35:29). But now it was Isaac and Ishmael who stood together at Abraham's grave. Note the word order. Isaac the younger is named first. He was the recognized firstborn in the eyes of God and his covenant people. But there were also blessings for Ishmael. His descendants would multiply "so that they cannot be numbered for multitude" (16:10). He would be made into a "great nation" (17:20). But in his own day Ishmael, son of Abraham, "would be a shadow, almost a parody of his father, his twelve princes notable in their times (17:20; 25:13) but not in the history of salvation; his restless existence was no pilgrimage but an end in itself; his nonconformism became a habit of mind, not a light to the nations."[7] Did Ishmael, this circumcised son of Abraham, ultimately come to faith? We do not know.

We do know that Isaac and Rebekah became the reigning patriarch and matriarch of Israel. "After the death of Abraham, God blessed Isaac his son. And Isaac settled at Beer-lahai-roi" (v. 11). "God blessed Isaac" will become the theme of the next ten chapters of Genesis (25:19 — 35:29). The area around Beer-lahai-roi was the place where Hagar was heard by God, and he delivered her. It was also where Isaac was meditating when he first saw Rebekah. It will be here that he will pray for his barren wife. Isaac dwelt in a place where he had met God — and where God blessed him.[8]

How faithful to the word of promise God had been. God had covenanted to Abraham that his offspring would be as the sand and the stars, that he would be the father of a multitude of nations, and that he would go to his fathers in peace and be buried at a good old age. God had also promised him that Isaac would become the sole heir of the covenant and that Ishmael would become greatly increased in numbers and the father of twelve rulers. And now, at the death of Abraham, we see that God had proved faithful in every word of his vast promise.

What a legacy this great man of faith has left us! Four famous New Testament passages expound the spiritual dimensions of his faith-legacy and together provide essential teaching about faith in the Christian life.

• *Faith* (Romans 4). When Abraham "believed the LORD, he counted it to him as righteousness" (Genesis 15:6), and his example became the reference point to understanding that salvation comes through faith. Thus in Romans 4, the apostle Paul demonstrates that Abraham was saved by faith (vv. 1-3), that King David was saved by faith (vv. 6-8), that the Gentiles were saved by faith (vv. 9-12), and that under the Law it was by faith that righteousness came (vv. 13-17).

• *Faith and works* (James 2). Whereas Paul uses Genesis 15:6 to prove that Abraham was justified by faith, James uses the story of Abraham's offering of Isaac in Genesis 22 (which took place over a quarter of a century later) to argue that Abraham was justified by works. And it is the revelation of the two passages together that is essential to understanding true faith. The fact that for twenty-five years Abraham had lived a life of faith shows that Genesis 22 is, as Griffith Thomas says, "the crown and culmination of that faith, and is proved by Abraham's act of offering Isaac. Faith wrought with his works, and by works was made perfect (Jas. ii. 22). Works are the essential proof of faith."[9]

• *Christ* (Galatians 3). Galatians 3 teaches us that the ultimate offspring of Abraham is Christ and that if we are saved by faith in Christ, we are then the true spiritual offspring of Abraham: "And the Scripture, foreseeing that God would justify the Gentiles by faith, preached the gospel beforehand to Abraham, saying, 'In you shall all the nations be blessed.' So then, those who are of faith are blessed along with Abraham, the man of faith" (vv. 8, 9). "Now the promises were made to Abraham and to his offspring. It does not say, 'And to offsprings,' referring to many, but referring to one, 'And to your offspring,' who is Christ" (v. 16). "In Christ Jesus you are all sons of God, through faith. For as many of you as were baptized into Christ have put on Christ. There is neither Jew nor Greek, there is neither slave nor free, there is neither male nor female, for you are all one in Christ Jesus. And if you are Christ's, then you are Abraham's offspring, heirs according to promise" (vv. 26-29).

• *Faithfulness* (Hebrews 11). Hebrews 11 uses Abraham's life to demonstrate how the faithful person lives. Through Abraham we see faith's *obedience* (v. 8), faith's *sojourn* (v. 9), faith's *hope* (v. 10), faith's *confidence* (vv. 11, 12), faith's *longing* (vv. 13-16), faith's *sacrifice* (vv. 17, 18), and faith's *reasoning* (v. 19).

Abraham is indeed the father of all who believe. The New Testament rides on the lyrics of belief. We come to Christ only by faith. And we live for Christ by faith.

We live by faith because every Word of God is true.

> *The God of Abraham praise,*
> *Who reigns enthroned above,*
> *Ancient of everlasting days,*
> *And God of love.*
> *Jehovah, Great I AM,*
> *By earth and heaven confessed;*
> *I bow and bless the sacred name,*
> *Forever blest.*
>
> THOMAS OLIVERS, 1770

40

Infamous Grace

GENESIS 25:19-34

Most of us probably do the same thing when we view rented videos —
we fast-forward through the previews and trailers that advertise other films.
And we likely do it for the same reasons. We are eager to get to the feature
film we have chosen. Even more, we like to avoid the junk that typifies so
many Hollywood trailers.

But here in Genesis, as we begin the lengthy main feature, *The Life
and Times of Isaac* (with its focus on his son Jacob), we want to resist fast-
forwarding through the opening verses because these sixteen verses (25:19-
34) are the informing trailer to the next ten chapters.[1] These brief verses
summarize in an unforgettable nutshell the future and significance of the
life of Isaac's son Jacob. As you may remember, Genesis is divided by ten
toledots (ten sections that begin with "These are the generations of"), five
of which frame primeval history and five patriarchal history. Here the Jacob-
Esau trailer casts brilliant light on this lengthy section. Here is essential and
unforgettable theological theater.

This compact preview teaches us about God and man in a frankly earthy,
morally unedifying story. The moral lessons that are here do not come from
observing the moral virtues of Jacob or Esau, but from their faults. Jacob and
Esau together dramatize the human predicament: Both the elect and non-
elect are hopelessly self-centered and incapable by themselves of doing
consistent good. Jacob is a scheming, Machiavellian figure, and Esau is a free
spirit who lives for his appetites.

Along with this we see that God's grace is not subject to our expectations, much less cultural conventions. God is sovereign. His grace cannot
be tamed. In fact, the uninformed heart may well find the exercise of God's

grace to be scandalous,[2] even infamous. But to those of faith it is a mysterious, blessed infamy.

The story opens with the focus on Isaac and Rebekah: "These are the generations of Isaac, Abraham's son: Abraham fathered Isaac, and Isaac was forty years old when he took Rebekah to be his wife, the daughter of Bethuel the Aramean of Paddan-aram, the sister of Laban the Aramean" (vv. 19, 20). Isaac was the miracle-child who arrived in Abraham's hundredth year and the ninetieth year of Sarah's barrenness. In obedience to God and in accordance with their joy they named him Laughter — "And Sarah said, 'God has made laughter for me'" (21:6). Up to this point, Isaac's great distinction came from his willingness to be obedient to death when he submitted to his father's offering him on Mt. Moriah. Scripture's brief glimpses of him suggest that he was of a retiring nature.

In contrast, there was nothing retiring about Rebekah. She was the woman who volunteered to water the ten camels of the bridal caravan — and did so for perhaps two sweaty hours! When Rebekah left with the caravan to marry Isaac, her family sang this blessing:

> *Our sister, may you become*
> *thousands of ten thousands,*
> *and may your offspring possess*
> *the gate of those who hate them! (24:60)*

So when Rebekah met her beloved Isaac and heard him reiterate the divine promise of offspring — that his seed would be as the stars — she fully expected to soon be pregnant. But it did not happen. And now twenty years had passed, Isaac was approaching sixty, and Rebekah was still barren (cf. v. 21)! Isaac's brother Ishmael had produced twelve sons to Isaac's zero.

Given who Isaac was, and given God's sovereign selection of Rebekah, given his lineage and her can-do magnificence, it should have been — well, easy! "But in the best possible arrangement there is barrenness" (Brueggemann).[3] Why? Because God was teaching his people that the promised blessing through the chosen seed of Abraham could not be accomplished by mere human effort. This is how it had been for Sarah. This is how it would be for her daughter-in-laws Rachael and Leah. And later it would be the same for the mother of Samson and for Hannah, the mother of Samuel. And ultimately the promise would culminate with Elizabeth, the mother of John the Baptist and (in a class by herself) Mary, the mother of our Lord.

EXTRAORDINARY BIRTH (vv. 21-26)

Effectual prayer. To Isaac's unending credit, he did not resort to a surrogate wife as had his father with Hagar. Rather, he engaged in passionate prayer.

"And Isaac prayed to the LORD for his wife, because she was barren" (v. 21a). The same word for "prayed" is used in Exodus to describe Moses' powerful entreaty of the Lord to remove the plagues (cf. Exodus 7 — 10).[4] To pray with such intense supplication shows that Isaac wholeheartedly believed that the promise through Abraham would be fulfilled. How long did he pray like this — five — fifteen — twenty years? Surely the latter, because the couple's distress would have been painfully immediate in ancient culture, especially when she had the expectation of a multitude of children.

So Isaac prayed and prayed, and his relentless intercession culminated in what had to be a delirium of joy when "the LORD granted his prayer, and Rebekah his wife conceived" (v. 21b). At last his magnificent wife was with child. Old Isaac (Laughter himself) must have taken his wife in his arms and whirled in dizzy peals of laughter. One thing was very clear after twenty years of barrenness: Rebekah's barrenness was ended by the direct intervention of God. Rebekah's womb bore the divinely given seed. Here we see God's sovereignty begin to visibly rise over the story.

Tumultuous pregnancy. No pregnancy is easy. But with the quickening, a tumultuous pregnancy ensued, and Rebekah's joy faded to dismay. "The children struggled together within her, and she said, 'If it is thus, why is this happening to me?'" (v. 22a). The Hebrew graphically says, "The children smashed themselves inside her."[5] She felt as if her womb had become a battlefield. According to Nahum Sarna, the sense of her dismay was something like "Why then did I yearn and pray to become pregnant?" or "Why do I go on living?"[6] Remember that Rebekah was no wilting flower. There was mayhem in her womb! *What on earth is going on?* she wondered. In her pain and perplexity she, like her husband, turned to God for the answer — "she went to inquire of the LORD" (v. 22b). Rebekah and Isaac were living in Beer-lahai-roi, the same place where God had informed Hagar about the birth and destiny of her son. Possibly Rebekah went to the same spot to seek God's word.

Perplexing prophecy. What she heard was of cosmic significance. The warfare in her womb would have far-reaching results. She learned that she would have twins and that they would father two nations that would divide and oppose each other.

> *Two nations are in your womb,*
> *and two peoples from within you shall be divided. (v. 23a)*

She also learned that the conventional rights of her firstborn would be overturned, as their roles would be reversed:

> *. . . the one shall be stronger than the other,*
> *the older shall serve the younger. (v. 23b)*

Rebekah learned that the tumult in her womb was not of her or Isaac's making but was part of a divine plan that God was working out for his own purposes and glory. The abiding fact is: "The order of nature is not necessarily the order of grace" (Griffith Thomas).[7]

This is repeatedly emphasized in Genesis. From the very first, the older brother Cain had his offering rejected while younger Abel's was accepted. The line of Seth, the even younger brother, was the chosen line (4:26 — 5:8). Young Isaac was chosen over Ishmael (17:18, 19). Joseph, the youngest of Jacob's sons, was chosen over his brothers (37:3). And Judah was likewise chosen over his older brothers (49:8).[8] Significantly, the New Testament is painstakingly clear that the order of nature does not determine the order of grace. "But God chose what is foolish in the world to shame the wise; God chose what is weak in the world to shame the strong; God chose what is low and despised in the world, even things that are not, to bring to nothing things that are, so that no human being might boast in the presence of God" (1 Corinthians 1:27-29). Tradition does not determine grace. Convention does not dictate grace. Neither does giftedness or natural endowments. Grace does not bow to social privilege or status.

Most significantly, Paul argues the principle in Romans 9:10-13 to show that natural descent (the Jewish bloodline) does not insure salvation by referring to the case of Jacob and Esau:

> *And not only so, but also when Rebecca had conceived children by one man, our forefather Isaac, though they were not yet born and had done nothing either good or bad — in order that God's purpose of election might continue, not because of works but because of his call — she was told, "The older will serve the younger." As it is written, "Jacob I loved, but Esau I hated."*

Jacob became the heir because of election, and not because of moral virtues or good works, because the twins were not even born when the choice was made. Not only that, but God's choice went beyond the individuals to nations. We know this because the context of the quotation from Malachi 1:2, 3 ("Yet I have loved Jacob but Esau I have hated") refers to the descendants of Jacob (the Jews) and of Esau (the Edomites) who spent long periods of bondage to the Jews. The selection of Jacob individually and the Israelites corporately was solely due to divine choice.

God's hatred must be understood in the relative sense. God did not hate Esau and the Edomites, but in comparison with his choice of Jacob and the Israelites they were hated. This relative use of hate was also employed by Christ himself. "If anyone comes to me and does not hate his own father and mother and wife and children and brothers and sisters, yes, and even his own life, he cannot be my disciple" (Luke 14:26). We must understand that "The Lord is not slow to fulfill his promise as some count slowness, but is patient toward you, not wishing that any should perish, but that all should reach repentance" (2 Peter 3:9). But at the same time we must understand, and John tells us, that "whoever does not obey the Son shall not see life, but the wrath of God remains on him" (John 3:36). God's wrath is the outworking of his hatred.

Notice in all of this that God offers no explanations, and certainly no apologies for his choice. The love of God transcends human convention. His sovereign grace will not bow to the order of nature or human expectations. His merciful election is a fact whether we understand it or not. God's purposes are as set as they are incomprehensible.

Dramatic birth. Rebekah's midwives witnessed a raw, earthy spectacle infused with divine theater.

> *When her days to give birth were completed, behold, there were twins in her womb. The first came out red, all his body like a hairy cloak, so they called his name Esau. Afterward his brother came out with his hand holding Esau's heel, so his name was called Jacob. Isaac was sixty years old when she bore them. (vv. 24-26)*

First there came a little furry, testosterone-redolent, redheaded male. As the midwives marveled at his appearance, they were further astonished by the fierce little hand of his twin grasping his heel as if to pull him back. The firstborn was given the name Esau ("red") by his proud parents. Interestingly, western Christianity picked up the Near East's prejudice against redheads so that medieval art pictured Judas as a redhead — a sinister figure in a curly, red fright wig![9] The second-born was named Jacob, a Hebrew word that sounded like "heel" and meant "protect" — for example, those who would follow at the heels of the rearguard of an army. As Jacob's scheming character developed, his conduct served to devalue his name, giving it the negative meaning of Heel-grabber or Overreacher.[10]

REMARKABLE CONTRAST (vv. 27, 28)

The boys were opposite to the extreme, and their parents' conduct served to worsen the divide. "When the boys grew up, Esau was a skillful hunter, a man of the field, while Jacob was a quiet man, dwelling in tents. Isaac loved Esau because he ate of his game, but Rebekah loved Jacob" (vv. 27, 28).

It was Esau's nature to love the outdoors. He liked to hunt. His pursuits made him strong and physically confident. Succeeding episodes reveal that he remained an unusually hairy specimen (cf. 27:17ff.) and that he smelled of the field (cf. 27:27). He was the prototype of a mountain man, a Near-Eastern Jeremiah Johnson. You might not hear him coming, but you could smell him!

Our text's rendering that "Jacob was a quiet man" translates a Hebrew word that has the idea of "sound" or "solid," which Derek Kidner calls "the level-headed quality that made Jacob, at his best, toughly dependable, and at his worst, a formidably cool opponent."[11] Jacob was self-contained, conventional, and controlled. Tragically, Isaac and Rebekah, who had prayed so long and persistently for offspring, chose sides. No doubt each loved both of his or her sons, even while each preferred one over the other. And, of course, their favoritism served to further exacerbate their boys' differences.

SHAMEFUL EXCHANGE (vv. 29-34)

Quite frankly, the exchange of birthright leaves neither Jacob nor Esau in a positive light, though in some respects Esau was more attractive than Jacob. Esau was a robust, brawny man who was indifferent to getting ahead. He was also frank and guileless. Years later, when Jacob returned from his miserable experience with Laban, and Esau had him at his mercy, Esau was astonishingly kind and generous to Jacob. "But Esau ran to meet him and embraced him and fell on his neck and kissed him, and they wept" (33:4). "Esau said, 'I have enough, my brother; keep what you have for yourself'" (33:9). It is probable that he was more likable than Jacob. At the same time, he was an immoral, unholy man, as Hebrews makes so clear:

> See to it that no one fails to obtain the grace of God; that no root of bitterness springs up and causes trouble, and by it many become defiled; that no one is sexually immoral or unholy like Esau, who sold his birthright for a single meal. For you know that afterward, when he desired to inherit the blessing, he was rejected, for he found no chance to repent, though he sought it with tears. (12:15-17)

Thomas Carlyle, the great man of letters, had this to say of Esau:

> He is the kind of man of whom we are in the habit of charitably saying that he is nobody's enemy but his own. But, in truth, he is God's enemy, because he wastes the splendid manhood which God has given him. Passionate, impatient, impulsive, incapable of looking before him, refusing to estimate the worth of anything which does not immediately appeal to his sense, preferring the animal over the spiritual, he is rightly called a "profane person."[12]

Esau was a shallow man, governed by his feelings. "Hey, you only go through life once, and you've got to grab all the gusto you can!" He was coarse, something of a backwoods lout.

At the same time cool, calculating Jacob invites a flood of negatives —

rascal, opportunist, cheating, ambitious, self-seeking, self-serving, grasping, scheming, heartless, exploitative — singularly unattractive. Indeed when you view them side by side, the wonder is that God could love either one of them!

When Esau came in from the field, he spoke like the coarse lout he was — literally, "Please let me swallow some of the red stuff, this red stuff, because I am exhausted."[13] Hence he earned another nickname — "Edom," which also means "red." The way Jacob pounced on his brother suggests a well-set trap: "Sell me your birthright now" (v. 31). In no way was Esau about to die. He was simply hungry and impertinent: "I am about to die; of what use is a birthright to me?" (v. 32). Jacob's three-word reply in the Hebrew — in English, "Swear to me now" (v. 33) — is the staccato response of a schemer. "Then Jacob gave Esau bread and lentil stew, and he ate and drank and rose and went his way. Thus Esau despised his birthright" (v. 34).

The closing line of the episode gives us the divine commentary because it does not say, "Thus Jacob took advantage of his brother, and Esau despised his birthright," but only that "Esau despised his birthright." Esau's own sin sealed his fate. He had little regard for the word of God and its promises. Therefore when he stands before God, he alone will be culpable.

At the very heart of Esau's demise is the sad reality that he did not believe the word of God. God's promise was, to him, intangible and unreal. In contrast, Jacob believed the promise and cherished it with all his being. Ironically, the stumbling in Jacob's life came because though he believed in the promise, he did not believe that God's promise could be his apart from his own sinful manipulation of Esau. Nevertheless, despite his faults and ungodly manipulation, Jacob stands as a man of faith.

Are you offended by this story, scandalized by God's exercise of sovereign choice? If you are, it is because, first, you do not know yourself. You do not know how profoundly sinful you are in every dimension of your personality (mind, speech, actions), as Paul makes so unmistakably clear in Romans 3:

• *Mind*: "As it is written: 'None is righteous, no, not one; no one understands; no one seeks for God. All have turned aside; together they have become worthless; no one does good, not even one'" (vv. 10-12).

• *Speech*: "'Their throat is an open grave; they use their tongues to deceive.' 'The venom of asps is under their lips.' 'Their mouth is full of curses and bitterness'" (vv. 13, 14).

• *Actions*: "'Their feet are swift to shed blood; in their paths are ruin and misery, and the way of peace they have not known'" (vv. 15-17).

Such are we if left to ourselves. In effect we are spiritually dead. "And you were dead in . . . trespasses and sins" (Ephesians 2:1-3). There is no way, unaided, that you either would or could turn to God. Indeed, apart from Christ, your status is that of an enemy to God (cf. Romans 5:10) — thoroughly sinful, spiritually dead. Enemies of God do not find grace, unaided.

Secondly, if you are scandalized by this, you do not understand God. He is King, not us! God does as he wants. "All the inhabitants of the earth are accounted as nothing, and he does according to his will among the host of heaven and among the inhabitants of the earth; and none can stay his hand or say to him, 'What have you done?'" (Daniel 4:35). He is not bound by our directions. He is not bound by our cultural conventions. He is not bound by unctuous, self-righteous moralizing. He is not bound by our limited knowledge. He is not tame and will not submit to the idolatrous captivity of our notions of what he should be or do. He is loving, righteous, just, and good in all that he does. And because we are so sinful and helpless to save ourselves, the only possible hope for us is the atoning death of his divine Son. Jesus did not want to drink the cup, but he did — because it was the only way we could be redeemed from sin (cf. Luke 22:39-46). God, in Christ, lovingly suffered and paid the price for our sin. He is thus free to dispense grace as he chooses.

And third, if you are scandalized by this, you do not understand grace. Grace that is earned is not grace at all. Grace goes to the undeserving. Grace comes at God's discretion, not our directives. And grace is there for you, if you will come to Christ. And if you do come, you will discover that it is all of God from beginning to end.

41

Weakness — God's Presence — Blessing

GENESIS 26:1-33

A. W. Tozer describes how we ought to think about the fact that God is all-present (omnipresent), that he is everywhere:

> We should never think of God as being spatially near or remote, for He is not here or there but carries here and there in His heart. Space is not infinite, as some have thought; only God is infinite and in His infinitude He swallows up all space. "'Do I not fill heaven and earth?' saith the LORD." He fills heaven and earth as the ocean fills the bucket that is submerged in it, and as the ocean surrounds the bucket so does God the universe He fills. "The heaven of heavens cannot contain thee." God is not contained: He contains.[1]

The mind-stretching reality is that if the hundred thousand million galaxies that form the ever-expanding universe were compressed in a bucket, that bucket would be as awash and fully saturated with God's presence as it would if lowered into the sea. God surrounds and fills the universe with the sea of his presence.

Tozer's explanation quoted one of the two great Old Testament passages on God's presence: "Am I a God at hand, declares the LORD, and not a God afar off? Can a man hide himself in secret places so that I cannot see him? declares the LORD. Do I not fill heaven and earth? declares the LORD" (Jeremiah 23:23, 24). The other grand text is the lyrical expression of David in Psalm 139:

> *Where shall I go from your Spirit?*
> *Or where shall I flee from your presence?*
> *If I ascend to heaven, you are there!*
> *If I make my bed in Sheol, you are there!*
> *If I take the wings of the morning*
> *and dwell in the uttermost parts of the sea,*
> *even there your hand shall lead me,*
> *and your right hand shall hold me. (vv. 7-10)*

All of God was present wherever David would go, not merely some aspect of God. God is present with his whole being everywhere. A classic expression of God's all-presence is: God does not have any size or spatial dimension and is present at every part of space with his whole being, and yet God acts differently in different places.[2] In respect to his people, while all of God is *spatially* present everywhere, he is *specially* present with his children. Indeed, he is with them and in them (cf. John 17:20, 21; 2 Corinthians 5:17). He is specially present with his people to protect and to bless them. David wrote:

> *You make known to me the path of life;*
> *in your presence there is fullness of joy;*
> *at your right hand are pleasures forevermore. (Psalm 16:11)*

Most of the time when the Bible speaks about God's presence, it refers to his presence to bless. The truth for believers is: All of God is always with us in every place and at all times to protect us and bless us. And when taken to heart this truth is elevating and life-altering. John Wesley, whose life and ministry so affected the church in Britain and America, died after calling out, "The best of all is, God is with us. The best of all is, God is with us."[3]

I have said all this because the life of Isaac, as it is presented in the brief compass of Genesis 26, had to do with his learning that God was present with him. We see this in three parallel declarations of God's presence at the beginning, middle, and end of the account. The first was *future*: "Sojourn in this land, and I will be with you" (v. 3). The second was *present*: "Fear not, for I am with you" (v. 24). And the third was *past*, as the pagan king Abimelech observed, "We plainly see that the LORD has been with you" (v. 28). How Isaac related to and appropriated the reality of God's presence had everything to do with how he lived. And so it is with us.

THE PROMISE OF GOD'S PRESENCE (vv. 1-5)

Famine. The specter of famine was never faraway for those dwelling in Palestine because it was (and is) an arid land. A year without rain, and many would necessarily be on the move. And Isaac was no exception. "Now there was a famine in the land, besides the former famine that was in the days of Abraham. And Isaac went to Gerar to Abimelech king of the Philistines" (v. 1). Just like his father before him, Isaac pulled up stakes with the intention of going down into Egypt where the sure waters of the Nile could water his flocks (cf. chap. 12). But on his way he passed through Gerar, where his father had had an earlier infamous encounter with King Abimelech.

As to whether this was the same Abimelech with whom Abraham had interacted eighty years earlier is not clear. Abraham had been dead only about five years, and a lifespan of 150 years was not a rarity.[4] On the other hand, names like Abimelech and Phicol could have been dynastic names.[5] Regardless of who this Abimelech was, Isaac was on his way to Egypt, the place where his father had originally gone in famine and where he misrepresented Sarah as his sister to save his own skin. But now, on his way to Egypt, Isaac stopped in Gerar, the second place where Abraham had lied — again passing Sarah off as his sister!

Promise. There in Gerar Isaac saw a theophany and heard the voice of God:

> And the LORD appeared to him and said, "Do not go down to Egypt; dwell in the land of which I shall tell you. Sojourn in this land, and I will be with you and will bless you, for to you and to your offspring I will give all these lands, and I will establish the oath that I swore to Abraham your father. I will multiply your offspring as the stars of heaven and will give to your offspring all these lands. And in your offspring all the nations of the earth shall be blessed, because Abraham obeyed my voice and kept my charge, my commandments, my statutes, and my laws." (vv. 2-5)

How Isaac must have thrilled at the reiteration of the promises of a people and land and blessing that had been given to his father. But there were two extra aspects that were sobering. The first, the command to forego going down to Egypt, was a substantial test of Isaac's faith because the famine was regional and thus included Gerar. Humanly speaking, to obey by staying in Gerar in time of famine was to court catastrophe. But God's word was explicit: "Sojourn in this land, and I will be with you and will bless you" (v. 3). Isaac was called to reside as an alien, devoid of legal status and totally dependent on the goodwill of the pagan community. And if he did, God said that he would be *specially* with him and bless him.[6]

Note, secondly, that this call to a dangerous, vulnerable sojourn in Gerar was driven home by an allusion to the faithful obedience of Isaac's father who obeyed (notice the five my's) "my voice and kept my charge, my commandments, my statutes, and my laws" (v. 5b). *Isaac, be like your great father at his best!* This challenge also promised a distinct benefit: "I will be with you and will bless you" (v. 3). God, who is always present, would specially be with him. Thus the key to Isaac's success was introduced by God himself.

What a spiritual landmark this was in Isaac's life. He obeyed at once and settled as an alien in Gerar. *Way to go, Isaac! Bravo!* Well, sort of.

SIN AND GOD'S PRESENCE (vv. 6-16)

You would think that the theophany with its promise of God's presence and blessing and pathos-filled call to obedience would have put some enduring steel into Isaac, but that was not to be. Isaac, so human and so frail, mingled fear with his faith — a combination that produces a shameful lowness and meanness in the sins of religious people.[7] And what follows is low.

Deception. "When the men of the place asked him about his wife, he said, 'She is my sister,' for he feared to say, 'My wife,' thinking, 'lest the men of the place should kill me because of Rebekah,' because she was attractive in appearance" (v. 7). When the local men began to show an interest in his magnificent, childless wife, Isaac adopted the disgraceful ruse that his father had twice succumbed to in his own weakness. Isaac did it despite his knowledge of Abraham's earlier scandal and ignominy. Isaac was ignoble to the *nth* degree. How cowardly, how selfish, how faithless! And that is the point. Isaac did not believe that God was with him. He might have theologically affirmed it, if asked, but he did not subjectively hold to it in his heart. If he had, he would never have succumbed to this scandalous, generational atavism.

And, believers, here is a window into our own souls. It is one thing to theologically affirm that God is omnipresent. But it is quite another to have it dominate and inform us day in and day out. To embrace the sure knowledge that God is spatially present and, more, specially present to bless and protect us — what a difference this makes in our lives. Recognizing God's presence crushes the temptation to compromise. God's presence puts our fears to flight. It instills confidence and steel. It protects us and our loved ones. It upholds the name of God.

Rebuke. Imagine the trouble that could have come if Abimelech had not "accidentally" discovered the truth from the window of his palace when he "saw Isaac laughing with Rebekah his wife" (v. 8). "Laughing" is a wordplay on Isaac's name. It leaves the details to the reader's imagination. Isaac was having fun with Rebekah in a most unsisterly way.[8]

Incensed by the couple's frolic, "Abimelech called Isaac and said, 'Behold, she is your wife. How then could you say, "She is my sister?"' Isaac said to him, 'Because I thought, "Lest I die because of her."' Abimelech said, 'What is this you have done to us? One of the people might easily have lain with your wife, and you would have brought guilt upon us'" (vv. 9, 10). What a sorry state of affairs when unbelievers rightly decry the conduct of believers. There are few things more pathetic. We must understand that we are being watched. When you sin, you may be sure that a nonbeliever is watching through some window. At times I have mused that even our dogs need to be converted and sanctified! Such scrutiny. The unbelieving see and do not forget — ever! Fifty years from now they will still be saying, "I used to go to church, until so-and-so lied to protect his sanctified self." The Apostle Paul mourned over God's name being blasphemed and his teaching reviled because of professing believers' conduct (cf. Romans 2:24; 1 Timothy 6:1). We must understand that "none of us lives to himself, and none of us dies to himself" (Romans 14:7).

What an irony. Due to his feeble faith Isaac put his wife and the promise in harm's way. But it was the pagan king Abimelech who protected Rebekah and the promise upon pain of death! "So Abimelech warned all the people, saying, 'Whoever touches this man or his wife shall surely be put to death'" (v. 11).

We have begun to see how desperately important it is that we truly believe that God is with us. Now the story moves on.

CONFLICT AND GOD'S PRESENCE (vv. 17-22)

From here on (though the text does not explicitly say it) we observe the actions of a chastened, repentant Isaac who truly believed that God was with him.

Prosperity and conflict. Now Isaac stayed put, as God had directed, and lived in obedience. The result was both prosperity and conflict.

> *And Isaac sowed in that land and reaped in the same year a hundredfold. The LORD blessed him, and the man became rich, and gained more and more until he became very wealthy. He had possessions of flocks and herds and many servants, so that the Philistines envied him. (Now the Philistines had stopped and filled with earth all the wells that his father's servants had dug in the days of Abraham his father.) And Abimelech said to Isaac, "Go away from us, for you are much mightier than we." (vv. 12-16)*

Isaac reaped a great harvest amidst a desperate famine. One hundredfold is rare but not unheard of in normal conditions. But this could only have been the hand of God. His bounty during the economic decline of famine made him immensely rich and powerful overnight. Understandably, the Philistines became intensely jealous and resorted to vandalism. Abimelech's command that Isaac go away may have been motivated not only by his fear of Isaac's sudden power, but also by the realization that he could not protect him.

Verses 17-21 recount a story of mounting prosperity amidst perpetual conflict. Isaac moved away from his antagonists at Gerar to the Gerar River

Basin and excavated the wells his father Abraham had dug. He gave them their original names as a way of affirming his ownership. And then he uncovered not a well but a fresh spring — a find of unusual value. Predictably, the range war reignited. He thus called the well "Esek" ("contention") and another new well "Sitnah" ("hostility"). Isaac again moved further out and dug another well that, this time, his enemies did not contest, and he called it "Rehoboth" ("room"), "for now the LORD has made room for us, and we shall be fruitful in the land" (v. 22).

The astonishing thing here is that Isaac kept finding water in time of famine! Clearly, God was with him and was blessing him. And now Isaac had Rehoboth — room to expand and rest and worship.

PROMISE AND GOD'S PRESENCE (vv. 23-25)

At peace, Isaac moved to Beersheba where his father had spent so many years. And there he immediately was graced with a second theophany: "And the LORD appeared to him the same night and said, 'I am the God of Abraham your father. Fear not, for I am with you and will bless you and multiply your offspring for my servant Abraham's sake'" (v. 24). Now note, and note well, that the declaration of divine presence ("I am with you") was much more prominent in this shortened version of the promise and that it was in the present tense, "I am."

There can be no doubt that Isaac believed with all his heart that God was with him because we read, "So he built an altar there and called upon the name of the LORD and pitched his tent there. And there Isaac's servants dug a well" (v. 25). The son echoed his great father as Isaac built an altar, just as Abraham had done when he first entered the promised land (cf. 12:8). Isaac also called on the name of the Lord, as Abraham and the godly Sethites before him had done (cf. 4:26). There in Beersheba he put down his tent stakes and dug another well. When God's children truly believe that God is with them, a deepening of both faith and obedience takes place.

I cannot vouch for the authenticity of the following delightful story, but the account still circulates of a young Chinese convert named Lo and his intense excitement when he first read Matthew 28:20 in the King James Version, "and, lo, I am with you alway, even unto the end of the world." Certainly, Lo understood the Chinese-English coincidence. But it nevertheless affirmed in a memorable and joyous way what is absolutely, eternally true for all believers. In a more sober vein, the King James language of Matthew 28:20 is the inscription that adorns my father's grave marker in Forest Lawn, California, where it was engraved over fifty years ago. Jesus' word to Graham W. Hughes is my father's eternal reality and joy in Heaven and my comfort in this world. Believing that God is always spatially and specially with you is life-altering if you believe it as Isaac came to believe.

PEACE AND GOD'S PRESENCE (vv. 26-33)

Now we come to the pinnacle of the passage: "When Abimelech went to him from Gerar with Ahuzzath his adviser and Phicol the commander of his army, Isaac said to them, 'Why have you come to me, seeing that you hate me and have sent me away from you?' They said, 'We see plainly that the LORD has been with you'" (vv. 26-28a). The first instance of the divine promise of God's presence was *future*: "I will be with you" (v. 3). Next it was *present*: "I am with you" (v. 24). And now it is *past*, as voiced in a retrospect by Isaac's unbelieving acquaintances: "The LORD has been with you." Abimelech's review was, of course, a materialistic deduction. Based on Isaac's agricultural bonanza, his repeated discovery of wells, and his increasing influence and power, Abimelech's conclusion was absolutely right — God was with Isaac.

Today God's presence in the lives of believers cannot be determined materially as it was with the patriarchs in the old economy, but by more profound, searching means. God's presence will be seen by unbelievers as we Christians navigate the ups and downs of life. I witnessed an entire nursing staff and several doctors seeing this as they observed the conduct of a godly couple throughout the illness and death of their infant son. I heard the attending physician voice the admiration of all, which was confirmed by their attendance at the memorial service. God was seen to be with the grieving couple. What is it that people see when they put us and our families under the microscope?

Rapprochement followed as Abimelech and Isaac and their fellows feasted together, exchanged promises, and departed in peace — very much as Isaac's father had done years before.

Observe at last that the story of Isaac that began with drought and famine ended with an abundance of water amidst drought: "That same day Isaac's servants came and told him about the well that they had dug and said to him, 'We have found water.' He called it Shibah; therefore the name of the city is Beersheba to this day" (vv. 32, 33). This is how God regards the life of the man who believes that God is with him.

An astonishing poem by Hildebert, the twelfth-century Archbishop of Tours, rhythmically chants about God's omnipresence.

> *First and Last of faith's receiving,*
> *Source and sea of man's believing,*
> *God, whose might is all potential,*
> *God, whose truth is truth's essential,*
> *Good supreme in thy subsisting,*
> *Good in all thy seen existing;*
> *Over all things, all things under,*

Touching all, from all asunder;
Centre thou, but not intruded,
Compassing, and yet included;
Over all, and not ascending,
Under all, but not depending;
Over all the world ordaining,
Under all, the world sustaining;
All without, in all surrounding,
All within, in grace abounding;
Inmost, yet not comprehended,
Outer still, and not extended;
Over, yet on nothing founded,
Under, but by space unbounded;
Omnipresent, yet indwelling. . . .[9]

This is Genesis reality. God is spatially all-present. There is no place where all of God is not. All of God is everywhere. We also believe that he is specially present to protect and bless us, his children. Any view other than this is reductionist and idolatrous. Bible-believing Christians, this is what the Scriptures teach and what we believe!

In the light of these dazzling realities, I must ask you three questions regarding future, present, and past. Do you believe that God *will be* with you? Do you believe that he will be with you in what you are facing this week, this month, this year? Do you believe that God *is* with you — spatially, specially, right now in your hurt, in your adversity? And do you believe that God *has been* with you all of these years in the ups and downs?

And more, do you believe it with all your soul, all your heart, all your being? Then do not fear.

Follow him with all your heart. And drink deeply from the wells of salvation.

42

Pilfered Blessing

GENESIS 27:1-40

The triple declaration of God's presence with Isaac during his extended encounter with the Philistine king Abimelech compassed the dimensions of Isaac's existence in respect to the *future* ("I will be with you"), the *present* ("I am with you"), and the *past* ("the LORD has been with you"). And Isaac's growth in awareness of the dynamic all-presence of God in his life lifted him from cowardice to confidence. Isaac recovered from the disgrace of passing off Rebekah as his sister as he stood tall amidst the hostile Philistines and prospered. During those remarkable years, Isaac came to live as the prince that he was, heir of the Abrahamic covenant.

But now as we continue the story of his life, years have passed, and he is quite old. And in the intervening decades something of Isaac's spiritual edge has dulled. Creature comforts have become center-place for him as represented in his love for food. Early on there had been a hint of this when we read, "Isaac loved Esau because he ate of his game" (25:28). We get the sense that wild game and savory delights were laid out by his servants to ease his pampered stomach through the night. And as he dreamed, his table was spread again with exotic dishes redolent with garnishes of leeks and onions — moist and succulent.

Aging had also left him visually impaired and dependent upon his family — and demanding. But most notably Isaac, notwithstanding his authentic faith, had come to oppose the revealed will of God regarding Jacob and Esau. He was well aware of the battle that had taken place between the twins in Rebekah's womb. He knew that God had said, "The one shall be stronger than the other, the older shall serve the younger" (25:23). Rebekah would not let him forget it. And the fact that Jacob had manipulated Esau to sell his birthright to him was a longstanding source of irritation to Isaac, and a subject of contention with his strong-willed wife. He was also painfully aware that Esau had married two Canaanite women — and that they had made life bitter for both him and Rebekah (cf. 26:34). But against the weight of all of this, Isaac was determined that though Esau had lost his birthright, he would now give him the firstborn's blessing. Isaac adored his manly, hairy, red-bearded hunter son. Esau's very smell intoxicated him. And dreams of a hunter's feasts filled his vacant eyes.

ISAAC PLOTS (vv. 1-4)

Isaac in his old age had given himself over to willfulness and self-gratification. And he determined to have his way despite God's word. Thus the story begins:

> When Isaac was old and his eyes were dim so that he could not see, he called Esau his older son and said to him, "My son"; and he answered, "Here I am." He said, "Behold, I am old; I do not know the day of my death. Now then, take your weapons, your quiver and your bow, and go out to the field and hunt game for me, and prepare for me delicious food, such as I love, and bring it to me so that I may eat, that my soul may bless you before I die." (vv. 1-4)

Isaac's desire that his "soul" would bless Esau indicates how intensely passionate he was about it. This is more than saying, "I desire with all my heart."[1] It was with his whole being. As Sarna explains, "Isaac summons from the very depths of his own soul all the vitality and energy at his command in order to invoke God's blessing upon his son."[2]

Isaac was willing to ignore God's word and the desires of his wife and his elect son (who now had the birthright) in order to bless his immoral, freebooting son. Isaac thus tossed a relational torch into the tents of his family. And because of his sin no one would do well — neither he, nor Rebekah, nor Isaac, nor Esau. There are no heroes in this story — only sinners. And old Isaac was chief.

REBEKAH COUNTERS (vv. 5-17)

Of course, Rebekah heard the whole plot. Tent walls hide nothing, especially when there is domestic strife. Besides, the blind and perhaps hearing-impaired old man's volume had likely increased a few notches over the years. As soon as Esau departed, artful Rebekah went into high gear. She rehearsed the gist of the plot to dutiful Jacob and sent him on his way to secure a couple of goats for a counter-feast to be served by Jacob instead of Esau (cf. vv. 5-13).

Jacob's hesitance about her plan was not moral (he had no compunction about deceit). Rather he feared the consequences if he could not pull it off. He might receive a curse instead of a blessing. But Rebekah was supremely confident and self-assured. "His mother said to him, 'Let your curse be on me, my son; only obey my voice, and go, bring them to me'" (v. 13). Rebekah knew the recipe well. She missed nothing. She knew that the way to Isaac's heart was through his stomach. Deftly she slaughtered the goats, dressed them out, and brought the meal to perfection.

But her greatest brilliance was disguising Jacob.

> *Then Rebekah took the best garments of Esau her older son, which were with her in the house, and put them on Jacob her younger son. And the skins of the young goats she put on his hands and on the smooth part of his neck. And she put the delicious food and the bread, which she had prepared, into the hand of her son Jacob. (vv. 15-17)*

She placed the best in Esau's wardrobe on Jacob, so as to imitate his profile and imbue Jacob with his smell. Esau was incredibly hairy — so hairy that goatskins had to be bound on the exposed parts of Isaac's body to imitate his feel. How absurd Jacob must have looked and felt as his mother placed the steaming meal in his hands. Jacob hoped no one would see him. Almost surely, Rebekah hovered in the background gesturing to her ridiculously costumed favorite.

But there is a deeper absurdity here — the mother and son's belief that God would not be able to accomplish his own purposes without their help. Mother and son believed that what they were doing helped God's revealed will along, and therefore their deceitful ways were justified. They believed that unrighteous acts were appropriate and good if they aided the righteous work of God.

In today's world many similarly believe that personal ethics are irrelevant if what you are doing helps effect the will of God. The variations of this ethical absurdity are endless: "It's God's will that I provide adequately for my family. Therefore a financial partial-truth told to a client is OK." "It's God's will that his Word be preached with power. So the use of made-up illustrations and personal stories is fine if they enhance the truth of the Word." "God wants people to be saved and come to a knowledge of the truth. So it's OK to utilize unbelievers as cameos and entertainers to get an audience." "World missions are at the very heart of God. So it's permissible to be deceptive about our intentions in order to get into a closed country."

Wrong! As Griffith Thomas said:

> Righteousness can never be laid aside, even though our object is yet more righteousness. In personal life, in home life, in church life, in endeavors

to win men for Christ, in missionary enterprise, in social improvement, and in everything connected with the welfare of humanity we must insist upon absolute righteousness, purity, and truth in our methods, or else we shall bring utter discredit on the cause of our Master and Lord.[3]

JACOB DECEIVES (vv. 18-29)

Jacob was a product of his mother's love and his own self-promoting heart. The "better angels" of Jacob's nature (to use Abraham Lincoln's words from his first inaugural address) were silenced. He was despicable here.

Domestic fraud. Jacob set his hesitations aside, and shouldering his ridiculous disguise, he played his part to the best of his abilities. Of course, his Esau imitations did not work. Tenors have difficulty singing bass! Thus we read:

> *So he went in to his father and said, "My father." And he said, "Here I am. Who are you, my son?" Jacob said to his father, "I am Esau your firstborn. I have done as you told me; now sit up and eat of my game, that your soul may bless me." But Isaac said to his son, "How is it that you have found it so quickly, my son?" He answered, "Because the LORD your God granted me success." Then Isaac said to Jacob, "Please come near, that I may feel you, my son, to know whether you are really my son Esau or not." So Jacob went near to Isaac his father, who felt him and said, "The voice is Jacob's voice, but the hands are the hands of Esau." And he did not recognize him, because his hands were hairy like his brother Esau's hands. So he blessed him. (vv. 18-23)*

Jacob lied three times. First, when he said to his father, "I am Esau your firstborn" (v. 19a). Did these lying words choke him? Did he hesitate? We wonder. And second, Jacob lied when he named the Lord as the reason for his good hunting: "Because the LORD your God granted me success" (v. 20b) — which was bald-faced blasphemy. He made God his accomplice.

The claustrophobic intimacy of the deception fascinates us. Covered with animal skins, Jacob came face-to-face with the unseeing eyes of his father as his father felt his goat-clad hands and neck. Old Isaac was satisfied enough to go ahead with the blessing. But in the last moment he was again gripped by a "vague disquiet"[4] and renewed his questioning. "He said, 'Are you really my son Esau?' He answered, 'I am.' Then he said, 'Bring it near to me, that I may eat of my son's game and bless you.' So he brought it near to him, and he ate; and he brought him wine, and he drank" (vv. 24, 25). Food first, blessing second! Now, with Jacob's third lie complete, the old gourmand commenced eating, smacking his lips, guzzling the vintage wine, and drizzling over his immense, white beard.

Authentic blessing. The meal over, Jacob was again drawn into stifling, terrifying intimacy with his father. "Then his father Isaac said to him, 'Come near and kiss me, my son.' So he came near and kissed him. And Isaac smelled the smell of his garments and blessed him" (vv. 26, 27a). Satisfied, Isaac laid his hands on pseudo-Esau and delivered a fiercely passionate blessing from the depths of his soul. The blessing is in the form of four poetic stanzas.

First stanza:

> *See, the smell of my son*
> *is as the smell of a field that the LORD has blessed! (v. 27b)*

The stolen garments, smelling of the country, called forth from Isaac the promise of the land, which produces abundantly.

Second stanza:

> *May God give you the dew of heaven*
> *and of the fatness of the earth*
> *and plenty of grain and wine. (v. 28)*

Dew is a favorite Hebrew metaphor for God's goodness in providing abundance and invigoration. Dew has always provided the main source of water during the rainless summer months when the water-laden air of the Mediterranean is condensed by the cool night temperatures to a life-giving mist.[5] "Dew," "fatness," and "plenty" formed an invocation of refreshment and prosperity upon his son.

Third stanza:

> *Let peoples serve you,*
> *and nations bow down to you.*
> *Be lord over your brothers,*
> *and may your mother's sons bow down to you. (v. 29a)*

"Isaac's fierce pride in Esau demanded an empire for him" (Kidner).[6] He utterly rejected God's word to Rebekah that "the older shall serve the younger" (25:23b). Isaac blessed pseudo-Esau with universal dominion.

Fourth stanza:

> *Cursed be everyone who curses you,*
> *and blessed be everyone who blesses you! (v. 29b)*

This final blessing reiterated God's words to Abraham invoking dynamic protection (cf. 12:2, 3).

So we see that Isaac's passionate hubris erupted to bless his Esau (Isaac disguised) with the covenant mantle of fertile land and God's good bounty, empire, and protection, and his word stood. He had thwarted God, so he thought. But Jacob, in Esau's clothing, slouched away in breathless excitement. He had displaced Esau — again.

ESAU'S DEFEAT (vv. 30-40)

Isaac's shattering. Isaac could have had no intimation of the earthquake that was coming.

> *As soon as Isaac had finished blessing Jacob, when Jacob had scarcely gone out from the presence of Isaac his father, Esau his brother came in from his hunting. He also prepared delicious food and brought it to his father. And he said to his father, "Let my father arise and eat of his son's game, that you may bless me." His father Isaac said to him, "Who are you?" He answered, "I am your son, your firstborn, Esau." Then Isaac trembled very violently and said, "Who was it then that hunted game and brought it to me, and I ate it all before you came, and I have blessed him? Yes, and he shall be blessed." (vv. 30-33)*

The seismic shock that tore through Isaac's body and soul signaled the fall of his willful opposition to the word of God. As Dr. Donald Grey Barnhouse so remarkably observed:

> Before a great work of grace, there must be a great earthquake. Isaac had put his personal love of Esau ahead of the will of God. Down came his idol, and the edifice of willful love collapsed before the shaking power that took hold of him. The arrogant pride which had slyly planned to thwart God toppled to the ground, broken beyond repair. When Isaac trembled exceedingly, all his desires were shattered.[7]

Isaac's submissive conclusion — "Yes, and he shall be blessed" (v. 33b) — declared that he had been defeated and that he accepted Jacob as blessed of God. Nothing now, or ever, would change Isaac's mind. Not even the tears of his beloved Esau.

Here it is instructive to note that Hebrews 11:20 says, "By faith Isaac invoked future blessings on Jacob and Esau." How so? Was his willful, sinful blessing of Jacob (who he thought was Esau) an act of faith? No. Rather, Isaac's "by faith" blessing of Jacob took place immediately after the shattering spiritual earthquake, when he affirmed of Jacob, "Yes, and he shall be blessed."

Esau's lament. Esau rued what had occurred but was helpless in its wake.

As soon as Esau heard the words of his father, he cried out with an exceedingly great and bitter cry and said to his father, "Bless me, even me also, O my father!" But he said, "Your brother came deceitfully, and he has taken away your blessing." Esau said, "Is he not rightly named Jacob? For he has cheated me these two times. He took away my birthright, and behold, now he has taken away my blessing." (vv. 34-36a)

Esau poured forth bitter sarcasm that reinterpreted Jacob's name as "cheat" as he mourned the loss both of his birthright and blessing.

But despite this accurate characterization of his brother, the ultimate culpability for losing his position remains Esau's, as Hebrews makes so clear:

See to it that no one fails to obtain the grace of God; that no "root of bitterness" springs up and causes trouble, and by it many become defiled; that no one is sexually immoral or unholy like Esau, who sold his birthright for a single meal. For you know that afterward, when he desired to inherit the blessing, he was rejected, for he found no chance to repent, though he sought it with tears. (Hebrews 12:15-17)

Esau's blessing. Esau continued to implore Isaac for a blessing.

Then he said, "Have you not reserved a blessing for me?" Isaac answered and said to Esau, "Behold, I have made him lord over you, and all his brothers I have given to him for servants, and with grain and wine I have sustained him. What then can I do for you, my son?" Esau said to his father, "Have you but one blessing, my father? Bless me, even me also, O my father." And Esau lifted up his voice and wept. (vv. 36b-38)

But all that was left for Esau was an anti-blessing,[8] a blessing that substantiated that the original blessing had gone to Jacob.

Then Isaac his father answered and said to him:

"Behold, away from the fatness of the earth shall your dwelling be, and away from the dew of heaven on high. By your sword you shall live, and you shall serve your brother; but when you grow restless you shall break his yoke from your neck." (vv. 39, 40)

Esau's destiny was not "dew" and "fatness" but to be "away" from such blessings. His descendants would live by the sword, from violence. And for a long time they would be subservient to Israel.[9] This was Esau's "bless-ing."

This story was real life. Everyone in the story sinned. No one looked good — not Isaac, not Rebekah, not Jacob, not Esau. The patriarch Isaac fought against God's word. The matriarch Rebekah, through her favorite son, attempted to manipulate life so as to ensure that God's promise would actu-ally happen. She and Jacob thought that God needed help, even if the help was dishonest and self-serving. Esau, the patriarch's favorite son, disre-garded God's word. Indeed, he despised the promise.

Everyone in the family sought the blessings of God without bending the knee to God. This little family was fraught with ambition, jealousy, envy, lying, deceit, coveting, malice, manipulation, stubbornness, and stu-pidity.

And everyone lost. Rebekah was forced to send her pet son to far-off Mesopotamia, away from his father's house, in a destitute condition. Jacob was gone for twenty years, and it appears that his mother never saw him again. Jacob's exile was just payment for his deceiving Esau as he experi-enced the extended miseries of conflict and exploitation at the hands of his Uncle Laban. Truly, blind old Isaac had tossed a torch into his families' tents by his fighting against God's word. And Esau, who despised his birthright, lost everything.

But in and above this is something of immense beauty and grandeur — the invincible determination of God to keep his word despite the prevailing unbelief and unfaithfulness of his people. God fulfilled his word despite Isaac's opposition, despite Rebekah and Jacob's manipulation, and despite Esau's indifference.

The invincible determination of God will see to it that his people are sanctified. Here the figurative earthquake in Isaac's life called him back to a life of faith. And Jacob was further pushed along the path that would result in his becoming Israel, a prince of God (cf. Genesis 32:28).

Fellow believers, amidst our sins and our stupidities, the invincible determination of God is set to bring us to completion — even when we resist it. This truth was given memorable voice in Paul's advice to Timothy in the surprising fourth line of this remarkable trustworthy saying:

> *If we have died with him, we will also live with him;*
> *if we endure, we will also reign with him;*
> *if we deny him, he also will deny us;*
> *if we are faithless, he remains faithful —*
> *for he cannot deny himself. (2 Timothy 2:11-13)*

The first two lines express assurance: "If we have died with him, we will also live with him; if we endure, we will also reign with him." Then the third line warns, "if we deny him, he also will deny us." So with the two lines of assurance and a line of warning ringing in our ears we come to the fourth line: "if we are faithless . . ." We expect the corollary, "he will be unfaithful." But surprisingly we read, "if we are faithless, he remains faithful" (v. 13a). God cannot and will not be anything but faithful to his unfaithful children. God will be faithful to his word and to his own — even when they manipulate and fight against his will. And more, his word will prevail.

Believer, are you playing games with God's word? Are you attempting to control its application? Are you engaging in unrighteous means to bring about its righteous end? Are you fighting against his word? If so, stop it! Give it up. Say with your Savior, "Your will be done." Yield to his invincible determination to fulfill his word.

Rest in this:

> *. . . if we are faithless, he remains faithful —*
> *for he cannot deny himself. (v. 13)*

43

An Angel-Freighted Ladder

GENESIS 27:41 — 28:22

As Isaac lifted his hands from Esau's head and Esau understood that the blessing that his father had just bestowed on him was, in effect, an anti-blessing because Jacob had stolen his blessing, a murderous hatred gripped Esau's soul. And he began to bide his time until his father's death when he would have the pleasure of killing his thieving brother with his own hands. His hatred was so deep that the thought of killing Jacob brought him comfort. *How do I hate thee? Let me count the ways.*

Esau was not a man who cared to keep his thoughts private, and his mother Rebekah was not one to miss much of anything. She did not doubt for a moment Esau's homicidal intent. So Rebekah took charge, commanding Jacob to flee to her brother Laban until Esau's fury cooled down and he forgot what Jacob had done to him. How would she ever get Isaac to agree to this? Easy, if you are as subtle as Rebekah. It was a bitter fact that Esau's two Hittite wives had made life miserable for Isaac and her (cf. 26:34, 35). So she suggested the possibility of new miseries for her and Isaac if Jacob followed Esau's example. "Then Rebekah said to Isaac, 'I loathe my life because of the Hittite women. If Jacob marries one of the Hittite women like these, one of the women of the land, what good will my life be to me?'" (27:46). Her suggestion so unnerved Isaac that he immediately grasped the logical alternative, imagining that it was his own idea, just as she knew he would.

Jacob was summoned and was commanded not to marry a Canaanite (i.e., Hittite) wife. He was instead told to tread the long journey to Paddan-aram and there marry a cousin from among the daughters of Rebekah's brother Laban. Isaac coupled this command with an extraordinary blessing — extraordinary because it represented a willing reversal of his pro-Esau attitude, now recognizing Jacob as the true heir of the Abrahamic covenant. In fact, the opening invocation of the blessing — "God Almighty [*El Shaddai*] bless you" (28:3) — bears the divine name first introduced in 17:1 when the covenant of circumcision was given to Abraham. And the language of the blessing here is covenantal in phraseology and scope: "God Almighty bless you and make you fruitful and multiply you, that you may become a company of peoples. May he give the blessing of Abraham to you and to your offspring with you, that you may take possession of the land of your sojournings that God gave to Abraham!" (vv. 3, 4). Isaac's blessing recognized Jacob as the third patriarch.

All hopes of Esau's elevation were now out of the picture. Parenthetically, the account tells us that Esau saw all of this (perhaps he had been watching in unseen malevolence) and that when Esau perceived that his Hittite wives were unpleasing to his father, he too decided to marry a cousin, a daughter of Isaac's half-brother Ishmael. Unspiritual, immoral Esau was slow to connect the dots. Esau was so clueless that he thought imitating Jacob's marriage might curry his father's blessing. Instead it demonstrated that he had no idea at all as to what God was about. An Ishmaelite wife (the daughter of Abraham's cast-out son) was not the way back to blessing! Kidner rightly comments, "Like most religious efforts of the natural man, [this was] superficial and ill-judged."[1]

Here we must remember that while it is true that neither Jacob nor Esau had acted well anywhere in the narrative, there was a polar difference between the two. Esau had only a surface interest in the promise and was faithless. But Jacob believed in God's word and treasured the promise. Yet his faith was incomplete, because he did not believe that the promise would be his apart from his own self-directed actions. As a result, the next twenty years were going to be necessarily hard on him.

JACOB'S FLIGHT (28:10, 11)

In fearful accord with his mother's command to "flee" to Haran (27:43), Jacob's journey was a flight. So we read, "Jacob left Beersheba and went toward Haran. And he came to a certain place and stayed there that night, because the sun had set." The psychic force of Esau's rage at Jacob's stealing both the birthright and the blessing ate at his heart. It is a terrible weight to be so hated. How bitter it must have been for Jacob to know that his misery had been unnecessary, that it was the creation of his own unbelieving deceit and stupidity, that the vulture that was eating his vitals was reared in his own nest. The mouth of God had promised Jacob the firstborn position, but Jacob had stolen it with his own lies.

Such pain. Jacob was now profoundly alone. He had no one to talk to. And he was in a dark howling wasteland full of real and present danger. His solitary state was palpable. Exhausted and despondent, Jacob settled for a stone pillow and fell fast asleep.

JACOB'S DREAM (vv. 12-15)

As he drifted off, he wondered if he would make it. He remembered every word of Isaac's blessing about the land and a people. But he was fleeing the land and was childless, indeed wifeless. What a mess he had made of his life. "And he dreamed, and behold, there was a ladder set up on the earth, and the top of it reached to heaven. And behold, the angels of God were ascending and descending on it! And behold, the LORD stood above it" (vv. 12, 13a). Jacob's dreaming eyes saw a ladder extending from the earth, on which he lay, far up to Heaven. Was it a staired ramp as on a ziggurat or a runged ladder? We do not know. But it makes no difference because it was a surreal dream ladder.

And there was more. It was freighted with angels. Some were rising from where he lay, and others were coming down. August emissaries of God were conducting commerce between Heaven and earth. The arrangement of the descriptions — from the ladder to the angels to the Lord — narrows the focus to the central point of the vision, which was God himself. The Hebrew suggests exclaiming with uplifted arm and open mouth in astonishment, "There, a ladder! Oh, angels! And look, *the Lord himself!*"[2] Yahweh presided over the commerce of Jacob's life. God was directing everything. There was heavenly activity in this desolate place on Jacob's behalf. Jacob's somnolent eyes were upturned to Yahweh in his splendor. Divine reality assaulted his quivering soul.

God speaks. Then from above the ladder, from Heaven, God himself spoke in grand covenantal terms:

> And behold, the LORD stood above it and said, "I am the LORD, the God of Abraham your father and the God of Isaac. The land on which you lie I will give to you and to your offspring. Your offspring shall be like the dust of the earth, and you shall spread abroad to the west and to the east and to the north and to the south, and in you and your offspring shall all the families of the earth be blessed." (vv. 13, 14)

The intent was to hearten the sleeping Jacob. The unconditional personal and national promises first made to Abraham were now made to Jacob by the Lord himself.

Indeed, he was the third patriarch. God had become the God of Abraham, the God of Isaac, and now the God of Jacob. This was the divine title that God would now bear throughout the Scriptures.

With the covenant promises affirmed, the Lord then explained the significance of the ladder: "Behold, I am with you and will keep you wherever you go, and will bring you back to this land. For I will not leave you until I have done what I have promised you" (v. 15). The dynamic presence of God, who directs commerce between Heaven and earth for his own people, would never leave Jacob. Jacob could never go beyond God's keeping. The angel-freighted ladder rising to God above would go with him on the thousand-mile trek to northern Mesopotamia, where it would accompany him for twenty years and return to the land with him. Always the ladder! Always the angels! Always God!

Fellow believers, this is all grace. Jacob, the conniving believer who was outcast and alone due to his own sin, who merited nothing from God, was met by God in his misery with an unparalleled revelation of God's care and assurance for the future. Jacob *was not* seeking God — he was fleeing the consequences of his deception. He was not expecting grace. But grace was unleashed upon his soul — and with not even a word of reproach. The vision and the voice of God only bore assurances.

> *Through many dangers, toils, and snares,*
> *I have already come;*
> *'Tis grace that brought me safe thus far,*
> *And grace will lead me home.*
>
> JOHN NEWTON, 1779

It was grace that had brought Jacob safe thus far, and grace would lead him home.

JACOB'S RESPONSE (vv. 16-22)

Amazement and fear. Jacob rose from his stone pillow astonished. "Then Jacob awoke from his sleep and said, 'Surely the LORD is in this place, and I did not know it'" (v. 16). He was astounded because he was like the rest of us who naturally forget that God is present when we are in trouble, especially when it is our own fault. Surprise, fleeing sinner, God is there! Surprise, sinful sufferer, God is there! Surprise, evil schemer, God is there! Surprise, faithless one, God is faithful!

Jacob's response evoked a very proper fear. "And he was afraid and said, 'How awesome is this place!'" (v. 17a). Terror and adoration were mixed, thus evoking a stunned awe, which was followed by the joyous declaration, "This is none other than the house of God, and this is the gate of heaven" (v. 17). The expression "the gate of heaven" was prompted by the vision of the ladder, and "the house of God" by the bracing reality that God was living in this desolate place. The spiritual truth is that "the house of God" and "the gate of heaven" are co-extensive with and encompass creation. The house (God's presence) and the gate (access to God) are everywhere!

Worship. Jacob's astonished declarations were followed by worship. "So early in the morning Jacob took the stone that he had put under his head and set it up for a pillar and poured oil on the top of it. He called the name of that place Bethel, but the name of the city was Luz at the first" (vv. 18, 19). When Jacob poured oil on his stone pillow-turned-pillar, it was a kind of gift-sacrifice. It demonstrated his love and devotion to God and consecrated the spot as holy to God (cf. Leviticus 8:10, 11). And by calling the desolation "Bethel" ("house of God"), he gave it a name that superseded the city's ancient name, Luz.

Vow. Jacob's amazement, fear, declarations, and worship were all so exemplary and make good models for us to imitate. But not so with his vow, because "if" and "then" are not the language of faith. Faith does not bargain with God, saying that "*If* God will do thus and so, *then* I will make him my God." Listen carefully to Jacob: "Then Jacob made a vow, saying, '*If* God will be with me and will keep me in this way that I go, and will give me bread to eat and clothing to wear, so that I come again to my father's house in peace, *then* the LORD shall be my God, and this stone, which I have set up for a pillar, shall be God's house. And of all that you give me I will give a full tenth to you'" (vv. 20-22, italics added). Jacob is a piece of work, a work in progress who has a long way to go. Jacob's amazed declaration remains immortal. His designations "house of God" and "gate of heaven" are laudable. His anointing of the stone pillow was a true act of worship. But his vow is vintage, conniving Jacob. "Jacob is still more scoundrel than saint" (Walton).[3]

Grace is truly amazing. It was Jacob's only hope. And it is our only hope. Our ifs and thens may be much more subtle, and we have been careful not to articulate them. But they are there, nevertheless.

And, may I say, we are far more culpable. The reason for this is: Jesus was and is the focus of the divine ladder. The New Testament revelation of this is truly stupendous. John's Gospel tells us that in response to Nathanael's faith, "Jesus answered him, 'Because I said to you, "I saw you under the fig tree," do you believe? You will see greater things than these.' And he said to him, 'Truly, truly, I say to you, you will see heaven opened, and the angels of God ascending and descending on the Son of Man'" (John 1:50, 51).

The telltale "Truly, truly" ("Amen, amen") calls us to pay close attention to a word of great importance. And what we learn is that here the focus of the ladder is not on Jacob but on Jesus, who designated himself as "the Son of Man." The title is of vast import because it at once speaks of Jesus' incarnate human life and also his awesome preexistence. It was an unparalleled messianic designation, used eighty-two times in the Gospels, and eighty-one of those times were by Jesus about himself. As the incarnate "Son of

Man," Jesus is the true Jacob (Israel), the one upon whom the angels ascended and descended as seen in his life, death, resurrection, and ascension.

Such was Jesus' human experience. But Jesus also made it very clear in John 1:51 that the angelic traffic would also be on him as the awesome "Son of Man" of Daniel's vision. In fact, it is from that vision that Jesus took his designation "Son of Man." Here is ultimate sovereignty!

> *I saw in the night visions,*
> *and behold, with the clouds of heaven*
> *there came one like a son of man,*
> *and he came to the Ancient of Days*
> *and was presented before him.*
> *And to him was given dominion*
> *and glory and a kingdom,*
> *that all peoples, nations, and languages*
> *should serve him;*
> *his dominion is an everlasting dominion,*
> *which shall not pass away,*
> *and his kingdom one*
> *that shall not be destroyed. (Daniel 7:13, 14)*

The glory is that today the ascended "Son of Man" mediates the commerce between Heaven and earth. As Paul says, "For there is one God, and there is one mediator between God and men, the man Christ Jesus, who gave himself as a ransom for all" (1 Timothy 2:5, 6a). Christ, our "Son of Man," is everywhere at all times, hearing our prayers and mediating the commerce of Heaven in our behalf. Think of this! He is at both ends of the ladder — as Jehovah at the top and Jesus ("Jehovah is salvation") at the bottom. The incarnate "Son of Man" is the ascended "Son of Man" whose dominion knows no end.

Even the old Bethel (i.e., "the house of God") has been superseded. It is no longer in Bethel where God reveals himself, but in Jesus. The temple is likewise obsolete, because Jesus *is* the temple (cf. Revelation 21:22). And, believers, there is nowhere we can go where he does not mediate commerce between Heaven and earth for us. His promises to us stand. He keeps his word. Everywhere we go is "the house of God" and "the gate of heaven." Furthermore, he is at work to conform us to himself, and we can be sure that "he who began a good work in you will bring it to completion at the day of Jesus Christ" (Philippians 1:6).

Now, you may be insulted when I suggest that we all are Jacobs. But if you are, you simply do not know yourself or your Bible. We are all people who often find ourselves in flight because of our sins. We are people who then imagine that God is not with us because of our sins. But the reality is that there is a ladder that extends between Heaven and earth for us, and the one who controls that ladder from top to bottom is the Lord himself. Astonishingly, he sends his angels to us as ministering spirits (cf. Hebrews 1:14). He directs our lives. He finds us in our solitary desolations and ministers to us.

Why? Because he is the God of grace. And he is not done with us. Truly, he will not be done with us in this life. We need to take these stupendous truths to heart. Our inner eye must perpetually behold the vision of the angel-freighted ladder superintended by the awesome Son of Man, who directs Heaven's traffic for our sanctification and his glory.

44

Deceiver Deceived

GENESIS 29:1-30

God's gift to Jacob, as he was fleeing from Esau to Haran, of the vision of an angel-freighted ladder between Heaven and earth, portraying that God was and would be with him wherever he went, was a gift that Jacob would carry with him the rest of his life. The mental picture of the busy ladder and the echo of God's voice affirming to Jacob that he was in the patriarchal succession of the Abrahamic covenant, plus the concluding declaration — "Behold, I am with you and will keep you wherever you go, and will bring you back to this land. For I will not leave you until I have done what I have promised you" (28:15) — would inform and energize his action throughout his decades-long sojourn in Haran, his frightened return to the land, and his wrestle in the night. He knew that everywhere he went, the ladder went, and that every place was therefore the house of God and gate of Heaven.

In practical terms, the ladder is an apt symbol for God's providential directing all of life for the believer. The God of Jacob is not simply a God of miracles who occasionally injects his power into our lives. He is far greater because he maintains and directs all of life to suit and effect his providence while rarely interrupting the natural order of life. The perpetual commerce of the ladder is always present animation.

Jacob's knowledge that the ladder of God's presence and provision was with him does not suggest, however, that Jacob's faith was complete or would not waver. Indeed, the old scheming, me-first Jacob remained alive and well, as was indicated by his conditional "If . . . then" vow, which said in essence, "If the Lord delivers me, then he shall be my God" (cf. 28:20-22). Notwithstanding this attitude, Jacob now proceeded from Bethel to Haran heartened and energized.

For sure, he was a piece of work, but he was also a work in progress. What takes place here and in the following episodes is the ongoing education, equipping, and completing of Jacob, the father of the twelve tribes of Israel.

JACOB ARRIVES IN HARAN (vv. 1-8)

The fact that Jacob was energized by his ladder-vision is indicated by the Hebrew behind the opening phrase, "Then Jacob went on his journey," which is literally, "Jacob lifted up his feet." Evidently he walked with a lighter step. In cinematic terms yellow bricks spread out before him as he sang, "I'm off to see my people, the wonderful people of Ur." At the very least, he hurried toward Mesopotamia in positive anticipation of what God would do "and came to the land of the people of the east" (v. 1) — a generic designation for his destination because it was here that he met his family.

Jacob knew by heart the story of how his mother Rebekah had been revealed to Abraham's servant Eliezer when he arrived in Mesopotamia and how Rebekah volunteered to water all ten of his camels — just as he had prayed she would if she was the appointed wife for Isaac (cf. 24:10-27).

Jacob knew this providence took place at a well. Wells had also been significant places in his father Isaac's life where important events had occurred (cf. 26:17-33). And therefore Jacob's expectation must have risen, because the first thing to meet his eyes was a well (vv. 2, 3). Would God now be pleased to bring about the answer to the promises made to him in Bethel? What was he to make of the situation?

Three flocks of sheep were lying around the well, along with their listless shepherds. A large stone plugged the well-mouth to prevent pollution and theft. And none of the shepherds had taken the trouble to greet him. So Jacob began with careful courtesy: "'My brothers, where do you come from?' They said, 'We are from Haran.' He said to them, 'Do you know Laban the son of Nahor?' They said, 'We know him.' He said to them, 'Is it well with him?' They said, 'It is well; and see, Rachel his daughter is coming with the sheep!'" (vv. 4-6).

These shepherds remind me of dock workers on their lunch break — little or no eye contact, grudging monosyllabic answers — and obvious relief when they spot Rachel coming. *Whew! Bother her, not us. Welcome to Mesopotamia, boy.* Of course, the unhelpful shepherds had underestimated Jacob, who could be a little aggressive himself, and he gave them a shot as the shepherdess approached. "He said, 'Behold, it is still high day; it is not time for the livestock to be gathered together. Water the sheep and go, pasture them'" (v. 7). The implication was, "It's midday. You should have watered your flock so your sheep could be grazing and fattening. You lazy bunch!" Stung, they managed to give a defensive reply: "We cannot until all the flocks are gathered together and the stone is rolled from the mouth of the well; then we water the sheep" (v. 8). The custom was that they would wait until the other flocks arrived and then the stone was removed. Evidently these listless shepherds with their flocks were first in the water line. Early to the well, early to sleep.

JACOB MEETS THE FAMILY (vv. 9-14)

Kissing cousin. Rachel means "ewe lamb." And there seems to be a word-play[1] on her name as she enters the story: "While he was still speaking with them, Rachel [ewe lamb] came with her father's sheep, for she was a shepherdess" (v. 9) — the lamb with her lambs.

There is no warrant for imagining as some do that Jacob's immediate enthusiasm means this was love at first sight. But his actions do certainly indicate that he believed that God's hand had guided him and that he was overwhelmed with joy. Every ounce of manliness rose in Jacob, so that we read, "Now as soon as Jacob saw Rachel the daughter of Laban his mother's brother, and the sheep of Laban his mother's brother, Jacob came near and rolled the stone from the well's mouth and watered the flock of Laban his mother's brother. Then Jacob kissed Rachel and wept aloud" (vv. 10, 11). The text has made it clear that removing the stone from the well was a communal task performed by the gathered shepherds, because of the stone's large size (vv. 2, 3). But in a burst of emotion Jacob strode up and wrenched it away single-handedly (indeed, he was from the same gene pool as Esau). Jacob was the man! Can you see the shepherds easing back in tense silence?

Jacob then watered Laban's flocks first. "Sorry, boys, but the lady goes first." It would have taken some time to water her sheep from this restricted source. But when the last sheep was satisfied, he planted a kiss on his cousin and wept out loud. This is the only place in biblical narrative where we read of a man kissing a woman who is not his wife or mother. But to attribute the kiss to sexual attraction is to read into the text. Jacob was simply overwrought with emotion. He had met his flesh-and-blood family. He had performed an extraordinary feat. He kissed his cousin — as he would soon kiss her father. He wept. At last he introduced himself. Jacob no doubt saw this as the beginning of the fulfillment of God's promises made to him at Bethel.

Scheming uncle. Rachel, of course, was astounded. "She ran and told her father. As soon as Laban heard the news about Jacob, his sister's son, he ran to meet him and embraced him and kissed him and brought him to his house. Jacob told Laban all these things, and Laban said to him, 'Surely you are my bone and my flesh!' And he stayed with him a month" (vv. 12b-14). Perhaps the memory of the riches that had come his way when Eliezer paid in gold for Laban's sister Rebekah enlivened Laban's footsteps as he ran to Jacob with an embrace and kiss and invitation. But when Jacob told Laban "all these things," his enthusiasm likely cooled. Forget the ten camels — Jacob didn't even have a donkey. As to gold? *Nada*. And as Jacob talked on, his revelations — if anything — diminished his position. Laban realized that Jacob was at his mercy — and highly exploitable. Gordon Wenham shows that Laban's ostensibly openhearted statement, "Surely you are my bone and my flesh" (which echoes Adam's words to Eve; cf. 2:23) more likely suggests the grudging admission, "You have convinced me that you are my nephew; so you may stay." Thus Laban intimated double-dealing. But Jacob, in his enthusiasm, may have missed it.[2]

From Jacob's perspective, the vision of the ladder and its promise of protection and provision now stood high over his life. God was directing the commerce of Heaven on his behalf. The gate of Heaven stood open over his life. And it was true and would remain true — but not as he expected. This third patriarch needed some substance. He needed some trimming. He needed a compassionate spirit. He needed to experience some pain. He needed to learn humility. He needed some added dimensions to his character. He needed to grow in faith. He needed to stop trusting in himself.

JACOB DECEIVED (vv. 15-30)

Seven years for Rachel. Uncle Laban slyly raised the subject of wages so that it sounded as if he were magnanimous. But an attentive reading indicates that the impetus came from his larcenous heart. "Then Laban said to Jacob, 'Because you are my kinsman, should you therefore serve me for nothing? Tell me, what shall your wages be?'" (v. 15).

Laban's introduction of the subject of money was followed by an ominous revelation. "Now Laban had two daughters. The name of the older was Leah, and the name of the younger was Rachel. Leah's eyes were weak, but Rachel was beautiful in form and appearance. Jacob loved Rachel" (vv. 16-18a). The *older-younger* sibling conflict introduced here is ominous, conjuring up the misery between Jacob and Esau. Jacob's past was catching up with him, and it would do so with a vengeance. Further portent lies in the contrast between the older and younger sister. Leah's eyes were "weak" (literally, "soft"), a description that most commentators think means no fire or sparkle or glow, which was much prized in the ancient East.[3] She was not, to use James Taylor's lyric, "a pretty señorita with fire in her eyes."

On the other hand, Rachel was a knockout in Jacob's estimation — though not necessarily beautiful by our standards, and probably not an anorexic model. In some cultures, strong-boned and plump defined beauty.[4] It was what *he* saw that counted.

Most ominously we are told that "Jacob loved Rachel." And what a love it was. Jacob offered to serve seven years for Rachel (v. 18) when, at the going dowry price, he could have served three or four years.[5] Such love! "So Jacob served seven years for Rachel, and they seemed to him but a few days because of the love he had for her" (v. 20).

Truly, Rachel became the love of Jacob's life, despite the fact that he would father children by Leah and the two wives' concubines when they used their maids as pawns in a birth war. Years later as Jacob lay dying he said to his sons, "As for me, when I came from Paddan, to my sorrow Rachel died in the land of Canaan on the way, when there was still some distance to go to Ephrath, and I buried her there on the way to Ephrath (that is, Bethlehem)" (48:7). And here, at the beginning of his love, the seven years (the double dowry) seemed like a day because he loved her so much. The angels were descending and ascending upon him. He could see it!

Deceiver deceived! Jacob's demand to Laban — "Give me my wife that I may go in to her, for my time is completed" (29:21) — strongly suggests that Laban was holding out, extorting as much as he could from Jacob. The absence of the courteous "Please give" and the presence of the solitary "Give" is the language of grievance.[6] And ostensibly Laban complied, doing the right thing in hosting a wedding feast. The typical wedding featured processions to and from the bride's dwelling. There was also the reading of the marriage contract. The feast was attended by both families and the community. And the first day's festivities ended with the groom wrapping his cloak around the bride and taking her to his tent where the marriage was consummated. Following that, the feast continued for six more days.[7]

Evidently Laban used the veiling of the bride, the lateness of the hour, and, likely, much wine to effect the switch — and it worked perfectly. As to what Laban did to restrain Rachel, we do not know. And more, Leah had to be a most willing bride. She must herself have loved Jacob and likely despised her beautiful sister. Nice work!

At any rate, when Jacob awoke to the morning glow of the sun illumining his tent and gazed upon his beloved, it was the uncomely Leah! What he said to Leah we can only imagine. He had whispered Rachel's name a hundred times to Leah in the night, and she had played her sister with passion. This was soap-opera ugly.

Leah was now his wife. There was no reversing the consummation. Oh, the betrayal, the hurt, the embarrassment, the rage. And then Jacob faced Laban. "What is this you have done to me? Did I not serve with you for Rachel? Why then have you deceived me?" (v. 25b). We wonder if he heard the irony in his own words. The verb "deceived" is the same stem used to describe Jacob's deception of Esau when he stole Esau's blessing (cf. 27:35).

At last Jacob knew what it was like to be on the receiving end! If anything, his agony and outrage exceeded that of Esau, because Esau's regard for his birthright was negligible, while Jacob here valued Rachel above all women. Now he understood Esau's pain to the *nth* degree.

Uncle Laban's self-righteous dig and further extortion was intended to cut Jacob to the quick. "It is not so done in our country, to give the younger before the firstborn. Complete the week of this one, and we will give you the other also in return for serving me another seven years" (vv. 26, 27). And cut it did. Jacob the younger had arrogated himself over older Esau. "Such a thing," Laban said, "would never do!" And the extortion was immense: "Complete the marriage week for Leah, then marry Rachel, and work seven more years to pay it off." Bottom line: a total of four full dowries and fourteen years of servitude for the wife he loved.

Jacob was beaten into silence. So we read, "Jacob did so, and completed her week. Then Laban gave him his daughter Rachel to be his wife. (Laban gave his female servant Bilhah to his daughter Rachel to be her servant.) So Jacob went in to Rachel also, and he loved Rachel more than Leah, and served Laban for another seven years" (vv. 28-30). And everyone lived happily ever after — in their dreams!

What a recipe for misery. Sister wives, one beautiful and the other less than beautiful. The less had savaged the favored. Most tellingly, one was loved, and the other was unloved. And then there were their maids, the concubines to be — eventually four competing future mothers. Two weeks earlier, Jacob was unmarried. Now all of this plus seven more years of servitude to Laban. Where was the angel-freighted ladder now?

It was where it had always been, extending upward into Heaven from the ground where Jacob stood. This place was "the house of God." His feet were at "the gate of heaven." God was with him. God was keeping him. God would bring him back to the land. God would never leave him until he had done what he had promised in the covenant. There was intense commerce between Heaven and earth for Jacob. The providence of God working in everyday life was in full effect, though Jacob could not see it.

Consider this: Twelve sons and one daughter would be born to the four women. Through unloved Leah and her maid Zilpah, eight of the twelve tribes would come. Leah would be the mother of Reuben, Simeon, Levi, Judah, Issachar, and Zebulun. Despised Leah was the hereditary mother of the kingly tribe of Judah and the priestly tribe of Levi. This makes her ultimate offspring Moses, David, and the Lord Jesus Christ! Indeed, God's work goes on and even thrives amidst human failure.

Was Jacob the father of the twelve tribes of Israel? Was God the God of Jacob? Yes. The divine ladder was there, and the Lord was keeping him. The heavenly commerce was free and flowing. But it is also true that although Jacob was the elect son, he did not escape the consequences of his own sins. Far from being immune to discipline, God's children are the object of special discipline.

The angel-freighted ladder disciplines and exalts. God had brought the arch-deceiver Laban into the life of the great patriarch-deceiver so that

Jacob's sin might be displayed before his eyes and he might be cut to the heart. Jacob's nemesis and greatest antagonist was an instrument of God. The ladder assured that it was so. And Jacob was going to change, not overnight but over time. He would become Israel, a prince of God.

Today for all believers the ladder is presided over and administered by the ascended Son of Man, as Jesus explained to Nathanael: "Truly, truly, I say to you, you will see heaven opened, and the angels of God ascending and descending on the Son of Man" (John 1:51). And the same Lord does the same thing for all his children. There is continual commerce between Heaven and earth for you and me. And like Jacob, we happily see it when everything is going well. But when life goes south, when our sins catch up with us and we are paying the piper, when hard times and hard people come into our lives, then the ladder seems remote. But the commerce is there. And if anything, it is more intense.

Perhaps, as it was for Jacob, there are difficult people in our lives — Laban-type nemeses — harsh people, judgmental people, deceitful people, untruthful people, arrogant people. And we cry for relief. But it just may be, as Allen Ross has suggested, that through them we "Take a long look at ourselves. It may be that some of those traits characterize us and that other people may be part of God's means of disciplining us."[8] One thing is for sure: The commerce on behalf of our souls will never cease until we are with the Son of Man.

And for this grace we must bless his name!

45

Birth Wars!

GENESIS 29:31 — 30:24

The creation account's explicit record that God created only one wife for Adam made it clear for all who would follow that anyone who takes an extra wife is going beyond what God intended. The famous creation ordinance is implicitly monogamous: "Therefore a man shall leave his father and his mother and hold fast to his wife, and they shall become one flesh" (2:24). In accord with this, the polygamous marriages in Genesis were darkly cast. Lamech's chest-thumping Sword Song before his wives Adah and Zillah exuded polygamous brutality (cf. 4:23ff.). Next, Abraham "listened to the voice" of his wife (an echo of Adam's listening to the voice of his wife at the fall; cf. 3:17) and took Hagar as his wife, thus acceding to the marital ethics of Mesopotamia (cf. 16:2ff.). The bitterness that followed is infamous. Ungodly Esau married two Hittite women (cf. 26:34) and added a third by taking an Ishmaelite wife (cf. 28:6-8). And in Genesis 29 the polygamy that Jacob was duped into can only be described as disastrous. It is true that the later Hebrew kings were scandalously polygamous. But their marriages were also catastrophic.

Clearly, the ideal for Hebrew marriage was always monogamy, despite the examples of royalty. So in the Old Testament polygamy was understood to be a violation of the covenantal faithfulness that God demanded of his bride Israel as dramatically portrayed, for example, in the book of Hosea.[1] And, of course, God spoke the final word in his Son who called his people to the joyous, monogamous love and fidelity that was emblematic of his love for his bride, the church (cf. Ephesians 5:25-33).

Now as we again take up Jacob's life, he is a *de facto* polygamist. Strictly speaking, it was not his fault. Certainly we know that it was not his choice! But there was a kind of equity here as the victimizer became the victim.

Jacob was made to drink his own duplicity-laced medicine. His marital situation was singularly unpromising. He was in pagan Mesopotamia at the mercy of his scoundrel uncle, Laban, to whom he was indentured for seven years and then for seven more years. He had a wife to whom he was not attracted and did not love. And this unloved wife had savaged her sister by masquerading as her on her wedding night and sexually engaging her groom. And more, this *ménage à trois* (this household of three, this triangle) was made up of difficult and unpromising human material. Jacob had demonstrated that he was an accomplished cheat. And, we shall see, the sister-wives were both sharp-tongued and shrill. Both women would use the births of their own and their surrogate children as opportunities to put their feelings into words, be it to celebrate or to gloat. This is messy — multiple wives, multiple births, sister hatred, brother hatred — all of which will be acted out over the years.

But despite all of this, we have here the genesis of the twelve tribes of Israel from one father and four mothers. Jacob did not know that he would father twelve sons. All he knew about his offspring was what he had heard the Lord say from above the angel-laden ladder at Bethel: "Your offspring shall be like the dust of the earth, and you shall spread abroad to the west and to the east and to the north and to the south, and in you and your offspring shall all the families of the earth be blessed" (28:14). Certainly Jacob did not know that his children would come in three sets of four. Initially, four would be born to Leah. Next, four would be born to the slave-maids Bilhah and Zilpah. And the last four would come from the sisters, two from Leah and two from Rachel. And, of course, Jacob had not the slightest intimation of the birth wars that lay ahead.

Imagine the interest with which this account would have been scrutinized when it was first written some five hundred years later by Moses upon the exodus from Egypt. The freshly delivered twelve tribes of Israel learned both about their origins and the ways of God. And for people of faith today there is likewise much to be learned here — about ourselves and about God.

FOUR BY LEAH (29:31-35)

As the focus of this section comes first upon Leah, we must understand that Jacob did not hate Leah as we normally use the word. "Hated" is used in 29:31 in the relative sense of "unloved," which is clear from the preceding verse: "So Jacob went in to Rachel also, and he loved Rachel more than Leah" (v. 30; cf. Deuteronomy 21:15ff.). This understood, we are ready for the essential revelations of the opening sentence of the passage under discussion: "When the LORD saw that Leah was hated, he opened her womb, but Rachel was barren" (v. 31). Of first importance we see that despite the sin and polygamy that had engulfed Jacob's marriage, the Lord had begun to work out his own purposes. God himself had closed beautiful, much-loved Rachel's womb and opened the womb of her lowly, unloved sister. He had bypassed Rachel and opened the womb of Leah in her humble estate.

Rachel was devastated. As Jacob's choice wife, she had rightly expected to be the matriarch who would fulfill the Bethel promises. And in the Mesopotamian context, barrenness was not so much pitied as disdained. In contrast, her older sister Leah was marvelously fertile, having one son after another while Jacob worked off his seven-year debt for Rachel.

Naturally, unloved Leah's hopes soared. Perhaps now, as this remarkable set of sons was developing, Jacob would come to love her. Barren Rachel, of course, felt increasingly diminished by her sister's successes. Thus we have two desperate women — one desperate for love and the other desperate for children. Oh, the joys of polygamy!

The barometer of Leah's pathetic hope of love is enshrined in her naming of the four boys. Reuben means "look, a son." So we read of boy number one, "And Leah conceived and bore a son, and she called his name Reuben, for she said, 'Because the LORD has looked upon my affliction; for now my husband will love me'" (v. 32). Significantly here, as in two other namings, Leah credited the Lord for the birth. There was no doubt in her mind that it was God's doing. Also, as in all the subsequent namings, she coupled the name's meaning ("look, a son") with an explanation of the significance of the name — "the LORD has looked upon my affliction." With this initial birth, her hope to be loved peaked — "now my husband will love me."

Simeon means "the Lord has heard." So of child two we read, "She conceived again and bore a son, and said, 'Because the LORD has heard that I am hated, he has given me this son also.' And she called his name Simeon" (v. 33). Perhaps this little boy would melt Jacob's hatred into love. The Lord had heard; so maybe Jacob would hear.

Levi means "attachment," and so we read of boy number three, "Again she conceived and bore a son, and said, 'Now this time my husband will be attached to me, because I have borne him three sons.' Therefore his name was called Levi" (v. 34). Here much-sobered Leah did not wish for love but attachment. This was a lonely, forlorn soliloquy. Her hope faded, and she demanded less.

Judah means "praise." So with boy four we have this sense: "And she conceived again and bore a son, and said, 'This time I will praise the LORD.' Therefore she called his name Judah. Then she ceased bearing" (v. 35). Here Leah made no plea for love or improved relations with her husband. She had given up. But though she might not ever enjoy Jacob's love, God had given her four sons, and she had to be thankful for that. And truly if Leah could have seen down the generations, she would have been astonished at how blessed she was, because her last two sons, Levi and Judah, would respectively father the *priestly* and *kingly* tribes of Israel. Leah's blood would flow in the veins of Moses and Aaron and David and Christ the Messiah!

As it stood, poor homely Leah remained unloved. Perhaps the musings of Sophie Tolstoy, another famous unloved wife, can tell us something of how she felt: "It is painful and humiliating. . . . I am nothing but . . . a useless creature with morning sickness, and a big belly, two rotten teeth, and a bad temper, a battered sense of dignity, and a love which nobody wants and which nearly drives me insane."[2]

FOUR BY THE SLAVE WIVES (30:1-13)

On the other hand, Rachel's barrenness became progressively intolerable with each of Leah's births. She was, of course, humiliated. But on top of that, Leah's beautiful little boys inflamed her maternal desires. Piteous envy gripped her soul. Envy's dark pathology diminished her own blessings and puffed Leah's blessings way beyond reality. In her bitterness, Rachel had forgotten that her barrenness was God's doing — that he is the giver of life. At this point, thoughts of God were far from her.

Thus the acrimonious exchange: "She said to Jacob, 'Give me children, or I shall die!' Jacob's anger was kindled against Rachel, and he said, 'Am I in the place of God, who has withheld from you the fruit of the womb?'" (vv. 1, 2). Rachel knew that children were a gift from God and that Jacob's sharp reply was deserved. But despite her husband's rebuke, Rachel decided to take matters into her own hands through the surrogate use of her maid Bilhah. Rachel knew all about the Sarah-Hagar fiasco. She knew of Esau's foolish unions. And, more, she had once treasured the ideal of a monogamous lifelong marriage to Jacob. But now she tossed it all aside as, taking up her own devices, she stepped up the birth wars. Perhaps she could catch up with Leah through Bilhah.

Two for Bilhah. Rachel's ploy was a smashing success. Bilhah bore her two sons in quick succession, Dan and Naphtali. Dan means "judged" or "vindicated." "Then Rachel said, 'God has judged me, and has also heard my voice and given me a son.' Therefore she called his name Dan" (v. 6). This was her declaration that God was beginning to set things right for her. Vindication at last! Naphtali means "wrestlings." "Then Rachel said, 'With mighty wrestlings I have wrestled with my sister and have prevailed.' So she called his name Naphtali" (v. 8). "Look, Leah, my tenacity is being rewarded." Rachel's surrogate was gaining.

Two for Zilpah. But Leah struck back by giving Zilpah to Jacob, and she in short time gave Leah two more sons, Gad and Asher. Gad means "good fortune," and Asher means "happy." "Bye, bye, Rachel. I'm leading 6 to 2! Don't you see, you poor infertile thing, that you're as close as you're going to get? God's fortune is smiling on me, not on you. What happy days!" Rachel was losing the war, and she knew it.

FOUR BY LEAH AND RACHEL (vv. 14-24)

Mandrake episode. Could the baby wars get any worse? They did, in fact, because we read, "In the days of wheat harvest Reuben went and found mandrakes in the field and brought them to his mother Leah" (v. 14). What boy number one found was an aphrodisiac-cum-fertility drug — a love potion. According to Genesis scholar Gordon Wenham, "The mandrake (*Mandragora autumnalis*) is a perennial Mediterranean plant that bears bluish flowers in winter and yellowish plum-sized fruit in summer. In ancient times, mandrakes were famed for arousing sexual desire (cf. Song of Solomon 7:13) and for helping barren women to conceive."[3] Indeed, the alleged powers are certainly seen here in Genesis and in the Song of Solomon, where the bride says,

> *The mandrakes give forth fragrance,*
> *and beside our doors are all choice fruits,*
> *new as well as old,*
> *which I have laid up for you, O my beloved. (7:13)*

Significantly, the Hebrew word translated "mandrakes" is almost the same as the Hebrew word for "love" (cf. Proverbs 7:18; Song 1:2; 4:10; 5:1).[4] Many ancients called mandrakes "love apples" or "May apples."[5]

The power of mandrakes was and is superstitious and not scientific. But what is clear here is that Rachel and Leah believed the mandrake myth and thus the mandrakes became coins for a desperate bargain.

Jacob hired. Tellingly, it is Rachel who again suggests the ungodly expedient, and "It is a further example, in this family, of trading in things that should be above trade, and resorting in trouble only half-heartedly to God" (Kidner).[6] The family ethics here seem more like those of a dog kennel!

> Then Rachel said to Leah, "Please give me some of your son's mandrakes." But she said to her, "Is it a small matter that you have taken away my husband? Would you take away my son's mandrakes also?" Rachel said, "Then he may lie with you tonight in exchange for your son's mandrakes." When Jacob came from the field in the evening, Leah went out to meet him and said, "You must come in to me, for I have hired you with my son's mandrakes." So he lay with her that night. (vv. 14b-16)

This is ugly. Leah, seeing she has the upper hand, speaks of Jacob as "my husband," notwithstanding her scandalous wedding night masquerade. And it is apparent in this sordid arrangement that Rachel controls which wife or slave-wife sleeps with Jacob and when. It seems that at Rachel's direction Leah has been shut out from her conjugal rights for some time.

The deal takes place, of course, because both women are now desperate for children. Leah gets her night, and Rachel gets the mandrakes.

Three for Leah. The Bible makes it clear that their beliefs in mandrakes are old wives' tales because Leah, who gives up the mandrakes, has two more children! And Rachel, who has the mandrakes, remains childless for three more years. So much for the love apples!

The text is explicit that Leah's renewed fertility comes from God: "God listened to Leah, and she conceived" (v. 17a). So again we see that God was accomplishing his divine purpose amidst the polygamous mess. As to Leah's two children, Issachar means "wages," a name that Leah ironically employs to denigrate Rachel's making her hire Jacob with the mandrakes.[7] The meaning of Zebulun is unclear, but Leah's upbeat mention of endowment and honor conveys the positive thrust of the name. This note of triumph is sustained as she calls her daughter Dinah — "judgment, vindication."[8]

Rachel's first! Meanwhile, Rachel, in the deep lowliness of her barrenness, had been praying for a child. Her petition was no doubt daily, and maybe even hourly. And God answered! "Then God remembered Rachel, and God listened to her and opened her womb. She conceived and bore a son and said, 'God has taken away my reproach.' And she called his name Joseph, saying, 'May the LORD add to me another son!'" (vv. 22-24).

Rachel had come to the end of herself. The beautiful, favored wife had given up on her devices. There were no surrogates and no mandrakes. Everything was of God, pure and simple. Here the words "opened her womb" duplicate the words that began the story in 29:31, forming a literary inclusion. Both Leah and Rachel had children only because God did it. Both had been visited in their low estate. This was grace alone. All was of God. The angel-freighted ladder with God's agents ascending and descending on Jacob had been fully operational throughout the scheming and manipulation, the surrogate competition, the love potions, the selling of intimacy, the celebrating and the gloating, the humiliations and the tears of the loveless and childless. Truly, God made "the wrath of man [to] praise [him]" (Psalm 76:10). Clearly, God would have no trouble using Jacob's sons, whether they were of Leah or Rachel or Bilhah or Zilpah.

With the birth of Joseph, joy almost leaps from the page. God had taken away Rachel's reproach. She called her son Joseph ("may he add"), saying, "May the LORD add to me another son!" (v. 24). And indeed God would one day do just that with Benjamin, son number twelve.

How fascinating this freshly written section must have been at the exodus when every man and woman could find his or her ancestral father and mother in this narrative. And how fascinating to see that human determination and cleverness would not, could not accomplish the work of God. In fact, God comes to the lowly as he did first to Leah in her humble condition and then to Rachel in her lowliness.

How fascinating this is for those of us who possess the revelation of Christ in the New Testament! When Martin Luther read this account, he asked, "Does God have no other occupation left than to have regard for the lowliness of the household?"[9] Luther's question was answered not only here but in the good news of the gospel, as we have it in Luke. When Mary heard Elizabeth confirm that her womb bore her Lord, Mary sang:

> *My soul magnifies the Lord,*
> *and my spirit rejoices in God my Savior,*
> *for he has looked on the humble estate of his servant.*
> *For behold, from now on all generations*
>   *will call me blessed. (Luke 1:46b-48)*

Upon the birth of Jesus, the angels voiced the Gloria to lowly shepherds (cf. Luke 2:8-20).

When Mary and Joseph brought Jesus to the temple, godly Simeon, who had been humbly waiting for the Lord, swept the baby into his arms, declaring:

> *Lord, now you are letting your servant depart in peace,*
> *according to your word;*
> *for my eyes have seen your salvation." (Luke 2:29, 30)*

And when Jesus initiated the preaching of the gospel, he quoted from Isaiah:

> *The Spirit of the Lord is upon me,*
> *because he has anointed me*
> *to proclaim good news to the poor.*
> *He has sent me to proclaim liberty to the captives*
> *and recovering of sight to the blind,*
> *to set at liberty those who are oppressed,*
> *to proclaim the year of the Lord's favor. (Luke 4:18, 19)*

46

The Greening of Jacob

GENESIS 30:25-43

Jacob's vision at Bethel of angels ascending and descending on a heavenly ladder on his behalf, coupled with God's three-dimensioned promise that the *land* of Canaan would be his, that a *people* as numerous as dust would spread from him to the four points of the compass, and that he would enjoy a *prosperity* that would bless the world — this stunning vision and multi-faceted promise became the informing, controlling, and heartening reality of Jacob's twenty-year sojourn in Haran in pagan Mesopotamia. We know this because angels frame his twenty-year sojourn beginning with the angel-filled ladder in 28:10ff. and concluding with the angels of God meeting him as he journeyed from Haran in 32:1.

The angelic bookends emphasized to Jacob their special care for him throughout his sojourn. Certainly the concluding assurance of the promise at Bethel echoed and reechoed in Jacob's heart over those twenty years: "Behold, I am with you and will keep you wherever you go, and will bring you back to this land. For I will not leave you until I have done what I have promised you" (28:15).

The unseemly genesis of Jacob's becoming a great people through twelve sons is something that neither he nor anyone else could have imagined. When he met Rachel and gallantly contracted to work seven years for her hand, he expected that she alone would be the matriarch through whom the dust of his descendants would spread. But then came polygamy as he was duped into marrying her sister Leah. This was followed by proud Rachel's barrenness and lowly Leah's four sons, which then eventuated in the infamous "birth wars" as the two women designated their maids as concubines and produced four more sons. And finally, after love potions and the selling of things that ought to be above sale, four more offspring were born — two of which were to Rachel, as God met her in her lowliness and gave her Joseph ("may he add") as her firstborn.

The polygamous intrigues of Jacob and his four wives had sown the wind, and they would reap the whirlwind in the tumultuous years that followed. But human sin could not thwart God's promise to Jacob. In fact, this sorry mess birthed the beginning of the twelve tribes of Israel. Leah's sons Levi and Judah would become the priestly and royal lines. Rachel's Joseph would be used to save the entire family. Father Jacob would be so harrowed and graced in the ensuing experiences that he would one day become Israel. And again we see that God was instructing his people (when he first opened Leah's womb and then at the end Rachel's womb) that he comes to the lowly — a principle that would obtain throughout salvation history right up to the humble birth of the Messiah and his eternal declaration, "Blessed are the poor in spirit, for theirs is the kingdom of heaven" (Matthew 5:3; cf. Luke 1:46-48).

But returning to the present situation, Jacob could now see that his offspring had the makings of a great *people*. However, as to the promise of his personal *prosperity* and of a *land*, he had nothing. So Jacob announced his departure for the promised land. "As soon as Rachel had borne Joseph, Jacob said to Laban, 'Send me away, that I may go to my own home and country. Give me my wives and my children for whom I have served you, that I may go, for you know the service that I have given you'" (vv. 25, 26). There was no love lost here. Though Jacob had married two of Laban's daughters and was entitled to parting gifts as he left Laban, which the later law would stipulate (cf. Deuteronomy 15:13, 14), he knew that Laban would send him away penniless if he could. Later Jacob would scold Laban, "If the God of my father, the God of Abraham and the Fear of Isaac, had not been on my side, surely now you would have sent me away empty-handed" (31:42). Laban's response confirmed his tightfistedness: "The daughters are my daughters, the children are my children, the flocks are my flocks, and all that you see is mine" (31:43).

So in declaring his departure, Jacob minced no words with his father-in-law. Jacob employed no "please" but just the unadorned imperative, "Send me away" — "let me go!" All Jacob asked for was his wives and his children.

DECEIVERS' DIALOGUE (vv. 27-34)

Departure disputed. Jacob's demand caught Laban flat-footed. Nevertheless, he was instinctively facile in his response (though perhaps more revealing than he would have liked to be). "But Laban said to him, 'If I have found favor in your sight, I have learned by divination that the LORD has blessed me because of you. Name your wages, and I will give it'" (vv. 27, 28). Laban momentarily groveled before Jacob as he sought a toehold. "If I have found favor in your sight" is a fawning way of addressing a superior. Flattery was second nature to Laban. Nevertheless, his next statement went right to the point: "I have learned by divination that the LORD has blessed me *because of you*" (emphasis added.) Whether he really did learn this by divination is not clear. If he did, then as Von Rad says, "This is one of the strangest confessions of Yahweh and his blessing in the Old Testament, a confession which even a Laban had arrived at by the dark process of his superstition!"[1] More likely instead of "divination" the Hebrew should read, "*I have become rich* and the Lord has blessed me because of you" — which plainly declares that his overriding interest was money, and that his prosperity was solely because God's blessing was on Jacob. Laban was not a man of faith. But he readily discerned and admitted that his blessing was because of association with Jacob. Did this make him hungry for God? Sadly, no. Laban's only desire was for the prosperity of association. Therefore, he cut to the bottom line: "Name your wages, and I will give it."

Vintage Laban. Uncle Scrooge had his wits about him here! Jacob had asked Laban for his wives and children, and Laban responded by talking about money. Laban knew the price of everything and the value of nothing. Sly Laban knew that he owed Jacob nothing, because Jacob already had received two wives given in exchange for fourteen years of labor. Obviously, if Jacob wanted even a penny more for travel expenses, he would have to indenture himself to more labor. Nice.

It is apparent that these two antagonists had rarely seen eye-to-eye. But Laban's crediting his blessing to Jacob was cause for Jacob's agreement and Jacob's God-glorifying application. "Jacob said to him, 'You yourself know how I have served you, and how your livestock has fared with me. For you had little before I came, and it has increased abundantly, and the LORD has blessed you wherever I turned'" (vv. 29, 30a). The application was to God's promise to Jacob at Bethel that "in you and your offspring shall all the families of the earth be blessed" (28:14b).

Also, Jacob's assertion that Laban's little had "increased abundantly" (literally, "teemed" as in teeming growth) is the same Hebrew used in the Bethel promise of Jacob's being "spread [teemed] abroad" (28:14a), and then later in the final verse of the present narrative it describes how Jacob "increased [teemed] greatly" (v. 43).[2] These three uses of the same word, first in the Bethel promise and twice in this story, serve to make the dominant point, which is this: *God is the giver of prosperity*. And more, what we are now going to see in the greening of Jacob will leave no doubt that it is God who brings prosperity.

Such a deal! Now Jacob took charge of the conversation, extending the dialogue with a question to Laban: "But now when shall I provide for my own household also?" (v. 30b). To which Laban asked in return, "What shall I give you?" (v. 31a), which then allowed Jacob to outline an amazing deal.

Jacob said, "You shall not give me anything. If you will do this for me, I will again pasture your flock and keep it: let me pass through all your flock today, removing from it every speckled and spotted sheep and every black lamb, and the spotted and speckled among the goats, and they shall be my wages. So my honesty will answer for me later, when you come to look into my wages with you. Every one that is not speckled and spotted among the goats and black among the lambs, if found with me, shall be counted stolen." (vv. 31b-34)

Such a deal indeed! Normally shepherds contracted to shepherd for 10 to 20 percent of the flock as payment as well as a percentage of the wool and milk products.[3] But this was extraordinarily generous — and apparently stupid. Most sheep are all white, and most goats are all one dark color, black or brown. Mottled and striped sheep and goats are comparatively rare. Incredibly, Jacob offered to remove the few multicolored sheep from Laban's flock as his compensation and then shepherd the plain colored animals for Laban. When they bred, the common, plain-colored would remain Laban's, and the rare variegated Jacob's. From every angle it was a deal for Laban. There were no loopholes. He could not lose! "Laban said, 'Good! Let it be as you have said'" (v. 34). Likely, when he got out of Jacob's sight he began to smile, then chuckle, and then roar with laughter. He tried not to look smug. But he could not help it. He inwardly sneered at the fool Jacob.

AMIDST DECEPTION GOD MAINTAINS HIS PROMISE (vv. 35-43)

Laban, in taking care to protect his own interests, immediately overstepped the spirit of the agreement as he himself removed all the variegated animals from his flock and sent them three days' journey away, with his sons tending them (vv. 35, 36). According to verse 32 Jacob, not Laban, was supposed to do this. And after that, only the occasional multicolored would be Jacob's as Laban's flocks multiplied. Again Laban must have felt smug about the arrangement. He had thought that Jacob was smarter than this. He was actually losing respect for the young man! All those mouths to feed. What a pity.

Jacob's countermeasures. Jacob's countermeasures were a combination of superstition and clever common sense. Superstitious folklore allowed that a vivid sight during mating would mark the outcome of the pregnancy. Such superstitions are not uncommon today as to human births, and sometimes birth anomalies are attributed to what a woman sees during her pregnancy. Here in the story Jacob's manipulation of sticks peeled to imitate stripes was intended to visually influence the plain animals to variegation. But Jacob was not wholly superstitious in the process, because his selective breeding was eminently reasonable. "Whenever the stronger of the flock were breeding, Jacob would lay the sticks in the troughs before the eyes of the flock, that they might breed among the sticks, but for the feebler of the flock he would not lay them there. So the feebler would be Laban's, and the stronger Jacob's" (vv. 41, 42).

Indeed, there may be a scientific basis for Jacob's success. The esteemed commentator Nahum Sarna cites an article from the *Jewish Encyclopedia* that argues that the more vigorous of the flock (in contrast to the feebler) were single-colored hybrids — that hybrids are characterized by what is called *heterosis* or hybrid vigor. Therefore, by careful observation as to which animals are more energetic, the breeder can determine which single-colored animals carry recessive genes for spottedness. Sarna goes so far as to suggest that Jacob may have gone through the elaborate procedure of arranging the peeled sticks to disguise his empirical technique.[4]

Also, it must be noted that Jacob received the breeding instructions from God in a dream:

> *In the breeding season of the flock I lifted up my eyes and saw in a dream that the goats that mated with the flock were striped, spotted, and mottled. Then the angel of God said to me in the dream, "Jacob," and I said, "Here I am!" And he said, "Lift up your eyes and see, all the goats that mate with the flock are striped, spotted, and mottled, for I have seen all that Laban is doing to you. I am the God of Bethel, where you anointed a pillar and made a vow to me." (31:10-13a)*

If Jacob was operating on largely superstitious beliefs (which is the likely view), we must keep in mind that the Bible is not teaching that animals are influenced by prenatal stimuli. It merely records that Jacob held the superstition along with general Mesopotamian culture. Jacob's peeled rods, then, are similar to Rachel's mandrakes. The mandrakes did not produce fertility, and neither did Jacob's rods. The Scriptures are explicit that God opened Rachel's womb (cf. 30:22). And they are also explicit that God intervened and gave the livestock to Jacob: "Thus God has taken away the livestock of your father and given them to me" (31:9). Therefore, however it happened and however informed Jacob was, God did it!

Jacob prospers. So right there in pagan Mesopotamia (Paddan-aram, Haran), Jacob prospered. "Thus the man increased greatly and had large flocks, female servants and male servants, and camels and donkeys" (v. 43).

How sweet it must have been! Money-loving, money-grubbing Laban was left comparatively destitute.

> *He catches the wise in their own craftiness,*
> *and the schemes of the wily are brought to a quick end. (Job 5:13)*

> The wicked man . . . makes a pit, digging it out,
> and falls into the hole that he has made. (Psalm 7:14, 15)

Jacob had become a rich, rich man. Like his grandfather Abraham, he also came to command a retinue of servants and flocks and camels (cf. 12:16 and 31:17, 18). Moreover, Jacob's prosperity did not rest on dishonesty. He was absolutely truthful and equitable in his dealings with Laban. And his wealth had come so quickly! Laban's sons complained that Jacob had taken their father's wealth, but that was not true (cf. 31:1ff.). It was the providence of God. In point of fact, this final verse again references the promises made to Jacob at Bethel in 28:14. Jacob had "increased greatly" ("*teemed* greatly," 30:43) — just as God had promised at the ladder.

As Jacob prospered in Paddan-aram, he knew that his success rested upon the revelations at Bethel. Through all the ups and downs in his battles with Laban, Heaven's commerce in his behalf had never ceased. The angels ascended and descended in both his humiliations and triumphs. God had been with him in every place. Along with this was the promise from the Lord of the ladder of a *people*, *prosperity*, and a *place*:

> And behold, the LORD stood above it [the ladder] and said, "I am the LORD, the God of Abraham your father and the God of Isaac. The land on which you lie I will give to you and to your offspring. Your offspring shall be like the dust of the earth, and you shall spread abroad to the west and to the east and to the north and to the south, and in you and your offspring shall all the families of the earth be blessed. Behold, I am with you and will keep you wherever you go, and will bring you back to this land. For I will not leave you until I have done what I have promised you." (28:13-15)

Jacob could see that despite the treachery and the domestic wars, he had begun to be a *people*, and that it was solely the work of God. There could be no other accounting for the incredible genesis of a people other than God's hand. Likewise, his *prosperity* rested solely upon God's blessing. Unbelieving Laban knew it, and Jacob knew it, and all history would know it. His prosperity was a glorious miracle. Soon Jacob would take his leave of Laban for the journey to the *land*. But again God would have to do it, as we will see.

What we have here in Jacob's life is a mini-preview of redemptive history, because Jacob's exile in Mesopotamia is a microcosm of what would happen in macrocosm to Israel in the later exile in Egypt. Just as Jacob's family multiplied in his exile, so the tribes of Israel would multiply to a vast multitude by the time of the exodus from Egypt. Just as Jacob would so prosper in his exile that Laban felt himself to be plundered, so also Israel would plunder the Egyptians in the exodus: "And the LORD had given the people favor in the sight of the Egyptians, so that they let them have what they asked. Thus they plundered the Egyptians" (Exodus 12:36). And just as God would have to protect and free Jacob from Laban and clear the way to the promised land, even so God would loose Israel from Pharaoh and open the way into Canaan in the exodus.

And more, it was the ultimate Israel (Christ himself) who would be called out of Egypt (Matthew 2:15).[5] And it is Christ who effects the ultimate spiritual exodus, who calls a *people*, who *prospers* their ways and leads them to the *land*.

We must never forget that the pattern for our salvation began long ago and is fulfilled in Christ.

All glory to his name.

47

Mesopotamian Exodus

GENESIS 31:1-55

Jacob's flight from Mesopotamia is framed by redemptive history. Looking back, it has parallels with Abraham's leaving the Mesopotamian city of Ur in obedience to God's call (cf. Genesis 12:1-9). Then Abraham took all his people and possessions and left for the land of Canaan. In Genesis 31 his grandson Jacob took all his people and possessions and returned to Canaan. Jacob's departure thus parallels Abraham's initial obedience.

Looking forward, Jacob's exodus from Mesopotamia provides a prophetic outline of Israel's exodus from Egypt. Here Jacob's large family flees from Laban; there a multitude of his descendants will flee Pharaoh. Here his family plunders Laban; there they will plunder Pharaoh and his people. Here Laban is forced to let Jacob's family go; there Pharaoh will be forced to let Jacob's descendants go. And all of this is prophetic of the glorious exodus that believers would find in Christ, the ultimate Israel, who plundered the power of evil and led them out of bondage to Satan.

The driving point of the narrative of Jacob's escape here in Genesis 31 is that God did it all — through his multiple interventions and constant protection. God would later do exactly the same in Moses' escape from Egypt. And so it now is in the ultimate exodus in Christ. All glory goes to God, "For from him and through him and to him are all things. To him be glory forever. Amen" (Romans 11:36).

One of the beautiful things about Jacob's flight is that we see that Jacob has made spiritual progress. He actually appears in a favorable light! He is now utterly faithful to God. He begins obediently and does not waver. Here this old deceiver is honest and rightly declares his integrity before Laban. Most significantly, this chronically self-sufficient man gives all the credit to God. Jacob's spiritual progress would also have its parallels in Moses' spiritual development preceding his leading Israel in its great exodus. Christ, the captain of the ultimate exodus, was, as we know, perfect in every way.

Now as we consider Jacob's exodus from Mesopotamia, everything is in place. He now has a *people* — some four wives and eleven children — the genesis of a vast people. His *possessions* are such that he is remarkably rich. He knows that his people and possessions are from God. God sees that he is ready.

JACOB ENLISTS HIS WIVES (vv. 1-16)

Laban's ugly mood did not bode well for Jacob. So when the Lord said to Jacob, "Return to the land of your fathers and to your kindred, and I will be with you" (v. 3), Jacob's response was unhesitating.

Jacob's case. But because the Mesopotamian legal code stipulated that he could not take his wives away without their consent, Jacob summoned them to the open field where he was shepherding, a place where they could not be overheard, and there he made his case. In the ensuing exchange in verses 4-16, Jacob and his wives reference God by name seven times, because God and his work was the controlling factor in their decision. Jacob began by reviewing for them Laban's unfair dealings, which God had just then nullified by making Laban's plain-colored flocks bear multicolored offspring. Jacob's conclusion was, "Thus God has taken away the livestock of your father and given them to me" (v. 9). Clearly God, not Jacob's machinations, was the reason for the transfer of wealth. And more, Jacob recounted how God had confirmed this in a dream during breeding season that concluded with this divine directive: "I am the God of Bethel, where you anointed a pillar and made a vow to me. Now arise, go out from this land and return to the land of your kindred" (v. 13). This called to Jacob's mind his sacred vow made in Bethel (amidst the promised land) that in response to God's faithfulness, the Lord would be his God (cf. 28:20-22). This was powerful.

The wives' response. Here for the first time we see Rachel and Leah in agreement. The two sisters, at once victims and victimizers, were in concert.

> Then Rachel and Leah answered and said to him, "Is there any portion or inheritance left to us in our father's house? Are we not regarded by him as foreigners? For he has sold us, and he has indeed devoured our money. All the wealth that God has taken away from our father belongs to us and to our children. Now then, whatever God has said to you, do." (vv. 14-16)

Particularly grievous to Laban's daughters was the ugly fact that their father had sold them and devoured the proceeds. The price of the bride (Jacob's fourteen years of wages) was supposed to be held in trust in the event that they were abandoned or widowed.¹ But Jacob's long labor had benefited their father alone. Thus the chorus of indignation — "Go for it, Jacob! What was his is now yours, which means ours. Do whatever God has said."

JACOB'S FLIGHT (vv. 17-21)

Stealth. Sheep-shearing in Mesopotamia was a springtime activity in which large flocks necessitated large shearing crews that would labor for extended periods away from their home. One of the famous Mari tablets record three to four hundred men working for a three-day period to complete a shearing. Others describe much longer periods.² Laban's wool-gathering absence provided a perfect time to escape.

> *So Jacob arose and set his sons and his wives on camels. He drove away all his livestock, all his property that he had gained, the livestock in his possession that he had acquired in Paddan-aram, to go to the land of Canaan to his father Isaac. Laban had gone to shear his sheep, and Rachel stole her father's household gods. And Jacob tricked Laban the Aramean, by not telling him that he intended to flee. He fled with all that he had and arose and crossed the Euphrates, and set his face toward the hill country of Gilead. (vv. 17-21)*

There is a wordplay here in verses 19, 20 that indicates the deep mutuality of Jacob and Rachel in their actions. The word "tricked" in verse 20 is literally (as the ESV margin has it) "*stole the heart of,*" which is an idiom for "tricked" or "deceived." So the Hebrew text reads, "And Rachel stole her father's household gods. And Jacob stole the heart of Laban the Aramean," which brilliantly "shows Rachel and Jacob to be of a kindred spirit" (Ross).³ Such solidarity. Watch out, Laban!

Theft. The *teraphim* or "household gods" that Rachel pilfered from her father were likely small, carved human figures. On a later occasion one of King David's wives took a life-sized image, put a wig on it, and placed it in David's bed to fool Saul's murderous emissaries (1 Samuel 19:13). Here the *teraphim* were small enough to hide in a camel's saddle cushion. As to why Rachel stole them, the Nuzi tablets suggest that the possession of the family gods strengthened your claim to an inheritance.⁴ Another possibility is that Laban used them for divination, and that Rachel was thwarting his ability to detect Jacob's escape.⁵ Perhaps it was just spite — so Rachel could demonstrate her contempt for Laban's gods. Significantly, the whole incident was bathed in alienation. Laban was now called "Laban the Aramean" (v. 20), emphasizing his ethnic identity. The alienation was becoming complete. Two distinct peoples were forming.

The tension began to peak. Rachel's secret theft had put both herself and unknowing Jacob in mortal danger.

LABAN ASSAILS JACOB (vv. 22-35)

However we account for Laban's not catching up to Jacob until he reached the hills of Gilead (perhaps he needed several days to equip for the pursuit,[6] or perhaps the numbers are symbolic[7]), one thing is sure: Laban's posse thundered after Jacob with murderous intent. The verbs in verses 22-25 — "fled," "pursued," "overtook," "pitched tents" — are militaristic.[8] Laban was on the warpath. If God had not come to "Laban the Aramean in a dream by night and said to him, 'Be careful not to say anything to Jacob, either good or bad'" (v. 24), there would have been violence.

Laban's speech. Jacob's long night awaiting Laban's confrontation must certainly have been terror-filled, notwithstanding God's promises to him. The meeting between the camps at Mizpeh and Mount Gilead was charged with uncertainty. What a relief for Jacob when the only things Laban hurled were words. And what a phony cascade it was as Laban played the part of the loving, wounded father who had come in injured innocence, a good man who had been sorely wronged.

> *And Laban said to Jacob, "What have you done, that you have tricked me and driven away my daughters like captives of the sword? Why did you flee secretly and trick me, and did not tell me, so that I might have sent you away with mirth and songs, with tambourine and lyre? And why did you not permit me to kiss my sons and my daughters farewell? Now you have done foolishly. It is in my power to do you harm. But the God of your father spoke to me last night, saying, 'Be careful not to say anything to Jacob, either good or bad.' And now you have gone away because you longed greatly for your father's house, but why did you steal my gods?" (vv. 26-30)*

Laban's buffoonery rings hollow and ineffectual, except for the final line — "But why did you steal my gods?" Jacob was not ready for this, and his concluding rejoinder unknowingly put his beloved Rachel under a sentence of death: "'Anyone with whom you find your gods shall not live. In the presence of our kinsmen point out what I have that is yours, and take it.' Now Jacob did not know that Rachel had stolen them" (v. 32).

Laban's search. Ignorance is bliss. So Jacob confidently watched Laban as he stormed through his tent and then Leah's and then the tents of Bilhah and Zilpah and then back through Leah's and then into Rachel's, where he met his match. "Now Rachel had taken the household gods and put them in the camel's saddle and sat on them. Laban felt all about the tent, but did not find them. And she said to her father, 'Let not my lord be angry that I cannot rise before you, for the way of women is upon me.' So he searched but did not find the household gods" (vv. 34, 35).

We must understand that the reason that wildly suspicious Laban never suspected that Rachel was sitting on his household gods is that he could not imagine such a sacrilege. Among the ancients "the way of women" was considered to be a state of impurity and thus contaminating. Rachel's recline was therefore a calculated act of withering contempt for the gods of Mesopotamia. She treated them as worthless and unclean. In doing this, Rachel foreshadowed the despoiling of Egypt's gods during the plagues of Egypt. This passage also announces future Israel's contempt for pagan gods. Very likely Laban's *teraphim* were among the gods that Israel would bury at Shechem (cf. 35:14).

JACOB BERATES LABAN (vv. 36-42)

Laban had ransacked Jacob's tents from top to bottom. And from Jacob's innocent viewpoint that was only a cheap pretext to search for other things that Laban suspected Jacob had stolen from him. Moreover, Laban offered no apology. So in an explosive moment all Jacob's pent-up anger over twenty years of deception and mistreatment erupted to give Laban the tongue-lashing of his life. According to Mesopotamian law, Laban's fruitless search of Jacob's tents constituted presumptive proof that Jacob was innocent.[9] Thus with the emotive leverage of wholehearted innocence, abused Jacob unloaded. "Then Jacob became angry and berated Laban. Jacob said to Laban, 'What is my offense? What is my sin, that you have hotly pursued me? For you have felt through all my goods; what have you found of all your household goods? Set it here before my kinsmen and your kinsmen, that they may decide between us two'" (vv. 36, 37). "Let's have a court right here and find out who's the real thief!"

My faithfulness! The bucolic, romanticized thoughts of the pastoral life have always been myths. Jacob's years had been filled with hardships and losses, and Jacob furiously described how he bore it all. "These twenty years I have been with you. Your ewes and your female goats have not miscarried, and I have not eaten the rams of your flocks. What was torn by wild beasts I did not bring to you. I bore the loss of it myself. From my hand you required it, whether stolen by day or stolen by night. There I was: by day the heat consumed me, and the cold by night, and my sleep fled from my eyes" (vv. 38-40). Indeed he had been a good shepherd. That is why Laban, by his own admission, had prospered by his association with Jacob.

Your dishonesty. "Me dishonest? You're the cheat." "These twenty years I have been in your house. I served you fourteen years for your two daughters, and six years for your flock, and you have changed my wages ten times.

If the God of my father, the God of Abraham and the Fear of Isaac, had not been on my side, surely now you would have sent me away empty-handed. God saw my affliction and the labor of my hands and rebuked you last night" (vv. 41, 42). God had rebuked Laban in the dream when he warned Laban not to harm Jacob. Laban was so low, he would have been content to rob his own daughters and grandchildren. Again Jacob credited God for everything. It was all the grace of God. Jacob's grateful spirit honored God alone.

This was pure triumph! Jacob, the man to whom God had given a *people* and *possessions,* stood high above Laban the Aramean. How sweet it was!

A NONAGGRESSION PACT (vv. 43-55)

Exposed for what he was, Laban tried to cover himself with bluster. "Then Laban answered and said to Jacob, 'The daughters are my daughters, the children are my children, the flocks are my flocks, and all that you see is mine. But what can I do this day for these my daughters or for their children whom they have borne?'" (v. 43). Laban indulged in legal fictions, filial posturing, and feigned benevolence. Empty words from a hollow man.

A covenant formed. Abashed and off-balance, Laban needed to do something. So he proposed a mutual covenant of nonaggression.

> *"Come now, let us make a covenant, you and I. And let it be a witness between you and me." So Jacob took a stone and set it up as a pillar. And Jacob said to his kinsmen, "Gather stones." And they took stones and made a heap, and they ate there by the heap. Laban called it Jegar-sahadutha, but Jacob called it Galeed. Laban said, "This heap is a witness between you and me today." Therefore he named it Galeed, and Mizpah, for he said, "The LORD watch between you and me, when we are out of one another's sight. If you oppress my daughters, or if you take wives besides my daughters, although no one is with us, see, God is witness between you and me." Then Laban said to Jacob, "See this heap and the pillar, which I have set between you and me. This heap is a witness, and the pillar is a witness, that I will not pass over this heap to you, and you will not pass over this heap and this pillar to me, to do harm." (vv. 44-52)*

This was an amazing about-face for the tightfisted, dominating Mesopotamian. In reality, Jacob did not need a treaty because God had already protected him from Laban. However, a treaty would officially keep them apart — and for that it was well worth it. The treaty would recognize Jacob as a separate, independent people by its dual representations: two stone memorials, two meals, two names for the memorials, two names of deity, and the delineation of two ethnic groups.[10]

Jacob's new stone pillar recalled for him the presence of God at Bethel.

He remembered the angel-freighted ladder and the eternal promises of the Lord of the ladder of a *people, possessions,* and a *place.*

The heap of stones was formed to bear witness to their mutual covenant. Laban gave the pile an Aramaic name, Jegar-sahadutha, and Jacob a Hebrew name, Galeed, both of which mean "the heap of witness." Mizpah means "watchpost." Interestingly, the careless reading of God's Word as it is represented in the King James Version ("The Lord watch between me and thee, when we are absent one from another," v. 49) has given rise to the popular so-called "Mizpah benediction" that has been used on Christmas cards, inscribed inside wedding bands, and even used as a title for an organization! The Mizpah benediction was ignorantly interpreted to invoke union, fellowship, and trust.[11] But this was the declaration of two men who neither trusted nor liked each other — "Because I don't trust you out of my sight, may God watch your every move."

The covenant solemnized. In solemnizing the treaty, Laban invoked two separate deities and then multiple deities: "The God of Abraham and the God of Nahor, the God of their father [literally, "the deities of their father"], judge between us" (v. 53a). Laban was a pagan indeed! But Jacob ignored Laban's formula and swore by the true God. "So Jacob swore by the Fear of his father Isaac, and Jacob offered a sacrifice in the hill country and called his kinsmen to eat bread. They ate bread and spent the night in the hill country" (vv. 53b, 54). The final covenant meal was sacrificed. Symbolically they bound themselves to keep it before their divine host.

So it was that "Early in the morning Laban arose and kissed his grandchildren and his daughters and blessed them. Then Laban departed and returned home" (v. 55).

Jacob was looking good, better than he ever had. He still had a considerable way to go, but this was not the heel-grabbing supplanter who double-dealt his brother and duped his father. Jacob was becoming a man of character who kept his word. His exodus from Mesopotamia had been characterized by his faithful obedience to God's word. Jacob understood that his entire deliverance had been wrought by God. Repeatedly he credited God with his success. His placing a stone pillar alongside the heap of stones declared his faith in the God of Bethel and his constant provision. Though far from perfect, Jacob had grown in grace, by God's grace.

And for any who have eyes to see, here is the work of an awesome, sovereign God who works amidst the compost of human sin to do his will. Amidst the swirl of deception and intrigue he birthed a people who would become the twelve tribes of Israel. God took a poor man who had been repeatedly enslaved and exploited and made him rich. And now God led him in a glorious exodus as a prelude to his return to the land of promise. Such an awesome God!

And all of this is merely a shadow of what Christ does for his people in the exodus of the cross. The shorthand for what we see in the history of redemption (in the lives of Abraham, Isaac, Jacob, and all true Israel) is this:

> *And we know that for those who love God all things work together for good, for those who are called according to his purpose. For those whom he foreknew he also predestined to be conformed to the image of his Son, in order that he might be the firstborn among many brothers. And those whom he predestined he also called, and those whom he called he also justified, and those whom he justified he also glorified. What then shall we say to these things? If God is for us, who can be against us? He who did not spare his own Son but gave him up for us all, how will he not also with him graciously give us all things? (Romans 8:28-32)*

What comfort for those who desire to grow in grace. Our part is to faithfully follow him.

> *If thou but suffer God to guide thee*
> *And hope in Him through all thy ways,*
> *He'll give thee strength, whate'er betide thee,*
> *And bear thee thro' the evil days.*
> *Who trusts in God's unchanging love*
> *Builds on the rock that naught can move.*
> GEORG NEUMARK, 1641

48

Jacob Becomes Israel

GENESIS 32:1-32

Jacob had substantial reason to be encouraged. Laban and Mesopotamia were history. Laban's parting word — "The LORD watch between you and me, when we are out of one another's sight" (31:49) — was not a benediction but a hostile malediction. And it was music to his son-in-law's ears. Never again would Jacob have to deal with his unctuous, manipulating father-in-law. Jacob was going home victoriously with eleven sons and immense wealth.

He was also further heartened because we read, "Jacob went on his way, and the angels of God met him. And when Jacob saw them he said, 'This is God's camp!' So he called the name of that place Mahanaim ["two camps"]" (32:1, 2). Twenty years earlier when he had left Canaan on the run, "the angels of God" had met him (cf. 28:12), and now as he returned to Canaan, "the angels of God" (the same designation) again met him. His joyful declaration of "Mahanaim" observed that there were two camps — a camp of angels was alongside his camp. Likely it was a vast throng of angels because elsewhere the phrase describes a large camp (cf. 1 Chronicles 12:22). So right there, about twelve to thirteen miles from the Jordan, Jacob was divinely refreshed by angelic realities that the psalmist would later celebrate in his own setting when he sang:

> The angel of the LORD encamps
> around those who fear him, and delivers them (Psalm 34:7)

> For he will command his angels concerning you
> to guard you in all your ways.
> On their hands they will bear you up,
> lest you strike your foot against a stone. (Psalm 91:11, 12)

All of this provided a marvelous retrospect upon Jacob's twenty-year sojourn in Mesopotamia and now, as he returned, the glorious prospect that angels would clear the way for his entrance back into Canaan. Further, Jacob's sighting of angels was visual confirmation of a deeper reality — namely, that Jacob had been and would continue to be the object of God's relentless grace — that an intrusive, tenacious, contending, renovating grace was at work on his life to make him to be the man that God intended him to be. This grace could not be shut out, would not let him go, and fought with him and for him at every turn.

JACOB'S MOUNTING FEAR (vv. 3-21)

Buoyed by the camp of angels, Jacob elected to first deal with a matter that had lain increasingly heavy upon his heart for those twenty years — his shabby dealings with his brother Esau and their broken relationship. We know that this was a heart-necessity because it was not a geographical must. Esau did not block his way, for he had settled far to the south at Mount Seir in Edom. Thus it was the spiritual necessity of making things right with his brother that drove Jacob. In support of this, Derek Kidner observes that the sequence of chapters 32 and 33, which culminates in 35:1-15, powerfully acts out the principles of spiritual reconciliation outlined in Matthew 5:23-25.[1]

Ominous developments. Jacob began with a peaceful overture. "And Jacob sent messengers before him to Esau his brother in the land of Seir, the country of Edom, instructing them, 'Thus you shall say to my lord Esau: Thus says your servant Jacob, "I have sojourned with Laban and stayed until now. I have oxen, donkeys, flocks, male servants, and female servants. I have sent to tell my lord, in order that I may find favor in your sight"'" (vv. 3-5). While the designations "my lord" and "your servant" were extravagantly humble in a brother relationship, they were not disingenuous but wholly sincere. These self-effacing terms were freighted with Jacob's repentance for his stealing ascendancy over his older brother. And Jacob's mention of his oxen, donkeys, flocks, and servants were more than a hint of his willingness to make reparations. Formerly larcenous, Jacob longed to make a generous payback to Esau.

The bare-facts report of the returning messengers — "We came to your brother Esau, and he is coming to meet you, and there are four hundred men with him" (v. 6) — does not indicate whether they had been able to convey Jacob's overture to Esau. All Jacob learned is the ominous number of four hundred men approaching with Esau in the lead, which was the standard size of a militia.[2] Jacob's fear and distress were eminently reasonable. The last he had heard from Esau was that Esau was biding his time to kill him (cf. 27:41). Now Esau was coming with a small army! This, mixed with the suprarational elements of the physical dominion of his big, hairy brother, made the memories of his brother's profile, even his smell terrifying.

The irony of Jacob's panicked response as he fearfully divided his people into two camps (Hebrew, *mahanaim*) could not have been missed by Jacob in retrospect. He simply was not thinking of the angels now. All that was on his mind was survival — and increasing the odds for at least half his camp. But while the Bible does not minimize using your head in difficult circumstances, it is implicit throughout the account that Jacob's actions would have proven futile apart from the ministries of God's camp.

Frightened prayer. Jacob's prayer in verses 9-12 is the first recorded prayer of Jacob and represents an advance in his spiritual growth. He includes within this prayer elements of *invocation, confession,* and *petition* and references to God's word at the beginning and end. His passionate confession of his unworthiness and lowliness — "I am not worthy of the least of all the deeds of steadfast love and all the faithfulness that you have shown to your servant, for with only my staff I crossed this Jordan, and now I have become two camps" (v. 10) — had not been characteristic of Jacob earlier. His newfound humility, like that of his wives before him, would now become the human ground for God's blessing, just as it had been for them.

Jacob's opening and concluding references to God's promises were also implicit statements of faith in his word. And we must note here that when Jacob concluded his prayer and engaged in further measures to control the situation, it was not Jacob's desperate measures that succeeded but his prayer!

Desperate measures. His measures bore a desperate brilliance. "So he stayed there that night, and from what he had with him he took a present for his brother Esau, two hundred female goats and twenty male goats, two hundred ewes and twenty rams, thirty milking camels and their calves, forty cows and ten bulls, twenty female donkeys and ten male donkeys" (vv. 13-15). All in all, Jacob assembled more than 550 animals that he arranged into five groups of goats, sheep, camels (and some calves), cattle, and donkeys. The size and admixture of the gift was fit for a king.

And Jacob staged the gift for maximum impact, spacing the droves out so that Esau would have just enough time to admire the animals and interact with the servants before the next group arrived. Jacob instructed his servants to say with each drove, "They belong to your servant Jacob. They are a present sent to my lord Esau. And moreover, he is behind us" (v. 18). So when the 220 goats arrived, Esau heard the spiel and the concluding words, "he is behind us." So it was with the 220 bleating sheep and rams. And again with the thirty camels and their young. And again with the fifty mooing cattle, and finally with the thirty braying donkeys. "They belong to your servant Jacob. They are a present sent to my lord Esau. And moreover, he is behind us." For the first time in Jacob's life he wanted to be last! Jacob's intention was forthright. "For he thought, 'I may appease him with the present that goes ahead of me, and afterward I shall see his face. Perhaps he will accept me'" (v. 20).

The scene became one of unmitigated nocturnal terror. "So the present passed on ahead of him, and he himself stayed that night in the camp" (v. 21). Was Jacob praying? Probably, though the text does not say. Clearly he was on the edge because he did a most dangerous thing by fording the ravine of the fast-moving Jabbok to place his wives and children on the other side. It was dangerous enough in the daylight, but in the black of night, most dangerous. In the morning he would be the first to meet Esau.

JACOB'S MORTAL COMBAT (vv. 22-32)

It was the darkest night of Jacob's life as he sat alone reflecting on the past and on what the sunlight might bring, alternately shivering in the mountain cold and trembling at the approach of Esau.

Combat and crippling. Then his heart seized as a hand fastened onto him — a powerful hand. Jacob was in the mighty hold of someone who seemed intent on taking his life. Jacob could see nothing. The assailant was silent and nameless. But Jacob, no pushover himself, rose mightily to the occasion. And that long night (six or seven hours?) became one of burning sweat, dripping hair and beard, and slipping appendages. There came brief periods of labored breathing, and then renewed fury, gouging, pulling, butting. And then more rage — and more pain and thirst — and smothering frustration.

Unknown to Jacob through most of that agonizing night, he was wrestling with a divine being, as the concluding verses make clear (vv. 29-31). Hosea 12:4 is unequivocal in his identification: "He strove with the angel." God was Jacob's ultimate and intimate enemy. Jacob was wrestling with God.

Certainly he did not see the wrestling for what it was — a parable of his entire life. Throughout the long narrative, Jacob's life has been characterized as a grasping struggle. Jacob had wrestled with his brother (25:22), and then with his father (chap. 27), and then with his father-in-law (chaps. 29 — 31), and now with God (chap. 32). Jacob had always struggled with both man and God.

As the two wrestled on, Jacob had no idea that he was in the grip of God's relentless grace. Hours passed, and we read, "When the man saw that he did not prevail against Jacob, he touched his hip socket, and Jacob's hip was put out of joint as he wrestled with him" (v. 25). Did the pain evoke an agonized howl? Jacob was reduced to a clinging doll, his disjointed leg dangling useless in the melee. But he hung on. His opponent had done it with a mere touch! A touch that dislocates suggests an opponent with superhuman power. Now perhaps Jacob began to wonder at the origin of his enemy. As the story will unfold, this was a crippling grace from the hand of God. We know that God accommodated his almighty strength to that of Jacob as he wrestled with him in human form. Only later would Jacob begin to understand.

Renaming and blessing. As the wrestlers became exhausted from their marathon match, they began to speak. The unknown assailant began: "'Let me go, for the day has broken.' But Jacob said, 'I will not let you go unless you bless me'" (v. 26). Jacob had already been given an intimation of the assailant's supernaturalness by the effortless dislocation, and his concern to remain unknown (v. 29) was another hint of his supernatural origin. Later Scripture would record that no man can see God and live (cf. vv. 30, 31; Exodus 33:20).[3] Jacob sensed the divine. Here Jacob, sensing the character of his opponent, seized the opportunity and insisted on a blessing. After all, he still is *Jacob*. We all know that the spirit of a man is not merely in the words he utters, but in the attitude in which he speaks. And here we discover Jacob's heart-attitude in the God-given interpretation of the story provided us in Hosea 12:4: "He strove with the angel and prevailed; he wept and sought his favor." It was not from proud dominance that Jacob asked for blessing, but with tears. His request came when he was at the end of himself, helpless. "I will not let you go unless you bless me" (v. 26) was a tear-choked plea.

In the context of the Bible, to disclose your name could be an act of self-disclosure, a revelation of your character, your deepest identity. So the assailant asked the question, "'What is your name?' And he said 'Jacob'" (v. 27). Here it was a confession of guilt — "I am fraud. I am deceiver. I am supplanter. I am rightly named Jacob, for I cheated my brother twice!" (cf. 27:36). This confession evoked amazing, transforming grace, because instead of merely blessing him, his assailant changed Jacob's name, announcing his new character. "Then he said, 'Your name shall no longer be called Jacob, but Israel, for you have striven with God and with men, and have prevailed'" (v. 28).

The name Israel literally means "God fights" or "God strives." But here the popular usage puts the emphasis on Jacob's fighting or striving — "Israel, for you have striven with God and with men." Popular etymologies or usages like this employ loose wordplays on the sound of a word to express its significance. As Allen Ross says, "The name 'God fights' and the popular explanation 'you fought and prevailed' thus obtained a significance for future struggles."[4] We must remember that Jacob fought in his weakness. The paradox continues to instruct. The day of failure through power was over, and the day of success through weakness had begun.

Encouraged by his new name, Jacob was emboldened to ask, "'Please tell me your name.' But he said, 'Why is it that you ask my name?' And there he blessed him" (v. 29). Such grace! Relentless grace — crippling grace — transforming grace — and now a gracious blessing.

Revelation about God and Jacob. At last Jacob realized that he had been wrestling with God, and his persistence turned to awe. "So Jacob called the name of the place Peniel, saying, 'For I have seen God face to face, and yet my life has been delivered'" (v. 30). Jacob's seeing God at daybreak suggests a dusky vision, dimly lit though face-to-face. Indeed, God withdrew at dawn to protect Jacob, because no man can see God's face and live (cf. Exodus 33:20). Thus the encounter ended as mysteriously as it had begun.

Now the sun shone brightly on Jacob. When Jacob had fled Canaan twenty years earlier, his flight was marked by an ominous sunset and darkness. But sunrise greeted him as he returned to Canaan — "The sun rose upon him as he passed Penuel, limping because of his hip" (v. 31). The bright morning sun revealed a stooped, bleeding, bruised man in tattered clothes, dark with soil and sweat, dragging a leg and grimacing with each step.

God had left his permanent mark on him. All Jacob's descendants were to remember this — thus the traditional avoidance of eating the sinew around the hip socket of an animal (cf. v. 32).

This blessed man sported two new distinctives — a new *name* and a new *crippling*. And here is the grand point: "The *new name* cannot be separated from the *new crippling*, for the crippling is the substance of the name"(Brueggemann).[5] Jacob (now Israel) prevailed when he came to the end of himself. His weakness birthed strength. His defeat wrought victory. His end was his beginning.

Jacob's life is the story of relentless grace — tenacious grace, contending grace, intrusive grace, renovating grace. Tenacious in that it would not let him go. Contending as it was always battling for his soul. Intrusive because it would not be shut out. Renovating because it gave him a new limp and a new name.

This is the God who has redeemed us. He wrestled Satan on the cross and won. He has given us new life. And now that we are his, he will not let us go. We must submit to him. We must understand with Luther:

> *Did we in our own strength confide,*
> *Our striving would be losing.*

How blessed we are when we yield to God at the beginning of God's call, the way Abraham and Joseph did. But so many of us are like Jacob. We struggle independently of the God whom we believe and love. We want to be part of his plan, but alas, we make our own plans — and we never truly succeed. Then a crisis comes through which he lays his hand upon us (life becomes dislocated — out of joint), and we have an appalling sense of our own incompetence and weakness. That is the great hour — the hour of grace, because from there on our walk is never the same.

God may be wrestling with some of you this very day. He may be saying to you (clever, astute, capable as you are), "You have believed in me, but you have always manipulated your own life and made your own arrangements. My child, what is your name?"

49

Brothers Reconciled

GENESIS 33:1-20

The dread that filled Jacob as he prepared to meet Esau was grounded in the mean facts of the life-altering humiliations that he had dealt his older brother — first, when he conned Esau, who while in a flippant mood sold him his birthright; and, second, when he dressed up as Esau and stole Esau's blessing from their father Isaac. These humiliating stratagems left Esau muttering, "Is he not rightly named Jacob? For he has cheated me these two times. He took away my birthright, and behold, now he has taken away my blessing" (27:36). He then tearfully pleaded, "Have you but one blessing, my father? Bless me, even me also, O my father" (v. 38). Witless Esau could only take dark comfort in visions of homicide. And now, for all Jacob knew, the twenty intervening years had only refined his brother's murderous intent.

Nevertheless, Jacob had to meet Esau. Making things right, and hopefully effecting reconciliation, had become a heart-necessity for Jacob. As Jacob had grown in grace, his conscience would not allow him to sidestep an attempt at reconciliation. Meeting Esau was a spiritual necessity. What a jolt, then, when the ominous answer to his peaceful and generous overture was that Esau was coming with four hundred men. Jacob did not know it, but as he prepared for the dreaded encounter, a greater dread would grip him throughout the long night until dawn in a titanic wrestling match. And further, he did not know that was preparation — necessary preparation — for meeting Esau. God had to first deal with Jacob before Jacob could deal with Esau.

As Jacob stood tottering in the rising light of the morning sun, he was awestruck by the revelation that he had been wrestling God in angelic form (who had accommodated himself to Jacob's puny strength). To use George MacDonald's words: "an angel too gentle to put out all his strength."[1] And

Jacob had acquired two new distinctives: a new crippling that would serve as a reminder of that night and his weakness, and a new name — Israel ("God fights") — that would come to celebrate him as one who fights with God. Jacob's strength, paradoxically, was in his weakness. The new name signaled his new character and was prophetic of his future development. The encounter was a transforming event, but Jacob had a long way to go. He was still Jacob as well as being Israel. But there had been spiritual advance. The relentless, intrusive, tenacious grace of God had him in its grip.

Now as the crippled, God-struck patriarch lifted his sleepless eyes, a further jolt rocked him. "Behold, Esau was coming, and four hundred men with him" (v. 1a). Though exhausted, Jacob frantically arranged his family for formal presentation to Esau. "So he divided the children among Leah and Rachel and the two female servants. And he put the servants with their children in front, then Leah with her children, and Rachel and Joseph last of all. He himself went on before them, bowing himself to the ground seven times, until he came near to his brother" (vv. 1b-3). Though hobbled, Jacob haltingly preceded his four wives and twelve children in a courtly greeting ceremony, bowing flat-out in prostration seven times as he approached Esau, as was fitting in a court of a Pharaoh.[2] Ironically, Jacob's bowing was the reverse of the blessing that he had stolen for himself, which stipulated to Jacob, "Be lord over your brothers, and may your mother's sons bow down to you" (27:29). Jacob's reversal here expressed his sorrow over his shameful theft of Isaac's blessing.

SURPRISE RECONCILIATION (vv. 4-11)

Brothers embrace. To Jacob's surprise, however, Esau would have no more of this bowing and scraping. "But Esau ran to meet him and embraced him and fell on his neck and kissed him, and they wept" (v. 4). Esau, his red beard flying, charged Jacob as he stood uncertainly, threw his arms around him, and kissed him! And in that brotherly embrace the two men wept uncontrollably. Esau was beautiful here. Whatever his intention had been up to that moment, the sight of Jacob made his natural affections take charge. He made no mention of the past. His hug and kiss said it all. Only the day before, Jacob had prayed, "Please deliver me from the hand of my brother, from the hand of Esau, for I fear him, that he may come and attack me, the mothers with the children" (32:11). And here was the direct answer to his prayer. God had changed Esau's heart. "Such is the result when 'God fights' in his way" (Ross).[3]

Family introduced. The first words from Esau's mouth were a question. "And when Esau lifted up his eyes and saw the women and children, he said, 'Who are these with you?' Jacob said, 'The children whom God has graciously given your servant.' Then the servants drew near, they and their children, and bowed down. Leah likewise and her children drew near and bowed down. And last Joseph and Rachel drew near, and they bowed down" (vv. 5-7). Jacob presented his wives in ascending order of their social status and affection. First Bilhah and Zilpah and their four boys (Dan, Naphtali, Gad, and Asher) bowed to the ground. Then Leah and her seven did likewise: Reuben, Simeon, Levi, Judah, Issachar, Zebulun, and daughter Dinah. And lastly Rachel with her baby Joseph. Significantly, Jacob saw this as the work of God and his grace — "the children whom God has graciously given your servant." Brother Esau had now been introduced to Israel and the genesis of the chosen people.

Gifts accepted. Esau's second question paved the way for rapprochement.

Esau said, "What do you mean by all this company that I met?" Jacob answered, "To find favor in the sight of my lord." But Esau said, "I have enough, my brother; keep what you have for yourself." Jacob said, "No, please, if I have found favor in your sight, then accept my present from my hand. For I have seen your face, which is like seeing the face of God, and you have accepted me. Please accept my blessing that is brought to you, because God has dealt graciously with me, and because I have enough." Thus he urged him, and he took it. (vv. 8-11)

Jacob's statement to Esau — "For I have seen your face, which is like seeing the face of God, and you have accepted me" (v. 10b) — indicates Jacob's awareness that seeing God's face at Peniel and seeing Esau's face here were connected.

From the onset Jacob had feared Esau's face. That is why he initially sent more than five hundred and fifty animals ahead in five droves with the announcement that he would bring up the rear. "For he thought, 'I may appease him with the present that goes ahead of me, and afterward I shall see his face. Perhaps he will accept me'" (32:20). But as God planned it, Jacob had to see God's face before that of Esau.

At the end of Jacob's night-long struggle in the dusky dawn, he'd had a dark glimpse of his divine assailant as he received the blessing. "So Jacob called the name of the place Peniel, saying, 'For I have seen God face to face, and yet my life has been delivered'" (32:30). Now facing Esau, Jacob declared to Esau, "For I have seen your face, which is like seeing the face of God, and you have accepted me" (v. 10). Jacob had seen the face of God and lived. And then he saw the face of Esau and lived — so that *to him* Esau's face was like that of God.

And there is more. Jacob had not been ready to see Esau's face until he had seen God's face. The divine encounter prepared the way for the human encounter. Jacob's rapprochement with God preceded and made possible his rapprochement with Esau. God's crippling of Jacob (Jacob's humbling) preceded his reconciliation with Esau. God's blessing upon Jacob preceded Esau's forgiveness of Jacob. The principle of God first, man second is written large in the language of love in the Scripture. It is in the very structure of the Ten Commandments. The first four command love for God; the second six command love for humanity. That is the order. Love God, and then you can love man. Jesus summed it up like this: "You shall love the Lord your God with all your heart and with all your soul and with all your mind. This is the great and first commandment. And a second is like it: You shall love your neighbor as yourself" (Matthew 22:37-39).

Jacob's awareness of God and his grace is all over the Genesis passage. Esau never once mentioned either grace or God directly. But Jacob references "the children whom God has graciously given your servant" (v. 5b) and his desire "to find favor [grace] in the sight of my lord" (v. 8b) and again, "If I have found favor [grace] in your sight" (v. 10a), and finally, "God has dealt graciously with me" (v. 11).

Etiquette in patriarchal times required that Esau make a show of refusing the gift and that Jacob insist he accept it — "Thus he urged him, and he took it" (v. 11). The fact that Esau accepted it and did not reciprocate tells us that this was not a mere exchange of civilities, but that the old score was settled.[4] Restitution had been made in full. This was no cheap forgiveness. It cost Jacob — and he joyfully paid the price, so to speak.

DISENGAGING ESAU (vv. 12-17)

With the restitution and reconciliation in effect, Esau's magnanimity overflowed as he offered to lead Jacob's clan to his home in Seir. But Seir was outside the promised land. God's word to Jacob at Bethel was that God would bring him back to the land (cf. 28:15). Moreover, God's chosen people were to remain separate from those who were not people of faith. The dangers in Esau's generous offer were therefore substantial.

So Jacob gently disengaged himself from Esau, which was all good and necessary. But he was ever so "Jacob" in his demurral. He began with exaggeration. "My lord knows that the children are frail, and that the nursing flocks and herds are a care to me. If they are driven hard for one day, all the flocks will die" (v. 13). But then he descended to deceit: "Let my lord pass on ahead of his servant, and I will lead on slowly, at the pace of the livestock that are ahead of me and at the pace of the children, until I come to my lord in Seir" (v. 14) — which he had no intention of doing! Likely, Esau sensed Jacob's intent, and it may have been fine with him. Nevertheless, Jacob's facile lie contradicted his stunning experience and affirmations of the previous day. He was both Jacob and Israel. Israel would have spoken the truth in love. Jacob rationalized that, well, one day he *might* go to Seir.

The upshot was that Esau left that very day for Seir. Esau and his four hundred marched off the pages of recorded history. Esau would make a brief appearance for Isaac's funeral (35:29) and in his genealogies (chap. 36), but that is all. But to our surprise Jacob, now rid of Esau, did not make the short trip to cross the Jordan into the promised land and up to Bethel, because we read, "But Jacob journeyed to Succoth, and built himself a house and made booths for his livestock. Therefore the name of the place is called Succoth" (v. 17).

Succoth was north back across the Jabbok and a step back spiritually. It is hard to reckon Jacob's sojourn to Succoth with God's clear call to Bethel. Succoth mean "stalls" or "booths," and therefore it may be that he built booths to husband his flocks and utilize the fertile valley lands to replenish what he had given to Esau before entering the promised land. Jacob was not transparent by any estimation. But his sojourn in Succoth suggests he was still a man who did things his own way. For this, Jacob and his family were going to pay dearly.

JACOB ENTERS CANAAN (vv. 18-20)

Settling in Shechem. Though crossing the Jordan over to Shechem was an historic event, the account records no fanfare. This may be because it represented only halfway obedience — he did not go to Bethel as God had directed. All we have are the bare facts.

> *And Jacob came safely to the city of Shechem, which is in the land of Canaan, on his way from Paddan-aram, and he camped before the city. And from the sons of Hamor, Shechem's father, he bought for a hundred pieces of money the piece of land on which he had pitched his tent. There he erected an altar and called it El-Elohe-Israel. (vv. 18-20)*

This was halfway, incomplete obedience. Yet at the same time, Jacob's purchase of land paralleled Abraham's purchase of land in Machpelah and Abraham's faith in God's promise that his descendants would inherit the land. So we have in Jacob faith mixed with partial obedience.

Moreover, Jacob built an altar in Shechem and gave it a magnificent name, El-Elohe-Israel, which means "the mighty God is the God of Israel." God had done mighty things for him over the course of his life. The altar celebrated that this mighty God was his God. But the altar should have been built in Bethel (cf. 28:22). Bethel is where he should have declared that this God was his God!

Why the halfway obedience? Professor Ian Duguid muses:

> Why was that? What was Jacob doing settling down at Shechem and raising an altar when he should have been continuing on to Bethel to raise the

altar there, where he had first had the dream? Did Jacob think that Shechem was a better site for trade and for his flocks? Perhaps he thought it didn't matter. After all, Bethel was now a mere twenty miles or so away; he could go there whenever it suited him, once he got settled. Why be so precise in these things? Shechem or Bethel — it's really all the same, isn't it? Indeed, it is not. Whatever his motivation, Jacob's compromise and his failure to follow through with complete obedience to what he had vowed would cost him and his family dearly, as we shall see in the following chapter. Almost obedience is never enough. Being in the right ballpark may be sufficient when watching a baseball game, but is not nearly enough when it comes to obeying God. Nothing short of full obedience is required.[5]

In tragic retrospect Jacob would come to see that his self-willed decision to settle in Shechem would result in the rape of his only daughter and the genocidal spree of his sons, resulting in Jacob and his family becoming a stench in the land. El-Elohe-Israel, Jacob's mighty God, would have to effect obedience in Jacob the *hard way* — through a fearsome grace.

We all understand the foolishness of halfway obedience from our life experiences. As both parents and children, we know that when a son is asked to take out the trash, his leaving it by the back door instead of in the trash barrel is unacceptable. In fact, it is disobedience because partial obedience is always disobedience. We also know that partial obedience can be dangerous, as, for example, when a child who is told not to play in the street plays alongside the roadway. Thus we insist on total obedience.

It is always a delusion to imagine that we have obeyed when we have partially obeyed. And this is eternally true when dealing with God. If God has called you to leave a relationship or a plan or a pursuit or a habit, do not imagine that you have obeyed by partial disengagement. Likewise, understand that if God has called you to a specific obedience, anything less than what he has directed is disobedience. Partial obedience is always disobedience, no matter what our rationalizations are. God will not be fooled or mocked. And his sweet grace can be brutal.

Self-sufficient Jacob had been brought to the end of himself that night at Peniel when as he wrestled with God, he became more and more aware of his helpless, hopeless state. Indeed he had become little more than a clinging, weeping cripple. Paradoxically, Jacob's prevailing with God had come through his growing weakness, as J. I. Packer explains: "The nature of Jacob's 'prevailing' with God was simply that he held on to God while God weakened him, and wrought in him the spirit of submission and self-distrust; that he had desired God's blessing so much that he clung to God through all this painful humbling, till he came low enough for God to raise him up by speaking peace to him and assuring him that he need not fear."[6] And as the narrative makes so clear in Jacob's encounter with Esau, it was in this God-induced, weakened, dependent state that Jacob prevailed with Esau. Truly God did it all — so that unbelieving Esau left his four hundred men, sprinted to Jacob, and forgave Jacob's grievous sins. Esau's face was like the face of God not only because he forgave Jacob, but because Jacob could see God's visage in his effecting his deliverance. In addition, Jacob's reconciliation with God put him in the way of reconciliation with Esau.

Jacob's new crippling and new name were the keys to a life of true power with man and with God. But almost immediately Jacob began to retreat from his humility and dependence. He lied to his godless, bighearted brother. He tarried in Succoth instead of entering the promised land. And then when he did enter, he continued in partial obedience. Jacob's altar in Shechem declared that the mighty God was his God — and he was right. But he built it in the wrong place, testifying that his knee was not bent to El-Elohe-Israel.

As we will see, Jacob would later go to Bethel humiliated and chastened — God's relentless, tenacious, intrusive grace would have its fearsome, loving way. But how much better it would have been if Jacob had gone in the glory of his new name and new crippling — in the power of his weakness.

The New Testament says it wonderfully: "[God] said to me, 'My grace is sufficient for you, for my power is made perfect in weakness.' Therefore I will boast all the more gladly of my weaknesses, so that the power of Christ may rest upon me" (2 Corinthians 12:9). May we remember that the crippled Jacob was the man who fought with God and prevailed. It is the strong who always lose. But in weakness there is victory.

Lord, hear our prayer:

> *O Love that wilt not let me go,*
> *I rest my weary soul in Thee;*
> *I give Thee back the life I owe,*
> *That in Thine ocean depths its flow*
> *May richer, fuller be.*
>
> GEORGE MATHESON, 1882

50

Fierce Grace

GENESIS 34:1-31

Among the distinctives of Flannery O'Connor's novels is the shocking ugliness of so many of her principal characters, the sheer cussedness of those who are the objects and conduits of grace. As to the reason behind her grotesque depictions, she wrote:

> The novelist with Christian concerns will find in modern life distortions which are repugnant to him, and his problem will be to make these appear as distortions to an audience which is used to seeing them as natural; and he may well be forced to take ever more violent means to get his vision across to this hostile audience. When you can assume that your audience holds the same beliefs you do, you can relax and use more normal means of talking to it; when you have to assume that it does not, then you have to make your vision apparent by shock — to the hard of hearing you shout, and for the almost-blind you draw large and startling figures.[1]

I can testify that she succeeds because I am among those who have turned the pages of her novels murmuring variations of "Oh my, oh my" at the absurdities of the likes of Hazel Motes in *Wise Blood* and Francis Tarwater of *The Violent Bear It Away*.

The life of Jacob in Genesis 25 — 35 has struck me much in the same way, and even more so because it is not fiction. Jacob's inveterate cussedness has continued to astound me, especially here in the sordid doings of chapter 34, which is full of "Oh mys." Personally, I have not found Jacob likable, though at times he has been admirable. He soared in his midnight wrestle and his crippling and renaming, and then in his turn toward Canaan and his making peace with Esau whom from youth he had so grievously cheated. But

Jacob's soar immediately turned into a slide when he deceived Esau as to his intent to return to Canaan, then dallied in Succoth, and finally settled twenty miles short of Bethel in Shechem in willful, halfway obedience. There his pious act of building an altar and naming it after God could not disguise the fact of his disobedience. The old Jacob was in full force. He was morally weak, unwilling to pay the cost of right actions, untrusting of God, and unmindful of the welfare of his children and the future of his people.

The cost of Jacob's turpitude was immense, as chapter 34 records — rape, degeneration, treachery, and genocide. Yet in all of this a fierce grace was at work. In Shechem, in the event we are about to consider, God allowed Jacob to experience the appalling weight of his sinfulness so he would return to his call. Divine grace will triumph despite human sin — fierce, fiery grace.

RAPE AND "PROPOSAL" (vv. 1-7)

Dinah's rape. There was only one girl among Jacob's children, Dinah, the daughter of unloved Leah. Leah's children, as compared to Rachel's, were less favored by Jacob, and Dinah appeared to have been of little interest at all to Jacob. This coupled with the fact that Jacob was not where God wanted him to be geographically or spiritually left her particularly vulnerable. And so here in Shechem young Dinah was pushing at the edges when she "went out to see the women of the land" (v. 1). Girls of marriageable age were not permitted to leave the tents of their people to go about visiting without a chaperone. In fact, the Hebrew term "went out" bears a sense of impropriety.[2] Likely she went out behind Leah's back. And the worst happened! Dinah became a victim of violent rape. "And when Shechem the son of Hamor the Hivite, the prince of the land, saw her, he seized her and lay with her and humiliated her" (v. 2). The three verbs ("seized . . . lay . . . humiliated") describe a progression of brutality — aggravated rape. Poor Dinah.

But unlike the case of Amnon's rape of Tamar when afterward Amnon despised his victim, "so that the hatred with which he hated her was greater than the love with which he had loved her" (2 Samuel 13:15), Shechem became consumed with Dinah. "And his soul was drawn to Dinah the daughter of Jacob. He loved the young woman and spoke tenderly to her. So Shechem spoke to his father Hamor, saying, 'Get me this girl for my wife'" (vv. 3, 4). Shechem's brutality was transmuted to tender affection. He was madly in love, though it is doubtful that he could distinguish passion from love. The young prince proposed a proper marriage. Pagan Shechem certainly was not all bad.

Family response. Shocking as Dinah's seduction was, we are equally shocked by Jacob's non-response: "Now Jacob heard that he [Shechem] had defiled his daughter Dinah. But his sons were with his livestock in the field, so Jacob held his peace until they came. And Hamor the father of Shechem went out to Jacob to speak with him" (vv. 5, 6). Though Jacob's silence might have been prudential in part, his apathy casts him in an unfavorable light. Consider his passionate love for Joseph and Benjamin and his distress at their misfortunes. The truth is, Jacob never cared for Leah, and his attitude trickled down to her daughter and six sons. Indeed, Leah's less-loved sons would be at the forefront of selling his favorite son, Joseph, into Egypt.

Here Jacob's callous indifference toward Dinah and her brothers fueled his sons' fury. "The sons of Jacob had come in from the field as soon as they heard of it, and the men were indignant and very angry, because he [Shechem] had done an outrageous thing in Israel by lying with Jacob's daughter, for such a thing must not be done" (v. 7). Amidst their fury, Jacob's sons responded properly to the demeaning of Israel as well as of Dinah. They understood that because Jacob had become Israel at Peniel, the rape of his daughter was a crime against Israel as a people, seeing that the relationship of Israel to God had been ignored and abused. Tragically, their father Jacob had neither stood up for his daughter or his God!

MARRIAGE ARRANGED (vv. 8-25)

Pagan proposals. Hamor and Prince Shechem addressed Jacob and his sons without apology. This was a little matter for which they believed that they had a reasonable and generous solution that Jacob's family would like. But note that they were careful not to mention two things: first, what Shechem had done to Dinah; and second, that they had Dinah in Shechem's house (cf. vv. 17, 26). They had the upper hand, notwithstanding that they were willing to make it "right."

Shechem's father spoke first. "But Hamor spoke with them, saying, 'The soul of my son Shechem longs for your daughter. Please give her to him to be his wife. Make marriages with us. Give your daughters to us, and take our daughters for yourselves. You shall dwell with us, and the land shall be open to you. Dwell and trade in it, and get property in it" (vv. 8-10). "No hard feelings. Let's all get married and be one big happy family" — a thing that Israel could never do. Hamor's offer pulsed with economic appeal — property in Canaan, grazing rights, the freedom to travel and dwell anywhere. In sum, Hamor promised what God had promised Israel. Very enticing. A shortcut to the promised land!

As Hamor finished magnanimously, Shechem assumed that Jacob's family was sufficiently placated to accept his offer. "Shechem also said to her father and to her brothers, 'Let me find favor in your eyes, and whatever you say to me I will give. Ask me for as great a bride price and gift as you will, and I will give whatever you say to me. Only give me the young woman to be my wife'" (vv. 11, 12). Impatient Shechem was extraordinarily gener-ous in his offer. The price of a bride was already fixed by custom, so that his "name the amount" offer was uncalled for. And the promise of a gift for the family was an added bonus.

Father and son expected immediate acceptance. But, of course, Hamor and Shechem did not understand with whom they were dealing — and espe-cially their God-given religious scruples.

The brothers' response. Now the writer warns the reader, "The sons of Jacob answered Shechem and his father Hamor deceitfully, because he had defiled their sister Dinah" (v. 13). Here the story becomes very dark. Jacob's sons justified their deceit by the heinous nature of the crime done to "their sister," and though this is not mentioned, she yet remained a hostage in Shechem's house. Dinah's brothers' speech is one of unabashed guile wor-thy of a Flannery O'Connor sketch.

> *They said to them, "We cannot do this thing, to give our sister to one who is uncircumcised, for that would be a disgrace to us. Only on this condi-tion will we agree with you — that you will become as we are by every male among you being circumcised. Then we will give our daughters to you, and we will take your daughters to ourselves, and we will dwell with you and become one people. But if you will not listen to us and be circum-cised, then we will take our daughter, and we will be gone." (vv. 14-17)*

The offer was plausible to the Shechemites because it reflected normal practice among the tribes of Israel. Genesis 17:9-14 installed circumcision as an indispensable rite of admittance into Israel. Likewise some pagans used it as an initiation into marriage. But Jacob's sons had no intention of extend-ing their religious influence, much less the knowledge of God, to the Shechemites. Genocide — not evangelism — was the goal. The irony of their deceit is supremely grotesque in that the aspect of Shechem used to perpe-trate the crime would serve to effect his death.

But more, there is here an abuse of the holy. Circumcision, Israel's most cherished symbol of faith, would now become a tool of inhumanity. The desecration of the covenant sign of circumcision as a means to gain revenge, and the widening of the revenge to the murder and plunder of a town, were immense crimes deserving condemnation.

But Jacob's sons were not thinking of anything but revenge — and cer-tainly not of God. And amorous Shechem was not thinking of anything but Dinah. So the deal was struck.

Consent obtained. All that remained was to get the consent of the male populace of Shechem, which was by no means a foregone conclusion! And here Hamor and his son showed themselves as masters of deceit as they concealed the Dinah factor and enumerated the domestic and financial pluses while making no mention of their promise to the Israelites. The bottom-line selling point was, "Will not their livestock, their property and all their beasts be ours? Only let us agree with them, and they will dwell with us" (v. 23).

What power avarice has! "And all who went out of the gate of his city listened to Hamor and his son Shechem, and every male was circumcised, all who went out of the gate of his city" (v. 24).

GENOCIDAL SPREE (vv. 25-31)

The birth order of Dinah's four full brothers was Reuben, Simeon, Levi, and Judah, and it was the middle two who effected the massacre. As to why Simeon and Levi did all the killing, we can only speculate. We do know that Reuben, the eldest, was the least murderous of the brothers, being the one who later convinced the others not to kill Joseph but to sell him into slavery (cf. 37:21, 22). But Judah's lack of participation remains a mystery, especially since he would show himself to be ethically challenged in the Tamar affair (cf. 38:12-26). But so was Reuben in his Bilhah affair (cf. 35:22). In any event, excepting Reuben, it was Dinah's two oldest big brothers who exacted the revenge.

Here now is bold biblical realism. The Bible does not spare its readers the awful truth. These two were cold and calculating. The third day following the crude operation would be the most painful and incapacitating. So Simeon and Levi counted the hours, whetting their swords. "On the third day, when they [the Shechemites] were sore, two of the sons of Jacob, Simeon and Levi, Dinah's brothers, took their swords and came against the city while it felt secure and killed all the males. They killed Hamor and his son Shechem with the sword and took Dinah out of Shechem's house and went away" (vv. 25, 26). In tandem, the brothers engaged in a genocidal spree, charging from house to house, shoving screaming wives and children aside and hacking their helpless victims to death. The murderous orgy ended with the executions of Hamor and the groom-to-be, after which the blood-soaked brothers led their trembling sister out of the wailing town.

This shocks us. But it was just as shocking to the ancient readers as it is to modern eyes and ears. The ancient law of *lex talionis* (an eye for an eye, a tooth for a tooth) had been trampled by Simeon and Levi. There had been no equity here, only exponential revenge. The brothers' actions offended every convention.

And then the remaining brothers swooped in "like vultures descending on lifeless corpses."[3] "The sons of Jacob came upon the slain and plundered the city, because they had defiled their sister. They took their flocks and their herds, their donkeys, and whatever was in the city and in the field. All their wealth, all their little ones and their wives, all that was in the houses, they captured and plundered" (vv. 27-29). This is a desolate picture. All that was left were the bones and barren homes of the Shechemites. Years later, as Jacob on his deathbed was blessing his sons, Jacob would pause and pronounce an anti-blessing on Simeon and Levi:

> *Simeon and Levi are brothers;*
> *weapons of violence are their swords.*
> *Let my soul come not into their council;*
> *O my glory, be not joined to their company.*
> *For in their anger they killed men,*
> *and in their willfulness they hamstrung oxen.*
> *Cursed be their anger, for it is fierce,*
> *and their wrath, for it is cruel!*
> *I will divide them in Jacob*
> *and scatter them in Israel. (Genesis 49:5-7)*

Actually, no one escaped censure on that infamous day in Shechem. No one looked good, not even one (cf. Romans 3:10).

Jacob's ignominy. But by far the worst was Jacob, as evidenced by his pathetic dressing down of the two sons. "Then Jacob said to Simeon and Levi, 'You have brought trouble on me by making me stink to the inhabitants of the land, the Canaanites and the Perizzites. My numbers are few, and if they gather themselves against me and attack me, I shall be destroyed, both I and my household'" (v. 30).

Jacob was pathetic — for what he did *not* say. He did not condemn the massacre. Neither did he condemn his sons for breaking the law of *lex talionis*. He did not mention that they violated his contract with Shechem. Jacob said nothing about their desecration of Israel's most precious symbol of faith. And, of course, there was not a word of concern about his just-raped daughter Dinah. Jacob's only concern was survival — to save his own skin and, by association, that of his family.

So there the patriarch stood, face-to-face with his bloody, glistening sons. And they were not buying it. They fiercely shouted back, "Should he treat our sister like a prostitute?" (v. 31). Despite the immorality of their genocide, they had assumed the moral high ground. Jacob was silenced.

What a mess! And the whole thing was Jacob's fault. Jacob's faith had peaked at Peniel. His triumph had been in his weakness. He had striven with God and prevailed. He became Israel ("strives with God"). Following his reconciliation with God, he was gloriously reconciled with his brother Esau.

But then came his lie and deception of Esau. And instead of traveling straight to Bethel as God had called him to do, he first sojourned in Succoth outside the promised land. Then when he did enter the land he did not settle in Bethel, but rather twenty miles away in prosperous Shechem. It was *almost* obedience, which is simply disobedience. If Jacob had gone to Bethel in full obedience, none of this would have happened. The rape, the desecration, the genocide, the disgrace were all due to *his* disobedience.

And more, the murderous deceit by his sons was rooted in *his* own deceitful ways. Why should they be concerned about deceiving the Shechemites when Jacob had deceived on so many occasions — the most recent being his deception of Esau when he broke his promise to visit Esau in Seir? What was wrong with their backing out of a commitment if it was okay for their father to do so? On top of this, Jacob had provoked his sons' revenge by his apathy about their sister Dinah.

Jacob's sole hope, and our only hope, lay in the ultimate Son of Jacob, the ultimate Israel, Christ the Savior who bore the wrath of God for our sin, turning it away from all who believe.

> *There for me the Savior stands,*
> *Shows His wounds and spreads His hands.*
> *God is love! I know, I feel;*
> *Jesus weeps and loves me still.*

Finally, the future would feature the outworking of the terrible fruit of his favoritism when the hatred of favored Joseph by Leah's sons would perpetrate his sale to Egypt.

The sky had fallen on Jacob. But through it all was a fierce grace. Jacob could see himself for what he was.

> *I have long withstood His grace,*
> *Long provoked him to His face,*
> *Would not hearken to His calls,*
> *Grieved Him by a thousand falls.*

Now the withering grace of God would spur Jacob on to Bethel. Sovereign grace would have its way. How absurd Jacob had been. How absurd we all are when we resist the Lord's will. How tragic the consequences.

> *Now incline me to repent,*
> *Let me now my sins lament,*
> *Now my foul revolt deplore,*
> *Weep, believe, and sin no more.*
> CHARLES WESLEY,
> "DEPTH OF MERCY," 1740

51

Residuals

GENESIS 35:1-29

O ne summer, while boating on one of Lake Michigan's northern bays, a sparkling forty-foot yacht slipped quietly into the bay and dropped anchor, where it then sat majestically riding the gentle swells with its radar in regal rotation. As her stern came around, I saw her name — *Residuals*. The message was instantaneous. The magnificent ship was the result of some very good investments. "Residuals" — those are the kind of returns that we like! But the word is defined by its context. On the back of a yacht, it announces good fortune. But written over a jail cell, it declares the opposite.

I have mentally inscribed "Residuals" over Genesis 35 because though the narrative conveys a positive change in Jacob's life, it records the residuals of his sin — as we say, "the chickens coming home to roost." Chapter 35 is so completely different from chapter 34. Donald Grey Barnhouse describes the contrast like this:

> Chapter 34 does not mention God, and is full of lust, murder, deceit, and wretchedness — but this chapter [35] is filled with God. His name appears ten times, plus once as God Almighty, *El Shaddai*, plus eleven times in the names *Bethel* and *Israel*. The contrast is striking, as it always must be in the life of a believer living out of the will of God, and again when he returns to the will of God.[1]

Happily, chapter 35 records Jacob's turnaround and newfound obedience, but it also chronicles the sad residuals. Yet even in this, there is hope because God had become the center of Jacob's life.

CALL AND OBEDIENCE (vv. 1-4)

Call. Some thirty years before, when God met Jacob at Bethel during Jacob's flight from Esau and encouraged him with a vision of angels ascending to and descending from Heaven on his behalf, Jacob had vowed, "If God will be with me and will keep me in this way that I go, and will give me bread to eat and clothing to wear, so that I come again to my father's house in peace, then the LORD shall be my God, and this stone, which I have set up for a pillar, shall be God's house. And of all that you give me I will give a full tenth to you" (28:20-22). This vow was followed by a twenty-year sojourn in Mesopotamia serving his Uncle Laban, at the end of which time God reminded Jacob of his obligation to leave Laban and return home (cf. 31:3).

But following his escape from Laban, Jacob willfully spent a decade doing much as he pleased, first dwelling for a time outside the promised land and then, when he did cross over into Canaan, settling in prosperous Shechem instead of traveling the twenty miles further to Bethel. This "I'll do it my way," halfway obedience brought tragedy. The catastrophic results (the desolation of Dinah, the desecration of Israel's most holy sign — circumcision, the massacre of the Shechemites, the degradation of his own children) rendered Jacob a stench in the land — and, most significantly, utterly ready to hear God's voice. Then "God said to Jacob, 'Arise, go up to Bethel and dwell there. Make an altar there to the God who appeared to you when you fled from your brother Esau'" (v. 1). It was a call to a religious pilgrimage, as the special use of "go up" suggests.[2] The pilgrimage was to culminate in the building of an altar at Bethel, which was a long-standing site of Canaanite worship, and by doing so to declare the name of the true God. The intent was to drive a stake into the heartland of Canaanite worship.

Obedience. The effects upon Jacob's family of their murder and plunder of the Shechemites were twofold: first, defilement through contact with the corpses of the dead, and, second, religious contamination by the taking and possession of the Shechemites' gold and silver-plated idols. So Jacob, now right with God, stepped up and took charge, giving explicit instructions. "So Jacob said to his household and to all who were with him, 'Put away the foreign gods that are among you and purify yourselves and change your garments. Then let us arise and go up to Bethel, so that I may make there an altar to the God who answers me in the day of my distress and has been with me wherever I have gone'" (vv. 2, 3).

The purification was effected by ritually washing their bodies, much as was done later by Israel at Sinai (cf. Exodus 19:10-15). Jacob's command to change clothes (unique in the Old Testament) dramatically symbolized the transition from one state to another.[3] Indeed, the symbolism may have been universally understood in the ancient world, because that is what Pharaoh had Joseph do when he entered his service (cf. 41:14). And here Jacob's command to Israel to change clothes likely is where Paul derived the metaphor for the changed life, exhorting believers "to put off your old self, which belongs to your former manner of life . . . and to put on the new self, created after the likeness of God in true righteousness and holiness" (Ephesians 4:22-24). From Shechem, Jacob and his people would pilgrimage to Bethel as a new people.

Their obedience was apparently immediate and full. "So they gave to Jacob all the foreign gods that they had, and the rings that were in their ears. Jacob hid them under the terebinth tree that was near Shechem" (v. 4). Teraphim and other idolatrous images were purged from their tents. The earrings were not everyday jewelry but amulets and talismans engraved with pagan symbols.[4] Most likely the earrings were largely from Shechem's booty.[5] Archaeological digs in other parts of Palestine have yielded crescent-shaped earrings that celebrated the moon god.[6] In any case, a rich cache of pagan idols and paraphernalia was unceremoniously buried under the terebinth tree at Shechem as God's people — washed, purged, and reclothed — set out for Bethel.

PILGRIMAGE AND WORSHIP (vv. 5-8)

Recall that after the massacre, faithless Jacob had angrily scolded his sons for their actions, not because they were immoral, but for fear that their terrible deeds would bring the surrounding Canaanites down upon their little band and annihilate it. But instead "a terror from God" (v. 5) fell upon the Canaanites, like the fear that later fell upon Canaan as Israel under Joshua prepared to cross the Jordan (cf. Joshua 2:9). So it was that Jacob's family and flocks, recently enlarged at the expense of the Shechemites, passed by in solemn pilgrimage under divine peace. At Bethel "he built an altar and called the place El-bethel ["God of Bethel"], because there God had revealed himself to him when he fled from his brother" (v. 7). Jacob then worshiped at the altar, offering joyful sacrifices to God. And as he fulfilled his thirty-year-old vow, he gratefully gave a tenth of all he had to God (cf. 28:22). At last Jacob was in the place where he was supposed to be — worshiping with a heart that was *right with God.*

Now, with the patriarch in Bethel, God began to effect a transition to a new generation with the death of aged Deborah. "And Deborah, Rebekah's nurse, died, and she was buried under an oak below Bethel. So he called its name Allon-bacuth ["oak of weeping"]" (v. 8). Deborah's 180 years bridged the lives of the first two patriarchs, "and her death reminded the people of the era that ended with the return of Jacob to Bethel" (Ross).[7] Change was in the air.

BLESSING AND CONSECRATION (vv. 9-15)

Blessing. The obedience and worship of Jacob and that of his people was followed by a theophany and a blessing direct from the mouth of God. The dazzling event was a divinely orchestrated parallel to what had happened to his grandfather Abraham when he was given the covenant of circumcision (cf. chapter 17). The parallels are four. First, just as Abram's original name ("exalted father") had been changed to Abraham ("father of a multitude"), now Jacob's given name ("deceiver") was changed to Israel ("fights with God"). In both cases the name-giving symbolized the transformation of the patriarch's character and destiny. Indeed, Abraham became the father of a multitude, and Israel strove and prevailed with God — not in his strength but in his weakness. And here, with the change of Jacob's name to Israel (which originally had been done on the other side of the Jordan at Peniel), he was now rehabilitated, confirmed, and validated by God himself *in* the promised land!

Second, the first use in the Bible of God's name *El Shaddai* ("God Almighty") was employed in confirming the promise to Abram (cf. 17:1). *El Shaddai* signifies God's power and sovereignty. It describes the God who makes things happen by means of his majestic power and might. He is the one who fulfills every promise. And it is *El Shaddai*, "God Almighty," who now blessed Jacob!

In the third of the parallels, *El Shaddai* blessed Jacob in terms similar to those used to bless Abraham in respect to *fruitfulness*, a *nation*, *kings*, and the *land*: "A nation and a company of nations shall come from you, and kings shall come from your own body. The land that I gave to Abraham and Isaac I will give to you, and I will give the land to your offspring after you" (vv. 11, 12). Abraham had been the first to learn that kings would come from him, and now Jacob heard the same. A thousand years hence the founding of a line of kings in the Davidic dynasty began the fulfillment of this promise, which would ultimately be fulfilled another thousand years later in the advent of Christ Jesus, the King of the Jews. Jacob had just heard the most categorical, most dramatic affirmation of the promises he would ever hear!

In the fourth and final parallel to Abraham's experience, the theophany ended as "God went up from him," as he had done with Abraham (v. 13; cf. 17:22).

Consecration. El Shaddai's stunning blessing evoked Jacob's consecration, which is described matter-of-factly. But it could only have been done with trembling passion, and not alone but with his entire clan as witnesses. "And Jacob set up a pillar in the place where he had spoken with him, a pillar of stone. He poured out a drink offering on it and poured oil on it. So Jacob called the name of the place where God had spoken with him Bethel"

(vv. 14, 15). The fact that the consecration ritual went beyond the original some thirty years earlier by adding a wine libation indicates that Jacob was rehabilitating the pillar and investing it with new meaning.[8] This was Bethel, "the house of God." And Jacob understood it with a depth and devotion that he was not capable of in his youth.

Jacob's experience of expanded understanding is common to all of us. As new, inexperienced Christians we learned some new truth, and it did us much good. Then years later, after the ups and downs of spiritual life, we reflect on the same truth — but with a far deeper level of application and understanding. Once again at Bethel, Jacob's understanding that it was "the house of God" penetrated the depths of his being and informed his way of life as never before. A different Jacob was rising.

The angel-freighted ladder extending up to Heaven from wherever Jacob dwelt had been perpetually busy in his behalf over the last thirty years. God's promise — that he would never leave Jacob until he had done what he had promised — remained unbroken (cf. 28:15). God had kept his word despite Jacob's self-focused scheming and halfhearted obedience. A constant grace rained upon him — most often as a gentle mist and sometimes as a fierce downpour. Grace had etched and watered his stubborn soul — and now he had grown. But life was passing quickly.

BIRTH AND DEATH (vv. 16-21)

For all Jacob's proclivities, Rachel had been the unchallenged love of Jacob's life. From the onset he had been wild about her, single-handedly moving the stone from the well's entrance so she could water her sheep, grandly volunteering to work seven years for her hand — and then laboring seven more years! He had shared the pain of her barrenness. And the unexpected joy of Joseph's birth had been so good.

How sweet it was when she conceived again, and especially because it took place in the promised land! Though she was well along in her pregnancy, neither she nor Jacob expected any trouble when they pulled up stakes to travel south to Hebron where Jacob's father Isaac lived. But somewhere, just a few miles north of Jerusalem, tragedy fell.

> *Then they journeyed from Bethel. When they were still some distance from Ephrath, Rachel went into labor, and she had hard labor. And when her labor was at its hardest, the midwife said to her, "Do not fear, for you have another son." And as her soul was departing (for she was dying), she called his name Ben-oni; but his father called him Benjamin. (vv. 16-18)*

Rachel was dying, and she knew it. Her midwife's attempt at consolation, affirming another son, brought little comfort, and as Rachel expired she named him after her misery, Ben-oni ("son of my sorrow"). But Jacob, who knew firsthand the power of a name, thought better and called him Benjamin ("son of the right") — the right-hand side being the favored side,[9] thus celebrating his beloved Rachel. Benjamin would become a favored son.

But a bitter irony always hung over the sad event. In her barrenness, Rachel had called out to Jacob, "Give me children, or I shall die!" (30:1) — and now it was the gift of children that killed her. Thus a second transitional death took place. "So Rachel died, and she was buried on the way to Ephrath (that is, Bethlehem), and Jacob set up a pillar over her tomb. It is the pillar of Rachel's tomb, which is there to this day. Israel journeyed on and pitched his tent beyond the tower of Eder" (vv. 19-21) — by a shepherd's watchtower somewhere between Bethel and Hebron.

Jacob's sorrow was deep. When he lay dying in old age he said, "As for me, when I came from Paddan, to my sorrow Rachel died in the land of Canaan on the way" (48:7). Jacob lived in tears to his dying day.

SIN'S RESIDUALS (vv. 22-26)

Incest. As it was, Jacob's past unfaithfulness meant that all his days would be full of trouble — sin's residuals. And this unadorned report of incest was at the top of the residuals: "While Israel lived in that land, Reuben went and lay with Bilhah his father's concubine. And Israel heard of it" (v. 22).

It may appear that Jacob's oldest son's incest came out of nowhere and was a sin of passion. Neither is true. Reuben's sin had its impetus in Jacob's favoring Rachel's children at the expense of the children of Leah, his unloved wife. We have already seen how Jacob's lack of concern for the honor of their sister Dinah fueled her brothers' anger and homicidal rampage. Here Reuben sensed that with Rachel's death, her servant Bilhah would become Jacob's favorite over his mother Leah. So Reuben seduced her to ensure that she could not rival Leah's position. The result of Reuben's liaison with Bilhah was that she was accorded the status of "living widowhood," just as happened to David's concubines when his son Absalom defiled them (cf. 2 Samuel 15:16; 16:20-23).[10]

And as Sarna points out, there was more because Reuben's incest was also a claim of authority over his father's inheritance. Near-Eastern custom held that the possession of the concubines of a man's father or vanquished enemies validated succession. That's why Saul's son Ish-bosheth was incensed when Abner seduced his father's concubines and why Abner had to defend his loyalty (2 Samuel 3:7, 8). The same rationale lay behind Absalom's taking his father's concubines.[11] Reuben's sin, therefore, centered in his attempt to ensure his mother's position by nullifying Bilhah and also to wrench power from his father.

Reuben lost. First Chronicles 5:1 says of Reuben, "for he was the firstborn, but because he defiled his father's couch, his birthright was given to the sons of Joseph the son of Israel." Jacob's anger toward Reuben burned until the end of his life, as his final words to Reuben attest:

> *Reuben, you are my firstborn,*
> *my might, and the firstfruits of my strength,*
> *preeminent in dignity and preeminent in power.*
> *Unstable as water, you shall not have preeminence,*
> *because you went up to your father's bed;*
> *then you defiled it — he went up to my couch! (49:3, 4)*

What bitter residuals.

Division. Apparently the residual bitterness extended to the entire family, as dramatized by the listing of Jacob's twelve sons according to their matriarchal origin rather than according to birth order: "Now the sons of Jacob were twelve. *The sons of Leah*: Reuben (Jacob's firstborn), Simeon, Levi, Judah, Issachar, and Zebulun. *The sons of Rachel*: Joseph and Benjamin. *The sons of Bilhah*, Rachel's servant: Dan and Naphtali. *The sons of Zilpah*, Leah's servant: Gad and Asher. These were the sons of Jacob who were born to him in Paddan-aram" (vv. 22b-24, italics added). There was animosity between Jacob and Leah's sons, and between the sons of Rachel and Bilhah and the sons of Leah and Zilpah. This would culminate in a plan to murder Joseph, which was avoided only by his sale into Egypt. Ugly residuals.

With a third transitional death, the generation passed on: "And Jacob came to his father Isaac at Mamre, or Kiriath-arba (that is, Hebron), where Abraham and Isaac had sojourned. Now the days of Isaac were 180 years. And Isaac breathed his last, and he died and was gathered to his people, old and full of days. And his sons Esau and Jacob buried him" (vv. 27-29). Isaac's estranged sons joined together to inter him in the ossuary at Machpelah beside the remains of his wife Rebekah and his parents Abraham and Sarah. Sarah's Laughter was laid to rest.

Due to sin's residuals, Jacob's long life would have many unexpected turns — the apparent death of Joseph, his sons' trip to Egypt, the custody of his beloved Benjamin in Egypt, Jacob's forced trip to Egypt, his death in Egypt, and the return of his embalmed remains by Joseph to Machpelah. The residuals kept coming in.

But there was also great grace in Jacob's life. Joseph, the son Jacob would receive back as if from the dead, would be used to effect the deliverance and salvation of his people. This Joseph, unlike his brothers, would lead a celebrated, exemplary life. In fact, he is seen as a type of Christ. There in Egypt a people would be formed who would come out in glorious exodus. All would be of grace. God would say to them:

*You yourselves have seen what I did to the Egyptians, and how I bore you
on eagles' wings and brought you to myself. Now therefore, if you will
indeed obey my voice and keep my covenant, you shall be my treasured possession among all peoples, for all the earth is mine; and you shall be to
me a kingdom of priests and a holy nation. These are the words that you
shall speak to the people of Israel. (Exodus 19:4-6)*

The life of Jacob is about Almighty God who delivers his sinful people
and fulfills his word amidst the residuals of sin. Jacob's life calls us to
repent of our sin and obey God's call and direction in our lives. That patriarch's life assures us of the triumph of grace.

Some sins that believers commit bear lifelong residuals. An ethical sin,
perhaps in business, though repented of, can bear lifelong residuals. A
Christian may enter into an adulterous relationship that destroys his marriage. Though he may later repent, the family residuals will follow him to
his death.

But there is always grace. God is written large all over this culminating
chapter that records Jacob's repentance and obedience. And more, God's
grace triumphs amidst sin's residuals and mediates their effects.

52

The Generations of Esau

GENESIS 36:1-43

Certainly Jacob was to blame for manipulating his older brother Esau into selling his birthright to him for a bowl of stew. But the great and eternal blame lay on Esau alone, to which the account leaves no doubt: "Thus Esau despised his birthright" (25:34). Does this suggest that Esau was a villain? Far from it. His failure lay in his young, attractive, unbridled nature. Scripture's brief glimpses suggest that Esau was a spontaneous, extroverted, impulsive outdoorsman — a good guy, as we say. Alexander Whyte, the eloquent nineteenth-century Scottish preacher, described him like this:

> Esau was full of the manliest interests and occupations and pursuits. He was a very proverb of courage and endurance and success in the chase. He was the ruggedest, the brawniest, and the shaggiest of all the rugged, brawny, and shaggy creatures of the field and of the forest, among whom he lived and died. Esau had an eye like an eagle. His ear never slept. His foot took the firmest hold of the ground. And his hand was always full both of skill, and strength, and success. Esau's arrow never missed its mark. He was the pride of all the encampment as he came home at night with his traps, and his snares, and his bows, and his arrows, and laden to the earth with venison for his father's supper. Burned black with the sun; beaten hard and dry with the wind; a prince of men; a prime favourite both with men, and women, and children, and with a good word and a good gift from the field for them all.[1]

The tragedy was, that was just about the sum total of who the man was. Esau was an easygoing "good time Charlie" who was accustomed to yielding to his appetites. The concept of delayed gratification had no place in his thinking. He lived for what was before him, be it a hunt or a meal or the company of women. Esau was singularly unreflective. He had no sense of the spiritual, no eye for the unseen, no vision, only earthbound dreams. Holy things? He never thought that deeply. And that is why he could so blithely sell his birthright for Jacob's stew with the facetious rhetoric of starvation. He cared not at all about the covenant's future glorious promises of Canaan and a multitude of descendants. What good were they in the present? Even the firstborn's entitlement to a double portion of the inheritance meant nothing *now*.

Jacob's maneuvering was reprehensible. But everyone knew that Esau disparaged his birthright, that it was up for sale. The sad reality was that Esau's dismissive neglect was a monumental insult to Jehovah, the God of his fathers Abraham and Isaac. He despised his birthright, and the Bible despises what he did: "See to it that no one fails to obtain the grace of God; that no 'root of bitterness' springs up and causes trouble, and by it many become defiled; that no one is sexually immoral or unholy like Esau, who sold his birthright for a single meal" (Hebrews 12:15, 16). Esau did this great sin with no repentance, no sorrow, and no regret. And his life went on unchallenged by consequences. He continued to stride the fields after game, eat under the sun and the stars, laugh and play as always. Nothing had changed — he thought.

Marriage. But his sensual nature pushed him further into sin. Marriage to the Canaanites of the land was strictly forbidden. His grandfather Abraham had gone to great lengths to find a proper wife for Isaac, making his servant Eliezer swear that he would not take a wife for Isaac from the daughters of the Canaanites (cf. 24:1-9). But Esau spat upon this when in open defiance he took wives from the idolatrous Hittites and brought them to his tents within the camp, where "they made life bitter for Isaac and Rebekah" (26:35). A man's choice in marriage showcases his values and is almost always the determining factor in the trajectory of his life. Esau had made his own bed — for life. So now, in his fortieth year, he had formally trashed both his birthright and his heritage.

Blessing. Nevertheless, this winsome free-spirited man's man remained his father's favorite. And in willful defiance of the birth oracle that "the older shall serve the younger" (25:23) and also in the face of the fact that the younger now possessed the birthright, Isaac and Esau covertly planned to take back what Esau had lost by having Isaac bestow upon Esau his patriarchal blessing. But Esau and his blind father were no match for mother and son, whose brilliant theatrics enabled Jacob to steal Esau's blessing as the old man intoned the covenantal blessings over his camouflaged head. Esau's pathetic cry and plea — "Have you but one blessing, my father? Bless me, even me also, my father" (27:38) — was answered with a necessarily diminished blessing:

Behold, away from the fatness of the earth shall your dwelling be,
and away from the dew of heaven on high.
By your sword you shall live,
and you shall serve your brother;
but when you grow restless
you shall break his yoke from your neck. (vv. 39, 40)

Esau's blessing was notably devoid of the spiritual blessings given to Jacob. Instead it prophesied where and how he would live, and that one day his servitude to his brother would be broken. Esau's sins had brought him much reduced, though substantial, blessings. And about this the writer of Hebrews pointedly observes, "For you know that afterward, when he desired to inherit the blessing, he was rejected, for he found no chance to repent, though he sought it with tears" (12:17).

The birthright and glorious covenantal blessing were gone forever. For Esau, the present was never as intoxicating as before. The hunt was less thrilling, life's pleasures muted.

The Moving Finger writes; and, having writ,
Moves on: nor all your Piety nor Wit
Shall lure it back to cancel half a Line,
Nor all thy Tears wash out a Word of it.
OMAR KHAYYAM[2]

Hatred. So it was that Esau was engulfed with homicidal rage so intense that his sole comfort was murderous fantasies. Jacob immediately fled to Mesopotamia with instructions to avoid Hittite women and marry one of the daughters of Laban (cf. 27:46 — 28:2). Esau clumsily countered. "So when Esau saw that the Canaanite women did not please Isaac his father, Esau went to Ishmael and took as his wife, besides the wives he had, Mahalath the daughter of Ishmael, Abraham's son, the sister of Nebaioth" (28:8, 9). But an Ishmaelite wife's mixed blood did not meet the covenantal ideal. So there Esau was — having despised and palmed off his birthright, polygamously wedded to pagan Canaanites, bereft of the covenantal blessing, married a third time amiss, and dreaming longingly of fratricide. Not a nice picture at all.

Not a word was written about Esau's life during the next two decades because the focus of Genesis turns to the Jacob/Laban saga in faraway Mesopotamia. There God's work in Jacob effected a sanctification in him that peaked at Peniel where he was renamed Israel, after which he succumbed to halfway obedience and its ensuing tragedies, finally eventuating in his chastened return to Bethel so that he came to be — at last — God's man in God's place.

As to Esau, we surmise that in keeping with his father's diminished blessing he began to dwell more regularly in Seir and that his family multiplied rapidly. Certainly he never broke fellowship with Isaac and Rebekah, as he remained Isaac's favorite, spending long periods with them at Hebron. And most certainly he and his pagan wives did not live in tranquillity those twenty long years. Recall Rebekah's complaint to Isaac: "I loathe my life because of the Hittite women. If Jacob marries one of the Hittite women like these, one of the women of the land, what good will my life be to me?" (27:46). Thus those silent decades graciously provided Esau plenty of time to reflect on his mistakes and his lot in life as he lived amidst the stresses of family and growing prosperity. And Esau began to change. Most notably, his rage cooled. With time, his natural ebullience returned.

Rapprochement. With the passing of those twenty years and Jacob's return, whatever had been Esau's intent when he came with four hundred men to meet Jacob was erased in an instant as "Esau ran to meet him and embraced him and fell on his neck and kissed him, and they wept" (33:4).

Esau's magnanimity shined. His demurrals were real, though he did ultimately accept Jacob's gift, thus officially erasing the offense. Esau had truly forgiven his brother. He opened both his heart and his home to Jacob. How beautiful the big man was! And when their father died and was gathered to his people, the brothers stood side by side to honor him as they interred him alongside their mother Rebekah and their loving grandparents Abraham and Sarah.

What are we to make of Esau? Most exegetes who address the matter believe that Esau was an unbelieving, lost soul. The main reason is found in the passage already cited in Hebrews:

> *See to it that no one fails to obtain the grace of God; that no "root of bitterness" springs up and causes trouble, and by it many become defiled; that no one is sexually immoral or unholy like Esau, who sold his birthright for a single meal. For you know that afterward, when he desired to inherit the blessing, he was rejected, for he found no chance to repent, though he sought it with tears. (12:15-17)*

But the question is, does this refer to Esau's entire life? Is it his life epitaph? Or does it apply to the event early in his life when he sold his birthright and lost his blessing — a time when his life was characterized by immorality and unholy conduct — a period in which he acquired his Canaanite and Ishmaelite wives — a graceless time in his life? As to the famous statement quoted in Romans 9:13, "Jacob I loved, but Esau I hated," which Paul uses to illustrate God's sovereign choice (particular, individual election) of Jacob over Esau, it must be remembered that it is a quotation from Malachi 1:2, 3, which is a centuries-later oracle of judgment against the Edomites for their abuse of Israel. In Genesis 33 there is no acrimony but rather forgiveness and mutual love and affection. And the brothers stood in solidarity at their father's death (35:29). One day the second table of the law would be summed up by the call to love your neighbor as you love yourself (cf. Leviticus 19:18), and here Esau appeared to be doing just that. Perhaps it was because he had first come to love God — and grace was effectual.

My point is that Genesis is ambiguous about Esau. The beginning of his life was certainly graceless, but he appeared as a different man after the twenty-year hiatus. Certainly his demotion from covenant-bearer did not mean that he was excluded from the benefits of the covenant.

Personally I have seen the pattern and ambiguities of Esau's chronicle traced in the lives of men I have buried over the years. They were born to godly, though imperfect, parents. Growing up, they were nurtured and catechized in God's Word. But Christian things meant little to them. Heaven was far-off, disconnected from real life. And as they matured, they came to despise their heritage — maybe not overtly but by neglect and dismissiveness. Some were ignorant despisers, others cultured despisers.

To their parents' great sorrow they married outside the faith and then went with the flow of culture in raising their children so that they became *de facto* pagans pursuing and even attaining the American dream.

But as these men passed through midlife, the emptiness of it all began to pummel their souls. They repented and came to faith. When they could, they made amends. But their families did not follow. So these men stayed at the fringes of the church, sometimes seeking counsel, engaging in benevolences, attending irregularly and alone, inarticulate as to their faith.

When they died, the family asked for a funeral in the church in respect to their father's wishes. And when I preached, it was to ignorant, unbelieving hearts — Edomites.

ESAU'S GENEALOGIES (vv. 1-8 and 9-43)

Here the genealogies of Esau are instructive. The brief genealogy of 36:1-8 begins with an emphasis on Esau's choice of Canaanite wives. "These are the generations of Esau (that is, Edom). Esau took his wives from the Canaanites: Adah the daughter of Elon the Hittite, Oholibamah the daughter of Anah the daughter of Zibeon the Hivite" (vv. 1, 2). Of this Sarna comments:

> On the surface, the raw data are presented objectively. In actuality, the epithet "Canaanite women" is undoubtedly derogatory, as a glance at 26:3, 37, and 27:46, and 28:1, 6, 8 shows. Esau's marriages violated the conventions of his family and flouted their values. . . . This explains why the order of wives in verses 2-3 differs from that in all subsequent lists in

this chapter. Adah and Oholibamah are here grouped together in order to emphasize their Canaanite — and hence unacceptable — origins.[3]

Esau's marital decisions had the tragic effect of cutting off his descendants from the chosen people.

The other momentous event of this genealogy is Esau's departure from the promised land.

> *Then Esau took his wives, his sons, his daughters, and all the members of his household, his livestock, all his beasts, and all his property that he had acquired in the land of Canaan. He went into a land away from his brother Jacob. For their possessions were too great for them to dwell together. The land of their sojournings could not support them because of their livestock. So Esau settled in the hill country of Seir. (Esau is Edom.) (vv. 6-8)*

The assertion that the land was not big enough to support both their flocks is questionable because chapter 34:21 indicates that the Shechemites thought there was adequate land for everyone. Likely, this was a convenient, face-saving spin for everyone involved. The result was that, like Lot before him, Esau abandoned the land of promise and, more, "walked out of the record of saving history" (Wenham).[4] Esau's departure was equally significant for Jacob, because it recognized Jacob's right to the promised land.

Tellingly, all this was done with the grace and magnanimity that had come to characterize Esau. There was no hassling over property. No stigma was attached to Esau. Like Ishmael before him, Esau is viewed kindly as a relative who walked out of the line of promise.

The result, however, was catastrophic as the bare bones of the expanded genealogy of verses 9-43 so clearly demonstrate. Positively, Esau prospered far beyond the Israelites, so that while Israel suffered famine and migration and captivity in Egypt, Edom expanded and even developed a succession of kings. Negatively, this came at the price of profound assimilation. In the first section of the enlarged genealogy (verses 9-14) intermarriage was tentative, and native wives were only accorded the status of concubines.[5] But the next section (verses 15-19) indicates that intermarriage had become *de jure* and that the indigenous people were accorded higher status. By the third section (verses 20-30), Esau had displaced the native people and had married into a leading family.[6] The picture here is one of violent invasion by Esau's clan followed by the absorption of the native populace into the "descendants of Esau."[7] Thus mutual absorption and assimilation moved into high gear.

The fourth section (verses 31-39) is not a genealogy but a list of eight kings who reigned in Edom prior to the monarchy in Israel. Edom became wealthy and powerful long before Israel. Here it seems that the promise to Abraham that kings would come from him (cf. 17:16) had an initial and partial fulfillment in these non-Israelite, Abrahamic kings.[8] Indeed, Esau prospered.

Finally, the fifth section (verses 40-43) emphasizes the spheres of ownership and influence of the leading Edomite families, all the way to "Elah" on the Gulf of Akaba.[9] Esau was flourishing by the sword in Edom, just as Isaac's "blessing" had predicted (cf. 27:39, 40).

Tragically, Esau's descendants would become inveterate enemies of Israel. Some five hundred years after Esau's departure when Moses was leading Israel's exodus from Egypt, the Edomites refused the peaceful overtures of Moses and would not allow Israel to pass through their territories (cf. Numbers 20:14-21). When Saul became king of Israel, he had to fight the Edomites (cf. 1 Samuel 14:47). King David subdued them for a time. The most infamous abuse came during Israel's deportation to Babylonia when the Edomites blocked the crossroads, cutting off the route of the fugitive Israelites, and delivered them back to the Babylonians (cf. Obadiah 14). Hence the fierce invective of Malachi and the entire book of Obadiah against the Edomites (cf. Obadiah 1-18; Malachi 1:2-5; Jeremiah 49:17, 18; Psalm 137:7-9).

And, finally, the tragic poetry of redemptive history is this: It was an Edomite king, Herod the Great, who exterminated the babies of Bethlehem in his attempt to kill the King of kings (cf. Matthew 2). The ultimate sons of Esau and Jacob (Herod the King and Christ the King) testified to the significance of the path we take up.

Young Esau could not see beyond what was in front of him. He possessed no vision, no spiritual imagination. He had no eyes or mind for God, or for Heaven, or for Hell. Spiritual realities were to him dull and opaque. He was a single-dimensional soul. Pleasure *now* was his guiding star. For him all that mattered was the excitement of the hunt, a hearty meal, a woman's company — all good things in the proper perspective and place. But pleasure is all that Esau could see. Thus he despised his birthright, selling it for a single meal, and likewise he despised his heritage for the pleasure of Canaanite women. Esau's blithe arrogance brutalized everything precious to life and fixed him on his tragic course.

For every generation, the challenge is the same — to see that there is more to life than a meal, or a video game, or baseball, or a party, or a movie, or an indulgence of some kind — to see, as Paul put it, that "the things that are seen are transient, but the things that are unseen are eternal" (2 Corinthians 4:18). The challenge is to "seek the things that are above, where Christ is, seated at the right hand of God," to "set your minds on things that are above, not on things that are on earth" (Colossians 3:1, 2). The challenge is to forgo the lazy brain death that comes so easily to the young who ignore the teaching and preaching of God's Word — and to listen with all you have. Do not sell what God has given you through his Word, your church, and your family for a cheap pleasure.

My heart's prayer for you is Paul's prayer, the prayer I pray for my own children and grandchildren:

> . . . that the God of our Lord Jesus Christ, the Father of glory, may give you a spirit of wisdom and of revelation in the knowledge of him, having the eyes of your hearts enlightened, that you may know what is the hope to which he has called you, what are the riches of his glorious inheritance in the saints, and what is the immeasurable greatness of his power toward us who believe, according to the working of his great might that he worked in Christ when he raised him from the dead and seated him at his right hand in the heavenly places. (Ephesians 1:17-20)

53

Joseph's Call

GENESIS 37:1-11

The story of Joseph is by far the longest and most masterful narrative in Genesis, if not the entire Bible. Thomas Mann, the celebrated German novelist and Nobel laureate, expanded the story line into an immense three-volume work: *Joseph and His Brothers*, *Young Joseph*, and *Joseph in Egypt*, which when published in 1930 some called "perhaps the greatest creative work of the 20th century." Agnes E. Meyer, writing in *The New York Times Book Review*, said, ". . . purely as narrative and background there is a magnificent story here which exceeds in drama, opulence, and movement anything that Hollywood has ever dreamed."[1] Andrew Lloyd Webber must have thought likewise when he composed the smash musical *Joseph and the Amazing Technicolor Dreamcoat*.

Be that as it may, the divinely inspired account exceeds its fictional renditions with a depth and theological subtlety beyond the intent and capacities of Mann and Webber. And because it is real-life theological drama, the inspired narrative has a power that exceeds art alone. The biblical account is at once theological narrative and heroic literature that will instruct and challenge all who seriously engage it.

Here is sweeping narrative that moves between the pastures of Palestine to the eighteenth-century B.C. courts of the Nile — with a hero for the ages. The majestic character of Joseph towers over it all, much like that of Daniel in Babylon. Indeed, both Joseph and Daniel displayed the wisdom of God, both men interpreted the dreams of their kings, both could not be compromised, both were jailed for their obedience, and both were made vice-regents of their adopted realms. And more, Joseph's actions sometimes foreshadowed those of Christ himself, whose rejection by men played an essential part in effecting our deliverance (cf. Isaiah 53:3; John 1:11; Mark 9:12).

The Joseph story also records the gestation of the nation of Israel as it chronicles the migration of Jacob's embryonic clan to Egypt, where it would grow to full-term in the womb of the Nile. Some four hundred years later, Israel burst fully formed from Egypt, fulfilling the Lord's prophecy to Abram: "Know for certain that your offspring will be sojourners in a land that is not theirs and will be servants there, and they will be afflicted for four hundred years. But I will bring judgment on the nation that they serve, and afterward they shall come out with great possessions" (15:13, 14). As God would have it, the microcosm of Joseph's life would be beautifully prophetic of the life of the nation of Israel in macrocosm. Allen Ross explains:

> . . . just as Joseph lived in bondage in Egypt before his deliverance and supremacy over Egypt, so would the nation. Just as suffering and bondage formed tests for Joseph to see if he kept his faith and was worthy of the promise, so too the bondage of the nation was a means of discipline and preparation for the nation's future responsibilities. Moreover, the climax of the story showed that the Hebrew slave served a God who was infinitely superior to Egypt, who controlled the economy of Egypt, and whose wisdom outstripped the wisdom of Egypt.[2]

Ultimately, and above all, the story of Joseph is about God working his will through the everyday events of life. There are no miracles here. God does not suspend his natural laws to make things happen. The story is about the hidden but sure way of God. God's hidden hand arranges everything without show or explanation or violating the nature of things. God is involved in all events and directs all things to their appointed end. Toward the conclusion of the great narrative, when Joseph reveals himself to his brothers, he says just this: "And God sent me before you to preserve for you a remnant on earth, and to keep alive for you many survivors. So it was not you who sent me here, but God" (45:7, 8). What a God he is — because he is not just a God of the extraordinary but a God of the ordinary. His power and infinitude take both the good and evil actions of Joseph's family, of Pharaoh and his servants, and of passersby and uses their actions for good (cf. 50:20).

As the story begins, God providentially brings about Joseph's rejection so that Joseph himself might ultimately be used to effect his people's salvation. God choreographed Joseph's rejection in two ways: first, by his father's favoring of Joseph over his brothers, and second, by God's giving Joseph a vision of his own future exaltation. Human sin and divine revelation combined to produce a hatred and rejection that ultimately created a way of salvation.

JACOB FATHERS JOSEPH'S REJECTION (vv. 1-4)

With Esau's departure from the land of promise, Esau had in effect acknowledged Jacob's right to the promised land. So Jacob settled down to stay. "The generations of Jacob" (v. 2), the next to the last *toledot* in Genesis, is the ninth occurrence of the phrase "These are the generations of." This is largely an account of the life of his son Joseph, just as "the generations of Isaac" were taken up with the life of his son Jacob. And here it is the life of Joseph that preserves and saves the generations of Jacob.

Joseph's evil report. The epic begins with teenaged Joseph shepherding his father's flocks along with Dan, Naphtali, Gad, and Asher, the sons of Jacob's secondary wives Bilhah and Zilpah. Though full sons, these men had a secondary status in Jacob's affections. We have already witnessed that there were hard feelings between Jacob and the sons of his unloved wife Leah, and these were heightened by Jacob's disregard for their sister Dinah (cf. 34:30, 31). And likely, Jacob felt even less affection for the sons of his slave wives, and these four sons of Bilhah and Zilpah knew it and resented it. Quite naturally, then, the four had little regard for young Joseph, the son of their father's favorite wife.

Now Joseph was far from perfect, notwithstanding his future greatness. Up until recently it has been customary for preachers to accord Joseph an almost sinless status because the Scripture records no overt sin or criticism of him. Such reckoning, of course, is contrary to what Scripture teaches about the sinful nature of all people and what we know about the daily sins and repentance of the most godly. At best, young Joseph was a good-boy sinner. Thus the elaborate attempts to say that Joseph did nothing wrong when he "brought a bad report of them to their father" (v. 2b) ring hollow. This is especially true in light of what the text actually says about the incident, because the word "report," *dibbâ,* is always used in the rest of Scripture in the negative sense of an *untrue* report, and here it is qualified by the adjective *rāʿâ,* "evil."[3] Thus Joseph misrepresented and so maligned his brothers.[4] Likely, his report was essentially true, but not perfectly so — due to exaggeration or inaccuracies. So young Joseph, in effect, became a tattler.

In the eyes of the disaffected sons of Bilhah and Zilpah, this was a monstrous offense. And when the rest of the older sons heard about what Joseph had done, they began to smolder with resentment. Joseph's offense grew larger with each retelling. On their relativized scale of morality, Joseph was the lowest.

Jacob's favoritism. Favoritism had become a generational sin in Jacob's family. Remember, Isaac loved Esau more than Jacob, and remember that Rebekah loved Jacob more than Esau, and recall that Jacob loved Rachel and her children more than Leah and her offspring. "Now Israel loved Joseph more than any other of his sons, because he was the son of his old age" (v. 3a). Jacob probably could not help his feelings of favoritism because Joseph was the son of Rachel, his deceased and never-forgotten first love, and Joseph had been born late in life after so many years of frustration. Along with this, young Joseph's freedom from the sins of his older sons made him a source of solace and joy to his father. Nevertheless, Jacob's blatant favoritism was unconscionable. The lifelong hurt inflicted by his own father's favoritism should have made him wary of even a hint of not being evenhanded with his children.

But father Jacob was in a relational fog, for we read, "And he made him a robe of many colors" (v. 3b). The designation "many colors" is arbitrary and derived from the Septuagint and Vulgate translations. The coat may well have been colored and ornamented. But likely the term describes a sleeved coat that reached to the wrists and ankles, thus setting Joseph apart as the one who would receive the double-portion of the inheritance. Joseph was the first son of Rachel, whom Jacob had chosen to marry before being deceived by Laban. And more, Reuben, the firstborn of Leah, had forfeited his birthright because of incest with Bilhah (cf. 35:22).

Young Joseph's sudden appearance in the distinctive robe ignited his brothers' hatred. "But when his brothers saw that their father loved him more than all his brothers, they hated him and could not speak peacefully to him" (v. 4). Joseph was already at the bottom of the brotherly chain because of his evil report, and now his lordly attire, announcing that he was "the wave of the future," inflamed their burning rage.[5] Sarna translates the phrase, "could not speak peacefully to him" as literally saying, "they could not abide his friendly speech" — that is, they rebuffed his every attempt to be friendly.[6] Joseph's brothers loathed his presence.

The human causes of this are so readily apparent: Joseph's sinful distortions and Jacob's sinful favoritism and blatant elevation of Joseph combined to harden his sons' rejection of and bitter hatred for Joseph.

Where was God in all of this? we may wonder. He was adding fuel to the fire.

GOD SEALS JOSEPH'S REJECTION (vv. 5-11)

The fuel came in the form of two Joseph-exalting dreams.

Joseph's harvest dream. The first dream utilized a pastoral motif and is described in "rhythmic, almost choreographic language."[7] Joseph was so full of the dream that he was compelled to pour it out to his brothers.

> *Now Joseph had a dream, and when he told it to his brothers they hated him even more. He said to them, "Hear this dream that I have dreamed: Behold, we were binding sheaves in the field, and behold, my sheaf arose and*

stood upright. And behold, your sheaves gathered around it and bowed down to my sheaf." (vv. 5-7)

No one, not even the dullest of his brothers, could miss the point. Joseph certainly must have understood it too. But the force of the dream, plus his naivete and self-focus (which came from being the center of his parents' affection), impelled him to spontaneously share it. After all, the dream was the real thing, and not a concoction. The dream, of course, foreshadowed the saving climax of the Joseph narrative when, because he had become ruler of Egypt, his brothers bowed down to him (cf. 42:6).

There is no way of knowing what response Joseph expected from his brothers, but there was truly only one possible response: "His brothers said to him, 'Are you indeed to reign over us? Or are you indeed to rule over us?' So they hated him even more for his dreams and for his words" (v. 8). Their ironic, sarcastic disgust throbs here: "This arrogant, pompous, ego-centered, self-focused brat is awash in megalomania. The spoiled little braggart." The refrain, "so they hated him" is the third repetition of this phrase in the account, marking the escalated intensity of their hatred.

Joseph's celestial dream. All dreams in the Joseph narrative come in pairs, because the pairing of dreams meant certainty of fulfillment. Later Joseph would explain to Pharaoh, "And the doubling of Pharaoh's dream means that the thing is fixed by God, and God will shortly bring it about" (41:32). So Joseph's second dream now sealed the matter.[8] God would sovereignly bring to pass the fulfillment of Joseph's dreams. This certitude may be the reason that Joseph had the audacity to inform his family of its contents.

The second of the dreams goes beyond the first in the grandeur of the emblems and also in the inclusion of his parents in bowing to him: "Then he dreamed another dream and told it to his brothers and said, 'Behold, I have dreamed another dream. Behold, the sun, the moon, and eleven stars were bowing down to me'" (v. 9). The vision was symbolic and surreal — a sky spangled with just eleven stars (his eleven brothers) and the crowning glories of a radiant sun and moon (his father and mother) — and they all do obeisance to him. How did they bow? Did the spheres momentarily flatten out like a westering sun? Did they blink obeisance in Morse code? We do not know. But one thing is sure: He saw them all bow to *him* — from Reuben to Benjamin to his father Jacob and his deceased mother Rachel.[9]

This was too much, even for his doting father.

But when he told it to his father and to his brothers, his father rebuked ["berated," Jewish Publication Society translation] him and said to him, "What is this dream that you have dreamed? Shall I and your mother and your brothers indeed come to bow ourselves to the ground before

you?" And his brothers were jealous of him, but his father kept the say-
ing in mind. (vv. 10, 11)

Jacob rebuked Joseph, but he did not hate him as did his sons. Something
in his soul gave him pause. Like Mary to come, he pondered the meaning
of what he heard in his heart (cf. Luke 2:19). Jacob was not dismissive.
Joseph was fortunate to have a father who, though he was the younger son,
had himself become heir of the birthright and blessing. What was God indicating about Joseph?

But the brothers' silence was ominous. Joseph's future was sealed. There
was no reversing his rejection. The epic course of his life had been set.

The hand of God was everywhere in this sweeping narrative as it orchestrated the creation of a preserver of his people. God's hidden hand had its
subtle way amidst the morass of human sin. Young Joseph's "bad report"
set him at odds with his brothers. Jacob's entrenched favoritism of Joseph
further incurred his sons' resentment and rejection of Joseph. God's visible
fingerprints were seen in the substance and choreography of Joseph's two
dreams. Their origin and meaning came from God's pleasure. God sovereignly sealed and insured the rejection of young Joseph. Human sin and
divine revelation were made to do his good work. As Walter Brueggemann
has said:

> The main character in the drama is Yahweh. Though hidden in the form
> of a dream, silent and not at all visible, the listener will understand that
> the dream is the unsettling work of Yahweh upon which everything else
> depends. Without the dream there would be no Joseph and no narrative.
> From the perspective of the brothers, without the dream there would be
> no trouble or conflict. For the father, without the dream there would be no
> grief or loss. The dream sets its own course, the father-brother-dreamer
> notwithstanding. And in the end, the dream prevails over the tensions of the
> family.[10]

The effect of the dream and its narration set in motion a chain of events
that were not disasters but the work of grace.

"God's work of providence is his most holy, wise, and powerful preserving and governing all his creatures, and all their actions," says the
Westminster Shorter Catechism, Question 11. Our great Creator uses his
creative power to keep all creation in existence, to involve himself in all
events, and to direct all things to their appointed end. That is why Joseph
would one day say, "As for you, you meant evil against me, but God meant
it for good, to bring it about that many people should be kept alive, as they
are today" (50:20).

Do you see what that tells us? It reveals that any of us who follow God will live a life that will sometimes become very tangled. At times complications will rise from our own sin (as with Joseph), from the sin of those around us, and from the sin of those in the wider spheres of our existence. We live in a world caught in a web of sin, and it is constantly casting new webs. But we know that amidst life's complexities the creative power of God is at work to do us good. This is true when we are ill, when we have trouble with our children or grandchildren, when professional problems engulf us.

Truly we have a God of providence, a God who sustains our souls in all of life, perpetually working good. This is a truth to learn now, because life is not going to get easier. In fact, the more you follow God, the more complicated life will become because your life's course will buck the currents of this world.

But take it to heart that God is at work to do you good, and rest your soul in that. Submit yourself to him in the great processes of life. Follow him. Listen to the life of Joseph, a hero for the ages, who became so much like Christ himself.

54

Sold into Slavery

GENESIS 37:12-36

The threads of Joseph's rejection by his brothers were woven fine. The sinful human strands of his father's favoritism and his own naive self-centeredness, plus the divine threads of the two Joseph-exalting dreams combined to create an ever-tightening noose for the gallows of Joseph's rejection. The noose was already around the young man's neck. And as we all know from the story line, the trapdoor would soon spring, sending young Joseph down to a living death of slavery in Egypt. We know, too, that God's plan was in full motion, though no human could see it. Israel's human savior, the future vice-regent of Egypt, was being put in place. Joseph's story would show how God's hidden providence works through men's evil for their ultimate good. Dark as the story is, it shines with hope and optimism. And we will duly note the glimmers of providence.

At the same time, because this is a real story of real brothers in an all-too-real family, we will miss much of what God has for us if we overly dwell on providence. We must listen to this story as it is and allow the events to speak for themselves in their own narrative power — life to life. As we listen, we will learn essential truth, both theological and personal.

JOSEPH SENT TO HIS BROTHERS (vv. 12-17)

Joseph sent. The story begins benignly enough with Jacob sending young Joseph to check on the well-being of his ten older brothers.

> *Now his brothers went to pasture their father's flock near Shechem. And Israel said to Joseph, "Are not your brothers pasturing the flock at Shechem? Come, I will send you to them." And he said to him, "Here I*

am." So he said to him, "Go now, see if it is well with your brothers and with the flock, and bring me word." So he sent him from the Valley of Hebron, and he came to Shechem. (vv. 12-14)

Hebron was twenty miles south of Jerusalem, and Shechem was thirty miles north of the holy city. So Joseph's brothers were fifty miles north, or approximately five days' journey away. This considerable distance to Shechem, coupled with the recent history of Simeon and Levi's bloody massacre of the Shechemites, was reasonable cause for Jacob's unease. We can certainly understand Jacob's concern for his sons, but it is difficult to understand his sending his favorite son decked out in his fabulous coat. The relational fact was that his brothers "hated him and could not speak peacefully to him" (v. 4). Possibly they had moderated their contempt for Joseph when their father was around. But the sense is that neither Jacob nor Joseph had any inkling of their malicious intent. Joseph seems to have gone out with the blithe presumption that though his brothers had been unhappy with him, they loved him like everyone else did. Thus Joseph naively made the five-day trek north.

Joseph searches. But when he arrived in Shechem, his brothers and their flocks were nowhere to be seen. A well-dressed Hebrew youth alone and roaming about a Canaanite killing field was not good. But God was watchful of his chosen instrument. "And a man found him wandering in the fields. And the man asked him, 'What are you seeking?' 'I am seeking my brothers,' he said. 'Tell me, please, where they are pasturing the flock.' And the man said, 'They have gone away, for I heard them say, "Let us go to Dothan."'" So Joseph went after his brothers and found them at Dothan" (vv. 15-17).

Dothan was another fourteen miles farther north, which would place Joseph sixty-four miles from home, far from his father's protective umbrella. And there the bottom would fall out — but not the net of God's care. In fact, as Kidner has pointed out, the two extremes of God's care occurred at Dothan. In the first instance, Joseph would cry for deliverance but to no apparent avail (cf. 42:21). But in the second instance in Dothan, when the prophet Elisha found himself surrounded by horses and chariots of the armies of Syria so that his servant called out in fear, "Elisha prayed and said, 'O LORD, please open his eyes that he may see.' So the LORD opened the eyes of the young man, and he saw, and behold, the mountain was full of horses and chariots of fire all around Elisha" (2 Kings 6:17).

The truth is, the angels were just as present for Joseph in Dothan as they later were for Elisha. If Joseph's eyes could have seen the unseen when he was pleading for help, what he would likely have seen would be the analogy of Jacob's ladder, because Heaven and earth were busily joined by divine activity on Joseph's behalf.[1]

JOSEPH ABUSED BY HIS BROTHERS (vv. 18-24)

Evidently, nine of the brothers (Reuben, the eldest, was absent) had been indulging in an orgy of hatred so intense that Joseph's approach sparked the will to murder — fratricide.

Murderous premeditation. One of the brothers observed a figure approaching across the expanse and called it to his brothers' attention. The gait was familiar, and then at once they all knew as they saw the shimmering of Joseph's magnificent coat.

> *They saw him from afar, and before he came near to them they conspired against him to kill him. They said to one another, "Here comes this dreamer. Come now, let us kill him and throw him into one of the pits. Then we will say that a fierce animal has devoured him, and we will see what will become of his dreams." (vv. 18-20)*

Thomas Mann imagined it like this: "And with one accord . . . their hearts beat with a wild rapid rhythm, like drums, so that a hollow concerted drumming noise arose in the breathless stillness."[2] Vile democracy reigned as each added his bit to the homicidal plan. When young Joseph arrived, the murder was set. The crowning wickedness was the plan to cast his murdered body into a cistern unburied — the supreme dishonor.[3]

Their eyes assessed him with bleary-red hatred. Joseph was alone in their hands. Let the murder begin. Would they all beat him formless into the dust? Or should one of them simply cut his throat? Simeon and Levi were experts at that.

Reuben's intervention. But such pleasures were not to be because Reuben got word of the plans. Reuben, so recently fallen from his father's favor for his Bilhah affair, could not afford further blame for the death of the favorite son. And as the eldest he would indeed bear the responsibility. So Reuben stepped up to the rescue.

His opening words — "Let us not take his life" (v. 21) — were not a suggestion. Rather, it was a forceful and decisive commitment — "We shall not take his life." His command to "Shed no blood" (v. 22) is in the second-person plural, having the sense, "*You* shed no blood," thus distancing himself from the very idea.[4] And Reuben's command to cast Joseph into the pit unharmed was a ploy so that he could return and rescue Joseph.

Joseph abused. The verbs of verses 23, 24 describe a brutal assault. "So when Joseph came to his brothers, they stripped him of his robe, the robe of many colors that he wore. And they took him and cast him into a pit. The pit was empty; there was no water in it." "They stripped him" is a term used to describe the skinning of animals (cf. Leviticus 1:6). Like a pack of dogs, his nine brothers were upon him, scratching and pulling the hated coat from him and likely his remaining clothing, finally dumping him like a dead body into a pit so deep and vertical that he could not climb out.[5]

Joseph lay bruised and bleeding and naked on the rocky floor of an empty water cistern. Their intent was to let him starve to death. They would have "shed no blood" in a twisted technical sense, and thus they wrongly reasoned that his blood could not cry out from the ground (cf. Genesis 4:10).

JOSEPH SOLD INTO SLAVERY (vv. 25-28)

The merciless lynch-mob callousness is obvious — "Then they sat down to eat" (v. 25a). "Nothing like administering a good beating to whet the appetite!" Likely, the meal came from the delicacies that Joseph had brought to them from their father (cf. 1 Samuel 17:17, 18). As to poor Joseph, the text here tells us nothing. But the brothers will tell us twenty years later in Egypt when they encounter Joseph, "In truth we are guilty concerning our brother, in that we saw the distress of his soul, when he begged us and we did not listen. That is why this distress has come upon us" (42:21).

Joseph's brothers laughed and joked and feasted while they listened to Joseph's piteous cries and pleadings. They acted as if they did not hear during their dreadful communion. But Joseph's ghostly wails and moans as he pled with each by name — "Simeon!" Levi!" Dan!" Zebulun!" — had relentlessly echoed in their souls over the years.

Judah's "better idea." The brothers' plan was to eat, move on, and leave Joseph to the birds of the air. But the hidden hand of providence deftly countered with a *deus ex machina* as a caravan unexpectedly appeared, offering a solution.

> *And looking up they saw a caravan of Ishmaelites coming from Gilead, with their camels bearing gum, balm, and myrrh, on their way to carry it down to Egypt. Then Judah said to his brothers, "What profit is it if we kill our brother and conceal his blood? Come, let us sell him to the Ishmaelites, and let not our hand be upon him, for he is our brother, our own flesh." And his brothers listened to him. Then Midianite traders passed by. And they drew Joseph up and lifted him out of the pit, and sold him to the Ishmaelites for twenty shekels of silver. They took Joseph to Egypt. (vv. 25-28)*

The Ishmaelite traders were made up of the descendants of Abraham through Keturah (cf. 25:1, 2) and also Midianites who were residents of the Arabah with whom the Ishmaelites had intermarried. The point is that both groups were outside the covenant. Joseph was sold to non-covenant people.

In the absence of Reuben, Judah (the fourth-born) bypassed the violent duo of Simeon and Levi and took charge, offering his "better idea" of selling Joseph into slavery. It is difficult to discern Judah's motivation. Was it for a few shekels? Or was it due to better motives — his recognizing that Joseph was their "own flesh" coupled with the lasting consequences of fratricide? However it was, Judah was responsible for saving Joseph's life. From here on Judah would play a more active role in leadership, and (notwithstanding the Tamar fiasco of chapter 38) he will have a more influential role in the covenant.[6] Ultimately Jacob would name him bearer of the messianic line (cf. 49:8-10).

Egypt was big in the international slave trade. So the Midianites looked to a profitable market on the Nile. Likely, they doubled their twenty-shekel investment in Egypt. And what about Joseph? Dragged naked from the pit and tethered to a beast of burden so that he too could carry some of the freight, he began the long trek to the Nile. He had begun the day a robed prince in Israel and ended it as a slave.

Joseph had a massive case for victimhood. Why not pity himself? He was indeed pitiful! He had not done anything to deserve this. His biggest sin was that he liked people — and he assumed that they liked him. How easy it would have been for him to fall into rage. How could his brothers do this? Their fists and their words were so brutal. He remembered their twisted faces, all so ugly, and now so easy to hate!

And where was God? Why did God not warn him at Shechem? Then Joseph could have easily gone home. And why the appearance of a caravan bound for Egypt? Reuben would have rescued him, had it not been for this. How treasured thoughts of revenge could have become for young Joseph.

JACOB'S MOURNING (vv. 29-36)

As the oldest of the brothers with the care of several flocks to supervise, Reuben was naturally on the go. No doubt he left briefly so that he could return at an opportune time and spirit Joseph away. But to his horror an unexpected caravan had come and gone with Joseph! Reuben's tearing of his robes and wretched cry to his brothers — "The boy is gone, and I, where shall I go?" — revealed how much he really did care for Joseph and his father. In agony Reuben wailed in effect, "Where shall I go to escape?" The only response from the brothers was silence.

Jacob deceived. Joseph's magnificent robe had been at the heart of the story. "The robe began in deep *love*. Then it was torn in deep *hate*. Now it is the main tool for a deep *deception*" (Brueggemann).[7]

> *Then they took Joseph's robe and slaughtered a goat and dipped the robe in the blood. And they sent the robe of many colors and brought it to their father and said, "This we have found; please identify whether it is your son's robe or not." And he identified it and said, "It is my son's robe. A fierce animal has devoured him. Joseph is without doubt torn to pieces."*
> *(vv. 31-33)*

There is bitter irony here as Jacob's sons used their brother's clothing and the blood of a slain goat to deceive Jacob, just as Jacob had long ago deceived his own father Isaac with his brother's clothing and the skin of a slain goat (cf. 27:9-17). Jacob's deceit had come full circle.

The full force of the pain descended upon Jacob's consciousness in three quick stages. First he identified "my son's robe." Second, its torn condition led him to conclude that "a fierce animal has devoured him." And third, a horrible mental image gripped his soul — "Joseph is without doubt torn to pieces."[8] Oh, the shock! His boy, his wonderful boy, was gone.

Jacob's sorrow. What relentless sorrow!

Then Jacob tore his garments and put sackcloth on his loins and mourned for his son many days. All his sons and all his daughters rose up to comfort him, but he refused to be comforted and said, "No, I shall go down to Sheol to my son, mourning." Thus his father wept for him. (vv. 34, 35)

Jacob insisted that he would publicly mourn for Joseph to his dying day. Conventional grieving lasted a week for a parent (cf. 50:10). And when Moses died, the people mourned for the extraordinary period of a month (cf. Deuteronomy 34:8). But Jacob refused to be comforted by his sons and daughters. And he may well have kept up something of his public mourning for two decades until the day he saw Joseph.

What a mess and mockery his sons had made of their filial devotion. Their comforts were hollow and ineffectual, because they had done the deed, and as they went through the motions, they all could hear Joseph's forlorn cries rising up out of Egypt.

Regarding Joseph, we have this postscript: "Meanwhile the Midianites had sold him in Egypt to Potiphar, an officer of Pharaoh, the captain of the guard" (v. 36). The providential threads of Joseph's rejection had effected his terrible sale into Egypt. Israel's human savior was in place. God had planned it all. The awesome God of the Bible and of all history was at work.

But Joseph was not an android or robot. He lived his life as you and I live ours — with God's word to guide him (though far less of it than we have, notwithstanding his dreams), with an imperfect understanding of life around him, with his own personal besetting sins, and with sinners framing his existence. Joseph lived a real life in real time.

As we have noted, Joseph had ample reason for self-pity, rage, anger with God, and revenge. He had immense reasons to become enslaved to victimhood. He had been relationally crippled by his father's overweening favoritism. He had suffered from the "yours, mine, ours" relational pathology of polygamy. He had been monstrously abused by his brothers. The scars were there to stay — their homicidal rage, his beating and humiliation, their demeaning piercing epithets, the agonizing trip to Egypt, and his naked humiliation on the slave block in Egypt. What an opportunity for enslavement to victimhood. But there is not a "poor me" hint anywhere in the entire Genesis account of Joseph! And in Egypt his treatment would become even worse. What the writer wants us to see is that though enslaved, *Joseph chose to reject the slavery of self-pity and victimhood.*

How and why? Like his great-grandfather Abraham, he believed the bare word of God (cf. 15:6). Joseph believed the promise handed down from Abraham, Isaac, and his father Jacob. He extended the continuity of their faith. He was a righteous man. He also believed God's word in the dream. He believed that one day his family would bow down to him as part of God's mysterious plan. Second, he had an immense view of God and thus reasoned that God was doing his will throughout the inscrutable drama and convolutions of his enslavement in Egypt.

So what does this have to do with us? Very much. We all carry wounds, some of which go all the way back to when we were young. For some that is recent history, for others antiquity! Nevertheless, for many of us all it would take to reopen those wounds is a high-school reunion — and behold, the rerun of old insecurities and hurts. Most can name those old wounds, with a vividness like it was yesterday. And some of the wounds are gaping — from irrational parenting, physical abuse, rejection or abandonment, and multiple violations. To the younger reader, it may be surprising to learn that date rape is not new with this decade. Many bear the scars of betrayal of their nearest and dearest in various ways.

And today's pop culture does not help us with its encouragement of the culture of victimhood. Victimhood is in. Just turn on the talk shows and you'll see it encouraged, be it economic victimhood or political victimhood or ethnic victimhood or social victimhood or domestic and religious victimhood. We must never minimize such wounds or imply that they are unreal. There must be sympathy, reparations, and rapprochement, if possible. But we must *never* allow victimhood to enslave our souls. Enslavement to victimhood is neither biblical nor Christian.

Joseph's life teaches us that life is full of inequities and unfairness and tragedies. But it also teaches us that we have a great God who works amidst the rich compost of human life to do his will. We must understand that as God's children, we are called to give everything to him, even the bitter things of the past. As believers, we have been set free from the bondage of sin and death (Romans 8:2). We must rest everything on the awesome God of the Bible. We must believe that the awesome God of Genesis is, and that he is a rewarder of those who diligently seek him — that he is good and equitable to all his children (cf. Hebrews 11:6). We must appropriate the freedom of Christ. "I have been crucified with Christ. It is no longer I who live, but Christ who lives in me. And the life I now live in the flesh I live by faith in the Son of God, who loved me and gave himself for me" (Galatians 2:20).

Here is reality. Real life is unfair. Real life deals out many inequities. Real life is filled with sin and sinners. Real wounds are everywhere. But the transcending eternal reality is that God is all-powerful and that his massive providence is at work in his children's behalf. Life brims with hope and optimism.

As God's children, we must believe his word — that God will work good out of past evils — and that trusting him we will one day say with Joseph to past evils, "As for you, you meant evil against me, but God meant it for good" (Genesis 50:20).

55

Tamar and Judah

GENESIS 38:1-30

It has been many years since I read Tolstoy's novels *War and Peace* and *Anna Karenina*, and now many of the details and minor characters have faded from memory. But what remains and still captivates me is Tolstoy's development of his main characters. Some began so well and then fizzled. Others, with seemingly no promise, rose to memorable heights. I read those long novels of the Napoleonic wars and the life of the rich in St. Petersburg with surprised fascination — and pleasure. Over the years I have learned more fully that is how life really is. People are not static. They are in process until they die. People surprise!

This is so true of the real-life drama of Jacob's descendants, and dramatically so right here with the account of Judah and Tamar. On one level it is about how Tamar single-handedly preserved the line of Judah. On a deeper level it is about the providential preservation of progeny for Judah. And on a still deeper personal level, it reveals how God's sovereign plan and purpose is bound up in the development of individuals as he shapes them to fulfill his ends.

The surprises begin to take place just after the opening of the Joseph story with the jarring interruption by the Judah-Tamar episode. This story is so unexpected that the older critical commentators argued it was an awkward editorial insertion.[1] But most today admit that the presence of this unusual story was intentional and actually argue that it was placed here for special purposes. In fact, a close comparison of chapters 37 and 38 shows that they have many literary and thematic parallels[2] — some of which we will note. Also, the Tamar story enlarges on a great theme of Genesis — the sovereign choice of the younger over the older. And more, the immoral conduct of Judah and Tamar in Canaan demonstrates how remarkable Joseph's chasteness was in pagan Egypt.

JUDAH'S SINS (vv. 1-11)

All Jacob's sons had long known that both Abraham and Isaac had warned against marrying the daughters of the Canaanites. Abraham had solemnly charged his servant Eliezer, "Swear by the LORD, the God of heaven and God of the earth, that you will not take a wife for my son from the daughters of the Canaanites" (24:3). And when Isaac sent Jacob off to Mesopotamia, he "called Jacob and blessed him and directed him, 'You must not take a wife from the Canaanite women'" (28:1). So Judah, Jacob's fourth-born son, who now occupied the place of birthright by virtue of his older three brothers' sins (cf. 35:22; chap. 34), knew full well that he must not marry a Canaanite. Yet despite his position and knowledge, Judah did just that before or during the time of Joseph's enslavement in Egypt. It happened when Judah went down to the area of Adullam, southwest of Jerusalem, and visited a Canaanite named Hirah and met an unnamed Canaanite woman, known only as the daughter of Shua. Evidently it was lust at first sight, or as Wenham wryly says, "a union based on chemistry rather than principle"[3] —because the language describing their relationship is minimalist and abrupt. "There Judah saw the daughter of a certain Canaanite whose name was Shua. He took her and went in to her" (v. 2). The woman was fertile, and she bore him three sons — Er, Onan, and Shelah. And when Er matured, Judah gave him a Canaanite wife named Tamar. Thus half-Canaanite Er and his Canaanite wife Tamar were set to carry on Judah's important line of inheritance.

Judah's sons' sins. But Judah's sons were "wicked" (vv. 6, 10). Er's wickedness was of such degree that the Lord put him to death. Onan's sin lay in this: The existing marital laws directed that if a husband died without an heir, his brother was to then marry his widow and produce an heir for him by proxy. The son would not be his but his deceased brother's son — and the legal heir to firstborn privileges. In fact, the son would be given the name of the dead man. Onan married Tamar but refused his duty because he wanted the rights of the firstborn for himself.[4] So the Lord also put him to death (cf. vv. 7-10). So poor, young, twice-widowed Tamar was childless.

To add insult to injury, Judah, as the father of his dead sons, sinned against his daughter-in-law Tamar. "Then Judah said to Tamar his daughter-in-law, 'Remain a widow in your father's house, till Shelah my son grows up' — for he feared that he would die, like his brothers. So Tamar went and remained in her father's house" (v. 11). Tamar took Judah at his word and quietly obeyed. But the reader knows what Tamar did not know — that Judah had effectively removed her from the picture and left her neutralized. Legal redress for a widow in Tamar's position was impossible. As Bible readers, we know that Judah would become the principal tribe in Israel, the royal tribe through which Israel's King would come. But at that time the line of Judah faced extinction. Er was dead. Likewise, Onan was no more. And Judah had manipulated Tamar away from Shelah. Of course, with the passing of time and Shelah's maturity, Tamar came to understand the bitter truth — she had been permanently sidelined.

What could she do?

TAMAR'S BOLD PLAN (vv. 12-19)

Tamar's ruse. Tamar's window of opportunity came when her father-in-law Judah became a widower himself. Knowing Judah for the kind of man he was, she discerned that when he was "comforted" (v. 12, meaning that the week's mourning was past), he would be seeking some female comfort. Tamar also knew that it was sheepshearing time and that he would be visiting his old friend Hirah. Also, as a Canaanite, Tamar knew that cultic prostitutes would be out selling their services as fertility magic to ensure the growth of the fields and herds.[5] In a flash Tamar disguised herself as a prostitute, seizing the opportunity to produce a child for her departed husband.

> *And when Tamar was told, "Your father-in-law is going up to Timnah to shear his sheep," she took off her widow's garments and covered herself with a veil, wrapping herself up, and sat at the entrance to Enaim, which is on the road to Timnah. For she saw that Shelah was grown up, and she had not been given to him in marriage. When Judah saw her, he thought she was a prostitute, for she had covered her face. (vv. 13-15)*

Her hurried disguise was reminiscent of Rebekah's busy assembly of a disguise for Jacob's deception of Isaac (cf. 27:14-17).

"Business" arrangement. Tamar was all business.

> *He turned to her at the roadside and said, "Come, let me come in to you," for he did not know that she was his daughter-in-law. She said, "What will you give me, that you may come in to me?" He answered, "I will send you a young goat from the flock." And she said, "If you give me a pledge, until you send it—" He said, "What pledge shall I give you?" She replied, "Your signet and your cord and your staff that is in your hand." (vv. 16-18a)*

Old Judah was despicable. As Robert Alter explains, "Judah takes the bait — his sexual appetite will not tolerate postponement though he has been content to let Tamar languish as a childless widow indefinitely."[6] Having no goat for payment, Judah readily gave Tamar his most personal items, which

GENESIS

declared his individual and corporate identity — in modern terms, his license and Social Security number. His "signet" was not a ring but a seal (likely cylindrical) that he wore on a cord around his neck. The staff, often carved, was equally distinctive.[7] Three generations of deceit were now complete, each involving an item of identity and a goat. Jacob deceived Isaac by wearing a goatskin. Judah deceived Jacob by dipping Joseph's robe in goat's blood. And now Tamar has deceived Judah, and the deceit involved disguise, items of identity, and a goat.[8]

Thus, the transaction between Judah and Tamar was brisk and businesslike. "So he gave them to her and went in to her, and she conceived by him. Then she arose and went away, and taking off her veil she put on the garments of her widowhood" (vv. 18b, 19). The child she conceived for Er was not a grandchild of Judah. Tamar was set to become the progenitress of the line of Judah, a principal matriarch in Israel, bearing the son of Judah himself.

TAMAR'S TRIUMPH (vv. 20-26)

Judah was not proud of his deed and predictably sent his Canaanite friend to settle up and get his identification back — in effect, to retrieve the license from the bordello. But the prostitute was gone, and the locals had no recollection of her. Both Judah and Hirah met and agreed to forget it so they would not become objects of local humor (cf. vv. 20-23).

More righteous! Infidelity during a betrothal period was counted as adultery and called for the death penalty. So when Tamar neared the end of her first trimester, the suspense and internal pressure must have been unbearable. "About three months later Judah was told, 'Tamar your daughter-in-law has been immoral. Moreover, she is pregnant by immorality.' And Judah said, 'Bring her out, and let her be burned'" (v. 24). Such "naked unreflective brutality" (Alter)![9] Judah's violent declaration suggests that he may have leapt at the opportunity to have her out of the way once and for all.

But now the moment of Tamar's triumph came because as she was being led out to judgment, she sent to Judah the symbols of his legal persona saying, "'By the man to whom these belong, I am pregnant.' And she said, 'Please identify whose these are, the signet and the cord and the staff'" (v. 25b). What a breathless moment as Judah was forced to own that each of the items was his!

And then came his declaration, "She is more righteous than I, since I did not give her to my son Shelah" (v. 26). Judah admitted that Tamar was justified in taking matters into her own hands. In doing so, he likewise admitted that his conduct had not been righteous. Tamar was exalted. Judah was humbled.

People do change. And this was the first hint of a change taking place in Judah as he publicly admitted his moral failure. Judah's admission to Tamar suggests that he had learned something. In fact, Judah would develop remarkably during the years leading up to chapter 44, where Judah would act as a righteous man before Joseph, pleading for the welfare of Benjamin and offering his life as a pledge to save his little half brother. For Judah the effects of his deep sin, plus the example of others, plus the hidden hand of God had been at work, so that at the end of his father Jacob's life, Jacob would confirm Judah as the scepter-bearing tribe through which would come the one to whom "shall be the obedience of the peoples" (49:10b). What surprises spring from changing grace! By God's grace Judah had become the man.

TAMAR PERPETUATES THE TRIBE OF JUDAH (vv. 27-30)

Just as the Jacob narrative began with the story of twins wrestling in their mother's womb, so now at the end of the Jacob narrative there is a similar struggle.

> *When the time of her labor came, there were twins in her womb. And when she was in labor, one put out a hand, and the midwife took and tied a scarlet thread on his hand, saying, "This one came out first." But as he drew back his hand, behold, his brother came out. And she said, "What a breach you have made for yourself!" Therefore his name was called Perez. Afterward his brother came out with the scarlet thread on his hand, and his name was called Zerah. (vv. 27-30)*

Again, just as with Jacob and Esau, the struggle resulted in the reversal of the right of the firstborn. In both cases the younger gained ascendance over the older, establishing again that God elects as he wills. The book of Ruth closes with a record of the ten generations from Perez to King David (4:18-22). Matthew later quoted these same ten generations leading to David (1:2-6) and then delineated the further generations to Christ.

Blessed be Tamar! Through her determination to have children of the promise, she scratched and clawed her way into Israel and secured for Judah the honor of fathering both David and the Savior of the world.

Here is a great surprise. Tamar the Canaanite, who began outside the people of God, turned out to be a heroine of God's people. Tamar aligned herself with the purposes of God, and through her God's promise to Abraham (blessing to all the peoples of the earth) was fulfilled. The Judah-Tamar story teaches us that God's purpose is bound up with the growth and development of his people, so that God is always at work in his children's lives, shaping them to serve his design, as he so marvelously did with Judah and Tamar. As Andrew Reid has so well said:

In this way it is possible to see all of life as the medium of God's activity. He is not just active when we read our Bible and pray. He is also active when we live in our world. Hence, when we wake up tomorrow we don't wake up to a day without God. Tomorrow is God's day, for he made it, formed it, and works in it. What's more, he wants you to enter tomorrow determined to be his person in it, and to let Christ be formed in you as you allow his word to interact with your situation.[10]

People are not static. And for we who believe this, there is cause for great optimism, "for it is God who works in you, both to will and to work for his good pleasure" (Philippians 2:13). So with proper fear and trembling we submit ourselves to God, believing that we will change, that surprising grace lies ahead.

A final word of encouragement. Tamar is the first of five women in the genealogy of Christ as we have it in Matthew 1. There is Tamar (v. 3), Rahab (v. 5), Ruth (v. 5), Bathsheba (identified as "the wife of Uriah," v. 6), and Mary (v. 16). Notably absent are the great mothers of Israel: Sarah, Rebekah, Leah, and Rachel. Why only the four, and then Mary? First, all four of Mary's predecessors were Gentiles. Tamar and Rahab were Canaanites, Ruth was a Moabitess, and Bathsheba was a Hittite. Thus Tamar and company declare that in Christ there is hope for the Gentile nations. This is why when Jesus' parents took him to the temple, Simeon swept the baby up in his arms and said:

> *Lord, now you are letting your servant depart in peace,*
> *according to your word;*
> *for my eyes have seen your salvation*
> *that you have prepared in the presence of all peoples,*
> *a light for revelation to the Gentiles,*
> *and for glory to your people Israel. (Luke 2:29-32)*

And this is also why Matthew bookends his Gospel with Gentile hope. Chapter 1 showcases Gentiles in Christ's genealogy, and the final chapter records Christ's charge to take the gospel to the Gentiles: "Go therefore and make disciples of all nations, baptizing them in the name of the Father and of the Son and of the Holy Spirit" (28:19).

There is one other reason for these women in the line of Christ, and it is so sweet. As Victor Hamilton explains:

Each of these four women had a highly irregular and potentially scandalous marital union. Nevertheless, these unions were, by God's providence, links in the chain to the Messiah. Accordingly, each of them prepares the way for Mary, whose marital situation is also peculiar, given the fact that she is pregnant but has not yet had sexual relations with her betrothed husband Joseph. Thus the inclusion of the likes of Tamar in this family tree on one hand foreshadows the circumstances of the birth of Christ, and on the other hand blunts any attack on Mary. God had worked his will in the midst of whispers of scandal.[11]

What a God is ours. He is so great that his hidden hand constantly surprises us as he works in history and in the hearts of his people for their benefit — always for their good.

> *Bless the LORD, O my soul,*
> *and forget not all his benefits,*
> *who forgives all your iniquity,*
> *who heals all your diseases,*
> *who redeems your life from the pit,*
> *who crowns you with steadfast love*
> * and mercy. (Psalm 103:2-4)*

56

Succeeding in Egypt

GENESIS 39:1-23

We left young Joseph trudging brokenhearted down to Egypt, a tethered slave, destitute of any human support, without a glimmer of external hope — and with plenty of reasons to hate. Joseph had been stripped of his clothing by his own brothers and tossed in a pit for a lingering death, though he had pleaded pitifully with them for mercy. His execution was only averted by the providential appearance of an Ishmaelite caravan bound for Egypt and the exchange of a few shekels. Joseph had been a naive, godly boy with a bright future. But now, from all appearances, he had been abandoned by God and man. Joseph possessed every human reason for distrust and bitterness. Common logic demanded that he cherish and nurture thoughts of revenge. In fact, feeding on such thoughts could sustain him, as they once had done for his Uncle Esau (cf. 27:42).

But Joseph made a different choice, a most remarkable choice, because as he shuffled through the dust to Egypt, he chose to trust God with his life and ultimately to forgive. This is astonishing but true, because a CAT scan of his soul reveals no spiritual malignancies anywhere. There is not a trace of the cancers of hatred or bitterness or vindictiveness no matter how close we look. Instead, we are awestruck when, years later in the story, we witness that though Joseph had his brothers in the palm of his hand with every terror possible, he wept and then lavished them with gifts and privileges. Joseph's soul was so extraordinary that even in the context of the greats of the Bible he towers — a skyscraper on the plains of spiritual history.

We have to willfully close our eyes not to see bold hints of Jesus in the life of Joseph, because Jesus too was sold and delivered up by sinful men with whom he lived. Also, when suffering untold agonies, he forgave them, even as he forgives our sins today. And today he calls his own people "brothers" and "sisters" and "fellow heirs," much like Joseph did with his own. Joseph was a monumental man living thousands of years before Jesus, but so much like him.

The long trek completed, Joseph descended to the storied Nile valley and the pyramids. Egypt's fifteenth dynasty was in full swing as the country prospered under its famous Hyksos rulers (*circa* 1720-1570 B.C.). Every morning the rising sun was greeted with the chanting of cultic hymns to awaken the gods from their slumber, after which the idols were ritually bathed and then sumptuously dressed and breakfasted with morning offerings.

Egypt's multiple gods were everywhere. There were *local* deities: Ptah, the artificer-god of Memphis; Thah, the god of learning and the moon, at Hermopolis; and Amon the hidden god of Thebes. There were *cosmic* gods: Re, the sun-god; Nut, the sky goddess; and three gods of the air — Shu, Geb, and Nu. And there was the pervasive cult of Osiris and its cyclical observances with the annual rise and fall of the Nile. Pharaoh was himself considered a god, the falcon sky-god Horus.[1]

All of this assaulted young Joseph his first day in Egypt as he stood alone in blinking wonder. And then, with a commercial nod, Joseph was cast into the dark, pulsing heart of that world. "Now Joseph had been brought down to Egypt, and Potiphar, an officer of Pharaoh, the captain of the guard, an Egyptian, had bought him from the Ishmaelites who had brought him down there" (v. 1). Joseph was at the epicenter of the darkness, an aristocratic house where the rulers of the land came and went — a penthouse of Egyptian opulence and culture.

Here in Potiphar's house, the world would come to ride on Joseph's shoulders. He had sensed something of his responsibility in his dream, that his destiny would yet involve his family bowing down to him. But the immensity and scope of the burden was beyond his knowledge. His dreams bore no hint that he would become their temporal savior two decades later.

SUCCESS IN THE PENTHOUSE (vv. 2-6a)

Of course, we know that Joseph would succeed spectacularly because we have heard the story referenced many times since we were children. But the question is, why would it happen? What would enable Joseph to succeed?

The ground of success. Happily the story of Joseph and Potiphar's wife leaves no doubt as to the answer because it is stated at both the beginning and the end of the story: *Joseph was successful because the Lord was "with" him.* Joseph's success is bracketed with two declarations that the Lord was "with" him. Look at the beginning: "The LORD was with Joseph, and he became a successful man, and he was in the house of his Egyptian master. His master saw that the LORD was with him and that the LORD caused all that he did to succeed in his hands" (v. 2, 3). Now note the end of the narrative in verses

21, 23: "But the LORD was with Joseph and showed him steadfast love and gave him favor in the sight of the keeper of the prison" (v. 21). "The keeper of the prison paid no attention to anything that was in Joseph's charge, because the LORD was with him. And whatever he did, the LORD made it succeed" (v. 23). Joseph's success story is preceded by two parallel declarations that the Lord was "with" him. So we understand that the theological centerpiece of the story is God, who was present and working on Joseph's behalf.

But there are also aspects here that we might not notice at first glance. Most important, the God who was with Joseph was "the LORD" (Yahweh), the personal covenant name of God, and this name is used eight times in this account (v. 2 once, v. 3 twice, v. 5 twice, v. 21 once, v. 23 twice), and then never again in the remaining eight chapters of Joseph's story, except for Jacob's use of it at the end on his deathbed (cf. 49:18). And more, no character in the story uses this personal name of God, not even Joseph. Here in our chapter, the narrator uses God's covenant name, Yahweh, eight times to tell the reader what is going on — and four of those eight times tell us that *Yahweh was with Joseph.*

Thus we are to understand that at the most uncertain time of Joseph's life, when he could see nothing of God, the covenant God of Israel was at work to effect his covenant promises through Joseph. Alone in Potiphar's house with the intimidating architecture of Egypt dwarfing him, living amidst idolatrous hymns, Joseph was not alone. Yahweh/Jehovah was with him to effect a mighty work for his covenant people and the blessing of the world.

Phenomenal success. Joseph experienced spectacular, surprising success and elevation.

> *So Joseph found favor in his [Potiphar's] sight and attended him, and he made him overseer of his house and put him in charge of all that he had. From the time that he made him overseer in his house and over all that he had the LORD blessed the Egyptian's house for Joseph's sake; the blessing of the LORD was on all that he had, in house and field. So he left all that he had in Joseph's charge, and because of him he had no concern about anything but the food he ate. (vv. 4-6a)*

Joseph's work ethic did not go unnoticed. So he advanced to Potiphar's personal attendant and then to overseer. And in promoting Joseph, Potiphar became the unwitting beneficiary of the covenant promise made to Abraham — "I will bless those who bless you" (12:3) — and so the Egyptian's favor to Joseph in turn brought blessing on everything he had. The more favor he showed to Joseph, the better things got. Joseph was such a super-slave that Potiphar realized that the best way to manage his affairs was to forget them and leave everything to Joseph. And he did, except for his food. This was likely because of ritual preparation at mealtimes.[2] Otherwise, everything was left in "Joseph's charge" (v. 6; literally, "hand"), meaning in Joseph's power. Potiphar was so confident that Joseph had his best interests at heart that even his wife was under Joseph's benign care. *Beware of Mrs. Potiphar's hand, Joseph!* Likely, Potiphar's chief slave was the envy of the Egyptian Riviera.

JOSEPH'S TEMPTATION (vv. 6b-10)

Joseph was at the pinnacle in Potiphar's penthouse estate. There was no doubt that God was with him. And he was handsome, extraordinarily handsome — "Joseph was handsome in form and appearance" (v. 6b).

It was the genes. The same phrase is used of his lovely mother Rachel (cf. 29:17). They are the only two people in Scripture to receive this double accolade. The Jewish Publication Society translation renders this, "Joseph was well built and handsome." What a magnificent spectacle he was in his Egyptian kilt — tan, broad-shouldered, cut, great abs! And it was here that the story turned, for with all his gifts, Joseph suffered from "one endowment too many" (Alter).[3]

Sexual siege. Here in Scripture is the prototype of all fatal attractions: "And after a time his master's wife cast her eyes on Joseph and said, 'Lie with me'" (v. 7). Lust-filled men and women are as old as the fall. And privileged sensualists, those who have had their every desire catered to, often become demanding and out-of-control. A modern case in point was Edwina Ashley, aka Lady Mountbatten, the wife of Lord Mountbatten, once the Viceroy of India. For sexual sport Lady Mountbatten shipped out on a trading schooner to the South Seas as an ordinary seaman, so she could gratify her lusts with fellow crewmen. Later she slept with Prime Minister Nehru during the time that her husband negotiated the terms of India's independence with Nehru.[4] Mrs. Potiphar also was in the habit of getting what she wanted. And after all, Joseph was a slave — hence her brusque demands. Actually, though, it was the mistress of the house who was a slave.

What an insidious temptation. Joseph was seventeen or eighteen years old (cf. 37:2), and his hormones were at full force; so he brimmed with sexual curiosity and drive. The rationalizations were so easy and logical. No one would ever know (cf. 39:11). His family would certainly never find out. They were on the other side of the Sinai and beyond. Moreover, Joseph was a slave (cf. 39:7-11). His life was not his own. Sexual promiscuity was a daily part of all slaveholding households. Besides, by giving in to Mrs. Potiphar's wishes, he could enhance his career. This is a time-honored political strategy. What is so wrong with a little "strategic adultery" if it furthers the cause? And face it, old Potiphar was gone all the time and was not meeting his wife's needs. She was entitled to a little caring affection. This would actually be the loving thing to do. In today's terms, the situation demanded this ethic. Even more, who could blame him? It was in his blood. Just look at his brothers Reuben and Judah! And again, not a soul would ever know.

Such powerful, reasonable rationalizations! And as Andrew Schmutzer explains:

> Add to this the fact that Joseph knew the dysfunction of a father's favoritism (37:3), the scorn of ten brothers' hatred (37:4-5, 8), the betrayal of being sold for profit by those responsible for him (37:27-28), the disdain of a slave's life as chattel (37:36; 39:1), and the dissolution of transplantation to foreign soil and culture (39:1). With this as his bio, Joseph had every reason to be angry, bitter, resentful, cynical, fearful, self-serving, and self-pitying. . . . Joseph had every human reason to find fleeting solace in an illicit embrace — frankly, to "act out!"[5]

Who could blame such a pitiful victim?

Joseph's speech. But Joseph did not go for it. And Mrs. Potiphar's two-word proposition (in the Hebrew) was met with his passionate thirty-five-word refusal.

> *But he refused and said to his master's wife, "Behold, because of me my master has no concern about anything in the house, and he has put everything that he has in my charge. He is not greater in this house than I am, nor has he kept back anything from me except yourself, because you are his wife. How then can I do this great wickedness and sin against God?"*
> *(vv. 8, 9)*

In short, Joseph refused to sin against a) the *trust* given him, b) the woman's *husband*, and c) *God himself.* Joseph's integrity was of one fabric. And because he was faithful in all relationships, he could resist being unfaithful in this instance. This story is not just about sexual fidelity — Joseph's life was a web of moral accountability. He saw his moral life as a unified, integrated whole. His overall faithfulness had helped him reject this massive temptation. We must understand that "little sins" pave the way to "big sins" — and that Joseph was on no such path. It was the power of this quality of his life as a whole that enabled him to resist the woman's advances.

Of course, the greatest deterrent to falling to the sexual siege was Joseph's awareness that God was with him — not because of the narrator's voice-over but because this is what God had repeatedly promised Joseph's forefathers and had been his personal awareness all of his life. The grand deterrent to Joseph's sinning was the awareness that God sees all and that a sin that no one knows about, committed behind locked doors in a dark room, is actually done in the presence of a holy God. Joseph believed this. And I am convinced that the personal realization and conviction of this truth is the strongest deterrent to sin that there is. King David invoked it after the horror of his own sin ravaged his soul: "For I know my transgressions, and my sin is ever before me. Against you, you only, have I sinned and done what is evil in your sight" (Psalm 51:3, 4a).

Persistent temptation. Great speech, Joseph, but the lady was not giving up. "And as she spoke to Joseph day after day, he would not listen to her, to lie beside her or to be with her" (v. 10). Her dialogue plumbed every angle, but he paid her no heed. And when she moderated her demands to "just lie beside me," he gave her wide berth. He never let his hand get near the cookie jar. His actions are parabolic and instructive to every man (and woman!) who wants to avoid sexual sin. The Mrs. Potiphars of today are at once material, phantasmal, and ubiquitous — in airbrushed photos, celluloid, videos, and luminous TV screens. Those who are wise refuse "to lie beside her or to be with her" (v. 10b).

JOSEPH IS FRAMED (vv. 11-20)

Flight from seduction. Perhaps Joseph should have seen this coming, but there was little he could do in that he had to be in the house to carry out his administrative duties. In any event, Mrs. Potiphar's ambush caught him unawares. "But one day, when he went into the house to do his work and none of the men of the house was there in the house, she caught him by his garment, saying, 'Lie with me.' But he left his garment in her hand and fled and got out of the house" (vv. 11, 12). There was surprise and violence here because the tunic Joseph was wearing was like a long T-shirt. There was a struggle as he sought to free himself. And then, having extricated himself, Joseph displayed an exemplary case of Biblical fear as he sprinted from her presence. The word is out, men: God is looking for a few good "cowards"!

Lies and more lies. Mrs. Potiphar was a skilled liar — in Robert Alter's words, a "subtle mistress of syntactic equivocation."[6] She tailored her lies first to enlist the servants' support and then altered them to incite her husband. Earlier Potiphar had left "all that he had in Joseph's hand" (v. 6, Hebrew). Now Joseph's garment was in Mrs. Potiphar's hand. The first testified to Potiphar's *trust* of Joseph (v. 6). The second testified to Joseph's *faithfulness* to Potiphar. Joseph was a good man.[7]

But never mind, the scorned woman assembled the men of her household and protested, falsely, "See, he has brought among us a Hebrew to laugh at us. He came in to me to lie with me, and I cried out with a loud voice. And as soon as he heard that I lifted up my voice and cried out, he left his garment beside me and fled and got out of the house" (vv. 14b, 15). All her lies were laced with prejudicial subtleties to elicit their wrath — for example, identifying Joseph as "a Hebrew" to evoke their national xenophobia, the fear of strangers.

And then, in preparation for her husband, she arranged Joseph's garment beside her and affected a ravished swoon, telling her husband, "The Hebrew servant, whom you have brought among us, came in to me to laugh at me. But as soon as I lifted up my voice and cried, he left his garment beside me and fled out of the house" (vv. 17b, 18). The "Hebrew" is now a "Hebrew servant [slave]." To be attacked by a Hebrew was bad enough, but to be attacked by a Hebrew slave was worse. Mrs. Potiphar implied that Potiphar was partially to blame, saying of Joseph, "whom *you* have brought among us," hoping that her husband's shame would turn to rage. She also altered "laugh at us" to "laugh at me" to underscore her personal devastation. No wonder Potiphar worked such long hours!

Prison. And her lies worked — to some extent. "As soon as his master heard the words that his wife spoke to him, 'This is the way your servant treated me,' his anger was kindled. And Joseph's master took him and put him into the prison, the place where the king's prisoners were confined, and he was there in prison" (vv. 19, 20). Apparently Potiphar was not completely convinced by his wife; otherwise he would have ordered Joseph's execution. Potiphar seems to have imprisoned Joseph out of necessity, leaving Joseph alive should more information come to light. We are left to wonder, at whom was Potiphar's anger really directed?

SUCCESS IN PRISON (vv. 21-23)

What an astounding turn of events! Joseph had gone from the pit in Shechem up to the penthouse of Potiphar's estate and now down to the prison-house of Egypt. Few situations could be worse than an Egyptian prison in 1500 B.C. — especially the lot of a manacled prisoner. Psalm 105 describes Joseph's incarceration: "Joseph . . . was sold as a slave. His feet were hurt with fetters; his neck was put in a collar of iron; until what he had said came to pass, the word of the LORD tested him" (vv. 17b-19).

But what a towering figure he had become. Never once, whether in prosperity or adversity, had Joseph doubted God. This is amazing. Ripped out of his house at seventeen years of age, hauled all the way down to Egypt, one thing after another happening to him, the emotional massage of all the ups and downs — and yet he believed God was with him. He had sensed and appropriated God's presence in every circumstance. And never had Joseph been more of a success than now. He dwarfed the monuments of the Nile.

God was "with" Joseph. Again Joseph did not hear the narrator's words that three times declare that Yahweh/Jehovah was with him and that he was a success.

But the LORD was with Joseph and showed him steadfast love and gave him favor in the sight of the keeper of the prison. And the keeper of the prison put Joseph in charge of all the prisoners who were in the prison. Whatever was done there, he was the one who did it. The keeper of the prison paid no attention to anything that was in Joseph's charge, because the LORD was with him. And whatever he did, the LORD made it succeed. (vv. 21-23).

Here we find the motifs that opened the story in verses 1-6 repeated, but at a new level. Here again we see phenomenal, astonishing, empirically verifiable success. Everyone could see that Yahweh was with Joseph. And Joseph had never stopped seeing this reality. He saw it in the pit, he saw it in the penthouse, he saw it amidst Mrs. Potiphar's lies, and he now saw it in the prison-house — and that is why he was and would be such an astonishing success.

How does Joseph's story intersect the lives of God's children today? Powerfully and substantially. Upon the conception of Christ the Messiah in the womb of the virgin Mary, the angel Gabriel explained to another Joseph, "That which is conceived in her is from the Holy Spirit. She will bear a son, and you shall call his name Jesus, for he will save his people from their sins" (Matthew 1:20b, 21). Jesus' divinely given name is the combination of two words — Yahweh/Jehovah and salvation — so that his name means "Yahweh saves" or "Jehovah saves" or "the Lord saves." In respect to the patriarch Joseph, Jesus is Yahweh, the one who was with Joseph and gave him great success in Egypt. Now consider the verses that follow in Matthew 1:

All this took place to fulfill what the Lord had spoken by the prophet: "Behold, the virgin shall conceive and bear a son, and they shall call his name Immanuel" (which means, God with us). (vv. 22, 23)

Our Messiah, Jesus, is Yahweh and bears the name Immanuel, "God with us." As believers, then, God is always with us, in all of life. In fact, when Jesus left this earth he said, "And behold, I am with you always, to the end of the age" (Matthew 28:20b).

Brothers and sisters, the key to our day-to-day success in this life is living in the reality that God is with us. The reality that we are called to embrace would have astonished Joseph. That God became one of us and now, ascended, remains "God with us" is the most sublime truth. May we own it with all our souls!

57

Preparation for Greatness

GENESIS 40:1-23

Among the most prized possessions of men of past centuries was a fine sword. In the East it was a Damascus blade that was valued for its strength and edge. During the Renaissance, the weapon of choice was a rapier cast and hammered through a secret process in Toledo, Spain. In the nineteenth century in the English-speaking world, nothing was thought better than a Wilkinson sword, used by British officers in the Battle of Omdurman, the last great cavalry charge. Swords have been immortalized in mythology as well, like King Arthur's broadsword Excalibur pulled from a cloven rock, which, of course, gave it magical powers. More recently there has been Frodo Baggins's miniature sword Sting, which often delivered him from his enemies. Even science fiction boasts its swords, like the lightsabers of the Jedi knights.

The sword is also a powerful biblical metaphor for the Word of God. "Take the . . . sword of the Spirit, which is the word of God" (Ephesians 6:17). "For the word of God is living and active, sharper than any two-edged sword, piercing to the division of soul and of spirit, of joints and of marrow, and discerning the thoughts and intentions of the heart" (Hebrews 4:12). John Bunyan's Pilgrim carries a "right true Jerusalem Blade" — his way of saying that the Christian is armed with God's Word.

But there is another kind of sword, and that is a human life so shaped and honed and tempered by God through the fires of life that it becomes a mighty blade of deliverance, a daunting instrument of salvation. This is what we have been seeing in Joseph — the sharpening of a life to such an edge that he became a singular instrument of redemption. It began when Joseph, as a callow, insensitive, innocently arrogant youth, was sold into Egyptian slavery. The bitterness of Joseph's experience, by God's grace, seasoned him with sweetness so that his arrogance deflated and he chose to forgive his brothers and trusted God that his God-given dreams would come true.

As we come to the point in the story where Joseph will interpret the dreams of two of Pharaoh's fallen servants, Joseph had already shown signs of spiritual greatness. Joseph remained uncompromised by Mrs. Potiphar's seductive siege, even though a whole library of human rationalizations was at his fingertips. The biblical writer, Moses, has written SUCCESS in large letters across Joseph's life at this juncture, as the beginning and end of Chapter 39 make so clear (39:2, 3, 23). This is because Yahweh was "with" him, as the text repeatedly states (39:2, 3, 21, 23). And more, Joseph's amazing dreams were still intact. Though he was far removed from his family, separated by the desolate expanse of the Sinai, immersed in another culture, speaking Egyptian and writing in hieroglyphics, and enduring the living death of a slave — despite all this Joseph held fast to his dreams that his family would one day bow down to him. About this, he had absolutely no doubt. Joseph was beginning to tower spiritually over the generational landscape of Genesis.

But huge challenges awaited him on the other side of his prison experience, when he would ascend to the vice-regency of Egypt. Just as it is today, the whole ancient world lay in the power of the wicked one (cf. 1 John 5:19) — and Egypt was at the center of the world's evil. And the ruling class where Joseph would be cast was caught in a web of unbridled ambition, sensuality, and intrigue — like any other aristocratic clan. And more, Joseph was the sole righteous man in Egypt. This meant that Joseph's tenure would be full of trouble. We must not imagine that his position put him above the junk. Rather, it put him in the middle of it. Joseph would suffer disappointments again and again, despite his skillful management. His pagan associates would be experts at returning evil for good — in spades. So on the eve of his ascent to power, Joseph needed some further honing to ensure greatness. And this is what his final stint in the Egyptian prison would provide.

PRISONERS ASSIGNED TO JOSEPH (vv. 1-4)

As we engage the story, eleven years have passed since Joseph was sold into slavery. We do not know how those eleven years were divided between serving in Potiphar's household and in prison. But we do know that Joseph is now twenty-eight years old, because two years after the events of this chapter, at the age of thirty, he will ascend to the service of Pharaoh (cf. 37:2; 41:1, 46).

So it is at this point that two high-profile prisoners join Joseph in "the pit," as he calls the prison (40:15). As the royal cupbearer and the royal baker, these two men had held the life of Pharaoh in their hands because they were charged with the purity and quality of his food. Egyptian cupbearers were sometimes called "pure of hands," referencing that a cupbearer must be a man of integrity because he tasted the wine before it came to the king.[1] Likely, the baker was responsible for the menu served to Pharaoh because his office can be rendered "royal table scribe."[2] Perhaps Pharaoh suspected them of plotting his demise, or perhaps he became ill after a meal and suspected that one or both of them were to blame.

However it was, the responsibility for their care fell to Joseph. "The captain of the guard appointed Joseph to be with them, and he attended them. They continued for some time in custody" (v. 4). Joseph became the servant of men accused of treason and attempted regicide. As the slave of these prisoners, Joseph was at the bottom of the bottom — a servant of infamous felons. Poor Joseph — he seemed destined to rise so that his dreams could be dashed!

PRISONERS' TROUBLING DREAMS (vv. 5-8)

Dual dreams. Understandably, prisoners in such straits were prone to bad dreams, and the dreams these men dreamed were certainly nightmarish — not because they were grotesque (for they were not), but for several other reasons. First, the ancient Egyptians put great stock in dreams because they believed that sleep put them in contact with another world.[3] Second, a pair of dreams, it was thought, indicated certainty of fulfillment. And third, due to their imprisonment they did not have access to professional interpreters whose "dream books" were thought essential to unlocking the symbolism of dreams.[4]

Thus we read, "When Joseph came to them in the morning, he saw that they were troubled. So he asked Pharaoh's officers who were with him in custody in his master's house, 'Why are your faces downcast today?' They said to him, 'We have had dreams, and there is no one to interpret them.' And Joseph said to them, 'Do not interpretations belong to God? Please tell them to me'" (vv. 6-8).

Joseph's response to the prisoners was deeply revelatory of what had been going on in his developing heart as God was preparing him for greatness.

Sensitive. Joseph's compassionate question to his sad charges displayed a striking contrast to what he had been as a seventeen-year-old, because (though he had been guileless and transparent) his interaction with his brothers revealed insensitivity on the level of a self-centered child. But now, though he had every reason to ignore the feelings of his fellow inmates, he was tender and solicitous of their feelings. It is apparent that what Joseph had experienced in the famous ups and down of his own life had made him unusually sensitive and compassionate toward others. This is the way life works. You may not feel for those who are lonely until you have suffered loneliness. If you have never suffered serious depression, your suggested cure may be, "Go shopping!" Ever broken a rib so that each breath is painful, and you live in terror that someone may tell you a joke? If so, you will truly sympathize when it happens to others. Through his life experiences, Joseph had been developing a redemptive edge. A sympathetic resonance for others welled in his soul. He knew where other people were and how they felt. And he cared. A great leader was emerging.

God-reflexed. But not only was he sensitive — he was also God-reflexed. As soon as the cupbearer and the baker stated their plights, Joseph referenced God — "Do not interpretations belong to God? Please tell them to me" (v. 8). We all know that what people do in reflex is very revealing of what is within. Consider the man who hung close to his pastor while they nailed up some wallboard so he could see what the pastor would do when he hit his thumb!

Joseph's split-second response revealed a profoundly God-dependent man. His decade of ups and, mostly, downs had created an intimate dependence on God. Turning to God was the habit of his mind (cf. 39:9; 41:16, 51, 52; 45:8) — an essential for godly leadership. In this, Joseph was also foreshadowing the way Christ himself would live.

Believing. How remarkable Joseph's response was. Yet there is even more here because Joseph's response — "Do not interpretations belong to God? Please tell them to me" — was an implicit declaration of belief that his own dreams would come true. If he had given up on his own dreams, he would never have given a thought to interpreting theirs! But he roundly volunteered to provide the meaning. Though more than a decade had passed since his dual dreams, first of a field at harvest where sheaves were being bound and his sheaf stood upright while the others bowed in obeisance to him, and then the second grander dream of a sky spangled with eleven stars (his brothers) and a radiant sun and moon (his parents) all bowing to him — though it had been eleven tumultuous years without a word as to whether his family was alive, eleven years of dressing like an Egyptian, speaking their language, and never meeting another believer — Joseph believed that his dreams would come true! He was supremely confident that every member of his family from Reuben to Benjamin would bow to him. Joseph's faith was like that of the greats in the Hebrews 11 "Hall of Faith": "Now faith is the assurance of things hoped for, the conviction of things not seen" (v. 1).

Joseph lived out this dynamic certitude regarding his dreams in the heart of Egypt's pyramids. And as Von Rad has noted, Joseph's statement — "Do not interpretations belong to God?" — was an in-your-face polemic to the idolatrous culture of Egypt.[5] Joseph declared that the interpretation of dreams was not a pseudo-science of the specialists with their dream books, but a gift that only God can give. The events of the future lay in Yahweh's power. And the only one who could interpret them was the one to whom he gave the interpretation — and that was to Joseph himself.

Joseph's preparation for leadership was in full effect. He was now graced with a sensitivity that was aware of and sympathetic to the plight of others. His demonstrated reflex was to first turn to God for wisdom and direction, which is essential to godly leadership. And Joseph tenaciously clung to his seemingly impossible dreams. He believed God's revelation. He knew what the future held. The brilliance of his leadership was firmly grounded.

JOSEPH INTERPRETS THEIR DREAMS (vv. 9-19)

The cupbearer's dream. Joseph set himself to hearing the cupbearer's dream, which was like a Home and Garden Television video on fast-forward. A three-branch vine appeared, budded, and sprouted blossoms that became clusters of grapes that were then plucked by the cupbearer and squeezed into Pharaoh's cup and placed in the sovereign's hand so he could drink up. The interpretation was easy and pleasant. "Then Joseph said to him, 'This is its interpretation: the three branches are three days. In three days Pharaoh will lift up your head and restore you to your office, and you shall place Pharaoh's cup in his hand as formerly, when you were his cupbearer'" (vv. 12, 13). To have your head lifted up signifies regaining your dignity, honor, and independence, just as hanging your head signifies shame and subjection.[6] Happy days were just three days away! By faith Joseph showed himself as singularly confident and awesomely authoritative.

Nevertheless he was in prison — the pit. And for all his ability to amaze others, he was in need. So he asked a simple favor of the royal cupbearer. "Only remember me, when it is well with you, and please do me the kindness to mention me to Pharaoh, and so get me out of this house. For I was indeed stolen out of the land of the Hebrews, and here also I have done nothing that they should put me into the pit" (vv. 14, 15). Joseph, who was absolutely confident in his interpretation, so that he said to the cupbearer, "when it is well with you," was himself in miserable straits. We see here that "The powerful man born to rule is also a needful one" (Brueggemann).[7] We must understand that these eleven long years had been an unrelenting test and that here Joseph uncharacteristically revealed his inner pathos. He had been stolen. He had done nothing deserving of "the pit."

Fellow believers, Joseph's dissonance is where the faithful often live. And this is where growth takes place. As the Apostle James would write to the persecuted church, "Count it all joy, my brothers, when you meet trials of various kinds, for you know that the testing of your faith produces steadfastness. And let steadfastness have its full effect, that you may be perfect and complete, lacking in nothing" (James 1:2-4). Joseph was on the way to being a man who lacked nothing — a leader to be emulated.

The baker's dream. Evidently the baker had been holding back (and for good reason as we shall see), but hearing the positive interpretation of the cupbearer's dream he ventured to share his. "He said to Joseph, 'I also had a dream: there were three cake baskets on my head, and in the uppermost basket there were all sorts of baked food for Pharaoh, but the birds were eating it out of the basket on my head'" (vv. 16, 17). In his dream, the baker bore in three baskets upon his head a veritable pastry feast for Pharaoh. His description, "all sorts of baked food" was common to kingly menus because the Egyptian dictionary lists thirty-eight kinds of cake and fifty-seven varieties of bread.[8] But ominously the gourmet's delight was pillaged by birds of prey, and none of the food got to Pharaoh.

Likely, in addition to interpreting the dream, Joseph was convinced of the baker's murderous culpability because he gave the interpretation a terrifying ironic twist. "And Joseph answered and said, 'This is its interpretation: the three baskets are three days. In three days Pharaoh will lift up your head — from you! — and hang you on a tree. And the birds will eat the flesh from you'" (vv. 18, 19). The baker would have his head lifted up all right — right off his body! And more, his body would be impaled so that the birds could have their own gourmet's feast. No happy days in three days!

DREAMS COME TRUE (vv. 20-23)

Heads up! Egyptian literature records the granting of amnesty on Pharaoh's birthday in later periods, but it was more common to grant amnesties on the anniversary of his accession to the throne, which was also described as the birth of a god.[9] So we read, "On the third day, which was Pharaoh's birthday, he made a feast for all his servants and lifted up the head of the chief cupbearer and the head of the chief baker among his servants. He restored the chief cupbearer to his position, and he placed the cup in Pharaoh's hand. But he hanged the chief baker, as Joseph had interpreted to them" (vv. 20-22).

Every interpretation of Joseph proved to be true. In fact, the specific words and phrases spoken to the cupbearer in verse 13 and the baker in verse 19 are echoed in the conclusion so as to underline the precision with which Joseph's predictions were fulfilled. How heartening for Joseph! For eleven years he had believed that his dreams would come true. He had never wavered in his conviction, despite his circumstances. And now he had solid objective evidence of his power, through God, to interpret dreams. He had brilliantly interpreted this pair of dreams. So now he was doubly sure that his own two dreams would be fulfilled.

Joseph, very likely, thought it would be soon. Now that the cupbearer was back in Pharaoh's good graces, he would certainly tell the king his story.

Disappointment. But it did not happen. Rather we read, "Yet the chief cupbearer did not remember Joseph, but forgot him" (v. 23) — that is, he completely forgot him.[10] Can you see Joseph as the grateful cupbearer joyfully departs? "Hey, royal cupbearer, remember me. God bless you!" "Sure, Joseph! How could I ever forget?" The next day, when the morning sun began its eastern ascent, Joseph stood at the prison's portals with rising expectancy. But when the sun reached its apex and began its western slide, Joseph's hopes descended. By the end of the first month, Joseph knew the truth. A year passed, and then another. It would be two more years until the cupbearer remembered, and only then because he reasoned that Pharaoh would be grateful for his commending Joseph's services.

The experience of delay is written large in the lives of God's greats. Abraham's long wait for a son — Moses' forty years of preparation in the desert — David's anointing as a boy, and then the long years of delay in the fields of Judea, and then the flight from Saul and hiding in the cave in Adullam. Hudson Taylor, the founder of China Inland Mission, knew the disappointment of delay. After six years of intensive service in China, he returned home as an invalid and settled with his little family in the poor east end of London. There his outside interests faded, friends began to forget, and five long years were spent in coal-blackened streets in London. But from those years he writes: "Yet without those hidden years, with all their growth and testing, how could the vision and enthusiasm of youth have been matured for the leadership that was to be?"[11] And as modern missionary history attests, when the delay ended, the great China Inland Mission emerged.

Joseph experienced disappointment after disappointment — his brothers' murderous rejection, evil for doing good in resisting Potiphar's wife, the withering disappointment from the forgetful cupbearer. Joseph's life teaches us that disappointments are essential to spiritual growth because they demand faith and resting all hope upon God. As V. Raymond Edman wrote, "Delay never thwarts God's purposes; it only polishes his instrument."[12]

In two years Joseph would be catapulted to life at the top, and it would be no picnic. Every morning of his existence, he would rise to the pagan wake-up hymns to the Egyptians' idols. Life would be lived amidst a swirl of sensuality. Mrs. Potiphars were everywhere. Open cookie jars adorned every mansion of the Nile. The chief baker's intrigues were a mere sampling of the deadly ambitions of the court. Lying and backbiting filled the air of Joseph's aristocratic existence. And he was the one righteous man in Egypt — and a Hebrew at that! Such righteousness was sure to offend the wicked, especially those who coveted his position. This has always been the response to the righteous in every age. As Peter would put it, "They are surprised when you do not join them in the same flood of debauchery, and they malign you" (1 Peter 4:4). If it were not for Pharaoh, Joseph would have been forced out.

But Joseph had been well-prepared for this, and for greatness. Joseph had his God-given dreams. And they had not faded in the least. Yahweh was "with" him, and that reality dominated his life. Young Joseph resisted the sensual siege of Mrs. Potiphar because he knew God was with him. Joseph had become a success because God was with him. And his greatest successes were not at the top, but in the pit in Egypt. Joseph's whole being had undergone the renovating grace of God. He had grown to become a man who was sensitive to others. His soul was God-reflexed; so it was to God that he instinctively turned. And though life was difficult those long years in the pit, he sent his delays and disappointments up to God. Notice: This episode ends in disappointment. But truly that disappointment never thwarted God's purposes; it only polished his instrument. And Joseph was being polished and stropped and honed to be a fine sword, a fine redemptive edge, which would make him a mighty instrument in the hand of God.

God could have conveyed these truths about Joseph's preparation by simply listing them. But instead he has chosen to illustrate them in the fabric and text of a human life, so that life can be pressed and impressed to ours — life to life. So this fortieth chapter of Genesis records the final living touches upon a man who would be mightily used by God. May we invite the Holy Spirit to infuse Joseph's virtues into us. May we humbly invite and embrace God's holy processes.

58

From Pit to Pinnacle

GENESIS 41:1-41

After I preached on Genesis 40, a father gave me a copy of his eight-year-old son's notes on that chapter that I found impressive:

> Joseh helped the buttler and baker with their dreams. He understood their dreams. Pharaoh had a feast on his birthday. He lifted up the buttler's head and lifted up the baker's head from his body! But the buttler forgot Joseph. Joseph never forgot his dreams. We should always know that God is always with us.

This young man captured the story line with admirable economy and clarity.

These final events of Joseph's imprisonment were arranged by God to make Joseph an extraordinary instrument for the preservation of his people. Amidst the disappointment and delay of being forgotten by the cupbearer, Joseph's trust in God had been further tempered and deepened. Joseph had become a radically God-centered man who believed that his God-given dreams would come true in God's good time. God would remain at the center of his vision through everything that was to come. At last Joseph was ready for the great work of his life.

PHARAOH'S TROUBLED DREAMS (vv. 1-8)

God's time came in Joseph's thirtieth year after two more years in prison, with nearly half his young life spent in Egypt. The occasion was a pair of bizarre nightmares that visited Pharaoh on the same night, both of which focused on cannibalism. Deep in his world of dreams he saw himself standing by the sacred Nile, where Egyptian cattle often stood almost submerged as a retreat from the heat and flies. And as he watched, "Behold, there came up out of the Nile seven cows attractive and plump, and they fed in the reed grass. And behold, seven other cows, ugly and thin, came up out of the Nile after them, and stood by the other cows on the bank of the Nile. And the ugly, thin cows ate up the seven attractive, plump cows. And Pharaoh awoke" (vv. 2-4). Violating nature and affinity, the "ugly and thin" cows (Hebrew, "evil in appearance and thin of flesh") attacked (killed, dismembered) and ate the "good in appearance and fat" cows (Hebrew).

The perversity and grotesqueness of the event so shocked Pharaoh that he awoke — perhaps with a start — like my own children did when they had night terrors. My boys, especially, would continue seeing their dream-monsters though their eyes were wide-open. Awake for a time, the king calmed himself and dosed off into a second fantastic dream in which seven "plump and good" ears of grain were devoured by seven thin, heat-shriveled ears of grain. The attack of the cannibal ears was again too much for Pharaoh, and he awoke a second time to discover that he was dreaming.

But consciousness and morning light gave him no comfort as "his spirit was troubled" (v. 8). Egyptian Pharaohs, supposedly gods themselves, were thought to live on the edge of the divine realms. So their dreams were given special credence. And these dreams were full of portent. They had come as a pair, signaling their importance and certitude. They were also closely parallel. Both featured cannibalism. Both ended in consuming violence. And both dreams were built on the number seven.

The dreams so stunned Pharaoh that the narrator uses an astonished "behold" six times (in the Hebrew) to indicate the king's response. So shook was Pharaoh that in the morning he assembled "all the magicians of Egypt and all its wise men" (v. 8) — a vast company of wizards and pagan priests with their dream books and priestcraft. "But there was none who could interpret them to Pharaoh" (v. 8). Certainly some attempted, but Pharaoh remained unsatisfied. Likely, some of the experts had an idea of what the dreams symbolized but didn't want to go there. The result was that Pharaoh was left anguished and nearly frantic.[1]

The reader of Genesis can see that God was moving because this was the third pair of God-given dreams that Joseph had been given to interpret. But Pharaoh did not know this. In fact, he did not believe in Israel's God. And besides, he thought he was himself a god.

PHARAOH SUMMONS JOSEPH (vv. 9-14)

It was not good for the king to be in such a state, and certainly not for anyone who worked closely with him, as did his cupbearer.

Joseph remembered. So at the opportune moment the cupbearer delicately volunteered that he knew of someone who could interpret Pharaoh's dreams. The man had been a fellow prisoner (not a particularly comfortable topic to raise with Pharaoh). So the cupbearer began with appropriate humility, saying to Pharaoh, "I remember my offenses today" (v. 9). Pharaoh understood him to be recalling the misdeeds that had landed him in prison. But the plural "my offenses" may also include his sin against Joseph in forgetting Joseph's poignant plea to remember him to Pharaoh (cf. 40:14).

With the subject introduced, the cupbearer recounted his prison experience.

> *When Pharaoh was angry with his servants and put me and the chief baker in custody in the house of the captain of the guard, we dreamed on the same night, he and I, each having a dream with its own interpretation. A young Hebrew was there with us, a servant of the captain of the guard. When we told him, he interpreted our dreams to us, giving an interpretation to each man according to his dream. And as he interpreted to us, so it came about. I was restored to my office, and the baker was hanged. (vv. 10-13)*

It was a fairly accurate account, except that the cupbearer, being the political animal that he was, did some selective editing. He neglected to mention that the young Hebrew actually claimed to have no power to interpret dreams and said that the power to interpret came from his Hebrew God. The cupbearer also gave the false impression that he took the initiative in getting Joseph to interpret his dream. And, of course, the cupbearer made no mention that he had failed to carry out his promise to mention Joseph to Pharaoh.

Joseph summoned. Nevertheless, the outcome was a bustle of activity, as the rush of verbs indicates: "Then Pharaoh sent and called Joseph, and they quickly brought him out of the pit. And when he had shaved himself and changed his clothes, he came in before Pharaoh" (v. 14).

Hebrew men, in contrast to Egyptians, wore beards. So in a flash Joseph was shaved, sanitized, Egyptianized, and presented to Pharaoh. The young Hebrew had gone from the pit to the palace in an instant. There handsome, well-built Joseph stood, looking more like an Egyptian than a Hebrew.

But Joseph was not standing alone because Yahweh was with him just as he had been with him in Potiphar's house and in prison (cf. 39:2, 3, 21, 23). Though God is not mentioned here, God was the convener. God had orchestrated the exquisite timing, first through the forgetfulness of the cupbearer and then through the cupbearer's self-serving recollection. Had the cupbearer's selective memory chosen to function earlier, it would likely have been lost on Pharaoh.

JOSEPH HEARS PHARAOH'S DREAMS (vv. 15-24)

From ground level Joseph's situation was, to say the least, intimidating. He had been yanked from the pit of powerlessness and placed before the personification of power in Egypt. Joseph had been living in filth but now stood amidst the scented finery of the court of the Nile.

The temptation to humbly moderate his views must have been intense — to say the acceptable thing, to tell Pharaoh what he thought Pharaoh wanted to hear. Charles Colson in his *Kingdoms in Conflict* describes how during his political career he used the aura of the White House to moderate and pacify visitors. He would begin by hosting his guests in the executive dining room of the West Wing. Colson would escort his guests past saluting guards and down a long corridor lined with dramatic photographs of the President in action. And then at the door of the dining room he would pause and point to the door at the right and say in hushed tones, "That's the situation room" — conjuring up visions of map-filled walls, computer screens, and busy generals when, in reality, those functions were at the Pentagon.

The ambience of the executive dining room was overwhelming with its rich, hand-rubbed mahogany walls lined with a waiting row of red-jacketed navy stewards and most of the Cabinet and senior staff huddled around the tables. Usually even the staunchest adversaries began to soften. If some needed more prodding, they were treated to a walk upstairs and a reverent tour of the Oval Office. And if the President was in, there was a prearranged impromptu greeting and a gift of gold-plated cuff links with the presidential seal. Colson summarized the effect:

> Invariably, the lions of the waiting room became the lambs of the Oval Office. No one ever showed outward hostility. Most, except the labor leaders, forgot their best-rehearsed lines. They nodded when the president spoke, and in those rare instances when they disagreed, they did so apologetically, assuring the president that they personally respected his opinion. Ironically, none were more compliant than the religious leaders. Of all people, they should have been the most aware of the sinful nature of man and the least overwhelmed by pomp and protocol. But theological knowledge sometimes wilts in the face of worldly power.[2]

So how did Joseph fare in Egypt's oval office in the face of the surprisingly solicitous and flattering remarks of Pharaoh — "I have had a dream, and there is no one who can interpret it. I have heard it said of you that when you hear a dream you can interpret it" (v. 15)? Would Joseph melt? Would he himself resort to flattery and a courteous, oblique answer?

No way! "Joseph answered Pharaoh, 'It is not in me'" (v. 16a). As Kidner remarks, "Joseph almost explosively disavowed this whole approach (the exclamation, *it is not in me*, is a single word)."[3] Joseph used a single word of deprecation. "Not me!" — "It is not in me!" And then he directed Pharaoh away from himself to God, saying, "God will give Pharaoh a favorable answer" (v. 16b).

No meltdown here! Joseph was all steel. Observe carefully that he told Pharaoh (who himself was considered to be a god incarnate) that God (*ha Elohim*, "the God") would explain his dream. Thus, to Pharaoh's face Joseph asserted that his God was superior to and sovereign over the gods of Egypt. Joseph's theological knowledge rose high against the face of worldly power. Joseph's speech to Pharaoh was the same here as it was to the prisoners in the pit. In prison he had declared, "Do not interpretations belong to God? Please tell [your dreams] to me" (40:8). Here he declared, "It is not in me; God [*ha Elohim*] will give Pharaoh a favorable answer" (v. 16). Joseph had not changed one whit in his trip from the pit to the palace. Those thirteen years of preparation were now paying huge dividends. Through Joseph, God was advertising and asserting himself in Egypt.

Those dreams again. Joseph had been unflinchingly direct with Pharaoh, but rather than being put off, Pharaoh unloaded his dreams on Joseph, only with more detail, as we see in verses 17-24. Pharaoh's embellishments emphasized the unparalleled ugliness of his dreams and his deep revulsion and alarm. Of the lean cows, he added that they were "poor and very ugly and thin, such as I had never seen in all the land of Egypt" (v. 19b). These seven bovines were a sorry lot — grotesque in their skeletal appearance. And further, when the flesh-eating cows cannibalized the fat cows, Pharaoh noted, "they were still as ugly as at the beginning" (v. 21b) — still horribly skeletal. The cannibalistic ears of corn did not repulse Pharaoh as much. But what alarmed him was that there was no one who could explain the dreams to him. This is all so very remarkable, because with immense subtlety the documenting of Pharaoh's helplessness and fear emphasizes "the mortality and finiteness of the dreamer, the pharaoh-god" (Hamilton).[4]

Pharaoh was a mere man. The God of Israel, the one and only true God, was rising high over the Nile.

JOSEPH INTERPRETS PHARAOH'S DREAMS (vv. 25-36)

Now as Joseph proceeded to interpret Pharaoh's dreams, the interpretation was wholly God-centered. Remember that Joseph had already twice declared that God is the source of interpretations, first to the royal cupbearer and baker ("Do not interpretations belong to God?" in 40:8), and then to Pharaoh with his initial word, "God [*Elohim*, "the God"] will give Pharaoh a favorable answer" (v. 16). Here Joseph's interpretation in verses 25-32 invoked God at the beginning, the middle, and the end of the interpretation. The opening line was unequivocally God-centered: "Then Joseph said to Pharaoh, 'The dreams of Pharaoh are one; God [*ha Elohim*] has revealed to Pharaoh what he is about to do'" (v. 25). The middle duplicates the God-centeredness: "It is as I told Pharaoh; God [*ha Elohim*, "the God"] has shown to Pharaoh what he is about to do" (v. 28). And the final sentence of Joseph's interpretation named God twice: "And the doubling of Pharaoh's dream means that the thing is fixed by God, and God [*ha Elohim*] will shortly bring it about" (v. 32). The interpretation that Joseph gave here announced to Pharaoh and to all of Egypt that the one true God controlled their existence.

Cyclic famine. As we know, the interpretation was one of cyclic famine, with the sevens representing years. There would be seven years of prosperity and seven cannibalizing years of famine, about which Joseph was grimly explicit: "There will come seven years of great plenty throughout all the land of Egypt, but after them there will arise seven years of famine, and all the plenty will be forgotten in the land of Egypt. The famine will consume the land, and the plenty will be unknown in the land by reason of the famine that will follow, for it will be very severe" (vv. 29-31). Joseph's language was that of a prophet and anticipated the prophets who would follow. The future of Egypt was established without any reference to Pharaoh. As Walter Brueggemann explains, "The future in Egypt does not depend upon Pharaoh. He does not get to decide. In fact, Pharaoh is irrelevant and marginal to the future of the kingdom. . . . Joseph has calmly announced to the lord of Egypt that the future is out of his hands. . . . In Gen. 41, it is clear that Pharaoh can cause no future. Nor can he resist the future that God will bring."[5]

Thus we are here confronted with the premise upon which all biblical history rests: Kings do not make history. Rather, God uses them to effect history. The prophet Isaiah would give this truth grand expression in Isaiah 45:4-7, where the Lord explains that the pagan king Cyrus was brought to power to bring about God's purposes for his people.

> *For the sake of my servant Jacob,*
> *and Israel my chosen,*
> *I call you by your name,*
> *I name you, though you do not know me.*
> *I am the LORD, and there is no other,*
> *besides me there is no God;*
> *I equip you, though you do not know me,*
> *that people may know, from the rising of the sun*
> *and from the west, that there is none besides me;*
> *I am the LORD, and there is no other.*
> *I form light and create darkness,*
> *I make well-being and create calamity,*
> *I am the LORD, who does all these things.*

Kings do not make history — they only serve history, as Jesus would declare in his answer to Pilate's question: "So Pilate said to him, 'You will not speak to me? Do you not know that I have authority to release you and authority to crucify you?' Jesus answered him, 'You would have no authority over me at all unless it had been given you from above'" (John 19:10, 11a).

We must remember this in these uncertain days — when evil regimes thumb their noses at justice, and millions cheer them on — when dark kings prevail with seeming impunity, and righteous people are engulfed by the night. Remember that these kings do not make history, but rather God uses them to effect his purposes.

Joseph's advice. To Pharaoh's credit, he did not discount the revelation from God but listened to Joseph's advice as he continued his response.

> *Now therefore let Pharaoh select a discerning and wise man, and set him over the land of Egypt. Let Pharaoh proceed to appoint overseers over the land and take one-fifth of the produce of the land of Egypt during the seven plentiful years. And let them gather all the food of these good years that are coming and store up grain under the authority of Pharaoh for food in the cities, and let them keep it. That food shall be a reserve for the land against the seven years of famine that are to occur in the land of Egypt, so that the land may not perish through the famine. (vv. 33-36)*

The brilliance of Joseph's "20 percent x 7 years saving plan" was at once obvious. The decentralization of the stored grain would, when the time came, allow for convenient distribution. And the storage of grain in centers of population provided for adequate protection should it be needed as the famine grew in severity. Fascinatingly, every aspect of Joseph's plan called for dynamic action. And here is what fascinates: Joseph's dynamic call to action was based on his knowledge of what God was about to do. So we see that the knowledge of what God is going to do does not produce passive resignation but aggressive action. The knowledge of God's purpose is not the end of human planning and action but the beginning of it. The fact that God has set the future is a mighty summons to action.

Today it is precisely this that undergirds the tremendous energy of world missions. We know how history is going to end — it will end with people redeemed from "every nation, from all tribes and peoples and languages" (Revelation 7:9). So we pray and give and go!

JOSEPH ELEVATED (vv. 37-41)

The key to Joseph's action plan was sound leadership and administration. As he put it, "select a discerning and wise man, and set him over the land of Egypt." But he never dreamed that he was commending himself. Joseph was not engineering a contrived "Who, me?" — a "*moi?*" moment. But that is how it all worked out. And Pharaoh led the way: "This proposal pleased Pharaoh and all his servants. And Pharaoh said to his servants, 'Can we find a man like this, in whom is the Spirit of God?'" (vv. 37, 38). Pharaoh did not know God or who *Elohim* was. And his phrase, "the Spirit of God" would have been colored by his polytheistic concepts.[6] Nevertheless, Joseph asserted repeatedly that "*God* has revealed to Pharaoh what he is about to do" and "*God* has shown Pharaoh what he is about to do" and "the thing is fixed by *God*, and *God* will shortly bring it about" — and these assertions were beginning to inform Pharaoh.

Pharaoh, however ignorantly, was giving praise to God. The man who thought himself a god was extolling the true God of Abraham, Isaac, Jacob, and Joseph. And along with this, he saw that God's faithful man, who had been a slave for all his grown years, was incomparable.

So Joseph was made viceroy by Pharaoh himself. "Then Pharaoh said to Joseph, 'Since God has shown you all this, there is none so discerning and wise as you are. You shall be over my house, and all my people shall order themselves as you command. Only as regards the throne will I be greater than you.' And Pharaoh said to Joseph, 'See, I have set you over all the land of Egypt'" (vv. 39-41). Joseph had gone from the pit to the pinnacle in a single day. The morning had begun in the pit as an imprisoned slave. And now he was second only to Pharaoh.

Indeed, the near future of Egypt lay in his hands. He was sure that his plan would save Egypt. But he did not know that it would also save his own people. A famine was coming — and with it Joseph would at last see his brothers.

As we look at the whole of Joseph's life, it is clear that the "oval office" never did get to Joseph. He knew who he was, and he knew who God was. He knew that there was no power in himself. Joseph understood that the future was determined by God, not by a mere human king.

And Joseph's own dreams were intact. He was confident that one day all his family would bow to him. He could now see that it was humanly feasible. But he would obediently wait for God to do it, in his time. From Palestine to the Sinai to Egypt — and truly around the world — Joseph's defining virtue was his massive concept of God. Joseph's view of God exceeded that of anyone on Planet Earth. And we must lay this to heart: God's choice servants have always been informed and defined by their view of God.

Robert Dick Wilson was one of the great professors at Princeton Theological Seminary. One of his students had been invited to preach in Miller Chapel twelve years after his graduation. Old Dr. Wilson came in and sat down near the front. At the close of the meeting, the old professor came up to his former student, cocked his head to one side in his characteristic way, extended his hand, and said:

"If you come back again, I will not come to hear you preach. I only come once. I am glad that you are a big-godder. When my boys come back, I come to see if they are big-godders or little-godders, and then I know what their ministry will be." His former student asked him to explain, and he replied, "Well, some men have a little god, and they are always in trouble with him. He can't do any miracles. He can't take care of the inspiration and transmission of the Scripture to us. He doesn't intervene on behalf of his people. They have a little god and I call them little-godders. Then, there are those who have a great God. He speaks and it is done. He commands and it stands fast. He knows how to show himself strong on behalf of them that fear him. You have a great God; and he will bless your ministry." He paused a moment, smiled, said, "God bless you," and turned and walked out.[7]

Are you a "little-godder" or a "big-godder"? So much rides on your answer, because those who embrace the God of the Scriptures embrace the God of Abraham and Isaac and Jacob and Joseph and Moses and David and Daniel and Paul and Peter — and that makes all the difference!

59

Life at the Top

GENESIS 41:42-57

Joseph stood alone and above every soul in the world in his massive under-standing of God. No one on earth saw God as he did or believed in God as he did. That is why he was so magnificent during the brief span when he was yanked from the pit, shaved and dressed, and thrust before Pharaoh. Indeed, his God-focus rendered him the same man both in the pit and in the palace as he declared to Pharaoh (who himself was thought to be a god) that the true God would provide the answer to his dreams (cf. 41:16). And then when Joseph interpreted Pharaoh's dreams, he three times named God as the source and sovereign arbiter of those dreams (cf. vv. 25, 28, 32).

Pharaoh, Egypt's god-king, was so overwhelmed that he reflexively extolled Joseph and his God, asking in amazement, "Can we find a man like this, in whom is the Spirit of God?" (v. 38). Unwittingly Pharaoh had lifted God's name up over the gods of the Nile. And with that he exalted Joseph, saying, "'Since God has shown you all this, there is none so dis-cerning and wise as you are. You shall be over my house, and all my people shall order themselves as you command. Only as regards the throne will I be greater than you.' And Pharaoh said to Joseph, 'See, I have set you over all the land of Egypt'" (vv. 39-41).

JOSEPH'S INVESTITURE (vv. 42-45)

Empowerment. On the spot Pharaoh ceremonially bestowed upon Joseph the paraphernalia of power. First, the king removed the signet ring from his own hand and slipped it onto Joseph's. The signet bore the name of Pharaoh in its cartouche (an oval surrounding his hieroglyphics).[1] The ring was used to press Pharaoh's seal upon official documents, therefore delegating to

Joseph the ability to operate with Pharaoh-like authority. Second, Joseph was decked out in garments of "fine linen," an almost transparent linen that was worn by court officials. Likely, as the robe of the viceroy it was a garment suspended from shoulder straps so that it hung straight from the chest to the ankles.[2] Henceforth Joseph would be clad in fine linen, the garments of the powerful and well-connected. Third, a gold chain was hung around his neck as a gift and a symbol of highest distinction. Because the gold was of great value, it served as Pharaoh's reward for the interpretation as well as a symbol of honor.

Having donned the visible signs of power, Joseph was then treated to an inaugural parade as Pharaoh made him ride in his second chariot, with runners preceding him and calling out "Bow the knee!" In present-day terms, "chariots were the limousines of the day, so it is arranged that Joseph will ride in style. The men going before him clearing the way are the equivalent of the Secret Service protection that is offered to important dignitaries and officers in the United States."[3]

What a rush that must have been for Joseph. He had been bowing and scraping to everyone for the last thirteen years of his life. He had been the "Hey, you" guy both in Potiphar's house and most recently in prison where he had served Pharaoh's servants. Now he rode in a royal chariot that plowed through masses that divided before him like a sea on bended knee.

Pretty heady stuff! And on top of all of this, Joseph received Pharaoh's formal words of investiture: "I am Pharaoh, and without your consent no one shall lift up hand or foot in all the land of Egypt" (v. 44) — that is, "no action will be taken without your OK."

Think of it. In the morning he was in a dirty, stinking pit. But at nightfall he was sitting in the palace, dressed in designer clothing, servants fanning him and brushing the flies away, his menu drawn from the haute cuisine of the Nile, and in the stable his chauffeured limo was ready to transport him everywhere through worshipful crowds.

Connection. It is evident that Pharaoh was intent on Egyptianizing Joseph because he gave him a new name and a wife. "Pharaoh called Joseph's name Zaphenath-paneah" (v. 45a), which is generally understood to mean "God speaks and lives."[4] But despite the fact that the name was Egyptian, it was an ongoing testimony to the superiority of Joseph's living, speaking God. Joseph's new name encapsulated divine reality. Now an Egyptian name is one thing, but an Egyptian wife is quite another — because we see how thoroughly Pharaoh intended Joseph to become identified with Egypt. Asenath was of aristocratic blood, "the daughter of Potiphera priest of On" (v. 45b). She was of such high-born lineage that the Pharaohs sometimes chose wives from this family.[5] The city of On, which is also known by the Greek name Heliopolis ("Sun City"), lies today about ten miles northeast of Cairo and was the center of worship of the sun-god Re. As priest of On,

Asenath's father presided over the temple-city of Heliopolis and officiated at all major festivals and supervised the other priests.

This ultra-aristocratic wife left Joseph well-connected — and ominously in danger of Egyptianization. His clothing was Egyptian, his name was Egyptian, his language was Egyptian, his wife was Egyptian, and his father-in-law was the leading Egyptian sun-worshiper. A novel written in the first century A.D. entitled *Joseph and Asenath* portrays Asenath as being converted to the worship of Yahweh.[6] Whether this is true or not, young Joseph began his married life listening to hymns sung to Re at the morning sunrise — in his own home.

Joseph's soul was in greater peril than at any other time in his short life. It is one thing to remain believing and God-centered and faithful in the pit; it is quite another to be faithful at the pinnacle. The pit instilled dependence upon God. Days, months, and years in the pit graced Joseph's soul with an ever-deepening sense of need and dependence upon God. There was only one way to look while in the pit, and that was up — to God. On the other hand, the pinnacle of Egyptian life inclined the soul toward pride and independence. At the top, looking up to God was not so natural. It was far easier then for Joseph to look down on humanity and to depend upon servants to meet his needs. And the fact that Joseph's name, speech, clothing, and wife were Egyptian all encouraged him to forget where he came from. Also, the undeniable brilliance of his interpretation of Pharaoh's dreams and his plan to spare Egypt could well have begun to give him a sense of mental and moral superiority. As economist and former ambassador John Kenneth Galbraith once quipped, "Wealth, in even the most improbable cases, manages to convey the aspect of intelligence."[7]

That is so true. Life at the top can make people imagine themselves so original and so wise — a one-of-a-kind that deserves all he or she has. Extended time at the top of society can work an incredible ugliness of soul, as it did in the proud English Duke of Somerset who gave commands to his servants by hand signals because he could not condescend to speak to such lesser beings.[8] Today we especially see this kind of ugliness in those who have had a meteoric rise — pro athletes, prodigies, media personalities, and children of the rich and famous. Accordingly, young Joseph, second only to Pharaoh at age thirty — a preternaturally handsome man with acute mental capacity — recently risen from nowhere and suddenly living in relentless luxury — was in great danger.

JOSEPH'S FAITHFULNESS (vv. 46-49)

But Joseph responded well. He did not assume the indolent lifestyle of the Nile's rich and famous. Rather he responded with the obedience that characterizes true faith. That is, he believed that Egypt would have just seven years of plenty to gather up grain for seven years of famine. So we see that his rise to power did not dull his response to God's word — because he gave himself wholly to hard work. The frenetic pace of Joseph's activity is underscored by the repetitions in the verses that describe Joseph's work:

> *Joseph was thirty years old when he entered the service of Pharaoh king of Egypt. And Joseph went out from the presence of Pharaoh and went through all the land of Egypt. During the seven plentiful years the earth produced abundantly, and he gathered up all the food of these seven years, which occurred in the land of Egypt, and put the food in the cities. He put in every city the food from the fields around it. And Joseph stored up grain in great abundance, like the sand of the sea, until he ceased to measure it, for it could not be measured. (vv. 46-49)*

The agriculture of the Nile is not based on rain that falls in Egypt because very little rain ever falls in the Nile Valley. Rather, the growing cycle is based on spring floods that come from rains faraway in the Upper Nile Basin. So Joseph quickly went out and surveyed the agricultural scene and the storage facilities (no doubt constructing new ones as needed) and then annually, for seven consecutive years, presided over storing 20 percent of the crops. The result was an immeasurable cache of grain in every strategic city. Joseph's work ethic was apparent to all. But what was not apparent is that it came from his deep belief in God's word. Joseph's faith had not shriveled with his rise to power. His belief remained constant and unflagging.

JOSEPH BLESSED (vv. 50-52)

Those seven years were also fruitful for Joseph in other ways, with the establishment of a nuclear family through the birth of two sons.

> *Before the year of famine came, two sons were born to Joseph. Asenath, the daughter of Potiphera priest of On, bore them to him. Joseph called the name of the firstborn Manasseh. "For," he said, "God has made me forget all my hardship and all my father's house." The name of the second he called Ephraim, "For God has made me fruitful in the land of my affliction." (vv. 50-52)*

Manasseh means "he who causes to forget" — and the birth of that little boy helped Joseph to forget the appalling hardship of his initial thirteen years in Egypt. And it also eased his intense longing for his father and siblings. Baby Manasseh brightened his life.

Ephraim means "fertile" and broadly celebrated not only the birth of his second son but the bounty Joseph was experiencing professionally in the ingathering of Egypt and in all of life. Joseph had been celebrating his blessings and was filled with gratitude, optimism, and hope.

But here is the great thing (and you must not miss it): Joseph declared his allegiance to God and his faith in God's word by giving his boys *Hebrew* names! Remember, Joseph had been renamed with an Egyptian name — Zaphenath-paneah — and his wife was Asenath, which means "she who belongs to the goddess Neit," referencing her idolatrous Egyptian ancestry. But the names of the sons of their union amidst the aristocracy of the Nile were blatantly Hebrew! Again, when all foreigners sought assimilation and welcomed Egyptianization, Joseph reasserted his ethnic, spiritual origin. And here, at this moment in history, Joseph not only understood the greatness of God as no other living person, but he also believed as no other person on earth! Significantly this was at the beginning of seven years of famine.

JOSEPH'S SUCCESS (vv. 53-57)

The Nile's agribusiness has always depended on flooding, as Nahum Sarna explains:

> Lower Egypt, the northern area of the country, is virtually rainless. Its entire economy, of which agriculture was the core in ancient times, has always depended upon the Nile floods caused by the river's periodic rise during three summer months. The swelling of the river results from the torrential rains in the Upper Nile Basin being carried down to the Delta by the Blue Nile. In ancient times an elaborate series of artificially constructed irrigation works controlled the distribution and utilization of the flood waters. The measurements of the maximum levels of inundation, as recorded by the Nilometers placed at strategic points along the river, were noted in the royal annals. Normally, the floods come with remarkable regularity. But there are years when the rainfall in the southern Sudan provides an insufficient volume of water. A shortfall of only a few inches could deny irrigation to the arid areas of the north, deprive the arable land of its productivity, and bring famine to the inhabitants of Egypt.[9]

Thus the monstrous seven cows and seven ears of grain were ready to cannibalize the seven plump cows and ears of grain.

The seven years of famine were as terrible as the seven years of bounty were wonderful. The Genesis description reiterates "famine" five times, twice saying that it was severe.

> *The seven years of plenty that occurred in the land of Egypt came to an end, and the seven years of famine began to come, as Joseph had said. There was famine in all lands, but in all the land of Egypt there was bread. When*

all the land of Egypt was famished, the people cried to Pharaoh for bread.
Pharaoh said to all the Egyptians, "Go to Joseph. What he says to you,
do." So when the famine had spread over all the land, Joseph opened all
the storehouses and sold to the Egyptians, for the famine was severe in
the land of Egypt. Moreover, all the earth came to Egypt to Joseph to buy
grain, because the famine was severe over all the earth. (vv. 53-57)

Whenever the Nile failed to rise, misery ensued. Egyptian records twice indicate that cyclic famine had become so bad that the Egyptians had resorted to cannibalism.[10] Now the Egyptian famine was rendered even more severe by the unusual combination of rains failing to fall in Palestine and surrounding lands. The crisis involved everyone in "all the earth." And had it not been for the execution of Joseph's great plan, mass death would have followed.

What storied success had come to Joseph! Not only did Joseph engineer the saving of Egypt, but "all the earth came to Egypt to Joseph to buy grain, because the famine was severe over all the earth" (v. 57). Money readily poured into Egypt's coffers, so that not only did the people have plenty to eat, but everyone actually prospered during the famine. And though he cared little about fame, Joseph became the hero of the Nile. All the earth named Joseph as its temporal savior.

Again there are glimmers here of the ultimate fulfillment of God's word to Abraham: "In you all the families of the earth shall be blessed" (12:3). And who can not help but see, in Joseph's faith in God's word and in his commitment to do God's work, shadows of the Savior of the world? And, of course (though Joseph had no idea), the coming of all the earth to Egypt to Joseph to buy grain set the scene for the dramatic fulfillment of his dreams. And on top of that, there would come a day when his father Jacob would call for his Hebrew grandsons, Manasseh and Ephraim, and would kiss and embrace them and lay his aged hands upon their hands and bless them to carry on his line as the progenitors of the tribes that would bear their names (cf. 48:8-20).

For those who believe, life at the top is a perilous pursuit. Many hearts forget God in the heights of prosperity and success. As the Puritan Cotton Mather said in his own day, "Religion begat prosperity and the daughter devoured the mother."[11] But Joseph not only survived life at the pinnacle — he prospered. Why was this? The answer lay in thirteen years of testing in which his soul was tempered in the downs and ups of life: down in the pit at Shechem — down in slavery — up in Potiphar's household — down in the pit in Egypt — down further when he was forgotten — and then up to the pinnacle in Egypt.

Through these wrenching extremes Joseph maintained at least three distinctives. At the base he had a transcending belief in the greatness of God. Joseph's understanding of God was that he controlled all of life, including the day-in, day-out events of life. He believed that God was at work in the rich compost of sinful life. In his day, Joseph maintained the greatest concept and understanding of God of any living soul. And he heroically declared that to Pharaoh (the pseudo-god man) — telling the king that God, not Pharaoh, controlled the destiny of the Nile.

Along with this Joseph believed God's word that had been revealed to him through Abraham, Isaac, and Jacob. He believed in God's covenant promises. He also believed in his God-given dreams. And he believed all this without exception as he stood alone in Egypt *contra mundum*. That is how Moses would stand before Pharaoh, that is how Daniel would stand before the King of Babylon, and that is how the Apostle Paul towered before the courts of Rome. That is how Martin Luther stood before the world. They all believed God's word. Joseph believed God's word as did no other soul in his day.

Furthermore, Joseph believed that Yahweh was with him both in the pit and at the pinnacle. That is why — in the face of every political, social, and spiritual force in Egypt — he gave his boys Hebrew names.

Joseph's belief in God's greatness, more than any other man — Joseph's belief in God's word, as no other man — Joseph's belief that God was with him, more than any of his contemporaries is a template for every soul in every age.

Christians, this is the age of affluence. And it is possible for a middle-class person to live with greater ease and independence than did Pharaoh in Egypt — insulated from the economy, insulated from the vicissitudes of nature, insulated from illness — so that he or she never looks up to God for anything.

So be warned and made wise by the God-given example of Joseph.

60

Guilt and Grace

GENESIS 42:1-38

Apart from Benjamin, Joseph's brothers were a miserable lot. Sons two and three, Simeon and Levi, were guilty of premeditated genocide in the slaughter of the unsuspecting Shechemites (cf. chap. 34). Number one son, Reuben, had committed incest with his father's concubine in an attempt to secure ascendancy over his father Jacob (cf. 35:22). Next, all ten of them had taken young Joseph and stripped him and beaten him and thrown him into a pit with fratricidal intent — which was only averted by a passing caravan and his sale into slavery in Egypt (cf. 37:12-28). Number four son, Judah, then impregnated his daughter-in-law, Tamar, who had disguised herself as a Canaanite prostitute (cf. chap. 38). So by any estimation these patriarchs-to-be were less than promising as bearers of the promise of Abraham and root stock for the covenant nation that would emerge from Egypt at the exodus.

These ten needed to be confronted with their guilt. They needed an awakening of conscience. They needed to mourn. They needed to genuinely repent. And they needed rapprochement with Joseph if they were to be preserved during the worldwide famine. Truly their future rested upon such changes. God could easily raise up new patriarchs if he so chose, as indeed he would do with Joseph's sons Ephraim and Manasseh (cf. 48:8-22). The brothers desperately needed grace, though they did not know it.

The famine was not just an Egyptian phenomenon but engulfed "all the earth" (41:57). So the lands around Egypt were also drought-stricken, and the people were starving. But because of Joseph's prescience and brilliance, Egypt had enough stored to save the world. As the drought reached a crisis level in Canaan, Jacob's sons were at best indecisive, at worst indolent. So Jacob got after them. "Why do you look at one another?" (42:1). In effect he was saying, "Come on, boys. Get with it!" as he charged them to make the trip down to Egypt. So they all went, with one exception. "But Jacob did not send Benjamin, Joseph's brother, with his brothers, for he feared that harm might happen to him" (v. 4). Jacob had no certain knowledge of what had actually happened to Joseph, but he knew the character of his sons, and he sensed that they were to blame for Joseph's death. And his sons felt it. So his charge to go to Egypt (where they had consigned Joseph), plus the withholding of Benjamin, likely stung their consciences.

AWAKENING GUILT (vv. 6-25)

So it was that thirteen years after selling Joseph into Egypt, Joseph's brothers made the trek across the Sinai and down into the Nile Valley. Never in their wildest and worst dreams did they imagine that they would ever meet him. If he was alive, he would be an obscure slave in some household or business, and they were themselves awash in a sea of desperate, hungry foreigners flooding into Egypt. But, of course, as God would have it, they did meet Joseph unwittingly and unawares. And Joseph had become virtually unrecognizable. He was beardless and clean-shaven and, likely, dressed in flowing white linen decked with gold and the color palette of the Nile aristocracy. And he spoke the language of the Egyptians. Thus they did what every other foreigner did — they "bowed themselves before him with their faces to the ground" (v. 6b) in a gesture of subordination. To them, this was a hateful gesture, but necessary to their survival.[1]

Recognition. Of course, Joseph recognized them in an instant. They were bearded Semites. And there were ten of them — all brothers! The older ones had grayed but were still recognizable by their profile and gait and, of course, their Hebrew dialect. Did Joseph momentarily freeze? Did he inwardly gasp? We do know that he recognized them and carried out his dealings with them with perfect regal composure.

Now Joseph had absolute and perfect advantage. They had no idea who he was, but he knew each one of them with a terrifying intimacy. And from their perspective he held over them the power of life and death. At the same time Joseph needed to know what was in his brothers' hearts. Were they the same callous, murderous lot? Were they as heartless as they had been thirteen years earlier? Did they still hate him? Would they resort to similar expedients among themselves when pressured? Would they sacrifice another to save their skins? Joseph needed to know the truth. And he knew that he might never know if he revealed who he was. Moreover, a pardon would allow the truth to be glossed over. So on the spot Joseph conceived a brilliant strategy — that of fierce, implacable interrogation.

Accusation. Remember, these were hard men who had massacred a whole people and had even sold their brother into slavery. So Joseph was tough with them.

> *He treated them like strangers and spoke roughly to them. "Where do you come from?" he said. They said, "From the land of Canaan, to buy food." And Joseph recognized his brothers, but they did not recognize him. And Joseph remembered the dreams that he had dreamed of them. And he said to them, "You are spies; you have come to see the nakedness of the land." They said to him, "No, my lord, your servants have come to buy food. We are all sons of one man. We are honest men. Your servants have never been spies." (vv. 7b-11)*

In the midst of the interrogation Joseph remembered his two dreams of them bowing to him, as they had now done. And a certain satisfaction came to him. But he also realized that his dreams were not yet fulfilled, because the dreams included not ten but eleven brothers, plus his parents. There was more to come! So he flung charges of espionage at them: "You are spies; you have come to see the nakedness of the land" — the weak points in Egypt's defenses.[2] As they countered with terror-stricken demurrals of honesty, he pressed harder: "'No, it is the nakedness of the land that you have come to see.' And they said, 'We, your servants, are twelve brothers, the sons of one man in the land of Canaan, and behold, the youngest is this day with our father, and one is no more.' But Joseph said to them, 'It is as I said to you. You are spies'" (vv. 12-14). Joseph's repeated accusations unnerved the ten. They revealed that there were really twelve brothers. They counted not only Benjamin among them but himself! Were their consciences coming to life?

Testing. At this point Joseph put his brothers to the test by afflicting them with what they had done to him. They had oppressed him; now he oppressed them. They had accused him of spying; now he accused them. They had thrown him into the pit; now he tossed them into prison. And most of all, he called them to bring forth their youngest brother, the favorite of their father who now occupied the place in their father's heart that had once been his. Note these subtle parallels as he lays out the test.

> *"By this you shall be tested: by the life of Pharaoh, you shall not go from this place unless your youngest brother comes here. Send one of you, and let him bring your brother, while you remain confined, that your words may be tested, whether there is truth in you. Or else, by the life of Pharaoh, surely you are spies." And he put them all together in custody for three days. (vv. 15-17)*

Those three days in an Egyptian prison provided time for terror-filled reflection over the wrenching parallels and the raising of conscience. And, of course, they discussed who would be the one to go and inform their father that Benjamin must come to Egypt if they were to receive help. Probably most chose to wait in prison rather than be the messenger.

Joseph had been brilliantly messing with their minds and hearts, and he continued to do so when, after three days, he surprised them with two new things. First, he stunned them by referencing God (*Elohim*): "On the third day Joseph said to them, 'Do this and you will live, for I fear God'" (v. 18). Thus far the ten brothers never once mentioned the name of God, but the Egyptian did. And he announced that he feared God! Such dissonance. God was intruded into their swirling, trembling thoughts by the pagan viceroy. And then, second, Joseph decided that only one brother would have to stay as hostage, while the nine others returned for Benjamin. Mercifully, this would allow them to carry adequate grain back to their families, but it also was suggestive of Joseph's original descent into Egypt. One brother was to remain in Egypt. And that subjected the brothers to a temptation familiar to Joseph. Would they abandon another brother as they once had abandoned Joseph?

Guilt. Joseph's strategy bore remarkable fruit in their corporate admission of guilt.

> *Then they said to one another, "In truth we are guilty concerning our brother, in that we saw the distress of his soul, when he begged us and we did not listen. That is why this distress has come upon us." And Reuben answered them, "Did I not tell you not to sin against the boy? But you did not listen. So now there comes a reckoning for his blood." (vv. 21, 22)*

Their confession was tinged with retrospective tenderness. Joseph, whom they had scorned as "this dreamer" (37:19), was now referred to as "our brother" and by the oldest brother Reuben as "the boy." Joseph learned here that Reuben had not consented to his sale. Joseph learned too that his macho, unfeeling brothers were not as hardened as some might think — that his pathetic pleas had been heard and had been haunting their souls during all the intervening years. And more, they believed that this distress had rightfully come upon them. Joseph's brothers were experiencing the grace of guilt — bloodguilt. They knew that they were guilty and deserving of death. God's ancient dictum to Noah rang in their consciences:

> *Whoever sheds the blood of man,*
> *by man shall his blood be shed,*
> *for God made man in his own image. (9:6)*

True guilt is a grace because it brings the guilty to seek forgiveness and to repent. It is especially a grace in a day when Freudian analysis has dismissed conscience and guilt as mere safety devices, collectively created to protect civilized order — an illusion of narrow minds.

Joseph's brothers were wracked with guilt that, in the context of the Bible, put them in the way of grace. This was good guilt, healthy guilt, graced guilt. Without guilt there could be no forgiveness and no resolution. And without guilt they could never assume their covenant mantles. Perhaps your growing knowledge of God's Word and your own heart is helping you understand and acknowledge your guilt. If so, embrace it because such an embrace can be a prelude to grace.

Relentless, ruthless Joseph is so beautiful here: "They did not know that Joseph understood them, for there was an interpreter between them. Then he turned away from them and wept" (vv. 23, 24a). He was so moved by their expressions of guilt and remorse that he could not control himself. There would be more tears — when he first saw Benjamin (cf. 43:30), and when Judah offered to take Benjamin's place (cf. 45:2), and finally when he met his father (cf. 46:29). But the great revelation of his initial tears right here was that Joseph had to turn away from his brothers to hide his sorrow for the pain his strategy was bringing upon them.

Yet there was still more probing that he had to do — a further test. So he composed himself. "And he returned to them and spoke to them. And he took Simeon from them and bound him before their eyes. And Joseph gave orders to fill their bags with grain, and to replace every man's money in his sack, and to give them provisions for the journey. This was done for them" (vv. 24b, 25). Of this St. Chrysostom wrote, "See how Joseph takes every means of putting fear into them so that, on seeing Simeon's bonds, they may reveal whether they manifested any sympathy for their brother. You see, everything he does is to test their attitude out of his wish to discover if they had been like that in dealing with Benjamin. Hence Joseph also had Simeon bound in front of them to test them carefully and see if they showed any signs of affection for him."[3]

With this, Joseph further tested his brothers by placing money in their sacks. Would they be happy to abandon Simeon for money, as they had once done to Joseph? How would they interpret Joseph's actions? As a gift? Or as an attempt to frame them as thieves?

RAISING GODLY FEAR AND SORROW (vv. 26-38)

The answers were soon to come. "Then they loaded their donkeys with their grain and departed. And as one of them opened his sack to give his donkey fodder at the lodging place, he saw his money in the mouth of his sack. He said to his brothers, 'My money has been put back; here it is in the mouth of my sack!' At this their hearts failed them, and they turned trembling to one another, saying, 'What is this that God has done to us?'" (vv. 26-28).

Godly fear. This is the first time ever in the narrative that the brothers mention the Lord. But because of their raging guilt, they were quick to see God in this.[4] They were traumatized, shocked, and terrified by a fresh and fearful awareness of the divine. However, this was not mere fear — it was *godly fear.* Joseph's brothers realized that their sins were against God. Fear is one thing, but godly fear comes from sensing that a holy God is the hand behind the circumstances of your life to bring you to where you ought to be. The brothers trembled in their awesome awareness.

Godly fear is a grace because the fearer knows where he or she must turn to have the fear assuaged. Fear alone (like guilt alone) is of little use. In fact, it can be debilitating. But godly fear is a fear that God blesses, for he comes to those who fear him. Good things were happening to those brothers. A godly fear is precisely what every child of God needs. Those who live with awed reverence find that God orders all their life to his glory and, ultimately, to his children's glory.

> *'Twas grace that taught my heart to fear.*
> JOHN NEWTON, 1779

When the long journey to Canaan was complete, Jacob's sons told him "all that had happened to them" — well, almost all (cf. vv. 29-34)! In an effort to persuade him to send Benjamin to Egypt, they neglected to mention some minor details — like their being imprisoned for three days, and the viceroy's threat to execute them, and the discovery of money in one of their sacks. But despite their tamed-down account Jacob remained unmoved and silent.

Fear and sorrow. But Jacob's silence was not for long.

> As they emptied their sacks, behold, every man's bundle of money was in his sack. And when they and their father saw their bundles of money, they were afraid. And Jacob their father said to them, "You have bereaved me of my children: Joseph is no more, and Simeon is no more, and now you would take Benjamin. All this has come against me." Then Reuben said to his father, "Kill my two sons if I do not bring him back to you. Put him in my hands, and I will bring him back to you." But he said, "My son shall not go down with you, for his brother is dead, and he is the only one left. If harm should happen to him on the journey that you are to make, you would bring down my gray hairs with sorrow to Sheol." (vv. 35-38)

Jacob's mention of his gray hairs indicates the toll that his grief and sorrow had taken upon him in his loss of Joseph. The loss of Benjamin would cause him to die of sorrow.

Jacob made it clear that his sadness was the work of his sons whom he believed were responsible for Joseph and Simeon being "no more" (v. 36). As the oldest, Reuben felt his father's pain and made an absurd promise. But nothing could lessen the pain exacted by his sons' sins. Thus the godly fear of Joseph's brothers was now matched by their godly sorrow — and that was a grace. As Paul would later advise the Corinthians, "Godly sorrow brings repentance that leads to salvation and leaves no regret, but worldly sorrow brings death. See what this godly sorrow has produced in you: what earnestness, what eagerness to clear yourselves, what indignation, what alarm, what longing, what concern, what readiness to see justice done" (2 Corinthians 7:10, 11, NIV). And that is what godly sorrow would effect in Joseph's brothers. Godly sorrow is a grace because it leads to repentance.

Israel's patriarchs would never become choirboys. They were always imperfect. And their past sins would continue to haunt them, as, for example, with Simeon and Levi when Jacob refused to bless them because they had been men of such violence (cf. 49:5, 6).

But this initial experience with their unrecognized brother was a redemptive grace to their souls.

• *Guilt*. Their admission of guilt, the acceptance of responsibility for their sins, this real guilt, this godly guilt, put them in the way of forgiveness.

• *Fear*. Next their godly fear, the realization that God was afflicting them, focused their souls on the only source of forgiveness and help.

• *Sorrow*. And their godly grief and sorrow then paved the way for repentance.

They had meant to do evil to Joseph, but God meant it for good — to preserve his people (cf. 50:20). And now godly guilt and godly fear and godly sorrow were going to effect a trio of graces on these impossible men.

Friends and sinners, do you desire God's grace? If so, accept the guilt for your own sin. Do not blame anyone else. Such guilt is good. It invites God's grace. Along with this, cultivate a godly fear that reverently trembles before him. Such fear will invoke a graced wisdom in your life. And then own a godly sorrow that will lead you to repentance.

May God bless you —

• — with guilt,
• — with sorrow,
• — and with fear.

Amen!

61

Mercy in Egypt

GENESIS 43:1-34

Philosopher Cornelius Plantinga, Jr., draws this distinction between the sins of covetousness and envy:

> Envy is a nastier sin than mere covetousness. What an envier wants is not, first of all, what another has; what an envier wants is for another not to have it. . . . To envy is to resent somebody else's good so much that one is tempted to destroy it. The coveter has empty hands and wants to fill them with somebody else's goods. The envier has empty hands, and therefore wants to empty the hands of the envied. Envy, moreover, carries overtones of personal resentment: an envier resents not only somebody else's blessing but also the one who has been blessed.[1]

Envy was what drove Joseph's brothers to their murderous deed. They cared nothing about owning Joseph's beautiful coat. They tore it in pieces. What the brothers resented was Joseph's having the coat. And they resented his person even more than his possession of it. That was why they stripped him naked and beat him and tossed him in a pit to die.

Envy's wreckage litters the biblical landscape — from Cain who envied Abel to Saul who envied David — and, indeed, the landscape of our own existence as well. There are the public infamies like the 1989 Iowa high school love triangle in which Miss Harvest Queen strangled Miss Homecoming with her leather belt for stealing her boyfriend.[2] And there are also the hidden envies of the church as are sometimes seen in the halls of denominational conventions, of which an observer wrote, "Most of the conversation in the hotel rooms and the halls was characterized either by envy of those who were doing well or scarcely concealed delight for those who were doing poorly."³ Envy is a particularly degenerating sin. As Iago remarked about Cassio:

> He hath a daily beauty in his life
> That makes me ugly.
> OTHELLO, V, I

And here in Egypt, where the covenant community would be gathered for preservation and the genesis of a great nation, it was essential that this deadly sin be eradicated. Thus Joseph had some very personal questions that needed answering. Were his brothers the same envious bunch that they were years earlier? If the conditions were "right," would they again descend to the same murderous depths? How did they regard Benjamin, who now occupied the place of favor? Would they sacrifice him if it were to their benefit? All this Joseph determined to find out when his brothers returned with Benjamin, as he was confident they would.

DRIVEN TO EGYPT (vv. 1-14)

The worldwide famine was just as severe in Canaan as it was in Egypt. So in a short time the provisions that the brothers had carried back from Egypt were nearly depleted. Apparently there was just enough grain left for their families to survive while the brothers made the trip. So father Israel initiated the forbidden subject (the subject he would not hear of!) with a mini-mizing, face-saving suggestion: "Go again, buy us a little food" (v. 2) — as if it were a trip to the corner store. Of course, his boys rose to the subject, asserting that another trip to Egypt was useless unless they took Benjamin with them (cf. vv. 3-7).

Decisive dialogue. It was then that Judah, who had already spoken, took charge. In fact, from here on Judah, the number four brother, remained in ascendancy because number one son Reuben had diminished himself by incest (cf. 35:22), and sons two and three, Simeon and Levi, had likewise dis-qualified themselves by their blood-lust (chap. 34). Judah's leadership was firm, thought through, and straight to the point.

> And Judah said to Israel his father, "Send the boy with me, and we will arise and go, that we may live and not die, both we and you and also our little ones. I will be a pledge of his safety. From my hand you shall require him. If I do not bring him back to you and set him before you, then let me bear the blame forever. If we had not delayed, we would now have returned twice." (vv. 8-10)

Judah stood tall. He would be the boy's pledge. And if he failed, he would assume ineradicable, personal guilt forever. But now there was no time to dally.

Swayed by Judah's appeal, Jacob once again became his directive old self, giving explicit orders about a gift, money, and his son.

> Then their father Israel said to them, "If it must be so, then do this: take some of the choice fruits of the land in your bags, and carry a present down to the man, a little balm and a little honey, gum, myrrh, pistachio nuts, and almonds. Take double the money with you. Carry back with you the money that was returned in the mouth of your sacks. Perhaps it was an oversight. Take also your brother, and arise, go again to the man." (vv. 11-13)

There was irony here. The gift was of the same produce that the original caravan bore that first took Joseph to Egypt, including the silver! Life was coming full circle.

Israel's prayer. At last, with every provision made, Israel offered a heartening prayer. "May God Almighty grant you mercy before the man, and may he send back your other brother and Benjamin. And as for me, if I am bereaved of my children, I am bereaved" (v. 14). The opening phrase — "May God Almighty grant you mercy" — is not perfunctory rhetoric, because mercy is the narrative key of this entire episode. In fact, the events that would take place on the day of the brothers' arrival in Egypt were a demonstration of God's mercy. Near the conclusion of this section, in verse 30, when Joseph sees Benjamin, we read, "Then Joseph hurried out, for his compassion [or mercy] grew warm."[4] It is the exact Hebrew word that is translated "mercy" in verse 14. So we see that mercy frames the account from beginning to end.

Along with this, note that Father Israel's prayer invoked mercy in the name of "God Almighty" (*El Shaddai*), because the special designation *El Shaddai* in Genesis is associated with blessing and promises and a revelation of himself.[5] So we must understand that "May God Almighty grant you mercy before the man" is not a mere phrase. With this benediction Jacob gave his sons something to take with them that would steel them for the terrifying encounter that lay ahead.[6] We must remember that for the pious Hebrew, God is the most real of all realities. The sons were charged to go down to Egypt with the expectation that God Almighty would show them mercy.

The old man's closing words — "And as for me, if I am bereaved of my children, I am bereaved" — evoke a sense of deep resignation. Old Jacob reconciled himself to the will of God.

A FEAST FOR THE BROTHERS IN EGYPT (vv. 15-34)

There is no record of how long the hurried journey took the brothers to complete. We do understand that when they arrived and "stood before

Joseph," this description apparently refers to their standing before Joseph's representatives, because there was no verbal exchange between the brothers and Joseph. At the same time, we are told that Joseph saw that Benjamin was with them but did all his communicating through his steward. And further, we see that what he communicated left the brothers shocked and terrified, because he invited them to his house to dine with him at high noon (cf. vv. 16-18).

The brothers' fear. With multiplied thousands of foreigners seeking sustenance, why would the viceroy single them out for special attention except that he had some evil in mind? It was common knowledge that ranking Egyptian officials maintained private dungeons in their homes. The brothers were sweating! Thus their nervous wordy explanations:

> *And the men were afraid because they were brought to Joseph's house, and they said, "It is because of the money, which was replaced in our sacks the first time, that we are brought in, so that he may assault us and fall upon us to make us servants and seize our donkeys." So they went up to the steward of Joseph's house and spoke with him at the door of the house, and said, "Oh, my lord, we came down the first time to buy food. And when we came to the lodging place we opened our sacks, and there was each man's money in the mouth of his sack, our money in full weight. So we have brought it again with us, and we have brought other money down with us to buy food. We do not know who put our money in our sacks." (vv. 18-22)*

Their father's benediction — "May God Almighty grant you mercy before the man" — was the right prayer, though it appears that none of them remembered it. Joseph's brothers expected only the worst. And as their fears mounted, out of the blue came a second shock (a good jolt). "[The steward] replied, 'Peace to you, do not be afraid. Your God and the God of your father has put treasure in your sacks for you. I received your money'" (v. 23). He said, "Peace to you." He said that the God of their fathers had put treasure in their sacks! What? Were they hearing correctly?

They were! The Hebrew-speaking steward had responded *Shalom lakem*, "Peace to you," the traditional Hebrew greeting for receiving guests. It meant that the arriving guests were received in concrete terms of "peace" and security.[7] As the Aussies say, "No worries!" Mercy was beginning to flow. Amazing! *Shalom lakem* from an Egyptian! The steward's declaration, "Your God and the God of your father has put treasure in your sacks for you. I received your money" was not describing a miracle, like God dropping money in their sacks during a flyover. The steward knew who put the money into the sacks and was not trying to deceive the brothers, who also knew, of course — it was the steward himself. His point was that their God had been at work through human agents.

Astonishing. The pagan Egyptian steward instructed Israel's sons about God's providential care for them through the actions of other people. We wonder, did Joseph tell his steward to say all of this? Likely, but it makes no difference because he was expressing the absolute truth. Their father Israel's prayer — "May God Almighty grant you mercy before the man" — was being answered. Did they recall it? Probably not. Life was swirling around them. There was little time to reflect. And amidst this, Simeon, who had been hostage for two years, was brought out — no longer a hostage (cf. v. 23b). His presence spoke forgiveness. The charges of theft had been dropped.

And so, in a wondering dizzy state, the brothers busied themselves in the remaining minutes before noon, preparing to meet the viceroy. "And when the man had brought the men into Joseph's house and given them water, and they had washed their feet, and when he had given their donkeys fodder, they prepared the present for Joseph's coming at noon, for they heard that they should eat bread there" (vv. 24, 25).

The brothers meet Joseph. At noon the viceroy entered the room, and the brothers presented their gift and bowed low to the ground. Joseph's greeting to his brothers is one of the most beautiful scenes in the entire story of Joseph. Joseph's theme is *shalom*, for the word is used three times. "And he inquired about their welfare [*shalom*] and said, 'Is your father well [literally, "Does your father have *shalom*?"], the old man of whom you spoke? Is he still alive?' They said, 'Your servant our father is well [has *shalom*]; he is still alive.' And they bowed their heads and prostrated themselves" (vv. 27, 28). Both the viceroy and his yet-to-be-enlightened brothers were awash in peace and well-being.

This was so lovely, and the beauty of the meeting further elevated as Joseph engaged Benjamin. "And he lifted up his eyes and saw his brother Benjamin, his mother's son, and said, 'Is this your youngest brother, of whom you spoke to me? God be gracious to you, my son!'" (v. 29). In addressing Benjamin, Joseph communicated tender, paternal affection. And his "God be gracious to you" is the same word found in the Aaronic benediction of Numbers 6:25 — "the LORD make his face to shine upon you and be gracious to you" — indicating a special blessing, because these words do not appear elsewhere in the Old Testament.[8] Joseph invoked grace upon Benjamin with a unique expression.

With this, the meeting peaked. "Then Joseph hurried out, for his compassion grew warm for his brother, and he sought a place to weep. And he entered his chamber and wept there" (v. 30). As we noted earlier, the same Hebrew word is translated "mercy" in verse 14 and "compassion" here in verse 30, so that we can read, "his mercy grew warm for his brother," or as the Hebrew literally reads, "his mercies were heated up for his brother."[9] Father Jacob's prayer that God Almighty would grant them mercy before the viceroy had been answered. Indeed, it had been answered in every event of the day. Hot, tender mercies were served in the house of Joseph! And in private, hot tears flowed from Joseph's eyes as he wept alone. Joy and sorrow were surely mixed in those tears. But the joy was in what had begun that day and what was yet to come.

The brothers feasted. After regaining his composure and washing his face, Joseph gave orders.

> *"Serve the food." They served him by himself, and them by themselves, and the Egyptians who ate with him by themselves, because the Egyptians could not eat with the Hebrews, for that is an abomination to the Egyptians. And they sat before him, the firstborn according to his birthright and the youngest according to his youth. And the men looked at one another in amazement. (vv. 31b-33)*

They ate in their separate groups — Joseph alone as a social superior, the Egyptians by themselves because of religious scruples, and the Hebrews alone by elimination.

Here was hidden irony as Joseph hosted a meal for his brothers who years earlier had sat down to a meal while he pleaded with them for his life.[10] Again, such mercy. But whereas in the first meal he was the victim, now he was the victor.[11]

The mysterious accuracy of Joseph's seating them from oldest to youngest astonished the brothers. Joseph, they imagined, had been supernaturally enlightened as to their family. The feasting was laced with awe. Claus Westermann writes:

> The meal has an exalted meaning in both the Old Testament and the New Testament. . . . The simple satisfaction of hunger would not be considered a meal in the Bible. One need only remember the shared meals of Jesus and his disciples, the last of which demonstrates this in a special way. The meal is not just an expression of a communion (*Gemeinschaft*), but engenders and preserves this commonality. The acceptance of a guest into the fellowship of the meal is therefore simultaneously the granting of participation in one's own existence.[12]

Joseph had welcomed his brothers into his own existence. It would not be long until his father and scores of his nieces and nephews would join him in Egypt. Their shared existence would become eternal.

It was a grand feast with plenty of food and drink. And as it progressed, "Portions were taken to them from Joseph's table, but Benjamin's portion was five times as much as any of theirs. And they drank and were merry with him" (v. 34). Joseph was generous to all his brothers, but five times more so to young Benjamin. Joseph wanted to see what they would do with such favoritism. Would those old animosities and envies resurface? Happily, they did not.

It was a great day. Good things had happened that day, as Allen Ross explains:

> In this chapter the brothers promised to take the blame for any catastrophe (responsibility); they acknowledged their culpability and made restitution for the money in their sacks (honesty); they retrieved their brother from prison in Egypt (unity); they recognized that God was at work in their midst (belief); and they rejoiced in their provisions, even when a brother was receiving more then they were (gratitude).[13]

Mercy is written large over this account from beginning to end.

Father Israel's prayer had been answered. Mercy rained down on his sons all the day long. Joseph boiled over with mercy for Benjamin, and hot tears streaked his face. The feast was one of grace and mercy. The celebration went on into the night — "And they drank and were merry with him." The time passed with hilarity and pleasure. Their fears proved groundless.

But morning was coming. And with it was coming a test over Benjamin that would try their mettle. The day of mercy had been a beautiful beginning. But there was much more to be done. A day of severer mercy was about to dawn.

GOD MOVES IN A MYSTERIOUS WAY

God moves in a mysterious way
His wonders to perform;
He plants His footsteps in the sea,
And rides upon the storm.

Ye fearful saints, fresh courage take;
The clouds you so much dread
Are big with mercy, and shall break
In blessings on your head.

Judge not the Lord by feeble sense,
But trust Him for His grace;
Behind a frowning providence
He hides a smiling face.

WILLIAM COWPER, 1774

62

Transformation in Egypt

GENESIS 44:1-34

During the two decades that began with Joseph's brothers selling him into Egypt, God was not only with Joseph, as chapter 39 so emphatically repeats, but was also with his brothers, though in a very different way. God never gave their consciences rest. When at the end of those two decades the brothers traveled to Egypt for their encounters with Joseph, we see that God was with Joseph in his brilliant handling of his brothers and with them as they came to terms with their guilt.

During their first visit, recounted in chapter 42, God graced the brothers with guilt, fear, and sorrow. I say graced because they knew they were guilty, their fear was a godly fear, and they mourned over the effects of their sin. The posture of grace was taking shape in their lives. Then, during the first day of their second visit to Egypt as told in chapter 43, the brothers experienced an unexpected shower of mercy as Joseph's steward greeted them with peace/*shalom*, assured them that the money in their bags was from God, and released Simeon to them. They were again greeted with peace by Joseph, incognito, and feasted long into the night. Unknown to them, mercy had so welled up in Joseph's soul for his brother Benjamin that he retired to his room and wept. God was effectively with both Joseph and his brothers in their encounters. Grace and mercy attended their ways.

Now, as we take up chapter 44, we will witness a life-altering transformation of the brothers that will variously involve conscience, repentance, enlarged sympathies, intercession, sacrifice, and substitution — all wrapped in a growing brotherly love that speaks of Christ.

Under God's direction, Joseph's method was to reconstitute the temptation to which the brothers succumbed when they sold him into slavery. The temptation was at once a test and a path to transformation. This story, which has so many parallels to our own existence, is most powerful when we allow the events to speak for themselves as we follow the story line.

JOSEPH FRAMES HIS BROTHERS (vv. 1-13)

The setup. The brothers had eaten and drunk to excess. So while they were sleeping off their merriment, Joseph and his steward set them up.

> *Then he commanded the steward of his house, "Fill the men's sacks with food,*
> *as much as they can carry, and put each man's money in the mouth of his*
> *sack, and put my cup, the silver cup, in the mouth of the sack of the youngest,*
> *with his money for the grain." And he did as Joseph told him. (vv. 1, 2)*

A silver cup was, of course, valuable. But its use here involved Joseph's personal recollection that his brothers had sold him into slavery for twenty pieces of silver, so that "now he harasses and tests them with silver" (Sarna).[1] This nuance indicates how carefully calculated Joseph was.

With the rising of the sun, the groggy brothers rose, saddled their donkeys, and set off for Canaan. How relieved and happy they must have been as they reminisced over the day and the party of all parties. And now they had bulging sacks of grain plus their brother Simeon and young Benjamin. Soon the pagan pyramids would be far behind them. But the brothers had not journeyed far out of the city when Joseph ordered his steward to form a posse to pursue the brothers and deliver a precisely worded accusation.

The capture. Joseph's steward coolly carried out his orders, and when he caught up to the happy group, he repeated the accusation word for word: "Why have you repaid evil for good? Is it not from this that my lord drinks, and by this that he practices divination? You have done evil in doing this" (vv. 4b, 5). Stunned, and instantly indignant, the brothers shot back, "Why does my lord speak such words as these? Far be it from your servants to do such a thing! Behold, the money that we found in the mouths of our sacks we brought back to you from the land of Canaan. How then could we steal silver or gold from your lord's house?" (vv. 7, 8). Excellent logic. Do thieves voluntarily return valuables only to steal again? *Come on, Mr. Steward!* The brothers were so certain of their innocence that they volunteered an extreme punishment on themselves: "Whichever of your servants is found with it shall die, and we also will be my lord's servants" (v. 9).

The steward, ever so cool, acceded, likely with an inner smile: "Let it be as you say: he who is found with it shall be my servant, and the rest of you shall be innocent" (v. 10). In this he was kind and reasonable. No death — only slavery — and that for the guilty man alone. Was he mocking them with his reasonableness? Actually Joseph was interested in one man, Benjamin, and in what choices his brothers would make over him.

Incrimination. So the search proceeded with the imperturbable steward calmly overseeing it, as if he had no idea of what was about to happen. The brothers' swift compliance conveyed confident annoyance. "Then each man quickly lowered his sack to the ground, and each man opened his sack. And he searched, beginning with the eldest and ending with the youngest" (vv. 11, 12a). Reuben's bag was opened first, and the steward found nothing. Reuben drew himself up in glowering indignation and crossed his arms. The ex-con Simeon's bag was opened next with the same result, and then Levi's, and then Judah's. *Take that, Mr. Steward!* Then followed the sons of concubinage Dan and Naphtali and Gad and Asher. Again no silver cup. All eight stood frowning righteously. Next, Issachar and Zebulun passed the test. Likely, the brothers had begun to smile and to murmur about the steward, hardly paying attention to Benjamin's bag check. But in a horrifying moment the steward lifted the gleaming object out of the grain and held the silver cup triumphantly as it flashed in the morning sun.

No words are recorded, but the brothers' actions tell all: "Then they tore their clothes" (v. 13a). Wenham remarks, "When Joseph disappeared, it was only Jacob who tore his clothes (37:34); now all the brothers do, the first sign of fraternal solidarity."[2] Something new was taking place. They were changing. What would they do now? Would they surrender Benjamin and save themselves? No; they would not abandon their father's favorite son. They were not the same men who once so blithely sold their favored brother into Egypt. So it was that the brothers tore their clothes and went back weeping to the house from which they had just departed rejoicing.

JOSEPH INDICTS HIS BROTHERS (vv. 14-17)

It was still early morning. Joseph had not yet left his home to do business in the marketplace. "When Judah and his brothers came to Joseph's house, he was still there. They fell before him to the ground" (v. 14). This was an act of abject, groveling submission. Again this is a very subtle touch. Joseph had dreamed that the brothers would bow before him. And as the dreams were fulfilled, the act of bowing varied, giving a different nuance on each occasion.[3] Initially, in 42:6, "Joseph's brothers came and *bowed themselves* before him with their faces to the ground" (italics added). Next, in 43:28, "they *bowed* their heads and prostrated themselves" (italics added). And here, in 44:14, "they *fell before him* to the ground" (italics added). The bows of Joseph's brothers demonstrated the dynamic fulfillment of Joseph's dream. "The dream is happening. The future is at work toward life. But in their fearfulness, the brothers do not notice it" (Brueggemann).[4]

With his brothers groveling before him, Joseph maintained his stern pagan persona: "What deed is this that you have done? Do you not know that a man like me can indeed practice divination?" (v. 15). As to whether

Joseph practiced divination with his cup, the text is not clear. Divination was forbidden later in Israel as a pagan custom (cf. Leviticus 19:26; Deuteronomy 18:10). It is also referenced in a declaration of judgment upon Egypt (cf. Isaiah 19:3). Likely, Joseph was not into reading tea leaves!

But here, as Joseph represented himself as an imperious pagan ruler with divine powers, the brothers did not doubt his powers. They were in an impossible fix. There was absolutely nothing they could do. And it was amidst this despair that Judah stepped up. "What shall we say to my lord? What shall we speak? Or how can we clear ourselves? God has found out the guilt of your servants; behold, we are my lord's servants, both we and he also in whose hand the cup has been found" (v. 16). In wrenching frustration Judah repeated himself: "What shall we say . . . What shall we speak?" There was no way they could clear Benjamin before the implacable viceroy. But in the excruciating angst of the moment, Judah confessed their great long-standing guilt — "God has found out the guilt of your servants."

As Judah admitted their guilt, he understood that it was not the viceroy who uncovered it but God! Though innocent of stealing the cup, they were guilty — ever so guilty, guilty, guilty! It was God who was assaulting them at their most vulnerable point — Benjamin, the one whom their father had entrusted to them with so many misgivings, all of which were due to their sins against the earlier favored son, Joseph. Thus, through Judah's declaration of guilt they all accepted that God had uncovered their sin. And since they had all offended together, they committed themselves to suffer together — "We are my lord's servants, both we and he also in whose hand the cup has been found" (v. 16b).

Joseph heard it all but with remarkable restraint maintained himself as he added an excruciating twist: "But he said, 'Far be it from me that I should do so! Only the man in whose hand the cup was found shall be my servant. But as for you, go up in peace to your father'" (v. 17). Everything rested on what they would do with Benjamin. Joseph would punish only Benjamin! The reconstitution of the original situation of the favored brother had been achieved. Joseph had restored the original grouping of the earlier betrayal. There the breach had taken place between the father, the brothers, and the youngest son.[5]

The conditions were all perfect for a second betrayal, but at a more enticing price than twenty pieces of silver. The lure was their liberty.[6] For men who had valued their own well-being above all else, the temptation to walk away was appallingly tantalizing.

JUDAH'S INTERCESSION (vv. 18-32)

At this critical juncture Judah stepped forward and at great personal risk asked the viceroy if he could speak further. "O my lord, please let your servant speak a word in my lord's ears, and let not your anger burn against your servant, for you are like Pharaoh himself" (v. 18). Receiving silent consent, Judah fervently interceded for Benjamin's freedom, first by reciting the history behind Benjamin's presence in Egypt, and then, second, predicting what would happen if Benjamin was not allowed to return home. The speech conveyed a compelling eloquence and passion. In effect Judah presented the whole story in a nutshell, which made it possible for the viceroy (and for us) to reflect on the narrative as a whole. Judah must have delivered it in tearful emotion.

Retrospect. In retrospect, he argued that Benjamin's presence in Egypt was due to the viceroy's persistent questioning and insistence.

> "My lord asked his servants, saying, 'Have you a father, or a brother?' *And we said to my lord, 'We have a father, an old man, and a young brother, the child of his old age. His brother is dead, and he alone is left of his mother's children, and his father loves him.'* Then you said to your servants, 'Bring him down to me, that I may set my eyes on him.' *We said to my lord, 'The boy cannot leave his father, for if he should leave his father, his father would die.'* Then you said to your servants, 'Unless your youngest brother comes down with you, you shall not see my face again.' *When we went back to your servant my father, we told him the words of my lord."* (vv. 19-24, emphasis added)

Judah's retrospect was meant to respectfully implicate the viceroy. He subtly called the ruler's integrity and fair play into question.[7] Next, having implicated the viceroy, Judah recounted his father's fear of losing Benjamin.

> *"And when our father said, 'Go again, buy us a little food,' we said, 'We cannot go down. If our youngest brother goes with us, then we will go down. For we cannot see the man's face unless our youngest brother is with us.' Then your servant my father said to us, 'You know that my wife bore me two sons. One left me, and I said, Surely he has been torn to pieces, and I have never seen him since. If you take this one also from me, and harm happens to him, you will bring down my gray hairs in evil to Sheol.'"* (vv. 25-29)

As Joseph listened, he gained vital, heretofore unknown information. For the very first time he learned what had happened at home twenty years earlier when his brothers returned without him. He learned of his father's heartbroken cry — "Surely he has been torn to pieces" — and that it still echoed in Judah's and his brothers' consciences. Judah, of course, had no idea how heartrending this revelation would be on Joseph. Joseph also learned that Judah and his brothers now spoke differently about the favoritism shown to Rachel and her two sons, because Judah cited his father's favoritism for Joseph and now for Benjamin as a reason for Joseph to let Benjamin go.

Judah's quoting his father as saying, "You know that my wife bore me two sons" could be taken as a delegitimization of himself and his other brothers.[8] But Judah and his brothers had come to terms with Jacob's favoritism. Beyond that, they simply could not bear the thought of their father's misery. That the sons of the hated wife Leah had come to terms with their father's special love for Rachel and her two boys was amazing. That Benjamin, the second of these children, should now be loved by the other brothers was astounding. And that Judah could reference his father's favoritism of Benjamin as the reason for freeing Benjamin meant that a transformation had taken place in his soul.

Prospect. As surely as Judah's retrospect gripped Joseph's heart, Judah's prospect (about what would happen to Jacob if Benjamin was not released) penetrated Joseph like an arrow.

> *"Now therefore, as soon as I come to your servant my father, and the boy is not with us, then, as his life is bound up in the boy's life, as soon as he sees that the boy is not with us, he will die, and your servants will bring down the gray hairs of your servant our father with sorrow to Sheol. For your servant became a pledge of safety for the boy to my father, saying, 'If I do not bring him back to you, then I shall bear the blame before my father all my life.'" (vv. 30-32)*

Judah quoted their father's own words, but along with his brothers he assumed the responsibility should his father's gray head go down to Sheol in sorrow. By making the old man's lament their own, we see that there had been a monumental change in the brothers' hearts. Transformation had been effected in Egypt. The fledgling covenant community was moving toward a loving solidarity. The brothers had repented of their sin against Joseph. They had forgiven the unfair favoritism of their father. They so loved their father and his favorite son that they would not forsake Benjamin though the cost was immense.

The transformation was astounding. These men were wretches who had committed abominations. Sons two and three, Simeon and Levi, had conceived and executed the horrific deception and genocide of the Shechemites and had stood bathed in blood before their father, unrepentant, declaring, "Should he treat our sister like a prostitute?" (34:31). Reuben, the eldest, had committed incest with his father's wife, Bilhah, in an effort to gain ascendancy over his father (cf. 35:22). And son four, Judah, was a whoremonger who impregnated Tamar, the wife of his deceased son, thinking she was a Canaanite prostitute (cf. chap. 38).

JUDAH'S SUBSTITUTION (vv. 33, 34)

How remarkable this transformation was. But there was more because Judah's intercession culminated in sacrificial substitution as Judah stepped out of the brotherly circle and spoke for himself: "Now therefore, please let your servant remain instead of the boy as a servant to my lord, and let the boy go back with his brothers. For how can I go back to my father if the boy is not with me? I fear to see the evil that would find my father" (vv. 33, 34).

Judah had been transformed by the love of God. Dr. Barnhouse summarizes beautifully:

> Here was the eloquence of true love. . . . Love so burningly manifest, so willing to take full responsibility before God, love which thought only of Jacob and Benjamin, melted the heart of Joseph. Such love moved Moses to ask God to blot his name out of the book of life (Exodus 32:32); such love prompted Paul to wish himself accursed for his brethren if only they could be saved. Judah was transformed by divine love.[9]

Judah's personal transformation was extraordinary. Though his name means "praise," his early life had been anything but that. He fully participated in the near murder and sale of his brother into Egypt (chap. 37). His sexual behavior with Tamar became an infamy (chap. 38). But God was at work in his life in ways both observable and hidden. Judah's humiliation became the ground for a deep work of God (cf. 38:26). Here we see him as a man with great force of character. And ultimately his father Jacob saw Judah as the bearer of the line when he prophesied:

> *The scepter shall not depart from Judah,*
> *nor the ruler's staff from between his feet,*
> *until tribute comes to him;*
> *and to him shall be the obedience of the peoples. (49:10)*

As God would have it, Judah's willingness to suffer as a substitute for his brother foreshadowed the substitutionary, vicarious atonement of his ultimate Son, Christ Jesus, the Lion of the tribe of Judah.

We must never underestimate the transforming grace of God. Just as God was with Joseph and his brothers across those two almost silent decades, so he is with all his children. Transformation is concomitant with the gospel. In fact, it fairly detonates at conversion. The Greek of 2 Corinthians 5:17 reads, "*If any man in Christ, new creation,*" indicating an explosive transformation. Boom — new creation! And that is the universal experience of every believer. At the same time, conversion introduces a process of ongoing transformation until he appears, because "we know that when he appears we will be like him, because we shall see him as he is. And everyone who thus hopes in him purifies himself as he is pure" (1 John 3:2, 3).

The New Testament calls us to commit ourselves to transformation. "I appeal to you therefore, brothers, by the mercies of God, to present your bodies as a living sacrifice, holy and acceptable to God, which is your spiritual worship. Do not be conformed to this world, but be transformed by the renewal of your mind, that by testing you may discern what is the will of God, what is good and acceptable and perfect" (Romans 12:1, 2). Our role, therefore, is to engage in a sublime complicity. "Therefore, my beloved, as you have always obeyed, so now, not only as in my presence but much more in my absence, work out your own salvation with fear and trembling, for it is God who works in you, both to will and to work for his good pleasure" (Philippians 2:12, 13).

So, brothers and sisters in Christ, just as Judah and his brothers came to see that God was caring for them all the way along, so must we. God has always been, and still is, about the utter transformation of his people.

63

Reconciliation in Egypt

GENESIS 45:1-28

Joseph had mercifully orchestrated his brothers' second visit to Egypt to both test and, hopefully, transform their hearts. His method was to create situations that at once tried and revealed their character. Upon the brothers' arrival in Egypt, Joseph activated their fears by inviting them to a meal at his home. Why would he invite them to a meal except to assault them and seize their possessions? thought the brothers. But the meal was an astonishing feast, with the viceroy generously supplying them with portions from his own table, and five times as much to Benjamin. What a day it turned out to be.

Thus they never anticipated the events of the next day, when Joseph set them up by having his servant plant a silver cup in Benjamin's bag. And then, when the brothers were just out of town, he sent a posse after them to arrest them and to deliver a carefully scripted accusation. Predictably, this evoked indignant declarations of innocence from the brothers, as well as their suggesting extreme punishments for the guilty. What terror seized them when the gleaming cup was lifted from Benjamin's sack as they groveled hopelessly before Joseph.

What would the brothers do in this terrible situation? Would they sacrifice Benjamin to save their skins, as they had done with Joseph twenty years before, and for a far lesser price? Would they engage in finger-pointing? No, they would not, because Judah stepped forward and confessed not to the cup, but that God had found out their long-standing guilt. And then, in a long, impassioned speech on behalf of the brothers, he unwittingly revealed to Joseph that a transformation had taken place in their lives. Not only did the brothers admit their guilt, but they affirmed their love for their father (mentioning him fifteen times) and his now favorite son Benjamin. They had implicitly forgiven their father's favoritism. They had proved their integrity and family loyalty. Transformation had happened in Egypt! Judah himself stepped forward to take Benjamin's place, foreshadowing what the ultimate son of Judah would do in effecting our salvation.

At this point, there was nothing that could be gained by further tests. Judah's heartrending speech was too much for Joseph. Twice before Joseph had broken down — on the brothers' initial visit when he heard Reuben recount his cries when they sold him into Egypt (cf. 42:24) and then on their second visit when he saw young Benjamin and retired to weep alone (cf. 43:30).

REVELATIONS (vv. 1-13)

Joseph! This was for the circle of brothers, not for the outsiders. "Then Joseph could not control himself before all those who stood by him. He cried, 'Make everyone go out from me.' So no one stayed with him when Joseph made himself known to his brothers. And he wept aloud, so that the Egyptians heard it, and the household of Pharaoh heard it" (vv. 1, 2). The brothers, amidst the magnificence of the viceroy's castle with its saturnine frescoes and artwork of gold and turquoise and lapis and carnelian, watched in astonished fear as the muscular, beardless, empyrean viceroy wailed uncontrollably.

They were clueless, helpless, and trembling. And then they were rocked: "And Joseph said to his brothers, 'I am Joseph! Is my father still alive?'" (v. 3a). Judah's repeated mentions of his father and the descriptions of his delicate state had so gripped Joseph that his words were more a run-together exclamation than a question. Racked and shocked, the dumbfounded brothers stood mute in speechless terror. "But his brothers could not answer him, for they were dismayed at his presence" (v. 3b). Of this, Chrysostom wrote, "I am surprised at the way they could stand there and gape without their soul parting company with their body, without their going out of their mind or hiding themselves in the ground."[1]

Speech. Through his tears, Joseph saw their paralyzing terror. "So Joseph said to his brothers, 'Come near to me, please.' And they came near. And he said, 'I am your brother, Joseph, whom you sold into Egypt'" (v. 4). His clarification of identity, while intended to comfort, must have increased their fear — *"whom you sold," remember?* Then Joseph hurried to calm them, continuing tenderly, "And now do not be distressed or angry with yourselves because you sold me here, for God sent me before you to preserve life. For the famine has been in the land these two years, and there are yet five years in which there will be neither plowing nor harvest. And God sent me before you to preserve for you a remnant on earth, and to keep alive for you many survivors. So it was not you who sent me here, but God. He has made me a father to Pharaoh, and lord of all his house and ruler over all the land of Egypt" (vv. 5-8). Notice that there was not a hint of reproach, but only encouragement. It was apparent that Joseph had already forgiven his brothers. His repeated soothing statement, "God sent me before you" qualifies and softens "you sold me," indicating that he had forgiven them and that he was attempting to ease their guilt.

It is evident that Joseph had spent the last two decades perpetually praying, thinking, and rethinking what had been going on — and that God had given him wisdom. Just as Joseph had been given insight about the divine plan in the dreams of Pharaoh, he knew the divine plan in the affairs of his brothers.[2] So now Joseph stripped away the superficial surface of human activity to reveal the hand of God. Most revealing were his four references to God: "God sent me before you to preserve life" (v. 5b); "God sent me before you to preserve for you a remnant" (v. 7a); "So it was not you who sent me here, but God" (v. 8a); and, "God has made me lord of all Egypt" (v. 9b).

These lines are a magisterial, theological declaration of divine providence — that God works his will in and through the actions of all people, whether good or bad. Providence is explicit in Joseph's juxtapositions "you sold me . . . God sent me" (v. 5) and "not you . . . but God" (v. 8). Joseph understood that every episode in his life's story, and that of his brothers, was under God's direct rule. As Donald Grey Barnhouse summarized:

> The jealous hatred of brethren; the dreams of a youth; the passage of a caravan bound for Egypt; the preparation of Joseph by a life of adversity; the anger of Pharaoh and the imprisonment of two officials; the strange dreams of these prisoners and Joseph's supernatural gift of interpretation; the dreams of Pharaoh; the change of rainfall in a fourth of Africa to bring about the two cycles of abundance and famine by the flood and failure of the Nile; the elevation of Joseph to the throne of Egypt — all of these things were brought about naturally by the supernatural work of God who is Lord of all, in order to fulfill the counsel of His will.[3]

Consider also some of God's proverbs: "The heart of man plans his way, but the LORD establishes his steps" (Proverbs 16:9). "A man's steps are from the LORD; how then can man understand his way?" (Proverbs 20:24).

Understand that Joseph was not giving his brothers a theological lesson to set them straight but rather sought to comfort their transformed yet trembling hearts. How comforting to know that their sins, though they had caused immense hurt to Joseph and their father and themselves and many others, had not thwarted the plan of God but actually had been used to bring it about "to preserve life" (v. 5) and "to preserve for you a remnant on earth, and to keep alive for you many survivors" (v. 7).

Joseph was effecting reconciliation with his brothers. It was being made possible by two things: first his brothers' admission of guilt and repentance; and second, by Joseph's forgiveness that had been encouraged and enabled by his knowledge of God's providential care — "As for you, you meant evil against me, but God meant it for good, to bring it about that many people should be kept alive, as they are today" (50:20). The difficult past underwent a kind of alteration as Joseph embraced God's providence and forgave his brothers from his heart. Believers who see and embrace who God is and what he is doing in life forgive! Hatred and unwillingness to forgive comprise the province of hearts that are ignorant of God and his Word.

Having calmed his brothers with the comfort of the knowledge of God and forgiveness, he commissioned them to bring back his father, and to do it quickly. The charge began and ended with the admonition to hurry:

> "Hurry and go up to my father and say to him, 'Thus says your son Joseph, God has made me lord of all Egypt. Come down to me; do not tarry. You shall dwell in the land of Goshen, and you shall be near me, you and your children and your children's children, and your flocks, your herds, and all that you have. There I will provide for you, for there are yet five years of famine to come, so that you and your household, and all that you have, do not come to poverty.' And now your eyes see, and the eyes of my brother Benjamin see, that it is my mouth that speaks to you. You must tell my father of all my honor in Egypt, and of all that you have seen. Hurry and bring my father down here." (vv. 9-13)

The land of Goshen was identified with the land of Rameses (cf. 47:11), which was in the eastern Nile delta, a very fertile district.[4] Here at the close of Genesis God was blessing his people with a shadow of Eden. When Pharaoh restated Joseph's promise, he twice gave them the "best" (literally, "good") of the land (45:18, 20; cf. 47:6), unconsciously echoing the repeated "goods" of the land given to Adam. "The picture of Joseph is a picture of restoration — not just the restoration of the good fortune of Jacob but, as a picture, the restoration of the blessing that was promised through the offspring of Jacob" (Sailhamer).[5] An earth-shaking arrangement had begun.

RECONCILIATION (vv. 14, 15)

Now came the emotional reconciliation: "Then he fell upon his brother Benjamin's neck and wept, and Benjamin wept upon his neck. And he kissed all his brothers and wept upon them. After that his brothers talked with him" (vv. 14, 15).

The reconciliation was with *all* his eleven brothers. He embraced his little brother Benjamin and wept on his neck and Benjamin on his. So many tears, and such joy! And it was the same with the older brothers Reuben,

Simeon, and Levi. Confessions were whispered or bawled. Forgiveness was reiterated. And whatever the order, it was the same with Judah and Dan and Naphtali and Gad and Asher and Issachar and Zebulun. Kisses and weeping, kisses and weeping.

All the guilt was gone. Joyous love enveloped all. And they talked and talked and talked. About twenty years times twelve — some 240 plus years of catching up.

PROVISIONS (vv. 16-24)

Royal generosity. The amazing news quickly traveled up and down the Nile.

> *When the report was heard in Pharaoh's house, "Joseph's brothers have come," it pleased Pharaoh and his servants. And Pharaoh said to Joseph, "Say to your brothers, 'Do this: load your beasts and go back to the land of Canaan, and take your father and your households, and come to me, and I will give you the best of the land of Egypt, and you shall eat the fat of the land.' And you, Joseph, are commanded to say, 'Do this: take wagons from the land of Egypt for your little ones and for your wives, and bring your father, and come. Have no concern for your goods, for the best of all the land of Egypt is yours.'" (vv. 16-20)*

Pharaoh exceeded Joseph's generosity, offering the "best" (literally, "good") of the land, and the cartage to bring everyone and everything down to Egypt.

Extraordinary departure. Joseph presided over the memorable departure.

> *The sons of Israel did so: and Joseph gave them wagons, according to the command of Pharaoh, and gave them provisions for the journey. To each and all of them he gave a change of clothes, but to Benjamin he gave three hundred shekels of silver and five changes of clothes. To his father he sent as follows: ten donkeys loaded with the good things of Egypt, and ten female donkeys loaded with grain, bread, and provision for his father on the journey. Then he sent his brothers away, and as they departed, he said to them, "Do not quarrel on the way." (vv. 21-24)*

The clothes (festive garments) were intentioned symbols of reconciliation. Joseph's clothing had been central to his rejection, and now, memorably, clothing was bestowed by Joseph in reconciliation — and five changes for Benjamin — and no one cared! Joseph was so like the Savior himself.

Joseph's parting shot, "Do not quarrel on the way," was so appropriate, despite the goodwill. Squabbling and recriminations could so easily come on the slow journey back. "You were the one who argued for the pit." "No, but it was you who thought of selling him to the caravan." "You never liked him anyway!" The brothers had been told to cool it. And so they journeyed loaded up with ten donkeys laden with good things, ten she-donkeys for milk, plus the Egyptian wagons.

REVIVAL (vv. 25-28)

Their journey took them from the Nile, across the Sinai, through the Arabah, and across the Jordan.

> *So they went up out of Egypt and came to the land of Canaan to their father Jacob. And they told him, "Joseph is still alive, and he is ruler over all the land of Egypt." And his heart became numb, for he did not believe them. But when they told him all the words of Joseph, which he had said to them, and when he saw the wagons that Joseph had sent to carry him, the spirit of their father Jacob revived. And Israel said, "It is enough; Joseph my son is still alive. I will go and see him before I die." (vv. 25-28)*

How revealing the little statement is that Jacob's "heart became numb, for he did not believe them." His sons' lies with which they had hidden their guilt had rightly poisoned his trust in them. Such sins soil everything. What self-serving cruelty were his sons perpetrating now, he wondered. Literally, Jacob's "heart became weak." He felt that he might die. But his repentant sons, including Simeon fresh from prison and Benjamin whole and enthused, told him the astonishing story of Joseph and all his honor in Egypt. And then when he saw the wagons and donkeys laden with good things far beyond their means, "the spirit of their father Jacob revived." The gray-beard suddenly took on new life. Chrysostom provides the image:

> Just as the light of the lamp, when the supply of oil runs out and the light is on the point of going out, suddenly emits a brighter flame . . . when some-one puts in a little oil, in just the same way this old man . . . on the point of expiring from disappointment . . . next learned that Joseph was alive and was in charge of Egypt. . . . From being old, Jacob became young; he put aside the cloud of disappointment; he repelled the storm in his mind and then found himself at peace, with God disposing everything so that the good man should enjoy relief from all these awful trials and share the happiness of his son.[6]

Likely, with the help of his sons, he recalled Joseph's dream and his own incredulous, "Shall I and your mother and your brothers indeed come to bow ourselves to the ground before you?" (37:10b) — and rejoiced! But more, his lament at the story's very beginning was finally stilled. Jacob would not go down in sorrow to Sheol, but he would journey to see his son and die in peace.

There is grand optimism in this story. "God sent me . . . to preserve life," says Joseph. "God sent me . . . to preserve for you . . . many survivors" (45:5, 7). And later we will read, "God meant it for good" (50:20). As Wenham says, "The God of Genesis is a God of mercy (43:14) and grace (44:29), who answered Jacob's forlorn prayer 'May God almighty grant you mercy from the man, so that he sends back your other brother and Benjamin' (43:14) beyond his wildest dreams. But in so doing, God is not just proving his control of events but keeping his promise to the patriarchs that they should have a multitude of descendants, or as Joseph puts it, 'a great number of survivors.'"[7]

It was God who informed Joseph's heart as to the ultimate good that would triumph over his brothers' evil deeds.

And it was God who gave him the grace to forgive. Without forgiveness there never would have been reconciliation, regardless of his brothers' repentance.

Today, on this side of the cross, we can be reconciled because Christ forgives all who come to him in faith and repentance.

> *All this is from God, who through Christ reconciled us to himself and gave us the ministry of reconciliation; that is, in Christ God was reconciling the world to himself, not counting their trespasses against them, and entrusting to us the message of reconciliation. Therefore, we are ambassadors for Christ, God making his appeal through us. We implore you on behalf of Christ, be reconciled to God. For our sake he made him to be sin who knew no sin, so that in him we might become the righteousness of God. (2 Corinthians 5:18-21)*

64

Preservation in Egypt

GENESIS 46:1-34

Some four hundred plus years following Israel's entrance into Egypt at Joseph's invitation (as is described here in chapters 46, 47), Israel's descendants would make their astonishing exodus as a substantial nation (cf. Exodus 12:40-42; 14:17-22; Numbers 1, 2). The duel between Moses and Pharaoh would cast all of Egypt into mourning for their firstborn, which then left Israel free to go. Moses' initial act in the exodus was to remember Joseph's final request that his mummified remains be buried in Canaan (cf. Genesis 50:25-26).

> Moses took the bones of Joseph with him, for Joseph had made the sons of Israel solemnly swear, saying, "God will surely visit you, and you shall carry up my bones with you from here." And they moved on from Succoth and encamped at Etham, on the edge of the wilderness. And the LORD went before them by day in a pillar of cloud to lead them along the way, and by night in a pillar of fire to give them light, that they might travel by day and by night. The pillar of cloud by day and the pillar of fire by night did not depart from before the people. (Exodus 13:19-22)

Joseph's catafalque bearing his sarcophagus and his centuries-old remains, overshadowed by the pillar of cloud during the day and illumined by the pillar of fire by night, dramatically commemorated God's preservation of Israel in Egypt through Joseph's faithful offices. So we see ironically that some four centuries *before* the exodus, God had nestled an ark of salvation and preservation, figuratively speaking, right in the midst of the intense paganism of Egypt, from which the covenant nation would emerge. The story before us is about how God got his people into the ark.

ASSURANCE ABOUT EGYPT (vv. 1-4)

The news that Joseph was alive had at first almost killed Jacob because he thought it was another of his sons' wicked fabrications. But his numbed heart was revived by the material evidence, and his trademark determination returned — "I will go and see him before I die" (45:28). Jacob was apparently living in Hebron, near his family tomb, Machpelah, when he heard the news and set out from there for Egypt by way of Beersheba, which was about twenty-five miles to the west at the beginning of the desert expanse that extends to Egypt.

Worship. And it was there at Beersheba that he worshiped. Beersheba was especially rich in patriarchal history and devotion because there Abraham had made a covenant with Abimelech, named the place Beersheba, planted a tree, and called on the name of the Lord (cf. 21:23, 24, 31-34). And it was there that Abraham's faith had shone brightest in his willingness to sacrifice Isaac (chap. 22). It was also there that his son Isaac later experienced a theophany, built an altar, and was three times assured that the Lord was with him (cf. 26:3, 24, 28). And Jacob himself knew Beersheba well because it had been his home in the early days before he journeyed to Haran (cf. 28:10).

Beersheba's history, plus its being on the edge of the land, plus the momentous action of Jacob's leaving the land that God had promised to Abraham and Isaac, plus fears of what could happen in Egypt drove Jacob to God. "So Israel took his journey with all that he had and came to Beersheba, and offered sacrifices to the God of his father Isaac" (v. 1). Jacob's sacrifices were not burnt offerings, but offerings of thanks that Joseph was alive and, likely, vows to follow God.[1]

Visions. Jacob's fear-driven devotion was then matched by God's direct revelation to him. "And God spoke to Israel in visions of the night and said, 'Jacob, Jacob.' And he said, 'Here am I.' Then he said, 'I am God, the God of your father. Do not be afraid to go down to Egypt, for there I will make you into a great nation. I myself will go down with you to Egypt, and I will also bring you up again, and Joseph's hand shall close your eyes'" (vv. 2-4). At once Jacob learned that the revelation was in continuity with that given to his father and that he must not fear going down to Egypt for four divine reasons.

First, do not be afraid, "for there I will make you into a great nation." It was the same promise that God had originally given to Abraham: "And I will make of you a great nation, and I will bless you and make your name great, so that you will be a blessing" (12:2). God reiterated this upon the promise of Isaac's birth (cf. 17:19) and then repeated it through Abraham's angelic guests (cf. 18:18) — all implicitly underscoring the other prophecies about his having innumerable descendants. But the fresh revelation to Jacob was that his family would become a great nation "there" — in Egypt. Astonishingly, Israel would *not* become a great nation in the land of promise but on the pagan Nile! This was amazing but encouraging. Great things would come out of his move to Egypt. Thus he must not fear.

Second, do not fear because, "I myself will go down with you to Egypt." This recalled Jacob's dream of a ladder extending between Heaven and earth with angels ascending and descending upon it (cf. 28:12) and God's words, "Behold, I am with you and will keep you wherever you go, and will bring you back to this land. For I will not leave you until I have done what I have promised you" (28:15). God knows no territorial constraints. He was with Jacob in Mesopotamia and likewise in Canaan (cf. 31:3; 35:3), and now in Egypt it would be the same. Not to fear.

Third, do not fear because "I will also bring you up again." The use of the personal pronoun "I" and the grammar of the Hebrew make this statement very emphatic: "It is I that shall surely bring you up" — an emphatic personal prophecy by the God of the exodus![2] Likely, Jacob did not immediately make the connection of this promise with God's earlier prophecy in his covenant to Abraham — "Know for certain that your offspring will be sojourners in a land that is not theirs and will be servants there, and they will be afflicted for four hundred years. But I will bring judgment on the nation that they serve, and afterward they shall come out with great possessions" (15:13, 14). Jacob may have not made the connection, but as time passed, his descendants saw it clearly and took heart.

Fourth, do not be afraid because "Joseph's hand shall close your eyes." So Jacob learned that his long-standing fear of a sorrowful death was groundless because his beloved Joseph would be at his side for his peaceful homegoing and would gently close his stilled eyes.

DOWN TO EGYPT (vv. 5-27)

In the morning, as Jacob looked off to the south and west over the wastes to Egypt, he understood that Egypt would provide an ark of preservation for his people, from which they would emerge as a great people. His gaze across the expanse was that of faith. By faith everything and everyone near and dear to him would be transported to Egypt. By faith he would entrust his drought-stricken family to the offices of Egypt. By faith he would abandon the land promised to Abraham and Isaac, leaving it to the Canaanites until the cup of the Amorites was complete (cf. 15:16). The reality was that apart from the family tomb in Hebron, not an inch of land belonged to Israel. Only once, for the burial of Jacob, would they return. Thereafter, until the exodus, no child of the covenant ever entered the land.

Into Egypt. Significantly, Wenham has pointed out that some of the phraseology of their departure echoes key terms from the flood story — for example, "into Egypt" (twice), which parallels the two occurrences of "into the ark" (cf. 6:18-20), as well as the similar emphasis on bringing the entire family (cf. 6:18).[3]

> *Then Jacob set out from Beersheba. The sons of Israel carried Jacob their father, their little ones, and their wives, in the wagons that Pharaoh had sent to carry him. They also took their livestock and their goods, which they had gained in the land of Canaan, and came into Egypt, Jacob and all his offspring with him, his sons, and his sons' sons with him, his daughters, and his sons' daughters. All his offspring he brought with him into Egypt. (vv. 5-7)*

So it was that Israel began the journey into the unlikely safety of the ark of Egypt.

Seventy. Because the event was so momentous, the writer gives an extended list of the "seventy" who went down to Egypt. The list has definite symmetries. Both Leah and Rachel bear twice as many descendants as their maids. Leah has thirty-three, and her maid Zilpah has sixteen. Rachel has fourteen, and her maid Bilhah has seven. These numbers, 33 plus 16 plus 14 plus 7 = 70 (v. 27). However, the writer notes that only sixty-six (v. 26) made the trip because Er and Onan were buried in Canaan (v. 12), and Joseph and Manasseh and Ephraim were already in Egypt (v. 27). This equals sixty-five; so evidently Dinah (v. 15) must be added on to get sixty-six.

Confusing? It gets even more so when we see that Exodus 1:5 lists seventy but excludes Jacob from the calculation, but Deuteronomy 10:22 includes him in the number. Thus virtually all the major commentators agree with Nahum Sarna that:

> There is no way of satisfactorily solving the problem and reconciling the differences unless 70 is understood here to be a typological rather than a literal number. It is here used, as elsewhere in biblical literature, to express the idea of totality. Thus it reiterates, in another way, the point made in verses 1 and 6-7, emphasizing the comprehensive nature of the descent to Egypt because this event is seen as the fulfillment of Genesis 15:13.[4]

Israel, then, was God's covenant people in round numbers — the hope of the world in microcosm to be lodged in the ark of Egypt.

REUNION IN EGYPT (vv. 28-30)

The Egyptian wagons laden with the aged patriarch, the women, and his children and grandchildren must have been a forlorn spectacle as they lurched across the drought-parched desolation toward Egypt. Judah rode scout, guiding them to Goshen, the best of the land of Rameses in the Nile Delta.

It had been twenty-two years since Jacob had been told that Joseph was dead. Now word sped ahead that Jacob's seventy were in Goshen. Both father and son must have welled with joyous anticipation and possibly some trepidation.

The language suggests that Joseph arrived in style. "Then Joseph prepared his chariot and went up to meet Israel his father in Goshen" (v. 29a), likely surrounded with a great retinue of servants and runners. The phrase "he presented himself" (v. 29b) is always used elsewhere in the patriarchal narratives of God appearing to man, and its use here "draws attention to the overwhelming impression on Jacob of the power, grandeur, and graciousness of Joseph in his own chariot attended by numerous servants" (Wenham).[5] Jacob's son, the magnificent, liveried viceroy of Egypt, dressed in the fine white linen of aristocracy, descended from his chariot and "fell on his [father's] neck and wept on his neck a good while" (v. 29c). The eleven brothers and their wives and their children's children looked on with joy. At length the old man lifted his head and looked upon his son, and "Israel said to Joseph, 'Now let me die, since I have seen your face and know that you are still alive'" (v. 30). Virtually all of Jacob's recorded words after the supposed death of Joseph had been about death, but after the revelation that Joseph was alive, that all changed (cf. 45:28). Jacob's words are the Old Testament *Nunc Dimittis* that aged Simeon in the Christmas story would voice when he held baby Jesus: "Lord, now you are letting your servant depart in peace" (cf. Luke 2:29ff.).

Here Jacob beheld his son, his temporal savior, and said he could now die. Later Simeon would behold *the* Son, his eternal Savior, and knew he would die in peace.

ENTERING THE ARK (vv. 31-34)

When Joseph regained his composure, "Joseph said to his brothers and to his father's household, 'I will go up and tell Pharaoh and will say to him, "My brothers and my father's household, who were in the land of Canaan, have come to me. And the men are shepherds, for they have been keepers of livestock, and they have brought their flocks and their herds and all that they have"'" (vv. 31, 32). Joseph's emphasis to Pharaoh regarding his family's pastoral vocation was intentionally nuanced. Since the seventy brought their own livestock, they would not be an economic burden. And more, their interests in husbandry would discourage nepotism. But most of all, Joseph was subtly telling Pharaoh that Goshen was the best place for his flock-keeping family, as it was pastureland and at the edges of Egyptian society. In this respect, what Joseph told the seventy to say to Pharaoh was somewhat of a masterpiece of diplomacy.[6] "When Pharaoh calls you and says, 'What is your occupation?' you shall say, 'Your servants have been keepers of livestock from our youth even until now, both we and our fathers,' in order that you may dwell in the land of Goshen, for every shepherd is an abomination to the Egyptians" (vv. 33, 34). And it worked brilliantly, as the next episode will show.

Egypt had been miraculously opened up for the sake of Israel's family because though the Israelites were never permitted to eat at the table of an Egyptian, they were given the very best part of the land! Thus they were afforded both separation and prosperity.

What a grace the ark of Egypt was. There at the fertile borders of Egypt, the people of Israel benefited from the prosperity and protection of Egypt without surrendering their distinctives. There they honed their spiritual and national identity. There they grew from a mere handful to a great nation. There they later fell out of favor with a new regime that "did not know Joseph" (Exodus 1:8) and underwent the sanctifying graces of suffering. There they birthed their greatest of all leaders, Moses. There they experienced the mighty power of God as he effected the exodus.

The exodus itself was a singular grace, as the metaphoric words of God through Moses so memorably declare: "You yourselves have seen what I did to the Egyptians, and how I bore you on eagles' wings and brought you to myself" (Exodus 19:4). The ark, the sojourn, the deliverance were all from God. So it is with the second Moses, the Messiah, Jesus. Just as there was no salvation outside Noah's ark, there is none outside of Christ (cf. the *Second Helvetic Confession,* chap. 27). In Christ there is salvation and deliverance in the second exodus: "'Out of Egypt I called my son'" (Matthew 2:15). Now, as then, it is all of grace.

Every word of God came true. When Jacob died, Joseph had his father's remains embalmed, and Joseph himself went up with him with chariots and horsemen to Canaan, to Hebron, to Machpelah and interred Jacob with Abraham and Sarah and Isaac (cf. Genesis 49:28 — 50:14). And when the 430 years of Israel's sojourn were completed, and the cup of the Amorites was made full, Joseph's coffin was brought forth *first* as the exodus began. And the glorious presence of God accompanied them. A cloud by day and a fire by night rose above his remains and over all Israel. And Moses sang this song to the Lord:

> *I will sing to the LORD, for he has triumphed gloriously;*
> *the horse and his rider he has thrown into the sea.*
> *The LORD is my strength and my song,*
> *and he has become my salvation;*
> *this is my God, and I will praise him,*
> *my father's God, and I will exalt him. (Exodus 15:1, 2)*

This is the mighty God of our salvation.
This is Christ our redeemer.
This is the gospel!

65

Prospering in Egypt

GENESIS 47:1-31

In the rough-and-tumble of the court politics of the Nile, Joseph had so honed his substantial people skills that he was the rarest of men — both a saint and a politician. Joseph knew how to get what he wanted because he was attuned to how others thought (and especially the thinking of his direct superior, Pharaoh). He studied their rationalities and irrationalities. He was careful of their blind spots and prejudices. In the ups and downs, the ins and outs of life in Egypt he had learned to choose his words well. As the book of Proverbs would later say, "Whoever keeps his mouth and his tongue keeps himself out of trouble" (21:23). Joseph also was a master of timing. He knew when to speak and when to hold his tongue. He remains proof that shrewdness is not alien to holiness.

Joseph brilliantly employed his subtlety in his successful attempt to persuade Pharaoh to grant his family the land of Goshen, a rich pastureland safely at the fringes of Egyptian society. Joseph's strategy was simple: Knowing that Egyptians abominated shepherds, he made sure that he mentioned to Pharaoh that his family were shepherds and then instructed them to emphasize the same at their royal audience. His strategy was truly a masterpiece of court diplomacy.

STANDING BEFORE PHARAOH (vv. 1-13)

Royal audience. And that is not all, because in arranging for a royal audience for his family, he presented Pharaoh with a subtle *fait accompli*, mentioning in passing that his family was already in Goshen. "So Joseph went in and told Pharaoh, 'My father and my brothers, with their flocks and herds and all that they possess, have come from the land of Canaan. They are now in the land of Goshen'" (v. 1). Joseph was a clever, artful man devoted both to the welfare of Pharaoh and that of his own people. Joseph's care is also evident because he took only five of his brothers (likely the most outstanding) to the royal audience. Just as Joseph predicted, Pharaoh inquired about their occupation, and they "spontaneously" chorused, "Your servants are shepherds, as our fathers were" (v. 3b).

Very good! But then, on their own, they pushed the edge of the envelope, asking the king directly for the land of Goshen. "They said to Pharaoh, 'We have come to sojourn in the land, for there is no pasture for your servants' flocks, for the famine is severe in the land of Canaan. And now, please let your servants dwell in the land of Goshen'" (v. 4). Happily their overreaching raised no royal ire. But, likely, Joseph had held his breath. *Whew!* Joseph's strategy could not have gone better because despite Pharaoh's phobic regard for shepherds, Pharaoh's response went far beyond expectations. Because of Joseph, virtually boundless favor was extended to Jacob's family as Pharaoh, in courtly decorum, spoke to Joseph. "Then Pharaoh said to Joseph, 'Your father and your brothers have come to you. The land of Egypt is before you. Settle your father and your brothers in the best of the land. Let them settle in the land of Goshen, and if you know any able men among them, put them in charge of my livestock'" (vv. 5, 6). Unbelievably, in addition to keeping his initial promise of the best of the land (cf. 45:18), Pharaoh even offered the brothers employment as superintendents of the royal cattle.[1]

With the initial audience a success, Joseph next proceeded with the presentation to Pharaoh of his aged father. "Then Joseph brought in Jacob his father and stood him before Pharaoh, and Jacob blessed Pharaoh" (v. 7). The tottering old patriarch before the imperial magnificence of the supposed god-man Pharaoh was a picture of lingering beauty. Hoisted to his feet, Jacob stood amidst what was to him alien and oppressive luxury populated by the gawking officials and sycophants of the court of the Nile. Undaunted, Jacob was "sovereign old age personified: unimpressed by rank . . . diffuse and deliberate" (Kidner).[2] He cared nothing about courtly ceremonies or conventions. The king of Egypt encountered the father of the promise and — the promise-bearer held court.[3] But before there was an exchange, Jacob blessed Pharaoh with the first of two blessings.

Though his words are not here recorded, the widespread custom of the ancient Near East would be to wish the king a long life with something like "Long live the king!" (cf. 2 Samuel 16:16; 1 Kings 1:31). That may be why Pharaoh then respectfully asked about Jacob's age. "And Jacob said to Pharaoh, 'The days of the years of my sojourning are 130 years. Few and evil have been the days of the years of my life, and they have not attained to the days of the years of the life of my fathers in the days of their sojourning'" (v. 9). Since Egyptian literature listed 110 years as an idealized old age,

Pharaoh could hardly have anticipated the less than enthusiastic response of a man whose life exceeded that by two decades.

But old Jacob was not there to bend the truth. His life had been hard — his flight to Mesopotamia, his miseries at the hand of Laban, the rape of his daughter Dinah, his beloved Rachel's death, his eldest son's power-seeking incest, his favorite son's apparent death. Moreover, his years were few when compared with Abraham's 175 years and Isaac's 180 years. "Few and evil" was the unadorned truth. At the same time he was the blessed bearer of the promised blessing. So the audience concluded with the leathery old shepherd from across the steppes bestowing a second blessing on the king of the Nile. Jacob's double blessing of Pharaoh here is most significant. Pharaoh had first blessed God's people with his generosity. He had spared and promoted Joseph. He had personally invited Joseph's family to Goshen. He had sent grain to preserve them, and wagons to transport them to Egypt. And when they arrived, Egypt had received them royally.

So Jacob's blessing of Pharaoh was proper and also divinely sanctioned because God had earlier said to Abraham at the very beginning, "I will bless those who bless you, and him who dishonors you I will curse, and in you all the families of the earth shall be blessed" (12:3). Here, through Joseph and Jacob, the promise to Abraham was being fulfilled in blessing the great nation of Egypt. Pharaoh's immediate response was to give Israel the very best land, which unwittingly brought further blessing upon Pharaoh and his people. "Then Joseph settled his father and his brothers and gave them a possession in the land of Egypt, in the best of the land, in the land of Rameses, as Pharaoh had commanded. And Joseph provided his father, his brothers, and all his father's household with food, according to the number of their dependents" (vv. 11, 12).

Astonishing! Amidst worldwide famine Jacob and his sons were granted a permanent possession in Egypt "in the best of the land, in the land of Rameses" — a later name for Goshen. So in the throes of a deepening world starvation, God prospered his people. Who but a young man in a coat of many colors could ever have dreamed such a thing? Now the pitcher of God's blessing was poised to pour out blessing upon Pharaoh (Egypt) and Israel.

But before we focus our democratized, critical western eyes on how God effected the blessing, we must listen to the advice of Gerhard Von Rad:

> The expositor must resist as much as possible the question of the extent to which Joseph's measures stand the test of modern opinion. The ancient narrator is honestly amazed and wants the reader also to be amazed at the way an expedient was found to save the people from a gigantic catastrophe.[4]

We must remember that there was no welfare system and no concept of entitlements. Moreover, this was not Israel but Egypt. In later Israel, family members would help destitute relations by buying their land and employing them as servants or slaves (cf. Leviticus 25:13-55). And those who were thus indentured received their land back in the year of Jubilee, which was supposed to occur every fifty years. Egypt was not as enlightened or humane as Israel. And later Pharaohs were not as magnanimous as the present Pharaoh. Finally, by the standards of all the people of Egypt, Joseph was hailed for what he did as their earthly savior — the man who saved Egypt (cf. v. 25). The Egyptians loved him!

PHARAOH PROSPERS (vv. 13-22)

Pharaoh prospered as Joseph effected a plan that nationalized the land and the livestock and turned the Egyptians into tenant farmers, serfs.

All their wealth. Because Joseph had created great stores of grain, the famine brought the populace to purchase rations from his storehouses — and soon Joseph had deposited all the money of Egypt and of the surrounding countries in Pharaoh's treasury. Then when the money dried up, the people brought their livestock and bartered them for food. Whether the livestock were exchanged for grain or were mortgaged is not clear. Mortgaging would have been more practical.[5] In any event, after a year Pharaoh owned all the money and livestock in Egypt.

All their land. Next, all the land of Egypt became Pharaoh's.

> And when that year was ended, they came to him the following year and said to him, "We will not hide from my lord that our money is all spent. The herds of livestock are my lord's. There is nothing left in the sight of my lord but our bodies and our land. Why should we die before your eyes, both we and our land? Buy us and our land for food, and we with our land will be servants to Pharaoh. And give us seed that we may live and not die, and that the land may not be desolate." (vv. 18, 19)

Tenant farming became the norm, with Pharaoh providing the seed.

All the people. Inevitably all the people became Pharaoh's servants.

> So Joseph bought all the land of Egypt for Pharaoh, for all the Egyptians sold their fields, because the famine was severe on them. The land became Pharaoh's. As for the people, he made servants of them from one end of Egypt to the other. Only the land of the priests he did not buy, for the priests had a fixed allowance from Pharaoh and lived on the allowance that Pharaoh gave them; therefore they did not sell their land. (vv. 20-22)

In short order, all of Egypt, except the pagan clergy, were serfs. Pharaoh was indeed blessed! He could not have prospered more. He was richer than Rockefeller.

EGYPT PROSPERS (vv. 23-26)

At the same time, given the alternative of starvation, all of Egypt prospered. That was the national interpretation of it.

> Then Joseph said to the people, "Behold, I have this day bought you and your land for Pharaoh. Now here is seed for you, and you shall sow the land. And at the harvests you shall give a fifth to Pharaoh, and four fifths shall be your own, as seed for the field and as food for yourselves and your households, and as food for your little ones." And they said, "You have saved our lives; may it please my lord, we will be servants to Pharaoh." So Joseph made it a statute concerning the land of Egypt, and it stands to this day, that Pharaoh should have the fifth; the land of the priests alone did not become Pharaoh's. (vv. 23-26)

Again, as Nahum Sarna explains:

> Joseph's actions cannot be measured by the moral standards that the Hebrew Bible, especially the prophetic tradition, has inculcated in Western civilization. Rather, they must be judged in the context of the ancient Near Eastern world, by whose norms Joseph emerges here as a highly admirable model of a shrewd and successful administrator. Nonetheless, a moral judgment on the situation is subtly introduced into the narrative by shifting the onus of responsibility for the fate of the peasants from Joseph to the Egyptians themselves. The peasants initiate the idea of their own enslavement (v. 19) and even express gratitude when it is implemented![6]

As royal serfs, the Egyptians paid 20 percent to the crown — which was a normal percentage and even low in its day. Forty percent was not uncommon in Mesopotamia. And there are examples as high as 60 percent.[7] The happy result in Egypt was that the coffers were overflowing with foreign wealth, bolstering the economy. As the famine worsened, everyone in Egypt was equitably fed. And the 20 percent? No one complained about it. Joseph was Egypt's national hero. They all would have been dead without him.

ISRAEL PROSPERS (vv. 27, 28)

Astonishingly, through the offices of Joseph during the depths of prolonged famine, Pharaoh enjoyed unparalleled prosperity. Egypt also prospered (in that the people did not starve like the adjacent world). And most astonishingly, tiny expatriate Israel prospered. "Thus Israel settled in the land of Egypt, in the land of Goshen. And they gained possessions in it, and were fruitful and multiplied greatly. And Jacob lived in the land of Egypt seventeen years. So the days of Jacob, the years of his life, were 147 years" (vv. 27, 28). To emphasize how extraordinary Israel's prosperity was, the story uses brief descriptions of Israel's acquiring possessions to bracket the reference to Pharaoh's and his people's prosperity. The initial bracket is in verses 11, 12, which mentions, "Then Joseph settled his father and his brothers and gave them a possession in the land of Egypt, in the best of the land." And the closing bracket is here in verse 27, which again emphasizes Israel's accumulation of possessions.

Israel's prosperity far outstripped that of the average Egyptian! But not only did they gain possessions, they also "were fruitful and multiplied greatly" — both during the famine and after. From the beginning, Israel so flourished that one day it would force their persecution and exodus. Astonishingly, "the time in Egypt is not an interruption of the covenant but an incubation of the covenant people" (Walton).[8] What Israel experienced in miniature in Egypt was a foretaste of the ultimate blessings of Canaan when the land and its fatness would be theirs. Here in Egypt their abundance was all of God, just as it would be in fulfillment of the covenant.

Significantly, Jacob would have seventeen years with his son Joseph, which is exactly the same number of years they had together in Canaan before the treachery. Genesis is silent about these years, but a fast-forward to his ultimate age of 147 years suggests uneventful, unruffled tranquillity for both father and son. How sweet it must have been for Jacob and Joseph. No doubt these years were used to further inform and deepen Joseph for the further role he would play in God's plan. We are meant to see that all of this was God's careful doing. The duplicate periods of seventeen years are but tiny windows into God's sovereign plan. Remember that it was God who also orchestrated the seven years of prosperity and the seven years of famine. He is the one who declared to Isaiah, "I form light and create darkness, I make well-being and create calamity, I am the LORD, who does all these things" (45:7). Thus we understand that God literally compelled Israel to move to Egypt by force of circumstances for a prosperous four-hundred-year period of incubation.

The truth that is written bold here in the history of God's people is given to us so that we might see something of God's hand as he works to prosper his people. This side of the cross we observe it in his sovereign arrangement in the life of someone like Zacchaeus as his heart was softened and prepared by life so that when Christ passed under the tree where he was sitting, the Savior looked up, locked eyes, and said, "Zacchaeus, hurry and come down" (Luke 19:5). That glad leap with which rich, little

Zacchaeus dismounted the tree began a life of true prosperity as he proclaimed, "Behold, Lord, the half of my goods I give to the poor. And if I have defrauded anyone of anything, I restore it fourfold" (v. 8). Such are the beginnings for all of us, though unseen and probably less dramatic.

As God's children, we become subjects of his persistent prosperity as he brings calamity and well-being to effect the prosperity of our souls. Everything we endure and enjoy — all our relationships, all our honors, all our defects, all our serendipities, all our disappointments, all our gains and losses — are meant for our ultimate prosperity.

Three great epigrams of this principle rise prominently across the landscape of Scripture. Joseph voiced it first in Genesis 50:20, "As for you, you meant evil against me, but God meant it for good, to bring it about that many people should be kept alive, as they are today." The apostle Paul's New Testament counterpart is, of course, Romans 8:28 — "And we know that for those who love God all things work together for good, for those who are called according to his purpose." The other memorable epigram is voiced by God himself through Jeremiah in Jeremiah 29:11: "For I know the plans I have for you, declares the LORD, plans for wholeness and not for evil, to give you a future and a hope." In that prophet's day, at the beginning of the hardships of the captivity, God assured his people that all his plans for them were for their wholeness (*shalom*). There was not an ounce of evil in the conception, implementation, and consummation of those plans. The apparent evil they suffered was for their good — to give them "a future and a hope" — ultimate prosperity! Seeing and believing this will change your life.

JACOB FACES DEATH (vv. 29-31)

At age 130 Jacob had almost died at the first news that Joseph was alive, but as he learned that it was really true, his spirit revived (cf. 45:27), and he lived for seventeen more years. But now came the end.

> And when the time drew near that Israel must die, he called his son Joseph and said to him, "If now I have found favor in your sight, put your hand under my thigh and promise to deal kindly and truly with me. Do not bury me in Egypt, but let me lie with my fathers. Carry me out of Egypt and bury me in their burying place." He answered, "I will do as you have said." And he said, "Swear to me"; and he swore to him. Then Israel bowed himself upon the head of his bed. (vv. 29-31)

Jacob so wanted to be buried in Canaan in the cave of Machpelah with the bones of Abraham and Isaac that he doubly bound his viceroy son to personally take his bones back to Canaan. In doing this he consciously imitated Abraham when he made his servant Eliezer place his hand under his thigh and swear that he would not take a wife for Isaac from among the Canaanites, but from his own kin in Mesopotamia (cf. Genesis 24:1-4). Here, after getting Joseph to swear that he would not bury him in Egypt, Jacob asked for a second oath from his son that in effect placed Joseph under God's wrath should he go back on his promise. This oath called for gravity and intense life-and-death resolve.[9] Upon Joseph's solemn oath, the old bedridden patriarch bowed as best he could and worshiped.

Why this almost desperate demand for assurance that his bones be interred in the promised land? Certainly Jacob knew that wherever he died, he would go to be with his fathers. The reason for the demand was that burying his remains in Canaan was a declaration of his faith in the promise of the land to Abraham and his seed forever (15:17ff.). Abraham had purchased the tomb for Sarah in faith, and he himself had been buried next to her in faith. And there Isaac's bones had been laid alongside theirs in faith. Like them, Jacob in faith looked to the ultimate prosperity.

One of the most famous chapters in the Bible, Ezekiel 37, gives dramatic reference to this great hope.

> The hand of the LORD was upon me, and he brought me out in the Spirit of the LORD and set me down in the middle of the valley; it was full of bones. And he led me around among them, and behold, there were very many on the surface of the valley, and behold, they were very dry. And he said to me, "Son of man, can these bones live?" And I answered, "O Lord GOD, you know." Then he said to me, "Prophesy over these bones, and say to them, O dry bones, hear the word of the LORD. Thus says the Lord GOD to these bones: Behold, I will cause breath to enter you, and you shall live. And I will lay sinews upon you, and will cause flesh to come upon you, and cover you with skin, and put breath in you, and you shall live, and you shall know that I am the LORD."
>
> So I prophesied as I was commanded. And as I prophesied, there was a sound, and behold, a rattling, and the bones came together, bone to its bone. And I looked, and behold, there were sinews on them, and flesh had come upon them, and skin had covered them. But there was no breath in them. Then he said to me, "Prophesy to the breath; prophesy, son of man, and say to the breath, Thus says the Lord GOD: Come from the four winds, O breath, and breathe on these slain, that they may live." So I prophesied as he commanded me, and the breath came into them, and they lived and stood on their feet, an exceedingly great army.
>
> Then he said to me, "Son of man, these bones are the whole house of Israel. Behold, they say, 'Our bones are dried up, and our hope is lost; we are clean cut off.' Therefore prophesy, and say to them, Thus says the Lord GOD: Behold, I will open your graves and raise you from your graves, O

my people. And I will bring you into the land of Israel. And you shall know that I am the LORD, when I open your graves, and raise you from your graves, O my people." (vv. 1-13)

Rest assured that everything that comes to us in this life, whether we regard it as good or evil, is meant to prosper us. And more, those who regard us with favor will be blessed as they heed our words about Christ. And finally, one day these old rattling bones will be on their feet dancing.

66

Faith and Blessing

GENESIS 48:1-22

Often when people of faith come to death, they see life with a greater clarity. As the poet Edmund Waller wrote:

> *The soul's dark cottage, battered and decayed,*
> *Lets in new light through chinks that time has made.*

We see this in an old barn whose roof and siding have begun to bow and sag so that shafts of light beam through like searchlights. This was certainly true in the life of the patriarch Jacob. His believing eyes afforded him a clear vision of the future for both himself and his sons. That is why he had demanded a double-oath from Joseph that he take his bones back to Canaan and inter them there — his eye of faith saw his people as one day returning to Canaan.

Thus as his death approached, old Jacob's soul rose above his material existence in Egypt to an exercise of faith so extraordinary that the New Testament's "Hall of Faith," Hebrews 11, selected it as the singular event that characterized him as a man of faith — namely, the blessing of Joseph's sons Ephraim and Manasseh. "By faith Jacob, when dying, blessed each of the sons of Joseph, bowing in worship over the head of his staff" (v. 21). Again, as earlier in his life, this would involve a surprising reversal that went against the natural order and expectations of this life.

Jacob's faith-blessing was occasioned when Joseph, his viceroy son, learned that he was ill (incidentally the first reference to illness in the Bible): "After this, Joseph was told, 'Behold, your father is ill.' So he took with him his two sons, Manasseh and Ephraim. And it was told to Jacob, 'Your son Joseph has come to you.' Then Israel summoned his strength and sat up in bed" (vv. 1, 2). With immense terminal resolve the dying patriarch sat up in his bed. And though there was no act other than the blessing recorded here, the Hebrews 11 reference describes it as worship. This is because to believe God's word, and to base everything in the future upon his word, is worship!

ADOPTION (vv. 3-13)

Joseph came to his dying father with his two half-Egyptian sons in expectation of obtaining the patriarch's blessing. Tellingly, Joseph's humble presence was itself an act of submissive faith because he had come to personally identify his boys with God's people. Such identification with the shepherd clan (so abominated by the Egyptians) would ultimately shut them off to Egyptian prominence. Joseph's presence with his sons was a by-faith exercise in downward mobility.

Promise recalled. As Joseph and Manasseh and Ephraim stood expectantly before Jacob, the patriarch recalled the promise that undergirded what he was about to do. "And Jacob said to Joseph, 'God Almighty appeared to me at Luz in the land of Canaan and blessed me, and said to me, "Behold, I will make you fruitful and multiply you, and I will make of you a company of peoples and will give this land to your offspring after you for an everlasting possession"'" (vv. 3, 4). God had appeared to Jacob twice in Luz, the old name for Bethel. The first appearance was when Jacob was fleeing the wrath of Esau, and God gave him the vision of heavenly angels ascending and descending on his behalf — accompanied with the verbal promise of the land on which he lay and offspring like the dust of the earth (cf. 28:12-14). The second appearance was again at Bethel when he returned after a twenty-year absence, and it is the source for the terminology that Jacob used here (cf. 35:11-15).

Those monumental affirmations of the promise at Bethel echoed the words of the promise made to Abraham and to his father Isaac and reflect the creation commandment to be fruitful and multiply (cf. 1:28). The point of Jacob's recollections of the promises here is that as heir to those promises, he had the right to decide to whom they would go with his blessing. This was a moment of immense power. Jacob's covenant recollections were redolent with faith that God would fulfill the promises through him.

Formal adoption. Having established his authority to bestow the blessing, Jacob then informed Joseph of his intentions. "And now your two sons, who were born to you in the land of Egypt before I came to you in Egypt, are mine; Ephraim and Manasseh shall be mine, as Reuben and Simeon are" (v. 5). The literal Hebrew reads, "Like Reuben and Simeon they will be to me" — that is, these boys would become the firstborn sons of Jacob.[1] Ephraim and Manasseh would become *not* Jacob's grandsons, but sons number one and two. They displaced Reuben and Simeon!

First Chronicles 5:1, 2 describes what happened: "The sons of Reuben the firstborn of Israel (for he was the firstborn, but because he defiled his father's couch, his birthright was given to the sons of Joseph the son of Israel, so that he could not be enrolled as the oldest son; though Judah became strong among his brothers and a chief came from him, yet the birthright belonged to Joseph)."

What an astonishing revelation. Jacob claimed them as twice "mine" (Genesis 48:5) — replacements for the senior uncles. Joseph had other children besides Ephraim and Manasseh. What of them? Jacob anticipated the question before Joseph could ask. "And the children that you fathered after them shall be yours. They shall be called by the name of their brothers in their inheritance" (v. 6). In the future, his other children would be incorporated into the tribes of Ephraim and Manasseh.

As we know, Joseph was the firstborn child of Jacob's beloved wife Rachel. And now Joseph's likeness to his mother (both he and his mother were unusually attractive) caused the dying old patriarch to recall an event painful to both himself and his son — the death of lovely Rachel (v. 7). As Jacob reminisced, his old frame coursed with emotion. As Barnhouse has it, "His mind was like an autumn when sun and shadows alternate across the valley. He had been out in the sun, and then came the clouds."[2] Jacob spoke poignantly. "As for me, when I came from Paddan, to my sorrow Rachel died in the land of Canaan on the way, when there was still some distance to go to Ephrath, and I buried her there on the way to Ephrath (that is, Bethlehem)."

Rachel had been the love of his life. He had worked fourteen years for her. And her untimely death cut her childbearing short and prevented his burying her in the family tomb. But now Rachel's firstborn son Joseph could extend her line by Joseph's giving his sons to Jacob as direct heirs.

Many scholars believe that the principal details of the interaction between Jacob and Joseph and his sons in verses 8-13 are specifics of a formal adoption process that began in verse 8 with Jacob's question, "Who are these?" — a question that functioned in a way similar to the question that begins modern-day marriages — "Who gives this woman to be married to this man?"[3] The ceremonial response, "Her mother and I do" is paralleled by Joseph's ceremonial response. Following this, Jacob's kiss and embrace of the boys were significant gestures in the adoption process (v. 10).[4] Lastly, Jacob's removal of his sons from his knees and bowing with his face to the earth was a consummating gesture of the adoption (v. 12).

This done, "Joseph took them both, Ephraim in his right hand toward Israel's left hand, and Manasseh in his left hand toward Israel's right hand, and brought him near him" (v. 13). Joseph's positioning of his sons made it convenient for his nearly blind father to place his right hand (the hand symbolic of action and power) on the head of the firstborn Manasseh and his left hand on Ephraim's head. The immense importance that this had for

Joseph is seen in the precision of the language, with the repeated use of "right" and "left" seven times in combination.[5]

BLESSING (vv. 14-20)

Here the drama intensifies as we follow every movement: "And Israel stretched out his right hand and laid it on the head of Ephraim, who was younger, and his left hand on the head of Manasseh, crossing his hands (for Manasseh was the firstborn)" (v. 14). Joseph, momentarily dumbfounded and speechless, was unable to respond as his father intoned the patriarchal blessing in a threefold invocation of God's name that recalled God's faithful dealings with his people.

And he blessed Joseph and said,

> *"The God before whom my fathers Abraham and Isaac walked,*
> *the God who has been my shepherd all my life long to this day,*
> *the angel who has redeemed me from all evil, bless the boys;*
> *and in them let my name be carried on, and*
> *   the name of my fathers Abraham and Isaac;*
> *and let them grow into a multitude in the midst of the earth." (vv. 15, 16)*

Such a lovely blessing in the name of the God who walks with, shepherds, and redeems his people.

Jacob's new sons had been mightily blessed!

REVERSAL

But now Joseph had recovered his wits. And he was not happy. Joseph did manage to control his language in deference to his father's age and infirmity. But his anger is indicated by his reflexive action, because the phrase "he took his father's hand" (v. 17) describes a firm grip, and his abrupt command, "Not this way, my father" (v. 18) exudes exasperation.

Joseph was appalled. His father had transgressed every tradition from the Nile to the Euphrates. Joseph knew his sons intimately, and there could be no logical reason for Jacob to elevate Ephraim over Manasseh. All Manasseh's years had been lived with the privilege and expectation of the firstborn. As Manasseh's father, Joseph had worked to instill firstborn character and a requisite sense of responsibility in his oldest boy. This humiliation was an undeserved wound. Why had the old man crossed his hands? Was it because of his near-blindness? Or was it his inveterate, heel-grabbing perversity?

In any event the deed was done. Blessings once uttered could not be undone (cf. 27:34-37). Since Isaac's unwitting blessing of Jacob could not be reversed (though Jacob had deceived his father), how much more immutable was Jacob's deliberate blessing of Ephraim over Manasseh. Jacob could not reverse it, even if he wanted to. And he did not wish to change a word — because the blessing did not originate with him, but with God. He was only the messenger. His crossed hands of blessing were an act of profound faith. That is the divine assessment. "By faith Jacob, when dying, blessed each of the sons of Joseph, bowing in worship over the head of his staff" (Hebrews 11:21).

It had taken Jacob a lifetime of divine discipline to learn that he must only speak and do the word of God. Now he dared to trust God and believe his plans were best. He dared to do God's will despite the wishes of his illustrious, godly son. Jacob had "cast his anchor into the will of God forever" (Barnhouse).[6]

Reversal confirmed. So now the faith-driven, old patriarch calmly continued with his right hand firmly placed upon the head of the younger son.

> *But his father refused and said, "I know, my son, I know. He also shall become a people, and he also shall be great. Nevertheless, his younger brother shall be greater than he, and his offspring shall become a multitude of nations." So he blessed them that day, saying,*

> > *"By you Israel will pronounce blessings, saying,*
> > *'God make you as Ephraim and as Manasseh.'"*

> *Thus he put Ephraim before Manasseh. (vv. 19, 20)*

The two boys' names would become the proverbial formula for invoking blessing — code words for wondrous destiny. And both sons were astonishingly blessed. Manasseh would become "a people," but Ephraim would become "a multitude of nations." In Egypt and at the exodus, Ephraim and Manasseh were great tribes indeed. At one time the name Ephraim was used as a synonym for the kingdom of Israel.[7] However, in the long run both tribes would apostatize, and the tribe of Judah would take on the mantle and ascendancy. Psalm 78 describes their tragic demise (cf. 2 Kings 17).

But here, in Jacob's handling of Ephraim and Manasseh, we see the crossed hands of blessing — and thus we clearly understand at the end of Jacob's life and the book of Genesis that God's grace must never become captive to position or privilege or heredity or expectation or tradition or convention or disposition. God's grace is sovereign. It cannot be tamed. The economy of grace operates on its own principles — humbling human wisdom and exalting the unlikely, so that the last are often the first, and the first last.

This is repeated again and again in Genesis. In primeval history, the older brother Cain had his offering rejected, while that of the younger, Abel, was accepted. Then with the line of Seth, the even younger brother became the chosen line (cf. 4:25 — 5:8). In patriarchal times, young Isaac was chosen over Ishmael (cf. 17:18, 19). Then Jacob was chosen over Esau (cf. chap. 27). Jacob's son Joseph was chosen over his older brethren (cf. 37:5-7, 9). And now Ephraim was chosen above Manasseh. Indeed, the last are often first, even for Christ. "He came to his own, and his own people did not receive him. But to all who did receive him, who believed in his name, he gave the right to become children of God, who were born, not of blood nor of the will of the flesh nor of the will of man, but of God" (John 1:11-13).

The crossed hands of blessing tell us that grace typically surprises. "But God chose what is foolish in the world to shame the wise; God chose what is weak in the world to shame the strong; God chose what is low and despised in the world, even things that are not, to bring to nothing things that are, so that no human being might boast in the presence of God" (1 Corinthians 1:27-29). This is what makes the gospel so wild and wonderful. Because no one is beyond God's grace, the proudest, baddest, meanest man in town can, and often does, find grace. There is a wildness to God's mercy!

And when it comes to living a life of faith, the crossed hands of blessing provide essential wisdom. Marcus Dods, Victorian-era principal of New College Edinburgh, comments about our common experience:

> Again and again, for years together, we put forward some cherished desire to God's right hand, and are displeased, like Joseph, that still the hand of greater blessing should pass to some other thing. Does God not know what is oldest with us, what has been longest at our hearts, and is dearest to us? Certainly he does: "I know it, My son, I know it," He answers to all our expostulations. It is not because He does not understand or regard your predilections, your natural and excusable preferences that He sometimes refuses to gratify your whole desire, and pours upon you blessings of a kind somewhat different from those you most earnestly covet. He will give you the whole that Christ hath merited; but for the application and distribution of that grace and blessing you must be content to trust Him.[8]

All this calls for faith, both for salvation and living. Just as Jacob pulled back from trusting his own wisdom and predilections and trusted God's word, so must we. God calls us to trust in him alone. This is what old Jacob did in the last hours of his life — and this is where he experienced the pleasure and praise of God as recorded in the "Hall of Faith" found in the book of Hebrews.

GIFT (vv. 21, 22)

And what of Joseph's faith?

It was remarkable. In giving his two sons to Jacob, he was virtually consenting to their being rejected in respect to a future and position in Egypt.

By identifying his sons with the despised sheepherding people, Joseph sealed them off from ascendancy. It was madness from the perspective of the Nile. But like his father Jacob, Joseph believed the word of promise — that God was building a great people who would one day return to the land of promise. Though Joseph apparently lived out his career as viceroy of Egypt, there is no record of any of his children attaining rank during the next four hundred years in Egypt. Thus, by faith Joseph lived without currying the favor of Egypt. In this he was very much like the future Moses, who is also celebrated in the Hall of Faith: "By faith Moses, when he was grown up, refused to be called the son of Pharaoh's daughter, choosing rather to be mistreated with the people of God than to enjoy the fleeting pleasures of sin. He considered the reproach of Christ greater wealth than the treasures of Egypt, for he was looking to the reward" (Hebrews 11:24-26). Joseph had made a similar choice, and he did it with like faith.

And understanding this, we understand something of the significance of Jacob's gift to Joseph. "Then Israel said to Joseph, 'Behold, I am about to die, but God will be with you and will bring you again to the land of your fathers. Moreover, I have given to you rather than to your brothers one mountain slope that I took from the hand of the Amorites with my sword and with my bow'" (vv. 21, 22). This "mountain slope" is almost certainly a reference to a plot in the land of Shechem inside the promised land. The Hebrew for "one mountain slope" is literally "one Shechem" — so that it can be translated, "And I, I give Shechem to you — O one above your brothers — which I took from the hand of the Amorites with my sword and my bow."[9] Jacob had purchased a plot of land from Hamor, the king of Shechem, for a hundred pieces of money (33:19) and had never approved of the subsequent violence with which his sons had taken Shechem, though their violence (his sword) made the land *de facto* doubly his to give.

Joseph accepted from his father the plot in Shechem in faith. And when Joseph died, his bones were carried out first in the exodus, and after the conquest of Canaan, Joshua buried them in Shechem — which was in Ephraim, the land of the blessed son (cf. Joshua 24:32).

Genesis 48 gives a remarkable portrait of an old man who took full charge of his own death. His faith on his deathbed was the singular triumph of his life. And there, while he did nothing that today is commonly referred to as worship, as there was no prayer or song, he intensely worshiped. This is because we worship when we, *by faith*, trust God for all of life and give ourselves to him (cf. Romans 12:1, 2). By faith Jacob crossed his hands in worship and blessed his adopted sons as he surrendered his life and the future of his people to God's word. And his sunset faith unleashed the wild grace of God to do its wondrous work in the generations to come.

67

The Testament of Jacob I

GENESIS 49:1-12

Jacob's death in his 147th year came expectedly. His health had been precarious before he was carted down to Egypt at age 130 (cf. 44:30, 31; 45:26). The past seventeen years in the land of Goshen where his beloved Joseph was viceroy of the Nile had been an unexpected grace. But now he could sense that life truly was slipping away, that he was rising above the material plane for his ascent. Thus Jacob had summoned his viceroy son and made him solemnly swear that he would carry his bones from Egypt and bury him with his fathers (cf. 47:29-31).

The viceroy had in turn brought his sons Ephraim and Manasseh to his father for what turned out to be an extraordinary blessing as the patriarch crossed his hands over the boys as he intoned their blessings (cf. 48:12-20). Now on his deathbed it was time for Jacob's final patriarchal blessing, which is introduced in chapter 49. "Then Jacob called his sons and said, 'Gather yourselves together, that I may tell you what shall happen to you in days to come'" (v. 1).

Confined to his bed, old Jacob had become accustomed to a new angle of sight, looking at his tent's ceiling and the distorted faces that swam in and out of his fading vision overhead, peering down at him like big, gawking fish. Now his twelve sons all gathered above him, walleyed and expectant. There were Leah's six oldest: Reuben, Simeon, Levi, Judah, Zebulun, and Issachar. There were the sons of Rachel's handmaid Bilhah: Dan and Naphtali. There were the sons of Leah's handmaid Zilpah: Gad and Asher. And there were his beloved Rachel's late-in-life sons: Joseph, in his regal attire, and Benjamin, the youngest. All of this swam undulating before Jacob's fading eyes.

The expectation of Jacob's sons was that their father was going to bless them and that his blessing would provide a glimpse of their future, much like Noah had given to his sons (cf. 9:18-27). Indeed, Jacob's oracle was a blessing, as is emphasized three times at the conclusion: "This is what their father said to them as he *blessed* them, *blessing* each with the *blessing* suitable to him" (49:28, emphasis added). This said, some of his sons' blessings contained no word of blessing and were, in fact, curses. This is because the broader blessing of all mankind was in view as the judgments passed upon certain of his sons opened the way of blessing through the lives of other of his sons. Jacob's blessings were at the very base of the blessings we enjoy in Christ today, as we will see.[1] Significantly, this long poem (by far the longest in Genesis) focuses on two grand figures, Judah and Joseph, ten of its twenty-five verses being about them. This study will culminate on Jacob's astonishing blessing upon Judah, his fourth son. It is again the gospel in Genesis — an explosive messianic prophecy.

OLDER BROTHERS DISQUALIFIED (vv. 2-7)

With his sons gathered close around him, Jacob began: "Assemble and listen, O sons of Jacob, listen to Israel your father" (v. 2). As they listened, no one was listening more intently than the eldest, Reuben, who lived with the memory that he had tried to usurp his father's power and place by sleeping with his father's concubine, Bilhah (cf. 35:22).

Reuben's disqualification. Likely Reuben involuntarily winced as his father addressed him directly. "Reuben, you are my firstborn, my might, and the firstfruits of my strength, preeminent in dignity and preeminent in power" (v. 3). Curiously, his father was heaping majestic descriptions on him — "firstborn," his parents' pride and joy — "my strength," the issue of Jacob's virility — "preeminent in dignity and power," terms that aptly describe God. For a second, Reuben's hopes welled, but then came the curse, "one of the fiercest denunciations in Genesis" (Wenham).[2] Old Jacob had been fearful of doing anything to Reuben in his lifetime, but he now cursed him from his deathbed: "Unstable as water, you shall not have preeminence, because you went up to your father's bed; then you defiled it — he went up to my couch!" (v. 4) Jacob's pent-up hurt and revulsion was driven into Reuben with a final switch to the distancing third person, "*he* went up to my couch!"

And Jacob's prophetic word came true. When Reuben's descendants settled in the Transjordan, they soon disappeared from history, and no prophet or judge or king would ever come from the tribe of Reuben. Reuben's descendants were characterized by a lack of leadership and resolve. The only time the tribe of Reuben appeared to exercise leadership was in the spiritual rebellion of Dathan and Abiram (cf. Numbers 16:1). How Jacob's revulsion and explosive rejection affected Reuben, we can only surmise. Now the brothers' eyes widened further with tremulous interest.

Simeon and Levi's disqualification. Having heard Jacob's fierce rejection of Reuben, it might be expected that the leadership would fall to the next in line, Simeon or perhaps Levi. But it is unlikely that these two held much hope of it because after their genocidal slaughter of the Shechemites, they had withstood their father's intense correction (cf. 34:30, 31). Jacob's rejection of these two was logical and predictable. "Simeon and Levi are brothers; weapons of violence are their swords. Let my soul come not into their council; O my glory, be not joined to their company. For in their anger they killed men, and in their willfulness they hamstrung oxen. Cursed be their anger, for it is fierce, and their wrath, for it is cruel! I will divide them in Jacob and scatter them in Israel" (vv. 5-7). And both tribes were divided and scattered, so that neither of them were given a portion of the land. The tribe of Simeon virtually disappeared after the time of the conquest of the promised land. And when the tribe of Levi was given the responsibility of the priesthood, its people were therefore disallowed from having their own territory.

So now it's son number four's turn, Judah, the one who impregnated Tamar, the wife of his deceased son, while thinking that he was visiting a Canaanite prostitute (chap. 38). Judah was an arch-sinner like his brothers. But unlike them, the Scripture records that a change had taken place in Judah's life. Evidently his infamy with Tamar had precipitated a deep humiliation of soul — "She is more righteous than I" (38:26) — which then provided the lowliness essential to an elevation in character. It was Judah who later pleaded before the viceroy for his brother Benjamin (cf. 44:18-32) and offered himself as Benjamin's substitute (cf. vv. 33-34) — a prophetic shadow of Christ's substitutionary death.

THE ELEVATION OF JUDAH (vv. 8-12)

As Judah awaited his father's words, it was precisely because of Judah's growth in humility, character, and love that he surely had no idea of the astonishing oracle that his father was about to pronounce — which would establish the kingly role of Judah until Messiah would come.

Lion-like dominance. The first words to him from his dying father prophesied an astonishing dominance:

> *Judah, your brothers shall praise you;*
> *your hand shall be on the neck of your enemies;*
> *your father's sons shall bow down before you.*
> *Judah is a lion's cub;*
> *from the prey, my son, you have gone up.*
> *He stooped down; he crouched as a lion*
> *and as a lioness; who dares rouse him? (vv. 8, 9)*

Judah's brothers' descendants would bow down to his descendants, just as they had bowed down to Joseph. The tribe of Judah would take its enemies by the neck. Judah would become a ferocious lion — here pictured as seizing its prey, hauling it back to its den, and fiercely crouching over it. The image of Judah as a lion would become common to biblical literature (cf. Numbers 24:9; Micah 5:8; Ezekiel 19:1-7).[3] King David's exploits in subduing Israel's enemies caused him to sing, "you gave me my enemies' necks" (cf. 2 Samuel 22:41, ESV margin; Psalm 18:40, ESV margin). His deeds gave rise to the messianic title, "Lion of Judah."

The Lion's coming. With the thrilling lion metaphor ringing in his ears and imagination, Judah heard his father's blessing move out to the distant future and the dawn of the messianic age.

> *The scepter shall not depart from Judah,*
> *nor the ruler's staff from between his feet,*
> *until tribute comes to him;*
> *and to him shall be the obedience of the peoples. (v. 10)*

Ancient Jewish and Christian commentators almost uniformly have interpreted this verse as messianic, though the second to last line — "until tribute comes to him" — is variously rendered. The King James Version reads "until Shiloh comes." The NIV has, "until he comes to whom it belongs." And similarly the NLT reads, "until the coming of the one to whom it belongs." All three translations list the various renderings in their margins.[4] Yet while there is no consensus as to what the exact wording should be, there is a unified understanding that the "scepter" and "ruler's staff" are symbolic of a kingship that would remain with Judah until the Messiah comes — "and to him shall be the obedience of the peoples" (the nations of the world). As the fourth-century A.D. Jewish Targum Onkelos had it, "until the Messiah comes, whose is the kingdom, and him shall the nations obey."[5]

His reign. So the scepter would not depart from Judah nor the ruler's staff from between his feet until the Lion's coming. And how will it be in his reign? It will be a golden age of extravagant abundance and celebration in which wine (the symbol of prosperity and blessing) will be as common as water. Thus Jacob prophesies of the Messiah:

> *Binding his foal to the vine*
> *and his donkey's colt to the choice vine,*
> *he has washed his garments in wine*
> *and his vesture in the blood of grapes. (v. 11)*

There will be such an abundance of grapes that the Messiah will tether his donkey to a choice grape vine with no concern as to his donkey's helping itself to the vintage. There will be such a surplus of wine that people will not worry about using it to wash clothes!

Regarding this coming king, Jacob concludes,

> *His eyes are darker than wine,*
> *and his teeth whiter than milk. (v. 12)*

He will be a picture of strength and power.

Such a prospect! An altogether lovely Messiah — vines used as hitching posts — wine as wash water. What dizzying, evocative imagery! Of this Derek Kidner writes, "In its own material terms it bids adieu to the pinched regime of thorns and sweat for 'the shout of them that triumph, the song of them that feast.' Jesus announced the age to come in just this imagery in His first 'sign' at Cana of Galilee."[6]

And indeed he did. As John's Gospel records it:

> *On the third day there was a wedding at Cana in Galilee, and the mother of Jesus was there. Jesus also was invited to the wedding with his disciples. When the wine ran out, the mother of Jesus said to him, "They have no wine." And Jesus said to her, "Woman, what does this have to do with me? My hour has not yet come." His mother said to the servants, "Do whatever he tells you." Now there were six stone water jars there for the Jewish rites of purification, each holding twenty or thirty gallons. Jesus said to the servants, "Fill the jars with water." And they filled them up to the brim. And he said to them, "Now draw some out and take it to the master of the feast." So they took it. When the master of the feast tasted the water now become wine, and did not know where it came from (though the servants who had drawn the water knew), the master of the feast called the bridegroom and said to him, "Everyone serves the good wine first, and when people have drunk freely, then the poor wine. But you have kept the good wine until now." This, the first of his signs, Jesus did at Cana in Galilee, and manifested his glory. And his disciples believed in him. (2:1-11)*

For a shimmering golden moment, donkeys were hitched to grape vines, and wine was as abundant as wash water. In fact, water was turned into wine! The abundance of wine signaled to Israel that the Messiah was present. Everyone knew that the scepter-bearing Messiah would come out of Judah. And at this initial sign, his disciples believed in him.

The first gospel promise of a deliverer from the seed of the woman who would crush the head of the serpent — in Genesis 3:15 — was preserved through the flood through righteous Noah, and then through Noah's son Shem (cf. 9:26), and then through Shem's son Abraham (cf. 12:3), and then through Abraham's son Isaac (cf. 21:12), and then through Isaac's son Jacob (cf. 25:23), and then through Jacob's son Judah (cf. 49:10). And then, beyond the history of Genesis, God chose a descendant of Judah, King David, to be the line through which Messiah would come (cf. 2 Samuel 7:12-16). When the Lion of the tribe of Judah came, he was born in Judah (his tribal territory) in the town of Bethlehem (cf. Micah 5:2).[7] No one but Jesus had these credentials. And when he changed the water to wine, his disciples knew that the Messiah was present! It was a day of intoxicating, exuberant abundance — and a taste of the eternal day when wine will be as common as water.

Readers, our faith is neither *ex nihilo* (from nothing) nor *de novo* (new). It was not some first-century notion that became popular in the ancient world. The Messiah was prophesied throughout the book of Genesis and became the unifying message of the Old Testament. The Messiah died and rose again, according to the Scriptures (cf. 1 Corinthians 15:1-3).

This side of the cross, we know that the means to the ultimate age of joy led through the cross. Jesus on the eve of his crucifixion offered a different cup to his followers — the cup of the new covenant in his blood that was to be shed for his people. So we understand that the exuberant, endless wine of the kingdom can only be ours through the shed blood of the Lion of the tribe of Judah.

The Messiah has come and has died and was resurrected. He has bound

> . . . *his foal to the vine*
> *and his donkey's colt to the choice vine,*
> *he has washed his garments in wine*
> *and his vesture in the blood of grapes.*
> *His eyes are darker than wine,*
> *and his teeth whiter than milk. (49:11, 12)*

He has given his blood for us. Believer, come to the cup and bread of remembrance with repentance and joy.

68

The Testament of Jacob II

GENESIS 49:13-33

The book of Genesis begins with blessing and ends with blessing. In the very first chapter, God crowns the creation of mankind with an extended blessing (cf. 1:28-31). In the penultimate chapter, the dying patriarch Jacob blesses his twelve sons who are destined to bear the blessing to mankind (chap. 49). So in sweeping terms we can say that the book of Genesis is concerned with the blessing (or gracing) of mankind. The great problem that Genesis addresses is the fall of man from the blessedness of fellowship with God and the regaining of that blessing.

The structure of Genesis, dividing into primeval history (from creation to Babel, 1 — 11) and patriarchal history (from Seth to Israel's sons, 12 — 50), is shaped by the problem of the fall and pursuit of a solution. Primeval history demonstrates the need for blessing and redemption. Man's fall was followed by an avalanche of sin that roared ever wider over the primeval world despite flashes of grace. The fall issued in Cain's murder of Abel and then the exponential violence and seventy-fold vengeance of Lamech. Both Cainite and Sethite civilization suffered demonization by the Nephilim, violent men, "men of renown." Man's corruption was universal and profound, so deep that "every intention of the thoughts of his heart was only evil continually" (6:5). Then came the flood, in which every soul, except righteous Noah and his family, perished. But even Noah succumbed to sin after the flood. And his descendants built the tower of Babel, demonstrating the folly of the greatest civilization of the day. So chapters 1 — 11 as primeval history give the reason for the patriarchal history of chapters 12 — 50. Chapters 1 — 11 teem with despair, while chapters 12 — 50 mount with hope. And we should note that the volume of patriarchal history (thirty-nine chapters) as compared with the size of primeval history (eleven chapters) indicates that the major concern of Genesis is how blessing and redemption are accomplished.

This is why the patriarchal section opens with God's grand declaration to Abraham that blessing would extend from him to the world: "Now the LORD said to Abram, 'Go from your country and your kindred and your father's house to the land that I will show you. And I will make of you a great nation, and I will bless you and make your name great, so that you will be a blessing. I will bless those who bless you, and him who dishonors you I will curse, and in you all the families of the earth shall be blessed'" (12:1-3).

Patriarchal history records how the blessing was passed on through Abraham, Isaac, Jacob, and then Judah. God's covenant with Abraham in Genesis 15 and the covenant of circumcision in chapter 17 further confirmed and defined the nature of God's promised blessing. The patriarchal narratives reveal that divine intervention was essential to the perpetuation of the blessing as all three matriarchs — Sarah, Rebekah, and Rachel — struggled with barrenness. God's grace to these women foreshadowed his gracious blessing to the Virgin Mary and her miraculous conception (cf. Luke 1:28-33). We also see that the blessing would be a work of God's autonomous grace as he repeatedly elevated the younger son over the older. Jacob's ill-conceived quest for the blessing provides the backdrop for the astonishing providential preservation of Jacob and his sons in Egypt through the offices of Joseph and the return of their children to the land of promise where one day there would emerge the ultimate blessing of the nations.

As now we take up Jacob's final blessing of his sons, we can sense how crucial this chapter is. Again we must emphasize that though some of the brothers were chastised and passed over and two were given ultimate leadership, *all* the sons of Jacob were blessed because they all became founders of tribes that would emerge victoriously from Egypt as the children of Abraham — and from them would come the blessing.

In the first part of Jacob's oracle, which exalted Judah, Jacob's first three sons (Reuben, Simeon, and Levi) were disqualified from leadership because of their sins, and number four son, Judah, was exalted as the source of the ultimate messianic line: "The scepter shall not depart from Judah, nor the ruler's staff from between his feet, until tribute comes to him; and to him shall be the obedience of the peoples" (v. 10). Indeed, after Messiah's death and resurrection, when he ascended, he proclaimed his rule: "All authority in heaven and on earth has been given to me" (Matthew 28:18). The poetic imagery Jacob used to describe Messiah's reign was evocative of extravagant abundance and joy — with grape-laden vines used as hitching posts and clothing washed in wine — images appropriated in Jesus' first miracle when he changed the water into wine at Cana in Galilee.

BROTHERS' BLESSINGS (vv. 13-21, 27)

As stunning as Jacob's prophecy about Judah was, Jacob continued right on with blessings suitable to each of his remaining eight sons, topped with a lavish blessing on Joseph, his other great son. Apart from the blessing on Joseph, the blessings are brief and a bit obscure, but the general sense of blessing is evident in two ways: prowess in battle and prosperity.[1]

Zebulun. Focusing on each of his sons in general birth order, Jacob now addressed son number five:

> *Zebulun shall dwell at the shore of the sea;*
> *he shall become a haven for ships. . . . (v. 13)*

Zebulun's prime location would siphon prosperity from the sea, though in fact the tribe had no ports of its own. International trade fueled Zebulun's prosperity.

Issachar. Then Jacob turned to Issachar:

> *Issachar is a strong donkey,*
> *crouching between the sheepfolds.*
> *He saw that a resting place was good,*
> *and that the land was pleasant,*
> *so he bowed his shoulder to bear,*
> *and became a servant at forced labor. (vv. 14, 15)*

Issachar settled in a fertile land and embraced a tarnished level of prosperity because her people chose to live as serfs rather than labor in a less fertile district. The descendants of Issachar traded their liberty for the humiliating comforts of slavery.

Dan. Next the patriarch addressed Dan:

> *Dan shall judge his people*
> *as one of the tribes of Israel.*
> *Dan shall be a serpent in the way,*
> *a viper by the path,*
> *that bites the horse's heels*
> *so that his rider falls backward. (vv. 16, 17)*

The tribe of Dan became the tribe of Samson, and medieval Jewish commentators understood the metaphor of the viper to be Samson, who by his stealth and trickery defeated the Philistines.[2] Dan's descendants would excel in stealth in battle.

Evidently, upon uttering this prophetic word Jacob, despite his infirmity, was heartened and cried, "I wait for your salvation, O LORD" (v. 18). The old man's hope effervesced. It was both a shout of longing and of faith — "I wait for your salvation, O LORD."

Gad, Asher, Naphtali, and Benjamin. Jacob's shout was followed by cleverly worded blessings that prophesied more victories and prosperity to Gad, Asher, and Naphtali:

> *Raiders shall raid Gad,*
> *but he shall raid at their heels.*
> *Asher's food shall be rich,*
> *and he shall yield royal delicacies.*
> *Naphtali is a doe let loose*
> *that bears beautiful fawns. (vv. 19-21)*

All three prophecies pulse with hope. And so did the final brief prophecy about Benjamin that characterized him as a wolf — a description parallel to Judah's being termed a lion.

> *Benjamin is a ravenous wolf,*
> *in the morning devouring the prey*
> *and at evening dividing the spoil. (v. 27)*

Like Judah, Benjamin would be fierce and successful in battle. In coming centuries, when Israel went to war, they cried out, "After you, O Benjamin!"

JOSEPH'S BLESSING (vv. 22-26)

As Jacob looked from his bed to his twelve sons, there was one profile distinct from them all — that of the viceroy of Egypt. Was he wearing his Egyptian headdress? Perhaps. But his unusually handsome son stood out regardless.

Just prior to Jacob's calling his sons to his deathbed, he had formally adopted Joseph's sons Ephraim and Manasseh as his own (cf. 48:5,6), and then he had blessed them. In bestowing the blessing, Jacob crossed his hands, so that his right hand (the hand reserved for the firstborn) was placed upon Ephraim, the second-born (cf. 48:13-20). When Joseph objected, Jacob explained that both boys would become great, but that Ephraim would be greater than Manasseh because his offspring would become a multitude of nations (cf. 48:19). Ephraim, appropriately, means "fruitful." And he would become the great tribe in the north — eminently fruitful.

Joseph's person. So now as Jacob began his blessing of Joseph, he celebrated Joseph's life and character with a pun on Ephraim's name.[3]

> *Joseph is a fruitful bough,*
> *a fruitful bough by a spring;*
> *his branches run over the wall. (v. 22)*

The metaphor is evocative of a well-watered tree that is so healthy and fruit-laden that its branches hang low over garden walls, offering its fruit to all who pass by. Certainly this is what Joseph had been for his family and the surrounding world during the famine. During the years that followed Jacob's death, he would remain a fruitful bough for Israel — until a new king arose in Egypt "who did not know Joseph" (Exodus 1:8). And certainly the tribe of his adopted son Ephraim would be a fruitful bough when Israel crossed into the promised land.

This image of the bough extends even further as the prophet Isaiah would describe the coming Messiah saying, "In that day the branch of the LORD shall be beautiful and glorious, and the fruit of the land shall be the pride and honor of the survivors of Israel" (Isaiah 4:2).

Joseph's conduct. Joseph's epic life had not only been a great benefit to his family and the world — he had done it under intense fire, as his father well knew.

> *The archers bitterly attacked him,*
> *shot at him, and harassed him severely,*
> *yet his bow remained unmoved;*
> *his arms were made agile*
> *by the hands of the Mighty One of Jacob. (vv. 23, 24a)*

Arrows are probably used here to represent wicked words that Joseph first experienced from his brothers and then from Mrs. Potiphar and then from those who resented his rise from prison to the court of Egypt. In all of this Joseph ably defended himself with the simple truth and no more. There was never a word of self-pity. His speech always glorified God. He had been grace under fire!

Joseph's God. The reason for Joseph's peerless conduct was God. And his father's blessing acknowledged this by a cascade of divine ascriptions unparalleled in Genesis.

Joseph's power came from "the Mighty One of Jacob." Jacob declared that God alone had saved Joseph. As Isaiah later used the terms:

> *Then all flesh shall know*
> *that I am the LORD your Savior,*
> *and your Redeemer, the Mighty One*
> *of Jacob. (Isaiah 49:26b)*

And you shall know that I, the LORD, am your Savior
and your Redeemer, the Mighty One of Jacob.
(Isaiah 60:16b; cf. Psalm 132:2, 5)

The God who empowered Joseph was also his Shepherd — "from there is the Shepherd" (v. 24), says Jacob. Ironically, up to now the only mention of *shepherd* in Genesis was that "every shepherd is an abomination to the Egyptians" (46:34b). But here Jacob tells his son (the *Egyptians'* viceroy) that God is his Shepherd — that he's been cared for as a sheep. What lavish care! Here is the initial inspiration for Psalm 23, the most comforting of all poems.

And even more, the God who had sustained him was "the Stone of Israel" (v. 24) — a metaphor probably inspired for Jacob when he set up a stone to honor God who had shepherded him up to Mesopotamia and back (cf. 28:10-22; 35:1-15).[4] Here again is the primary source of the great biblical metaphor of a rock as indicating the unchanging dependability of God — elsewhere "the Rock of Israel" (2 Samuel 23:3; Isaiah 30:29).

And further, the assertion that this God is "the God of your father" (v. 25) recalls all of God's dealings with Joseph's father Jacob — from Bethel's angel-freighted ladder to Peniel where God left him as a cripple named Israel. This same caring, superintending God had been with Joseph in Dothan and in Potiphar's house and in the prison and now in the palace.

Lastly, God is "the Almighty" (v. 25) — *El Shaddai*, the name of God most associated with blessing by giving prosperity and offspring (cf. 28:3; 35:11; 43:14; 48:3).

So we see that Jacob invoked a waterfall of divine names over his son: "Mighty One of Jacob" — "Shepherd" — "Stone" — "God of your father" — "*El Shaddai*." Thus, we cannot miss the point: It was God in the full significance of these names and metaphoric appellations who had delivered Joseph and sustained him — and who would effect further blessing in his life. And for us his children, God has "blessed us in Christ with every spiritual blessing in the heavenly places, even as he chose us in him before the foundation of the world" (Ephesians 1:3, 4a). The promise of his care for us is equally astonishing. Our awesome God will effect our care and blessing!

The book of Genesis is about blessing, about grace. The book of Genesis is about getting blessing out to the world. And in Christ we have every spiritual blessing. I write these words pastorally because I am positive after forty years of ministry that at least 50 percent of my parishioners and readers are experiencing difficulties in some way — either professionally or relationally or domestically or physically or a combination of these stresses. Some are concerned about losing their job. Some feel abandoned and friendless. Others are reeling from an ominous diagnosis. Parents worry over their children, and children over their parents. And I am always aware that a hurting heart needs to understand and believe that God's gracious plan is one of blessing and that despite circumstances his people are always blessed.

Fellow Christian, whatever your situation — and it may seem impossible — God is with you to effect your care and blessing.

Jacob's blessing. If the names of God came in a divine cascade, the blessing was "like the finale of a fireworks display" (Wenham)[5] as the blessing occurred six times:

> *. . . by the Almighty who will bless you*
> *with blessings of heaven above,*
> *blessings of the deep that crouches beneath,*
> *blessings of the breasts and of the womb.*
> *The blessings of your father*
> *are mighty beyond the blessings of my parents,*
> *up to the bounties of the everlasting hills.*
> *May they be on the head of Joseph,*
> *and on the brow of him who was set apart from*
> *   his brothers. (vv. 25b, 26)*

The blessings of the future far outstrip those already experienced. We have been blessed, and we do indeed have every spiritual blessing in Christ Jesus right now in the heavenly places. But the consummation of the blessing will go beyond this — because it is God's intent to bless you eternally.

Thus ended Jacob's blessing of his sons. The prophetic blessing left the patriarch exhausted. But with his final strength,

> *he commanded them and said to them, "I am to be gathered to my people; bury me with my fathers in the cave that is in the field of Ephron the Hittite, in the cave that is in the field at Machpelah, to the east of Mamre, in the land of Canaan, which Abraham bought with the field from Ephron the Hittite to possess as a burying place. There they buried Abraham and Sarah his wife. There they buried Isaac and Rebekah his wife, and there I buried Leah — the field and the cave that is in it were bought from the Hittites." When Jacob finished commanding his sons, he drew up his feet into the bed and breathed his last and was gathered to his people. (vv. 29-33)*

The specificity of the dying man is remarkable. Jacob must have been lucid up to his final minutes. He was more specific here than in his earlier directives for burial. Jacob was determined to be buried in the promised land along with his ancestors and family. The reason was quite simply that he believed the words of the blessings he had just invoked — with all his heart! Jacob believed that blessing and redemption would come through Abraham, Isaac, himself, and Judah. He believed that the time was coming when the tribes his sons fathered would depart from Egypt and settle in the promised land.

And it all came true. Joseph immediately bore Jacob's bones back to the family tomb in Canaan. And when Joseph died, he made his sons promise to carry his remains back to the promised land. And some four hundred years later his bones were indeed carried out in the exodus.

True to Jacob's prophecy, the descendants of Joseph's son Ephraim became a major source of blessing in the promised land. But with time, as apostasy gripped the northern kingdom, the ascendancy switched from Ephraim to the tribe of Judah. And the blessing, so long promised in Genesis, passed down through Judah to David to the Messiah. And two thousand years ago godly Simeon, who was "waiting for the consolation of Israel" (Luke 2:25), took the baby Jesus, the Messiah, in his arms and blessed God and said:

> *Lord, now you are letting your servant depart in peace,*
> *according to your word;*
> *for my eyes have seen your salvation*
> *that you have prepared in the presence of all peoples,*
> *a light for revelation to the Gentiles,*
> *and for glory to your people Israel. (Luke 2:29-32)*

Fellow believers, one day we will join "every creature in heaven and on earth and under the earth and in the sea, and all that is in them, saying, 'To him who sits on the throne and to the Lamb be blessing and honor and glory and might forever and ever!'" (Revelation 5:13).

The entire book of Genesis is about blessing and how grace is going to go out to the world. And through the Lion of the tribe of Judah it has come to you, and you have been blessed with every spiritual blessing in the heavenly places in Christ Jesus, and his intent for you is further blessing. You may be going through hard days, but understand what God is about — and trust him.

Or perhaps you do not yet know God. Please understand that his desire for you according to the revelation of God's Word is to be blessed — to have fellowship with him, to be freed of your sins and destined for blessing in eternity.

69

Jacob's Exodus

GENESIS 50:1-14

The very first thing promised to Abraham was the land, followed in quick succession by the promise of a people. God said, "Go from . . . your father's house to the land that I will show you. And I will make of you a great nation . . ." (12:1, 2). So Abraham set out for the land, and when he arrived in the promised land, the Lord familiarized him with its parameters, commanding him, "Lift up your eyes and look from the place where you are, northward and southward and eastward and westward, for all the land that you see I will give to you and to your offspring forever. . . . Arise, walk through the length and the breadth of the land, for I will give it to you" (13:14, 15, 17). Triumphantly, Abraham began the tour of the land by building an altar in Hebron, its very heart.

But life did not go as Abraham expected. Sarah was barren, and their small clan lived among many other dwellers in the land. Abraham became discouraged. Thus God took Abraham out under the stars affirming, "So shall your offspring be. And he believed the LORD, and he counted it to him as righteousness" (15:5, 6). Abraham's faith was followed by an astonishing theophany and ratification of the covenant as the flaming presence of God passed between the flayed parts of sacrificed animals, confirming the promise that Abraham's descendants would possess the land after a four-hundred-year sojourn in a foreign land and then depart with great possessions that they would carry back to the promised land (cf. 15:7-21). Abraham's defining quality was that he believed both aspects of the promise with all his heart — the certainty of a people and of a land. At the covenant of circumcision, God again affirmed his promise of a people and land (cf. 17:8) — but with the added revelation that aged Sarah would be the mother (cf. 17:15-19)!

The birth of Isaac served to further confirm Abraham's faith. So sure did he become of God's promise that when God called him to sacrifice Isaac, he did it because he reasoned "that God was able even to raise him from the dead" (Hebrews 11:19). As to the promise of the land, Abraham believed it all the more! The miraculous birth of Isaac left him in no doubt that his children would possess the land, notwithstanding four hundred years of captivity in a foreign nation. He was as sure of the land as he was sure that Isaac had been born. Though he was only a sojourner in the land, Abraham possessed a massive certitude about the land.

And that is why when Sarah died, he purchased a family tomb in the heart of the promised land. Abraham was so sure that his descendants would one day possess the land that he wanted Sarah's bones to be there when they arrived! His beloved wife's body entombed in Hebron, the center of the land, was his public stake in God's promise — against all the present circumstances.

The tomb in Hebron became a monument to the faith of Abraham and his children in God's sure word of promise. By faith Abraham embraced God's promise that his descendants would inherit the land. By faith Abraham sojourned in the promised land for about a century, living as a man to whom it belonged. By faith Abraham purchased the cave at Machpelah in Hebron. By faith he buried Sarah in the cave. By faith his beloved son Isaac buried him with Sarah at Hebron.

By faith his grandson Jacob buried his father Isaac at Hebron. And Jacob, whose sons would father the tribes of Israel, lived his life in full assurance of the promise of the land. At Bethel, in flight from Esau, Jacob dreamed of the angel-freighted ladder with the Lord standing above it and heard him say, "I am the LORD, the God of Abraham your father and the God of Isaac. The land on which you lie I will give to you and to your offspring" (28:13).

And when he returned to Bethel after his flight and a twenty-year sojourn, God appeared to him again and blessed him:

> *"Your name is Jacob; no longer shall your name be called Jacob, but Israel shall be your name." So he called his name Israel. And God said to him, "I am God Almighty: be fruitful and multiply. A nation and a company of nations shall come from you, and kings shall come from your own body. The land that I gave to Abraham and Isaac I will give to you, and I will give the land to your offspring after you." Then God went up from him in the place where he had spoken with him. And Jacob set up a pillar in the place where he had spoken with him, a pillar of stone. He poured out a drink offering on it and poured oil on it. So Jacob called the name of the place where God had spoken with him Bethel. (35:10-15)*

Jacob believed that the land would be his descendants' with an intensity equal to that of Abraham. That is why he made Joseph twice promise to bury him there, the last being with his dying breath as "he drew up his feet into the bed and breathed his last and was gathered to his people" (49:33; cf. 47:29-31; 49:29, 30). Jacob may well have sensed that the four-hundred-year captivity was in the making, even though Egypt under Joseph was so welcoming and benign (cf. 46:1-4).

PREPARATIONS FOR BURIAL (vv. 1-3)

Because of the failures of the three oldest brothers, Joseph had risen to headship of the twelve, though the future leadership and hope would be through Judah (cf. 1 Chronicles 5:1, 2). And during the last seventeen years in Egypt Jacob's pleasure in his favorite son, who had in effect returned from the dead, was intense. How proud Jacob was of his viceroy son — and especially that though he reigned in Egypt, Egypt was not in him. Joseph's stand-alone character had prepared him well for life at the top. He was unphased. He was proud to be Jacob's son. Joseph drank in every word from his father about his people's history and the words of God. Though viceroy, he sat at his father's feet.

Joseph's sorrow. It was understood between father and son that Joseph would close Jacob's eyes in death because God had so promised (cf. 46:4). And when Jacob breathed his last, Joseph did just that as his brothers looked on. "Then Joseph fell on his father's face and wept over him and kissed him" (v. 1). Seventeen years earlier, when Joseph was reunited with his father, we read that he fell on his father's neck (cf. 46:29). Now he literally fell on his father's face and bathed it with his tears.

How beautiful Joseph was. The only tears recorded in his life were not for himself but for the plight of his brothers and now the loss of his father. Surely his brothers wept too, but Joseph set the heart-example.

Joseph's command. Joseph took charge, and his command was ostensibly very Egyptian. "And Joseph commanded his servants the physicians to embalm his father. So the physicians embalmed Israel. Forty days were required for it, for that is how many are required for embalming. And the Egyptians wept for him seventy days" (vv. 2, 3). Egyptian religion, under the influence of the cult of Osiris, required that the body be preserved so that the deceased could enjoy the afterlife; so every dead body in Egypt was treated with care. But how much attention a body received was determined by how much money the family had. The poor were simply washed and dried in the sun. Some were packed with salt. Those with a little more means were injected with juniper oil to dissolve and ease the removal of organs and to scent the body before salting. But neither of these options included a mummy wrap. However, the rich got a total redo as well as a body wrap. All organs were extracted. The body was soaked in niter and then bound in linen and laid out for an eternal good time. Ah, the life of the rich and pious![1]

However, such superstitions did not inform Joseph's actions. Jacob's mummification was purely utilitarian — much like the salting of David Livingstone's body to ship it from Africa to London's Westminster Abbey for interment. This is subtly emphasized by the mention that "the physicians embalmed Israel," not professional mortuary priests.[2] The seventy days of mourning may have consisted of forty days of embalming and thirty days of Hebrew mourning, as thirty days was the amount of time that Israel would later mourn for Aaron and Moses (cf. Numbers 20:29; Deuteronomy 34:8). But the statement that "the Egyptians wept for him seventy days" indicates that national mourning was ordered by Pharaoh as a sign of respect for Joseph. Seventy days was two days short of the mourning for the death of a Pharaoh.

BURIAL (vv. 4-14)

Though Joseph was on the best of terms with Pharaoh, he thought better of going directly to him. Perhaps this was because of his recent contact with his father's dead body. Or, even more likely, he was in an unshaven, disheveled state from mourning. So Joseph submitted his tactfully worded request through courtiers (notice that he took care not to mention that his father abominated the thought of being buried in Egypt).

> *And when the days of weeping for him were past, Joseph spoke to the household of Pharaoh, saying, "If now I have found favor in your eyes, please speak in the ears of Pharaoh, saying, My father made me swear, saying, 'I am about to die: in my tomb that I hewed out for myself in the land of Canaan, there shall you bury me.' Now therefore, let me please go up and bury my father. Then I will return." (vv. 4, 5)*

Cortege. What followed was an affair of state, a grand state funeral conducted with national pomp and ceremony. The father of the man to whom Egypt owed so much, who had saved them from starvation, who used the occasion to consolidate Egyptian power and empire, must not be buried as a common man. Jacob was honored by an immense cortege that accompanied his bier to Canaan. The procession was made up of three groups.

First, the elite of Egypt. "So Joseph went up to bury his father. With him went up all the servants of Pharaoh, the elders of his household, and all the elders of the land of Egypt" (v. 7). They were all there — the rich and famous, the glitterati of the Nile — in their finery and with their train of servants. The repeated "all" suggests that there were no no-shows.

Second came Jacob's family — "all the household of Joseph, his brothers, and his father's household. Only their children, their flocks, and their herds were left in the land of Goshen" (v. 8). Joseph's sons Ephraim and Manasseh, his eleven brothers from Reuben to Benjamin, and his father's household including his surviving wives and older grandchildren joined the train.

Third came the military. "And there went up with him both chariots and horsemen. It was a very great company" (v. 9). Charioteers were unusual in Egyptian funeral processions and were therefore present for security reasons, because Jacob's burial would take place far beyond the borders of Egypt.

Can you see the procession decked out in the color palette of Egypt (gold and turquoise and the blood-red of carnelian) gleaming in the sun as it wound along the blue of the Nile and up across the steppes of the Sinai to Canaan? The sequence of the text suggests the order of the procession. Joseph, accompanying the catafalque bearing his father, rode in front of the van attended by the clean-shaven leadership of Egypt in their flowing, diaphanous linens. Next come bearded patriarchs and their families — motley in comparison. And then, in the vanguard, came the prancing mounts of the military and chariots emblazoned with hieroglyphs and deities of Egypt. Indeed, "It was a very great company" (v. 9).

Here we have a bright flash of God's initial promise to Abraham — "and I will bless you . . . so that you will be a blessing" (12:2). Now all of Egypt stopped and paid homage with great pomp and circumstance at the passing of Abraham's grandson.[3] A vast blessing issued from Abraham's grandson to Egypt and the world. It was a glimpse of a worldwide blessing that would have its fulfillment in Abraham's ultimate Son.

Along with this, the procession from Egypt to Canaan was a mini-rehearsal of Israel's grand exodus from Egypt. Many of the words and descriptives used here to portray the procession — "servants of Pharaoh," "flocks," "herds," "chariots," "horsemen," and "great company" — occur again in the story of the exodus.[4] Now Joseph bore the bones of Jacob to the promised land, but then Joseph's bones would be carried in the exodus to the land (cf. Exodus 13:19). Now the Egyptian horses and chariots helped the procession; then they would oppose it (cf. Exodus 14:9, 17, 18, 26, 28). Now Israel's children were left behind; then they would join in the exodus.

The fact that the whole company mourned at the "threshing floor of Atad, which is beyond the Jordan" means that the funeral procession, for some unknown reason, took the long circuitous way around the bottom of the Dead Sea and up the east side of the Jordan — which is the same round-about way the Israelites would take four hundred years later under Moses' leadership.[5] It was a proto-exodus, a dress rehearsal indeed!

Mourning. With the route completed, the procession set up camp just short of Canaan and held a last great public ceremony of mourning.

> *When they came to the threshing floor of Atad, which is beyond the Jordan, they lamented there with a very great and grievous lamentation, and he made a mourning for his father seven days. When the inhabitants of the*

land, the Canaanites, saw the mourning on the threshing floor of Atad, they
said, "This is a grievous mourning by the Egyptians." Therefore the place
was named Abel-mizraim; it is beyond the Jordan. (vv. 10, 11)

Hebrew mourning was characterized by loud weeping that variously included the tearing of clothing and the donning of sackcloth, fasting, and going bareheaded and barefooted. To what extent the Egyptians joined in we do not know. But we do know that the Canaanite observers were amazed at the Egyptians' mourning and named the place Abel-mizraim — "mourning of Egypt." Was their sorrow from the heart or because of Pharaoh's order? Surely the latter. But it was a remarkable outpouring nevertheless.

Interment. With the formal Egyptian part of the mourning completed, the family proceeded to Hebron and Machpelah for the interment.

Thus his sons did for him as he had commanded them, for his sons car-
ried him to the land of Canaan and buried him in the cave of the field at
Machpelah, to the east of Mamre, which Abraham bought with the field
from Ephron the Hittite to possess as a burying place. (vv. 12, 13)

Machpelah was their land! They owned it outright. The heart of Canaan was theirs. Jacob's bier was gently placed before the ossuary. The stone was removed by the strong among the twelve. And as they peered in, there they saw the grinning remains of Abraham and his beloved princess Sarah, and their beloved son Isaac, the laughter of their life, and his Rebekah and Jacob's Leah. And there they reverently interred their father's remains.

Thus Joseph and his brothers declared against all appearances their faith in God's word that the land would be theirs — that an exodus was in their future.

As Joseph and his brothers left Hebron and forded the Jordan to join the procession back to Egypt, they took their last look at the promised land. None of them would see it again. Joseph and his brothers were to walk by faith and not by sight. By faith Joseph led them away from the home of their ancestors and their future.

Traveling from the Transjordan down the Arabah and across to Egypt, they must have dwelt long and hard on their great-grandfather's experience that dark night when the fiery presence of God glided between the pieces of sacrifice as God sealed his unilateral covenant confirming these words:

Know for certain that your offspring will be sojourners in a land that is
not theirs and will be servants there, and they will be afflicted for four
hundred years. But I will bring judgment on the nation that they serve,
and afterward they shall come out with great possessions. As for yourself,
you shall go to your fathers in peace; you shall be buried in a good old age.

And they shall come back here in the fourth generation, for the iniquity of the Amorites is not yet complete. (15:13-16)

Mysterious as it was, the faithful among them, the likes of Joseph and Judah, believed it wholeheartedly. In fact, a train of wholehearted belief extended over the next four hundred years to the exodus.

By faith Joseph, at the end of his life, made mention of the exodus of the Israelites and gave directions concerning his bones. By faith Moses, when he was born, was hidden for three months by his parents, because they saw that the child was beautiful, and they were not afraid of the king's edict. By faith Moses, when he was grown up, refused to be called the son of Pharaoh's daughter, choosing rather to be mistreated with the people of God than to enjoy the fleeting pleasures of sin. He considered the reproach of Christ greater wealth than the treasures of Egypt, for he was looking to the reward. By faith he left Egypt, not being afraid of the anger of the king, for he endured as seeing him who is invisible. By faith he kept the Passover and sprinkled the blood, so that the Destroyer of the firstborn might not touch them. By faith the people crossed the Red Sea as if on dry land, but the Egyptians, when they attempted to do the same, were drowned. By faith the walls of Jericho fell down after they had been encircled for seven days. (Hebrews 11:22-30)

Today as we look back to the exodus, we see that it was effected through the blood of the Passover lamb. Those who by faith daubed the blood of the slain lamb over their door were delivered from death and then from Egypt. The same fiery presence of God that passed among the sacrificed pieces four hundred years earlier now stood as a pillar of fire between Egypt and Israel to effect Israel's deliverance (cf. Exodus 13:17-22).[6]

All this pointed down the centuries to the new exodus in Christ. In New Testament terminology, "Christ, our Passover lamb, has been sacrificed" (1 Corinthians 5:7). Those who by faith come under his blood experience deliverance. And as a redeemed people they find a place in him. Their promised land is the new Eden where Christ dwells.

Have you made the exodus? Have you by faith rested all your hope of deliverance on his blood? Have you passed through the sea? Do you know the protection of his fiery presence? Are you destined for the place he has prepared for you?

If not, come! By faith come to Christ — your atonement, your Savior, your exodus, and your destiny.

70

Good Providence

GENESIS 50:15-26

When you fear that the worst will happen, your mind can do strange things — like the Chicagoan who was driving on a lonely country road one dark and rainy night and had a flat. He opened the trunk — no lug wrench. The light from a farmhouse could be seen dimly up the road. So he set out on foot through the driving rain. Surely the farmer would have a lug wrench he could borrow, he thought. Of course, it was late at night — the farmer would be asleep in his warm, dry bed. Maybe he would not answer the door. And even if he did, he would be angry at being awakened in the middle of the night.

The city boy, picking his way blindly in the dark, stumbled on. By now his shoes and clothing were soaked. Even if the farmer did answer his knock, he would probably shout something like, "What's the big idea waking me up at this hour?"

This thought made the city boy angry. What right did that farmer have to refuse him the loan of a lug wrench? After all, here he was stranded in the middle of nowhere, soaked to the skin. The farmer was a selfish clod — no doubt about that!

The man finally reached the house and banged loudly on the door. A light went on inside, and a window opened above. A voice cried out, "Who is it?" His face white with anger, the man called out, "You know who it is. It's me! And you can keep your lug wrench. I wouldn't borrow it now if you had the last one on earth!"[1] Ah, negative expectations.

Something not dissimilar to this had been going on with Joseph's brothers as they returned to Egypt after burying their father in the family tomb in Canaan, for they feared the worst. "When Joseph's brothers saw that their father was dead, they said, 'It may be that Joseph will hate us and pay us back for all the evil that we did to him'" (v. 15). Their fears were utterly unfounded and irrational. No clear-thinking person would forget, much less dismiss their stunning reconciliation with Joseph and Joseph's comforting words, "do not be distressed or angry with yourselves because you sold me here, for God sent me before you to preserve life" (45:5), which was followed by his outpouring of affection as "he kissed all his brothers and wept upon them" (45:15). The seventeen years following their reconciliation had been prosperous and peaceful due to Joseph's caring for them. And now they had just come from a fresh display of family solidarity and hope at their father's tomb. Joseph had done nothing to fan their fears. Clearly it was guilt that drove their apprehension.

Though Joseph had forgiven them, they had never confessed their sins to him, much less asked his forgiveness, with the result that their consciences had never been assuaged. They had hated Joseph when he was a boy, and now they could not believe that he did not hate them. The brothers feared that Joseph's benign smiles masked a malevolence that would effect their destruction now that their father was gone. Hearts like this are slow to recognize grace.

Thus they unnecessarily sought Joseph's forgiveness.

So they sent a message to Joseph, saying, "Your father gave this command before he died, 'Say to Joseph, Please forgive the transgression of your brothers and their sin, because they did evil to you.' And now, please forgive the transgression of the servants of the God of your father." Joseph wept when they spoke to him. His brothers also came and fell down before him and said, "Behold, we are your servants." (50:16-18)

As you might expect, given his brothers' checkered past, this plea for forgiveness was messy and, frankly, twisted — because it was introduced with a lie. Jacob had given no command to Joseph to forgive his brothers. There is no hint of this anywhere. In fact, there is no evidence that Joseph had done anything to cause his father to even imagine that he would harm his brothers. This cloaked their entire plea for forgiveness with a lie because not one word of it came from the lips of Jacob.

However, though the brothers sinfully attributed the request that they be forgiven to their father, the plea contained a full confession of their sin and accurately described their desperate desire for forgiveness. Twice they pled for forgiveness. And they described their wickedness in such forthright terms as "transgression" (twice), "sin," and "evil." They employed no euphemisms. They did not call their sin a mistake or a lapse or an error in judgment, as is so common today. And Joseph saw their plea for what it was: Despite their deception and obfuscation, it was the cry of their guilt-ridden hearts for forgiveness. And poor "Joseph wept when they spoke to him."

It was as if all he had done had been in vain. Despite their sins against him, he had loved them and forgiven them. Everything he had done had been with an eye to their well-being. How pitiful as his eleven brothers groveled before him as if he had just threatened to take their lives.

And Joseph could not hold back his tears.

JOSEPH'S COMFORT (vv. 19-21)

Joseph could not bear their pathetic groveling, and the first and last words from his mouth were, "Do not fear." He then ministered comfort to his brothers. And in his brief words of comfort, he gave three heartening reasons not to fear.

First, Joseph had no desire to play God. "But Joseph said to them, 'Do not fear, for am I in the place of God?'" (v. 19) He certainly was in a position to be "god" in their lives if he so chose. He had been hailed as the savior of Egypt, and in fact the world. And he had earned it. And more, at that very moment he may have had more actual power than Pharaoh. Thus to play God in his brothers' lives and administer a little "divine justice" in behalf of God could have been tempting. But Joseph had a clear view of who God was, and he matched it with a clear understanding of who he himself was not. He had no desire to be God in their lives. Bless Joseph's name forever!

How much of our relational trouble comes from our attempting to be God in other peoples' lives. Oh, if we were only God for a day — we would set so many evils right! In our bad moments we imagine that we know what God ought to do with others. And at our very worst moments, we take correction into our own hands — because God apparently has not had the wisdom to do so. Joseph left all the righting of his *personal* wrongs to God and set the example for the faithful in every age. As Paul would later write, "Beloved, never avenge yourselves, but leave it to the wrath of God, for it is written, 'Vengeance is mine, I will repay, says the Lord'" (Romans 12:19). And again, "See that no one repays anyone evil for evil, but always seek to do good to one another and to everyone" (1 Thessalonians 5:15).

Second, Joseph told his brothers not to fear because in addition to his having no desire to play God, he discerned God's good providence in their evil. "As for you, you meant evil against me, but God meant it for good, to bring it about that many people should be kept alive, as they are today" (v. 20).

This is the mysterious heart of the Joseph story: Through the sins of wicked men, God works good. Joseph's unforgettable declaration here bookends the earlier and similar explanation to these same fearful brothers:

And now do not be distressed or angry with yourselves because you sold me here, for God sent me before you to preserve life. For the famine has been in the land these two years, and there are yet five years in which

there will be neither plowing nor harvest. And God sent me before you to
preserve for you a remnant on earth, and to keep alive for you many sur-
vivors. So it was not you who sent me here, but God. (45:5-8a)

Though no man could see it, God was holding all the strings, pulling them to effect his good purposes. "Don't fear," said Joseph in effect, "you did intentional evil to me, but God has used it for good — to keep you alive as well as many others." This astonishing revelation informs all of Genesis: God created everything "good" (cf. 1:4-31) and then — through all his dealings with his people before and after the flood and in the life of Joseph — he worked out his good plan.

The prophet Jeremiah voiced this same truth to encourage his people when they were about to go into captivity in evil Babylon: "For I know the plans I have for you, declares the LORD, plans for wholeness and not for evil, to give you a future and a hope" (Jeremiah 29:11). When it appeared that life was out of control, that the darkness was just about to engulf God's people, when a wicked culture was in the driver's seat, God said, "I know the plans I am literally planning for you. No one else knows them, but I know them fully." And these plans were good — that is, for "wholeness" (*shalom*, peace, well-being), and "not for evil." From this we understand that God can have no evil thoughts toward his own — no thoughts of calamity. He never has had an evil thought toward a child of his, and he never will. Theodore Laetsch, the Old Testament scholar, makes a most perceptive comment regarding this:

> His plans concerning his people are always thoughts of good, of blessing. Even if he is obliged to use the rod, it is the rod not of wrath, but the Father's rod of chastisement for their temporal and eternal welfare. There is not a single item of evil in his plans for his people, neither in their motive, nor in their conception, nor in their revelation, nor in their consummation.[2]

He has never had an evil thought toward his children, and he never will! This does not mean that God's servants are shielded from hardship or misery. What it does mean is that God's plans are never for evil in the believer's life, but with an eye to their well-being and wholeness — always. Even the apparent evil we suffer is for our good. This means that as believers, whatever our lot, we can and must be optimistic because we have "a future and a hope."

The grand New Testament expression of this truth is, of course, Romans 8:28 — "And we know that for those who love God all things work together for good, for those who are called according to his purpose." This is followed by Romans' Golden Chain of linked events that culminate in glory and the astonishing declaration, "What then shall we say to these things? If God is for us, who can be against us? He who did not spare his own Son but gave him up for us all, how will he not also with him graciously give us all things?" (vv. 31, 32). The truth is that everything that happens to those who love God, whether we consider it good or bad, works together for their good.

Now when you pile these three great texts together — Genesis 50:20, "As for you, you meant evil against me, but God meant it for good" — Jeremiah 29:11, "For I know the plans I have for you, declares the LORD, plans for wholeness and not for evil, to give you a future and a hope" — and Romans 8:28, "And we know that for those who love God all things work together for good, for those who are called according to his purpose" — when you stack them theologically, they teach that the God of the Bible is so great that he not only breaks into life to do miracles but is involved concurrently and confluently in all that occurs in this world — without violating the nature of things. In other words, he is involved non-miraculously in everyday life, using all events for the good of his people. Any thoughts scaled down from this are not the God of the Bible but are idolatrous diminutions.

And there is more: All the goodness is mediated through Christ Jesus, for he is the co-Creator with the Father and the Sustainer of the universe (cf. John 17:2; Colossians 1:16, 17; Hebrews 1:1-3). So, if you are "in Christ," you can be sure that everything (even the apparent evil that comes your way) will work out for your good. "The doctrine of providence tells us that the world and our lives are not ruled by fate but by God, who lays bare his purposes of providence in the incarnation of his son" (T. H. L. Parker).[3]

If you have never truly believed this, it will change your life if you take it to heart. Joseph believed it and therefore comforted his brothers. He knew that all their evil to him and indeed all he suffered in this life was meant for good. The question I must ask is, *do you truly believe this?*

Joseph comforted his brothers because he had no desire to stand in the place of God and because he rested in God's providential goodness, which led him to a third concrete expression of comfort: "'So do not fear; I will provide for you and your little ones.' Thus he comforted them and spoke kindly to them" (v. 21). The brothers had insulted him with their fears; he wept and then comforted them with his reflections about God. Now he spoke kindly to them.

How like Jesus he was! It was the Savior who said, "But I say to you who hear, Love your enemies, do good to those who hate you" (Luke 6:27).

JOSEPH'S EXODUS (vv. 22-26)

Ninety-three of Joseph's 110 years were lived in Egypt — and most of those years he reigned as viceroy.

His remaining years were blessed. "So Joseph remained in Egypt, he and his father's house. Joseph lived 110 years. And Joseph saw Ephraim's children of the third generation. The children also of Machir the son of Manasseh were counted as Joseph's own" (vv. 22, 23). To have seen his grandchildren was a crowning joy, as it is today. Proverbs declares, "Grandchildren are the crown of the aged" (Proverbs 17:6). Joseph wore his crown joyfully. His grandchildren gave him such pleasure that even as Jacob had adopted Ephraim and Manasseh as his own, Joseph adopted some of his grandchildren as his own — the children of Machir.

Joseph's last words sparkled with faith, as the writer of Hebrews comments: "By faith Joseph, at the end of his life, made mention of the exodus of the Israelites and gave directions concerning his bones" (11:22). So it was with luminous faith that

> Joseph said to his brothers, "I am about to die, but God will visit you and bring you up out of this land to the land that he swore to Abraham, to Isaac, and to Jacob." Then Joseph made the sons of Israel swear, saying, "God will surely visit you, and you shall carry up my bones from here." (vv. 24, 25)

Unlike his father Jacob who had made Joseph promise to take his bones upon death back to Canaan, Joseph was content to have his people take his bones back to Canaan in the future when they all departed at the exodus. Thus there was no grand funeral procession when Joseph died. His father Jacob's immediate interment in the family tomb in Canaan had rightly expressed his solidarity with Abraham and Isaac and his sure hope in the land. But Joseph's temporary interment in Egypt also rightly expressed his identification with the future generations in Egypt and their hope of returning to the land.

Certainly there was a great state funeral held for Joseph, the savior of Egypt, though the text makes no mention of it. We read simply, "So Joseph died, being 110 years old. They embalmed him, and he was put in a coffin in Egypt" (v. 26). Like it or not, the great man was duly embalmed and placed in a coffin — literally "*the* coffin," specifying a sarcophagus like those used in Egypt for high-ranking officials.[4] Such a coffin would then have been placed in a monumental building in the heart of Egypt. The Egyptians would have seen it as an eternal shrine, but the Israelites saw it much differently — as a temporary monument to the coming exodus. The shriveled, colorless lips that lay in it, wrapped with folds of linen, had left this last utterance: "God will surely visit you, and you shall carry up my bones from here." To believing hearts, Joseph's bones spoke of great hope.

With the passing of some thirty plus generations, Pharaoh let Israel go. And Moses and his people removed the sarcophagus (the ark) bearing Joseph's bones, and as they bore his bones along, the pillar of cloud shaded them by day, and the pillar of fire illumined them at night. During Joseph's life he had suffered immense evil and hurt, "but God meant it for good, to bring it about that many people should be kept alive" (Genesis 50:20).

The theme that emanates from Joseph's life has its clearest expression in the life, death, resurrection, and exaltation of our Lord. Christ suffered far more evil in his life on earth than did Joseph, and in his death the wickedness of us all fell upon him, "but God meant it for good, to bring it about that many people should be kept alive."

Genesis ends with Joseph's coffin awaiting the exodus, and the story continues in the second book of the Pentateuch. Even more important, the Old Testament ends with the expectation of the Messiah who, when he came, by grace led his people in a second exodus from the bondage of this world.

71

Man and Sin in Genesis

A potential drawback to a close and lengthy exposition of Genesis as this has been is that you may not see the forest for the trees. Examining the forest's remarkable trees has been beneficial, but you need to step back so that you can see the magnificence of the forest itself, which is what we are now going to do.

Close study has revealed that Genesis is so carefully crafted that in some places key words like a name of God are numbered in multiples of seven. There are also numerous literary chiasms where stories build to a point and then conclude with parallel events in the inverse order. The theological contours of Genesis are so primary and reflective of reality that they find resonance in the contours and structure of the book of Romans, Paul's magisterial masterpiece. This literary and theological intentionality is also seen in the overall structure of the book into pre-flood and post-flood history and the sustaining of grand themes through both epochs.

So in these final chapters we are going to consider, in turn, Man and Sin in Genesis, Faith and Righteousness in Genesis, Grace in Genesis, Messiah in Genesis, and God in Genesis.

From beginning to end, the book of Genesis delivers a relentless portrayal of the human predicament of fallen, inveterately sinful humanity. And it is appropriate to begin with the problem of man because the following subjects of faith and righteousness, grace, Christ, and God provide the answer to man's predicament. Our method will be to examine the theme in primeval history and then in patriarchal history.

MAN AND SIN IN PRIMEVAL HISTORY (CHAPTERS 1 — 11)

When we meet the first man, Adam, in Genesis, he has been "formed" by God (2:7). He is the product of divine intentionality — the brilliant creation of the infinite mind that designed the atom and the cosmos. God has kissed

life into Adam as he puffed into his nostrils the breath of life (cf. 2:7). Adam
was no afterthought. He came from the mind and breath of God.

Man's excellency, Genesis 2. As the very first poetic line in the Bible
has it, God created Adam in his own image:

> *So God created man in his own image,*
> *in the image of God he created him;*
> *male and female he created them. (1:27)*

Made in God's image, he was "a personal, self-conscious, Godlike
creature with a capacity for knowledge, thought and action" (Packer).[1]
Because Adam and Eve were in God's image, they could do what no other
creature could — they could hear God's word. They could live nuanced lives
of the deepest devotion and morality. They could even speak his word. Being
made in God's image rendered them creative beings. God intended man
and woman, within their limits, also to be creative beings. So humanity's
music and art and homemaking and architecture and sonnets came from
God's image. The first couple even had a God-given immortality. Though
they were not eternal but created, they would exist as immortal souls for all
eternity — endless creations. And the earth was theirs to rule: "And God
blessed them. And God said to them, 'Be fruitful and multiply and fill the
earth and subdue it and have dominion over the fish of the sea and over the
birds of the heavens and over every living thing that moves on the earth'"
(1:28). On top of rulership, Adam and Eve walked with God in deepest intimacy. They were sinless. Nothing separated them from God or one another.

Adam and Eve lived in Eden as vicegerents of creation in a stunning
state of spiritual, social, and ecological perfection.

This tilts the imagination and is so mind-boggling that C. S. Lewis
invented another cosmology in his novel *Perelandra* as an attempt to get
his readers to engage the wonder of the Genesis story. The planet Perelandra
sat under a golden canopy of sky, beneath which rose an emerald sea dotted
with floating pink islands that required sea legs for new arrivals. The floating islands were forested, and when the first couple walked under the forests,
bubbles burst from the foliage, showering the couple with refreshment super-
nal. Among the gentle animals of Perelandra were porpoises to ride and little dragons with red and green scales who liked to have their tummies
scratched — all of this providing for us an imaginary world to reengage the
realities of Eden — ecological, social, and, most of all, spiritual.

Genesis presents us with no small view of man and is the basis for the
Bible's radical humanism. Humanism is essentially the pursuit of the full
realization of our potential as humans. Such realization will only be accomplished through the radical effect of God's grace and living under the pre-
cepts of his word as we await the ultimate redemption and the full

denouement of our humanity in Christ. Secular humanism is a "philosophy that asserts the dignity and worth of man and his capacity for self-realization through reason and that often rejects supernaturalism."[2]

But secular humanism never truly works because it forfeits the wisdom of the God who made us in his image and because it regards no authority except the sinful urgings of all-too-human hearts. Today's humanism as it works out in popular culture often leads to animalism. True humanism, full humanity, comes from knowing God and doing his will.

What stunning humanism we find in the garden as Adam and Eve lived out the image of God.

Man's fall, Genesis 3. But, of course, there came the fall when, in a fatal act of moral autonomy, the word of God was shoved aside. During Eve's tragic dialogue with the serpent, Satan perverted God's word. Then Eve revised it by *minimizing* the freedom God had given to eat from the trees of the garden, by *adding* her own strictness to God's word that was not there, and finally by *softening* God's word in regard to the certainty of death should they sin.

Adam, who had been given God's word directly, witnessed everything that transpired between Eve and the serpent without saying a word. And when he saw that she did not die, he then sinned too, willfully taking the fruit she offered him, assuming there would be no consequences.

Paradise was lost! Guilt coursed through their naked bodies as they fumbled to cover themselves. The sacred rustle of God's step brought dread as they resorted to slouching around paradise. Guilty Adam admitted no wrong but indicted both Eve for giving him the fruit and God for giving him Eve. How wicked! As a result both the man and the woman were cursed by God at the very center of their existences and were cast together out of Eden. Thus Adam and Eve fell from a very great height. Their fall was a catastrophic crash.

The authoritative apostolic interpretation and application of what happened is this: "Sin came into the world through one man, and death through sin, and so death spread to all men because all sinned" (Romans 5:12). Adam and Eve, in fact, both died right there at the tree of the knowledge of good and evil, while the taste of the fruit was yet on their lips. Theologian Henri Blocher explains: "In the Bible, death is the reverse of life — it is not the reverse of existence. To die does not mean to cease to be, but in biblical terms it means, 'cut off from the land of the living.' . . . It is a diminished existence, but nevertheless an existence."[3] Adam and Eve's existence, as they stumbled from the garden in animal skins, was now one of death. And not only that, in a nanosecond sin penetrated every sphere of their being, like a drop of dye diffusing in a pail of water. They were at once utterly sinful. The original couple had passed from life to death, from sinlessness to sin, from harmony to alienation, from trust to distrust, from ease to dis-ease. And thus it has been for every man and woman who has ever lived.

Man's sinfulness, Genesis 4 — 11. The physics of an avalanche involve an ever-growing mass of snow and an ever-increasing speed of descent that sweeps over and around and through everything in its path. And Adam's sin began an avalanche of sin in its full metaphoric dimensions as it rolled over primeval history.

Cain, 4:1-16. The real difference between the offerings of Cain and Abel was in the attitude of their hearts. Cain came to God on his own self-prescribed terms, while Abel came on God's terms. The rejection of Cain's offering and God's poignant plea for his soul left Cain at the edge of Hell. And he stepped off.

Cain's murder of Abel was not only a homicide but a fratricide. The two brothers were direct offspring of the mother and father of the human race and must have been very twin-like. Abel's flesh felt the same as Cain's. Abel's eyes were mirrors of his own. Abel's breath bore the same aroma. There was no technology to depersonalize Cain's murder of his little brother. Did he crush his skull and watch him die like a bug in the dust? Did he cut Abel's throat and bleed him like a sacrifice? Did he choke him with his own hands until Abel's eyes lost their light?

Wit became the murderer's refuge — "Am I my brother's keeper?" And when Cain went out from the Lord's presence, his head was "bloody, but unbowed" (from "Invictus" by William Ernest Henley). Though he bore God's mark of protection, he left Eden full of disdain for God. The taste of anger bitter and sweet clung to his palate and energized him. He would show God. He would show them all! His founding his own city was a declaration that he was still captain of his soul.

Lamech, 4:19-24. The story of Lamech, sixth from Cain, is a story of exponential violence and vengeance. Lamech's chest-thumping "Me Tarzan, You Jane" song to his hapless wives Adah and Zillah is a primeval gangster rap:

Lamech said to his wives:

> *"Adah and Zillah, hear my voice;*
> *you wives of Lamech, listen to what I say:*
> *I have killed a man for wounding me,*
> *a young man for striking me.*
> *If Cain's revenge is sevenfold,*
> *then Lamech's is seventy-sevenfold." (4:23, 24)*

God's vengeance upon anyone killing Cain was sevenfold, meaning a perfect measure — appropriate to the crime. But Lamech would outdo God — seventy-sevenfold, a roaring waterfall of vengeance. Today Lamech's seventy-sevenfold vengeance is still the reigning paradigm for the Middle East — and in fact the whole world.

Men of renown, 6:1-8. Just prior to the flood we find the account of "the sons of God" — the scriptural designation for angels, though here in Genesis 6 for fallen angels, demons, who commandeered the bodies of men in what we term demon-possession. These "sons of God" had married the daughters of normal men, thus demonizing both marriage and primeval culture itself. The result of such unions was the birth of the Nephilim (literally, "fallen ones"): "The Nephilim were on the earth in those days, and also afterward, when the sons of God came in to the daughters of men and they bore children to them. These were the mighty men who were of old, the men of renown" (6:4). These fallen ones, the mighty men of renown, were men of violence. The same word is used to describe Nimrod who was a mighty warrior on the earth (cf. 10:8). So we see that "the men of renown," the idols of pre-diluvian culture, were violent men and, even more, sexually violent men, as their crude treatment of the daughters of men suggests.

How did God assess this? "The LORD saw that the wickedness of man was great in the earth, and that every intention of the thoughts of his heart was only evil continually. And the LORD was sorry that he had made man on the earth, and it grieved him to his heart" (6:5, 6). It is hard to conceive of a more emphatic statement of the wickedness of the human heart. The words "every . . . only . . . continually" leave nothing out. The term "every intention" is literally, "every forming" and comes from the metaphorical sense of the verb that describes a potter in the act of forming and molding his vessel (cf. Isaiah 29:16; Genesis 2:7, 8). "It means even the reflections of fantasy, the rising and freely formed movements of the will were 'only evil continually'" (Von Rad).[4]

Human depravity was not a temporary state. There were no relentings, no repentances, no hesitations. Lust was their medium, violence their method. This was total, inveterate depravity. The tragic bookend to this universal depravity came shortly in the indictment of the earth as wholly corrupt and subject to judgment (note the reiteration of forms of "corruption" three times):

> Now the earth was corrupt in God's sight, and the earth was filled with violence. And God saw the earth, and behold, it was corrupt, for all flesh had corrupted their way on the earth. And God said to Noah, "I have determined to make an end of all flesh, for the earth is filled with violence through them. Behold, I will destroy them with the earth." (6:11-13)

Sin's avalanche was roaring down upon the earth unimpeded.

Noah, chaps. 7 — 9. Amidst this depravity there was one righteous man: "Noah was a righteous man, blameless in his generation. Noah walked with God" (6:9). Righteous, faithful Noah obeyed God and built an ark through which he and his family were saved. But Noah, that singular righteous man, disappointed after the flood: "Noah began to be a man of the soil, and he planted a vineyard. He drank of the wine and became drunk and lay uncovered in his tent" (9:20, 21). Righteous, rescued Noah lay passed out in a drunken stupor on the floor of his tent. The old man wrought his own degradation — he literally "uncovered himself."

Oh, the awful virulence of sin! Noah's righteous life had been a thing of wonder in the depraved pre-diluvian world. Nevertheless when Noah stepped into the new world washed clean by the flood, he brought sin with him, for sin was in him. His son Ham then made his father's sin the occasion for his own savage, sensual delight and the desecration of his family. Sobered, Noah saw the same sin welling in Ham's son, Canaan, and uttered a curse that foresaw the degradation of the Canaanites as future enemies of God's people.

The virulence of human sin astonished in the freshly cleansed world.

Babel, 11:1-9. The apex of primeval sin and rebellion came with the tower of Babel: "Then they said, 'Come, let us build ourselves a city and a tower with its top in the heavens, and let us make a name for ourselves, lest we be dispersed over the face of the whole earth" (v. 4). The drive behind building "a tower with its top in the heavens" was to displace God. The ziggurat was a multistage structure, like giant porch steps to Heaven. Its builders had come to imagine that God was localized, in direct contradiction to Genesis and primeval history.

They had created a god in their own image. "Human beings regarded themselves as the measure of all things, able to control the course of their world, able to build better worlds!" (Dumbrell).[5] Presumptive sin gripped their perverse hearts. And when God scattered them, they took their Babylonian hearts with them. The scattering was, by and large, a scattering of pagans. Thus an avalanche of apostasy blanketed the world in darkness, like an ink bottle inverted on the globe.

Primeval history grows ever darker from Adam's sin to Cain's murder of Abel to Lamech's exponential violence and revenge to the Nephilim, the vile icons of the pre-diluvian world, to Noah's debacle to Babel's hubris and folly. And the story of Babel lacks any resolution or even a glimmer of hope. The blessing of creation, the blessing of the garden, was lost.

MAN AND SIN IN PATRIARCHAL HISTORY (CHAPTERS 12 — 50)

Hope only resurfaced with the advent of patriarchal history and the call of Abraham to be a blessing to the whole world (cf. 12:1-3). Patriarchal history concerns itself with the application of faith and righteousness and blessing in and through God's covenant people to the world. But the best of the patriarchs are helpless, hopeless sinners.

Abraham's life, 11:27 — 25:11. Abraham's monumental faith enabled him to leave Ur and travel to Canaan in obedience to God's word (cf. 12:1-9). But not long after arriving, during a drought-induced visit to Egypt, he lied to Pharaoh, saying Sarah was his sister (cf. 12:10-20). The result was his disgraceful exit from Egypt, in which Pharaoh appears the saint and Abraham the sinner.

Did Abraham learn from this? No! Decades later, just prior to Isaac's birth, he lied to King Abimelech, again saying Sarah was his sister (cf. 20:1-18). We have a word for this today — recidivism. And that is not all — his son Isaac did the same thing when he passed off Rebekah as his sister to Abimelech (cf. chap. 26). The word for this is atavism. Recidivism and atavism haunted patriarchal culture!

The infamous Hagar affair rendered Abraham, Hagar, and Sarah all as ignoble. But Abraham was the worst, as he in *listening* to his wife abdicated his patriarchal responsibility, much as Adam did when he listened to Eve (cf. 16:2; 3:17).

The assimilation of Abraham's righteous nephew Lot into the life of Sodom left him so entrenched that he only escaped when angels gripped the hands of Lot and his wife and his daughters — and then his wife was lost anyway. Here Noah's history was replayed in miniature as the entire population of Sodom was destroyed. Nevertheless, Sodom was reborn in the lives of his daughters, resulting in unspeakable sins (cf. 19). Again we see sin's virulence.

Lives of Jacob and Esau, 25:19 — 50:14. Abraham's son Isaac tossed a relational torch into the tents of his family by his grievous sin of favoritism for Esau. The result was that everyone in the family sinned, while his son Jacob became the arch-deceiver (cf. 27).

Deceit became the currency of Jacob's life. And he got back as good as he gave. Laban, in league with Leah, deceived Jacob on what he thought was his wedding night with Rachel. But "behold, it was Leah!" (cf. 29). Jacob's sons Simeon and Levi would go on to deceive the Shechemites as a prelude to genocide (cf. 34). Jacob's eldest son Reuben committed incest with Jacob's concubine Bilhah in an effort to gain ascendancy over his father (cf. 35:22). All his sons banded together to sell Joseph into slavery (cf. 37). And Judah, son number four, impregnated his widowed daughter-in-law as she disguised herself as a Canaanite prostitute (cf. 38).

So what are we to conclude? Principally this: The book of Genesis, which is the sole record of creation and primeval history and patriarchal history, teaches us that man is both *wonderful* and *awful* and spends most of its pages confirming his awfulness. Genesis teaches that humanity left to itself is thoroughly sinful and helplessly and hopelessly lost. Genesis also informs all of subsequent Old Testament history, which repeatedly confirms the conclusions of primeval and patriarchal history. And more, the New Testament's view of man, and particularly that of Paul, is not a novel twist. Rather, it is in radical continuity with the contours and conclusions of Genesis. Paul's statements are not so much Pauline as primeval and patriarchal.

Romans 3:10-12 — "'None is righteous, no, not one; no one understands; no one seeks for God. All have turned aside; together they have become worthless; no one does good, not even one'" — is profoundly primeval and patriarchal.

Romans 3:23 — "for all have sinned and fall short of the glory of God" — is likewise rooted in earliest history.

Romans 1:22-25 — "Claiming to be wise, they became fools, and exchanged the glory of the immortal God for images resembling mortal man and birds and animals and reptiles. Therefore God gave them up in the lusts of their hearts to impurity, to the dishonoring of their bodies among themselves, because they exchanged the truth about God for a lie and worshiped and served the creature rather than the Creator, who is blessed forever! Amen" — is a reprise of Sodomite history.

Ephesians 2:1-3 — "And you were dead in the trespasses and sins in which you once walked, following the course of this world, following the prince of the power of the air, the spirit that is now at work in the sons of disobedience — among whom we all once lived in the passions of our flesh, carrying out the desires of the body and the mind, and were by nature children of wrath, like the rest of mankind" — is not Pauline but primeval and patriarchal.

Original sin. We must understand that the doctrine of original sin is as old as biblical history — that "sinfulness marks everyone from birth, and is there in the form of a motivationally twisted heart, prior to any actual sins" (Packer).[6] We sin because we are sinners. Vance Havner told of a preacher who was preaching on original sin, and at the end of his sermon one of his listeners came up and said, "Preacher, I can't swallow what you say about original sin." The preacher responded, "That's all right. It's already in you!" As G. K. Chesterton said, the doctrine of original sin is the only philosophy empirically validated by centuries of recorded human history.[7] It is a source of constant wonderment how any rational person could deny original sin. Yet that is precisely what the elites do — in unwitting testimony to the reality they so vehemently deny.

The phrase *total depravity*, while not a biblical term, describes the full implications of original sin. Again as Dr. Packer says, "It signifies a corruption of our moral and spiritual nature that is total not in degree (for no one is as bad as he or she might be) but in extent. It declares that no part of us is untouched by sin, and therefore no action of ours is as good as it should be."[8] This is why none of us can turn to God in a sincere, wholehearted way on our own.

This is foundational to everything the Bible teaches. Our following expositions on Faith and Righteousness and Grace and Christ and God find their full understanding in relation to what man is. This is particularly true of the cross because the cross only makes sense in the light of man's radical sinfulness and lostness.

Humanism. Man is *awful*, and he is *wonderful*. Shakespeare's Hamlet says, "What a piece of work is a man, how noble in reason! how infinite in faculties! in form and moving how express and admirable, in action how like an angel! in apprehension how like a god: the beauty of the world, the paragon of animals!"[9] Well, yes, if he heeds the "better angels" of his nature, as Abraham Lincoln put it. But the problem is, he cannot.

That is why Christ came. "Therefore, if anyone is in Christ, he is a new creation. The old has passed away; behold, the new has come" (2 Corinthians 5:17). What awaits the Christian is the likeness (*eikon*, "image") of Christ. "Just as we have borne the image of the man of dust, we shall also bear the image of the man of heaven" (1 Corinthians 15:49). Ultimate humanity. True humanism!

72

Faith and Righteousness in Genesis

GENESIS 15:1-6

In biblical studies the word *Pauline* is used to identify the writings and theology of the Apostle Paul. In general it is used as a positive descriptive for the magisterial doctrinal formulations in the book of Romans and the rest of Paul's epistles that underpin his desire to bring the gospel to the nations.

But in liberal-humanist circles *Pauline* is often used as a sneering term of opprobrium that characterizes Paul as the apostle of gloom, or his writings as nothing less than what went wrong with Christianity. Such people mourn that the wonderful teachings of Christ came under the doleful shadow of Paul and were thus emptied of their sunshine. "If only we had Christ without Paul!" they say.

Never mind that the doctrines of original sin and human depravity did not originate with Paul but are, in fact, primeval and patriarchal — that the oldest Scriptures give these doctrines repeated, unforgettable illustrations in the lives of Cain and Lamech and the violent "men of renown," plus in the most incisive expressions — for example, "The LORD saw that the wickedness of man was great in the earth, and that every intention of the thoughts of his heart was only evil continually" (Genesis 6:5). Never mind what the most ancient Scriptures say. Never mind that the good news of the gospel is based on the same bad news that Paul echoes from Genesis — that the reason Christ came and suffered the death that he did was because humanity was so desperately sinful and lost — that the radical sinfulness of us all demanded the radical work of the cross. Never mind that Jesus knew the sinfulness of man far better than Paul.

Never mind that Paul was from the beginning a propagandist for biblical humanism. "The first man was from the earth, a man of dust; the second man is from heaven. As was the man of dust, so also are those who are of the dust, and as is the man of heaven, so also are those who are of heaven. Just as we have borne the image of the man of dust, we shall also bear the image of the man of heaven" (1 Corinthians 15:47-49). Believers will bear the *eikon*, the image, of the ultimate man, in Heaven. That is dizzy, wild humanism! Apostle of gloom? No! Paul was the apostle of optimism!

The purpose of this second overview of Genesis is to show that just as original sin and depravity were not Pauline inventions but are wholly from Genesis, so likewise is the New Testament's teaching that salvation comes not by works but from the righteousness that comes by faith. Again our method will be to examine this in primeval history and in patriarchal history.

FAITH AND RIGHTEOUSNESS IN PRIMEVAL HISTORY (CHAPTERS 4 — 11)

The so-called "Hall of Faith" in Hebrews 11 calls our attention to three prediluvian men of faith — Abel, Enoch, and Noah.

Abel's faith, chap. 4. The Genesis account of Abel's offering to God mentions neither his faith nor his righteousness, but the summary evaluation in Hebrews 11:4 does, by twice referencing his faith: "By faith Abel offered to God a more acceptable sacrifice than Cain, through which he was commended as righteous, God commending him by accepting his gifts. And through his faith, though he died, he still speaks." So how do we discern Abel's faith from the Genesis account? We do so by noting that he brought the very best he could offer, "the firstborn of his flock and of their fat portions" (4:4) — everything prime grade, A-1. But Cain's produce was generic, nothing special, simply "the fruit of the ground" (4:3) — no firstfruits. God had evidently instructed the brothers on what to bring — the very best of their occupations. Abel's excellent offering revealed his believing, righteous heart. But Cain's lackluster offering uncovered his faithless, unbelieving heart.

Abel's offering was "by faith" from beginning to end. So from the beginning of primeval history, faith and righteousness were inseparably bound together.

Enoch's faith, chap. 5. Following Cain's expulsion from the garden, Cain founded a city and began to propagate his evil Cainite line. Adam and Eve also bore a third son, Seth, who replaced Abel and fathered the godly Sethite line.

Of course, death reigned in both the godly and ungodly lines. The Sethite genealogy is recorded in Genesis 5 with a stately cadence that repeats after each name, "and he died." But when the genealogy comes to Enoch, the seventh in the Sethite genealogy (the parallel antithesis to the seventh in the

Cainite genealogy, wicked Lamech), we read, "Enoch walked with God after he fathered Methuselah 300 years and had other sons and daughters. Thus all the days of Enoch were 365 years. Enoch walked with God, and he was not, for God took him" (vv. 22-24). How did God take him? Maybe it was similar to the translation of Elijah as he walked with his successor, Elisha, and suddenly they were separated by chariots and horses of fire, and as Elisha gazed after Elijah, he saw him ascend in a whirlwind (cf. 2 Kings 2:11, 12). Awesome! Or perhaps Enoch just disappeared, was "beamed up," so to speak.

We do know *why* God took him. It was because he "walked with God," a term that describes closest communion with God — as if walking side-by-side with God, as his forefather Adam once had done. And we know that Enoch's walk was charged by his faith because Hebrews 11:5 tells us, "By faith Enoch was taken up so that he should not see death, and he was not found, because God had taken him. Now before he was taken he was commended as having pleased God."

So again, primeval history links faith and righteousness together and then adds the dramatic translation of Enoch to Heaven, demonstrating that faith-righteousness was the sole ground of salvation from earliest creation.

Noah's faith, chaps. 6, 7. It is not a stretch to characterize our present age in pre-diluvian terms because much of what we see is demonized in ways analogous to the pre-flood world, both in real life and in media culture. In comic books and in real life our heroes promote a world of steroids and spittle and blood and violence. The most sacred things of life are blasphemed before laughing audiences. And terrorists lurk in the shadows waiting for their chance. But as bad as things may be, there is nothing quite to match the Genesis description of wholesale depravity: "The LORD saw that the wickedness of man was great in the earth, and that every intention of the thoughts of his heart was only evil continually" (6:5).

Righteous Noah. But amidst this churning depravity, Noah stood as a righteous man, the *only* righteous man on the earth: "Noah was a righteous man, blameless in his generation. Noah walked with God . . . 'for I have seen that you are righteous before me in this generation'" (6:9; 7:1). We must let this settle into our thinking. Noah was the only righteous man in existence at that time. He stood alone.

Of course, Noah had been preceded by righteous Abel and righteous Enoch and many others, but this is the first instance of the word "righteous" (*tsadiq*) in the Bible. And like Adam and Enoch, he "walked" with God in intimate communion. In fact, like Enoch, he was "a herald [preacher] of righteousness" (2 Peter 2:5; cf. Jude 14, 15). He stood up and preached righteousness to his culture, and that without a single convert in 120 years!

Faith-righteousness. Astonishing. But what we must see, most of all, is that his righteousness was not a self-generated righteousness, as the writer of

Hebrews makes so clear: "By faith Noah, being warned by God concerning events as yet unseen, in reverent fear constructed an ark for the saving of his household. By this he condemned the world and became an heir of the righteousness that comes by faith" (11:7).

Note well that Noah's righteousness was credited to him by faith — and this, centuries before God's grand declaration to Abraham.

Righteous obedience. And faith-righteousness produced a towering obedience in Noah. Four times the flood story gives variations of the declaration that "Noah did everything just as God commanded him" (6:22; cf. 7:5, 9, 16). So we see that the person God saves is the one who believes the bare word of God, so that it changes his life. Whenever we read this story, we must see above the churning drama the arching faith and obedience of the one righteous man on earth!

The evidence is most clear from the lives of three great pre-diluvians — Abel and Enoch and Noah — that it is faith that produced righteousness and obedience and effected their redemption.

FAITH AND RIGHTEOUSNESS IN PATRIARCHAL HISTORY (CHAPTERS 12 — 50)

Abraham's life. As we move past the flood and the tower of Babel to patriarchal times, we must understand that Abraham's obedience in leaving Mesopotamia was a monumental act of faith.

He was, until that time, a pagan. He was also advanced in years. And he was prosperous and settled in his pagan world. But Abraham was the only person in his culture who heard God's word. And on the basis of hearing alone, he risked all to follow God.

None of us has ever done anything comparable to this. We trivialize what Father Abraham did if we imagine that we have.

Faith and obedience. Abraham's obedience was immediate. It was an outward evidence of his inward faith. His obedience was so prompt (as described in Hebrews 11:8 — "[he] obeyed . . . And he went out") that he seems to have set out while the command still rang in his ears. In fact, we know that it was not until later that he learned that his destination was Canaan because the whole sentence in Hebrews reads, "And he went out, not knowing where he was going." Abraham was asked to believe the bare word of God, "the naked Word" as Calvin put it. And he did. Thus his lifelong pilgrimage began with faith and was lived out in faith (cf. Hebrews 11:9, 10).

Faith and courage. The curve of Abraham's faith graphs unevenly, because he was a sinful, sometimes faithful, sometimes unfaithful man. The curve soars when he hears God's word and leaves Ur, traveling across the Fertile Crescent and down to Canaan. It spikes higher when Abraham travels the land building altars and calling on the name of the Lord. But the curve dives dramatically in his disastrous folly in Egypt. After Egypt it gently rises when he returns to Canaan repentant and rises more in his generous faith-graced dealings with Lot. Then in chapter 14 the faith-curve again sweeps upward in his incredible rescue of Lot from the kings of the east. Abraham drew out 318 choice men from his household to pursue the kings and save Lot. Swords were whetted, and spears were thrust into the sky. One hundred and twenty miles later, Abraham caught up with the coalition of kings, and his swords prevailed in the night, and Lot was delivered.

How had Abraham done this? Where did he get the courage? It was because of his faith. He believed God's promise that the land would go to his descendants and that God was with him. Even if he met defeat, Abraham knew that God would keep his promise.

Faith and righteousness. It is common to human experience that fear and doubt often follow great victories, as it was with Elijah after his triumph at Mt. Carmel. In the aftermath of victory, Abraham's heart slowed and spasmed with doubt. Despite his faithful life and heroics, he had no heirs. His servants had children. But his faithfulness had not brought him heirs to take up God's promises to him.

Restless doubt gripped his faltering heart. Thus began the divinely initiated dialogue with Abraham:

> *After these things the word of the LORD came to Abram in a vision: "Fear not, Abram, I am your shield; your reward shall be very great." But Abram said, "O Lord GOD, what will you give me, for I continue childless, and the heir of my house is Eliezer of Damascus?" And Abram said, "Behold, you have given me no offspring, and a member of my household will be my heir." And behold, the word of the LORD came to him: "This man shall not be your heir; your very own son shall be your heir." And he brought him outside and said, "Look toward heaven, and number the stars, if you are able to number them." Then he said to him, "So shall your offspring be." (15:1-5)*

Abraham, the former moon worshiper, was familiar with the planets and the astral trails. He was humbled, awed, and hushed under the skies. He said nothing. He was speechless. There were only stars and silence. But though Abraham did not speak, Scripture does: Abram "believed the LORD" (v. 6a). The exact sense is that he believed and kept on believing. The Hebrew for "believed" comes from a root word from which we derive "Amen." So we might paraphrase it, "Abraham inaudibly said Amen to the Lord" — "It is so, Lord." The silence remained unbroken as Abraham believed with all his heart that myriads would come from his yet childless body.

This was not the first time that Abraham had put his faith in God's word. He had trusted God for over a decade. But here his faith was defined.

The clarification was a landmark to our understanding of faith. Abraham "believed the LORD, and he counted it to him as righteousness" (v. 6). Our various English translations all have adequate variations of this: "he credited it to him as righteousness" or "reckoned it to him as righteousness" or "imputed to him as righteousness." Abraham, who was originally destitute of righteousness, was now counted as righteous through faith in God. As Von Rad has said, "But above all, his righteousness is not the result of any accomplishments, whether of sacrifice or acts of obedience. Rather, it is stated programmatically that belief alone has brought Abraham into a proper relationship with God."[1]

This understanding is revolutionary! Circa 2000 B.C., Abraham was declared righteous because of his belief. This understanding is in profound accord with the faith-righteousness of primeval fathers Abel, Enoch, and Noah. It was not *de novo* but rooted in history that began right after the fall. Righteousness has always come by faith. This understanding has remained operative through both primeval and patriarchal history and, as we shall see, the old-covenant era and is rooted in the new covenant in Christ.

The very next night Abraham's faith was further strengthened as God confirmed his promise of a land for Abraham's offspring with a theophany as the blazing furnace of God's presence glided down the aisle of glistening sacrifices in unilateral covenant (cf. 15:12-20). What elevation this brought to Abraham's faith! First, under the stars Abraham had believed that a countless people would come from his own body, and God counted it to him as righteousness. Now, with the same faith, he believed that the land would go to his people. All was light. His fears and doubts were gone.

Faith extraordinary. The great man of faith was, to use Luther's term, "at the same time justified and a sinner" (*simul justus et peccator*), and his faith and conduct were not perfect in the following years. There were setbacks, and yet overall Abraham experienced substantial growth. And Genesis 22 records the most extraordinary demonstration of faith in the Bible apart from that of Christ himself — Abraham's sacrifice of Isaac. In obedience to God's word Abraham reached for the blade, his trembling fingers convulsing as they tightened about the handle for the sacrificial plunge. Abraham's will was in motion. In a split second the sacrifice would be done. "But the angel of the LORD called to him from heaven and said, 'Abraham, Abraham!' And he said, 'Here am I.' He said, 'Do not lay your hand on the boy or do anything to him, for now I know that you fear God, seeing you have not withheld your son, your only son, from me'" (22:11, 12). Abraham's aching heart soared to relief and ecstasy, as did that of young Isaac.

How could Abraham do this? The answer is, he believed that he and Isaac, after the sacrifice, would return down the mountain together.

Hebrews explains, "By faith Abraham, when he was tested, offered up Isaac, and he who had received the promises was in the act of offering up his only son, of whom it was said, 'Through Isaac shall your offspring be named.' He considered that God was able even to raise him from the dead" (11:17-19a).

True faith produces amazing works. Real faith is a faith that works. As the Apostle James memorializes in commenting on Abraham's faith:

Was not Abraham our father justified by works when he offered up his son Isaac on the altar? You see that faith was active along with his works, and faith was completed by his works; and the Scripture was fulfilled that says, "Abraham believed God, and it was counted to him as righteousness" — and he was called a friend of God. You see that a person is justified by works and not by faith alone. (James 2:21-24)

The faith of Sarah, Isaac, Jacob, and Joseph. Time will not permit exposition of the real but faltering faiths of Sarah and Isaac and Jacob — and the model faith of Joseph. The assessments by the writer of Hebrews will suffice.

Though Sarah had initially laughed in disbelief at God's promise that she would bear a son, Hebrews records, "By faith Sarah herself received power to conceive, even when she was past the age, since she considered him faithful who had promised" (11:11).

Though Isaac had attempted to counter God's word and bless Esau alone, God sovereignly dealt with him, so that Hebrews states, "By faith Isaac invoked future blessings on Jacob and Esau" (11:20).

Though Jacob sought God's blessing the wrong way, he came to believe and submit to God's will, so that, as Hebrews says, at the end of his life, "By faith Jacob, when dying, blessed each of the sons of Joseph, bowing in worship over the head of his staff" (11:21).

Joseph, of course, was a paragon of faith as he rested everything on God's promise to him and dramatized it by ordering that his body be mummified for the exodus. As Hebrews has it, "By faith Joseph, at the end of his life, made mention of the exodus of the Israelites and gave directions concerning his bones" (11:22).

Thus we see that from beginning to end the redemptive principle of the patriarchal age was faith. The principal characters of that age were men and women who lived, or came to live, by faith. Furthermore, Abraham's life and the divine dictum that Abraham "believed the LORD, and he [God] counted it to him as righteousness" (Genesis 15:6) was in fact the operative principle for the major players in primeval history — Abel, Enoch, and Noah — as well as for the partriarchs — and their offspring.

FAITH AND RIGHTEOUSNESS IN HISTORY

Paul quotes Genesis 15:6 in two of his letters, Romans and Galatians, to demonstrate that salvation comes by faith, and not by works. In Romans 4 he quotes it to show, first, that Abraham, the grand patriarch of Israel, was counted righteous by faith, not by works (vv. 1-5), and, second, that King David was likewise counted righteous apart from works, as Psalm 32 proves (Romans 4:6-8), and, third, that Gentiles are saved by faith, because Abraham was a Gentile when he believed God, and it was counted to him as righteousness (vv. 9-12), and, lastly, that the faith-righteousness principle preceded the Law, and there is no way the Law could invalidate it or restrict it (vv. 13-15). Thus the faith principle is universal.

This universality is the theme of Paul's other quotation of Genesis 15:6 in Galatians 3:5-9.

> *Does he who supplies the Spirit to you and works miracles among you do so by works of the law, or by hearing with faith — just as Abraham "believed God, and it was counted to him as righteousness"? Know then that it is those of faith who are the sons of Abraham. And the Scripture, foreseeing that God would justify the Gentiles by faith, preached the gospel beforehand to Abraham, saying, "In you shall all the nations be blessed." So then, those who are of faith are blessed along with Abraham, the man of faith.*

The universal gospel is the good news that salvation comes not by works, but by faith!

So what must we conclude? Solely this: Just as original sin was not a Pauline invention but is primeval and patriarchal and universal, so also faith-righteousness is not something that Paul cooked up, but it too is primeval and patriarchal and universal.

The logic that connects these two doctrines of original sin and righteousness through faith is clear and indisputable. It is this: Original sin is a radically sinful state in which every part of our being is tainted by sin, so that the innate inclinations of the heart and mind and will are sinful. Therefore, "'no one understands; no one seeks for God. All have turned aside; together they have become worthless; no one does good, not even one'" (Romans 3:11, 12). There is no way that radically sinful people can achieve the radical righteousness that God requires. This demands a radical solution that is the gift of righteousness that comes by faith — the gift that Abraham received when he believed God. And going deeper, ultimately this righteousness rested and rests on the radical atonement of the cross when Christ who knew no sin became sin for us: "For our sake he made him to be sin who knew no sin, so that in him we might become the righteousness of

God" (2 Corinthians 5:21). There is only one way that redemption can come, and that is by faith. Every works system is doomed by who and what we are.

Here is the gospel from the lips of Paul: "But now the righteousness of God has been manifested apart from the law, although the Law and the Prophets bear witness to it — the righteousness of God through faith in Jesus Christ for all who believe" (Romans 3:21, 22). And again, "For we hold that one is justified by faith apart from works of the law" (v. 28). The desire of Paul's heart for himself (and others) was that he might gain Christ "and be found in him, not having a righteousness of my own that comes from the law, but that which comes through faith in Christ, the righteousness from God that depends on faith" (Philippians 3:9).

And here's the *how* of the good news from Paul:

> *"The word is near you, in your mouth and in your heart" (that is, the word of faith that we proclaim); because, if you confess with your mouth that Jesus is Lord and believe in your heart that God raised him from the dead, you will be saved. For with the heart one believes and is justified, and with the mouth one confesses and is saved. (Romans 10:8-10)*

It was these words that the Holy Spirit used to give me life. I recall like yesterday when I was a boy reading these lines slowly in the King James Version — "That if thou shalt confess with thy mouth the Lord Jesus, and shalt believe in thine heart . . ." And as I read, I believed. It was as if the words of the text lifted off the page and the phrase entered my eyes and then journeyed to my heart. And I was saved!

So my question as a pastor and commentator is one of faith, *not* of works.

Do you *believe* Jesus is Lord?

Do you *believe* in your heart that he died for you?

Do you *believe* in your heart that God raised him from the dead?

If so, I tell you on the authority of God's Word, you have been saved. Here is why: "For with the heart one believes and is justified, and with the mouth one confesses and is saved" (Romans 10:10).

73

Grace in Genesis

GENESIS 6:7, 8

Many Christians unconsciously adopt a view of grace that focuses on saving grace but delimits grace to the grace of salvation. Their thoughts of grace are capsulated by today's most popular hymn, "Amazing Grace!" "Amazing grace! — how sweet the sound — that saved a wretch like me!" And it is certainly true that we are saved by grace. "For by grace you have been saved through faith. And this is not of your own doing; it is the gift of God" (Ephesians 2:8). All so wondrous and true.

But there is much more in the word *grace*, as the rest of John Newton's hymn bears out. The second verse sings of preparatory or, as the theologians say, *prevenient grace*: "'Twas grace that taught my heart to fear, and grace my fears relieved; how precious did that grace appear the hour I first believed!" Newton's third verse is about sustaining, *enabling grace*: "Thro' many dangers, toils, and snares, I have already come; 'tis grace hath brought me safe thus far, and grace will lead me home." And the final stanza is about *glorifying grace*: "When we've been there ten thousand years, bright shining as the sun, we've no less days to sing God's praise than when we've first begun."

So we see that grace is a far more expansive term than many suppose. In the Old Testament it is the Hebrew word *ḥnn,* which is most often translated "grace" or "favor" and describes the favor of a superior to another. In general, grace is the good pleasure of God that inclines him to freely bestow blessing on undeserving people.

According to God's good pleasure, there are saving graces (prevenient grace, efficacious grace, regenerating grace), sanctifying graces (renovating grace, gifting grace, enabling grace, discomfiting grace, preserving grace, dying grace), and glorifying grace — to name just some of the facets of grace. For our purposes, we are going to look at grace in two large categories under which these aspects of grace can be subsumed — *saving* grace and *sanctifying* grace. Our method will be to look at grace in primeval history (from creation to the flood) and then in patriarchal history (from Abraham to the death of Joseph). And then we will look at the universal implications of grace.

GRACE IN PRIMEVAL HISTORY (CHAPTERS 1 — 11)

What we need to see above all is that just as the doctrines of sin and faith-righteousness came with the fall, so did the doctrine of grace. Grace was a major theme in pre-flood history that cycled repeatedly through earth's earliest epochs. In fact, the five principal stories that make up pre-flood primeval history (the stories of the fall, of Cain, of universal depravity, of the flood, and of Babel) all have a similar structure, which is: a) Sin, b) Speech, c) Grace, and d) Judgment.[1] Man sins, God delivers a speech about the sin, God freely gives a mitigating grace, and then God effects a judgment.

Fall and grace, Genesis 3. The fall of Adam and Eve courses with grace that is even evident in the *sin* and *speech* sections of the story. On the occasion of Adam's sin, God did not destroy him but graciously engaged the fallen man in conversation. Also, the ensuing judgment speech to the snake and to the woman shined with grace. God cursed the snake, but that curse contained "the first gospel" indicating that the woman's seed would crush the serpent's head (cf. 3:15). In addition, God's judgments on Eve's and Adam's fundamental roles would mean that nothing in their lives would satisfy them apart from God himself. Their perpetual discomfort in life was a grace insofar as it would drive them to God (cf. 3:14-19).

But with the *sin* and *speech* parts of the story of the fall complete, God performed an act of mitigating *grace* as he executed their *punishment*. "And the LORD God made for Adam and for his wife garments of skins and clothed them" (3:21). Here is amazing, astounding, abounding grace — primeval and eternal. It is clear that this covering of the couple was a sovereign work of God's grace conceived and executed by God alone. It was a work that Adam and Eve could not, as yet, have conceived of because it involved the unprecedented taking of life. Their self-made attempts to cover themselves in inadequate fig-leaf loincloths were replaced by clothing made by God himself. Adam and Eve had attempted to cover themselves, but this covering was from God — a tunic that reached to their knees or ankles.[2]

God's provision here of robes of animal skin both recognized their sin and was an act of grace. Marcus Dods, the famous nineteenth-century Scottish preacher and scholar and principal of New College, Edinburgh University, makes these remarkably penetrating observations:

It is also to be remarked that the clothing which God provided was in itself different from what man had thought of. Adam took leaves from an inanimate, unfeeling tree; God deprived an animal of life, that the shame of His creature might be relieved. This was the last thing Adam would have thought of doing. To us life is cheap and death familiar, but Adam recognized death as the punishment of sin. Death was to early man a sign of God's anger. And he had to learn that sin could be covered not by a bunch of leaves snatched from a bush as he passed by . . . but only by pain and blood.[3]

God's action here in primeval history was a gracious foreshadowing of his sovereign provision for sin. Certainly the first couple would have only understood this in faint principle. But the foundation was mightily laid. Later no Levitical priest could read this passage without making the connection with the blood of atonement because the skins of the animals slain in sacrifice were given to the priests for their use (cf. Leviticus 7:8).[4] God's provision of coverings was a telling illustration of the method of grace in response to sin and its consequences.

God covers sin and its degradation. The Biblical picture of justification is the gift of the robe of righteousness (cf. Zechariah 3:4ff.; Matthew 22:11-13; Luke 15:22). Believers are described as clothed with Christ (cf. Galatians 3:27). At the wedding of the Lamb and his bride we read how God's righteousness produces the saints' righteousness:

> ". . . it was granted her to clothe herself
> with fine linen, bright and pure" —
> for the fine linen is the righteous deeds of
> the saints. (Revelation 19:8)

This is grace abounding! This is the gospel in Genesis.

Cain and grace, Genesis 4. Next, the *sin, speech, grace, punishment* pattern is very clear in the story of Cain and Abel. There, following Cain's horrendous sin of fratricide and God's speech, Cain fell to pieces, crying out that his punishment was too great to bear. There was no remorse over killing his brother, but only self-pity and fear for his own life. Yet, amazingly God heard him. "Then the LORD said to him, 'Not so! If anyone kills Cain, vengeance shall be taken on him sevenfold.' And the LORD put a mark on Cain, lest any who found him should attack him" (4:15). God promised Cain that any vigilante seeking revenge would be severely judged and then marked Cain with a distinctive sign. Cain's fear of a violent death was at once removed.

The nature of Cain's sign has been the subject of much speculation. Some have supposed a tattoo, others a special hairstyle. One ancient rabbi suggested that the sign was a dog that accompanied Cain on his wanderings, assuring Cain of God's protection and frightening his attackers.[5] I picture a giant bull mastiff with a spiked collar! By all estimates God's mark, whatever it was, was an amazing grace. Death was stayed. Cain was cursed and separated from God, yet guarded by God. There is astounding grace right here in darkest Genesis. God was so gracious to Cain.

Observe that the Lord did not abandon guilty Cain. When Cain arrogantly brought his sparse offering to God, and God saw his anger, God did not turn away from him. That is grace. God, in fact, engaged Cain in a fatherly manner with probing, remedial questions. God did not leave him exposed to Satan without recourse. Such grace. God then exhorted Cain to withstand temptation. Again, grace. And after the murder, the Lord listened to Cain's unrepentant, self-pitying plea. Finally, God placed a sign upon Cain that protected him for the remainder of his natural life. Amazing grace!

Depravity and grace, Genesis 6. The extraordinary depths to which the pre-flood world descended when fallen angels commandeered the bodies of men in demon-possession, so that they could then marry the daughters of men, thus producing thoroughly depraved offspring and a culture of violence, is a matter of spiritual record. "The LORD saw that the wickedness of man was great in the earth, and that every intention of the thoughts of his heart was only evil continually" (6:5). And God's speech minced no words. "So the LORD said, 'I will blot out man whom I have created from the face of the land, man and animals and creeping things and birds of the heavens, for I am sorry that I have made them'" (v. 7).

But amidst the black rain of pre-diluvian culture there was a burst of grace. "But Noah found favor in the eyes of the LORD" (6:8) — or as the King James Version has it, "Noah found grace in the eyes of the LORD." This is the very first occurrence in Genesis of the Hebrew word *ḥnn*, which underlies our renderings "favor" and "grace." The significance of this is further heightened because the following verse declares that Noah was a "righteous man," which is also the first use of that word in Scripture. And both words are focused on Noah. This grace or favor was saving grace! Noah and his family (under his godly umbrella) were the only ones who entered the ark of salvation. By faith, Noah obeyed. In sum, this was all due to God's gracious favor! "Noah found grace in the eyes of the LORD." Amazing grace.

The flood and grace, Genesis 6, 7. The story of pre-flood depravity and grace combines with that of the flood so that the worldwide judgment was framed by grace. Going into the flood, Noah found gracious favor in the eyes of the Lord, and because of God's favor he was preserved. On the other side of the flood, we see Noah emerge as he stepped into a virgin world washed clean by judgment — amidst colorful birds filling the air and great animals lumbering forth and busy creatures scurrying about. By grace alone Noah stood with his family in the sunlight of a new world.

It was glorious. And the first thought of Noah was Godward. "Then Noah built an altar to the LORD and took some of every clean animal and some of every clean bird and offered burnt offerings on the altar" (8:20). Joyous worship, surrender, and atonement were in this offering. The whole burnt offering represented Noah's total surrender and dedication to God (cf. Leviticus 1). The offering was totally incinerated to picture the total giving of himself. At the same time it was wholly celebratory, thanking God for the grace just rendered. As the sacrifice disintegrated to ashes, he was in effect saying, "All of my life is yours."

God's response to this offering was one of grace. "And when the LORD smelled the pleasing aroma, the LORD said in his heart, 'I will never again curse the ground because of man, for the intention of man's heart is evil from his youth. Neither will I ever again strike down every living creature as I have done'" (8:21). God responded to Noah's sacrifice with grace to all humanity for reasons totally within himself. Today we all live under this primeval grace, though the world's sins compound.

Babel and grace, Genesis 11. When we come to Babel, we again observe the primeval pattern of *sin, speech,* and *judgment,* but *grace* is missing. This lack serves to set up the continuation of grace during the patriarchal section in chapters 12 — 50. The salvation history of the patriarchal narratives functions as the gracious answer to mankind's scattering at Babel.

Primeval history was about grace — grace to Adam and Eve — grace to Cain — grace to Noah — grace through the flood. Paul's aphorism, "but where sin increased, grace abounded all the more" (Romans 5:20) sums up the theme of primeval history. Grace was rooted in creation and chronicled in pre-flood history. From the beginning it has been our only hope.

And as we will now briefly see, grace was at the heart of patriarchal history as well, beginning with Abraham.

GRACE IN PATRIARCHAL HISTORY (CHAPTERS 12 — 50)

Abraham and grace, Genesis 12. In the patriarchal section, Abraham received the gracious promise that through him all the peoples of the earth would be blessed (cf. 12:3). And then patriarchal history unfolds the fulfillment of that promise — largely through the sanctifying grace of God as God prepared a people to take his blessing to the world.

Abraham, as a man of faith, was subject to a polishing process wherein God worked through the ups and downs of life to make him more usable to him. The process was one of grace from beginning to end. We have spent considerable space chronicling Abraham's two steps forward, one step back — two steps back, one step forward — progress. From the narrative we saw a man who had twice palmed off his wife to a king because of a lack of faith rise to such heights of faith that he could offer his son because he believed that God would raise his son up on the spot.

Faith does not grow in a hothouse but in the uneven climates of life. When we believe and step out to follow God, we step into a process in time and space under his gracious tutelage — which is meant to infuse repeated mercies and grace into our lives that will then enable us to trust more in him.

Our calling is the same as those of old — to submit to the friction and polishing for what it is — the sweet sanctifying grace of God.

Isaac and grace, Genesis 27. Every patriarch had to undergo the renovating grace of God. At first the patriarch Isaac had put his personal love for Esau ahead of the will of God when he attempted to disregard God's word and bless Esau with the primary blessing. But when Jacob (the rightful heir) stole it, old Isaac acceded to the will of God and with renewed faith blessed Jacob (cf. 27:33).

Isaac's shattering humiliation was a grace because it drove him back to faith and aligned him with the glory of God. Often before a work of grace there must first come an earthquake.

Jacob and grace, Genesis 28 — 32. The patriarch Jacob was, by all estimates, a piece of work. His faith-informed instincts were right. He believed the words of God's promise about a people and a land. But he was sinfully unbelieving that God could and would give him the promises apart from his own self-help and deception. Jacob was desperately in need of God's sanctifying grace, and that was what he got!

At the beginning when Jacob was fleeing from Esau, he was given a vision of God's care for him — and it was all of grace. Jacob was not seeking God at that moment — he was fleeing the consequences of his having deceived Esau. He was not expecting grace. But grace was unleashed on his soul in the vision of a ladder extending from where he lay to Heaven. This vision was meant to steel him for what lay ahead with Laban and Leah and Rachel far to the north in his twenty-year sojourn in Mesopotamia. There God's sanctifying grace plowed him as he met his double-dealing match in Rachel's brother Laban and her pathetic sister Leah. Twenty years later when Jacob returned, he was much improved. Jacob had grown in grace by God's grace.

Back from Mesopotamia, his sanctification continued when in the middle of the night Jacob was gripped by an unknown assailant. He had no idea that he was in the grip of God's relentless grace. That night Jacob was crippled and renamed and blessed. Such grace!

Jacob's life was one of relentless, sanctifying grace — tenacious grace, contending grace, intrusive grace, renovating grace. Tenacious in that it would not let him go. Contending as it was always battling for his soul.

Intrusive because it would not be shut out. Renovating because it gave him a new limp and a new name.

Significantly, when Jacob was reunited with Esau, Esau never once mentioned either grace or God. But Jacob referenced "the children whom God has graciously given your servant" (33:5b) and his desire "to find favor [grace] in the sight of my lord" (v. 8b). He also said, "If I have found favor [grace] in your sight" (v. 10a), and finally, "God has dealt graciously with me" (v. 11). Jacob now lived in the awareness of the need of grace.

Jacob still had miles to go, but the sanctifying grace of God was doing its work so that at the end he would by faith bless each of his sons (49; cf. Hebrews 11:21).

Joseph and grace, Genesis 39. And what will we say of Jacob's son Joseph, the viceroy of Egypt, whose sons Ephraim and Manasseh were granted patriarchal status? Obviously, Joseph's life was one of remarkable grace from beginning to end. A brief snapshot from Genesis 39, which records Joseph's abuse by Mrs. Potiphar and his unfair incarceration, is fragrant with grace. Four times in the story we are told that the Lord (*Yahweh*) was "with" Joseph (cf. vv. 2, 3, 21, 23). Joseph's knowledge that God was with him evoked his immortal response, "How then can I do this great wickedness and sin against God?" (v. 9). The text also declares three times (twice in the beginning in Potiphar's house and once at the end in prison) that he was successful because God was "with" him (cf. vv. 2, 3, 23).

Joseph's achievement was astonishing and truly the result of amazing grace. God's grace in helping Joseph to succeed gave him favor (grace) both with Potiphar (v. 4) and then with his jailer (v. 21). Verse 21 brings it all together: "But the LORD was with Joseph and showed him steadfast love [*hesed,* covenantal love] and gave him favor [*hnn,* grace] in the sight of the keeper of the prison."

The word *grace* is expansive indeed, as it denotes the good pleasure of God that inclines him to freely bestow blessing upon his people. Certainly it is bound up with *salvation.* But grace also encompasses *sanctification* and all that the process entails.

Broadly speaking, the primeval narratives of Genesis, with their Sin — Speech — Grace — Punishment structure, are concerned with *saving grace.* In each instance — with the fall, with Cain, with depravity, with the flood — God injects grace amidst judgment.

And broadly speaking, the patriarchal narratives concern themselves with *sanctifying* grace as God calls and develops a covenant people to bless the nations. The lives of Abraham, Isaac, Jacob, and Joseph demonstrate God's determination to shower favor on his people.

So the grand point is that grace was at the root of creation and recurrent in primeval history and was then lavished upon God's people in patriarchal history.

Saving grace. God has always saved his people by grace — and no other way. Salvation has always been the free gift of God. The grand statement of Ephesians 2:8, 9 ("For by grace you have been saved through faith. And this is not your own doing; it is the gift of God, not a result of works, so that no one may boast") is consonant with God's way of salvation in primeval and patriarchal history. Grace has always been "Amazing grace . . . that saved a wretch like me!"

If you have not yet come to faith, one of the best things you can do is read Ephesians 2:8 with significant pauses: "For by grace — you have been saved — through faith — and this is not your own doing — it is the gift of God." I know of a man who came to Christ simply by hearing this text read this way in church.

Sanctifying grace. And, of course, when saving grace is effectual, it begins relentless, sanctifying grace. It is as if the pitcher of God's blessing remains ever tilted over the lives of his children as he makes room for more grace — with a tenacity that will not let us go — with a contention that is always battling for our souls — with an intrusiveness that will not be shut out — with a love that will not let us go.

74

Messiah in Genesis

GENESIS 3:14, 15

Arturo Toscanini had just finished conducting Beethoven's Ninth Symphony. It was a brilliant performance. At the end the audience went wild. They clapped, they whistled, and they stamped their feet, absolutely caught up in the greatness of the moment. As Toscanini stood there, he bowed and bowed and bowed and then acknowledged his orchestra.

When the ovation finally began to subside, Toscanini turned and looked intently at his musicians. He was almost out of control as he whispered, "Gentlemen! Gentlemen! Gentlemen!" The orchestra leaned forward to listen. Was he angry? They could not tell.

In a fiercely enunciated whisper Toscanini said, "Gentlemen, I am nothing." That was an extraordinary admission since Toscanini had an enormous ego. Then he added, "Gentlemen, you are nothing." They had heard that same message before in rehearsal. "But Beethoven," said Toscanini in a tone of adoration, "is everything, everything, everything." And by way of analogy (notwithstanding that we are created in the image of God and are endowed with creator-like capacities and, as believers, even bear Christ's image), we are nothing, and he is everything!

Messiah Jesus is the first and last, the Alpha and Omega, the beginning and end of our faith. He is the grand theme of the Old and New Testaments, the focal point who brings coherence to the whole Bible. As the venerable Old Testament scholar Alec Motyer explains it:

> There is an old jingle which is certainly simple and verges on the simplistic, but our forebears were fundamentally right when they taught that: the Old Testament is Jesus predicted; the Gospels are Jesus revealed; Acts is Jesus preached; the Epistles, Jesus explained; and the Revelation, Jesus

expected. He is the climax as well as the substance and centre of the whole. In him all God's promises are yea and amen (2 Cor. 1:20).[1]

This reality is written large in Genesis, as we have seen over the course of our studies in pre-flood and patriarchal history. The book of Genesis, rightly understood, is the genesis of Christology. As we examine the Christ/Messiah in Genesis, we will not attempt to highlight the many allusions to Messiah and his work but merely the major signposts along the way.

MESSIAH IN PRIMEVAL HISTORY (CHAPTERS 1 — 11)

The Apostle John makes it very clear with the opening words of his Gospel that the creation account of Genesis 1 is full of Christ: "In the beginning was the Word, and the Word was with God, and the Word was God. . . . All things were made through him, and without him was not any thing made that was made" (John 1:1-3). Though the creation account is full of Christ, it is not until after the fall when God cursed the serpent that we have a major prophecy of Christ in Genesis.

The first gospel. The initial part of the curse fell upon the serpent itself.

> *The LORD God said to the serpent,*
> *"Because you have done this,*
> *cursed are you above all livestock*
> *and above all beasts of the field;*
> *on your belly you shall go,*
> *and dust you shall eat*
> *all the days of your life." (3:14)*

But as God cursed the reptile, his speech moved beyond the snake, and the cursed became Satan himself.

> *"I will put enmity between you and the woman,*
> *and between your offspring and her offspring;*
> *he shall bruise your head,*
> *and you shall bruise his heel." (v. 15)*

The "offspring" (literally, "seed") mentioned in this verse became the "'mother prophecy' that gave birth to all the rest of the promises" (Kaiser).[2] The messianic significance of this is that "he [Christ/Messiah] shall bruise your [Satan's] head, and you [Satan] shall bruise his [Messiah's] heel." And more, this significance was understood some three hundred years before Christ, when the Jewish translators of the Septuagint, the Greek Old

Testament, interpreted the word "seed" ("offspring" in the ESV) as a *single individual* — "*he* shall bruise your head." The Septuagint translators, totally free from Christian controversy, understood the seed of the woman to be a future individual who would deal a crushing blow to the serpent. Today's scholarship supports the Septuagint rendering that God's curse predicted that an individual man would engage the snake in combat and win.[3]

So what we have here (right after the fall!) is what the second-century A.D. fathers Justin Martyr and Irenaeus called the "first gospel" (*protoevangelium*). Genesis 3:15 promised that one was coming who would defeat the serpent who had perpetrated the fall. Here is the gospel in paradise just lost! God cursed Satan and in the process proclaimed victory through his Son, the second Adam, who crushed Satan by his great work on the cross.

Thus we see, amidst the inconsolable bleakness and despair of the fall and the divine curses, a curse that radiates the first light of the gospel. A mighty deliverer is coming. That is good news!

Seed preserved. How God preserved the line of the Deliverer is a marvel of primeval history. Adam had, of course, listened closely to God's oracle to the serpent. He understood that one of Eve's offspring would bruise the head of the snake. Thus Adam "called his wife's name Eve, because she was the mother of all living" (3:20). Eve means "life." Hope of a Deliverer welled in the primeval couple. And then when Eve gave birth to her first son, Cain, she said, "I have gotten a man with the help of the LORD" (4:1). Eve's words were an implicit declaration of faith. Adam had believed the promise of 3:15 and named her "Life." And now the young mother of life praised God with a freshly charged faith for her newborn son, a man just like Adam. Later the birth of Abel again buoyed the couple's hopes of an offspring who would conquer the serpent.

But all was not well. A dark shadow moved over the sons. And as life faded from murdered Abel's eyes, darkness enveloped humanity. With Abel's death and Cain's degeneration there was no heir, no seed who would challenge, much less strike the head of the serpent. Cainite civilization went "the way of Cain" (Jude 11), as epitomized by the brutal song of Lamech. Darkness had gone to midnight. Exponential violence became a way of life.

But amidst the couple's violent, seedless night there flashed light — "And Adam knew his wife again, and she bore a son and called his name Seth, for she said, 'God has appointed for me another offspring instead of Abel, for Cain killed him'" (4:25). Eve's faith shined here because her term "another offspring" referenced the promise of 3:15 — that her seed would crush the snake's head. How sweet it was for the mother of all living to hold the promised baby Seth in her arms. And the grace of God was effectual because Seth and his family called on the name of the Lord in worship (cf. 4:26). Their hope was that one day a child would come through Seth's descendants who would crush the snake.

Both Cainite and Sethite lines multiplied. The apex of the long-lived Sethite patriarchs was righteous Enoch who "walked with God, and he was not, for God took him" (5:24). However, despite the elevating example of Enoch, wicked Cainite civilization increased in dominance over the Sethites. And universal depravity covered civilization so that man's mind became "only evil continually" (6:5).

So it came about that the hope of a godly line was reduced to a single pinpoint in all humanity — one man. Only one of Seth's descendants remained untarnished: "Noah was a righteous man, blameless in his generation. Noah walked with God" (6:9). When the flood was over, Noah and his three sons remained as the only hope for the promise of Genesis 3:15.

But the promise was hardly safe! Noah's subsequent drunken display demonstrated the danger for all to see (cf. 9:20-23). And the danger was further confirmed by Ham's leering delight in his father's folly. Divine judgment followed as Noah cursed the descendants of Ham's youngest son Canaan, the father of the infamous Canaanites. If Shem and Japheth had followed Ham in his sin, the Sethite line would have been vitiated. Instead, the two covered their father's nakedness. And Noah's oracle to Shem was, "Blessed be the LORD [Yahweh], the God of Shem" (9:26). Noah's blessing and affirmation that Yahweh was "the God of Shem" indicates that Shem was already in special relationship with God. And the grand fact is that it was through Shem that the godly line of Adam's son Seth would go on to be extended to the great patriarch Abraham (cf. 11:10-26).

The primeval preservations of God's promise to Eve of a Deliverer-offspring who would bruise the head of Satan astound us. The promise appeared to be finished with Cain's murder of Abel. But then came baby Seth, and people "called on the name of the LORD" (4:26). Seth's line, however, became all but buried by the demonized Cainite civilization. But God answered with righteous Noah and the flood. Noah and his three sons and their spouses were all that survived. And then the promised line was narrowed to Shem (the Semites). Finally, the promise of Genesis 3:15 was given to one man, father Abraham. It was through his seed that Messiah would come, and he would crush the head of Satan. What we must see here is that all pre-flood history is tied together by a singular concern — the preservation of the promise to Eve of a descendant who would do battle with Satan and would be wounded before crushing him. Thus we have the genesis of the great messianic hope of the Bible — the arrow that points us to Jesus Christ.

MESSIAH IN PATRIARCHAL HISTORY
(CHAPTERS 12 — 50)

So now we come to patriarchal times with Abraham, the descendant of Shem, living in a pagan, moon-worshiping culture. It was through Abraham's offspring that God had elected to effect Genesis 3:15's promise of the Messiah-deliverer.

Promise to Abraham. Abraham's call was wrenching in that it called for him to fully abandon his roots: "Leave your country — leave your people — and leave your father's household" (nuclear family).

At the same time God's great promise to him was laced with reiterated blessing. The first half of God's promise prophesied *personal* blessings upon Abraham: "And I will make of you a great nation, and I will bless you and make your name great, so that you will be a blessing" (12:2).

The promises assaulted reality because Abraham was childless and Sarai (Sarah) was barren. But Abraham believed God's bare word.

The second half of the promise moved from personal blessings for Abraham to specific *global* blessings: "I will bless those who bless you, and him who dishonors you I will curse, and in you all the families of the earth shall be blessed" (12:3).

The final soaring line is fragrant with the gospel's good news for the world, for the blessing includes the fulfillment of the promise of 3:15, which would be effected by Christ's life, death, and resurrection. Significantly, the Apostle Paul would reference this promise of worldwide blessing when he explained to the Galatians that faith is the universal principle through which the blessings of righteousness come: "And the Scripture, foreseeing that God would justify the Gentiles by faith, preached the gospel beforehand to Abraham, saying, 'In you shall all the nations be blessed.' So then, those who are of faith are blessed along with Abraham, the man of faith" (3:8, 9). Thus the gospel blessings spoken of in Genesis will go to those who, like Abraham, believe the word of God. This is good news!

The high point in Abraham's faith came in his offering of Isaac, which evokes ready images of Christ. Very significantly, a pre-Christian Jewish midrash (commentary) on Genesis, the *Genesis Rabbah*, commented that Isaac, bearing the wood for his own sacrifice on his back, was like a condemned man, carrying his own cross.[4] Truly the image was, and is, prophetic of Jesus, whom John's Gospel describes as "bearing his own cross, to the place called the place of a skull" (19:17). Isaac's utter trust also foreshadowed the greater partnership of the cross. The phrase, "they went both of them together" (repeated in Genesis 22:6, 8) twice emphasizes the victim and the offerer ascending the hill together — a dramatic shadow of Calvary. Moreover, it is clear that Abraham could not have offered Isaac without Isaac's cooperation. Thus Isaac had decided to obey his father whatever the cost, just as his father had decided to obey God whatever the cost!

Isaac's obedience calls to mind Christ's words to the Father before the Incarnation:

> *"Sacrifices and offering you have not desired,*
> *but a body have you prepared for me;*
> *in burnt offerings and sin offerings*
> *you have taken no pleasure.*
> *Then I said, 'Behold, I have come to do your will, O God,*
> *as it is written of me in the scroll of the book.'"*
> *(Hebrews 10:5-7, paraphrasing Psalm 40:6, 7)*

The Suffering Servant passages in Isaiah also come to mind. "He was oppressed, and he was afflicted, yet he opened not his mouth; like a lamb that is led to the slaughter, and like a sheep that before its shearers is silent, so he opened not his mouth" (53:7).

Here also, in Abraham's offering of Isaac, is a fitting place to consider what it was that Jesus had in mind when he declared to the Jews, "Your father Abraham rejoiced that he would see my day. He saw it and was glad" (John 8:56). To which the hearers replied incredulously to Jesus, "You are not yet fifty years old, and have you seen Abraham?" (v. 57). So we ask, when could Abraham actually have seen something of the day of Christ? Likely it was when he took his son Isaac up the mountain to offer him, and God provided a substitute offering — a ram caught in a thicket. Observe that Abraham named the place "The LORD will provide" (Genesis 22:14). As Walter Kaiser explains, "Abraham saw that God himself would provide a substitute, someone in that coming 'seed' who would somehow be connected with the sacrifices and deliverance of Isaac, the son of promise."[5] Thus he saw Christ's day and rejoiced.

In retrospect we also see that Isaac's bearing the wood anticipated Christ's bearing the wood of the cross and that Isaac's trusting obedience was evocative of the obedience of Christ unto death.

Promise to Judah. Now trace the life of Isaac's son Jacob all the way to the end of Genesis, when from his deathbed he intoned his patriarchal blessings to his twelve sons, bestowing the messianic promise upon Judah and his descendants because Judah's older brothers Reuben, Simeon, and Levi had disqualified themselves.

Jacob's oracle began by prophesying that Judah's descendants would achieve a lion-like dominance over his brothers as well as over his enemies. But then, with the lion imagery ringing in Judah's ears and imagination, Judah heard his father's blessing expand out to the distant future and the dawn of the messianic age:

> *"The scepter shall not depart from Judah,*
> *nor the ruler's staff from between his feet,*
> *until tribute comes to him;*
> *and to him shall be the obedience of the peoples." (49:10)*

Ancient Jewish and Christian commentators almost uniformly interpreted this prophecy as messianic. "The scepter" and "the ruler's staff" are plainly symbolic of kingship, which would remain with Judah until Messiah comes — "and to him shall be the obedience of the peoples," meaning the nations of the world. Indeed, the fourth-century A.D. Jewish Targum Onkelos reads, "until the Messiah comes, whose is the kingdom, and him shall the nations obey."[6]

And what will Messiah's reign be like? It will be a golden age of extravagant abundance and celebration in which wine (the symbol of prosperity and blessing) will be as common as water. Thus Jacob further prophesies of the Messiah:

> *"Binding his foal to the vine*
> *and his donkey's colt to the choice vine,*
> *he has washed his garments in wine*
> *and his vesture in the blood of grapes.*
> *His eyes are darker than wine,*
> *and his teeth whiter than milk." (vv. 11, 12)*

There will be such an abundance of grapes that the Messiah will tether his donkey to a choice grape vine with no concern as to his donkey's helping itself to the vintage. The surplus of wine will be such that people will not worry about using it to wash their clothes. The Messiah will be a handsome picture of strength and power.

Such a prospect! An altogether lovely Messiah — vines used as hitching posts — wine as wash water. What dizzying, evocative imagery! It says good-bye to life as it has been and welcomes a new age. Jesus' contemporaries understood it this way. This is how they read the Hebrew Scriptures. And this is how Messiah Jesus understood it, because Jesus announced the age to come in just this imagery in his very first "sign" at Cana of Galilee. Do you recall the moment of discovery when the master of the feast tasted the water turned to wine? "The master of the feast called the bridegroom and said to him, 'Everyone serves the good wine first, and when people have drunk freely, then the poor wine. But you have kept the good wine until now.' This, the first of his signs, Jesus did at Cana in Galilee, and manifested his glory. And his disciples believed in him" (John 2:9b-11).[7]

For a shimmering golden moment, donkeys were hitched to grape vines, and wine was as abundant as wash water. In fact, water was turned into wine! The abundance of wine signaled to Israel that the Messiah was present. This was the Lion of the tribe of Judah. And at this initial sign, his disciples believed in him. They simply connected the dots!

MESSIAH IN GENESIS AND THE BIBLE

The first gospel's promise in Genesis of a Deliverer from the seed of the woman who would bruise the head of the serpent was preserved through the birth of Seth when God gave Eve another seed to replace Abel (cf. Genesis 4:25). Seth's line was then preserved in righteous Noah through the flood. And after the flood the Sethite line was preserved through Noah's son Shem (cf. 9:26), and through Shem's descendant Abraham (cf. 11:10 — 12:3), and then through Abraham's son Isaac (cf. 21:12), and through Isaac's son Jacob (cf. 25:23), and through Jacob's son Judah (cf. 49:10).

And then, beyond the history of Genesis, God chose a descendant of Judah, Jesse's son David, to be the line through which Messiah would come (2 Samuel 7:12-16). When Jesus Christ, the Lion of the tribe of Judah, came, he was born in Judah in the town of Bethlehem (cf. Micah 5:2). No one but Jesus had these credentials. And when Jesus changed the water to wine, his disciples knew that the Messiah was present! It was a day of intoxicating, exuberant abundance — a taste of the eternal day when wine will be as common as water.

Christians, our faith is not something new. It was not some first-century notion that by chance became popular in the ancient world. No. Rather, the Messiah was prophesied at the beginning of primeval history, and the hope of his coming was wonderfully preserved through primeval and patriarchal history and thus became the unifying message of the Old Testament.

For us, Christ is everything. He is everything — *everything* — *EVERYTHING!*

75

God in Genesis

GENESIS 2:1, 2

There is a myth abroad that suggests that too much knowledge of the Bible is not good because it tends to cool the heart and stunt devotion. Christians who think this way encourage a simple saving faith in Christ but caution against too much learning lest it spoil your faith. And they have a point, if their concern is about imbibing the destructive biblical criticism of liberal theologians or speculative, academic, ivory-tower theology. But sadly, all too often what they discourage is the rigorous study of the Scriptures, which then delimits their knowledge of God.

Author and publisher Frank Sheed describes the folly of such thinking, saying:

> A virtuous man may be ignorant, but ignorance is not a virtue. It would be a strange God Who could be loved better by being known less. Love of God is not the same thing as knowledge of God; love of God is immeasurably more important than knowledge of God; but if a man loves God knowing a little about Him, he should love God more from knowing more about Him: for every new thing known about God is a new reason for loving Him.[1]

Therefore our study of the Bible, which is our primary and infallible source of knowledge about God, is everything to our spiritual health.

And we must take this logic even further, because the single most important thing about you is what you believe about God. Your belief about God defines you. Your belief about God shapes the way you live. Right now, your belief about God is controlling your life.

The truth of this makes the book of Genesis crucial to our existence because Genesis is about God from first to last. It is no accident that God is the subject of the first sentence of the Bible: "In the beginning, God [*Elohim*] created the heavens and the earth" (v. 1). And it is no accident that the name *Elohim* occurs thirty-five times in the creation account (which is five times seven, the biblical number of perfection). There is a great intentionality here. Genesis also reveals a careful intentionality in its introduction and use of God's names as is appropriate to each account. For example, following creation, when God interacts with man, the covenant name of God, *Yahweh*, is joined with *Elohim* as *Yahweh-Elohim*, "the LORD God." It is *Yahweh-Elohim* who interacts with Adam and Eve and Cain and Abel. The names *El Shaddai* ("God Almighty"), *El Olam* ("Eternal God"), *Yahweh Jireh* ("the Lord will provide"), and others are used with the same revelatory intentionality. So when you read Genesis with its epics and grand stories and characters, remember that the book is about God from first to last.

As we consider God in Genesis, we will do so in the order of his power, his presence, his knowledge, his sovereignty, and his providence.

GOD ALL-POWERFUL

As to God's power, *Elohim* is the singular word for the majestic expression of God as Creator of the universe because *Elohim* signifies his omnipotent deity. The five times seven instances of *Elohim* in the creation account give metered sevenfold praise to the perfect creation of the all-powerful Creator.

Elohim. God is so all-powerful that he merely spoke everything into existence, beginning with light and ending with man. The psalmist summarized God's all-power saying:

> *By the word of the LORD the heavens were made,*
> *and by the breath of his mouth all their host. (Psalm 33:6)*

Such power! He spoke matter and the universe and light into existence — from the fires of Arcturus to the coruscations of the firefly. All that *Elohim* employed was his word, his breath.

Thus the first page of the Bible reveals God who existed "in the beginning," before time itself, as a self-existent Creator of limitless power, the source of all power. That is to say, he is omnipotent. Genesis flashes with this power in cosmic events like the universal flood in the age of Noah, the destruction of Sodom and Gomorrah in Abraham's day, and the famine in Joseph's day.

The logic of God's all-power as we have it in Genesis is this:

Since He has at His command all the power in the universe, the Lord God omnipotent can do anything as easily as anything else. All His acts are done without effort. He expends no energy that must be replenished. His self-sufficiency makes it unnecessary for Him to look outside of Himself for a renewal of strength. All the power required to do all that He wills to do lies in undiminished fullness in His own infinite being. (A.W. Tozer)[2]

Fellow believers, how you relate to this truth about God defines you. If you doubt it, or hedge it with conditions, or rationalize it as theological hyperbole, or refuse to engage this truth because you are lazy, you abuse and defile yourself. Remember, the single most important thing about you is what you believe about God.

GOD ALL-PRESENT

While the all-presence of God (what we call his omnipresence) is implicit throughout Genesis, the references in Genesis to God's presence are anecdotal and largely from the life experiences of the patriarchs Isaac, Jacob, and Joseph. For each of them the reality of God's presence was both encouraging and sanctifying.

Isaac and God's presence. Isaac's experience of God's presence came when he was sojourning in Gerar among the Philistines and was assured of God's presence in the *future*, the *present*, and the *past* (Genesis 26). God appeared to him, declaring first, "I will be with you" (v. 3), and the second time, "I am with you" (v. 24). Then the Philistines observed that "the LORD has been with you" (v. 28).

This is Genesis reality: God is *spatially* and *specially* present. There is no place that God is not. All of God is everywhere to specially protect and bless his children. The dual promises of God's presence lifted Isaac out of generational deceit and disgrace and brought glory to God's name among the Philistines and blessing to Isaac (vv. 28-33).

Jacob and God's presence. Jacob's life-altering experience of God's presence occurred as he fled from Esau and found himself alone at night in a howling waste full of danger, then fell into an exhausted sleep on a pillow. "And he dreamed, and behold, there was a ladder set up on the earth, and the top of it reached to heaven. And behold, the angels of God were ascending and descending on it! And behold, the LORD stood above it" (28:12, 13a). Then, from above the ladder, God spoke in grand covenantal terms, reaffirming the promise through Jacob (cf. vv. 13, 14). From this Jacob learned that God was present with him and that traffic was being carried on between Heaven and earth for his sake.

Jacob rose from his pillow astonished. "Then Jacob awoke from his sleep and said, 'Surely the LORD is in this place, and I did not know it'" (v. 16). He was astounded because he was so like us who forget that God is present, especially when we are in trouble. Jacob responded in reverence and awe, "How awesome is this place! This is none other than the house of God, and this is the gate of heaven" (v. 17). Jacob learned the spiritual truth that the "house of God" and "the gate of heaven" are coextensive with and encompass creation. The house (God's presence) and the gate (access to God) are everywhere!

God's ministering presence went with Jacob all his life through the twenty succeeding years in Mesopotamia and beyond. In fact, after two decades, during his journey back to the promised land, "the angels of God met him. And when Jacob saw them he said, 'This is God's camp!' So he called the name of that place Mahanaim" (32:1, 2). Twenty years earlier when he had left Canaan on the run, "the angels of God" met him on the ladder between Heaven and earth, and now as Jacob returned, "the angels of God" (identical phrase) again met him. His joyful declaration of "Mahanaim" ("two camps") heralded that there were two camps — his camp and a camp of angels.

God's presence had been with him, was now with him, and would be the abiding reality as he entered Canaan, and for the rest of his life.

Joseph and God's presence. Later it was the certainty of God's presence that enabled Jacob's son Joseph to resist Mrs. Potiphar's advance as in that story we are told four times that the Lord was "with" Joseph (39:2, 3, 21, 23). It was the sanctifying awareness of God's presence that compelled Joseph to declare when alone with the temptress, "How then can I do this great wickedness and sin against God?" (v. 9b).

Genesis gives us the genesis of the grand doctrine of God's abiding presence everywhere. Jeremiah would record God's words, "'Am I a God at hand, declares the LORD, and not a God afar off? Can a man hide himself in secret places so that I cannot see him? declares the LORD. Do I not fill heaven and earth? declares the LORD'" (Jeremiah 23:23, 24; cf. Psalm 139:9, 10). The mind-stretching reality is that if our universe of a hundred thousand million galaxies were all compressed into a bucket, that bucket would be as awash and fully saturated with God's presence as if it were immersed in the sea. God surrounds his people and the whole universe with his presence. God "is present at every part of space with his whole being" (Grudem).[3] All of God is present wherever we go — *spatially* and, for his children, *specially*.

Again, the most important thing about you is what you believe about God. That is what defines you. It is one thing to blithely affirm that God is present. But it is quite another to have it dominate and inform us in all our moments. The knowledge that God is spatially present and, more, specially present to bless and protect us — what a difference this makes in our lives. God's presence quells the temptation to compromise. God's presence puts our fears to flight. It instills confidence and steel.

Truly, what you understand and believe about God determines who you are.

GOD ALL-KNOWING

Though the creation account and the story of the fall posit an all-knowing God, the first explicit reference to this comes prior to the flood: "The LORD saw that the wickedness of man was great in the earth, and that every intention of the thoughts of his heart was only evil continually" (6:5). No human could make such an assessment — only the universal consciousness of a divine mind could do this. This one statement encapsulates a stupendous revelation about God — his omniscience (all-knowledge).

Later when Hagar was fleeing the wrath of her mistress Sarah and was alone in the wilderness of Shur, she was encountered by the angel of the Lord, who comforted her with a directive to return to Sarah and the revelation that she was pregnant with a son. Hagar's response was remarkable. "So she called the name of the LORD who spoke to her, 'You are a God of seeing,' for she said, 'Truly here I have seen him who looks after me.' Therefore the well was called Beer-lahai-roi" (16:13, 14).

Surprisingly, Hagar did not revel in the revelation of her pregnancy but rather in God. In amazed gratitude she bestowed two names — the first upon God, and the second upon the place. Both names celebrate the same reality — that God sees all (his omniscience). She named God "You are a God of seeing." And she named the place "Beer-lahai-roi," which means "well of the living one who sees me." Hagar's lips created an enduring double celebration of God's omniscience. In doing so she became the only person, male or female, in the Old Testament to confer a name on God.

The truth that God knows all became especially poignant later for Hagar's mistress Sarah when she overheard from an adjacent tent one of Abraham's angelic guests (actually Yahweh himself) tell Abraham that his aged wife would bear a son within the year (cf. 18:10). *Absurd*, thought Sarah. Her response was silent and inward. "So Sarah laughed to herself, saying, 'After I am worn out, and my lord is old, shall I have pleasure?'" (v. 12). It was melancholy, hopeless, and nonbelieving laughter — hidden unbelief. Her laughter echoed nowhere but in her soul. But in a blessed moment her unbelief was stripped away. "The LORD said to Abraham, 'Why did Sarah laugh and say, "Shall I indeed bear a child, now that I am old?"'" (v. 13). In a graced instant old eavesdropping Sarah understood that her unuttered thoughts were fully known to the Lord. Whereas Sarah's maid Hagar had learned that God sees her, Sarah now learned that God saw *inside* her. Sarah was doused with the reality of God's omniscience, that he is all-knowing.

Sweetly and ironically, Sarah's future son David would put this reality into unforgettable verse.

O LORD, you have searched me and known me!
You know when I sit down and when I rise up;
you discern my thoughts from afar. . . .
Even before a word is on my tongue,
behold, O LORD, you know it altogether. (Psalm 139:1, 2, 4)

Similarly, the apostle John would say, "God is greater than our heart, and he knows everything" (1 John 3:20). And the writer of Hebrews gives this truth classic expression: "And no creature is hidden from his sight, but all are naked and exposed to the eyes of him to whom we must give account" (4:13).

God knows all inner thoughts, whether they be the thoughts of humans or angels. No human, whether in a dark rain forest or atop a Manhattan skyscraper, has a thought that is not known to God. God perfectly knows all things. He has never wondered about anything. He has never been taken by surprise. He has never forgotten anything. He will never be mistaken. How sweet this is for God's children. As J. I. Packer wrote:

> What matters supremely, therefore, is not, in the last analysis, the fact that I know God, but the larger fact which underlies it — the fact that *he knows me*. I am graven on the palms of his hands. I am never out of his mind. All my knowledge of him depends on his sustained initiative in knowing me. I know him, because he first knew me, and continues to know me. He knows me as a friend, one who loves me; and there is no moment when his eye is off me, or his attention distracted from me, and no moment, therefore, when his care falters.[4]

Fellow Christians, do you truly believe this? The answer is crucial — because the most important thing about you is what you believe about God.

GOD'S SOVEREIGNTY

The great Genesis truths that God is all-powerful and all-present and all-knowing coalesce in the truth that he is sovereign over all — that he is on the throne ruling over all.

As sovereign King his rule is total and unexceptionable. God does as he chooses, and none can stay his hand, inhibit his plans, or even question what he has done (cf. Daniel 4:34, 35). God's sovereignty resounds in every episode in Genesis and would require several books to give adequate exposition.

Sovereign in history. So we can only mention briefly that God revealed himself to Abraham as sovereign over history when he told Abraham, "Know for certain that your offspring will be sojourners in a land that is not theirs and will be servants there, and they will be afflicted for four hundred years.

But I will bring judgment on the nation that they serve, and afterward they shall come out with great possessions" (Genesis 15:13, 14). This divine preview of history with its precise dating that extends out four centuries taught Abraham that God is sovereign in history. Process Theology and Openness Theology are refuted here. God controls every detail of history. The forty-fifth chapter of Isaiah, which so magnificently chronicles God's sovereign direction of history, records this divine question:

> *Who told this long ago?*
> *Who declared it of old?*
> *Was it not I, the LORD? (Isaiah 45:21)*

Sovereign in life. Genesis also reveals that God is the sovereign giver of life. The incredulous, unbelieving laughter of first Abraham and then Sarah underwent a believing rebirth as they both laughed together when baby Isaac (Hebrew, "laughter") was born. God had taken the old couple who were "as good as dead" (Romans 4:19) in respect to childbearing and gave them a son whose descendants would be as numerous as the stars. Then when Isaac grew and married, his wife Rebekah was barren. "And Isaac prayed to the LORD for his wife, because she was barren. And the LORD granted his prayer, and Rebekah his wife conceived" (Genesis 25:21). Old Isaac (Laughter himself) must have taken his pregnant wife in his arms and whirled in dizzy peals of laughter.

One thing was clear after twenty years of barrenness — Rebekah's barrenness was ended by the sovereign intervention of God. When baby Jacob matured and took Rachel as his wife, barrenness was also her lot — until God gave life to her womb and gave her Joseph.

Sovereign in grace. But here, with Rebekah's divinely granted pregnancy, we begin to see God's sovereign grace rise over the story. As her pregnancy progressed, Rebekah discerned a struggle in her womb. So she went and inquired of the Lord.

What she heard was of cosmic significance. She learned that she would have twins and that they would father two nations that would divide and oppose each other. She also learned that the conventional rights of her firstborn would be overturned, as their roles would be reversed.

> *. . . the one shall be stronger than the other,*
> *the older shall serve the younger. (v. 23b)*

Rebekah learned that the tumult in her womb was not of her or Isaac's making but was part of a divine plan that God was working out for his own purposes and glory and that "The order of nature is not necessarily the order of grace" (Griffith Thomas).[5]

This is repeatedly emphasized in Genesis, from the very first. The older brother Cain had his offering rejected, while younger Abel's was accepted. After Cain murdered Abel, the line of Seth, the even younger brother, became the chosen line (4:26 — 5:8). Young Isaac was chosen over his older brother Ishmael (17:18, 19). Joseph, the youngest of Jacob's sons, was chosen over his brothers (37:3ff.). And Judah was likewise chosen over his older brothers Reuben, Simeon, and Levi (49:8).

Significantly, the New Testament is likewise clear that the order of nature does not determine the order of grace.

> *But God chose what is foolish in the world to shame the wise; God chose what is weak in the world to shame the strong; God chose what is low and despised in the world, even things that are not, to bring to nothing things that are, so that no human being might boast in the presence of God. (1 Corinthians 1:27-29; cf. Romans 9:6-13)*

Tradition does not determine grace. Convention does not dictate grace. Neither do giftedness or natural endowments. Grace does not bow to social privilege or status. God is not bound by our self-righteous moralizing. God is not bound by our limited knowledge. God is not tame and will not submit to the captivity of our notions of what he should be or do. So we see in Genesis that God is sovereign in history, in life, and in grace — and, lastly, in providence.

GOD'S PROVIDENCE

The sweet doctrine of God's providence is this: God sovereignly works in and through the everyday, non-miraculous events of life to effect his will. Such a God, of course, is great beyond our imaginings because he *maintains* all of life, *involves* himself in all events, and *directs* all things to their appointed end while rarely interrupting the natural order of life.[6] He is far greater than our imaginings because he arranges all of life to suit and effect his providence. This makes all of life a miracle. God provides and controls in three grand arenas — history, nature, and the lives of individual people. God's providential control of life is illustrated by virtually every narrative in the Bible. His providence is an axiom for all biblical narrative.[7]

Above all, the story of Joseph is about God working his will through the everyday events of life. There were no miracles here. God did not suspend his natural laws to make things happen. The story was about the hidden but sure way of God. God's hidden hand arranges everything without show or explanation or violating the nature of things. God is involved in all events and directs all things to their appointed end.

Toward the conclusion of the great narrative, when Joseph reveals himself to his brothers, he says exactly this: "And God sent me before you to preserve for you a remnant on earth, and to keep alive for you many survivors. So it was not you who sent me here, but God" (45:7, 8).

What a God he is — because he is not just a God of the extraordinary but a God of the ordinary! His power and infinitude took both the good and evil actions of Joseph's family, of Pharaoh and his servants, and of passersby and used their actions for good, so that at the end Joseph declared to his brothers, "As for you, you meant evil against me, but God meant it for good, to bring it about that many people should be kept alive, as they are today" (50:20). The compounded providences of Joseph's life stagger the mind.

> The jealous hatred of brethren; the dreams of a youth; the passage of a caravan bound for Egypt; the preparation of Joseph by a life of adversity; the anger of Pharaoh and the imprisonment of two officials; the strange dreams of these prisoners and Joseph's supernatural gift of interpretation; the dreams of Pharaoh; the change of rainfall in a fourth of Africa to bring about the two cycles of abundance and famine by the flood and failure of the Nile; the elevation of Joseph to the throne of Egypt — all of these things were brought about naturally by the supernatural work of God who is Lord of all, in order to fulfill the counsel of His will. (Barnhouse)[8]

The sweet providence of God is the province of God's people. The prophet Jeremiah sang of it: "For I know the plans I have for you, declares the LORD, plans for wholeness and not for evil, to give you a future and a hope" (Jeremiah 29:11). Paul gave it this cherished expression: "And we know that for those who love God all things work together for good, for those who are called according to his purpose" (Romans 8:28).

Christians, the most important thing about you is what you believe about God. What you believe defines you. What you believe determines how you live.

So I must ask, do you believe with your whole mind and heart that God is all-powerful? Do you believe with everything in you that God is spatially and specially present with you? Do you believe wholeheartedly that he knows everything, even your inarticulate words and thoughts before you say them? Do you believe that God is absolutely sovereign in all of life? Do you believe that God's providence is working in and through your life to effect your good?

If so, you have embraced the God of Genesis and the Christ of the Bible because "in him the whole fullness of deity dwells bodily" (Colossians 2:9). And you are ready to live.

And we know that for those who love God all things work together for good, for those who are called according to his purpose. For those whom he foreknew he also predestined to be conformed to the image of his Son, in order that he might be the firstborn among many brothers. And those whom he predestined he also called, and those whom he called he also justified, and those whom he justified he also glorified. (Romans 8:28-30)

Soli Deo Gloria!

Notes

CHAPTER ONE: BEGINNING

1. 1) 2:4a: "of the heavens and the earth"; 2) 5:1a: "of Adam"; 3) 6:9a: "of Noah"; 4) 10:1a: "of the sons of Noah"; 5) 11:10a: "of Shem"; 6) 11:27a: "of Terah"; 7) 25:12a: "of Ishmael"; 8) 25:19a: "of Isaac"; 9) 36:1a, 9a: "of Esau"; and 10) 37:2a: "of Jacob."

2. Victor P. Hamilton, *The Book of Genesis: Chapters 1—17,* New International Commentary on the Old Testament (Grand Rapids, MI: Eerdmans, 1990), pp. 2, 3.

3. See D. J. A. Clines, *Catholic Biblical Quarterly,* No. 38 (1976), pp. 487, 488. Clines explains that Gerhard Von Rad initially observed a pattern of *sin, mitigation,* and *punishment.* Then Claus Westermann discerned another element, that of divine *speech.* Though he did not include it in the pattern, Clines does. Thus the following chart:

	I. **Sin**	**II.** **Speech**	**III.** **Grace**	**IV.** **Punishment**
1. Fall	3:6	3:14-19	3:21	3:22-24
2. Cain	4:8	4:10-12	4:15	4:16
3. Sons of God	6:2	6:3	6:8, 18ff.	7:6-24
4. Flood	6:5, 11f	6:7, 13-21	6:8, 18ff.	7:6-24
5. Babel	11:4	11:6f	10:1-32	11:8

4. *Ibid.,* p. 490.

5. *Ibid.,* pp. 502, 503.

6. Gleason Archer, Jr., *A Survey of Old Testament Introduction* (Chicago: Moody Press, 1964), p. 257 explains:

    Only chapter 34 is demonstrably post-Mosaic, since it contains a short account of Moses' decease. But this does not endanger in the slightest the Mosaic authenticity of the other thirty-three chapters, for the closing chapter furnishes only that type of obituary which is often appended to the final work of great men of letters. An author's final work is often published posthumously (provided he has been writing up to the time of his death). Since Joshua is recorded to have been a faithful and zealous custodian of the Torah, Moses' literary achievement, it is quite unthinkable that he would have published it without appending such a notice of the decease of his great predecessor.

7. Ronald Youngblood, *The Book of Genesis* (Grand Rapids, MI: Baker, 1991), pp. 14, 15 writes:

    . . . archaeological evidence (primarily from Ebla in northern Syria) has tended to push back the dating of the patriarchal period. These factors in particular have strengthened the position of those who hold to the 1445 date — a date that, in any case, fits better with a literal understanding of the internal biblical chronology than the 1290 date does. According to 1 Kings 6:1, Solomon began to build the temple in the fourth year of his reign over Israel, which was "the four hundred and eightieth year after the Israelites had come out of Egypt." The fourth year of Solomon's reign was about 966 B.C., and 480 years before that would give us a date of 1445 for the exodus.

    Israel's wanderings in the Sinai desert, under the leadership of Moses, would then have taken place during the forty years immediately following 1445 B.C. It would therefore seem safe to assume that Moses — a man suitably qualified for the task in terms of possessing the necessary education, motivation, energy, and time — wrote the Pentateuch, including the book of Genesis, late in the fifteenth century before Christ.

8. Bruce Waltke, "The Literary Genre of Genesis Chapter One," *Crux*, Vol. XXVII, No. 4 (1991), pp. 2, 3.

9. U. Cassuto, *A Commentary on the Book of Genesis* (Jerusalem: The Magnes Press, 1989), p. 7.

10. Derek Kidner, *Genesis: An Introduction and Commentary,* Tyndale Old Testament Commentaries (Downers Grove, IL: InterVarsity Press, 1975), p. 43.

11. Youngblood, *The Book of Genesis*, p. 23.

12. Gordon J. Wenham, *Genesis 1—15*, Vol. 1, Word Biblical Commentary (Waco, TX: Word, 1987), pp. 13, 14 explains:

בְּרֵאשִׁית "beginning" is an abstract noun etymologically related to רֹאשׁ "head," and רִאשׁוֹן "first." In temporal phrases it is most often used relatively, i.e., it specifies the beginning of a particular period, e.g., "From the beginning of the year" (Deut 11:12) or "At the beginning of the reign of" (Jer. 26:1). More rarely, as here, it is used absolutely, with the period of time left unspecified; only the context shows precisely when is meant, e.g., Isa 46:10. "Declaring the end from the beginning from ancient times (מִקֶּדֶם) things not yet done" (cf. Prov. 8:22). The contexts here and in Gen 1 suggest בְּרֵאשִׁית refers to the beginning of time itself, not to a particular period within eternity (cf. Isa 40:21; 41:4; H. P. Müller, *THWAT* 2:711-12).

13. Gerhard Von Rad, *Genesis: A Commentary,* Old Testament Library (Philadelphia: Westminster, 1972), p. 49.

14. Phillip E. Johnson, *Objections Sustained: Subversive Essays on Evolution, Law, and Culture*, chapter 7, "The Unraveling of Scientific Materials" (Downers Grove, IL: InterVarsity Press, 1998), pp. 71, 72.

15. William A. Dembski, ed., *Mere Creation* (Downers Grove, IL: InterVarsity Press, 1998), pp. 29, 30.

16. Youngblood, *The Book of Genesis*, p. 23.

17. Wenham, *Genesis 1—15*, Vol. 1, p. 15.

18. Stephen W. Hawking, *A Brief History of Time* (New York: Bantam, 1990), p. 37.

19. *Ibid.*

20. *Ibid.*, pp. 38, 39.

21. *Ibid.*, 50:

The final result was a joint paper by Penrose and myself in 1970, which at last proved that there must have been a big bang singularity provided only that general relativity is correct and the universe contains as much matter as we observe. There was a lot of opposition to our work, partly from the Russians because of their Marxist belief in scientific determinism, and partly from people who felt that the whole idea of singularities was repugnant and spoiled the beauty of Einstein's theory. However, one cannot really argue with a mathematical theorem. So in the end our work became generally accepted and nowadays nearly everyone assumes that the universe started with a big bang singularity. It is perhaps ironic that, having changed my mind, I am now trying to convince other physicists that there was in fact no singularity at the beginning of the universe — as we shall see later, it can disappear once quantum effects are taken into account.

22. Wenham, *Genesis 1—15*, Vol. 1, p. 15.

23. Cassuto, *A Commentary on the Book of Genesis*, p. 23.

24. *Ibid.*, p. 25 writes:

". . . to fly to and fro, flutter," the sense in which it is used in Deut. xxxii 11: *Like an eagle that stirs up its nest, that* FLUTTERS *over its young.* Likewise in the Ugaritic writings, the meaning of the stem *rhp* is "to flutter" . . . the young eaglets, which are not yet capable of fending for themselves, are unable by their own efforts to subsist and grow strong and become fully-grown eagles, and only the care of their parents, who hover over them, enables them to survive and develop, so, too, in the case of the earth, which was still an unformed, lifeless mass, the paternal care of the Divine Spirit, which hovered over it.

CHAPTER TWO: FORMING THE EARTH

1. Bryan Chapell, Covenant Theological Seminary '98-'99 President's Goals and Report prepared for December 5, 1997 Executive Committee Meeting with revisions from the January 30, 1998 full Board Meeting, p. 1.
2. *Ibid.*, p. 3.
3. U. Cassuto, *A Commentary on the Book of Genesis* (Jerusalem: The Magnes Press, 1989), p. 12.
4. *Ibid.*, p. 15.
5. Joseph Pipa, Jr. and David Hall, eds., *Did God Create in Six Days?*, chapter 6, C. John Collins, "Reading Genesis 1:1 — 2:3 as an Act of Communication: Discourse Analysis and Literal Interpretation" (Taylors, SC: Southern Presbyterian Press/Oak Ridge, TN: Covenant Foundation, 1999), pp. 131, 132.
6. *Ibid.*, p. 139.
7. Francis Schaeffer, *Genesis in Time and Space* (Downers Grove, IL: InterVarsity Press, 1972), p. 15.
8. Pipa, Jr. and Hall, eds., *Did God Create in Six Days?*, p. 141, where Collins explains:
   That is to say, whatever length those six days are, and whatever the degree of overlap and topical arrangement, still they are "broadly sequential," and extend over some span of elapsed time. The sequentiality comes from the combined effect of the use of the *wayyiqtol* tense for the main narrative events, and from the march of the numbered days.
9. Derek Kidner, *Genesis: An Introduction and Commentary* (Downers Grove, IL: InterVarsity Press, 1975), p. 54.
10. Bruce Waltke, "The Literary Genre of Genesis Chapter One," *Crux*, Vol. XXVII, No. 4 (1991), p. 3.
11. Douglas F. Kelly, *Creation and Change* (Ross-shire, Great Britain: Christian Focus Publications, 1997), p. 51.
12. Pipa, Jr. and Hall, ed., *Did God Create in Six Days?*, p. 147. Collins explains:
   Some have maintained that the days of Genesis 1 must be "literal" days, because whenever the Hebrew word *yom* "day" has a number in the rest of the Old Testament, it is a "literal" day. The statistic cited may in fact be accurate, but statistics alone are not enough to establish an inductive argument (which is what this argument is). We would need, not just a statistic, but an explanation of *why* the statistic demonstrates a principle. For a lexical argument such as this one, this explanation would be in terms of the combinational rules of the Hebrew word *yom* "day" and the kinds of words with which it is being combined. For this argument to be good, then, we must propose a combinational rule for the Hebrew word *yom* when it is modified by a number. We would then have to show that the rule applies in every case; and to do that we would have to show that it was the *rule*, and not the *context* of the other usages, which secured the interpretation of *yom*. To do so we would have to compare like with like, i.e. we would need a context comparable to that of Genesis 1 where the proposed rule overrode any contextual factors which pointed away from a strictly "literal" understanding of *yom* (unfortunately I do not know of such a context in the Hebrew Bible).
13. Phillip E. Johnson, *Objections Sustained: Subversive Essays on Evolution, Law, and Culture* (Downers Grove, IL: InterVarsity Press, 1998), p. 51, quoting Richard Dawkins, *The Blind Watch Maker* (New York: W. W. Norton, 1996), pp. 2, 3.
14. Kidner, *Genesis: An Introduction and Commentary*, p. 46.
15. C. S. Lewis, *The Magician's Nephew* (New York: Harper & Row, 1955), pp. 123-139.

16. Victor P. Hamilton, *The Book of Genesis: Chapters 1—17* (Grand Rapids, MI: Eerdmans, 1990), p. 121, who quotes John Calvin (1554) (*Commentaries on the First Book of Moses Called Genesis,* trans. John King, 2 vols. [Grand Rapids, MI: Eerdmans, 1948], 1:76).

17. Cassuto, *A Commentary on the Book of Genesis*, p. 31.

18. Sukkah 5:2-3, *The Mishna*, trans. Herbert Danby (Oxford: Oxford University Press, 1933). See also R. Kent Hughes, *John* (Wheaton, IL: Crossway Books, 1999), pp. 227, 228.

CHAPTER THREE: FILLING THE EARTH

1. Gordon J. Wenham, *Genesis 1—15*, Word Biblical Commentary 1 (Waco, TX: Word, 1987), pp. 21, 22 notes the "well-organized concentric structure" with this chart:

A	to divide the day from the night (14a)
B	for signs, for fixed times, for days and years (14b)
C	to give light on the earth (15)
D	to rule the day (16a) } God made the
D'	to rule the night (16b) } two lights
C'	to give light on the earth (17)
B'	to rule the day and the night (18a)
A'	to divide the light from the darkness (18b)

2. Charles Colson, "This Beautiful System — God's Handiwork in Space," *BreakPoint Commentary*, April 28, 1999.

3. Gerard Manley Hopkins, *Hopkins — Poems and Prose* (New York: Alfred A. Knopf, 1995), p. 15.

4. Derek Kidner, *Genesis: An Introduction and Commentary* (Downers Grove, IL: InterVarsity Press, 1975), p. 50.

5. William Blake, "The Tyger," in *Poetry and Prose*, ed. David V. Erdman (Garden City, NY: Doubleday, 1965), p. 24.

6. Henri Blocher, *In the Beginning*, trans. David G. Preston (Downers Grove, IL: InterVarsity Press, 1984), p. 84.

7. U. Cassuto, *A Commentary on the Book of Genesis* (Jerusalem: The Magnes Press, 1989), p. 57.

8. Gerhard Von Rad, *Genesis: A Commentary* (Philadelphia: Westminster, 1972), p. 57.

9. Blocher, *In the Beginning*, p. 94.

10. Kenneth A. Mathews, *Genesis 1—11:26* (Nashville: Broadman & Holman, 1996), pp. 170, 171.

11. Blocher, *In the Beginning*, p. 94.

12. Blaise Pascal, *Pensées*, #425, trans. W. F. Trotter (New York: E. P. Dutton & Co., 1958), pp. 113, 114.

What is it, then, that this desire and this inability proclaim to us, but that there was once in man a true happiness of which there now remain to him only the mark and empty trace, which he in vain tries to fill from all his surroundings, seeking from things absent the help he does not obtain in things present? But these are all inadequate, because the infinite abyss can only be filled by an infinite and immutable object, that is to say, only by God Himself. He only is our true good, and since we have forsaken Him, it is a strange thing that there is nothing in nature which has not been serviceable in taking His place; the stars, the heavens, earth, the elements, plants, cabbages, leeks, animals, insects, calves, serpents, fever, pestilence, war, famine, vices, adultery, incest. And since man has lost the true good, everything can appear equally good to him, even his own destruction, though so opposed to God, to reason, and to the whole course of nature.

CHAPTER FOUR: GOD RESTS

1. Donald Brownlee and Peter Ward, *Rare Earth* (New York: Springer Verlag, 2000), pp. 27-29.

2. Kenneth A. Mathews, *Genesis 1—11:26* (Nashville: Broadman & Holman, 1996), p. 176.
3. *Ibid.*, p. 177.
4. Claus Westermann, *Genesis 1—11*, trans. John J. Scullion (Minneapolis: Fortress Press, 1994), p. 173.
5. C. F. Keil, and F. Delitzsch, *Biblical Commentary on the Old Testament, The Pentateuch*, Vol. 1, trans. James Martin (Grand Rapids, MI: Eerdmans, n.d., pp. 69, 70.
6. Westermann, *Genesis 1—11*, p. 172.
7. Mathews, *Genesis 1—11:26*, p. 178, where he quotes A. Heschel, *The Earth Is the Lord's and the Sabbath* (New York: Harper Torchbooks, 1966), p. 10.
8. *Ibid.*, p. 179.
9. *Ibid.*, p. 177.
10. Dr. and Mrs. Howard Taylor, *Hudson Taylor's Spiritual Secret* (Philadelphia: China Inland Mission, 1932), p. 147.
11. Philip Schaff, ed., *The Nicene and Post-Nicene Fathers*, Vol. 1, *The Confessions of St. Augustine*, Book 1.1.1., trans. J. G. Pilkington (Grand Rapids, MI: Eerdmans, 1974), p. 45.

CHAPTER FIVE: EAST, IN EDEN

1. Gordon J. Wenham, *Genesis 1—15*, Word Biblical Commentary 1 (Waco, TX: Word, 1987), p. 57.
2. Kenneth A. Mathews, *Genesis 1—11:26* (Nashville: Broadman & Holman, 1996), p. 191. See also Wenham, *Genesis 1—15*, p. 58.
3. *Ibid.*, p. 191 explains:

    By using the vocabulary of 1:1, v. 4 echoes the creation narrative's beginning affirmation; it also recalls from 1:1 — 2:3 the frequent word "made" *(āśâ)*. Verse 4 is an independent sentence (as in 1:1), and vv. 5-7 are a distinctive syntactical unit. Verses 5-6 present a series of circumstantial clauses describing the condition of the land when God formed the first man (2:7). This syntactical arrangement is similar to the pattern of 1:2-3, but not exactly the same since 1:2 is a positive description whereas 2:5 is negative. In 1:2 the interest lies with the "earth," but here the sense is uncultivated "land."

4. New International Version, New Revised Standard Version, New Jewish Publication Society translation, New Jerusalem Bible, New American Bible, New Living Translation.
5. U. Cassuto, *A Commentary on the Book of Genesis*, Part One (Jerusalem: The Magnes Press, 1989), p. 102.
6. *Ibid.*
7. Wenham, *Genesis 1—15*, p. 59.
8. Ronald Youngblood, *The Book of Genesis* (Grand Rapids, MI: Baker, 1991), p. 35.
9. Allen P. Ross, *Creation and Blessing* (Grand Rapids, MI: Baker, 1998), p. 122.
10. *Ibid.*
11. John Calvin, *Genesis*, trans. and ed. John King (Carlisle, PA: Banner of Truth Trust, 1965), p. 111.
12. Derek Kidner, *Genesis: An Introduction and Commentary* (Downers Grove, IL: InterVarsity Press, 1975), p. 60.
13. Wenham, *Genesis 1—15*, Vol. 1, p. 60.
14. Geoffrey Bromiley, ed., *The International Standard Bible Encyclopedia*, Vol. 2 (Grand Rapids, MI: Eerdmans, 1982), p. 17.
15. *Ibid.*
16. Youngblood, *The Book of Genesis*, p. 37.
17. Wenham, *Genesis 1—15*, pp. 66, 67.
18. Mathews, *Genesis 1—11:26*, p. 201.
19. Dietrich Bonhoeffer, *Creation and Fall* (New York: Macmillan, 1959), p. 49.
20. Ross, *Creation and Blessing*, p. 124 explains:

The vocabulary in verses 15-17 strikingly points to the spiritual nature of the man's responsibility. First, the word translated "placed" is actually from the word for "rest" *(nûah)*. It means "placed" in this passage, but the choice of a word with overtones of "rest" is important (cf. *śim*, "put," in 2:8). The word is cognate to "rest" *(mᵉnûhâ)*, which is used in Psalm 95:11 to refer to rest in the Promised Land. Genesis 2:15 thus must have some connection with the biblical teaching of Sabbath rest in the Bible (see vv. 1-3 and Heb. 3:7—4:11).

21. Calvin, *Genesis*, p. 127.
22. Wenham, *Genesis 1—15*, p. 64.

CHAPTER SIX: MAN AND WOMAN

1. U. Cassuto, *A Commentary on the Book of Genesis*, Part One (Jerusalem: The Magnes Press, 1989), pp. 126, 127.
2. Henri Blocher, *In the Beginning* (Leicester, England: Inter-Varsity Press, n.d.), p. 97 says, "Our thoughts should turn to the undoubted analogy between the non-solitude of God and the communal structure of humanity."
3. Gordon Wenham, *Genesis 1—15*, Word Biblical Commentary 1 (Waco, TX: Word, 1987), p. 68.
4. Allen P. Ross, *Creation and Blessing* (Grand Rapids, MI: Baker, 1998), p. 124.
5. Kenneth A. Mathews, *Genesis 1—11:26* (Nashville: Broadman & Holman, 1996), p. 214.
6. C. F. Keil and F. Delitzsch, *The Pentateuch*, Vol. 1, trans. James Martin (Grand Rapids, MI: Eerdmans, n.d.), p. 88.
7. Gerhard Von Rad, *Genesis: A Commentary* (Philadelphia: Westminster, 1972), p. 84.
8. Blocher, *In the Beginning*, pp. 98, 99.
9. Wenham, *Genesis 1—15*, p. 69.
10. Von Rad, *Genesis: A Commentary*, p. 84.
11. Wenham, *Genesis 1-15*, p. 70.
12. Claus Westermann, *Genesis 1—11*, trans. John J. Scullion (Minneapolis: Fortress Press, 1984), p. 231 writes:

    They are perceptively different: the double beat in the first line forms the purely emotional, joyful cry, the triple beat in the second the announcement and fulfillment which require the broader rhythm of the triple beat. P. Humbert has explained the difference accurately: the first verse "finds its meter in the joyful surprise and has an almost explosive meter, while in the second the grouping of 3:3 broadens the rhythm and gives the thought solemnity and harmony."

13. John Calvin, *Genesis*, trans. and ed. John King (Carlisle, PA: Banner of Truth Trust, 1965), p. 125.
14. Wenham, *Genesis 1—15*, p. 71.
15. Blocher, *In the Beginning*, pp. 105, 106 explains:

    In biblical times the event the Bible calls marriage involved the whole society. The idea of a purely private marriage is simply a recent aberration, the result of individualism and of the disintegration of traditional communities. The marriage feast assured that the marriage was a public event. For Scripture the marriage bond is a part of those social realities supervised by the civil authority; it is the law (Jewish or Roman, the commentators are uncertain) which binds a woman to her husband (Rom. 7:2; *cf.* Dt. 22). The commitment of the new couple consequently takes place under the eye of the magistrate, within his area of jurisdiction.

CHAPTER SEVEN: PARADISE LOST: THE FALL

1. See the author's exposition of this in R. Kent Hughes and Brian Chapell, *1, 2 Timothy and Titus: Guard the Deposit* (Wheaton, IL: Crossway Books, 2000).

2. Kenneth A. Mathews, *Genesis 1—11:26* (Nashville: Broadman & Holman, 1996), p. 220. Mathews gives an excellent synopsis of the arguments for the pre-fall order on pp. 220-222.

3. C. S. Lewis, *The Problem of Pain* (New York: Macmillan, 1962), chapter 5, p. 78.

4. Gordon J. Wenham, *Genesis 1—15,* Vol. 1, Word Biblical Commentary (Waco, TX: Word, 1987), pp. 90, 91.

5. Allen P. Ross, *Creation and Blessing* (Grand Rapids, MI: Baker, 1998), p. 134.

6. Wenham, *Genesis 1—15*, p. 72.

7. G. C. Aalders, *Genesis*, Vol. 1, trans. William Heynen (Grand Rapids, MI: Zondervan, 1981), pp. 98, 101.

8. Derek Kidner, *Genesis: An Introduction and Commentary* (Downers Grove, IL: InterVarsity Press, 1975), p. 67.

9. Some have suggested that attributing such blatant revisions to Eve imputes too much intention to her. After all, Adam may not have clearly communicated the divine prohibitions to her, and paraphrasing God's word is something all believers have done. However this ignores two facts: 1) Moses wrote under the inspiration of the Spirit with immense literary care and intentionality (witness the literary structure and literary-numerical distinctives thus far). And 2) Adam and Eve lived in an unhindered, uncluttered state of communication. And more, their history was recent and simple. No doubt they had discussed the trees and the prohibitions more than casually at least once! Moses wants us to see the subtle revisions.

10. Ross, *Creation and Blessing*, p. 135.

11. Gerhard Von Rad, *Genesis: A Commentary* (Philadelphia: Westminster, 1972), p. 90.

12. Mathews, *Genesis 1—11:26*, p. 238.

13. C. S. Lewis, *Preface to Paradise Lost* (New York: Oxford University Press, 1970), p. 117.

14. *Ibid.*, p. 119.

CHAPTER EIGHT: PARADISE LOST: THE CONFRONTATION

1. Dietrich Bonhoeffer, *Temptation* (London: SCM Press Ltd., 1961), p. 33.

2. Henri Blocher, *In the Beginning* (Leicester, England: Inter-Varsity Press, n.d.), p. 171.

3. Gerhard Von Rad, *Genesis: A Commentary* (Philadelphia: Westminster, 1972), p. 91.

4. U. Cassuto, *A Commentary on the Book of Genesis*, Part One (Jerusalem: The Magnes Press, 1989), p. 156.

5. Von Rad, *Genesis: A Commentary*, p. 91 says: "Fear and shame are henceforth the incurable stigmata of the Fall of man."

6. Dietrich Bonhoeffer, *Creation and Fall* (New York: Macmillan, 1959), p. 81.

7. Kenneth A. Mathews, *Genesis 1—11:26* (Nashville: Broadman & Holman, 1996), p. 241 writes: "God first addresses the man, who evidently bears the greater responsibility, then the woman and the serpent. This inverts the order of the participants in the act (serpent, woman, and man) and indicates God's chief interest in the state of the human couple. It is not until the man points to Eve that God addresses her; it is the first time in the Edenic narrative that Eve and God converse." Similarly Cassuto, *A Commentary on the Book of Genesis*, p. 155 writes: "The man was the first to be tried, because the primary responsibility rested upon him, and he was the first to receive the Divine command." See also Derek Kidner, *Genesis: An Introduction and Commentary* (Downers Grove, IL: InterVarsity Press, 1975), p. 70: "God, by addressing man, woman and serpent in that order, has shown how He regards their degrees of responsibility."

8. Robert Johnstone, *Lectures Exegetical and Practical on the Epistle of James* (Minneapolis: Klock & Klock, 1978), p. 104.

9. Charles Krauthammer, *Chicago Tribune*, "A True Test for True Justice When the Victim Is the Victimizer" (February 7, 1994), Section 1, p. 11.

CHAPTER NINE: PARADISE LOST: CURSE AND JUDGMENT

1. By Bill Watterson. Distributed by Universal Press Syndicate, 1993.
2. C. F. Keil and F. Delitzsch, *The Pentateuch*, Vol. 1, trans. James Martin (Grand Rapids, MI: Eerdmans, n.d.), p. 99.
3. Derek Kidner, *Genesis: An Introduction and Commentary* (Downers Grove, IL: InterVarsity Press, 1975), p. 70.
4. John Calvin, *Genesis*, trans. and ed. John King (Carlisle, PA: Banner of Truth Trust, 1965), p. 167.
5. Keil and Delitzsch, *The Pentateuch*, pp. 99, 100, who quote E. W. Hengstenberg, *Christology of the Old Testament*, Vol. 1, p. 15: "While all the rest of creation shall be delivered from the fate into which the fall had plunged it, according to Isa. lxv. 25, the instrument of man's temptation is to remain sentenced to perpetual degradation in fulfillment of the sentence, 'all the days of thy life,' and thus to prefigure the fate of the real tempter, for whom there is no deliverance."
6. Kenneth A. Mathews, *Genesis 1—11:26*, Vol. 1 (Nashville: Broadman & Holman, 1996), p. 247 explains that the Septuagint version (LXX) may be the earliest attested interpretation of "seed" as an individual. It translates the Hebrew *zera* ("seed") with the Greek *sperma*, a neuter noun. The expected antecedent pronoun is "it" — "it *[auto]* will crush your head," but the Greek has "he" *(autos)*, which suggests that the translators interpreted "seed" as an individual. The Targums, Jewish pseudepigrapha, and later rabbinic commentators, however, generally viewed the "seed" as collective for humankind.
7. Jack Collins, "A Syntactical Note (Genesis 3:15): Is the Woman's Seed Singular or Plural?" *Tyndale Bulletin*, 48.1 (1997), pp. 139-148.
8. Victor P. Hamilton, *The Book of Genesis: Chapters 1—17*, Vol. 1 (Grand Rapids, MI: Eerdmans, 1990), pp. 197, 198 argues that the word "crush" or "strike" must be translated the same in its two occurrences in 3:15 and concludes:

    In order to maintain the duplication of the Hebrew verb, whatever English equivalent one decides on must be used twice. We have already suggested a reason why "crush" would not be appropriate. *Strike at* covers adequately the reciprocal moves of the woman's seed and the serpent's seed against each other rather than something like: "He shall lie in wait for your head" and "you shall lie in wait for his heel."
9. John Sailhamer, *The Pentateuch as Narrative* (Grand Rapids, MI: Zondervan, 1992), p. 56.
10. Saint Augustine, *Confessions*, trans. R. S. Pine-Coffin, Book VII, 8 (London: Penguin, 1961), p. 144.

CHAPTER TEN: PARADISE LOST: JUDGMENT AND SIN

1. Gerhard Von Rad, *Genesis: A Commentary* (Philadelphia: Westminster, 1972), p. 94.
2. Henri Blocher, *In the Beginning* (Leicester, England: Inter-Varsity Press, n.d.), p. 187.
3. See Kenneth A. Mathews, *Genesis 1—11:26*, Vol. 1 (Nashville: Broadman & Holman, 1996), p. 253.
4. Gordon J. Wenham, *Genesis 1—15*, Vol. Word Biblical Commentary 1 (Waco, TX: Word, 1987), p. 84, writes:

    More likely חוה is a by-form of חיה and means "life" (BDB [*Brown, Driver & Briggs Hebrew and English Lexicon*], 295b); at least this is how LXX translates "Eve," *Zoe* — "life," and it fits in with the explanation offered in the text itself.
5. Victor P. Hamilton, *The Book of Genesis: Chapters 1—17*, Vol. 1 (Grand Rapids, MI: Eerdmans, 1990), pp. 205, 206 explains,

    Indeed, her name may reflect a primitive form of the Hebrew verb "to live" with medial *w* instead of *y*. The evidence here is the Ugaritic verb "to live": *hwy/hyy*. What is clear from the Ras Shamra texts is that the verb there appears with the medial *y* only in the Qal stem. By contrast, in the Piel stem the verb appears only with medial w. Furthermore, the Piel stem has a factitive meaning — "to give life, preserve." The same is true in Phoenician. Thus it is quite possible that Heb. *Hawwa* reflects this feature and as a *qattal* type noun means "life-giver."

6. Blocher, *In the Beginning*, p. 192.
7. Hamilton, *The Book of Genesis: Chapters 1—17*, Vol. 1, p. 205.
8. Blocher, *In the Beginning*, p. 192.
9. Wenham, *Genesis 1—15*, Vol. 1, pp. 84, 85.
10. Marcus Dods, *The Book of Genesis* (New York: A.C. Armstrong and Son, 1903), pp. 24, 25.
11. Allen P. Ross, *Creation & Blessing* (Grand Rapids, MI: Baker, 1998), p. 151.
12. Blocher, *In the Beginning*, p. 191.
13. *Ibid.*, p. 190.
14. Wenham, *Genesis 1-15*, Vol. 1, p. 86.
15. Mathews, *Genesis 1—11:26*, Vol. 1, p. 257.
16. *Ibid.*, p. 258.
17. *Ibid.*, p. 255.

CHAPTER ELEVEN: THE WAY OF CAIN

1. *Chicago Tribune*, February 2, 1991, Section 1, p. 3.
2. Paul Johnson, *Modern Times: From the Twenties to the Nineties* (New York: HarperCollins, 1991), p. 783.
3. Rich Soll, "The Killing Fields," *Chicago Magazine* (March 1993), pp. 56, 57.
4. Gordon J. Wenham, *Genesis 1—15*, Vol. 1, Word Biblical Commentary (Waco, TX: Word, 1987), p. 96.
5. Allen P. Ross, *Creation & Blessing* (Grand Rapids, MI: Baker, 1998), p. 156.
6. Wenham, *Genesis 1—15*, Vol. 1, p. 103.
7. *Ibid.*
8. Kenneth A. Mathews, *Genesis 1—11:26*, Vol. 1 (New York: Broadman & Holman, 1996), pp. 269, 270 writes:
    Despite the problems, we can achieve a credible understanding of the passage. "Accepted" translates the Hebrew word for "a lifting up" or an "exaltation"; this literal rendering is found in the awkward translation of the NJPS: "Surely, if you do right, there is uplift. . . ." The implication is made explicit in the NASB's "If you do well, will not *[your countenance]* be lifted up?" and the REB's emended option, "You hold your head up." In this understanding the expression reverses the earlier imagery of Cain's "downcast" face. When Cain practices what is right, there will be an uplifted face, meaning a good conscience before God without shame. Most versions offer the metaphorical sense "accepted," referring to Cain and his offering (e.g., Vg; NIV, AV, RSV, NRSV). It is best to take the expression "lifting up" as figurative referring to the uplifted face, indicating acceptance from God that comes with a pure heart.
9. Dietrich Bonhoeffer, *Creation and Fall: Temptation* (New York: Macmillan, 1959), p. 93.
10. Henri Blocher, *In the Beginning* (Leicester, England: Inter-Varsity Press, n.d.), p. 199.
11. Robert Atwan and Laurence Weider, *Chapters into Verse*, Vol. 1 (Oxford, England: Oxford University Press, 1993), p. 51, from William Blake's *The Ghost of Abel*.
12. Gerhard Von Rad, *Genesis: A Commentary* (Philadelphia: Westminster, 1972), p. 106.
13. Wenham, *Genesis 1—15*, Vol. 1, p. 109.

CHAPTER TWELVE: THE SONG OF LAMECH

1. Louis Untermeyer, ed. *Modern British Poetry* (New York: Harcourt, Brace and World, 1962), p. 53.
2. Allen P. Ross, *Creation & Blessing* (Grand Rapids, MI: Baker, 1998), p. 164.

3. Derek Kidner, *Genesis: An Introduction and Commentary* (Downers Grove, IL: InterVarsity Press, 1975) p. 78.

4. Ross, *Creation & Blessing*, p. 167 explains:
    This cultural growth brings delight to the families, as is seen by the names using *yûbāl* (note the possible etymological connection to Israel's delightful concept of Jubilee) and the mention of Naamah *(na'ămâ)*, a name similar to Naomi. The exegete must be very careful in interpreting such names. We must not make too much out of the meanings of names if there is no convincing evidence. In this passage, however, there may be some etymological connection with words that indicate joy and happiness.

5. Kenneth A. Mathews, *Genesis 1—11:26*, Vol. 1 (Nashville: Broadman & Holman, 1996), p. 288 says:
    The name "Jubal," the father of musical instruments, also corresponds closely in sound to the melodic ram's horn *(yôbēl)*, which in later Israel announced the Year of Jubilee and other special occasions (e.g., Exod 19:13; Lev 25:9). Specifically, however, the text refers only to the widely known harp (lyre) and flute (pipe).

6. *Ibid.*, p. 287.

7. Paul Johnson, *Modern Times: From the Twenties to the Nineties*, rev. ed. (New York: HarperCollins, 1991), p. 424.

8. Kidner, *Genesis: An Introduction and Commentary*, p. 76.

9. Mathews, *Genesis 1—11:26*, Vol. 1, p. 288.

10. Kidner, *Genesis: An Introduction and Commentary*, p. 78.

11. Anastasia Toufexis, "Dances with Werewolves," *Time*, April 4, 1994, pp. 65, 66.

12. U. Cassuto, *A Commentary on the Book of Genesis*, Part One (Jerusalem: The Magnes Press, 1989), p. 243.

13. Henri Blocher, *In the Beginning* (Leicester, England: Inter-Varsity Press, n.d.), p. 200.

14. Mathews, *Genesis 1—11:26*, Vol. 1, p. 290.

15. *Ibid.*, pp. 290, 291.

16. Ross, *Creation & Blessing*, p. 169 explains:
    Usage of this expression in the Pentateuch supports the idea of proclamation more than praying (cf. Gen. 12:8; Exod. 34:6; Lev. 1:1). The meaning of *šēm*, "name," also requires interpretation, since the word is actually followed by the name itself. The word "name" often refers to characteristics or attributes (see Isa. 9:6). The idea of this line is that people began to make proclamation about the nature of the Lord ("began to make proclamation of the Lord by name").

CHAPTER THIRTEEN: HE WAS NO MORE

1. Allen P. Ross, *Creation & Blessing* (Grand Rapids, MI: Baker, 1998), p. 169, writes:
    The verb *qārā*, "call," can be used for naming (cf. 4:17, 25), reading, proclaiming, summoning, and praying. Usage of this expression in the Pentateuch supports the idea of proclamation more than praying (cf. Gen. 12:8; Exod. 34:6; Lev. 1:1). The meaning of *šēm*, "name," also requires interpretation, since the word is actually followed by the name itself. The word "name" often refers to characteristics or attributes (see Isa. 9:6). The idea of this line is that people began to make proclamation about the nature of the Lord ("began to make proclamation of the Lord by name").

2. Kenneth A. Mathews, *Genesis 1—11:26*, Vol. 1 (Nashville: Broadman & Holman, 1996), pp. 303, 304. The author further explains that Matthew's genealogy of Jesus is selective, though it uses another structure, three sets of fourteen names. Here in Genesis some names (such as Adam and Seth) leave no gap. Seth is the third son of Adam (Genesis 4:25), and Lamech names his son Noah (5:29); so the Sethite genealogy selectively mixes actual descent and gapping side by side.

3. *Ibid.*, p. 309.

4. Mike Mason, *The Mystery of Marriage* (Portland: Multnomah, 1985), p. 170.
5. Derek Kidner, *Genesis: An Introduction and Commentary* (Downers Grove, IL: InterVarsity Press, 1975), p. 8, quoting *The Interpreter's Bible*, Vol. I, p. 530.
6. C. F. Keil and F. Delitzsch, *The Pentateuch*, Vol. 1, trans. James Martin (Grand Rapids, MI: Eerdmans, n.d.), p. 125.
7. Ross, *Creation & Blessing*, pp. 174, 175.
8. Luci Shaw, *The Secret Trees* (Wheaton, IL: Harold Shaw Publishers, 1976).

CHAPTER FOURTEEN: GREAT SIN, GREATER GRACE

1. Robert Atwan and Laurence Wieder, eds. *Chapter and Verse*, Vol. 1 (New York: Oxford, 1993), p. 53.
2. Alan M. Stibbs, *The First Epistle General of Peter* (London: The Tyndale Press, 1966), pp. 142, 143 explains:

> Many have wished to interpret the phrase *the spirits in prison* as a reference to departed human spirits; but it fits in with the linguistic usage of Scripture, and with the reference to the days of Noah, to understand it as a reference to fallen angels (cf. Gn. vi. 1-4; 2 Pet. ii. 4, 5). The word *pneumata, spirits,* alone and without qualification, is not thus used anywhere else in the Bible to describe departed human spirits. Note, for example, 'the spirits of just men' (Heb. xii. 23). But the word is thus used of supernatural beings, both good and bad (see Heb. i. 14; Lk. x. 20). To quote E.G. Selwyn, 'The facts that the word *pneumata* is used absolutely of supernatural beings, that Jewish tradition spoke of such beings . . . as disobeying God and transgressing their due order, and being punished by imprisonment, that the period of this transgression was always reckoned as immediately prior to the Flood; and that these beliefs are undoubtedly alluded to in 2 Pet. ii. and Jude 6, 7 — these facts tell strongly in favour of this interpretation here.'

3. Gordon J. Wenham, *Genesis 1—15*, Vol. 1, Word Biblical Commentary (Waco, TX: Word, 1987), p. 139, says:

> The "angel" interpretation is at once the oldest view and that of most modern commentators. It is assumed in the earliest Jewish exegesis (e.g., the books of 1 Enoch 6:2ff; Jubilees 5:1), LXX, Philo (*De Gigant* 2:358), Josephus (*Ant.* 1.31) and the Dead Sea Scrolls (1QapGen2:1; CD 2:17-19). The NT (2 Pet 2:4, Jude 6,7) and the earliest Christian writers (e.g., Justin, Irenaeus, Clement of Alexandria, Tertullian, Origen) also take this line.

4. Allen P. Ross, *Creation & Blessing* (Grand Rapids, MI: Baker, 1998), p. 182.
5. Wenham, *Genesis 1—15*, Vol. 1, p. 141.
6. Nahum M. Sarna, *The JPS Torah Commentary: Genesis* (Philadelphia: The Jewish Publication Society, 1989), p. 46.

> The NIV makes an interpretive error in rendering spirit with a capital "Spirit" thus making it concomitant with the Spirit of God. Sarnach describes it as "the life force that issues from God, corresponding to 'the breath of life' in 2:7." So also Wenham, p. 141 writes, "My spirit." Though Skinner argued this referred "to the divine substance" common to Yahweh and the angels (145), it seems much more likely that it denotes the life-giving power of God, on which every creature is entirely dependent for its life. It is called the "breath of life" (2:7) or "the spirit of life" (6:17; 7:15) and the phrase "my spirit" is used again in Ezek 37:14.

7. Wenham, *Genesis 1—15*, Vol. 1, p. 142.
8. Nahum M. Sarna, *The JPS Torah Commentary: Genesis*, p. 4, writes:

> Significantly, the verb *y-d'* is not used, as in 4:1, 17, and 25, but a coarser term, as befits the circumstances. Also Wenham, p. 143, "When they went in . . ." etc., it is more natural (with Skinner, König, Gispen) to take the imperfect "went" and perfect preceded by *waw* ("bore . . . children") as frequentative. To "go in to" is a frequent euphemism for sexual intercourse (cf. 30:16; 38:16).

9. Gerhard Von Rad, *Genesis: A Commentary* (Philadelphia: Westminster, 1972), p. 117.

10. Gordon J. Wenham, *Genesis 1—15,* Vol. 1, pp. 144, 145, explains:
     "He felt bitterly indignant." The root צב is used to express the most intense form of human emotion, a mixture of rage and bitter anguish. Dinah's brothers felt this way after she was raped; so did Jonathan when he heard Saul planned to kill David; and David reacted similarly when he heard of Absalom's death (34:7; 1 Sam 20:34; 2 Sam 19:3[2]). A deserted wife feels this way (Isa 54:6). The word is used of God's feelings in only two other passages (Ps 78:40; Isa 63:10). Only here is the verb supplemented by the phrase "to his heart" (in our translation "bitterly"), underlining the strength of God's reaction to human sinfulness.
11. C. F. Keil and F. Delitzsch, *The Pentateuch,* Vol. 1, trans. James Martin (Grand Rapids, MI: Eerdmans, n.d.), p. 140.

CHAPTER FIFTEEN: DE-CREATION: THE BIBLICAL FLOOD

1. Kenneth A. Mathews, *Genesis 1—11:26,* Vol. 1 (Nashville: Broadman & Holman, 1996), p. 350.
2. Allen P. Ross, *Creation & Blessing* (Grand Rapids, MI: Baker, 1998), p. 191.
3. Mathews, *Genesis 1—11:26,* Vol. 1, p. 351.
4. Ronald Youngblood, *The Book of Genesis* (Grand Rapids, MI: Baker, 1991), p. 89.
5. John H. Sailhamer, "Genesis," Vol. 2, *The Expositor's Bible Commentary* (Grand Rapids, MI: Zondervan, 1990), p. 85.
6. Philip Edgecumbe Hughes, *A Commentary on the Epistle to the Hebrews* (Grand Rapids, MI: Eerdmans, 1977), p. 464, quoting *Sibylline Oracles,* 1.125ff.
7. Sailhamer, *Genesis,* Vol. 2, p. 83 supplies abundant fascinating details about ancient shipbuilding.
8. Derek Kidner, *Genesis: An Introduction and Commentary* (Downers Grove, IL: InterVarsity 1975), p. 89.
9. John Calvin, *Genesis,* trans. and ed. John King (Carlisle, PA: Banner of Truth Trust, 1965), pp. 259, 260.
10. Kidner, *Genesis: An Introduction and Commentary,* p. 87.
11. Mathews, *Genesis 1—11:26,* Vol. 1, p. 374, referencing the *Genesis Rabbah,* 32:7.
12. *Ibid.,* p. 279.
13. James Pritchard, ed., *Ancient Near Eastern Texts,* 2nd edition (Princeton, NJ: Princeton University Press, 1955), p. 94.

CHAPTER SIXTEEN: RE-CREATION: THE WORLD RESTORED

1. Gordon J. Wenham, *Genesis 1—15,* Vol. 1, Word Biblical Commentary (Waco, TX: Word, 1987), p. 157.
2. Ronald Youngblood, *The Book of Genesis* (Grand Rapids, MI: Baker, 1991), p. 101 explains:
     In a very real sense, the period after the flood marks a new beginning for the human race. It is again the first day of the first month of the first year of a man's new life (**8:13**). And in a remarkable way the events of Genesis 8 parallel the events of Genesis 1 in their literary order:
     8:1: God "sent a wind over the earth" (see 1:2; the Hebrew word for "wind" is the same as the word for "Spirit").
     8:2: "The springs of the deep and the floodgates of the heavens had been closed" (see 1:7: God "separated the water under the expanse from the water above it").
     8:5: "The waters continued to recede . . . and . . . the tops of the mountains became visible" (see 1:9: "Let the water under the sky be gathered . . ., and let dry ground appear").
     8:6: Noah "sent out a raven, and it kept flying back and forth" (see 1:20: "Let birds fly above the earth").

8:17: "Bring out every kind of living creature that is with you — the birds, the animals, and all the creatures that move along the ground" (see 1:25: "God made the wild animals . . ., the livestock . . . ., and all the creatures that move along the ground").

3. Allen P. Ross, *Creation & Blessing* (Grand Rapids, MI: Baker, 1998), p. 197, quoting B. S. Childs, *Memory and Tradition in Israel*, p. 34.

4. Kenneth A. Mathews, *Genesis 1—11:26,* Vol. 1 (Nashville: Broadman & Holman, 1996), p. 388.

5. John H. Sailhamer, "Genesis," Vol. 2, The Expositor's Bible Commentary (Grand Rapids, MI: Zondervan, 1990), p. 91, quoting Francis Andersen, *Sentence in Biblical Hebrew*, p. 39.

6. Wenham, *Genesis 1—15*, Vol. 1, p. 190 explains:

   "I shall not curse the soil any further." It is important to note the position of עוד in this sentence, coming after לקלל to "curse," not after אסף "do again" as in the parallel clause "Never again shall I smite." This shows that God is not lifting the curse on the ground pronounced in 3:17 for man's disobedience, but promising not to add to it. The flood was a punishment over and above that decreed in 3:17.

7. *Ibid.*, p. 193.

8. Derek Kidner, *Genesis: An Introduction and Commentary* (Downers Grove, IL: InterVarsity Press, 1975), p. 101.

9. U. Cassuto, *A Commentary on the Book of Genesis,* Vol. 2 (Jerusalem: The Magnes Press, 1989), p. 127.

10. Mathews, *Genesis 1:11-26,* Vol. 1, p. 404.

11. Claus Westermann, *Genesis 1—11*, A Continental Commentary, trans. John J. Scullion (Minneapolis: Fortress Press, 1994), p. 471.

CHAPTER SEVENTEEN: NOAH: CURSE AND BLESSING

1. C. F. Keil and F. Delitzsch, *The Pentateuch,* Vol. 1, trans. James Martin (Grand Rapids, MI: Eerdmans, n.d.), p. 155.

2. Nahum M. Sarna, *The JPS Torah Commentary: Genesis* (Philadelphia: The Jewish Publication Society, 1989), p. 63 explains:

   The narrative is also separated from the account of the Flood by a time lapse equivalent to the years it takes for a newly planted vine to yield its grape harvest. This span of time is clearly indicated by the fact that Noah by now has a grown grandson. Nevertheless, a sense of continuity with the foregoing is conveyed by the connectives of verses 18-19, as by the unstated but pertinent historical fact that the vine and viticulture were highly developed in the region of Armenia, where the ark grounded.

3. Kenneth A. Mathews, *Genesis 1—11:26,* Vol. 1 (Nashville: Broadman & Holman, 1996), p. 417, says:

   Noah degraded himself by drunken stupor and concomitant nakedness. "Lay uncovered" (*yitgal*) describes his state in the tent; he is visibly naked. The verb occurs in the same Hebrew stem *(hithpael)* once more and is clearly reflexive (Prov 18:2), thus "uncovered himself" (NJPS) is meant.

4. Graeme Goldsworthy, *According to Plan* (Leicester, England: Inter-Varsity Press, 1991), pp. 139, 140.

5. Marcus Dods, *The Book of Genesis*, The Expositor's Bible, ed. W. Robertson Nicoll (New York: A. C. Armstrong and Son, 1903), p. 76.

6. Allen P. Ross, *Creation & Blessing* (Grand Rapids, MI: Baker, 1998), pp. 215, 216.

7. John H. Sailhamer, "Genesis," The Expositor's Bible Commentary, Vol. 2 (Grand Rapids, MI: Zondervan, 1990), p. 96.

8. Victor P. Hamilton, *The Book of Genesis, Chapters 1—17,* The New International Commentary on the Old Testament (Grand Rapids, MI: Eerdmans, 1990), p. 323.

9. Mathews, *Genesis 1—11:26*, p. 415.

10. Keil and Delitzsch, *The Pentateuch,* Vol. 1, p. 157.

11. Ross, *Creation & Blessing*, p. 217.

12. Hamilton, *The Book of Genesis, Chapters 1—17*, p. 325.

13. Derek Kidner, *Genesis: An Introduction and Commentary* (Downers Grove, IL: InterVarsity Press, 1975), p. 104 writes:

> Of the three oracles, only that on Shem uses God's personal name Yahweh (*the Lord*); the significance of the fact begins to emerge at 12:1, and will dominate the Old Testament (*cf.* Dt. 4:35). Since Shem means 'Name', there may well be a play on words here; *cf.* on 27. The traditional text, *Blessed be the Lord, the God of Shem* (RV, *cf.* AV), suggests that Shem is himself already in covenant with Yahweh and that his blessing is wholly found in his Lord.

See also G. C. Aalders, *Genesis*, Bible Students Commentary, trans. William Heynen (Grand Rapids, MI: Zondervan, 1981), p. 208:

> Admittedly, we must be on guard against reading something into this use of the name "Lord" that actually belongs to a later period of revelation. Thus, we cannot pour into the name "Lord" when it is used here, immediately after the Deluge, a meaning that is not revealed until the time of Moses. We must also again remind ourselves that we are still dealing with the period before the confusion of languages and, as such, the Hebrew language did not yet exist. At the same time, it must be granted that the Hebrew name "Lord," which later was designated as God's personal name "Jahweh," placed in the mouth of Noah, must have a special significance. We can safely say that this indicates that Shem's special relationship to God is indicated by the use of this name. God would be Shem's personal Lord. When we recognize this, we catch a glimpse of the essence of the blessing that was pronounced on Shem. To stand in a special, personal relationship to God is certainly the highest and greatest blessing anyone can experience.

14. John Calvin, *Genesis*, trans. and ed. John King (Carlisle, PA: Banner of Truth Trust), 1975, p. 309.

CHAPTER EIGHTEEN: HOPE FOR THE NATIONS

1. John H. Sailhamer, "Genesis," Vol. 2, The Expositor's Bible Commentary (Grand Rapids, MI: Zondervan, 1990), p. 99.

2. Ronald Youngblood, *The Book of Genesis* (Grand Rapids, MI: Baker, 1991), pp. 129-131 provides a remarkably clear delineation of the geographical destinies of Noah's three sons — which have been followed in the subsequent paragraphs. See also J. D. Douglas, ed., *The New Bible Dictionary* (Grand Rapids, MI: Eerdmans, 1962), pp. 855-860 for helpful charts and maps of the Table of Nations.

3. Walter Brueggemann, *Genesis*, Interpretation (Atlanta: John Knox Press, 1982), p. 83 says: "The 'map' offers an unparalleled ecumenical vision of human reality. In a sweeping scope, the text insists that there is a network of interrelatedness among all peoples. They belong to each other. As ecumenists are fond of saying, we have to do not with a unity to be achieved, but with a unity already given among us."

4. Sailhamer, *Genesis,* Vol. 2, p. 98.

5. Derek Kidner, *Genesis: An Introduction and Commentary* (Downers Grove, IL: InterVarsity Press, 1975), p. 105 writes: "Possibly the seventy names (LXX, 72) influenced our Lord's choice of the apparently symbolic numbers of emissaries in Luke 10:1."

CHAPTER NINETEEN: ALL MAN'S BABYLONS

1. "Behold! Gordon Hall's Millions Shall Make of Him a God," *Arizona Republic*, January 17, 1986, p. A2.

2. Francis Thompson, "The Heart," *Poems of Francis Thompson* (New York: D. Appleton-Century, 1941), p. 267.

3. Gordon J. Wenham, *Genesis 1—15,* Vol. 1, Word Biblical Commentary (Waco, TX: Word, 1987), p. 235.

4. Allen P. Ross, *Creation & Blessing* (Grand Rapids, MI: Baker, 1998), p. 237 explains:

   The word plays in the passage strengthen the ideas. E. W. Bullinger calls such word plays "paronomasia," which he describes as the employment of two words that are different in origin and meaning but similar in sound and appearance to emphasize two things by calling attention to the similarity of sound *(Figures of Speech Used in the Bible* [London: Eyre and Spothiswoode, 1898; reprint, Grand Rapids: Baker, 1968], p. 307). One is placed alongside the other and appears to be a repetition of it. Once the eye has caught the two words and the attention concentrated on them, one discovers that an interpretation is put on the one by the other.

   While this description gives the general nature of word plays, it is too broad for distinguishing the types of word plays within the group known as paronomasia. To be precise, it should be said that paronomasia involves a play on similarity of sound and some point in the meaning as well; those that have no point of contact in meaning are best classified as phonetic word plays such as assonance, rhyme, alliteration, or epanastrophe (the repetition of words from the end of one sentence at the beginning of another).

5. Kenneth A. Mathews, *Genesis 1—11:26* (Nashville: Broadman & Holman, 1996), p. 467.

6. Wenham, *Genesis 1—15,* Vol. 1, p. 244, and Ross, *Creation & Blessing,* p. 248.

7. Mathews, *Genesis 1—11:26,* p. 478.

8. Ross, *Creation & Blessing,* p. 244.

9. Wenham, *Genesis 1—15,* Vol. 1, p. 239.

10. Nahum M. Sarna, *The JPS Torah Commentary: Genesis* (Philadelphia: The Jewish Publication Society, 1989), p. 82.

11. *Ibid.*

12. Lawrence Wieder, "The Tower of Babel," from *Chapters into Verse,* Vol. 1, eds. Robert Atwan and Lawrence Wieder (New York: Oxford, 1993), p. 67.

13. *Creation & Blessing,* p. 245, quoting Alan Richardson, *Genesis I-XI,* p. 128.

14. C. F. Keil and F. Delitzsch, *The Pentateuch,* Vol. 1, trans. James Martin (Grand Rapids, MI: Eerdmans, n.d.), p. 175.

15. Gerhard Von Rad, *Genesis: A Commentary* (Philadelphia: Westminster, 1972), p. 149, who quotes Procksch but gives no reference.

CHAPTER TWENTY: FROM SHEM TO ABRAHAM

1. John H. Sailhamer, "Genesis," The Expositor's Bible Commentary, Vol. 2, (Grand Rapids, MI: Zondervan, 1990), p. 108 explains how the symmetries work:

   Numbering from Shem to Terah, the list has only nine names. The LXX has a tenth name in the list (Καιναν, *Kainan*), the father of xlv (*šelah* "Shelah," v. 12). This appears to be a secondary attempt to adapt the list to the scheme of ten names. Jacob (p. 304) suggests that the number ten was intended by reading Noah with both the list in chapter 5 and (from 9:28) the list in chapter 11. The number ten is also obtainable by reading Abraham as the last name (11:26b). That, of course, appears to arbitrarily exclude Nahor and Haran, who are listed after Abram at the close of the list.

   As is often the case with the numerical symmetry of the Genesis lists, the numbers are close, but some adding and subtracting is often necessary in the end. One might be tempted to draw the conclusion that if the numbers are not always perfect, it means that the apparent symmetry was not intentional. However, the fact that some adding and subtracting is necessary even when the narrative itself does the final counting (e.g., 46:27) shows that a purpose lies behind such numerical symmetry, even though that symmetry is not always perfect.

2. Allen P. Ross, *Creation & Blessing* (Grand Rapids, MI: Baker, 1998), p. 252.

3. Kenneth A. Mathews, *Genesis 1—11:26* (Nashville: Broadman & Holman, 1996), p. 491.

4. Merrill C. Tenney, ed., *The Zondervan Pictorial Encyclopedia of the Bible,* Vol. 5 (Grand Rapids, MI: Zondervan, 1975), pp. 847, 848.

5. Ross, *Creation & Blessing*, p. 258, and Victor P. Hamilton, *The Book of Genesis: Chapters 1—17* (Grand Rapids, MI: Eerdmans, 1990), p. 363.

6. Nahum Sarna, *The JPS Torah Commentary: Genesis* (Philadelphia: The Jewish Publication Society, 1989), p. 78 explains that "elder brother of Japheth" is correct: "Because an adjective does not usually modify a proper name in biblical Hebrew, this is the natural meaning required by the syntax." See also Kenneth A. Mathews, *Genesis*, Vol. 2 (Nashville: Broadman & Holman, 2002), p. 461 who explains:

    > Jewish tradition and some modern commentators interpret the Hebrew of 10:21 so as to make Japheth the elder brother to Shem (so NIV, AV). Most English versions, however, interpret Shem as "Japheth's older brother." Thus our author has shown in yet another way that Shem has priority among the three sons, despite coming third in the table, with the actual chronological order of birth Shem, Japheth, and Ham.

7. Philo, *The Migration of Abraham*, Vol. 4, trans. F. H. Colson and G. H. Whitaker, The Loeb Classical Library, 43, 44 (Cambridge, MA: Harvard, 1985), p. 157.

    > There is a deliberate intention when his words take the form of a promise and define the time of fulfillment not as present but future. He says not "which I am shewing" but "which I will shew thee" (Gen. xii.1). Thus he testifies to the trust which the soul reposed in God, exhibiting its thankfulness not as called out by accomplished facts, but by expectation of what was to be. For the soul, clinging in utter dependence on a good hope, and deeming that things not present are beyond question already present by reason of the sure steadfastness of Him that promised them, has won as it [exercised] faith, a perfect good; for we read a little later "Abraham believed God" (Gen. xv.6).

CHAPTER TWENTY-ONE: THE LIFE OF ABRAHAM: FAITH ANSWERS THE CALL

1. Richard L. Zettler and Lee Horne, *Treasures from the Royal Tombs of Ur* (Philadelphia: University of Pennsylvania Museum, 1998), p. 9.

2. *Ibid.*

3. John Calvin, *Genesis*, trans. and ed. John King (Carlisle, PA: Banner of Truth Trust, 1965), p. 344. Note that I have modernized the translation of the quotation by changing "thee" to "you."

4. U. Cassuto, *A Commentary on the Book of Genesis* (Jerusalem: The Magnes Press, 1989), p. 306.

5. Victor P. Hamilton, *The Book of Genesis: Chapters 1—17* (Grand Rapids, MI: Eerdmans, 1990), p. 371.

6. *Ibid.*, p. 372.

7. Gordon J. Wenham, *Genesis 1—15,* Word Biblical Commentary 2 (Waco, TX: Word, 1987), pp. 276, 277.

    > 12:3 uses a milder term קלל "disdain" instead of ארר "curse" to describe those opposed to Abram. Traditional English translations fail to bring out the difference between these words, usually translating both "curse." However, קלל "disdain" generally covers illegitimate verbal assaults on God or one's superiors, e.g., Exod 21:17; Lev 24:22; 2 Sam 16:5-13, whereas the latter term ארר refers to a judicial curse pronounced on evildoers (3:14, 17; 9:15; Deut 27:15-26.) Balak wanted Balaam to "curse" Israel (Num 22:6), but in the event he merely "disdained Israel (Deut 23:5 [4]; Josh 24:9). כבד "make heavy, honor" is the opposite of קלל "disdain," whereas ברך "bless" is the antonym of ארר "curse."
    >
    > The formula as used elsewhere, "cursed are those who curse you," preserves a balance between evildoers and their reward. The cursers are cursed, just as the blessers are blessed; this is a literary formulation of the talion principle ("eye for eye," etc., as in Exod 21:24; Lev 24:20) which makes the punishment fit the crime.

Here, however, the punishment is heightened. Those who merely "disdain" Abram will be "cursed" by God himself.

8. *Ibid.*, p. 278.

9. Derek Kidner, *Genesis: An Introduction and Commentary* (Downers Grove, IL: InterVarsity Press, 1975), p. 114.

10. Yohanan Aharmi and Michael Avi-Yonah, *The Macmillan Bible Atlas* (New York: Macmillan, 1977), p. 28.

11. Cassuto, *A Commentary on the Book of Genesis*, pp. 320, 321.

And the SOULS [נֶפֶשׁ *nepheš*] that they had WON [עָשׂוּ *'āśu*] in Haran נֶפֶשׁ *nepheś* ['soul', 'person'] as a word can denote male and female slaves, but that does not appear to be the meaning here, for several reasons:

(a) The slaves and handmaids are already included in *all the possessions which they had gathered.*

(b) The verb עָשׂוּ *'āśu* [literally, 'made'] is not the correct term for acquiring slaves.

(c) The 'making of the souls' is limited to Haran only, whereas if the reference were to slaves, male and female, there is no reason to exclude those that were acquired in Ur of the Chaldees or in other places. The rabbinic sages explained it as an allusion to proselytes (Abram converted the men, and Sarah the women). In this form it is certainly a homiletical exposition, but it seems that this haggadic interpretation approximates to the actual meaning of the text, and that we have here one of those verses that point to the theme of an ancient tradition that was not indeed incorporated in the Torah in its entirety, but was known to the Israelites, and hence a passing allusion to it sufficed (see above, the general introduction to the Pentateuchal narratives concerning Abraham, ß 5). Possibly the old tradition related that Abram, since he acknowledged his Maker, and hearkened to his voice, which spoke to him, and attained to the belief that He was the supreme God, the Creator of all things and the Lord of all, began to proclaim in *Haran* the basic principles of his faith, and succeeded in winning for it a number of souls.

12. Walter Brueggemann, *Genesis* (Atlanta: John Knox Press, 1982), p. 122.

13. Nahum Sarna, *The JPS Torah Commentary: Genesis* (Philadelphia: The Jewish Publication Society, 1989), p. 91.

14. Hamilton, *The Book of Genesis: Chapters 1—17*, p. 366.

15. Sarna, *The JPS Torah Commentary: Genesis*, p. 92.

16. Allen P. Ross, *Creation & Blessing* (Grand Rapids, MI: Baker, 1998), p. 267.

17. *Ibid.*

CHAPTER TWENTY-TWO: STARTING AND STUMBLING

1. Gordon J. Wenham, *Genesis 1—15*, Vol. 1, Word Biblical Commentary (Waco, TX: Word, 1987), p. 287 cites *ANET* (*Ancient Near Eastern Texts*), p. 251.

2. *Ibid.*, p. 188 explains: "Gunkel suggested there was a natural tendency to glorify the national mother figures (cf. 24:16; 29:17)."

3. James Boswell, *The Life of Samuel Johnson* (London: Penguin, 1979), pp. 70, 71.

4. Derek Kidner, *Genesis: An Introduction and Commentary* (Downers Grove, IL: InterVarsity Press, 1975), p. 117.

5. Robert S. Candlish, *Commentary on Genesis*, Vol. 1 (Grand Rapids, MI: Zondervan, n.d.), p. 190.

6. Nahum M. Sarna, *The JPS Torah Commentary: Genesis* (Philadelphia: The Jewish Publication Society, 1989), p. 95.

7. D. A. Carson and John D. Woodbridge, *Letters Along the Way* (Wheaton, IL: Crossway, 1993), p. 252.

8. Sarna, *The JPS Torah Commentary: Genesis*, p. 96 explains:

The riding animals are placed last. The separation of female from male asses reflects the experience of ass-herders. The male has a very powerful sex drive that asserts itself when he scents the presence of a female of the species, even from afar. He then becomes almost uncontrollable. For this reason, the female affords superior convenience and greater ease of handling as a riding animal. Possession of many she-asses was a sign of much wealth, as may be seen, for example, in Job 1:3 and 42:12.

9. *Ibid.*, explains:

A solution to the problem may perhaps be sought along other lines. Certain bilingual Sumerian-Akkadian lexical texts from Mesopotamia equate a domesticated animal called "a donkey-of-the-sea-land" with a dromedary, thus proving a knowledge of the latter in southern Mesopotamia in Old Babylonian times (ca. 2000-1700 B.C.E.) Moreover, the scribes knew to differentiate between the dromedary and the Bactrian camel, and a Sumerian text from that period mentions the drinking of camel's milk. The original habitat of the camel seems to have been Arabia. It is likely that the domesticated camel at first spread very slowly and long remained a rarity. A wealthy man might acquire a few as a prestige symbol for ornamental rather than utilitarian purposes. This would explain their presence in Abraham's entourage, their nonuse as beasts of burden, and their special mention in situations where wealth and honor need to be displayed, as, for instance, in Genesis 24.

10. Allen P. Ross, *Creation & Blessing* (Grand Rapids, MI: Baker, 1998), p. 276.

11. Wenham, *Genesis 1—15*, Vol. 1, p. 290.

12. *Ibid.*

13. Victor P. Hamilton, *The Book of Genesis: Chapters 1—17* (Grand Rapids, MI: Eerdmans, 1990), p. 382.

14. Wenham, *Genesis 1-15*, Vol. 1, p. 289.

15. Ross, *Creation & Blessing*, p. 277.

16. Hebrews 5:8, 9 explains: "Although he was a son, he learned obedience through what he suffered. And being made perfect, he became the source of eternal salvation to all who obey him" (cf. 2:10). This does not mean Jesus passed from disobedience to obedience. Nor does it mean that he developed from imperfection to perfection. The idea is that he became *complete* in his human experience. Enduring trials was essential to his perfection as our Savior.

17. Iain M. Duguid, *Living in the Gap Between Promise and Reality* (Phillipsburg, NJ: P & R Publishing, 1999), pp. 24-27 explains the biblical theological connection between Genesis 12:7 and Galatians 3:16. His work on Abraham repeatedly demonstrates the connection between his life and the gospel. The book is well-written and full of application.

CHAPTER TWENTY-THREE: MAGNANIMOUS FAITH

1. U. Cassuto, *A Commentary on the Book of Genesis*, Vol. 2 (Jerusalem: The Magnes Press, 1989), p. 363, 364 explains:

Now Abram was very RICH [כָּבֵד *kābhēd*] in cattle, in silver, and in gold. The word כָּבֵד *kābhēd* [literally, 'heavy'] is in antithetic parallelism to what is narrated at the commencement of the section (xii 10: for the famine was SEVERE [כָּבֵד *kābhēd*]): then Abram suffered because the famine was כָּבֵד *kābhēd* ['heavy', 'severe']' now he is very כָּבֵד *kābhēd* ['heavy', 'laden', 'rich'] with possessions.

2. Gordon J. Wenham, *Genesis 1—15*, Vol. 1, Word Biblical Commentary (Waco, TX: Word, 1987), p. 297.

3. Cassuto, *A Commentary on the Book of Genesis*, Vol. 2, p. 364.

4. *Brown, Driver & Briggs Hebrew and English Lexicon (BDB)* (Peabody, MA: Hendrickson Publishers, 1996), p. 609.

5. Wenham, *Genesis 1—15*, Vol. 1, p. 297 explains:

"Men and brothers." It is unusual to have "men, brothers" in apposition like this. It would have made good sense to say simply, "We are brothers." The wording seems to imply, "Men should not quarrel, let alone brothers." "Brothers," אחים, is used here in the sense of "kinsmen"; cf. 32:32; Lev. 10:4. Lot was in fact Abram's nephew, his brother's son. Abram's ideal is no doubt summed up by Ps 133:1: "How good and pleasant it is when *brothers dwell* [שֶׁבֶת]" *in unity* [יחד]" (cf. v 6).

6. Walter Brueggemann, *Genesis* (Atlanta: John Knox Press, 1982), p. 133.

7. Alexander Maclaren, *Expositions of Holy Scripture, Genesis* (Grand Rapids, MI: Baker, 1974), p. 89.

8. Nahum M. Sarna, *The JPS Torah Commentary: Genesis* (Philadelphia: The Jewish Publication Society, 1989), p. 98.

9. Allen P. Ross, *Creation & Blessing* (Grand Rapids, MI: Baker, 1998), p. 286 explains:

   The tenth verse elaborately describes how Lot chose the best for himself. "Lot lifted up [*nāśā*] his eyes and saw" [*rā'â*] reflects his intense survey of the region of the Jordan.

10. U. Cassuto, *A Commentary on the Book of Genesis,* Vol. 2, p. 366.

11. *Ibid.*

12. Ross, *Creation & Blessing,* explains:

   The motif of evil (*ra'*) is compounded in this note about Sodomites; the construction uses it adverbially (the hendiadys translates "wicked and sinners" as "wicked sinners"), as if to say that these sinners were a step below the normal sinners.

And Wenham, *Genesis 1—15,* Vol. 1, p. 298 also enlarges:

   וחטאים מאד "great sinners" is used only here. "Sinners" in the Pentateuch face sudden death (cf. Num 17:3 [16:38]). The rare phraseology implies the extreme seriousness of Sodom's sin.

13. Sarna, *Genesis,* p. 100. Also Wenham, *Genesis 1—15,* Vol. 1, p. 298.

14. Sarna, *The JPS Torah Commentary: Genesis,* p. 100 explains:

   Compare Joshua 24:3. Early Jewish exegesis (Targ. Jon.) understood this traversing of the length and breadth of the land to be a symbolic act constituting a mode of legal acquisition termed *hazakah* in rabbinic Hebrew. The validity of the formality is discussed in tannaitic sources in connection with this passage. The existence of this practice, in one form or another, is attested over a wide area of the ancient world. In both the Egyptian and Hittite spheres, the king had to undertake a periodic ceremonial walk around a field or a tour of his realm in order to symbolize the renewal of his sovereignty over the land. In Nuzi, in order to enhance the validity of property transfer, the former owner would "lift up his own foot from his property" and place the foot of the new owner on it. A reflex of this practice appears to lie behind the ceremony recounted in Ruth 4:7-9 and behind the phrasing of some biblical passages relating to Israel's acquisition of its land, such as Deuteronomy 11:24 and Joshua 1:3f. The same symbol of acquiring land by walking through it is also known from ancient Roman law.

CHAPTER TWENTY-FOUR: MAGNANIMOUS LIVING

1. *Webster's Seventh New Collegiate Dictionary* (Springfield, MA: C. & C. Merriam, 1971), p. 508.

2. Gordon J. Wenham, *Genesis 1—15,* Vol. 1, Word Biblical Commentary (Waco, TX: Word, 1987), p. 311 explains:

   "El-Paran" (tree of Paran) is mentioned only here. However, the southward thrust of Chedorlaomer along the king's highway must have brought him toward Eilat (Deut 2:8; 1 Kgs 9:26) at the head of the gulf of Akaba. Since the next verse speaks of their turning, it seems most likely that Eilat is meant here. Paran is the largest of the wildernesses south of Canaan, covering much of the Sinai peninsula and part of the Negeb and Arabah (cf. 21:21; Num 10:12; so M. Harel, *Masei Sinai* [Tel Aviv: Am Oved, 1968] 208-9). Aharoni (*EM* 6:433-34) believes the whole Sinai peninsula is meant.

3. *Ibid.*, p. 312.
4. Nahum M. Sarna, *The JPS Torah Commentary: Genesis* (Philadelphia: The Jewish Publication Society, 1989), p. 107.
5. John Calvin, *Genesis*, trans. and ed. John King (Carlisle, PA: Banner of Truth Trust, 1965), p. 382.
6. Iain M. Duguid, *Living in the Gap Between Promise and Reality* (Phillipsburg, NJ: P & R Publishing, 1999), pp. 41, 42.
7. Wenham, *Genesis 1—15*, Vol. 1, p. 314.
8. James E. Hewett, ed., *Illustrations Unlimited* (Wheaton, IL: Tyndale, 1988), pp. 129, 130.
9. Duguid, *Living in the Gap Between Promise and Reality*, p. 44.
10. James Hastings, ed., *The Speaker's Bible*, Vol. 17 (Grand Rapids, MI: Baker, 1971), p. 655.
11. Victor P. Hamilton, *The Book of Genesis: Chapters 1—17* (Grand Rapids, MI: Eerdmans, 1990), p. 408.
12. Derek Kidner, *Genesis: An Introduction and Commentary* (Downers Grove, IL: InterVarsity Press, 1975), p. 121.
13. Hamilton, *The Book of Genesis: Chapters 1—17* pp. 409, 410 explains:

    Melchizedek is connected with the city of *Salem*, traditionally identified as Jerusalem. Ps. 76:3 (Eng. 2) explicitly connects Salem with Jerusalem (Zion). But how can we connect Salem (*šālēm*) with Jerusalem (*y⁽ʳûšālayim*)? For it was not customary among the Hebrews to shorten a compound name by dropping the first element. Hypocorism (i.e., abbreviation) is done most often by apocopation (i.e., omission of the last sound or syllable of a word) or by the omission of sounds from a name's interior. The connection between the two names may be clarified by the fact that the first element of "Jerusalem" (*y⁽ʳû-*) is the word for "city" in Sumerian (*uru*), as is evidenced by the Sumero-Akkadian name for Jerusalem, *uru-salim*. This indicates that a Sumerian name was given to Jerusalem long before David appeared, possibly when Jerusalem was an outlying trading post of the Sumerians. The Genesis Apocryphon (1QapGen 22:13) clearly connects Salem and Jerusalem with its reading, "he came to Salem, that is, Jerusalem," but of course this is a reflection of first-century A.D. tradition.

14. Wenham, *Genesis 1—15*, Vol. 1, p. 322.
15. Ralph P. Martin and Peter H. Davids, eds., *Dictionary of the Later New Testament & Its Developments* (Downers Grove, IL: InterVarsity Press, 1997), p. 729 explain:

    Melchizedek is named only one other time in the OT, in Ps 110:4. Here, in what appears to be a royal psalm of coronation, the Davidic king in Jerusalem is said to be "a priest for ever after the order of Melchizedek." In other words, because Melchizedek was a king and priest in Jerusalem, the Jewish king, who also has priestly functions, can be likened to Melchizedek. The Psalm came to read as properly messianic (as in the NT and the targum).

16. Walter Brueggemann, *Genesis,* Interpretation (Atlanta: John Knox Press, 1982), p. 137.
17. Wenham, *Genesis 1—15*, Vol. 1, p. 318.
18. Brueggemann, *Genesis,* p. 138.

CHAPTER TWENTY-FIVE: MELCHIZEDEK THE PRIEST-KING

1. *Facts on File: World News Digest with Index*, Volume 36, No. 1, 1861, July 10, 1976 (New York: Facts on File), pp. 485, 486.
2. Geoffrey W. Bromiley, ed., *The International Standard Bible Encyclopedia,* Vol. 3 (Grand Rapids, MI: Eerdmans, 1986), p. 313.
3. *Ibid.*, where D. W. Burdick explains:

    The verb *aphomoioō* always assumes two distinct and separate identities, one of which is a copy of the other. Thus Melchizedek and the Son of God are represented as two separate persons, the first of which resembled the second.

4. Gerhard Von Rad, *Genesis: A Commentary* (Philadelphia: Westminster, 1972), p. 181.

5. J. D. Douglas, ed., *The New Bible Dictionary* (Grand Rapids, MI: Eerdmans, 1962), p. 806 explains:

   In Ps. cx. 4 a Davidic king is acclaimed by divine oath as 'a priest for ever after the order of Melchizedek'. The background of this acclamation is provided by David's conquest of Jerusalem *c.* 1000 BC, by virtue of which David and his house became heirs to Melchizedek's dynasty of priest-kings.

6. F. F. Bruce, *The Epistles to the Colossians, to Philemon, and to the Ephesians* (Grand Rapids, MI: Eerdmans, 1984), pp. 137, 138 explains:

   The important consideration was the account given of Melchizedek in holy writ; to him the silences of Scripture were as much due to divine inspiration as were its statements. In the only record which Scripture provides of Melchizedek — Gen. 14:18-20 — nothing is said of his parentage, nothing is said of his ancestry or progeny, nothing is said of his birth, nothing is said of his death. He appears as a living man, king of Salem and priest of God Most High; and as such he disappears. In all this — in the silences as well as in the statements — he is a fitting type of Christ; in fact, the record by the things it says of him and by the things it does not say has assimilated him to the Son of God.

7. Simon J. Kistemaker, *Hebrews* (Grand Rapids, MI: Baker Book House, 1984), p. 189 says:

   A priest might assume his priestly duties "as soon as the first signs of manhood made their appearance," but according to rabbinical tradition "he was not actually installed till he was twenty years of age." The period of service for a priest might cover twenty to thirty years, but the end would come.

Kistemaker also references Emile Schurer, *History of the Jewish People,* Vol. 1, Div. 2, p. 215 and comments, "Note also that the following passages imply that a priest was installed at age thirty and served until he reached the age of fifty: Num. 4:3, 23, 30, 35, 39, 43, 47; also see I Chron. 23:3. Num 8:23-26 speaks of Levites twenty-five years of age. And I Chron. 23:24, 27; II Chron. 31:17; and Ezra 3:8 mention the twenty year old priest."

8. William L. Lane, *Hebrews: A Call to Commitment* (Peabody, MA: Hendrickson, 1988), p. 106.

9. Leon Morris, *The Expositor's Bible Commentary*, Vol. 12 (Grand Rapids, MI: Zondervan, 1981), pp. 63, 64 writes:

   And it is the Son of God who is the standard, not the ancient priest-king. The writer says that Melchizedek is "made like" (*aphomoiomenos*) the Son of God, not that the Son of God is like Melchizedek. Thus it is not that Melchizedek sets the pattern and Jesus follows it. Rather, the record about Melchizedek is so arranged that it brings out certain truths that apply far more fully to Jesus than they do to Melchizedek. With the latter, these truths are simply a matter of record; but with Jesus they are not only historically true, they also have significant spiritual dimensions. The writer is, of course, speaking of the Son's eternal nature, not of his appearance in the Incarnation.

10. Bruce, *The Epistles to the Colossians, to Philemon, and to the Ephesians*, p. 142, writes:

    Reverting for a moment to the tithe receiving tribe of Levi, our author points out that Levi, the ancestor of that priestly tribe and the embodiment of its corporate personality, may be said himself to have paid tithes to Melchizedek (thus conceding the superiority of the Melchizedek priesthood) in the person of his ancestor Abraham. Levi was Abraham's great grandson, and was yet unborn when Abraham met Melchizedek; but an ancestor is regarded in biblical thought as containing within himself all his descendants. That Levi may be thought of thus as paying tithes to Melchizedek is an afterthought to what has already been said about the significance of this particular payment of tithes; lest it should be criticized as far-fetched, our author qualifies it with the phrase "so to say" ("it might even be said," NEB).

CHAPTER TWENTY-SIX: FAITH AND RIGHTEOUSNESS

1. Nahum M. Sarna, *The JPS Torah Commentary: Genesis* (Philadelphia: The Jewish Publication Society, 1989), p. 112.

2. Victor P. Hamilton, *The Book of Genesis: Chapters 1—17* (Grand Rapids, MI: Eerdmans, 1990), p. 418, explains:

   Yahweh's method of communicating with Abram was through a vision (*maḥ⁽ᵉ⁾zeh*), or literally "in the vision" (*bammaḥ⁽ᵉ⁾zeh*), a word that occurs only three more times in the OT (Num. 24:4, 16; Ezek. 13:7). But related words which also mean "vision," such as *ḥāzôn* (35 times), *ḥāzût* (5 times), and *ḥizzāyôn* (9 times), appear frequently. What is transmitted from God to a mortal in such visions is not a visual image but a word from God. This is what distinguishes a vision from a dream. . . . That God's word was revealed most frequently to the prophets through a vision may suggest that in Gen. 15:1 Abram is represented as a prophet, a designation specifically attached to him in 20:7. What follows in the vision is an oracle of assurance.

3. Sarna, *The JPS Torah Commentary: Genesis*, p. 113.

4. Hamilton, *The Book of Genesis: Chapters 1—17*, p. 420, explains:

   Scholars have noted that Abram's suggestion reflects an adoption procedure known from the Nuzi texts. A childless couple adopts a son, sometimes a slave, to serve them in their lifetime and bury and mourn them when they die. In return for this service they designate the adopted son as the heir presumptive. Should a natural son be born to the couple after such action, this son becomes the chief heir, demoting the adopted son to the penultimate position.

5. Derek Kidner, *Genesis: An Introduction and Commentary* (Downers Grove, IL: InterVarsity Press, 1975), p. 123.

6. Gordon J. Wenham, *Genesis 1—15*, Vol. 1, Word Biblical Commentary (Waco, TX: Word, 1987), p. 329 explains: "The verbal form וְהֶאֱמִן (waw + perfect) 'he believed' probably indicates repeated or continuing action. Faith was Abram's normal response to the Lord's words."

7. W. H. Griffith Thomas, *Genesis* (Grand Rapids, MI: Eerdmans, 1946), p. 138.

8. Walter Brueggemann, *Genesis*, "Interpretation" (Atlanta: John Knox Press, 1982), p. 144.

9. *Ibid.*, p. 145.

10. Hamilton, *The Book of Genesis: Chapters 1—17*, p. 425, 426 explains,

    The verb *ḥāšab* has two basic meanings throughout the OT. One is "count, value, calculate." The second is "plan, think out, conceive, invent." The first encompasses the bringing together of numbers and quantities and values with an eye to weighing or evaluating or calculating. The second encompasses the bringing together of ideas and plans for some intended project. In addition, the OT provides instances of *ḥāšab* with an impersonal accusative object and a dative of the person involved, who is introduced by the preposition *lᵉ*, "to"; the meaning of this construction is "to reckon or credit something (as something) to someone's account." This idiom appears in both active and passive constructions. This is what one finds in Gen. 15:6: (1) the verb *ḥāšab* ("he credited or reckoned"); (2) double impersonal accusative object, *-hā* ("it") and *ṣ⁽ᵉ⁾dāqā* ("righteousness"); and (3) dative of the person involved, who is introduced with the preposition *lᵉ* ("to him"). Thus our translation, *he credited* (or reckoned, imputed) *it to him as righteousness*. A second instance of this construction appears in 2 Sam. 19:20 (Eng. 19). Shimei, the Benjamite secessionist who had led a revolt against David, now comes before a restored David and pleads for mercy. His plea to the king is "let my lord not reckon [*al-yaḥ⁽ᵃ⁾šāb*] to me [*lî*] [my] wrongdoing [*'āwōn*]." Again, we have the verb *ḥāšab*, followed by the dative of the person involved, introduced with the preposition *lᵉ*, and then the impersonal accusative object. This illustration is very close to Ps. 32:2, "blessed is the man whom Yahweh does not impute [*lōyaḥšōb*] to him [*lô*] iniquity [*'āwōn*]."

11. Gerhard Von Rad, *Genesis: A Commentary* (Philadelphia: Westminster, 1972), p. 180.

12. C. E. B. Cranfield, *A Critical and Exegetical Commentary on the Epistle to the Romans*, Vol. 1 (Edinburgh: T. & Clark Limited, 1975), p. 323.

13. A. A. Anderson, *The Book of Psalms*, Vol. 1 (Grand Rapids, MI: Eerdmans, 1981), p. 401 writes regarding Psalm 51:

> In verse 16 the underlying thought is, so it seems, that the Law simply does not prescribe any atoning sacrifices for such things as murder and adultery, and since these or similar grave offences may have been the cause of the Psalmist's downfall, it is clear that the only alternative was penitence (see verse 17; 2 Sam. 12:13ff.). Even so, the cleansing is not the inevitable end-product of man's contrition, but it depends upon the faithfulness of God. Sacrifice, as a God-given means, functions only within the setting of the Covenant; if the Covenant relationship is broken by man, then also sacrifice and any other cultic means have lost their significance (cf. Eichrodt, TOT, 1, p. 168).

14. F. F. Bruce, *The Epistle of Paul to the Romans* (London: The Tyndale Press, 1966), p. 111.

CHAPTER TWENTY-SEVEN: GOD'S COVENANT WITH ABRAM

1. Meredith G. Kline, "Abram's Amen," *Westminster Journal of Theology*, Vol. 31 (1968), pp. 2, 3 argues that הֶאֱמִן ("and he believed") is "delocutive," indicating a spoken formula or stock phrase had been verbalized. Says Kline:

> This verse will then state not (explicitly) that Abram's inner attitude was one of faith but that his "Amen" (אָמֵן) is audible response to the word of God.

The fact that that statement appears in the context of a form of response adds plausibility to the interpretation presented here. Genesis 15 is the account of a solemn covenant ritual and an "Amen" response by the covenant vassal in such ceremonies is attested in the records of both biblical and extrabiblical covenants. Also indicative of the external-procedural rather than internal-psychological level of Genesis 15:6 is the terminology of its second clause. The verb חָשַׁב, "reckon," is employed for the rendering of decisions in cultic-judicial process (*cf.* Lev. 7:18; 17:4; Num. 18:27). And the substance of the divine reckoning, "righteousness," points to the judicial locution, "You are in the right." Thus, in the case of Yahweh's act, too, intimations of an outward occurrence are present in Genesis 15:6 itself.

2. Nahum M. Sarna, *The JPS Torah Commentary: Genesis* (Philadelphia: The Jewish Publication Society, 1989), p. 114.

3. *Ibid.*, pp. 114, 115 explains:

> In the Mari texts "to kill a donkey foal"(*hayarum/ayarum qatālummm/šuqqtu-lum*) is to conclude a covenant. At Alalakh they "cut the neck of a sheep" (*kišad/immerum ithuh*) for the same purpose. All these analogues demonstrate that the cutting up of the animal was a crucial element in the treaty-making procedure. Its retributive meaning is suggested by the only other biblical parallel (Jer. 34:17-20). The cutting of the animals is thus a form of self-imprecation in which the potential violator invokes their fate upon himself. This is confirmed by the above cited Sfire treaty, which includes the following clause; "As this calf is cut up, thus Matti'el and his nobles shall be cut up" (1:40). A similar clause occurs in a treaty between Ashurnirari V of Assyria and Matti'ilu of Arpad. The fate of the animal is explicitly projected upon the violator.

4. Victor P. Hamilton, *The Book of Genesis: Chapters 1—17*, Vol. 1 (Grand Rapids, MI: Eerdmans, 1990), p. 434 lists references that associate fright with divine pressure: Exodus 15:16, where it is parallel to *pahad*; 23:27; Deuteronomy 32:25; Psalm 88:16 (Eng. 15); Job 9:34 and 13:21.

5. *Ibid.*, p. 435, explains:

> The *four hundred years* of exile mentioned here (which Stephen quotes in Acts 7:6) seems not to match the four hundred and thirty years of exile mentioned in Exod. 12:40-41 (which Paul quotes in Gal. 3:17). We take it that the *four hundred*

years refers to both the period of sojourning and the eventual enslavement. The best way to reconcile these different numbers is to see that "the 400 years is a round figure in prospect, while the 430 years is more precise in retrospect."

6. Sarna, *The JPS Torah Commentary: Genesis*, p. 115 explains:

   Hebrew *'ayit*, here taken as a collective "birds of prey," is most likely the carrion-eating falcon (cf. Isa. 18:6; Ezek. 39:4). In Egyptian art this bird represents the important god Horus with whom the living king was identified. It is possible, therefore, that the sudden appearance of the birds of prey, and of Abram successfully warding them off, symbolically portends the sharp and menacing change that is to take place in the fortunes of the Israelites at the hands of the Egyptians while it also prefigures their rescue through the merit of the patriarch.

7. Derek Kidner, *Genesis: An Introduction and Commentary* (Downers Grove, IL: InterVarsity Press, 1975), p. 125. See also Sarna, *The JPS Torah Commentary: Genesis,* p. 116 for a fuller explanation.

8. W. F. Albright, *Archaeology and the Religion of Ancient Israel,* 4th ed. (Baltimore: Johns Hopkins, 1956), pp. 74, 75.

9. Kidner, *Genesis: An Introduction and Commentary,* p. 125.

10. Sarna, *The JPS Torah Commentary: Genesis*, p. 117.

11. Donald Grey Barnhouse, *Genesis: A Devotional Commentary* (Grand Rapids, MI: Zondervan, 1975), p. 118.

12. Hamilton, *The Book of Genesis: Chapters 1—17*, Vol. 1, p. 438, explains,

    God obliges himself to give to Abram's descendants the land of ten nations, all of which fall within the land of Canaan proper. The *river of Egypt* (see Num. 34:5; Josh. 15:4, which use *nahal* instead of *nāhār*)is not the Nile but the modern Wadi el-Arish, the dividing lines between Palestine and Egypt. The geographical extremes of the promise obviously extend beyond Canaan, witnessed especially by the phrase *to the great river, the river Euphrates*. In fact, only during the apogee of David's reign, many hundreds of years later, was this promise actualized. But even then the empire was maintained only for a generation. By Solomon's time cracks appeared in the empire, and portions of the empire rebelled and reclaimed their own land for themselves.

13. Iain M. Duguid, *Living in the Gap Between Promise and Reality* (Phillipsburg, NJ: P & R Publishing, 1999), p. 59.

CHAPTER TWENTY-EIGHT: *SHORTCUTTING FAITH*

1. Donald Grey Barnhouse, *Genesis* (Grand Rapids, MI: Zondervan, 1973), p. 123.

2. Gordon J. Wenham, *Genesis 16—50,* Vol. 2, Word Biblical Commentary (Dallas: Word, 1994), p. 7.

3. E. A. Speiser, *Genesis* (Garden City, NY: Doubleday, 1964), p. 120.

4. W. H. Griffith Thomas, *Genesis* (Grand Rapids, MI: Eerdmans, 1946), p. 146.

5. John H. Sailhamer, "Genesis," Vol. 2, The Expositor's Bible Commentary (Grand Rapids, MI: Zondervan, 1990), pp. 134, 135.

6. Gerhard Von Rad, *Genesis: A Commentary* (Philadelphia: Westminster, 1972), p. 191.

7. Victor P. Hamilton, *The Book of Genesis: Chapters 1—17* (Grand Rapids, MI: Eerdmans, 1990), p. 447.

8. James E. Pritchard, ed., *Ancient New Eastern Texts* (Princeton, NJ: Princeton, 1955), p. 172 reads:

   146: When a seignior married a hierodule and she gave a female slave to her husband and she has then borne children, if later that female slave has claimed equality with her mistress because she bore children, her mistress may not sell her; she may mark her with the slave-mark and count her among the slaves.

9. Wenham, *Genesis 16—50,* Vol. 2, pp. 9, 10.

10. Von Rad, *Genesis: A Commentary*, p. 194.

11. Hamilton, *The Book of Genesis: Chapters 1—17*, p. 453.

12. Gordon J. Wenham, *Genesis 16—50*, Vol. 2, p. 11.

13. Derek Kidner, *Genesis: An Introduction and Commentary* (Downers Grove, IL: InterVarsity Press, 1975), p. 127.

14. Hamilton, *The Book of Genesis: Chapters 1—17*, p. 455.

CHAPTER TWENTY-NINE: COVENANT CONFIRMED

1. Ronald Youngblood, *The Book of Genesis* (Grand Rapids, MI: Baker, 1991), p. 168.

2. Allen P. Ross, *Creation & Blessing* (Grand Rapids, MI: Baker, 1998), p. 330.

3. Marcus Dods, *The Book of Genesis* (New York: A.C. Armstrong and Son, 1903), p. 161.

4. Nahum M. Sarna, *The JPS Torah Commentary: Genesis* (Philadelphia: The Jewish Publication Society, 1989), p. 124.

5. Youngblood, *The Book of Genesis*, 1991), p. 170.

6. Iain M. Duguid, *Living in the Gap Between Promise and Reality* (Phillipsburg, NJ: P & R Publishing, 1999), p. 75. Note: The application that surrounds this quotation is either from this writer or is inspired by his thought.

7. Ross, *Creation & Blessing*, p. 335.

CHAPTER THIRTY: IS ANYTHING TOO HARD FOR THE LORD?

1. Allen P. Ross, *Creation & Blessing* (Grand Rapids, MI: Baker, 1998), p. 342.

2. Gordon J. Wenham, *Genesis 16—50,* Vol. 2, Word Biblical Commentary (Dallas: Word, 1994), p. 46.

3. *Ibid.*

4. Robert S. Candlish, *Commentary on Genesis,* Vol. 1 (Grand Rapids, MI: Zondervan, n.d.), p. 296.

5. Ross, *Creation & Blessing*, p. 343.

6. Iain M. Duguid, *Living in the Gap Between Promise and Reality* (Phillipsburg, NJ: P & R Publishing, 1999), pp. 85, 86.

7. Wenham, *Genesis 16—50,* Vol. 2, p. 48.

8. A. W. Tozer, *The Knowledge of the Holy* (New York: Harper & Row, 1961), p. 63.

9. Ross, *Creation & Blessing*, p. 346.

CHAPTER THIRTY-ONE: GOD, RIGHTEOUS AND JUST

1. Victor P. Hamilton, *The Book of Genesis: Chapters 18—50*, Vol. 2 (Grand Rapids, MI: Eerdmans, 1990), p. 17.

2. *Ibid.*, p. 21.

3. Nahum M. Sarna, *The JPS Torah Commentary: Genesis* (Philadelphia: The Jewish Publication Society, 1989), p. 132.

4. Gordon J. Wenham, *Genesis 16—50,* Vol. 2, Word Biblical Commentary (Dallas: Word, 1994), p. 60.

5. David F. Wells, *No Place for Truth or Whatever Happened to Evangelical Theology?* (Grand Rapids, MI: Eerdmans, 1993), p. 58.

6. A. W. Tozer, *The Knowledge of the Holy* (New York: Harper & Row, 1961), p. 62.

7. Alexander Maclaren, *Expositions of Holy Scripture, Genesis* (Grand Rapids, MI: Baker, 1974), p. 135.

8. *Ibid.*, p. 141.

9. Wenham, *Genesis 16—50,* Vol. 2, p. 53 explains:

    31 Though Abraham's request has the same polite diffidence as in v 27, the reply has a slightly ominous ring. The Lord himself introduces the word "ruin" in his reply to Abraham, whereas on the previous occasion he had used the more colorless "do," perhaps giving a hint that he cannot be pressed much further.

32 Clearly Abraham feels he has reached the limit of what he dare ask. He opens with the conciliatory "Do not be angry" (v 30) and asks to speak "just once more." And again his request is granted, albeit with the same threatening formula as in v 31: "I shall not *ruin* it."

33 As the Lord had hinted in v 21 that he wanted intercession for Sodom, so he now closes the prayer by going on his way.

CHAPTER THIRTY-TWO: MOLTEN RAIN

1. Gordon J. Wenham, *Genesis 16—50,* Vol. 2, Word Biblical Commentary (Dallas: Word, 1994), p. 54.
2. Francis Brown, *The Brown-Driver-Briggs Hebrew and English Lexicon* (Peabody, MA: Hendrickson, 1999), p. 1059.
3. Nahum M. Sarna, *The JPS Torah Commentary: Genesis* (Philadelphia: The Jewish Publication Society, 1989), p. 135.
4. Gerhard Von Rad, *Genesis: A Commentary* (Philadelphia: Westminster, 1972), p. 217.
5. Wenham, *Genesis 16—50,* Vol. 2, p. 55.
6. Sarna, *The JPS Torah Commentary: Genesis*, p. 136 explains:
   Lot is not appealing to the passions of the men of Sodom but is underscoring the seriousness with which he treats the value of hospitality. Verse 14 shows that the two girls were betrothed but not yet married. The Mesopotamian law codes make it clear that betrothal was as sacrosanct as a consummated marriage. The Akkadian phrase corresponding to our Hebrew is *ša zikaram la idū*, "who has not known a male." It is similarly used in legal formulation to describe a woman engaged to be married and still living in her father's house. Her violator incurs the death penalty.
7. Derek Kidner, *Genesis: An Introduction and Commentary* (Downers Grove, IL: InterVarsity Press, 1975), p. 134 explains:
   The rare word for *blindness* probably indicates a dazzled state, as of Saul on the Damascus Road. The same word recurs in 2 Kings 6:18, also in the context of angels. *Cf.* Speiser, *in loc.*; also in *JCS*, VI, 1952, pp. 81ff.
   Similarly, Sarna, *The JPS Torah Commentary: Genesis*, p. 136:
   . . . *blinding light* Hebrew *sanverim* occurs again only in 2 Kings 6:18 in a similar context. The Aramaic targums understand it to mean a dazzling brightness. The people of Sodom did not suffer the usual kind of sightlessness (*ivvaron*) but a sudden, immobilizing, blazing flash of light.
8. Wenham, *Genesis 16—50,* Vol. 2, p. 57 explains:
   "At crack of dawn," lit. "as dawn rose." שַׁחַר "dawn" is the time when the blackness of night starts to lighten before sunrise (cf. v 23; Judg 19:25-26).
9. Kidner, *Genesis: An Introduction and Commentary*, p. 135.
10. John H. Sailhamer, "Genesis," Vol. 2, The Expositor's Bible Commentary (Grand Rapids, MI: Zondervan, 1990), pp. 156, 157 explains:
    God had promised not to destroy the city "on behalf of" the righteous in it (18:26, 28, 29, 30, 31, 32). So now, though Sodom was destroyed, Zoar was saved from the destruction on account of Lot (v. 21). Thus by including this episode the writer has headed off an interpretive problem between chapters 18 and 19: namely, if Lot was the "righteous one" whom Abraham had in mind in his prayer in chapter 18, why did the Lord not save the city of Sodom on his behalf? Whatever the specific answer given to that question (see discussion on ch. 18), the point of vv. 17-22 is that Abraham's prayer was specifically answered, and God did save the city of Zoar on account of the righteous one living in it.
11. Marcus Dods, *The Book of Genesis* (New York: A.C. Armstrong and Son, 1903), p. 195.
12. *Josephus Jewish Antiquities*, 1.203, Vol. 4, trans. H. St. J. Thackeray (Cambridge, MA: Harvard University Press, 1978), p. 101:

But Lot's wife, who during the flight was continually turning round towards the city, curious to observe its fate, notwithstanding God's prohibition of such action, was changed into a pillar of salt: I have seen this pillar which remains to this day.

13. Sailhamer, *Genesis,* Vol. 2, The Expositor's Bible Commentary, pp. 158.
14. *Ibid.*

CHAPTER THIRTY-THREE: FINISHING UN-WELL

1. Robert H. Gundry, "A Paleofundamentalist Manifesto for Contemporary Evangelicalism," *Books & Culture*, Vol. 7, No. 5, pp. 27, 28.
2. *Ibid.*
3. Donald Grey Barnhouse, *Genesis* (Grand Rapids, MI: Zondervan, 1973), p. 171.
4. Harry A. Hoffner, ed., "Incest, Sodomy and Bestiality in the Ancient Near East," *Orient and Occident*, (Kevelaer: Verlag Butzon & Bereker Kevelaer, 1973), pp. 81-90.
5. Gordon J. Wenham, *Genesis 16—50,* Vol. 2, Word Biblical Commentary (Dallas: Word, 1994), p. 61.
6. Nahum M. Sarna, *The JPS Torah Commentary: Genesis* (Philadelphia: The Jewish Publication Society, 1989), p. 140.
7. C. F. Keil, and F. Delitzsch, *Biblical Commentary on The Old Testament, The Pentateuch*, Vol. 1, trans. James Martin (Grand Rapids, MI: Eerdmans, n.d.), pp. 37, 38.
8. John H. Sailhamer, "Genesis," Vol. 2, The Expositor's Bible Commentary (Grand Rapids, MI: Zondervan, 1990), p. 159.
9. Sarna, *The JPS Torah Commentary: Genesis*, p. 140.

CHAPTER THIRTY-FOUR: OLD SINS

1. Nahum M. Sarna, *JPS Torah Commentary: Genesis* (Philadelphia: The Jewish Publication Society, 1989), p. 141.
2. "Man's Weakness — God's Strength," *Missionary Crusader* (December 1964), p. 7.
3. Allen P. Ross, *Creation & Blessing* (Grand Rapids, MI: Baker, 1998), p. 371.
4. Iain M. Duguid, *Living in the Gap Between Promise and Reality* (Phillipsburg, NJ: P & R Publishing, 1999), p. 118.
5. Chambers, "Man's Weakness — God's Strength," p. 7.
6. Duguid, *Living in the Gap Between Promise and Reality*, p. 119.

CHAPTER THIRTY-FIVE: TWO LAUGHTERS

1. Nahum M. Sarna, *JPS Torah Commentary: Genesis* (Philadelphia: The Jewish Publication Society, 1989), p. 146, observes:

   This utterance of Sarah has the form of a song. It consists of three short clauses of three words each. The forms of the verbs as well as the rare stem *m-l-l* seem to indicate that the words of Sarah had their origin in an ancient poem.
2. *Ibid.*
3. Derek Kidner, *Genesis: An Introduction and Commentary* (Downers Grove, IL: InterVarsity Press, 1975), p. 140 says:

   RSV's *playing* (implying that Sarah was insanely jealous) is unfair: it should be translated *mocking* (AV, RV). This is the intensive form of Isaac's name-verb 'to laugh', its malicious sense here demanded by the context and by Galatians 4:29 ('persecuted'). RSV itself renders it 'jesting' (19:14) and 'to insult' (39:14, 17).
4. W. H. Griffith Thomas, *Genesis* (Grand Rapids, MI: Eerdmans, 1946), p. 187.
5. Kenneth A. Mathews, *Genesis*, Vol. 2 (Nashville: Broadman & Holman, 2002), p. 23.
6. *Ibid.*
7. Frederick Buechner, *Telling Secrets* (San Francisco: HarperSanFrancisco, 1991), p. 36.

CHAPTER THIRTY-SIX: THE LORD WILL PROVIDE

1. John H. Walton, *Genesis,* NIV Application Commentary (Grand Rapids, MI: Zondervan, 2001), p. 509.
2. John S. Sailhamer, *Genesis,* Vol. 2, The Expositor's Bible Commentary (Grand Rapids, MI: Zondervan, 1990), p. 168 explains:

   "Take" (*qah-nā*), "go" (*wᵉlek*), and "sacrifice him" (*wᵉha "ᵃlēlû*). Furthermore, the reader is given no reason to believe that Abraham himself had any further explanation.
3. Walton, Genesis, p. 510.
4. Gordon J. Wenham, *Genesis 16—50,* Vol. 2, Word Biblical Commentary (Dallas: Word, 1994), p. 114.
5. *Ibid.,* p. 108.
6. *Ibid.,* p. 109.

CHAPTER THIRTY-SEVEN: PROMISE AND PURCHASE

1. Walter Brueggemann, *Genesis,* "Interpretation" (Atlanta: John Knox Press, 1982), p. 197.
2. John H. Walton, *Genesis*, The NIV Application Commentary (Grand Rapids, MI: Zondervan, 2000), p. 528 explains:

   It is difficult to determine whether the Hittites mentioned here are related to those of the Hittite empire known from Anatolia a few centuries later. Abraham's era is far too early to coincide with the dissemination of the Hittites into Syro-Palestine that took place in the aftermath of the turmoil associated with the Sea Peoples around 1200 B.C. Genesis knows of Hittites that were distinct from the Indo-European empire builders (see 10:15, which mentions Hittites from the family of Heth, a descendant of Canaan). These Genesis Hittites have Semitic names and appear to possess a thoroughly Semitic culture. That they appear to own substantial amounts of land suggests they are part of the indigenous population rather than a merchant colony from far-away Anatolia.
3. Brueggemann, *Genesis,* p. 196:

   1. There is a suggested incongruity between Abraham's self-effacing identity (v. 4) "a stranger and a sojourner," and the title the Hittite commander uses for Abraham (v. 6), "a prince of God." The RSV offers an alternative rendering of the address as "a mighty prince." Such a rendering is, of course, possible; but it cannot be unimportant that the Hebrew adjective is *"'elohim"* — "God." If this translation be accepted, it suggests that for the narrative, it is the *landless sojourner* who is *God's prince.* It is the landless one who bears all the promises and lives in hope. It is the very incongruity which intensifies the main concern of Genesis.
4. Kenneth A. Mathews, *Genesis,* Vol. 2 (Nashville: Broadman & Holman, 2002), p. 2.
5. Ronald Youngblood, *The Book of Genesis* (Grand Rapids, MI: Baker, 1991), p. 193.
6. *Ibid.,* pp. 192, 193.
7. Derek Kidner, *Genesis: An Introduction and Commentary* (Downers Grove, IL: InterVarsity Press, 1975), p. 145.
8. Allen P. Ross, *Creation & Blessing* (Grand Rapids, MI: Baker, 1998), p. 412.

CHAPTER THIRTY-EIGHT: FAITH AND PROVIDENCE

1. Nahum M. Sarna, *JPS Torah Commentary: Genesis* (Philadelphia: The Jewish Publication Society, 1989), p. 112.
2. John Calvin, *Genesis,* Vol. 2, trans. and ed. John King (Carlisle, PA: Banner of Truth Trust, 1965), p. 16.
3. J. I. Packer, *Concise Theology* (Wheaton, IL: Tyndale, 1993), p. 56.
4. *Ibid.,* p. 54.
5. Derek Kidner, *Genesis: An Introduction and Commentary* (Downers Grove, IL: InterVarsity Press, 1975), p. 146.

6. Sarna, *JPS Torah Commentary: Genesis*, p. 163.

7. *Ibid.*, p. 164.

8. John H. Walton, *Genesis,* The NIV Application Commentary (Grand Rapids, MI: Zondervan, 2001), p. 530.

9. Sarna, *JPS Torah Commentary: Genesis*, p. 166.

10. John H. Sailhamer, "Genesis," Vol. 2, The Expositor's Bible Commentary (Grand Rapids, MI: Zondervan, 1990), p. 177 explains:

> Another striking feature of this story is that after introducing the new characters of Laban and his household, the writer allows the servant again to retell the narrative (vv. 34-49). But as with most repetitions in biblical narrative, the retelling is not a mere repeating. It is rather a reassertion of the central points of the first narrative. The point of the retelling can be seen in the fact that the servant adds to what was originally reported by Abraham (v. 7). Originally we heard Abraham say, only generally, that God would send a messenger and that the servant would find a wife for Isaac (v. 7). When he retold the story to Laban, however, the servant included the idea that God would send the angel and also added that the angel would make his journey a success by gaining a wife for Isaac from his own family (v. 40). As we overhear the servant recount more details, we see that the miracle of God's provision was even more grand than that suggested in the narrative itself.

> It should also be noted that the servant also deletes Abraham's refusal to allow Isaac to return to his homeland, because he did not wish to imply an insult to Laban and Bethuel.

11. *Ibid.*, p. 178.

12. Sarna, *JPS Torah Commentary: Genesis*, p. 170.

13. Leland Ryken, James C. Wilhoit, Tremper Longman III, eds., *Dictionary of Biblical Inquiry* (Downers Grove, IL: InterVarsity Press, 1998), p. 681.

14. Ian M. Duguid, *Living in the Gap Between Promise and Reality* (Phillipsburg, NJ: P & R Publishing, 1999), p. 155.

CHAPTER THIRTY-NINE: THE DEATH OF ABRAHAM

1. Marvin R. O'Connell, *Blaise Pascal: Reasons of the Heart* (Grand Rapids, MI: Eerdmans, 1997), p. 76.

2. Nahum M. Sarna, *JPS Torah Commentary: Genesis* (Philadelphia: The Jewish Publication Society, 1989), pp. 171, 172.

3. Derek Kidner, *Genesis: An Introduction and Commentary* (Downers Grove, IL: InterVarsity Press, 1975), p. 150.

4. David Remnick, "Letter from Moscow: Deep in the Woods," *New Yorker,* August 6, 2001, pp. 23-40.

5. Gerhard Von Rad, *Genesis: A Commentary* (Philadelphia: Westminster, 1972), p. 262 writes:

> The expression "old man and full of years" shows that in ancient Israel one accepted life not with a defiant claim to endlessness but from the start in resignation, as something limited, something assigned to one man, in which then the state of satisfaction was to be reached (cf. ch. 35.29; Job 42.17; I Chron. 23.1; 29.28; II Chron. 24.15).

6. Robert S. Candlish, *Commentary on Genesis,* Vol. 1 (Grand Rapids, MI: Zondervan, n.d.), p. 418.

7. Kidner, *Genesis*, p. 150.

8. Allen P. Ross, *Creation & Blessing* (Grand Rapids, MI: Baker, 1998), p. 427.

9. W. H. Griffith Thomas, *Genesis* (Grand Rapids, MI: Eerdmans, 1946), p. 221.

CHAPTER FORTY: INFAMOUS GRACE

1. Gordon J. Wenham, *Genesis 16—50*, Vol. 2, Word Biblical Commentary (Dallas: Word, 1994), p. 172.

2. Walter Brueggemann, *Genesis*, "Interpretation" (Atlanta: John Knox Press, 1982), pp. 204, 217.

3. *Ibid.*, p. 212.

4. Allen P. Ross, *Creation & Blessing* (Grand Rapids, MI: Baker, 1998), pp. 438, 439 explains:

   Isaac knew that the only recourse for such a problem was to entreat the Lord. That this is the predominant point may be seen from the repetition of the verb: "Isaac entreated [*wayye'tar*] the LORD . . . and the LORD was entreated [*wayy'āter*]." The verb *'ātar* thus warrants a closer study as part of the exegetical procedure. Such a study will discover that the verb occurs frequently in the narratives of the plagues of Egypt (Exod. 8-10), in which Moses entreated the Lord to remove the plagues. There may not be sufficient evidence to determine all that went into Isaac's supplication, but it is interesting to note that the Arabic cognate of the verb meant "to slaughter for sacrifice," and the Hebrew cognate noun (*"ātār*) was used in Zephaniah 3:10 to describe worshipers or suppliants who would bring offerings. Some form of ritual perhaps accompanied Isaac's prayer. At any rate, a study of the verb's usage shows that God is always the one being entreated for deliverance or relief. Here, the result of the entreaty was that Rebekah's barrenness was removed.

   See also Wenham, *Genesis 16—50*, Vol. 2, pp. 174, 175.

5. Wenham, *Genesis 16—50*, Vol. 2, explains:

   Isaac's prayer is answered by a multiple pregnancy, which, though a tribute to the efficacy of the prayer, is extremely painful for Rebekah. "The children" (number unspecified) "smashed themselves inside her." The verb רצץ "smash, crush" is most frequently used figuratively of the oppression of the poor. Literally, it is used to describe skulls being smashed (Judg 9:53; Ps 74:14) or reeds being broken (e.g., Isa 36:6). The use of such a term here vividly indicated the violence of the struggle within Rebekah's womb.

6. Nahum M. Sarna, *JPS Torah Commentary: Genesis* (Philadelphia: The Jewish Publication Society, 1989), p. 179.

7. W. H. Griffith Thomas, *Genesis* (Grand Rapids, MI: Eerdmans, 1946), p. 226.

8. John H. Sailhamer, "Genesis," Vol. 2, The Expositor's Bible Commentary (Grand Rapids, MI: Zondervan, 1990), pp. 182, 183.

9. Wenham, *Genesis 16—50*, Vol. 2, p. 176.

10. Ross, *Creation & Blessing*, p. 441 explains:

    The name Jacob likely had a positive connotation at the time of the naming. There is evidence for a meaning "protect" rather than "overreach, assail" (see *PN*, pp. 177-178; Albright, *From the Stone Age to Christianity* [Garden City, N.Y.: Doubleday, 1957], p. 237). The name may have been contracted from *ya'ăqōb 'ēl*, "may God protect." Its connection with "heel" probably was that of the following at the heels as a rearguard — but it would not be necessary for the parents to know the actual etymology when they chose the name.

    The name seems to have been in existence from an early stage. Because the name sounded like the word for heel, the parents chose it to commemorate the unusual event, the grabbing of the "heel" (*'āqēb*). Later events then showed how his name took on the negative significance of assailant or overreacher. Tradition loved to tell of those incidents that verified his name, as Driver puts it. It is quite unlikely, however, that parents would have named a baby "assailant, overreacher," or "deceiver."

11. Derek Kidner, *Genesis: An Introduction and Commentary* (Downers Grove, IL: InterVarsity Press, 1975), p. 152.

12. Griffith Thomas, *Genesis*, p. 232, quoting Strachan, *Hebrew Idioms*, p. 23.
13. Wenham, *Genesis 16—50*, Vol. 2, p. 178.

CHAPTER FORTY-ONE: WEAKNESS — GOD'S PRESENCE — BLESSING

1. A. W. Tozer, *Born After Midnight* (Harrisburg, PA: Christian Publications, 1959), pp. 119, 120.
2. Wayne Grudem, *Systematic Theology, An Introduction to Biblical Doctrine* (Grand Rapids, MI: Zondervan Publishing House, 1994), p. 173.
3. Herbert Lockyer, *Last Words of Saints and Sinners* (Grand Rapids, MI: Kregel, 1969), p. 64.
4. C. F. Keil, and F. Delitzsch, *Biblical Commentary on The Old Testament, The Pentateuch*, Vol. 1, trans. James Martin (Grand Rapids, MI: Eerdmans, n.d.), pp. 270, 271. Keil writes:

    The name proves nothing, for it was the standing official name of the kings of Gerar (cf. 2 Sam. xi.21 and Ps. xxxiv.), as Pharaoh was of the kings of Egypt. The identity is favoured by the pious conduct of Abimelech in both instances; and no difficulty is caused either by the circumstance that 80 years had elapsed between the two events (for Abraham had only been dead five years, and the age of 150 was no rarity then) . . . whereas the first Abimelech had Sarah taken into his harem, the second not only had no intention of doing this, but was anxious to protect her from his people, inasmuch as it would be all the easier to conceive of this in the case of the same king, on the ground of his advanced age.

5. Nahum M. Sarna, *JPS Torah Commentary: Genesis* (Philadelphia: The Jewish Publication Society, 1989), p. 183.
6. *Ibid.*
7. Derek Kidner, *Genesis: An Introduction and Commentary* (Downers Grove, IL: InterVarsity Press, 1975), p. 153 writes:

    Typically human, Isaac mixes faith . . . and fear, an incompatible combination which can give a special quality of meanness to the sins of the religious; and nowhere more so than here.

8. Gerhard Von Rad, *Genesis: A Commentary* (Philadelphia: Westminster, 1972), p. 271 explains:

    Details are left to the reader's imagination; the narrator veils it with an etymological allusion to Isaac's name (*yishaq—sāhaq*), "jest."

9. George Dana Boardman, *The Ten Commandments* (Philadelphia, Chicago, Los Angeles: The Judson Press, 1952), pp. 48, 49.

CHAPTER FORTY-TWO: PILFERED BLESSING

1. Allen P. Ross, *Creation & Blessing* (Grand Rapids, MI: Baker, 1998), p. 476.
2. Nahum M. Sarna, *JPS Torah Commentary: Genesis* (Philadelphia: The Jewish Publication Society, 1989), p. 190.
3. W. H. Griffith Thomas, *Genesis* (Grand Rapids, MI: Eerdmans, 1946), p. 252.
4. Sarna, *JPS Torah Commentary: Genesis,* p. 192.
5. *Ibid.*, pp. 192, 194.
6. Derek Kidner, *Genesis: An Introduction and Commentary* (Downers Grove, IL: InterVarsity Press, 1975), p. 156.
7. Donald Grey Barnhouse, *Genesis* (Grand Rapids, MI: Zondervan, 1973), p. 71.
8. Ross, *Creation & Blessing,* p. 480.
9. C. F. Keil, and F. Delitzsch, *Biblical Commentary on the Old Testament, The Pentateuch*, Vol. 1, trans. James Martin (Grand Rapids, MI: Eerdmans, n.d.), p. 279.

CHAPTER FORTY-THREE: AN ANGEL-FREIGHTED LADDER

1. Derek Kidner, *Genesis: An Introduction and Commentary* (Downers Grove, IL: InterVarsity Press, 1975), p. 157.

2. Allen P. Ross, *Creation & Blessing* (Grand Rapids, MI: Baker, 1998), p. 488, writes:

   Jacob was surprised by what he dreamed, a reaction that the reader is vividly made aware of. Fokkelman points out that the particle *hinnēh* functions deictically; it is pre- or paralingual. It goes with a lifted arm and open mouth: "There, a ladder! Oh, angels! And look, the Lord Himself!" (*Narrative Art*, pp. 51-52).

3. John Walton, *Genesis,* The NIV Application Commentary (Grand Rapids, MI: Zondervan, 2001), p. 574.

CHAPTER FORTY-FOUR: DECEIVER DECEIVED

1. Nahum M. Sarna, *JPS Torah Commentary: Genesis* (Philadelphia: The Jewish Publication Society, 1989), p. 202.

2. Gordon J. Wenham, *Genesis 16—50,* Vol. 2, Word Biblical Commentary (Dallas: Word, 1994), p. 231, explains:

   "You are truly my flesh and blood" is more ambiguous than it sounds. It is apparently an openhearted admission that Jacob is indeed Laban's close relative (cf. *Comment* on 2:23), which the particle אך "truly" reinforces. So it could be taken as a warm welcome to Jacob to stay. However, אך may suggest a rather grudging admission on Laban's part of kinship. "You have convinced me that you are my nephew, so you may as well stay" (cf. Jacob; Ehrlich; Fokkelman, *Narrative Art*). On this view, Laban's double-dealing is already being hinted at, even though Jacob must have understood the comment entirely positively and have been reassured by it.

   "He stayed with him a month" echoed his mother's injunction, "Stay with him a few days" (27:44). (The phrase "a few days" is found in 29:20.) It seems therefore unlikely that "stay with" meant that Laban legally acknowledged Jacob as a co-heir (*pace* D. Daube and R. Yaron, *JSS* 1 [1956] 61). Thus staying with his uncle, Jacob has begun to fulfill his parents' instructions. Will he now succeed in marrying one of Laban's daughters and returning home as they had also instructed him?

3. *Ibid.*, p. 235, explains:

   What makes eyes "soft" (רך) is unclear; most commentators think it means they had no fire or sparkle, a quality much prized in the East. Whether her eyes were the only features that let her down is not said, but the glowing description of Rachel as having "a beautiful figure and a lovely face" suggests Leah was outshone by her sister in various ways.

   See also Gerhard Von Rad, *Genesis: A Commentary* (Philadelphia: Westminster, 1972), p. 291, who explains:

   What is meant is probably their paleness and lack of luster. The Oriental likes a woman's eyes to be lively, to glow, and therefore eye make-up was used from most ancient times.

4. John Walton, *Genesis,* The NIV Application Commentary (Grand Rapids, MI: Zondervan, 2001), p. 586.

5. *Ibid.*

   In texts from Nuzi the typical bride price was thirty to forty shekels. Since a shepherd's annual wage was ten shekels a year, Jacob is in effect paying a premium by working seven years, but he is in no position to negotiate. Theoretically, Laban will garner Jacob's would-be wages and secure them into a bride-price account of some sort.

6. Wenham, *Genesis 16—50*, Vol. 2, p. 234.

7. *Ibid.*

8. Allen P. Ross, *Creation & Blessing* (Grand Rapids, MI: Baker, 1998), p. 504.

CHAPTER FORTY-FIVE: BIRTH WARS!

1. Geoffrey W. Bromiley, ed., *The International Standard Bible Encyclopedia*, Vol. 3 (Grand Rapids, MI: Eerdmans, 1986), pp. 901, 902.

2. Carol Gilligan, *In a Different Voice* (Cambridge, MA: Harvard University Press, 1982), p. 124.
3. Gordon J. Wenham, *Genesis 16—50*, Vol. 2, Word Biblical Commentary (Dallas: Word, 1994), p. 247.
4. *Ibid.*
5. G. C. Aalders, *Genesis*, Vol. 2, trans. William Heynen (Grand Rapids, MI: Zondervan, 1981), p. 119.
6. Derek Kidner, *Genesis: An Introduction and Commentary* (Downers Grove, IL: InterVarsity Press, 1975), p. 162.
7. Allen P. Ross, *Creation & Blessing* (Grand Rapids, MI: Baker, 1998), p. 513.
8. Wenham, *Genesis 16—50*, p. 248, writes:

> This note of triumph is carried through in calling her daughter "Dinah," "judgment, vindication" (cf. Dan v 6). In fact, no etymology is offered for her name, perhaps because it is too obvious or because she was merely a daughter. It is, of course, extraordinary to mention the birth of daughters; it is done only if they are going to have an important role to play later (cf. Rebekah in 22:23). Dinah's appearance does not just make the number of children born to Jacob up to twelve; it signifies that she too will be an actor of note in a tale of judgment and vindication (chap. 34).

9. Walter Brueggemann, *Genesis*, "Interpretation" (Atlanta: John Knox Press, 1982), pp. 255, 256.

CHAPTER FORTY-SIX: THE GREENING OF JACOB

1. Gerhard Von Rad, *Genesis: A Commentary* (Philadelphia: Westminster, 1972), p. 300.
2. Gordon J. Wenham, *Genesis 16—50*, Vol. 2, Word Biblical Commentary (Dallas: Word, 1994), p. 256.
3. John Walton, *Genesis,* The NIV Application Commentary (Grand Rapids, MI: Zondervan, 2001), p. 589.
4. Nahum M. Sarna, *JPS Torah Commentary: Genesis* (Philadelphia: The Jewish Publication Society, 1989), p. 212:

> One account has it that he first segregates the feebler animals. Then he subjects the sturdier ones to visual impressions at mating time, in this way influencing the character of the progeny. Of course, this interpretation rests on folkloristic beliefs and fallaciously assumes the inheritability of acquired characteristics.
>
> Another explanation is given in 31:8-12. Here the preferred characteristics are obtained through controlled propagation and transmitted from parent to progeny. Scientifically, the required results could be achieved by the successive interbreeding of the monochrome heterozygotes, or the single-colored animals that carried recessive genes for spottedness. Such animals are detectable by the characteristic known as heterosis, or hybrid vigor.
>
> It should be noted that Jacob claims to have received the idea in a dream. The entire action is thus attributed to divine intervention, not to Jacob's ingenuity. This process made it necessary for Jacob to find a way to advance the mating season so that the rare types would be induced to engage in reproductive activity before they were segregated, which they were when the normal mating time approached. If this is the true explanation, then the varied accounts need not be contradictory. The first would describe the elaborate display put on by Jacob in order to mask his secret technique. It is also possible that the three plants placed in the watering troughs, each known to contain toxic substances and used in the ancient world for medicinal purposes, could have had the effect of hastening the onset of the estrous cycle in the animals and so heightened their readiness to copulate.

5. T. Desmond Alexander, Brian S. Rosner, D. A. Carson, Graeme Goldsworthy, eds., *New Dictionary of Biblical Theology* (Leicester, England: Inter-Varsity Press, 2000), pp. 584, 585 explain:

Jesus appears, not just as the Saviour of Israel in fulfillment of prophetic expectation, but also as an embodiment of Israel as they should be. Matthew makes this point dramatically in his opening chapters, first by applying the Exodus verse Hosea 11:1 to Jesus (Matt. 2:15), and then by telling the story in a way that makes Jesus re-enact Israel's history: the Exodus from Egypt (2:19-20), the crossing of the Red Sea (3:13-17), the temptations (see Testing) in the desert (4:1-11), even the arrival at Mt. Sinai to receive the law (5:1-2). Perhaps most pointedly, it is Jesus on whom the Spirit descends (Matt. 3:16), although the prophetic expectation was of an outpouring of the Spirit upon Israel (Is. 44:2-3; Ezek. 36:25-27). Where Israel had failed the temptations in the desert, Jesus now remains faithful to God.

CHAPTER FORTY-SEVEN: MESOPOTAMIAN EXODUS

1. John Walton, *Genesis,* The NIV Application Commentary (Grand Rapids, MI: Zondervan, 2001), p. 590.
2. Nahum M. Sarna, *JPS Torah Commentary: Genesis* (Philadelphia: The Jewish Publication Society, 1989), p. 216.
3. Allen P. Ross, *Creation & Blessing* (Grand Rapids, MI: Baker, 1998), pp. 530, 531.
4. Derek Kidner, *Genesis: An Introduction and Commentary* (Downers Grove, IL: InterVarsity Press, 1975), p. 165.
5. Sarna, *JPS Torah Commentary: Genesis,* p. 216.
6. Walton, *Genesis,* p. 591, writes:

   The only conceivable solution that explains Laban's not catching up to Jacob before the area of Gilead is to assume that it takes Laban a week or ten days to prepare for the trip before he can set out and that he cannot travel very fast (after all, he is over 150 years old now).
7. Sarna, *JPS Torah Commentary: Genesis,* p. 217, writes:

   These are symbolic numbers indicative of significant segments of time. A literal understanding would mean that Jacob covered the approximately 400-mile (640 km.) distance between Haran and Gilead in ten days, thus sustaining an average rate of travel of about forty miles (64 km.) a day, despite the encumbrance of vast flocks and a considerable entourage, which included women and children. Comparative evidence from the ancient Near East suggests that daily progress of about 6 miles (9.65 km.) would be realistic in these circumstances.
8. Ross, *Creation & Blessing,* p. 532. Also Sarna, *JPS Torah Commentary: Genesis,* p. 217.
9. Sarna, *JPS Torah Commentary: Genesis,* p. 219.
10. *Ibid.,* p. 221.
11. W. H. Griffith Thomas, *Genesis* (Grand Rapids, MI: Eerdmans, 1946), p. 287.

CHAPTER FORTY-EIGHT: JACOB BECOMES ISRAEL

1. Derek Kidner, *Genesis: An Introduction and Commentary* (Downers Grove, IL: InterVarsity Press, 1975), p. 167.
2. Nahum M. Sarna, *JPS Torah Commentary: Genesis* (Philadelphia: The Jewish Publication Society, 1989), p. 224.
3. Gordon J. Wenham, *Genesis 16—50,* Vol. 2, Word Biblical Commentary (Dallas: Word, 1994), p. 296.
4. Allen P. Ross, *Creation & Blessing* (Grand Rapids, MI: Baker, 1998), p. 555 explains:

   The popular etymology in Genesis is giving the significance of the name. Most of these other suggestions, however, are no more compelling than the popular etymology given in the text of Genesis. The concept of God's fighting with someone is certainly no more of a problem than the passage itself. And the reversal of the emphasis (from "God fights" to "fight with God") in the explanation is due to the nature of popular etymologies which are satisfied with a loose word play on the sound or meaning of the name to express its significance.

The name served to evoke the memory of the fight. It was freely interpreted to say that God was the object of Jacob's struggle. Hearing the name *yiśrā'ēl,* one would recall the incident in which Jacob wrestled with God and prevailed. Dillmann says that ever after the name would tell the Israelites that when Jacob contended successfully with God, he won the battle with man (*Genesis,* vol. 2, p. 279). The name "God fights" and the popular explanation "you fought and prevailed" thus obtained a significance for future struggles.

5. Walter Brueggemann, *Genesis,* "Interpretation" (Atlanta: John Knox Press, 1982), p. 270.

CHAPTER FORTY-NINE: BROTHERS RECONCILED

1. John Walton, *Genesis,* The NIV Application Commentary (Grand Rapids, MI: Zondervan, 2001), p. 613, quoting George MacDonald, *The Wise Woman and Other Fantasy Stories* (Grand Rapids: Eerdmans, 1980), p. 42.
2. Gerhard Von Rad, *Genesis: A Commentary* (Philadelphia: Westminster, 1972), p. 327.
3. Allen P. Ross, *Creation & Blessing* (Grand Rapids, MI: Baker, 1998), p. 565.
4. Nahum M. Sarna, *JPS Torah Commentary: Genesis* (Philadelphia: The Jewish Publication Society, 1989), p. 230.
5. Ian M. Duguid, *Living in the Gap Between Promise and Reality* (Phillipsburg, NJ: P & R Publishing, 1999), pp. 126, 127.
6. J. I. Packer, *Knowing God* (Downers Grove, IL: InterVarsity Press, 1974), p. 85.

CHAPTER FIFTY: FIERCE GRACE

1. Flannery O'Connor, *3 By Flannery O'Connor,* Introduction (New York: Signet Classic, 1983), p. xxi.
2. Gordon J. Wenham, *Genesis 16—50,* Vol. 2, Word Biblical Commentary (Dallas: Word, 1994), p. 310.
3. Victor Hamilton, *The Book of Genesis, Chapters 18—50* (Grand Rapids MI: Eerdmans, 1995), p. 370.

CHAPTER FIFTY-ONE: RESIDUALS

1. Donald Grey Barnhouse, *Genesis* (Grand Rapids, MI: Zondervan, 1973), p. 142.
2. Gordon J. Wenham, *Genesis 16—50,* Vol. 2, Word Biblical Commentary (Dallas: Word, 1994), p. 323.
3. Nahum M. Sarna, *JPS Torah Commentary: Genesis* (Philadelphia: The Jewish Publication Society, 1989), p. 240.
4. *Ibid.*
5. Wenham, *Genesis 16—50,* Vol. 2, p. 324, explains:

A comparison with Num 31:48-54 suggests a quite different possibility. After the battle with the Midianites, the Israelites had to purify themselves (Num 31:19-20). Part of their purification process included donating to the sanctuary booty consisting of "articles of gold, armlets and bracelets, signet rings, earrings, and beads, to make atonement for ourselves before the Lord" (Num 31:50). This suggests that the rings removed by Jacob's sons may well have been part of the booty captured by them from the Shechemites; indeed it is possible that the outer garments and the foreign gods (gold-plated idols?) were part of the spoil (cf. Num 31:20; Josh 7:21; Deut 7:25). We have already noted the close parallels between Gen 34 and Num 31:1-9 (*Comment* on 34:27-29). These further parallels strengthen the case for reading all of 35:1-4, not merely v 5, in the light of chap. 34. 35:5 is not a late gloss or extract from a different source, but it flows naturally out of the preceding verses.

6. John Walton, *Genesis,* The NIV Application Commentary (Grand Rapids, MI: Zondervan, 2001), p. 631.

7. Allen P. Ross, *Creation & Blessing* (Grand Rapids, MI: Baker, 1998), p. 581.

8. Sarna, *JPS Torah Commentary: Genesis,* p. 242, explains:

> On this occasion, unlike the earlier, Jacob pours upon it a libation. Hebrew *nesekh* usually means a wine offering and is nowhere else found in Genesis. Moreover, it is here poured on the pillar, not on the altar. This combination of anomalies indicates that the ceremony Jacob here performs is not simply a duplication of the earlier one but has an added dimension. He is rehabilitating the original stela, which is now invested with new meaning. An interesting parallel may perhaps be drawn from an inscription by Sennacherib, king of Assyria and Babylonia (704-681 B.C.E.): "When that palace shall have become old and ruined, may some future prince restore its ruins, look upon the stele with my name inscribed [on it], anoint it with oil, pour out a libation upon it, and return it to its place."

9. Wenham, *Genesis 16—50,* Vol. 2, pp. 326, 327.

10. Sarna, *JPS Torah Commentary: Genesis,* p. 244.

11. *Ibid.,* pp. 244, 245.

CHAPTER FIFTY-TWO: THE GENERATIONS OF ESAU

1. Alexander Whyte, *Bible Characters* (Grand Rapids, MI: Zondervan, 1973), p. 100.

2. James Hastings, ed., *The Greater Men and Women of the Bible, Adam-Joseph* (London: T & T Clark, 1913), p. 455.

3. Nahum M. Sarna, *JPS Torah Commentary: Genesis* (Philadelphia: The Jewish Publication Society, 1989), p. 247.

4. Gordon J. Wenham, *Genesis 16—50,* Vol. 2, Word Biblical Commentary (Dallas: Word, 1994), p. 337.

5. Sarna, *JPS Torah Commentary: Genesis,* p. 250, explains:

> *Timna . . . Amalek.* Behind this parenthetical note lies social and political history. According to verse 22, Timna was "the sister of Laton," an indigenous Horite. This means that the Edomites who migrated to Seir began to intermarry with the natives but that such alliances were not socially acceptable, which explains Timna's inferior status here as a concubine rather than as a wife. It also means that, at some period, the Amalekites joined the Edomite tribal confederation and attached themselves to the Eliphaz clans in a subordinate relationship.

6. Derek Kidner, *Genesis: An Introduction and Commentary* (Downers Grove, IL: InterVarsity Press, 1975), p. 178, explains:

> Chiefs of the Horites. Deuteronomy 2:12 records that Esau's group dispossessed the Horites, as Israel dispossessed the Canaanites; but Esau married into a leading family, that of Anah son of Zibeon (cf. 2 with 24, 25). Anah's family is called Hivite in verse 2, but Horite here, which indicates either that the terms overlap, or that Hivite may be, here and elsewhere, a copyist's error for Horite. The terms Horites usually seems to denote the Hurrians, a non-Semitic people widely dispersed in the Ancient Near East; the Semitic names in these verses however suggest that the Horites of mount Seir were of different stock. The word could mean cave-dwellers, possibly miners.

7. Sarna, *JPS Torah Commentary: Genesis,* p. 251.

8. Victor P. Hamilton, *The Book of Genesis: Chapters 18—50,* Vol. 2 (Grand Rapids, MI: Eerdmans, 1990), p. 401.

9. Sarna, *JPS Torah Commentary: Genesis,* p. 253.

CHAPTER FIFTY-THREE: JOSEPH'S CALL

1. Thomas Mann, *Joseph in Egypt* (New York: Knopf, 1939), from the jacket of the cased set.

2. Allen P. Ross, *Creation & Blessing* (Grand Rapids, MI: Baker, 1998), p. 590.

3. Gordon J. Wenham, *Genesis 16—50,* Vol. 2, Word Biblical Commentary (Dallas: Word, 1994), p. 350, explains:

> It is not clear whether Joseph's report about his brothers was true or not, but the term דבה "tales" is always used elsewhere in a negative sense of an untrue report, and here it is qualified by the adjective "evil" (cf. Num 13:32; 14:36-37). So it seems likely that Joseph misrepresented his brothers to his father, his father believed him and his brothers hated him for his lies. If his account was true, it would doubtless have enraged his brothers, especially since their father had never held them in high regard anyway.

4. Victor P. Hamilton, *The Book of Genesis: Chapters 18—50* (Grand Rapids, MI: Eerdmans, 1990), p. 406, explains:

> For some undisclosed reason, Joseph *maligned* his brothers to Jacob. To describe Joseph's malignment of his bothers the narrator uses *dibbâ rā'â.* In Ps. 31:14; Jer. 20:10; and Ezek. 36:3 *dibbâ* is the whispering of hostile people (see also Prov. 10:18; 25:10). The closest parallel to its use in Gen 37:2 is Num. 12:32; 14:36, 37 to refer to the bad report of the land that the returning spies spread throughout the camp. *dibbâṭām rā'â* of Gen. 37:2 is close to *dibbâṭ hā'āres rā'â* of Num. 14:37. n. 25. R. Gordis (*The Word and the Book* [New York: Ktav, 1976], pp. 348-49) suggests that the verb *dābab* ("speak") and the noun *dibbâ* (cf. Akk. *dabâbu*, "speak, charge") have a cognate *ṭōb, ṭbb*, which he detects in Hos. 14:3 (*wᵉqah ṭôb*: "accept our speech"). He supports this view by observing that Targ. Onqelos renders *bibbāṭām* in Gen. 37:2 by *ṭyb*, Pesh. by *'ṭ'bhwn.*

5. Walter Brueggemann, *Genesis,* "Interpretation" (Atlanta: John Knox Press, 1982), p. 300.

6. Nahum M. Sarna, *JPS Torah Commentary: Genesis* (Philadelphia: The Jewish Publication Society, 1989), p. 256, explains:

> *speak . . . to him* Hebrew *dabbero* is unique. Usually the suffix attached to this verb carries a possessive sense, meaning "his speech." The passage would then be translated, "They could not abide his friendly speech." In other words, they rebuffed every attempt by Joseph to be friendly.

7. Claus Westermann, *Genesis 37—50,* trans. John J. Scullion (Minneapolis: Fortress Press, 1994), p. 38.

8. John H. Sailhamer, "Genesis," Vol. 2, The Expositor's Bible Commentary (Grand Rapids, MI: Zondervan, 1990), p. 256.

9. Wenham, *Genesis 16—50,* Vol. 2, p. 352, explains:

> "Sun, moon" is taken by Jacob to be "I and your mother," which raises the question as to whether Rachel is still alive at this point in the story, even though her death was reported in 35:19. It is clear that Genesis does not relate everything in strict chronological order, especially deaths (cf. *Comments* on 11:32 and 24:65-66; 25:1-4). But the presence of eleven stars seems to imply Benjamin's existence, so it would seem more likely that Rachel is assumed to have died and that the moon is included just to complete the picture of the heavenly bodies (cf. Coats, *Canaan to Egypt,* 14).

10. Brueggemann, *Genesis,* p. 299.

CHAPTER FIFTY-FOUR: SOLD INTO SLAVERY

1. Derek Kidner, *Genesis: An Introduction and Commentary* (Downers Grove, IL: InterVarsity Press, 1975), p. 181.

2. Thomas Mann, *Joseph and His Brothers,* trans. H. T. Lowe-Porter (London: Random House Vintage, 1999), p. 372.

3. Nahum M. Sarna, *JPS Torah Commentary: Genesis* (Philadelphia: The Jewish Publication Society, 1989), p. 259.

4. *Ibid.*

5. Gordon J. Wenham, *Genesis 16—50,* Vol. 2, Word Biblical Commentary (Dallas: Word, 1994), p. 354.

6. John Walton, *Genesis,* The NIV Application Commentary (Grand Rapids, MI: Zondervan, 2001), p. 666, explains:

   Judah is the one who offers the idea of selling Joseph rather than killing him. This is the first appearance of a number of significant actions by Judah in the narrative as he begins his own personal journey. It is probably significant that in all three of the narrative contexts of the Joseph story where Judah plays a role, he successfully persuades others to do as he suggests (whether his suggestions are commendable or not; 37:26-27, 43:3-10; 44:16-34). Each speech is longer than the previous one, and each one is more commendable than the previous one. As modern readers we must be aware of the role Judah is already playing to most of the ancient audience.

7. Walter Brueggemann, *Genesis,* "Interpretation" (Atlanta: John Knox Press, 1982), p. 305.

8. Sarna, *JPS Torah Commentary: Genesis,* p. 262.

CHAPTER FIFTY-FIVE: TAMAR AND JUDAH

1. Gerhard Von Rad, *Genesis: A Commentary* (Philadelphia: Westminster, 1972), p. 357.

2. Victor P. Hamilton, *The Book of Genesis: Chapters 18-50,* New International Commentary on the Old Testament (Grand Rapids, MI: Eerdmans, 1995), p. 433.

   In addition to these linguistic parallels, note the following thematic parallels and contrasts. (1) Ch. 38 highlights Tamar's deception of Judah by disguising herself as a harlot. This theme of deception parallels ch. 37, where the sons deceive Jacob through the bloodied coat, and ch. 39, where Potiphar's wife attempts to deceive her husband about Joseph. In chs. 37 and 38 the deception is perpetrated by a relative (sons, daughter-in-law). (2) In all three chapters evidence is presented by one party (the bloodied coat, ch. 37; Judah's seal, cord, and staff, ch. 38; Joseph's coat, ch. 39) to another party to establish either facticity (ch. 37) or culpability (chs. 38, 39). (3) Tamar the seductress balances Potiphar's wife the seductress, and the seduced Judah contrasts with the chaste Joseph. (4) Jacob's grief over the alleged death of one son (37:34, 35) contrasts with the absence of any grief displayed by Judah over the death of two sons. (5) In ch. 37 Joseph has a dream which provokes this question:. Shall you rule over us? and the rest of the Joseph story shows Joseph, so to speak, ruling over his brethren. In ch. 38 the focus is on Judah out of whose line will come the kings who will rule over God's people. (6) In both chs. 37 and 38 we observe fraternal rivalry. [See J. Goldin, "The Youngest Son or Where does Genesis 38 Belong," *JBL* 96 (1977) 27-44.] Onan feels about Er as Joseph's brothers feel about him. (7) In both episodes the law of primogeniture is set aside. A younger son (Joseph) is his brothers' salvation, and a younger son (Perez) continues the messianic line (Ruth 4:18; Matt. 1:3).

3. Gordon J. Wenham, *Genesis 16—50,* Vol. 2, Word Biblical Commentary (Dallas: Word, 1994), p. 369.

4. John Walton, *Genesis,* The NIV Application Commentary (Grand Rapids, MI: Zondervan, 2001), p. 668.

5. Derek Kidner, *Genesis: An Introduction and Commentary* (Downers Grove, IL: InterVarsity Press, 1975), p. 188.

6. Robert Alter, *The Art of Biblical Narrative* (New York: Basic Books, 1981), p. 8.

7. Kidner, *Genesis: An Introduction and Commentary,* p. 189.

8. Andrew Reid, *Salvation Begins* (Sydney: Aquila, 2000), p. 251.

9. Alter, *The Art of Biblical Narrative,* p. 9.

10. Reid, *Salvation Begins,* p. 255.

11. Hamilton, *The Book of Genesis: Chapters 18—50,* p. 455, 456.

CHAPTER FIFTY-SIX: SUCCEEDING IN EGYPT

1. J. D. Douglas, ed. *The New Bible Dictionary* (Grand Rapids, MI: Eerdmans, 1962), p. 351.

2. Victor P. Hamilton, *The Book of Genesis: Chapters 18-50* (Grand Rapids, MI: Eerdmans, 1995), p. 461, explains:

> The only thing Potiphar does not delegate to Joseph is the preparation of his food, perhaps because of a general Egyptian concern that non-Egyptians were unaware of how properly to prepare food (see 43:32); or more likely, because of ritual separation at mealtimes.

3. Robert Alter, *The Art of Biblical Narrative* (New York: Basic Books, 1981), p. 108.
4. William Manchester, *The Last Lion* (Boston: Little Brown, 1983), p. 87.
5. Andrew J. Schmutzer, "Digging Deeper. Learning Character Over Comfort: The Purification of Temptation" (unpublished paper, 2003), p. 2.
6. Alter, *The Art of Biblical Narrative*, p. 110.
7. Hamilton, *The Book of Genesis: Chapters 18-50*, p. 465.

CHAPTER FIFTY-SEVEN: PREPARATION FOR GREATNESS

1. J. D. Douglas, ed., *The New Bible Dictionary* (Grand Rapids, MI: Wm. B. Eerdmans, 1962), p. 283.
2. *Ibid.*, p. 685.
3. Gordon J. Wenham, *Genesis 16—50,* Vol. 2, Word Biblical Commentary (Dallas: Word, 1994), p. 382.
4. John Walton, *Genesis,* The NIV Application Commentary (Grand Rapids, MI: Zondervan, 2001), p. 673, writes:

> In the ancient Near East, dream interpretations were sought from experts who had been trained in techniques and methods of the day. Both the Egyptians and Babylonians compiled what are called "dream books," which contain sample dreams along with a key to their interpretation. Though some of the interpretations in the biblical accounts may seem transparent or self-evident, dreams often depended on symbolism, and the symbols might not stand for what was most logical. The dream books preserved the empirical data concerning past dreams and interpretations and therefore offered the security of scientific documentation. It was believed that the gods communicated generally through dreams but that they revealed the meanings of dreams by giving wisdom in the expert's research.

5. Gerhard Von Rad, *Genesis: A Commentary* (Philadelphia: Westminster, 1972), p. 371, explains:

> By contrast, Joseph's answer, "Interpretations belong to God," is completely polemic. It is again one of those splendid statements which our narrator loves and which go far beyond the situation in the programmatic, doctrinal form in which they are spoken (cf. at ch. 39.9). Spoken by a very lowly foreign slave, whom the two prisoners had not dreamed of questioning, the statement contains a sharp contrast. Joseph means to say that the interpretation of dreams is not a human art but a *charisma* which God can grant. In everything that concerned the interpretation of the future, ancient Israel's faith reacted very strongly. The events of the future lay in Yahweh's hand only, and only the one to whom it was revealed was empowered to interpret.

6. Nahum M. Sarna, *JPS Torah Commentary: Genesis* (Philadelphia: The Jewish Publication Society, 1989), p. 278.
7. Walter Brueggemann, *Genesis,* "Interpretation" (Atlanta: John Knox Press, 1982), p. 324.
8. Wenham, *Genesis 16—50,* Vol. 2, p. 324.
9. Walton, *Genesis,* p. 673.
10. Sarna, *JPS Torah Commentary: Genesis*, p. 280.
11. Dr. and Mrs. Howard Taylor, *Hudson Taylor's Spiritual Secret* (London, Philadelphia, Toronto, Melbourne, Shanghai: China Inland Mission, 1935), pp. 75, 76.
12. V. Raymond Edman, *The Disciplines of Life* (Wheaton, IL: Scripture Press Foundation, 1972), p. 80.

CHAPTER FIFTY-EIGHT: FROM PIT TO PINNACLE

1. Victor P. Hamilton, *The Book of Genesis: Chapters 18-50* (Grand Rapids, MI: Eerdmans, 1995), p. 486, explains:

   . . . *his spirit* [was] *perturbed* (*wattippāʿem rûḥô,* v. 8). This same expression is used with Nebuchadnezzar and his baffling dream (Dan. 2:1, Hithpael; 2:3, Niphal), as well as by the anguished psalmist in Ps. 77:5 (Eng. 4): "I am so troubled that I cannot speak" (RSV) or "I am bewildered, yet I will not speak." The latter reference provides the only instance in the OT in which the subject of the verb is not *rûaḥ.*

2. Charles Colson, *Kingdoms in Conflict* (New York/Grand Rapids, MI: William Morrow/Zondervan, 1987), pp. 306, 307.

3. Derek Kidner, *Genesis: An Introduction and Commentary* (Downers Grove, IL: InterVarsity Press, 1975), p. 195.

4. Hamilton, *The Book of Genesis: Chapters 18-50,* p. 494.

5. Walter Brueggemann, *Genesis,* "Interpretation" (Atlanta: John Knox Press, 1982), p. 331.

6. Kidner, *Genesis: An Introduction and Commentary,* p. 196.

7. John Huffman, *Who's in Charge Here?* (Chappaqua, NY: Christian Herald Books, 1981), p. 63.

CHAPTER FIFTY-NINE: LIFE AT THE TOP

1. John Walton, *Genesis,* The NIV Application Commentary (Grand Rapids, MI: Zondervan, 2001), p. 676.

2. Gordon J. Wenham, *Genesis 16—50,* Vol. 2, Word Biblical Commentary (Dallas: Word, 1994), p. 396.

3. Walton, *Genesis, The NIV Application Commentary,* p. 676.

4. Allen P. Ross, *Creation & Blessing* (Grand Rapids, MI: Baker, 1998), p. 643.

5. G. C. Aalders, *Genesis,* Vol. 2, trans. William Heynen (Grand Rapids, MI: Zondervan, 1981), p. 216.

6. Ross, *Creation & Blessing,* p. 643.

7. *Forbes* Magazine, "Thoughts on the Business of Life," October 11, 1999, p. 452.

8. C. H. Spurgeon, *Lectures to My Students* (rpt., Grand Rapids, MI: Zondervan, 1969), p. 167.

9. Nahum M. Sarna, *JPS Torah Commentary: Genesis* (Philadelphia: The Jewish Publication Society, 1989), p. 290.

10. Derek Kidner, *Genesis: An Introduction and Commentary* (Downers Grove, IL: InterVarsity Press, 1975), p. 198, referencing J. Vandier, *La Famine dans L'Egypte Ancienne* (Cairo: n.p., 1936), p. 8ff.

11. Leland Ryken, *Worldly Saints* (Grand Rapids, MI: Zondervan/Academic Books, 1986), p. 63, citing *Magnalia Christi Americana* [p. 21].

CHAPTER SIXTY: GUILT AND GRACE

1. Claus Westermann, *Joseph: Eleven Bible Studies on Genesis,* trans. Omar Kaste (Minneapolis: Fortress Press, 1996), p. 65.

2. Gordon J. Wenham, *Genesis 16—50,* Vol. 2, Word Biblical Commentary (Dallas: Word, 1994), p. 407.

3. Mark Sheridan, ed., Thomas Oden, gen. ed., *Ancient Christian Commentary on Scripture,* Vol. 2 (Downers Grove, IL: InterVarsity Press, 2002), p. 277.

4. John H. Sailhamer, "Genesis," Vol. 2, The Expositor's Bible Commentary (Grand Rapids, MI: Zondervan, 1990), p. 246.

CHAPTER SIXTY-ONE: MERCY IN EGYPT

1. Cornelius Plantinga, Jr., *Not the Way It's Supposed to Be: A Breviary of Sin* (Grand Rapids, MI: Eerdmans, 1995), p. 162.
2. *Ibid.*, pp 157, 158.
3. John R. Claypool, *The Preaching Event* (Waco, TX: Word, 1980), p. 68.
4. John H. Sailhamer, "Genesis," Vol. 2, The Expositor's Bible Commentary (Grand Rapids, MI: Zondervan, 1990), p. 250, explains:

   Jacob's farewell words provide the narrative key to what follows: "May God Almighty grant you mercy [*raḥ°mîm*] before the man" (v. 14). As so often in the patriarchal narratives, the events that follow seem to be guided by just these words. At the conclusion of the narrative, when the sons reached Joseph and he saw Benjamin, we are told that "his mercy" (*raḥ°māyw*, v. 30; untr. in NIV) was kindled toward his brother. It is important that in these words of Jacob the compassion (*raḥ°mîm*) that Joseph was to find toward his brothers was given by "God Almighty." Again in these subtle and indirect ways the writer informs the reader of the power of God in directing the lives of his people and in carrying his plans to completion.

5. Victor P. Hamilton, *The Book of Genesis: Chapters 18-50* (Grand Rapids, MI: Eerdmans, 1995), p. 545.
6. Claus Westermann, *Joseph: Eleven Bible Studies on Genesis*, trans. Omar Kaste (Minneapolis: Fortress Press, 1996), p. 76.
7. *Ibid.*, p. 77.
8. *Ibid.*, p. 76.
9. Nahum M. Sarna, *JPS Torah Commentary: Genesis* (Philadelphia: The Jewish Publication Society, 1989), p. 302.
10. *Ibid.*
11. Hamilton, *The Book of Genesis: Chapters 18-50*, p. 555.
12. Westermann, *Joseph*, p. 79.
13. Allen P. Ross, *Creation & Blessing* (Grand Rapids, MI: Baker, 1998), p. 122.

CHAPTER SIXTY-TWO: TRANSFORMATION IN EGYPT

1. Nahum M. Sarna, *JPS Torah Commentary: Genesis* (Philadelphia: The Jewish Publication Society, 1989), p. 303, explains:

   In the present instance, the goblet serves both as a drinking vessel and as a divining instrument (v. 5). The fact that we are told it is made of silver is not meant solely to emphasize its preciousness; the offense would be grave enough no matter what the composition of the goblet might have been. The main point here is that Hebrew *kesef*, "silver, money," is a key word, reiterated twenty times in the accounts of Joseph and his brothers in Egypt (chaps. 42-45). The brothers had sold Joseph into slavery for twenty pieces of silver (Gen. 37:28); now he harasses and tests them with silver.

2. Gordon J. Wenham, *Genesis 16—50,* Vol. 2, Word Biblical Commentary (Dallas: Word, 1994), p. 425.
3. Claus Westermann, *Genesis 37—50*, trans. John J. Scullion (Minneapolis: Fortress Press, 1986), p. 133.
4. Walter Brueggemann, *Genesis*, "Interpretation" (Atlanta: John Knox Press, 1982), p. 338.
5. Westermann, *Genesis 37-50*, p. 134.
6. Derek Kidner, *Genesis: An Introduction and Commentary* (Downers Grove, IL: InterVarsity Press, 1975), p. 205.
7. Sarna, *JPS Torah Commentary: Genesis*, p. 306.
8. Wenham, *Genesis 16-50*, Vol. 2, p. 427.
9. Donald Grey Barnhouse, *Genesis* (Grand Rapids, MI: Zondervan, 1973), p. 200.

Chapter Sixty-three: *Reconciliation in Egypt*

1. Mark Sheridan, ed., *Genesis 12—50*, Vol. 2, Ancient Christian Commentary on Scripture (Downers Grove, IL: InterVarsity Press, 2002), p. 290.

2. John H. Sailhamer, "Genesis," Vol. 2, The Expositor's Bible Commentary (Grand Rapids, MI: Zondervan, 1990), p. 257.

3. Donald Grey Barnhouse, *Genesis* (Grand Rapids, MI: Zondervan, 1973), p. 208.

4. Derek Kidner, *Genesis: An Introduction and Commentary* (Downers Grove, IL: InterVarsity Press, 1975), p. 207, writes:

    Goshen is a name which remains unattested, so far, in Egyptian remains; but 47:11 gives us the name it bore in later times, 'the land of Rameses'. This name, coupled with the fact that the district was fertile (47:6) and *near* to Joseph at court, suggests that it was in the eastern part of the Nile delta, near Tanis, the seat of the Hyksos kings of the seventeenth century and of the Ramessides of the thirteenth century, the probable periods of Joseph and Moses respectively.

5. Sailhamer, *Genesis*, p. 257.

6. Sheridan, ed. *Genesis 12—50*, Vol. 2, p. 298.

7. Gordon J. Wenham, *Genesis 16—50,* Vol. 2, Word Biblical Commentary (Dallas: Word, 1994), p. 433.

Chapter Sixty-four: *Preservation in Egypt*

1. Gordon J. Wenham, *Genesis 16—50,* Vol. 2, Word Biblical Commentary (Dallas: Word, 1994), p. 441, explains:

    זבח "sacrifice" is a general term for sacrifice, often restricted to peace offerings (see Lev. 3), which could be offered in making vows, or as acts of thanksgiving. Such motives would be appropriate here. The offering of sacrifice sometimes is seen as a preliminary to prophetic inspiration (Num 23:1, 14, 29; Ps 50:5; Isa 6:6).

2. *Ibid.*, p. 448.

3. *Ibid.*, p. 442.

4. Nahum M. Sarna, *JPS Torah Commentary: Genesis* (Philadelphia: The Jewish Publication Society, 1989), p. 317.

5. Wenham, *Genesis 16—50,* Vol. 2, p. 445.

6. Gerhard Von Rad, *Genesis: A Commentary* (Philadelphia: Westminster, 1972), p. 403.

Chapter Sixty-five: *Prospering in Egypt*

1. Nahum M. Sarna, *JPS Torah Commentary: Genesis* (Philadelphia: The Jewish Publication Society, 1989), p. 319, provides interesting details:

    Hebrew *sarei mikneh*, literally "officers of cattle," that is, superintendents of the royal cattle. This office is mentioned frequently in Egyptian inscriptions since the king possessed vast herds of cattle. Ramses III is said to have employed 3,264 men, mostly foreigners, to take care of his herds.

2. Derek Kidner, *Genesis: An Introduction and Commentary* (Downers Grove, IL: InterVarsity Press, 1975), p. 210.

3. Walter Brueggemann, *Genesis*, "Interpretation" (Atlanta: John Knox Press, 1982), pp. 354, 355.

4. Gerhard Von Rad, *Genesis: A Commentary* (Philadelphia: Westminster, 1972), p. 410.

5. Gordon J. Wenham, *Genesis 16—50,* Vol. 2, Word Biblical Commentary (Dallas: Word, 1994), p. 448.

6. Nahum M. Sarna, *JPS Torah Commentary: Genesis*, pp. 322, 323.

7. Von Rad, *Genesis: A Commentary*, p. 411, explains:

    Judged by conditions of that time, a tax of about 20 per cent must be considered normal. In private business transactions the interest rates were often considerably higher. In the Babylonian economy the interest rates for the purchase of seed corn went as high as 40 per cent; in the Jewish military colony at Elephantine in the fifth century B.C. they went even to 60 per cent. Nevertheless, it must be emphasized that the vocation of merchant was not followed in Israel, which had settled in Palestine, until the late postexilic period. The law forbade every form of usury (Ex. 22.25; Deut. 23.20f.). It is significant that the term "Canaanite" became the word for "dealer" (Isa. 23.8; Zech 14.21; Prov. 31.24). Only in the Diaspora did Judaism give up its ties with the vocation of agriculture.

8. John Walton, *Genesis,* The NIV Application Commentary (Grand Rapids, MI: Zondervan, 2001), p. 709.

9. Victor P. Hamilton, *The Book of Genesis: Chapters 18—50* (Grand Rapids, MI: Eerdmans, 1995), pp. 624, 625.

CHAPTER SIXTY-SIX: FAITH AND BLESSING

1. John Walton, *Genesis,* The NIV Application Commentary (Grand Rapids, MI: Zondervan, 2001), p. 710.

2. Donald Grey Barnhouse, *Genesis* (Grand Rapids, MI: Zondervan, 1973), p. 223.

3. Walton, *Genesis, The NIV Application Commentary,* p. 711.

4. Nahum M. Sarna, *JPS Torah Commentary: Genesis* (Philadelphia: The Jewish Publication Society, 1989), p. 327. Note: Sarna has the fullest discussion of the adoption process.

5. *Ibid.*

6. Barnhouse, *Genesis,* p. 227.

7. Sarna, *JPS Torah Commentary: Genesis,* p. 329.

8. W. Robertson Nicoll, ed., *The Expositor's Bible, Genesis* (New York: A.C. Armstrong, 1903), p. 424.

9. Walton, *Genesis,* p. 712.

CHAPTER SIXTY-SEVEN: THE TESTAMENT OF JACOB I

1. John H. Sailhamer, "Genesis," Vol. 2, The Expositor's Bible Commentary (Grand Rapids, MI: Zondervan, 1990), pp. 274, 275.

2. Gordon J. Wenham, *Genesis 16—50,* Vol. 2, Word Biblical Commentary (Dallas: Word, 1994), p. 471.

3. Allen P. Ross, *Creation & Blessing* (Grand Rapids, MI: Baker, 1998), p. 703.

4. Almost all modern scholars and many ancient scholars and versions (e.g., the Septuagint [LXX]) reject the rendering "Shiloh," although Delitzsch argues for it. For evenhanded discussions of the various views, see Wenham, *Genesis 16—50* and Hamilton. Proponents of the "tribute" translation include Speiser, Sarna, Wenham, and Walton. The "until he come to whom it belongs" rendering is supported by Kidner, Ross, and Sailhamer. Though all three are possible, I favor "until tribute comes to him" for reasons too complex to recite in a public exposition.

5. Ross, *Creation & Blessing,* p. 703.

6. Derek Kidner, *Genesis: An Introduction and Commentary* (Downers Grove, IL: InterVarsity Press, 1975), p. 219.

7. William C. Varner, *Jacob's Dozen* (Bellmawr, NJ: Friends of Israel, 1987), pp. 47, 48 provides further detail on Judah's messianic line.

CHAPTER SIXTY-EIGHT: THE TESTAMENT OF JACOB II

1. John H. Sailhamer, "Genesis," Vol. 2, The Expositor's Bible Commentary (Grand Rapids, MI: Zondervan, 1990), pp. 278, 279.

2. Gordon J. Wenham, *Genesis 16—50,* Vol. 2, Word Biblical Commentary (Dallas: Word, 1994), p. 481, writes:

   And this is what the Targums do (e.g., *Tg. Neof.,* "The venomous serpent . . . He is Samson bar Manoah"), as do most of the medieval Jewish commentators (see Leibowitz, 548-54). Through his own strength and various tricks, Samson defeated the Philistines on various occasions (Judg 13-16). Later the small tribe of Dan migrated northwards and sacked the unsuspecting town of Laish (Judg 17-18). Yet despite the prominence of Danites in the Book of Judges, modern commentators are strangely reluctant to link these sayings about Dan here with exploits of Samson or his tribe. Only Delitzsch, Dillmann, Driver, and König do so cautiously. Though it is unfashionable, I agree with this linkage.

3. Ronald F. Youngblood, *The Book of Genesis: An Introductory Commentary*, 2nd ed. (Grand Rapids, MI: Baker Book House, 1991), pp. 280, 281, writes:

It underscores the importance of the tribes that would some day descend from Joseph's sons, Manasseh and Ephraim. It also illustrates, however incidentally, Jacob's insistence that Ephraim should be more powerful than Manasseh because it makes a pun on Ephraim's name (the Hebrew word for "fruitful," used twice in 49:22, is similar to the word "Ephraim," which means "twice fruitful").

4. Wenham, *Genesis 16—50,* Vol. 2, p. 486.

5. *Ibid.*

CHAPTER SIXTY-NINE: JACOB'S EXODUS

1. "The Treasures of Egypt," *National Geographic Collector's Edition*, Vol. 5, July 2003, p. 97.

2. Nahum M. Sarna, *JPS Torah Commentary: Genesis* (Philadelphia: The Jewish Publication Society, 1989), p. 347.

3. John Walton, *Genesis,* The NIV Application Commentary (Grand Rapids, MI: Zondervan, 2001), p. 720.

4. Gordon J. Wenham, *Genesis 16—50,* Vol. 2, Word Biblical Commentary (Dallas: Word, 1994), p. 489.

5. Victor P. Hamilton, *The Book of Genesis: Chapters 18-50* (Grand Rapids, MI: Eerdmans, 1995), p. 697 explains:

The site *Goren-ha-atad* is unidentifiable. This is the only place in the OT where it is mentioned. It is described as being *bᵉēḇer hayyardēn,* for which most translations have "beyond the Jordan," that is Transjordan or East Jordan. If we retain that translation, then that means that the funeral march did not take the normal route from Egypt to Canaan, but — for some unknown reason — took a detour and traveled around the Dead Sea and up the east side of the Jordan, much as a later march of Jacob's descendants did under Moses' leadership. After the seven-day grieving period, the party continued on to Hebron, by either crossing the Jordan or by swinging around the lower tip of the Dead Sea.

6. T. Desmond Alexander, Brian S. Rosner, D. A. Carson, Graeme Goldsworthy, eds., *New Dictionary of Biblical Theology* (Leicester, England: Inter-Varsity Press, 2000), pp. 478, 479, explains:

The confirming theophany of a smoking brazier and a flaming torch passing through the split animals adumbrates the pillar of fire and cloud (Exod. 13:21) and (possibly) Yahweh's causing Israel to pass through the split sea (Ps. 136:13-14).

CHAPTER SEVENTY: GOOD PROVIDENCE

1. James S. Hewitt, ed., *Illustrations Unlimited* (Wheaton, IL: Tyndale, 1988), pp. 205, 206.

2. Theodore Laetsch, *Bible Commentary on Jeremiah* (St. Louis: Concordia, 1965), pp. 234, 235.

3. Walter A. Elwell, ed., *Evangelical Dictionary of Theology* (Grand Rapids, MI: Baker, 1984), p. 891.

4. Victor P. Hamilton, *The Book of Genesis: Chapters 18-50* (Grand Rapids, MI: Eerdmans, 1995), p. 712.

CHAPTER SEVENTY-ONE: MAN AND SIN IN GENESIS

1. J. I. Packer, *Concise Theology* (Wheaton, IL: Tyndale, 1993), p. 72.
2. *Webster's*, seventh edition.
3. Henri Blocher, *In the Beginning* (Leicester, England: Inter-Varsity, n.d.), p. 71.
4. Gerhard Von Rad, *Genesis: A Commentary* (Philadelphia: Westminster, 1972), p. 117.
5. William J. Dumbrell, *The Faith of Israel* (Leicester, England: Apollos, 1993), p. 23.
6. Packer, *Concise Theology*, p. 83.
7. Charles W. Colson, 1993, Templeton Address, "The Enduring Revolution," p. 5.
8. Packer, *Concise Theology*, pp. 83, 84.
9. William Shakespeare, *Hamlet*, Act 2, Scene 2, lines 273-277.

CHAPTER SEVENTY-TWO: FAITH AND RIGHTEOUSNESS IN GENESIS

1. Gerhard Von Rad, *Genesis: A Commentary* (Philadelphia: Westminster, 1972), p. 180.

CHAPTER SEVENTY-THREE: GRACE IN GENESIS

1. D. J. A. Clines, *Catholic Biblical Quarterly*, No. 38 (1976), pp. 487, 488. Clines explains that Gerhard Von Rad initially observed a pattern of *sin, mitigation,* and *punishment*. Then Claus Westermann discerned another element, that of divine *speech*. Though he did not include it in the pattern, Clines does. Thus the following chart:

	I. Sin	II. Speech	III. Mitigation Grace	IV. Punishment
1. Fall	3:6	3:14-19	3:21	3:22-24
2. Cain	4:8	4:10-12	4:15	4:16
3. Sons of God	6:2	6:3	6:8, 18ff.	7:6-24
4. Flood	6:5, 11f	6:7, 13-21	6:8, 18ff.	7:6-24
5. Babel	11:4	11:6f	10:1-32	11:8

2. Gordon J. Wenham, *Genesis 1—15,* Vol. 1, Word Biblical Commentary (Waco, TX: Word, 1987), pp 84, 85.
3. Marcus Dods, *The Book of Genesis* (New York: A.C. Armstrong and Son, 1903), pp. 24, 25.
4. Allen P. Ross, *Creation & Blessing* (Grand Rapids, MI: Baker, 1998) p. 151.
5. Wenham, *Genesis 1—15*, Vol. 1, p. 109.

CHAPTER SEVENTY-FOUR: MESSIAH IN GENESIS

1. Alec Motyer, *Look to the Rock: An Old Testament Background to Our Understanding of Christ* (Leicester, England: Inter-Varsity, 1996), p. 22.
2. Walter C. Kaiser, *The Messiah in the Old Testament* (Grand Rapids, MI: Zondervan, 1995), pp. 37, 38.
3. Jack Collins, "A Syntactical Note (Genesis 3:15): Is the Woman's Seed Singular or Plural?" *Tyndale Bulletin* 48:1 (1997), pp. 139-148.
4. Gordon Wenham, *Genesis 16—50*, Vol. 2, Word Biblical Commentary (Dallas: Word, 1994), p. 108.
5. Kaiser, *The Messiah in the Old Testament*, p. 50.
6. Allen P. Ross, *Creation and Blessing* (Grand Rapids, MI: Baker, 1986), p. 703.
7. Derek Kidner, *Genesis: An Introduction and Commentary* (Downers Grove, IL: InterVarsity Press, 1975), p. 219.

CHAPTER SEVENTY-FIVE: GOD IN GENESIS

1. F. J. Sheed, *Theology and Sanity* (New York: Sheed & Ward, 1946), pp. 9, 10.
2. A. W. Tozer, *The Knowledge of the Holy* (New York: Harper & Row, 1961), p. 73.

3. Wayne Grudem, *Systematic Theology: An Introduction to Biblical Doctrine* (Grand Rapids, MI: Zondervan, 1994), p. 173.
4. J. I. Packer, *Knowing God* (Downers Grove, IL: InterVarsity Press, 1973), p. 37.
5. W. H. Griffith Thomas, *Genesis* (Grand Rapids, MI: Eerdmans, 1946), p. 226.
6. J. I. Packer, *Concise Theology* (Wheaton, IL: Tyndale, 1993), p. 54.
7. Leland Ryken, James C. Wilhoit, Tremper Longman III, eds., *Dictionary of Biblical Imagery* (Downers Grove, IL: InterVarsity Press, 1995), p. 681.
8. Donald Grey Barnhouse, *Genesis* (Grand Rapids, MI: Zondervan, 1973), p. 208.

Scripture Index

General Index

Index of
Sermon Illustrations

About the Book Jacket

The design of the book jacket brings together the talents of several Christian artists. The design centers around the beautiful banners created by artist Marge Gieser. They are photographed here on the jacket at about one-twentieth of their original size.

Concerning the symbolism used in the banners for *Genesis*, Marge Gieser writes:

> Genesis — Banner I
>
> This banner makes a bold statement about the origin of creation. "In the beginning . . ." God created everything we see in the world. The entire border of the banner is a display of created beings — both animal and plant life. It is intended to depict the variety and lushness of God's creation. The banner is three-dimensional by design, using several thick layers to give it a sculptural look. The animals and plant life are cutouts from a tapestry fabric.
>
> Genesis — Banner II
>
> The book of Genesis starts out with the origin of creation. However, most of the book is about the "everlasting covenant" between God and Abraham and his descendants. The stars on the banner are a reference to Genesis 15:5, when God says to Abraham, "Look toward heaven, and number the stars. . . . So shall your offspring be." Again, the banner is three-dimensional, using thick layers to create a sculptural look.

The other artists contributing their talents to the creation of the jacket were: Bill Koechling, photography; Paul Higdon, design and typography; and David LaPlaca, art direction.